The Sust

FX Plus Library

This book provides the first systematic and accessible text for students of hospitality and the culinary arts that directly addresses how more sustainable restaurants and commercial food services can be achieved.

Food systems receive growing attention because they link various sustainability dimensions. Restaurants are at the heart of these developments, and their decisions to purchase regional foods, or to prepare menus that are healthier and less environmentally problematic, have great influence on food production processes. This book is systematically designed around understanding the inputs and outputs of the commercial kitchen as well as what happens in the restaurant from the perspective of operators, staff and the consumer. The book considers different management approaches and further looks at the role of restaurants, chefs and staff in the wider community and the positive contributions that commercial kitchens can make to promoting sustainable food ways.

Case studies from all over the world illustrate the tools and techniques helping to meet environmental and economic bottom lines. This will be essential reading for all students of hospitality and the culinary arts.

Stefan Gössling is a Professor in the Department of Service Management and Service Studies, Lund University, Sweden, as well as the School of Business and Economics, Linnaeus University, Sweden. He is also the research coordinator for tourism studies at the Western Norway Research Institute. He is interested in the sustainability of food, owns a farm and has made various attempts at running a restaurant that have made him aware of the many difficulties entrepreneurs face in implementing sustainable practices.

C. Michael Hall is a Professor in the Department of Management, Marketing and Entrepreneurship, University of Canterbury, New Zealand, Docent in Geography, University of Oulu, Finland, a Visiting Professor in Tourism at Linnaeus University, Sweden, and a Guest Professor in the Department of Service Management and Service Studies, Lund University, Sweden, and the Department of Food, Nutrition and Culinary Science, Umeå University, Sweden. He has written widely on tourism, regional development, policy, World Heritage, global environmental change and food, as well as growing tree crops on his family's regenerative farming property.

The Sustainable Chef

The Environment in Culinary Arts, Restaurants, and Hospitality

Stefan Gössling and C. Michael Hall

LONDON AND NEW YORK

First published 2022
by Routledge
2 Park Square, Milton Park, Abingdon, Oxon OX14 4RN

and by Routledge
605 Third Avenue, New York, NY 10158

Routledge is an imprint of the Taylor & Francis Group, an informa business

© 2022 Stefan Gössling and C. Michael Hall

The right of Stefan Gössling and C. Michael Hall to be identified as authors of this work has been asserted by them in accordance with sections 77 and 78 of the Copyright, Designs and Patents Act 1988.k

All rights reserved. No part of this book may be reprinted or reproduced or utilised in any form or by any electronic, mechanical, or other means, now known or hereafter invented, including photocopying and recording, or in any information storage or retrieval system, without permission in writing from the publishers.

Trademark notice: Product or corporate names may be trademarks or registered trademarks, and are used only for identification and explanation without intent to infringe.

British Library Cataloguing-in-Publication Data
A catalogue record for this book is available from the British Library

Library of Congress Cataloging-in-Publication Data
Names: Gössling, Stefan, author. | Hall, C. Michael, author.
Title: The sustainable chef: the environment in culinary arts, restaurants, and hospitality / Stefan Gössling and C. Michael Hall.
Description: Abingdon, Oxon; New York, NY: Routledge, 2022. | Includes bibliographical references and index.
Identifiers: LCCN 2021028162 (print) | LCCN 2021028163 (ebook)
Subjects: LCSH: Restaurant management. | Hotel management. | Hospitality—Environmental aspects. | Food service—Environmental aspects. | Environmental protection.
Classification: LCC TX911 .G668 2022 (print) | LCC TX911 (ebook) | DDC 647.95068—dc23
LC record available at https://lccn.loc.gov/2021028162
LC ebook record available at https://lccn.loc.gov/2021028163

ISBN: 978-1-138-73370-1 (hbk)
ISBN: 978-1-138-73373-2 (pbk)
ISBN: 978-1-315-18748-8 (ebk)

DOI: 10.4324/9781315187488

Typeset in Frutiger
by codeMantra

Contents

List of figures — vii
List of tables — viii
List of boxes — x
Preface and acknowledgements — xiii
List of abbreviations — xiv

1 Introduction: the advantages of a sustainable kitchen — 1
2 Where does our food come from? — 31
3 Climate-friendly food — 57
4 Local foods — 77
5 Organic food — 90
6 Sustainable foods: the importance of standards and certification — 107
7 Purchasing strategies and supply chains — 121
8 Healthy and sustainable foods — 134
9 Menu marketing, portions and presentation — 152
10 Making the most of your food; nose-to-tail and leaf-to-root eating, and packaging — 168
11 Efficient restaurants and kitchens — 179
12 The intelligent kitchen: using management systems to promote sustainability — 199
13 Minimizing waste: technology and management — 210
14 Minimizing waste: behaviour — 233
15 The restaurant in the community — 250

| 16 | Conclusions and futures: expanding the restaurants and foodservice sustainability menu | 263 |

References 275
Index 319

Figures

1.1	Assessing the sustainable restaurant and foodservice operation	27
2.1	From farm to plate: the food consumption and production system	40
2.2	Food loss and waste by region and reason	46
2.3	Water embodied in various foodstuffs	51
3.1	Global warming relative to 1850–1900, and pathways	60
3.2	Emissions from different subsectors	58
3.3	Emissions from different subsectors, European Union	60
3.4	Emissions of greenhouse gases associated with food, kg CO_2-eq/kg	64
3.5	Dietary implications for climate change	68
5.1	The ten European countries with the largest organic production	92
5.2	Global overview of organic land area by continent	100
5.3	Complexity of organic food choices	102
8.1	A healthy and sustainable food environment	135
9.1	Where food is purchased/consumed and where choices can be influenced	152
9.2	Five steps in the design of healthy and sustainable menus	167
12.1	Interrelationships between systems in the development of sustainable restaurant management systems	200
12.2	Potential EMS system architecture for a restaurant	205
13.1	The food system supply chain	213
13.2	Food waste prevention hierarchy	214
13.3	Overview of options for food waste avoidance management	217
13.4	Food waste as share of food purchases	220
14.1	Per capita food losses in different world regions	235

Tables

1.1	Number of premises and food waste arising by hospitality and food services sector in the UK, 2015 and 2018	2
1.2	Plastics and health	6
1.3	The top 20 products in shoreline waste data: merged datasets	8
1.4	Restaurant sustainability strategies	12
1.5	Adoption of environmental sustainability practices by US restaurants	13
1.6	Dimensions of sustainable restaurant and foodservice schemes	16
1.7	Approaches to sustainable culinary systems	19
1.8	Contribution of food supplies, food storage, food preparations and operational support	26
2.1	Top five food staples produced worldwide, 2016	34
2.2	Live animal numbers, 2016	34
2.3	The world's largest retailers, 2019	37
2.4	Global consumption of meat and milk products	44
2.5	Livestock disease	53
3.1	Livestock ratio of energy input to protein output	63
3.2	Foodstuff energy intensity depending on transport mode	75
5.1	External costs to farm gate, UK (2000)	95
5.2	German organic label criteria	97
5.3	Organic certifications	98
5.4	Comparative cost of conventional, organic and Fairtrade produce, Germany	104
6.1	Components of sustainable wine certification programmes	119
7.1	Sectors and segments included in 'social food service'	127
7.2	Main environmental hotspots and causes from food procurement and catering services	128
7.3	List of the environmental criteria in reviewed procurement schemes	131
8.1	Cost of a healthy diet per person per day (US$ equivalents)	148
8.2	Planetary diet focused on health, 2,500 kcal/day	150
9.1	Results of changes in a children's menu	155
9.2	Types of food-related certifications and consumer-relevance	158
9.3	Overview of studies on food labelling and their outcomes	159
9.4	Examples of media supporting meat-free food choices	161
9.5	Examples of foodstuffs that should be choice-edited	162

11.1	Average energy use in US foodservice operations and full-service restaurant	180
11.2	Annual energy consumption in gastro-pub by business (physical) area	183
11.3	Annual energy consumption in gastro-pub by end function	183
11.4	Top restaurant operating costs and profitability	186
11.5	Economic impacts of the adoption of different forms of lighting for a Vancouver pub	187
11.6	Average monitored kitchen consumption composition (%) of different appliances	190
11.7	Proportion of Energy Star-rated appliance type in US restaurant operations	191
11.8	Example of average end use of water in US restaurants	193
11.9	Proportion of US restaurant operators, by type of operation, use water-saving equipment	194
11.10	KPIs and technical details of best practice in small-medium sized, or larger, commercial kitchens	195
11.11	Change in pot washing per annum following installation of new dishwashing technology	197
12.1	Off-premise options in US restaurants	202
12.2	Gap between consumer demand and availability	202
12.3	US restaurant consumer likeliness of using, if available	203
12.4	Potential components of EMS packages	205
12.5	Proportion of restaurant operators, by type of operation, who report they use efficient lighting, programmable thermostats or start-up, shut-down schedules	208
12.6	Use of food waste-specific software	209
13.1	Operational and waste characteristics of different foodservice businesses	215
13.2	Catalysts and barriers to food waste avoidance	216
13.3a	Seasonal calendar for fruit in Northern Italy	225
13.3b	Seasonal calendar for fruit in Canterbury, New Zealand	226
13.4	Examples of websites and apps reducing food waste	228
14.1	Modernization's effects on food systems	234
14.2	Generations characteristics with respect to food and consumption	237
14.3	Estimated average cost of food being wasted in the UK hospitality and foodservice sector (HaFS)	247
16.1	Contribution of farmed animal products at global scale	268

Boxes

1.1	Food waste hot spots	4
1.2	The plastic problem	5
1.3	EU citizens perceptions of what constitutes sustainable food	10
1.4	Epicurious food website drops new beef recipes for environmental reasons	27
1.5	The move towards vegetable-based restaurant cuisine: Eleven Madison Park and ONA	28
2.1	One percent of the world's farms operate 70% of the world's farmland	35
2.2	Market concentration in the beer market	38
2.3	Market concentration in coffee markets	39
2.4	COVID-19 and the food supply chain	41
2.5	Reducing pesticide use in farming	49
2.6	Definitions of water required for agriculture and food production	52
2.7	FAO's global challenges facing food and agriculture	55
3.1	Dietary shifts to mitigate the climate crisis	62
3.2	The environmental value of vegetarian diets	67
3.3	How much CO_2 is sustainable? And what contribution does a meal make?	68
3.4	The carbon footprint of 'milk': is non-dairy better for the climate?	70
3.5	Beverages: should restaurants offer beer from the tap or in bottles?	71
3.6	Animal or plant protein: is lab-grown meat or plant-based meat more climate friendly?	72
3.7	Home food delivery systems	76
4.1	Grower definition of local food	80
4.2	The Sportsman	83
4.3	Short food supply chains and local food in the EU	86
5.1	Definitions of 'organic' agriculture	91
5.2	Organic food sales boomed during COVID-19	93
5.3	The cost of pesticide use	95
5.4	Certified organic restaurants in the USA	100
5.5	The Swedish KRAV certification for restaurants	103
5.6	Mainstreaming organic food in public kitchens and canteens	105
6.1	Environmentally friendly food packaging	109
6.2	IFOAM – Organics International	111
6.3	Fairtrade standards	115
6.4	Certified sustainable wine	118

7.1	Barriers to local procurement by wholesale distributors	126
8.1	Definitions of healthy foods and diets	137
8.2	Patterns of global obesity	138
8.3	Choose Health LA Restaurants Program	139
8.4	Restaurant staff and responses to food allergies	143
8.5	Labelling unhealthy foods: examples from Chile and Ecuador	146
8.6	The WHO recommendations for healthy diets	147
9.1	A win-win in the revision of a children's menu	154
9.2	The importance of taste in the provision of healthy eating alternatives	156
9.3	Scandic choice-editing of giant prawns	163
9.4	Reinventing fast food: Max Burgers	164
9.5	Promoting healthy eating in the African American community	165
10.1	Hugh's *War on Waste*	169
10.2	Using more of the fish	173
10.3	Disrupting the 'to-go culture'	177
11.1	Pacific Gas & Electric (PGE): ten ways foodservice businesses can become more energy efficient	180
11.2	Energy performance and cost analysis for the nZEB retrofit of a typical UK hotel	184
11.3	How do you get restaurants excited about efficiency?	185
11.4	Energy efficiency websites	188
11.5	Water usage and costs for casual dining restaurants in Kansas	193
11.6	Behavioural measures with staff and management to encourage better water use	196
11.7	Kempinski Hotel Corvinus, Budapest	197
11.8	Water-saving websites	198
12.1	Features to look for in restaurant management systems	203
13.1	Definitions related to FLW	210
13.2	Industrial food production and contamination-related losses in the USA	212
13.3	Monklands Hospital, Airdrie, Scotland	219
13.4	Food losses in fuel stations	221
13.5	Food waste management on cruise ships	222
13.6	Food remains as surprise menu	224
13.7	Waste distribution charities	230
13.8	FAO food loss and waste database	232
14.1	Saudi Arabian and Indian attitudes towards leftover food	235
14.2	The Guardians of Grub	239
14.3	Reducing plate waste	241
14.4	"Clean dish, clean conscience!"	241
14.5	Which nudges work best in reducing food waste?	243
14.6	Does being vegetarian reduce food waste? The case of Korean restaurant diners	244
14.7	Overview of steps in strategic food waste (avoidance) management	248
15.1	Food for Soul	253
15.2	Chefs in School	258
15.3	Mainstreaming organic food in public kitchens and canteens	259

Boxes

16.1	Mark Bittman on the true costs of our cheap food and the American diet	265
16.2	The influence of chefs on sustainability	267
16.3	The professional kitchen is not a TV set	269
16.4	Alternative food delivery platforms	272

Preface and acknowledgements

Michael would like to acknowledge colleagues in the Department of Management, Marketing and Entrepreneurship, University of Canterbury, New Zealand; the Geography Research Unit, University of Oulu, Finland; Tourism, Linnaeus University, Kalmar, Sweden; Department of Service Management and Service Studies, Lund University, Helsingborg, Sweden and the Department of Food, Nutrition and Culinary Science, Umeå University, Sweden. In addition, Michael would like to specifically thank a number of colleagues and friends with whom he has undertaken food-related conversations and research over the years, including Amelia Bryden, Bailey Adie, Alberto Amore, Tim Baird, Paul Ballantine, Dorothee Bohn, Chris Chen, Tim Coles, Hervé Corvellec, David Duval, Alexandra Gillespie, Martin Gren, Dikte Grønvold, Johan Hultman, Muhammad Azman Ibrahim, MJ Kim, Tyron Love, Val Marquez, Dieter Müller, Jan-Henrik Nilsson, Yuri Oh, Girish Prayag, Yael Ram, Hiran Roy, Jarkko Saarinen, Anna Dóra Sæþórsdóttir, Dan Scott, Liz Sharples, Allan Williams, Kimberley Wood and Maria José Zapata Campos for their thoughts, as well as for the stimulation of Fiona Apple, Ann Brun, Beirut, Paul Buchanan, Bill Callahan, Nick Cave, Bruce Cockburn, Dimmer, Ebba Fosberg, PJ Harvey, Hennessy, Mark Hollis, Aimee Mann, Larkin Poe, Vinnie Reilly, Henry Rollins, Emma Swift, TISM, Henry Wagon and The Guardian, BBC6, JJ and KCRW – for making the world much less confining. Special mention must also be given to the Malmö Saluhall; Balck, Packhuset and Postgarten in Kalmar; Bertels Salon in Copenhagen; Campbell's Butchery, Dalante Artisan Bakery, Decant, Deutsches Eck German Butchery, Emilio's Cheese, Evansdale Cheese, Karikaas Cheese, Star and Garter, Tees Street Café, Vinbrux Bakery, Whitestone Cheese and the Tai Tapu Milk Company in Te Waipounamu; and Nicole Aignier and the Hotel Grüner Baum in Merzhausen. Finally, and most importantly, Michael would like to thank the Js and the Cs who stay at home and mind the farm.

We also wish to gratefully acknowledge the help and support of Jody Cowper-James for her indispensable proofreading and editing and Thu Ha Nguyen who prepared several of the graphs in the book. Finally, we would both like to thank Emma Travis, Lydia Kessell and all at Routledge for their continuing support in trying circumstances.

Abbreviations

APEO	alkylphenolethoxylates
APD	alkylphenol derivatives
B&I	business and industry
BAU	Business as Usual
CEM	Comprehensive Energy Management
CFL	compact fluorescent lamps
CIEL	Center for International Environmental Law
CO_2-eq	carbon dioxide equivalent
DADMAC	dialkyl dimethyl ammonium chloride
DCKV	demand-controlled kitchen ventilation
DBP	di-n-butylphthalate
DEHP	di(2-ethylhexyl)phthalate
DHW	domestic hot water
EMS	Energy Management System
FAFH	food away from home
FAH	food at home
FAO	Food and Agricultural Organisation of the United Nations
FOG	fat, oil and grease
FLW	food loss and waste
FUSIONS	Food Use for Social Innovation by Optimising Waste Prevention Strategies
GHG	greenhouse gas
HaFS	hospitality and food service sector
HVAC	heating, ventilation and air conditioning
IEA	International Energy Agency
IFAD	International Fund for Agricultural Development
IFOAM	International Federation of Organic Agriculture Movements
ILC	International Land Coalition
IPCC	Intergovernmental Panel on Climate Change
L	litre (2.11 pints)
LAS	linear alkylbenzene sulphonates
LCA	Life Cycle Assessment
LED	light-emitting diode
NRA	National Restaurant Association
NZEB	net-zero energy buildings
nZEB	near-zero energy buildings
PAHs	polycyclic aromatic hydrocarbons

PCBs	polychlorinated biphenyls
PEC	primary energy consumption
PFAS	per- and polyfluoroalkyl substances
POS	point of sale
POPs	persistent organic pollutants
RABDF	Royal Association of British Dairy Farmers
RMS	restaurant management system
SDGs	Sustainable Development Goals
SRA	Sustainable Restaurant Association
UNICEF	United Nations International Children's Emergency Fund
USDA	United States Department of Agriculture
WEF	World Economic Forum
WFP	United Nations World Food Programme
WHO	World Health Organization
WRI	World Resources Institute

Chapter 1

Introduction

The advantages of a sustainable kitchen

Introduction

'Green', 'sustainable', 'local' and 'organic' foods are major menu items for many restaurants and are a focal point not only of positioning and promotion but also of consumer demand. But what do these terms mean, especially when they seem to be used so widely? And, if they are speaking to how the hospitality and food services sector responds to issues of climate and environmental change then how do managers, chefs and staff know how to apply these concepts in the kitchen? This chapter provides an introduction to these issues by highlighting how concepts of sustainability are important not only for a greener kitchen but also for the bottom line. The chapter provides an explanation for the design of the book, the inherent difficulties that emerge when it comes to examining sustainability in the kitchen and in the front of house and discusses how it can be used by stressing that there are many ways in which any kitchen, restaurant or foodservice operation can reduce its impact on the environment.

In this book, we will often use the terms 'sustainable restaurant' or 'sustainable food services'. This, in part, reflects the wide range of food-related businesses and organizations that exist. This book focuses on the sustainability of the hospitality and food services sector, which includes all outlets that serve food and/or drinks for immediate intake in an out-of-home setting (Dhir et al., 2020). This means that the notion of food services includes both profit/commercial and cost-driven/non-commercial organizations (Marthinsen et al., 2012; WRAP, 2020). The wide range of foodservice operations that this includes is illustrated in Table 1.1, which shows the estimates of food waste for premises in the UK by the different sectors.

In general terms, the profit sector includes hotels, restaurants and cafés (HORECA), and commercial catering. Restaurants include establishments serving different cuisines and food styles, as well as quick-service restaurants (QSR) also referred to as fast-food outlets that offer both eat-in or takeaway at various locations, as well as cafés. Hotels include accommodation providers such as luxury, business or budget hotels, bed & breakfasts, catered apartments and hostels. Both restaurants and hotels also cover catering services. Other for-profit foodservice businesses include commercial catering, such as that available at events and convention centres as well as for clients. Cost-driven or institutional foodservice operations include the health care sector (hospitals, nursing homes and care centres); education (preschools, primary and secondary schools, tertiary

Table 1.1 Number of premises and food waste arising by hospitality and food services sector in the UK, 2015 and 2018

Source: WRAP (2020)

Sector	Number of premises 2015	Number of premises 2018	Food waste 2015 (t)	Food waste 2018 (t)
Profit sector				
Quick-Service Restaurant	37,000	39,000	103,000	106,000
Restaurants	56,000	63,000	253,000	289,000
Pubs and clubs	40,000	46,000	202,000	234,000
Hotels	13,000	13,000	83,000	88,000
Leisure, transport and sport	14,000	15,000	60,000	61,000
Total profit sector			702,000	779,000
	Number of people or other unit 2015	Number of people or other unit 2018		
Cost sector				
Education, of which:			125,000	127,000
Primary schools (all sizes)	5,356,000	5,575,000	66,000	68,000
Secondary schools (all sizes)	3,790,000	3,869,000	28,000	28,000
Further education (all sizes)	1,362,000	940,000	5,000	4,000
Higher education (all sizes)	2,092,000	2,343,000	2,000	3,000
Other education			24,000	25,000
Health, of which:			120,000	120,000
Nursing and residential	535,000	535,000	59,000	59,000
Hospitals (catering units)	1,000	1,000	61,000	61,000
Services, of which:			65,000	62,000
Prisons	95,000	85,000	19,000	17,000
Military bases (number)	1,000	1,000	46,000	46,000
Staff catering (number of premises offering)	8,000	8,000	22,000	21,000
Total cost sector			332,000	331,000

education institutions, colleges and universities) and staff catering such as canteens and cafeterias located in workplaces for feeding employees (Dhir et al., 2020).

The wide range of businesses, organizations and institutions involved in food services means that the sector is inherently complex with different drivers that will affect how notions of sustainability can be implemented (Filimonau & De Coteau, 2019). For example, while restaurants can consider food donation as a way of dealing with waste, hospitals will usually not have that option available to them due to the risk of infection (Dhir et al., 2020). A further complicating factor is that as a result of outsourcing many of the food services in public hospitals and educational facilities are now provided by commercial catering businesses (Gray et al., 2017; Carino et al., 2020). Therefore, Dhir et al. (2020) suggest that hospitality and food services comprise three main segments: (a) a business segment, including accommodations and food service at hotels, restaurants, cafés, workplace canteens, inflight catering, snack bars, coffee shops and pubs; (b) an education segment, including nurseries, primary schools, secondary schools, tertiary education centres, colleges and universities and (c) a health care segment, comprising hospitals, elder care, retirement homes and nursing homes. In this book, we will primarily concentrate on the business segment, although, given the substantial overlap that exists, we will also be referring to examples from the education and health care segments.

Environmentally friendly eating

There is no single definition of environmentally friendly eating, but usually environmentally friendly eating is regarded as something that leads to one or all of the following:

- a reduction in the throughput of resources (e.g., energy, water and other resources);
- the conservation of biodiversity; and/or
- reduced production of waste and/or GHG emissions (Vanhonacker et al., 2013).

Consideration of environmentally friendly eating means that attention is given not only to food preparation and waste reduction in foodservice operations but also to the supply chain (Pirani & Arafat, 2016; Wang et al., 2017). The latter is extremely important because agriculture uses almost two-fifths of the world's land area and almost a third of fish stocks are presently overfished (Food and Agriculture Organization of the United Nations (FAO), 2016, 2018b, 2019c) (see Chapter 2). Crippa et al. (2021) estimated that in 2015, food-system emissions amounted to 18 Gt CO_2 equivalent per year globally, representing 34% of total GHG emissions with the largest contribution to this figure coming from agriculture and land use/land-use change activities (71%), with the remaining from supply chain activities. If food waste were a country, it would have the third biggest carbon footprint after the USA and China. Meat and dairy production is a major contributor to GHG emissions, water use and nutrient pollution of waterways (Vanhonacker et al., 2013; McCabe, 2017). As a result, the adoption of more plant-based diets may provide substantial reductions in GHG emissions and environmental change relative to non-vegetarian diets (Berners-Lee et al., 2012; Turner-McGrievy et al., 2016). Therefore, a substantial challenge to the restaurant and foodservice industry is how to make vegetarian and vegan food more exciting to consumers, especially to those for who perceive meat as being an essential part of any meal or even as denoting some form of status in food consumption (Kim et al., 2020).

Nevertheless, what is perceived as environmentally friendly eating and the relative environmental impact of food services can vary between different locations as well as different types of foodservice providers. For example, while food waste is usually identified as the most recognized environmental impact of hospitality operations (Filimonau & Magklaropoulou, 2020), a study by Filimonau and Sulyok (2021) of restaurant managers in Hungary found that plastic waste was the most mentioned in interviews, followed by energy with food waste coming third. According to Filimonau and Sulyok (2021),

> high managerial awareness of energy use as an environmental impact of foodservices can be explained by the relative 'tangibility' of its consumption.

> Indeed, energy use has a clear monetary value .... In contrast, [food waste] was seen as an indirect, 'hidden', operational expense, which was partially covered by customers, or even as the operational necessity. The immediate availability and affordability of municipal FW collection services was mentioned as another reason for why the issue of FW was insufficiently recognised by restaurateurs.

Similarly, sustainability behaviours and priorities can differ between institutional foodservice sectors. Huang et al. (2011) examined hospital foodservice sustainable practices from the perspective of foodservice director and found that the most common sustainable practices were recycling practices such as recycling fat, oil and grease, cardboard, paper and using permanent cutlery. In contrast, in the case of sustainable practices in college and university dining services, Chen (2008) found that the most frequently implemented sustainable practices were recycling cardboard; using recycled paper products; recycling aluminium; and recycling fat, oil and grease. Eighty-nine percent of her respondents had purchased energy-saving equipment such as light bulbs, refrigerators and dishwashers. Significantly, the most important factor identified in the adoption of sustainable practices was not a desire from within the kitchen for change but social pressures from university administrators and students to have a more sustainable kitchen (Chen et al., 2011). Interestingly, Raab et al. (2018) found that restaurant managers were most influenced by pressures from their suppliers, customers and to a lesser extent from their employees and by expectations of society at large.

Box 1.1   Food waste hot spots

The type of cuisines, meals and foodservice provider can all influence whether some food items are wasted more than others, and these are collectively referred to as food waste hot spots (Dhir et al., 2020). Some of the main food waste hot spots in foodservice outlets, including schools, day-care centres, workplace canteens, petrol stations, restaurants and diners, include salads and side dishes such as pasta, potatoes, vegetables and rice (Silvennoinen et al., 2015). However, there can be substantial differences between countries. For example, in a study of the Delish restaurant chain in Canada by Charlebois et al. (2015), plate waste was much more likely to be starches, which are low-cost items, as opposed to meat which is a high-cost protein. In contrast, a study of a hotel restaurant in Malaysia identified fruits, vegetables, sauces, oils and fats as the hot spot (Papargyropoulou et al., 2016).

Inflight service on airlines provides another example of a food waste hot spot. For Egypt Airlines economy class, the breakfast snack meal generated the highest weight of waste of all meals which recorded an average of 265 g. Interestingly, plastic waste generated varied from 39.6% to 64.6% by weight for the various types of meals served (El-Mobaidh et al., 2006). A study by Blanca-Alcubilla et al. (2018) as part of a European Union zero cabin waste project found that, from a Life Cycle Assessment (LCA) approach, menus with a greater amount of foods of vegetable origin will have a lower carbon footprint than those that have meat, especially beef. However, in terms of waste, a study by Thamagasorn and Pharino (2019) of halal food airline catering found that vegetable wastes accounted for 40%–50% of the total food waste generated.

Box 1.2 The plastic problem

The term plastic is used to refer to various types of polymers, which are synthesized from monomers that are polymerized to form macromolecular chains. Plastics have become a ubiquitous part of both the food services industry and the environmental problems facing the planet. Plastics are having a major impact on the environment and also on human health and wellbeing:

> Roughly two-thirds of all plastic ever produced has been released into the environment and remain there in some form—as debris in the oceans, as micro- or nanoparticles in air and agricultural soils, as microfibers in water supplies, or as microparticles in the human body.
> (Center for International Environmental Law (CIEL), 2019, p. 5)

More than 99% of plastic produced is manufactured from fossil fuels, primarily ethylene and propylene which are derived from natural gas, or from naphtha, a by-product of crude oil refining; and propylene which can also be derived from coal. As of 2015, of the approximately 6,300 Mt of plastic waste generated, around 9% had been recycled, 12% incinerated and 79% accumulated in landfills or the natural environment (Geyer et al., 2017), with the oceans often being an end point for the accumulation of plastic wastes. Plastic is hydrophobic, meaning it tends to absorb hydrophobic persistent organic pollutants (POPs), such as polychlorinated biphenyls (PCBs) and polycyclic aromatic hydrocarbons (PAHs) while circulating in marine waters (Ogata et al., 2009). The accumulated pollutants can concentrate to as much as 100 times background levels in sea water (Mato et al., 2001). Some of these chemicals have also been found to desorb into the tissues of marine species when ingested, therefore posing threats to species and environmental health, including humans and other animals at the top of the food chain (Browne et al., 2013; Eerkes-Medrano et al., 2015; Rochman et al., 2015; Auta et al., 2017; CIEL, 2019). The different stages in the production of plastic and their implications for human health are indicated in Table 1.2.

It is so common for chemicals to migrate from packaging into food that the US *Food Drug and Cosmetics Act* defines food packaging chemicals as indirect food additives (21 U.S.C. §321(s) in CIEL, 2019). Migration of chemicals from food packaging, including plastic wraps, into food and beverages is regarded as the main source of human exposure to plastic contaminants (Grob et al., 2006). At least 175 chemicals that are known to be hazardous (i.e., endocrine disrupters, reproductive toxics, mutagens or carcinogens) are used in food contact materials in the USA and the European Union (EU) (Geueke et al., 2014). Of the 4,000 chemicals approved in the USA to be intentionally added in food packaging, only about a quarter of them have been evaluated for health risks, and even then often only in a very limited way (Geueke et al., 2014; Muncke et al., 2017; CIEL, 2019).

Swan and Colina (2021) highlight the dangers of chemicals in plastic with respect to human (and other animals) reproductive health because they can interfere with or mimic sex hormones, such as testosterone and oestrogen. Phthalates, used to make plastic soft and flexible, are used in food manufacture, processing and packaging. They lower testosterone and therefore diminish sperm count in men, while in women they have been shown to decrease libido and

Table 1.2 Plastics and health

Source: CIEL (2019)

Stage of plastic life cycle	Emissions	Exposure	Health
Extraction & transport	Include benzene, volatile organic compounds (VOCs) and 170+ toxic chemicals in fracking fluid. Pipelines emit methane, ethane, benzene, toluene, xylene, carbon monoxide, ozone and other pollutants	Inhalation and ingestion (air and water)	Affects the immune system, sensory organs, liver and kidney; impacts include cancers, neuro-, reproductive and developmental toxicity
Refining & manufacture	Include benzene, polycyclic aromatic hydrocarbons (PAHs) and styrene	Inhalation, ingestion and skin contact (air, water and soils)	Impacts can include cancers, neuro-toxicity, reproductive toxicity, low birth weight, and eye and skin irritation
Consumer use	Include heavy metals, persistent organic pollutants (POPs), carcinogens, endocrine disrupting chemicals (EDCs) and microplastics	Inhalation, ingestion and skin contact	Affects renal, cardiovascular, gastro-intestinal, neurological, reproductive and respiratory systems; impacts include cancers, diabetes and developmental toxicity
Waste management	Include heavy metals, dioxins and furans, PAHs and toxic recycling	Ingestion and inhalation (air, ash and slag)	Impacts include cancers, neurological damages, and damages to immune, reproductive, nervous and endocrine system
Environmental exposure to microplastics (e.g., tyre dust and textile fibres) and toxic additives: including POPs, EDCs, carcinogens and heavy metal		Inhalation and ingestion (air, water and food chain)	Affects cardiovascular, renal, gastro-intestinal, neurological, reproductive and respiratory systems; impacts include cancers, diabetes, neuro-, reproductive and developmental toxicity

increase the risk of early puberty, miscarriage and premature birth (Swan & Colina, 2021). Bisphenol A (BPA), which is used to harden plastic and is found in the lining of some canned-food containers, mimics oestrogen and therefore affects women's fertility while men that are occupationally exposed to BPA have been shown to have decreased sperm quality, reduced libido and higher rates of erectile dysfunction (Swan & Colina, 2021). In terms of reducing exposure Shanna Swan advocates, "To the extent possible, eat unprocessed foods – a bunch of carrots, potatoes that you cook yourself – as this should reduce exposure through plastic. Also, when cooking, don't use Teflon or anything coated and don't microwave in plastic" (quoted in Corbyn, 2021).

The different sizes of plastic in the environment are also defined by size. Macroplastics are generally defined as plastic items larger than 5 mm. A compilation by the CIEL (2019) of the top 20 most common products found in six different international sets of shoreline data well illustrates the different types of plastic products reaching the environment and being found on beaches (Table 1.3). Importantly for the food services sector with respect to sustainability and human health, 75% of the listed items are some type of food and beverage packaging (wrappers, bottles and bottle caps, straws, stirrers, lids, utensils, containers, cups and plates) (Table 1.3). Microplastics are generally recognized as synthetic organic polymer particles less than 5 mm at their longest point. Microplastics can be detected in environmental sampling down to 1 micron in size, but few studies identify particles smaller than 50 microns. Nanoplastics are generally defined as 1–100 nm (Imhof et al., 2016). Macro-, micro- and nanoplastics are increasingly entering the human food chain from what humans eat and drink, including via bottled water (European Food Safety Authority (EFSA), 2016; CIEL, 2019).

In restaurants, plastics are to be found in plastic food wrapping and storage containers, especially commercial-grade food storage containers, as the containers for cleaning products, and most damaging of all as the containers for takeaway food and drink, carry bags and plastic knives and forks. Per- and polyfluoroalkyl substances (PFASs) are highly persistent synthetic chemicals, some of which have been associated with cancer, developmental toxicity, immunotoxicity and other health effects. PFASs in grease-resistant food packaging can leach into food and increase dietary exposure. Schaider et al. (2017) collected samples of food contact papers, paperboard containers and beverage containers from fast-food restaurants throughout the USA and measured total fluorine. They found that 46% of food contact papers (dessert and bread wrappers 56%, sandwich and burger wrappers 38%) and 20% of paperboard samples contained detectable fluorine (>16 nmol/cm^2). Paper cups had low concentrations, although previous studies had noted their presence (Trier et al., 2011). Plastic wrapping and containers are also extensively used in prepared foods that are often used in catering. Cirillo et al. (2011) evaluated the levels of di(2-ethylhexyl)phthalate (DEHP) and di-n-butylphthalate (DBP) and the influence of the packaging process on meal contamination in pre-packed school meals. The packaging consisted of polyethylene-coated aluminium (PE/Al) dishes thermally welded by a polyethyleneterephthalate-coated aluminium (PET/Al) foil. Ninety-two percent of foodstuffs employed in meal preparation contained DEHP, and 76% of them DBP, at detectable levels. The mean increases in median concentrations of DEHP in cooked foods before and after packaging were 113% and 125% for DBP.

Table 1.3 The top 20 products in shoreline waste data: merged datasets
Source: CIEL (2019)

Plastic product	Source dataset					Project aware	Total	%
	ICC	NOAA	MoT	Heal the Bay	COA			
Food wrappers (candy, chips, etc.)	318,880.0	272.0	16,315.0	307.0	14,827.0	217.0	350,818.0	18.6
Bottle caps (plastic)	273,089.0	779.0	11,735.0	27,352.0	2,328.0	205.1	315,488.1	16.7
Beverage bottles (plastic)	206,993.0	122.0	7,809.0	6,297.0	5,508.0	289.0	227,018.0	12.0
Bags (plastic)	157,702.0	39.0	6,970.0	5,249.0	7,871.0	313.0	178,144.0	9.4
Straws, stirrers	125,635.0	172.0	4,645.0	4,026.0	8,102.0	165.0	142,745.0	7.5
Lids (plastic)	75,921.0	186.9	409.0	5,829.5	15,347.0	57.9	97,751.2	5.1
Utensils	42,599.0	33.0	1,848.0	47,133.0	1,864.0	352.0	93,829.0	4.9
Cigarette butts[a]	51,550.5	25.3	2,337.9	6,775.9	643.0	9.1	61,341.7	3.2
Take-out/away containers (foam)	41,805.0	102.9	537.7	17,696.0	548.0	8.3	60,697.8	3.2
Take-out/away containers (plastic)	49,973.0	123.0	37.0	5,624.0	1,021.7	9.9	56,788.6	3.0
Cups, plates (plastic)	48,559.0	14.6	732.6	1,862.2	1,766.0	9.6	52,943.9	2.8
Cigar tips	41,211.0	47.0	328.0	6,243.0	2,351.0	16.0	50,196.0	2.6
Cups, plates (foam)	42,047.0	12.4	4,495.7	690.0	2,021.0	8.3	49,274.5	2.6
Tobacco packaging/wrap	33,434.0	82.3	604.5	352.0	694.0	19.0	35,185.8	1.8
Balloons	23,492.0	19.0	1,442.0	5,263.0	480.3	13.0	30,709.3	1.6
Other plastic bottles	17,548.0	62.0	1,578.0	4,769.6	1,429.0	9.0	25,395.6	1.3
Cigarette lighters	10,750.0	24.0	676.5	10,750.0	405.0	3.0	22,608.5	1.2
Personal care products (condoms & tampon applicators)	11,555.0	37.4	827.5	2,213.2	1,875.1	14.0	16,522.2	0.8
6-pack holders	8,224.0	3.0	180.0	641.0	130.0	10.0	9,188.0	0.4
Diapers	3,938.0	12.5	276.8	2,150.6	82.0	7.0	6,466.9	0.3
Total	1,584,905.5	2,169.3	63,785.2	161,223.9	69,293.0	1,735.1	1,883,112.0	100

[a] Counts of cigarette butts were divided by 20 to represent packs rather than individual cigarettes.

High volumes and often short usage phases make food and drink packaging highly visible. Fast-food restaurants are already positively associated with the consumption of ultra-processed foods. However, because of their packaging and the emphasis on takeaways they are also major users of sources of plastics (Souza & Louzada, 2020). In a report on public perceptions of plastic post-COVID-19, *The Grocer* (2021) presented the results of a January 2021 UK survey of 1,000 people. One in three (33%) said solving plastic pollution has become more important to them since the COVID-19 outbreak with just 8% saying it is now less important. More than one in five (21%) respondents said that plastic remains the most important environmental issue to them with 75% reporting plastic pollution as one of many issues of equal importance (The Grocer, 2021).

Much of the opposition to plastics is based on visual pollution and growing awareness of the impacts of microplastics. However, plastics are also a significant contributor to greenhouse gas and other emissions at various stages of their life cycle. For example, of the 46 studies that were conducted on fracking between 2009 and 2015 and that dealt with air quality, 87% of these indicated elevated air pollution emissions (Hays & Shonkoff, 2016). Overall,

> the toxic impacts of the plastic lifecycle on human health are over-whelming. While many actions will be necessary to confront this threat to human life and human rights, it is clear that urgent, global action is needed to reduce the production and consumption of plastic and associated toxic chemicals.
> (CIEL, 2019, p. 64)

can potentially contribute to other social goals (Higgins-Desbiolles & Wijesinghe, 2019). For example, in recent years the interrelationships between environmental, public and individual health in food consumption have become increasingly highlighted (e.g., van Dooren & Aiking, 2016; McCabe, 2017; Fresán et al., 2018; Kaljonen et al., 2019; Willett et al., 2019b). Unhealthy diets are the largest global burden of disease with "2.1 billion adults overweight or obese and the global prevalence of diabetes almost doubling in the past 30 years" (Willett et al., 2019b, p. 449). Reductions in red meat and sugar consumption and increases in plant-based foods, such as fruits, vegetables, nuts and legumes, can improve personal health as well as produce environmental benefits (McCabe, 2017; Willett et al., 2019b).

Much of shifts in what we eat to include more meat, sugar and salt and less raw fruit and vegetables is a result of the changes that have taken place in the industrialization of the global food system. As a result, and given the effects on obesity and health, there has been a significant response to counter the industrialization of food by championing pre-industrial era diets that encouraged greater food diversity as well as the use of unprocessed foods. Importantly, chefs and restaurants have been at the forefront of such movements (Kim et al., 2020). Therefore, there has been promotion of, for example, the Mediterranean diet as an environmentally friendly eating because of its ecosystem, nutritional, sociocultural and economic benefits (Fresán et al., 2018). Other pre-consumerism diets have also attracted interest. For example, van Dooren and Aiking (2016) quantified the historical Dutch 'Low Lands' diet of circa 1930s and used a life cycle analysis to compare it with the present Dutch, Mediterranean and New Nordic Diets. They found that an optimized Low Lands diet has almost the same healthy nutritional characteristics as the Mediterranean diet but resulted in a lower environmental impact than the Mediterranean and New Nordic diets.

Introduction

Interest in environmentally friendly eating is also growing in the restaurant and catering sector with increased attention to menu offerings (Kaljonen et al., 2019) as well as the provision of meat substitutes (Kearney, 2019). For example, McDonald's development of plant-based meat alternatives, the McPlant burger, therefore not only shows responsiveness to consumer demand but can also potentially have a positive effect on the food chain. According to Matei,

> no matter what you think of the fast food chain's marketing department, the McPlant actually represents a meaningful milestone for plant-based protein products. This is a real step toward a greener world. While other chains, such as Burger King and Dunkin' Donuts, have already launched plant-based meat items, the impact of the planet's most popular fast food chain – which sells a dizzying 75 burgers every second – could be decisive in allowing plant-based meat alternatives to catch on in the mainstream.
>
> Simply put, the more accessible meat alternatives are, the better, given the need for humans to change the ways we consume and produce food to ensure a sustainable future.
>
> (Matei, 2020)

Defining the sustainable restaurant

There is no single definition of a sustainable restaurant or foodservice operation (Kim & Hall, 2020). Different countries and regions have different emphases on strategies and practices as do different types of food businesses and individual businesses (National Restaurant Association (NRA), 2018; Raab et al., 2018; Higgins-Desbiolles et al., 2019). The range of sustainability practices and strategies is illustrated in Jang's (2016) survey of top-level restaurant managers, i.e., those with the ultimate management discretion, in all types of restaurants (e.g., stand-alone establishments or part of a hotel or chain) in the

---

Box 1.3 EU citizens perceptions of what constitutes sustainable food

For Europeans, food is 'sustainable' when it is nutritious and healthy (41%), it has been produced with little or no use of pesticides (32%) and when it is affordable for all (29%). Nearly a quarter consider 'local or short supply chains' (24%) as an important characteristic of sustainable food and over one in five cite the 'low environmental and climate impact' of food (22%).

Europeans consider food being healthy for them (74%) as the most important aspect of a sustainable diet, far above all other items. For nearly 60% of Europeans, a healthy and sustainable diet involves eating a 'variety of different foods, having a balanced diet' and 'eating more fruit and vegetables' (both 58%). While nearly 50% mention eating seasonal, local (47%), at least 40% of respondents mentioned 'eating more home-cooked meals' (43%), 'little or no pesticides' (43%), 'avoiding wasting food' (42%), and 'avoiding or not eating too much food high in fat, sugars and/or salt' (40%). In addition to health concerns, Europeans identify a number of other elements as important with respect to sustainable food. Half refer to food choices that support the local economy while around 40% consider that sustainable diets 'minimize waste' (40%), address social concerns (such as fair 'wages and workers' rights' (39%)) and protect the environment ('what you eat is good for the planet' (37%)) are also important (BEUC, 2020; Eurobarometer, 2020).

USA that had implemented environmental practices (e.g., recycling, using local food, using energy-efficient equipment). Jang's (2016) sample differed slightly from those of the nationwide population of US restaurant managers and had a higher proportion of female (47.1%) and younger managers (average age of 38). Results of the survey are illustrated for all restaurants as well as whether they are chain-affiliated or not, as well as by the type of restaurant (Tables 1.4 and 1.5). The nature of ownership of a restaurant is regarded as significant as it can affect the capacity of individual managers and staff to make decisions (Park & Kim, 2014; Park et al., 2014). For example, managers of independent restaurants have more discretionary power than managers of chain restaurants to develop environmental initiatives (Park & Kim, 2014), such as purchasing local food (Roy, 2016). The survey is also useful as it includes a larger number of strategies and practices than that used in the US National Restaurant Association (NRA) sustainability survey (2018).

Jang (2016) found that most restaurants were performing the six environmental sustainability strategies (Table 1.4) and 16 environmental sustainability practices (Table 1.5) he evaluated on to a modest degree. The most widely adopted strategy was purchasing environmentally friendly (e.g., biodegradable, reusable, recyclable) products. The most frequently implemented environmental practice was the use of energy-efficient lighting, followed by separating waste for recycling, using energy-efficient products and equipment, donating food leftovers to a food bank or equivalent organization and recycling. The least-utilized practice was the implementation of renewable energy programmes.

Significant differences exist between independent and chain restaurants with respect to commitment to environmental sustainability strategies and practices. Chain restaurants were found to be more active in informing stakeholders about their environmental practices than independent restaurants via annual reports or by their websites. However, such a result should not be surprising given the corporate nature of chain enterprises, regulatory requirements for reporting for public companies and the increasing significance of sustainability issues for corporate brand equity (Namkung & Jang, 2013; Jang et al., 2015; Kang & Namkung, 2018; Sung et al., 2020). In terms of environmental practices, significant differences were found between independent and chain restaurants with respect to purchasing locally grown food, purchase foods grown without use of toxic synthetic pesticides, composting of kitchen waste, use of reusable items (e.g., cloth napkins, glass cups, ceramic dishes), recycling measures and support for local communities. Independent restaurants displayed significantly higher mean scores than chain-affiliated restaurants for purchasing environmentally friendly foods, purchasing locally grown foods and purchasing foods grown without use of toxic synthetic pesticides and composting kitchen waste. Independent restaurants showed higher involvement in reuse and recycling practices as well as being more likely to support the environmental activities of local communities.

In terms of environmental strategies, compared to casual and fast-food restaurants, upscale restaurants were shown to be significantly more likely to monitor and record environmental performance; implement employee environmental training programmes and recognize and reward environmental initiatives of employees. With respect to environmental sustainability practices, significant differences were found among the three types of restaurants (Table 1.5). Upscale and casual restaurants were more likely to purchase locally grown food and support local communities than fast-food restaurants. Compared to casual and fast-food restaurants, upscale restaurants implemented more renewable energy programmes, used more water-saving faucets, composted more kitchen waste and handled more FOG waste and also used more reusable items. The sustainability activities of upscale restaurants led Jang (2016, pp. 60–61) to conclude, "the commitment of upscale restaurants to environmental

Table 1.4 Restaurant sustainability strategies

Source: Adapted from Jang (2016)

Environmental sustainability strategies	All restaurants		Chain affiliation						By restaurant type						
			Independent		Chain				Upscale		Casual		Fast food		
	Mean	SD	Mean	SD	Mean	SD	t-value		Mean	SD	Mean	SD	Mean	SD	F-value
Incorporates environmental management into policy	5.36	1.320	5.38	1.28	5.34	1.37	0.254		5.43	1.33	5.35	1.26	5.18	1.38	0.606
Monitors and records our environmental performance	4.72	1.801	4.61	186	4.81	1.76	−0.800		4.98^a	1.60	4.73^{a,b}	1.82	4.23^b	1.93	3.130*
Gives priority to purchasing environmentally friendly products (e.g., biodegradable, reusable, recyclable) over other environmentally harmful alternatives	5.65	1.337	5.61	1.36	5.67	1.32	−0.354		5.87	1.26	5.41	1.41	5.47	1.36	2.613
Implements employee environmental training programmes	4.74	1.736	4.75	1.76	4.74	1.73	0.007		5.15^a	1.67	4.73^{a,b}	1.61	4.10^b	1.73	6.984**
Recognizes and rewards environmental initiatives of employees	4.62	1.856	4.73	1.81	4.51	1.90	0.836		5.02^a	1.70	4.62^{a,b}	1.84	4.00^b	1.95	5.565**
Publishes regular external reports about environmental impacts or provides those information on website	4.02	2.026	3.71	2.07	4.32	1.93	−2.243*		4.35^a	1.95	4.06^{a,b}	2.10	3.53^b	1.88	2.968
Overall mean/SD	4.85	1.679													

Note: *$p < 0.05$; **$p < 0.01$.
[abc] indicates Tukey post-hoc comparisons; means that have different superscripts significantly differ.
Scale: 1 (To no extent) to 7 (To a very great extent).

Table 1.5 Adoption of environmental sustainability practices by US restaurants

Source: Adapted from Jang (2016)

Environmentally sustainability practices	All restaurants		By chain affiliation						By restaurant type						
			Independent		Chain				Upscale		Casual		Fast food		
	Mean	SD	Mean	SD	Mean	SD	t-value		Mean	SD	Mean	SD	Mean	SD	F-value
Purchases locally produced foods	5.35	1.841	5.90	1.34	4.86	2.07	4.338***		5.65	1.65	5.67	1.34	4.42	2.29	10.373***
Purchases foods grown without use of toxic synthetic pesticides or fertilizers	5.17	1.687	5.41	1.45	4.95	1.85	2.038*		5.33	1.56	5.32	1.51	4.85	1.96	1.733
Uses energy-efficient products and equipment (e.g., cooler, freezer, air conditioner, ice machine or steamer)	5.62	1.390	5.62	1.43	5.60	1.37	0.083		5.74	1.22	5.51	1.51	5.53	1.47	0.620
Uses high-energy-efficient lighting	5.83	1.200	5.76	1.29	5.87	1.12	0.623		5.88	1.30	5.73	1.13	5.85	1.12	0.302
Implements renewable energy programmes (e.g., use of wind or solar power)	3.26	2.055	3.09	2.05	3.41	2.05	−0.141		3.77	2.05	3.27	1.99	2.63	1.97	5.646**
Has water-efficient devices and equipment (e.g., water-efficient dishwashers)	5.23	1.753	5.19	1.78	5.25	1.75	−0.255		5.57	1.54	5.06	1.84	4.90	1.87	3.011
Uses water-saving faucets	4.98	1.998	5.08	1.82	4.89	2.14	0.677		5.51	1.66	4.81	2.01	4.43	2.19	5.830**
Gives food leftovers, e.g., to a food bank or food shelter	5.52	1.923	5.41	1.98	5.61	1.88	−0.756		5.74	1.74	5.59	1.84	5.38	2.15	0.614
Composts kitchen waste	5.09	2.037	5.57	1.64	4.68	2.28	3.245**		5.90	1.40	5.44	1.73	3.63	2.31	29.298***

Table 1.5 continued

Environmentally sustainability practices	All restaurants		By chain affiliation						By restaurant type						
			Independent		Chain				Upscale		Casual		Fast food		
	Mean	SD	Mean	SD	Mean	SD	t-value		Mean	SD	Mean	SD	Mean	SD	F-value
Collects fat, oil, grease (FOG) waste and gives it to a qualified company for recycling	4.10	2.291	4.31	2.28	3.84	2.29	1.518		4.58	2.15	4.03	2.27	3.32	2.30	5.633**
Uses reusable items (e.g., cloth napkins, glass cups, ceramic dishes)	4.43	2.323	4.82	2.24	4.07	2.36	2.395*		5.04	2.21	4.11	2.19	3.80	2.38	5.982**
Purchases used or recycled-content products (e.g., napkins or take-out containers made with post-consumer products)	5.38	1.686	5.56	1.55	5.19	1.79	1.621		5.63	1.57	5.10	1.65	5.15	1.84	2.312
Implements recycling programmes	5.51	1.510	5.78	1.40	5.25	1.58	2.627**		5.67	1.52	5.65	1.31	5.15	1.68	2.444
Sets recycling spot in order to properly classify waste and garbage	5.66	1.528	5.91	1.31	5.42	1.68	2.390*		5.82	1.43	5.78	1.39	5.33	1.77	2.033
Educates guests on environmentally friendly practices and policies	4.16	1.918	4.29	1.82	4.03	1.99	1.022		4.21	2.01	4.48	1.66	3.67	1.97	2.917
Supports local communities to enhance the local environment (e.g., participate in activities concerned about the environment, caring for the community)	5.22	1.742	5.55	1.43	4.91	1.94	2.718**		5.50	1.63	5.44	1.50	4.60	1.98	5.665**
Overall mean/SD	5.03	1.805													

Note: * $p < 0.05$; ** $p < 0.01$; *** $p < 0.001$.
Scale: 1 (To no extent) to 7 (To a very great extent).

performance appears indispensable to their profitability". While not examining profitability, Kim and Hall (2020) also highlighted the good business sense of restaurants adopting sustainable practices and found that sustainable restaurant practices enhanced customer loyalty, which is clearly valuable in the competitive restaurant market.

Differences in approaches to sustainable or green restaurants are also clearly illustrated in Table 1.6 which provides an overview of seven different sustainable restaurant and foodservice organizations and accreditation programmes around the world. The only common criterion is the use of sustainably harvested fish. Criteria which more than half of the programmes share include organic and local meat and/or vegetables; animal welfare in meat purchasing; certified ethically produced products; energy and water reduction; providing healthy eating/portion meals, offering vegetarian meals; waste reduction, reuse and recycling; community engagement and local partnerships and staff education and training on sustainable practices. While some criteria are not mandatory, most of the programmes also support restaurants that engage in food redistribution/food bank donation schemes (Hall et al., 2018).

The UK based and world-leading Sustainable Restaurant Association (SRA) does not provide a definition of a sustainable restaurant per se, but its aims suggest the direction in which it seeks to shift the restaurant, hospitality and foodservice sector: "The choices we make around the food we grow, cook, serve and eat are our biggest impact on the natural world. The problems facing our food system are complex and urgent. Where we eat out matters". The SRA's vision is "Eating out is good for everyone and has a restorative impact on the planet", while their mission is "We bring together progressive people working in food & empower them to change the system faster" (SRA, 2021). What is arguably significant in the SRA's approach is that they consider the entire food system in framing their approach to sustainability. As such the SRA's approach reflects the importance of developing sustainable culinary systems, in which combining concerns for present and future generations a sustainable culinary system seeks to demonstrate that it can optimize food output and consumption without compromising the stock of natural capital and ecosystem services (Gössling & Hall, 2013). Therefore, in order to reduce their environmental footprint, restaurant and foodservice operations need to become part of a circular economy rather than a linear one, so that inputs of virgin raw material and energy and outputs in the form of emissions and waste requiring disposal are reduced. However, from a system-wide perspective, and as will be highlighted in this book, at least three different approaches exist towards developing sustainable culinary systems each with a different emphasis (Table 1.7), while sustainability in relation to food is more than just an environmental problem because it is also shaped by social and economic concerns (Vidergar et al., 2020). Nevertheless, it is becoming increasingly clear that a Business as Usual (BAU) approach to food and business by the restaurant, catering and foodservice sector is no longer appropriate given the wide-ranging negative impacts of the modern, industrialized food system.

Assessing the sustainable restaurant and foodservice operation and becoming a sustainable chef: from farm to fork and beyond

How you conduct analysis and where you draw the boundaries can substantially affect the results you get when examining sustainability. This can be accurately restated in terms of an old computer programming term – GIGI – 'Garbage In, Garbage Out'. In the case of examining sustainable restaurants and foodservice operations, GIGO is an extremely important idea as while what happens in the kitchen is clearly significant, if

Table 1.6 Dimensions of sustainable restaurant and foodservice schemes

Source: After Hall et al. (2018)

	Sustainable Restaurant Association	Dine Green	Green Tourism	Sanitas Per Escam (Health through food)	REAL by US Healthful Foods Council	London Food Link: 'Good food for London'	Green Meeting Industry Council
Main objective	Build a community of passionate professionals and consumers working together to make food good for people and the planet.	Provide a transparent way to measure each restaurant's environmental accomplishments while providing a pathway for the next steps each restaurant can take towards increased environmental sustainability.	Encourage and enable people to make sustainable choices that reduce their impact on the planet.	Provide a universal, trusted standard for healthy and delicious dining outside the home.	Provide a trusted, nationally recognized mark of excellence for food and foodservice operators committed to holistic nutrition and environmental stewardship.	Working for a healthy, sustainable and ethical food system for the capital. Through our projects and campaigns we strive for a food system that benefits all Londoners.	Transform the global meetings industry through sustainability practices and provide advocacy, education, resources, industry research and recognition of industry leadership.
Primarily operating in	UK	North America	UK, Canada, Africa, Italy	Canada	USA	London, UK	USA, Canada, Singapore, Hong Kong
Products/services certified	Restaurants	Restaurants	Restaurants, lodging, tourism providers	Restaurants, hotels	Restaurants	Restaurants, catering, food system	Catering, food and beverage industry, Hotels
Scheme launch	2010	1990	1997	2001	2011	2011	2003

Introduction

	Sustainable Restaurant Association	Dine Green	Green Tourism	Sanitas Per Escam (Health through food)	REAL by US Healthful Foods Council	London Food Link: 'Good food for London'	Green Meeting Industry Council
Supply chain sourcing and procurement							
Sustainably harvested fish	●				●	●	●
Organic meat and/or vegetables		●	●		●		●
Local/regional meat and/or vegetables	●	●	●	●	●		●
Antibiotic free meats		●		●	●		
Animal welfare in meat purchasing	●	●			●		
Fair Trade products	●		●			●	
Certified ethically produced products	●		●				●
Sustainably/eco-certified products			●		●		●
Environmental practices							
Energy reduction	●	●	●				●
Water reduction	●	●	●				●
Water recycling	●	●					●
Healthy eating/portion size control				●	●	●	

Introduction

Table 1.6 continued

	Sustainable Restaurant Association	Dine Green	Green Tourism	Sanitas Per Escam (Health through food)	REAL by US Healthful Foods Council	London Food Link: 'Good food for London'	Green Meeting Industry Council
Vegetarian		•		•	•		
Low-carbon menu options		•					•
Sustainable restaurant design (recycled materials, passive energy, renewables, etc.)		•	•				
Sustainable kitchen design		•	•				•
Waste reduction, reuse and recycling	•	•	•		•		•
Food redistribution		•					•
Composting		•					•
Air quality		•					•
Social, economic and work practices							
Community engagement & local partnerships	•		•			•	•
Responsible marketing & communication	•						
Living wage				•	•	•	
Staff education and training on sustainable practices	•	•		•			
Food redistribution		•					•
Local/regional meat and/or vegetables	•	•	•	•	•		•

Table 1.7 Approaches to sustainable culinary systems

Source: Gössling and Hall (2013)

Elements of consumption and production	'Business as Usual' (BAU)	'Green growth'	'Traditional sustainable'	'Steady-state'/sustainable consumption
Concept of sustainability	The sustainability "problem" is defined in economic terms and the need for the reduction of regulatory barriers to the development of international food trade in order to allow market solutions to operate.	Although the approach seeks to balance the economic, environmental and social foundations of sustainability, sustainability is primarily defined in technical-rational economic terms that seek to encourage greater efficiency. Promotion of "green" economic growth via market and technological solutions.	Based on the development of 'traditional' methods of food production in Less Developed Countries in order to encourage food security on rural poor. 'Sustainable agriculture' as an alternative model for rural development. Limited attention to urban issues. Promotes sufficiency as well as efficiency.	Sustainability is understood as being grounded in the constraints of natural capital/natural systems. Includes aspects of sustained yield approaches together with environmental conservation (degrowth). Recognized as dependent on natural capital. Sufficiency more important than efficiency for sustainable consumption.
General characteristics	Based on 'Fordist' principles of seeking high labour productivity and economies of scale in all elements of the culinary system. Food consumption is based on a wide variety of mass commodities and is especially high in meat products. It is also characterized by high scientific input into food product and process innovation, including genome modification.	Responds to criticisms of the environmental effects of BAU approaches by looking to use technological and scientific approaches to encourage greater efficiencies in the industrial ecology of food, thereby reducing waste per capita as well as maintaining or increasing food output per capita. Genome modification is regarded as the most economical and environmentally friendly solution in many cases.	Emphasis on small-scale agricultural production and innovation that is culturally and ecologically sensitive to local needs and foodways.	Focused on food production that engages with natural systems and cycles in agriculture and processing in order to achieve social and economic sustainability goals. Cultural significance is given to 'natural' and 'organic' products and production methods as a means of ensuring human, plant, animal and ecosystem health. Strategy is focused on local food systems/foodsheds regarding production-consumption relations, although spatially extended short supply chains may be appropriate for some products, such as Fair Trade.

Table 1.7 continued

Elements of consumption and production	'Business as Usual' (BAU)	'Green growth'	'Traditional sustainable'	'Steady-state'/Sustainable consumption
Energy use	High-energy use along with high-energy efficiency in crop production.	High-energy use along with high-energy efficiency in crop production.	Renewable energy is used wherever possible.	Renewable energy use wherever possible. Renewable energy is subsidized and non-renewables taxed to reduce GHG emissions.
Control of pests and diseases	Application of pesticides or other agrochemicals, use of genome knowledge in the development of new strains.	Application of pesticides or other agrochemicals, use of genome knowledge in development of new strains. Biological methods employed where economically viable or regulation or public pressure requires its use.	Non-chemical solutions encouraged and use of natural pests.	Use of non-chemical solutions including overall management of cultivated ecology so as to encourage natural pests.
Overcoming soil fertility constraints	Application of chemical fertilizers.	Application of chemical fertilizers. Organic farming methods used for high-end niche markets only.	Limited chemical inputs together with nutrient recycling, natural nitrogen fixation and soil regeneration.	Closed nutrient cycles with much waste recycling.

Elements of consumption and production	'Business as Usual' (BAU)	'Green growth'	'Traditional sustainable'	'Steady-state/sustainable consumption
Solving water problems	Construction of large-scale water storage, supply and irrigation systems and genetic manipulation of crops and stock.	Construction of irrigation systems and genetic manipulation of crops and stock. Use of grey water where economically viable and public perceptions allow.	Small-scale water storage along with selection of appropriate local food species.	Small-scale water storage along with selection of appropriate food species for climate. Strong focus on water management.
Biodiversity	Loss of genetic diversity unless immediately economically valuable.	Potential long-term economic value of genetic diversity recognized for private sector innovation and wealth generation. Market approaches favoured for biodiversity conservation.	Substantial emphasis on maintaining and increasing local biodiversity; GM seeds based on local seed improvements and local genome ownership.	High emphasis on maintaining and increasing natural and cultivated biodiversity; no GM seeds or livestock.
Farm size	Large with small labour forces and high productivity of uniform products for mass markets. Animal welfare not a focus. Extremely high meat production. Potential transfer of farming approach to biofuel production.	Large with small labour forces and high productivity of a range of mass customized products. Animal welfare issue only when affects brand values. High levels of meat production as well as non-food production, such as biofuels and pharmaceuticals.	Small farms, based on traditional rural communities; high labour inputs and local intellectual capital. Limited meat production.	Smaller farms that BAU or green economy and more labour intensive. Production is primarily for local food system although some may be exported. Strong focus on animal welfare. Limited meat production.

Table 1.7 continued

Elements of consumption and production	'Business as Usual' (BAU)	'Green growth'	'Traditional sustainable'	'Steady-state/sustainable consumption
Food manufacture, processing and packaging	High levels of automation and processes. Focused on mass markets and increasing use of packaging to attract consumers.	High levels of innovation in food products, e.g., functional foods, processing methods, energy reduction and packaging. Focused on a large increase in demand for processed foods and meat products in developing countries. Quality developed via branding and industry self-regulation.	Primary focused on production improvement for local consumption, with limited processing. Regional food surpluses are exported.	Focus on certification and regulation throughout the food chain; as well as food quality criteria include waste management, packaging systems and energy-saving and emissions reduction systems in processing and transport.
Food distribution, wholesaling, retail and transport	Distribution based on flexible and intelligent *production-led* supply chains. Extended supply chains based on air, sea, rail and road transport. Increasing growth of supermarkets.	Distribution based on flexible and intelligent *co-produced* supply chains. Extended supply chains based on air, sea, rail and road transport. Limited changes for niche markets only. Increasing growth of supermarkets along with a small number of specialist food stores. Both supermarkets and specialist stores respond to highly specialized *consumption-led* supply chains, e.g., organic and local foods.	Distribution is localized with accompanying job creation and skills development. Use of traditional farmers markets. Surplus can be distributed to other regions.	Emphasis on environmental costs. Growth in organic products and more *local* food distribution. Shift to seasonal and regional foods with reductions in international trade in food products. Where international trade does occur social justice principles are a major consideration.

Elements of consumption and production	'Business as Usual' (BAU)	'Green growth'	'Traditional sustainable'	'Steady-state'/sustainable consumption
Food storage and preparation	High capital and energy intensity, with dependence on packaging and refrigeration.	High capital and energy intensity, with dependence on packaging and refrigeration. Some high-end market driven intelligent energy-saving devices.	Improvements in local storage by better pest management. Limited use of food storage and preparation equipment run on renewable energy.	Seeks to reduce energy intensity and therefore environmental and resource impacts while preserving nutritional quality.
Hospitality and Foodservice	Continued rise in out-of-home consumption of food in all countries. Continued encouragement of mass international tourism and hospitality. Significant standardization. High levels of media promotion of foodservice products.	Continued rise in out-of-home consumption of food in all countries. Mass customization of food and hospitality. Development of niche food tourism experiences, including international 'slow tourism' and gastronomic tourism to high-end markets. Branding that links food and visitor economy used for regional promotion. High levels of media convergence between food and visitor economy as part of lifestyle promotion.	Limited development of food services based on local foodways and notions of hospitality. International tourism encouraged as part of pro-poor tourism strategies; visitor economy remains an important component of regional economic development.	Growth of organic and other appropriate specialized hospitality services encouraged. High levels of local leisure related mobility tied to food and lifestyle and part of a reshaping of the visitor economy. Strong domestic tourism focus. Some international tourism encouraged but with costs of emissions accounted. Branding remains significant.

Table 1.7 continued

Elements of consumption and production	'Business as Usual' (BAU)	'Green growth'	'Traditional sustainable'	'Steady-state/sustainable consumption
Household food activities	High capital and energy intensity in food preparation and clearing up. Continued growth in the use of prepared foods as well as internationalization of food products. Majority of shopping based on car-dependent supermarkets as well as supermarket-based Internet shopping.	High capital and energy intensity in food preparation and clearing up. Continued growth in use of prepared foods as well as growing internationalization of food products but little increase in overall food consumption. Majority of shopping based on car-dependent supermarkets as well as supermarket-based Internet shopping.	Improvements in household cooking and storage practices, including more fuel and energy efficiency. Encouragement of regional markets.	Focus on local food system and short supply chains means an emphasis on direct sales, farmers markets, locally owned stores and retail diversity. Cooperative and community-owned supermarkets supported. Opposition to transnational food retail and foodservice chains. Internet use encouraged to promote food localism.
Disposal and recycling of food and packaging wastes	Limited recycling for packaging where economically viable for market to operate. Household food waste recycling limited to home composting.	Installation of good systems of packaging and household recycling. Some subsidy of private initiatives or managed under public–private partnerships.	Food wastes recycled for agriculture.	Strong focus on reduced packaging of foods, although recycling is integral along with waste food disposal for agriculture/composting.

the attention is just focused, there we fail to understand what the issues are in the wider food system and how the restaurant influences that. In other words, if taking a system-wide perspective we want to understand not only what happens from farm to fork, but also the implications of the leftovers and waste left behind. These impacts may also be significant. For example, in a study to assist in the development of the Green Seal Standard for Restaurants and Food Services, GS-46, in the USA, Baldwin et al. (2011) found that procurement of food accounted for 97.2% of the impact of restaurants and food services on land use and 94.7% of total environmental impacts (Table 1.8). Such findings are supported by more recent research (see also Chapter 2). For example, Taylor (2020) reported that the global food system is on course to drive rapid and widespread ecological damage with 87.7% of land animals likely to lose some of their habitats by 2050 as a result of agricultural expansion unless there is a transition away from Business as Usual (Williams et al., 2021) in which the restaurant and food services sector is clearly embedded (see Table 1.8).

Nevertheless, Dai et al. (2020) suggested that the environmental sustainability of the growth in dining out, termed by them as food away from home (FAFH), had received insufficient attention. The size of and growth in FAFH is substantial. In the USA, FAFH consumption doubled from 1997 to 2017 (Okrent et al., 2018). Between 1997 and 2017, nominal sales for limited- and full-service restaurants in the USA grew an average of about 5.5% and 5.3% per year respectively, but slowed for limited-service restaurants with FAFH expenditures overtaking food at home (FAH) expenditures in share of total food expenditures in 2010 (Okrent et al., 2018). However, potentially significantly given changes in food ordering, home delivery of food is counted as FAH. In South Korea, as with many countries that have undergone rapid economic transition and developed strong consumer cultures, Choi et al. (2017) estimated that the foodservice industry grew seven-fold from 1986 to 2012.

Dai et al. (2020) argued that previous studies, including that of Baldwin et al. (2011) noted above, had actually underestimated the environmental impacts of eating out because they did not sufficiently address the embodied environmental impact of food items (see Chapter 2 for a further discussion of this important concept). Estimates of the GHG emissions of FAFH meals range from 0.134 kg CO_2 e/meal (de Laurentiis et al., 2019) to 13.2 kg CO_2 e/meal (Benvenuti et al., 2016) for school canteen meals, and from 0.60 kg CO_2 e/meal (Pulkkinen et al., 2016) to 9.6 kg CO_2 e/meal (Saxe et al., 2019) for other catering services. Nevertheless, a consistent finding in studies of eating out, and which further supports some of the concerns discussed above regarding the food system, is that meat ingredients are the most important contributor to GHG emissions, and the food production stage usually accounts for more than half of the total GHG emissions in the FAFH life cycle (Dai et al., 2020).

However, often missing from assessments of the sustainability of eating out and the impacts of food supply chains is the role of socio-economic effects, which is significant as food life cycles include societal and economic functions as well as circular economy options, during production or end-of-life processes (Vidergar et al., 2020). Therefore, in this book, we also seek to bring in some of the social and economic dimensions of sustainability to provide a broader understanding of both the concept of the sustainability of restaurants and food services and also to highlight some of the tensions and tradeoffs that potentially exist in sustainability decision-making. Figure 1.1 illustrates the approach we use in this book in terms of assessing the sustainable restaurant and foodservice operation. Chapters 2–8 focus on different aspects of procurement and what goes into restaurant from the wider food system. Chapter 7 focuses on purchasing strategies, and Chapters 9–12 focus more on what happens within the restaurant or foodservice operation and the strategies and practices that are utilized to be efficient yet also satisfy customers. Chapters 13–16 examine ways in which

Table 1.8 Contribution of food supplies, food storage, food preparations and operational support

Source: Baldwin et al. (2011)

Foodservice subsystem	Carcinogens (%)	Respiratory inorganics (%)	Climate change (%)	Ecotoxicity (%)	Land use (%)	Fossil fuels (%)	Acidification/ eutrophication (%)	Total environmental impacts (normalized results) (%)
Food procurement – the purchase of food and beverages (and related waste)	23.9	84	52.6	13.6	97.2	32.5	65.1	94.7
Food storage – energy used in storing food, beverages and other products in the restaurant or food service (it did not include food)	5.6	0.8	2.5	7.1	0.05	3.43	3.4	0.7
Food preparation and cooking – energy used in preparing food, beverages and other products at the restaurant or food service and water use (it did not include food)	0.6	1.4	3.4	0.2	0.8	4	3.02	1.2
Food service and operational support – energy used for lighting, heating, ventilation and air conditioning, water use, supplies (restroom, cleaning, disposable products) and administrative support (paper)	69.9	13.8	41.6	79	2.0	60.1	30.1	3.4

Introduction

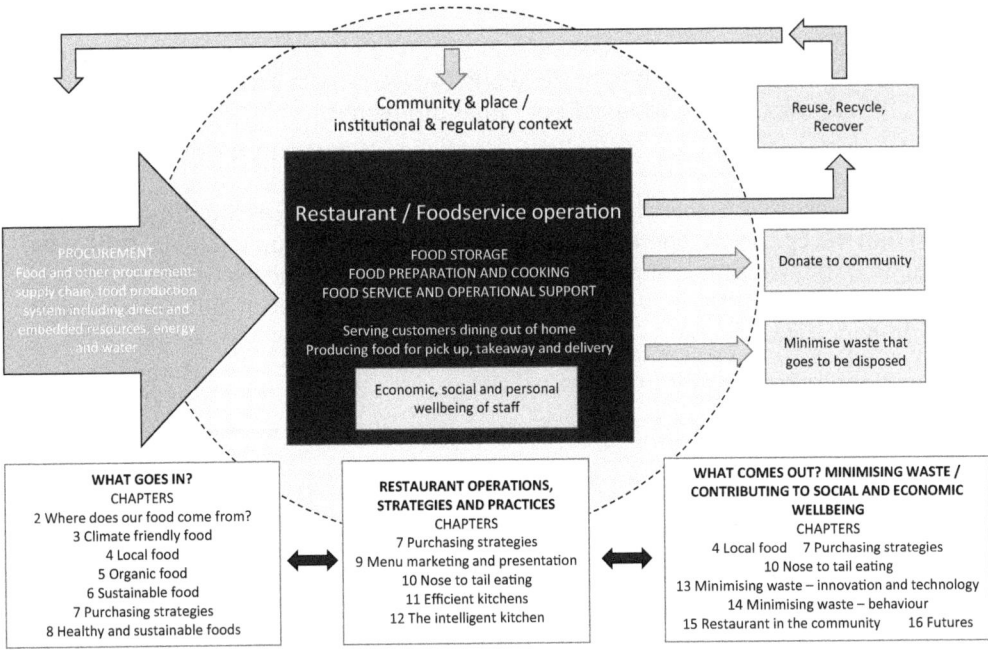

Figure 1.1 Assessing the sustainable restaurant and foodservice operation

---

Box 1.4 Epicurious food website drops new beef recipes for environmental reasons

Epicurious, an online publisher specializing in recipes and cooking owned by Condé Nast, began in 1995, and comes in the form of a website, an app, a YouTube channel, a series of newsletters as well as a Facebook Group and has 8.4 million digital users and 8.5 million followers on social networks (BBC, 2021). In April 2021, the Epicurious website announced that it will no longer publish new recipes containing beef "in an effort to encourage more sustainable cooking": "We've cut out beef. Beef won't appear in new Epicurious recipes, articles, or newsletters. It will not show up on our homepage. It will be absent from our Instagram feed" (Tamarkin & Hoffmann, 2021).

> For any person—or publication—wanting to envision a more sustainable way to cook, cutting out beef is a worthwhile first step. Almost 15 percent of greenhouse gas emissions globally come from livestock (and everything involved in raising it); 61 percent of those emissions can be traced back to beef. Cows are 20 times less efficient to raise than beans and roughly three times less efficient than poultry and pork. It might not feel like much, but cutting out just a single ingredient—beef—can have an outsize impact on making a person's cooking more environmentally friendly. … We know that some people might assume that this decision signals some sort of vendetta against cows—or the people who eat them. But this decision was not made because we hate

hamburgers (we don't!). Instead, our shift is solely about sustainability, about not giving airtime to one of the world's worst climate offenders. We think of this decision as not anti-beef but rather pro-planet.

(Tamarkin & Hoffmann, 2021)

Epicurious assured readers that the beef recipes that were on the site would stay and that the Epicurious agenda in terms of inspiring cooks would remain, "The only change is that we now believe that part of getting better means cooking with the planet in mind. If we don't, we'll end up with no planet at all" (Tamarkin & Hoffmann, 2021).

Epicurious: www.epicurious.com

Box 1.5 The move towards vegetable-based restaurant cuisine: Eleven Madison Park and ONA

Eleven Madison Park in New York (www.elevenmadisonpark.com), which has won three Michelin stars and is one of the top restaurants in Manhattan announced in May 2021, that in reopening after COVID-19 it would abandon meat dishes and serve a plant-based menu. However, at the time of writing its pick-up menu still included ethically produced meat as well as a contribution to the donation of meals to those in New York experiencing food insecurity. In announcing its reopening in June 2021, chef patron, Daniel Humm, expressed why this shift had occurred in a letter on the restaurant's website:

> we've evolved our business model. When we reopen … every dinner you purchase will allow us to provide five meals to food-insecure New Yorkers. This food is being delivered by Eleven Madison Truck, which is operated by our staff in partnership with Rethink Food. We've created a circular ecosystem where our guests, our team, and our suppliers all participate.
>
> In the midst of last year, when we began to imagine what EMP would be like after the pandemic – when we started to think about food in creative ways again – we realized that not only has the world changed, but that we have changed as well. We have always operated with sensitivity to the impact we have on our surroundings, but it was becoming ever clearer that the current food system is simply not sustainable, in so many ways.
>
> We use food to express ourselves as richly and authentically as our craft allows – and our creativity has always been tied to a specific moment in time. In this way, the restaurant is a personal expression in dialogue with our guests.
>
> It was clear that after everything we all experienced this past year, we couldn't open the same restaurant.
>
> With that in mind, I'm excited to share that we've made the decision to serve a plant-based menu in which we do not use any animal products — every dish is made from vegetables, both from the earth and the sea, as well as fruits, legumes, fungi, grains, and so much more.

> We've been working tirelessly to immerse ourselves in this cuisine. It's been an incredible journey, a time of so much learning. We are continuing to work with local farms that we have deep connections to, and with ingredients known to us, but we have found new ways to prepare them and to bring them to life.
>
> I find myself most moved and inspired by dishes that center impeccably-prepared vegetables, and have naturally gravitated towards a more plant-based diet. This decision was inspired by the challenge to get to know our ingredients more deeply, and to push ourselves creatively. It wasn't clear from the onset where we would end up. We promised ourselves that we would only change direction if the experience would be as memorable as before.
>
> … All this has given us the confidence to reinvent what fine dining can be. It makes us believe that this is a risk worth taking.
>
> It is time to redefine luxury as an experience that serves a higher purpose and maintains a genuine connection to the community. A restaurant experience is about more than what's on the plate. We are thrilled to share the incredible possibilities of plant-based cuisine while deepening our connection to our homes: both our city and our planet.
>
> (Humm, 2021)

The change in menu of Eleven Madison Park is reflective of wider food trends and the growth of vegetarian and vegan restaurants and offerings, which even includes fast-food conglomerates such as Burger King. In 2021, the restaurant Origine Non-Animale (ONA) in the city of Ares, near Bordeaux in France became the first animal-free products/vegan restaurant to win a Michelin star. The restaurant also won a green star, which Michelin introduced in 2000 to reward establishments with a strong record of ethical practices. ONA's chef patron, Claire Vallée, offered seven dishes on her gourmet menu before she had to close ONA because of COVID-19 restrictions with her favourite combinations involving pine, boletus mushroom and sake; and celery, tonka and amber ale. Vallée secured financing for the restaurant through crowdfunding, without the need for collateral, and through La Nef, a bank that specializes in lending to green and ethical projects. Vallée did this as traditional banks would not give her a loan to start the restaurant as, "They said the outlook for veganism and plant-based food was too uncertain" (quoted in Agence France-Presse, 2021).

waste are minimized as well as the contribution of restaurants and foodservice operations to social and economic wellbeing, both in the community and for staff.

Conclusions

The modern, industrial, food system is increasingly unsustainable. The Business as Usual thinking that favours the lowest common denominator (direct cost minimization) approach to food without consideration of the externalities that arise from such supply chains have provided substantial amounts of processed food together with substantial harm to environmental and public health. The restaurant, catering and foodservice sector is a major and growing part of that food system. Yet, simultaneously, it is also a significant actor for change both with respect to industry associations and networks as well as the activities of independent restaurants and cafés and their commitment to quality food and experiences and being a positive part of the communities and places in which they are located.

The act of "eating out" has far greater consequences than most people would believe (Hall & Gössling, 2013). There is no single common metric or analytic process of judgement with which to establish that some food is quality food, and everyone has their own taste (Harvey et al., 2004). However, it is possible to determine the impacts of what we eat and where we eat and purchase from. While some people may therefore potentially decry environmental or health challenges to how much steak or ice cream they consume when they go out to dine, it would be surprising if they also actively advocated for biodiversity loss, global heating, land use change and increased waste as a result of their consumption. Restaurant and foodservice businesses as well as their consumers are nevertheless at the forefront of transitions to a more sustainable food and culinary system. Chefs, cook and kitchen staff more than anyone else should have the capacity to change the menu and make it palatable. This book is designed to help understand why that is important and some of the strategies and practices by which it can be done. Although it does not provide one universal recipe, it does hopefully provide insights into some of the ways each chef, establishment and staff can start to focus on particular elements to improve sustainability and, as is pointed out frequently in this book many such measures make very good business sense, especially given growing consumer concern over sustainability issues.

A sustainable chef, and the restaurants and food services in which they operate, therefore provides dining services and related dishes and food products which respond to a customer's desire for good food and positive sensory and dining experiences while minimizing the use of natural resources and toxic materials as well as waste, pollutants and emissions. This is done in a manner that seeks to maximize staff and community social and economic wellbeing and environmental and public health over the life cycle of the food service so as not to jeopardize the needs of the future. We hope this book, even in some small way, makes such a contribution.

Chapter 2

Where does our food come from?

Introduction

For many people their understanding of where their food comes from barely goes beyond what they purchase from the supermarket or store, or from the restaurant or fast-food outlet. However, as highlighted in the introduction, understanding the supply chain of foodservice businesses is crucial to reducing their environmental impacts and maximizing social and economic benefits, both for the business as well as the wider community. This chapter provides an overview of where food comes from and details the structures and systems within which food is produced for eventual consumption and provides an understanding of the context within which the supply chains of specific food businesses are located.

Structures of food production and consumption

Food provision structures vary significantly in the world. While most people in industrialized countries visit supermarkets, grocery stores, drug stores or farmers' markets to purchase foods, a majority of humanity continues to independently produce a significant share of the food they consume. Small-scale subsistence farming, as well as hunting and gathering, remains highly relevant for billions of people, who are thus highly dependent on the integrity of local agricultural systems and ecosystems (Robinson & Bennett, 2000). For example, in regions including Central America, Eastern and Central Africa, India, Pakistan, Nepal or Bhutan as well as large parts of East Asia, a majority of the population continues to engage in small-scale agriculture and is officially considered farmers (FAO, 2018a; Figure 2.1). In the Amazon, as well as many African and Asian forest areas, food is directly derived through hunting, fishing or slash-and-burn agriculture (e.g., Robinson & Bennett, 2000; Tremblay et al., 2015). Coastal ecosystems in many countries remain highly important as sources of marine protein (Cinner et al., 2018). Overall, the Food and Agriculture Organization (FAO) estimates that in 2016, about 45% of the world's population lived in rural areas (3,374 million people), and roughly one in four people (26.7%) are still employed in agriculture worldwide (FAO, 2018a).

It is in industrialized countries and emerging economies that food systems have become increasingly complex, mostly as a result of opportunities to transport foodstuffs over large distances, in combination with industrial food preparation, packaging and preservation. Highly processed foods have become very common, in a global food system that is increasingly in the hands of a limited number of transnational agro-food corporations, which, according to Weis (2007, pp. 13–14):

> are controlling, refining, combining, distributing and marketing what is being produced on farms in expansive new ways, and systematically detaching food consumption patterns from time, space and cultural traditions with long-distance sourcing and distribution networks, sophisticated processing and packaging systems that reduce perishability …

Weis (2007) describes this as the de-spatialization and de-culturation of food, in wider processes of diet change that leave large parts of the poor reliant on food durables (flour, cornmeal and rice). In comparison, supermarkets in affluent countries offer a wide range of fresh and processed foods sourced from all over the world. These foods are often flown over vast distances, and sometimes in reverse flows: For example, it is common for New Zealand kiwi fruits to be exported to Europe in the European summer/autumn, while the country imports Italian kiwis in the European winter/spring. The journey involves transportation by ship over close to 20,000 km. Another example is Norwegian exports of salmon and trout, totalling one million tonnes worth €6.6 billion (NOK 65 billion) to 146 countries (in 2016) (Norwegian Seafood Council, 2017). A large share of exports is by air, with for example hundreds of tonnes of salmon per week being flown to Asia (Svenska Yle, 2014). Notably, China, one of the major recipients of Norwegian salmon, is itself one of the world's leading countries exporting fish products (OECD & FAO, 2018).

Global flows in agricultural products can be illustrated on the basis of the value of trade, as well as the calories traded. As Macdonald et al. (2015) outline, about one-quarter of the value of global agricultural production (26%) is traded, representing some 20% of global calorie production. Wheat, soybean and maize represent about 50% of the calories traded, but only 21% of the value. In contrast, meat and animal products, along with fruits and nuts, account for 44% of the value traded, but less than 10% of the calories.

Geographically, trade flows mainly occur within the European Union, between the EU and North America and between North America and Mexico. About 41% of the global value of exports is exchanged between EU countries, and another 21% between the USA, Canada and Mexico. The USA also exports considerable value to Japan and China. The caloric trade pattern is different, though, with 24% of exports and 30% of imports being associated with EU countries, and 9%–10% of the caloric flows with exports from Southeast Asia and South America to China. The USA also exports considerable amounts of food to Japan and China (Macdonald et al., 2015).

Apart from agricultural produce, meats and animal products, fish is one of the most traded international commodities. About one-third (35%) of all fish products are being traded internationally. Developing countries account for 59% of exports of fish and 46% of imports, indicating a net 'loss' of fish protein in these countries. Asia is the world's major fish-producing region, with expectations that by 2030, 89% of all aquaculture production will take place here. China alone accounts for 62% of current production, as well as 38% of global fish consumption. China also has the world's highest fish consumption, at 41 kg per capita and year (FAO, 2018b).

As outlined, the globalization of foods and their marketing and distribution through transnational corporations has meant that a growing share of foods are refined or processed, often involving several production steps, ingredients sourced from a wide range of countries, a considerable transport demand as well as the development of associated industries producing preservatives, antioxidants, stabilizers, baking powder, flavours or sweeteners. As Weis (2007) notes, the proliferation of 'junk food' (soft drinks, snacks) as well as convenience foods containing fats, sweeteners, artificial flavours and colouring has significantly changed the global food system. In a study of food consumption in Australia, Hadjikakou (2017, p. 120) found that discretionary foods and drinks represented a significant share, i.e., foods not providing essential nutrients to humans and having "significant overlap" with ultra-processed and refined foods. These discretionary foods account for 35%–39% of the environmental impact of Australian food consumption, if measured in terms of water and energy use, as well as CO_2 emissions and land use.

Other industries are concerned with packaging and waste management. A major challenge with processed foods is their shelf life, which retailers like to extend in order to reduce the share of very perishable foods going to waste, ultimately measures designed to increase profitability. Packaging technologies consequently seek to control oxidation and respiration, microbial growth and moisture migration (Restuccia et al., 2010). Waste management, on the other hand, is about dealing with effluents and waste from food production, preparation and consumption; it is equally about reducing economic losses (Martin-Ríos et al., 2018).

Food waste has received much attention in recent years, as the negative impacts of food production have been noted globally, including their implications for food security and climate change (Gustavsson et al., 2011; FAO, 2019c). These are challenges that also need to be seen in the light of the current and future world population. At a current net growth of about 85 million people per year, the world population is expected to reach 10 billion by 2050, while the corresponding food demand will increase by 50% (2013–2050) (FAO, 2017). The higher growth in food demand is a result of population growth as well as a dietary transition towards higher consumption of meat, fruits and vegetables, all of which require shifts in output compared to cereals.

As this short introduction highlights, structures of food production and provision are complex, and interwoven with a wide range of challenges such as population growth; dietary change; land use, land use change and access to land; production and consumption; food security and environmental change. These aspects are discussed in more detail in the following sections.

Global food production structures

Agriculture requires about one-third of total global land area, though this is more than 50% of the total land in Asia and less than 25% in Europe. Some 40% of all arable cropland is located in five countries: India, the USA, Russia, China and Brazil (FAO, 2018a). The total harvested area in the world is 1,385 million ha in 2016 and has grown by more than 200 million ha since 1995 (FAO, 2018a). The top five food items produced in the world are sugar cane, maize, wheat, rice/paddy and potatoes (Table 2.1). For these staples, production has increased significantly between 2006 and 2016. In the future, production is expected to change, as outlined by FAO (2018a, p. 28):

> External factors, such as rising incomes and urbanization, are causing diets to become higher in protein, fats and sugar. In addition, livestock and biofuel production have grown at a faster rate than crop production, and will probably continue to do so. This is causing a shift away from crops such as wheat and rice, towards coarse grains and oilseeds to meet demands for food, feed and biofuel.

Livestock numbers are growing rapidly, as a result of diets increasingly based on animal products such as meat, milk and dairy (FAO, 2018a; Table 2.2). Worldwide, humanity collectively holds almost 28 billion animals (chicken, cattle, ducks, sheep, goats), i.e., close to four animals per person. Fisheries and aquaculture are not contained in this total, even though fish provides 3.2 billion people with close to 20% of their animal protein. On a

Table 2.1 Top five food staples produced worldwide, 2016

Source: FAO (2018a)

Staple	2006 ('000 t)	2016 ('000 t)	% increase
Sugar cane	1,417,376	1,890,662	33
Maize	707,932	1,060,107	50
Wheat	614,538	749,460	22
Rice, paddy	640,706	740,961	16
Potatoes	297,111	376,827	27
Total	2,260,287	4,818,017	113

Table 2.2 Live animal numbers, 2016

Source: FAO (2018a)

Staple	2006 ('000 heads)	2016 ('000 heads)	% increase
Chicken	17,591,486	22,705,417	29
Cattle	1,382,836	1,474,888	7
Ducks	1,102,437	1,241,388	13
Sheep	1,098,662	1,173,354	7
Goats	840,371	1,002,810	19
Total	22,015,792	27,597,857	25

global scale, protein production in aquaculture (some 80 million tonnes) is now approaching the scale of wild catches (some 90 million tonnes per year); (FAO, 2018a, 2018b), with an estimated total of 153 million tonnes in 2017 (OECD & FAO, 2018).

The land currently used for agricultural production is equivalent to one-third of the world's total land area. It covers more than 50% of all land in Asia and less than 25% in Europe. As a result of population growth and agriculture expansion, pressure on lands is increasing. For example, forest ecosystems worldwide face clear-cutting as a result of the growing demand for agricultural land. Given the lack of new land that can be cultivated, there are also trends for transnational corporations to purchase land use rights in developing countries. This process, also referred to as land grabbing, is widespread. Non-governmental organization GRAIN reports that in 78 countries, some 491 land deals cover an area of 30 million ha (GRAIN, 2016). The implications of land deals can be significant. In 2008, Jung-a et al. (2008) reported on an impending deal between Daewoo Logistics and Madagascar to farm maize and palm oil. The deal, which foresaw a lease of 1.3 million ha – almost half the country's arable land of 2.5 million ha – would have had the objective of meeting food demand in Korea, through Daewoo Logistics. The deal also implied the development of new agricultural land, which would likely have involved deforestation. It was never implemented, however, because the Malagasy government was overthrown before contracts could be signed.

Agriculture continues to be an important employment sector, in which about a quarter of the world population is active (FAO, 2018a). Even though this share has significantly declined since 1995, when 41.3% of the world population were employed in the sector, agriculture still provides work for more than 50% of people in all of central Africa, in excess of 80% of the male workforce in Burundi, Mali, Chad or Central African Republic, as well as more than 90% of the female workforce in Burundi, Chad, Somalia and Central African Republic (FAO, 2018a). Agriculture also continues to be highly important in East Asia, and in particular India. As the FAO (2018a, p. 6) outlines, "Much labour in agriculture is informal, characterized by high levels of pluri-activity and seasonality. […] As a large share of the working poor are involved in agriculture, developments in this sector have a major impact on welfare". The situation is fundamentally different in industrialized countries, where employment in agriculture has continuously declined. For example, Swinnen (2009) shows that in Belgium, Netherlands, France and Germany, the share of people employed in agriculture declined from 30%–50% in 1875 to 10%–20% in 1965. Today, agriculture stands for all but a few percent of employment in the European Union (EC, 2018).

These developments are also a result of structural change. In the EU-28, the number of small agricultural holdings has declined by about 0.7% per year. Farms of up to 5 ha of utilized agricultural area represented 70.3% of holdings in 2007 and 66.3% in 2013. Farms with 100 ha or more, on the other hand, increased from 2.2% to 3.1% over the same period (EC, 2018). In Africa, the smallholder agricultural model is the norm and is likely to persist even though it has been questioned in terms of its effectiveness in reducing poverty (Collier & Dercon, 2014). Globally, the family farm model continues to dominate, with estimates that up to 98% of all farms, and 53%–75% of agricultural land, are family-owned (Graeub et al., 2016; Lowder et al., 2016). As a consequence, food is often still sourced very locally. As an example, a study in Romania found that a large share of food provisions is sourced from home gardens (24%), farmers' markets (17%), the extended family's farm (11%), local farmers (11%), own animals (10%) and fishing/hunting (1%). Only a small share of food provisions was bought in supermarkets (18%), or in other stores or online (8%) (Kónya & Gergely, 2016).

Box 2.1 One percent of the world's farms operate 70% of the world's farmland

A report by the International Land Coalition (ILS) (2020) highlighted the substantial inequalities of land ownership and the corporatization of agriculture. The ILC estimated that there are approximately 608 million farms in the world, with the majority still being family farms. They found that the largest 1% of farms operate more than 70% of the world's farmland and that these farms are strongly integrated into the corporate food system. In contrast, over 80% of farms are smallholdings of less than 2 ha and that these are generally excluded from global food chains. Patterns vary significantly from region to region but, since 1980, in all regions land concentration has been increasing, with high rates in North America, Europe, Asia and the Pacific slower rates in Africa and Latin America. However, in most low-income countries, there is an increasing number of farms in combination with ever decreasing average farm sizes, while in higher-income countries large farms continue to get bigger.

Changes in farm size are also related to increasing corporatization of agriculture and the growing role of the financial market in determining how land is used. The ILC concludes:

> In the agri-food sector, corporate organisation is linked to industrial modes of primary production, which seek advantages of scale. In addition, through horizontal and vertical integration, these actors control large sections of specific value chains, often all the way from seeds via inputs to retail, enabling them to exercise significant control over the land to reap maximum value, and contributing indirectly to land inequality.
>
> Concentration of control is compounded by increased interest in agricultural land from the financial sector. Parts of the world's farmland are now considered financial assets, with no known physical owner, subject to decision-making processes that may be external to the farm. Instruments such as shareholdings and the use of derivative values detach investments from their material base, and can bring greater instability to agricultural markets and put speculative pressures on land and agricultural products.
>
> (ILC, 2020, p. 11)

Transnational corporations and concentration in food production

> [...] we expect serving sizes to be large, [and] we also expect the price to be cheap. Owing to the distortions of our industrial food system, it is often cheaper to buy a hamburger than a head of broccoli, cheaper to get a bottle of soda than a bottle of water. [...] It is a demand made by a generation of people that is spending the smallest percentage of income on food we have ever known.
>
> (Bahnson & Wirzba, 2012, p. 118)

Expanding demand is a major driver in the development of the global food system, specifically for animal protein and highly processed foods. Of equal importance are large corporations supporting market concentration processes while forcing producers to reduce production cost (Berne Declaration (BD) & EcoNexus, 2013). As national studies show, 'cost' is the most important factor when considering food purchases (Hartikainen et al., 2014; Emberger-Klein & Menrad, 2018). This increases pressure on food producers, and continues to encourage the industrialization and globalization of food production and consumption. As illustrated in Table 2.3 for food retailers, the process is driven by the US and European companies. Out of the leading retailers, Walmart dwarfs all other corporations, with sales of US$524 billion – exceeding the GDP of Spain or Australia. Of the remaining largest food retailers, six are based in the USA, five in Germany and four in France (Deloitte, 2021). A notable number of food retailers are also operating globally, i.e., in up to 27 different countries.

The Forbes Global 2000 list (McGrath, 2018a) shows that the most powerful food companies, measured in terms of revenue, profit, assets and market value, also include Nestlé, Pepsi and Coca-Cola. Anheuser-Busch reported US$56 billion in revenue and US$7.9 billion in profit. In comparison, Nestlé reported US$91 in revenue, with US$7.3 billion in profit, followed by Pepsico, with US$64 billion in revenue and US$4.9 billion in profit. Among the restaurant chains, McDonald's, Starbucks and Restaurant Brands International are the most valuable brands in the world (McGrath, 2018b). Notably, McGrath (2018b), in discussing the success of McDonald's becoming the world's leading restaurant chain, suggests that the company's "value offer" of $1, $2, $3 menus was key in regaining market share, highlighting both foodstuff cost pressure (purchases) and low profit margins (sales) as competitive strategies. Changes in the food market

Table 2.3 The world's largest retailers, 2019
Source: Deloitte (2021)

Name of company	Country	2019 retail revenue (million US$)	No. of countries of operation
Walmart	USA	523,964	27
Costco	USA	152,703	12
Schwarz Group	Germany	126,124	33
The Kroger Co.	USA	121,539	1
Aldi	Germany	106,326	19
Tesco	UK	81,347	8
Target	USA	77,130	1
Ahold Delhaize	Netherlands	74,160	10
Aeon	Japan	72,711	11
Albertsons Companies	USA	62,455	1
Edeka	Germany	61,221	1
Seven & Holdings Co.	Japan	58,552	18
Rewe	Germany	55,772	13
Auchan	France	51,264	14
Centres Distributeurs E. Leclerc	France	43,426	6
Woolworths	Australia	41,778	3
Casino	France	38,775	27
Publix Super Markets	USA	38,463	1
J Sainsbury	UK	36,303	2
Loblaw	Canada	35,493	3
ITM Développment (Intermarché)	France	35,435	4
H-E B Grocery Company	USA	28,200	2
X5 Retail Group	Russia	26,791	1
Mercadona	Spain	26,146	2
Metro AG	Germany	25,350	24
Coles Group	Australia	25,063	1
Migros	Switzerland	24,968	3

are also visible in the types of food consumed. For example, in the USA, highly processed food sales are on the increase, a phenomenon linked to the expansion of drug stores and their food offers (Ruhlman, 2017). In Europe, furniture chain IKEA is a major retailer of processed foods, also setting a global social norm regarding desirable foods including

> **Box 2.2   Market concentration in the beer market**
>
> Anheuser-Busch Inbev is, measured in turnover and profitability, one of the largest food companies in the world. The company is known for its share of global beer production, totalling 433.9 million hL in 2016, or about 5.6 L per person if averaged by the world's population. It is also an example of the vast concentration in markets, as the company owns breweries in many parts of the world. Individual brands owned by Anheuser-Busch include: Ten Barrel, Aguila Light, Aguila Cero, Aleston, Alexander Keith's, Andes, Antarctica, Archibald, Bagbier, Barrilito, Bass, BBC, Beck's Blue, Beck's Red Ale, Becker, Beer House, Belle-Vue, Birra del Borgo, Blue Point, Boddingtons, Bohemia, Brahma, Brahma 0.0%, Bud Light, Budweiser Magnum, Budweiser Prohibition, Budweiser Supreme, Busch, Busch Light, Cafri, Camden Town, Carlton Draught, Carlton Dry, Cass, Castle Lite, Chernigivske, Club Colombia, Club Colombia Trigo, Colorado, Corona Cero, Corona Extra, Corona Light, Corona SunSets, Corona This Is Living, Coronita, Cristal, Cubanisto, Cubanisto Mojito, Cusqueña, Cusqueña Quinua, Deus, Devils Backbone, Diebels, Diekirch, Double Deer, Eagle Lager, Elysian, Estrella, Estrella Jalisco, Franziskaner, Ginette, Ginsber, Golden Road, Goose Island, Great Northern, Guaraná Antarctica, Haake-Beck, Harbin, Hasseröder, Hertog Jan, Hoegaarden Radler, Jinling, Jinlongquan, Julius, Jupiler, Jupiler 0.0%, Jupiler Blue, Kaiba, Karbach, King of Beers, KK, Klinskoye, Kakonee, Kwak, Labatt, Lakeport, Land Shark Lager, La Virgen, Leffe Royale, Leffe Royale Spring, Leon, Liberty, Löwenbräu, Lucky, Mackeson, Mexicali, Michelob Ultra, Mill Street, MixxTail, Modelo, Modelo Especial, Modelo Trigo, Montejo, Mountain Series, Natty Daddy, Natural Light, Negra Modelo, Norte, O'Doul's, OB, Oculto, Oland, Original, Paceña, Pacifico, Patagonia, Patricia, Pilsen, Pony Malta Plus, Presidente, Pure Blonde, Quilmes, Redd's Apple, Rogan, Saison d'Alliance, Sedrin, Shiliang, Shock Top, Sibirskaya Korona, Skol, Skol Beats Secrets, Skol Beats Senses, Skol Beats Spirit, SmartBarley, Spaten, SpikedSeltzer, Stanley Park, Stella Artois Be Legacy, Stella Artois Buy A Lady A Drink, Stella Artois Cidre, Stella Artois Le Savoir, Sunbru, T, Tijuana, Tolstiak, Tripel Karemeliet, Tropical, Vieux Temps, Victoria, Victoria Bitter, Victoria Chelada, Victoria Oro, Wäls, Whitbread, Yantar.
>
> Source: Anheuser-Busch Inbev (2016)

Swedish meatballs. The furniture retailer is also Sweden's largest food exporter (Jonsson & Foss, 2011), with a 5% share of food-related revenue (Holbrook, 2013).

Market concentration processes are also visible in other domains. Swiss NGO Public Eye (BD & EcoNexus, 2013) outlines, for example, how feeds, stock breeding, seeds, fertilizer and pesticide production are increasingly concentrated among a few companies. According to the NGO, the animal feed market was worth US$350 billion in 2011, out of which the ten largest corporations had a share of 16% (in 2009). Livestock breeding, which is focused on livestock genetics to develop hybrid animals fattening faster, is also concentrated in the hand of a few corporations: "Just three companies supply the world market for turkey genetics, and worldwide only two companies breed the ducklings and day-old chicks that are flown around the world packed in cartons for fattening and egg production factories" (BD & EcoNexus, 2013, p. 7).

Box 2.3 Market concentration in coffee markets

An estimated 500,000 million consumers drink coffee, mostly in developed countries. This coffee is produced by some 25 million farmers in developing countries. In other words, 20 coffee consumers secure employment for one person. However, the global coffee trade is in the hands of a very limited number of wholesalers: three roasters – Nestlé, Kraft and Sara Lee – controlling 40% of global coffee roasting. Five transnational corporations – Neumann, Volcafe, ECOM, Kraft and Nestlé – control 55% of the global trade in coffee. As highlighted by Public Eye (BD & EcoNexus, 2013), there is a tendency for further concentration. Nestlé controlled 21.4 million coffee plants in 13 countries in 2013, with plans to increase this number to 220 million coffee plants by 2020. However, it is not only the amount of coffee controlled by Nestlé, as the brand also exerts considerable power over coffee consumer culture. In order to gain market share, the company invented the Nespresso brand, which features a coffee machine that requires coffee packaged in specific aluminium capsules. Aluminium is a highly problematic metal produced out of Bauxite, a sedimentary rock compound with a high aluminium content, that is the world's primary source of the metal. Considerable amounts of bauxite are produced through strip mining, and in tropical or subtropical regions, such as Brazil, Guinea, Sierra Leone and Indonesia. The production of aluminium not only opens up new rainforest tracts, it also requires high amounts of energy for smelters. As the example illustrates, coffee culture has indirect environmental implications that can be highly significant for resource extraction.

Source: BD and EcoNexus (2013); Menzie et al. (2013)

For seeds, 26% of global production is with Monsanto and another 18.2% with DuPont (both US corporations). Together with Syngenta in Switzerland (9.2%), these three corporations managed more than three-quarters of the global proprietary seed market. Similarly, 55% of the global fertilizer market is controlled by the world's ten largest producers. In 2010, this included a total amount of fertilizer comprising 100 million tonnes of nitrogen, 39 million tonnes of phosphate and 30 million tonnes of potassium. Perhaps the most concentrated market in the food system is pesticides. Here the largest ten corporations managed 95%, with global sales of US$44 billion per year (BD & EcoNexus, 2013).

According to the FAO (2019c, p. 5) a food system, "gathers all the elements (environment, people, inputs, processes, infrastructures, institutions, etc.) and activities that relate to the production, processing, distribution, preparation and consumption of food along with the outputs of these activities, including socioeconomic and environmental outcomes". Figure 2.1 illustrates the complexity of the flow of materials as well as inputs and outputs of the food system, also indicating where resources are wasted, or where the system generates effluents or solid waste. Emissions occur at every stage of the food production, supply and consumption chain. The food supply chain is usually defined as consisting of the following elements (FAO, 2019c):

i *agricultural production and harvest/slaughter/catch operations* which refer to activities where produce is still on the farm or the producer's premises;
ii *post-harvest/slaughter/catch operations* including cleaning, grading, sorting and treatments (e.g., for disinfestation on the farm or in a packing facility);

Where does our food come from?

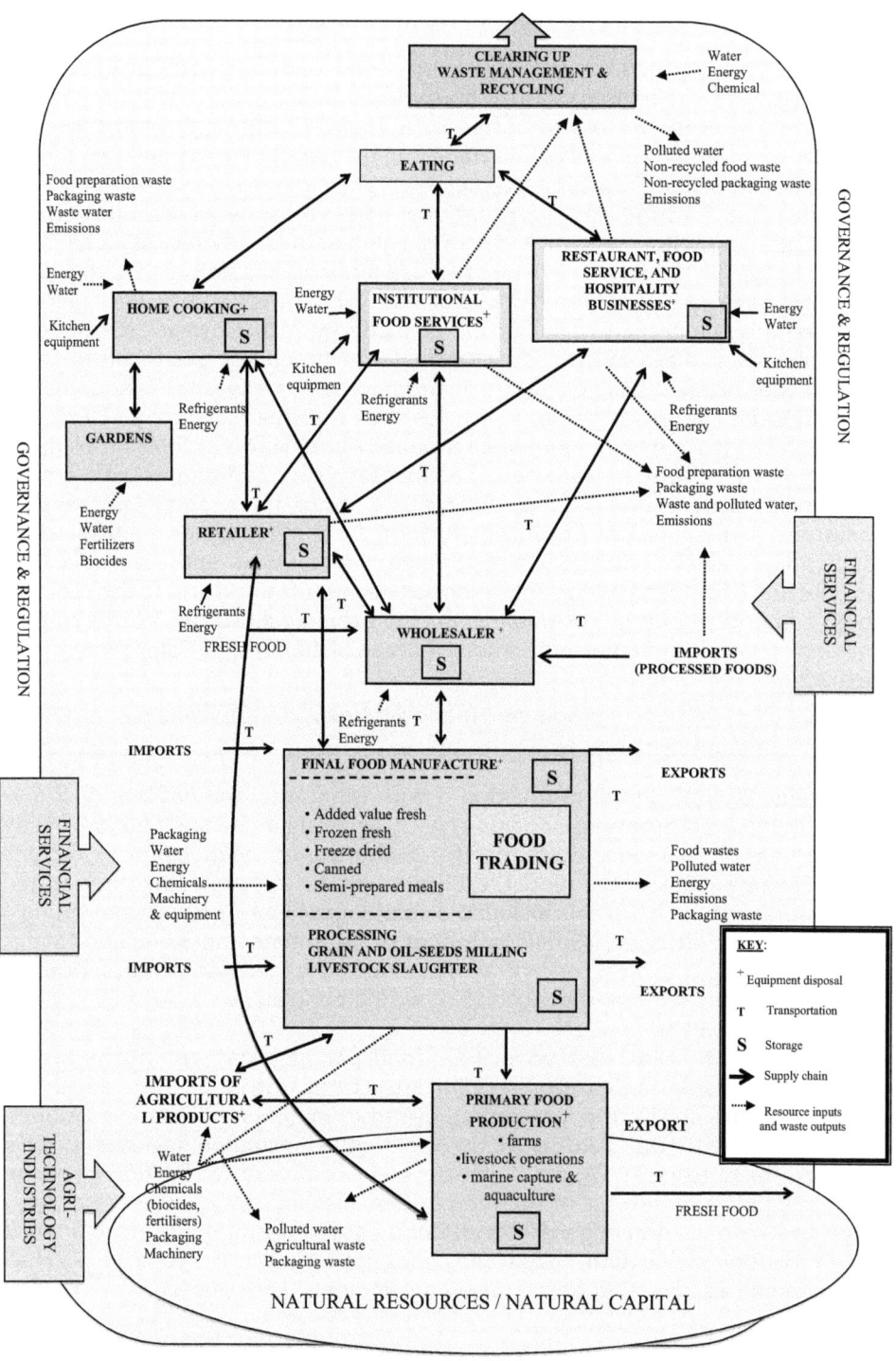

Figure 2.1 From farm to plate: the food consumption and production system

iii *storage*;
iv *transportation*;
v *processing*, which includes primary processing operations (e.g., drying, dehusking, deshelling), which often take place on the farm and secondary processing (product transformation);
vi *wholesale and retail;* and
vii *consumption* by households and food services, such as restaurants and catering.

Importantly, Figure 2.1 also shows that food production is embedded in a complex network of financial services, regulation, distribution, wholesale and retail, waste management and recycling (Hall & Gössling, 2013).

Box 2.4   COVID-19 and the food supply chain

The application of non-pharmaceutical interventions to restrict the spread of COVID-19, such as social distancing and restrictions on the numbers of people that could be together in a single space, had a huge effect on restaurants and cafés both in terms of closure and/or restrictions on trade as well as on consumer demand. In December 2020, the imposition of a tier 3 lockdown in London and South East England led the chief executive of the British Hospitality Association, Kate Nicholls, to observe:

> As with previous short-notice lockdowns, this is going to cause a glut of wasted food and drink. It's not possible to just turn on and off a hospitality business. Beer will go down the drain, fresh food will have to be thrown away and there will be impacts throughout the supply chain of cancelled orders. This stop-start approach to hospitality is disastrous.
>
> (quoted in Smithers, 2020)

The culinary director of the Norma and the Game Bird restaurants in London, Ben Tish, said:

> Sadly there's going to be an immense amount of food wasted across the restaurants in the capital. We were due to have full restaurants this week, including booked-out private dining rooms, and we had ordered a load of produce in. We were also booked up on Christmas Day at the Stafford – with about 100 guests due – and had already ordered and received 100 lobster tails costing about £25 each. Those will freeze but not for long. We have also got a lot of special ingredients which we love to serve during the festive period – truffles, for example. These don't freeze, so that's another financial loss.
>
> (quoted in Smithers, 2020)

These measures clearly impacted the income of businesses and employment in the sector, but they also had substantial downstream impacts on the food supply chain and illustrate the way that the food services sector is a critical element of the food system.

After many years of strong growth, the USA, the world's biggest cafe market, experienced a drop in sales at specialist tea and coffee shops of almost 11% in 2020, while in China, the world's second biggest market sales growth was expected to fall from just over 40% per annum to just 1.6%. As sales of coffee and tea at cafés contracted, net imports by coffee-buying countries dropped nearly 6% in the three months to the end of June compared with the same period in the previous year (Butler, 2020). As a result, the price of coffee fluctuated wildly with its effects throughout the supply chain. Coffee roasters who supplied retailers or sold online did much better than those who primarily sold to the hospitality and food services sectors. However, fluctuating prices will "have a wide-ranging impact on producers who are already struggling to cope with depressed coffee prices and the effects of climate change which has made growing crops more difficult by, for example, increasing incidence of disease in some regions". According to Becky Forecast, supply chain manager at Fairtrade, changes in price made it difficult to plan ahead and cover costs, making the Fairtrade way of conducting business, which guarantees a minimum price for producers, more important than ever:

> Volatility of coffee prices has been a big problem and the Covid crisis has exacerbated that. [The] safety [of a guaranteed minimum price] is not only crucial for farmer but for the long-term sustainability of coffee. If they are not covering the cost of production there is little incentive to carry on [farming].
>
> (quoted in Butler, 2020)

The cascade effect of the COVID-19 that ran through the food system with respect to coffee was also experienced in the farming sector. Seal (2020) described the problem extremely accurately:

> When the hospitality industry shut down, many people assumed farmers and producers could simply sell their food through shops. But hyper-efficient, inflexible supermarket systems are not built to absorb excess food from elsewhere. And if you usually produce 30cm square catering packs of sticky toffee pudding, it is very hard to change all the packaging, let alone set that pudding in front of a retail buyer.

Non-aesthetic or standard size fruit and vegetables can be managed and used by chefs and cooks, but they do not meet the criteria that are usually set by supermarkets and retail chains – and which have also strongly influenced perceptions of what fruits and vegetables should look like. Sometimes produce also can't be easily used in other ways. For example, because of the closure of fish and chip shops, a traditional British business, and other fast-food outlets during lockdowns along with social distancing measures that reduce how many can be in premises at the one time, sales of bagged potatoes for the chipping market declined enormously with substantial flow on effects down the supply chain all the way through to UK potato farmers. According to the Agriculture and Horticulture Development Board (AHDB) estimates even in a best-case scenario, there were 95,000 tonnes of spare chipping potatoes in storage across Britain at the end of the farming season before new potatoes began to be harvested in July (Bailey, 2020). With no ready market growers were donating part of the supply to food banks and charities, some of the potatoes would become cattle feed where possible, and small amounts were to be broken down by anaerobic digestion to generate electricity, but it was still expected that the majority of the potatoes would be dumped. According to the National Farmers Union's Alex Godfrey, "the closure of fish and chip shops and fast-food outlets at the end of March deprived hundreds of thousands of tonnes of potatoes already in store of their planned routes to market", while a spokesperson for the Potato Processors Association stated: "We have seen volumes of chilled and frozen products, which were intended for food service, fall dramatically. Out-of-home sales have completely stopped" (quoted in Payne, 2020). A similar situation also existed in other countries, with potato farmers in Belgium requesting people to eat fries twice a week because 750,000 tonnes of potatoes were in storage in Belgian warehouses (BBC, 2020).

Potatoes were not the only product in surplus as a result of the closure of foodservice outlets, beef, milk and wheat also rapidly went into surplus. The Royal Association of British Dairy Farmers (RABDF) (2020a) estimated that foodservice sector orders dropped by approximately 70%–80% during the first COVID lockdown in the UK, and this equates to about one million litres of milk per day. Up to the middle of May 2020 results from the RABDF (2020b) dairy losses survey showed over 17 million litres of milk had received a reduced value with milk production reduction amounting to almost three million litres and milk not collected and thrown away approximately 1.15 million litres. The closure of restaurants, cafés and coffee shops also meant that other dairy products also suddenly lost their markets. World champion cheese producer the Cornish Cheese Company (www.cornishcheese.co.uk) had to sell off 10 tonnes of surplus Cornish blue cheese in consumer-friendly 1 kg pieces which it did thanks in part to the food waste app Too Good To Go (https://toogoodtogo.co.uk/en-gb), Some specialist producers of goat's curd and burrata for chefs were facing 100% income loss and there were concerns that some livestock would be culled (Seal, 2020), as happened in the USA (Kevany, 2020).

Specialist vegetable growers also faced problems. Peter Ascroft, a beetroot and cauliflower grower in Lancashire, UK, commented. "We supply beetroot to the catering industry … We had a good crop this year. We've probably lost 100 tonnes of beetroot [in sales], which to us is significant". Some of his unusual candied and yellow beetroot was gleaned by volunteers for redistribution, but most was simply ploughed back into the soil. As Seal (2020) noted, "Chefs love speciality beetroot, but it is of little interest to most supermarkets".

Some readers may wonder why couldn't the excess production be stored and used later where possible? However, the food supply chain has developed to increasingly cut costs by reducing storage and providing supplies by using a just-in-time model wherever appropriate. By mid-2020 cold storage warehouses in the UK were full. According to Shane Brennan, chief executive of the Cold Chain Federation industry body.

> No one is taking on new business. The peak was in April when we had things backing up like frozen vegetables and meat, especially the expensive cuts that normally go into restaurants. Fast-food restaurants opening up drive-throughs means frozen meat and potatoes will begin to move, but we don't know what demand will be like because you can't serve as many people.
>
> (quoted in Seal, 2020)

Global food security

Food production and dietary needs are not aligned, with estimates of 800 million people being chronically hungry and two billion suffering micronutrient deficiencies (FAO, 2018a, p. xi). Various organizations, including the FAO (2018a) and the World Resources Institute (WRI), have repeatedly highlighted the importance of food security, specifically for those directly depending on their own food production (Ranganathan, 2013). As the FAO (2018a) underlines, world hunger is on the rise again – after a prolonged decline – and will likely be exacerbated by climate change. Impacts are already felt, as is evident in food price inflation, which has fluctuated by 10%–240% in a wide range of countries in 2017, specifically in Africa (FAO, 2018a, p. 13). Importantly, food insecurity should also be measured in terms of the share of income spent on food, which is as low as 6.4% in the USA, and less than 10% in countries including Singapore, the UK, Switzerland, Canada, Ireland, Australia and Austria. In comparison, populations in Azerbaijan, Guatemala, Pakistan, Philippines, Algeria, Kazakhstan, Cameroon and Kenya spend more than 40% of their income on food, and 56% in Nigeria (Gray, 2016).

To maintain food security is a Sustainable Development Goal (SDG), though one that is fraught with enormous challenges. The global food gap, i.e., the amount of food in calories needed by 2050 in comparison to 2010/2013 is large, with estimates of a necessary 50%–56% increase in production (Searchinger et al., 2018; FAO, 2018a) (see Table 2.4). The WRI estimates that by 2050, 20,500 trillion calories will be consumed by humanity, compared to 13,100 trillion in 2010 (Searchinger et al., 2018). To provide these food calories, a further 593 million ha of agricultural land are needed, in a scenario already considering further intensification of livestock and pasture productivity

Table 2.4 Global consumption of meat and milk products

Source: Ranganathan (2013)

Region	Livestock (kcal/person/day)			Beef and mutton (kcal/person/day)		
	2006	2050	% change	2006	2050	% change
European Union	864	925	7	80	75	−6
Canada & USA	907	887	−2	117	95	−19
China	561	820	46	41	89	116
Brazil	606	803	33	151	173	15
Former Soviet Union	601	768	28	118	156	32
Other OECD	529	674	27	64	84	31
Latin America (e.g., Brazil)	475	628	32	59	86	45
Middle East and North Africa	303	416	37	59	86	45
Asia (e.g., China, India)	233	400	72	24	43	79
India	184	357	94	8	19	138
Sub-Saharan Africa	144	185	29	41	51	26
World	413	506	23	50	56	30

as seen over the period 1961–2010. As the WRI summarizes, the development of yield growth is difficult to project, though it is clear that the world faces a very significant challenge (Searchinger et al., 2018).

Key reasons for the increase in calories include population growth and dietary change, as outlined earlier. These processes are enrooted in more complex societal changes, however. Urbanization is a major driver in the demand for processed foods, and specifically animal protein sources, because these formerly restricted diets become affordable with higher incomes paid in cities (FAO, 2018a). Urbanization is also a reason for shifts in employment within the food system, where a decline in the number of people working in agriculture has been met by an increase in the number of people employed in transport, wholesaling, retailing, food processing and vending (FAO, 2018a). Yet, urbanization also means that fertility rates decline, with repercussions for population growth (White et al., 2008).

A rarely discussed issue is that urbanization also means that people are exposed to new social norms, many of which are mediated through forms of advertisement. On the most basic level, this includes processed foods, which are readily available in supermarkets and marketed in various media. As an example, Fuller et al. (2006) highlight the growth in China's dairy consumption, which more than tripled to 18.6 kg per person and year among the urban top ten income percentile, within the period 1996–2003. In 2015, dairy consumption had increased to an average of 30 kg per capita and year among urban residents in China (Cui et al., 2016). This growth in demand is likely induced, as global corporations heavily market dairy products, specifically in new markets such as China. As Nestlé (2019) notes on its website: "Dairy is our single biggest category by volume […]", and "Unlike many of our ingredients, dairy is sourced from around the world". Hence, global corporations not only provide a growing share of foodstuffs, they also create the social norms of 'normal' or aspirational diets. This is a notable paradox given the global push towards reductions in the use of animal protein, which is not only considered quintessential in meeting greenhouse gas emission reduction needs but also in terms of providing healthier diets. These development objectives for global society are also reflected in the SDGs (Goal 2: Zero Hunger, Goal 3: Good Health and Well-Being, Goal 13: Climate Action).

Food waste and food loss also contribute to food insecurity (FAO, 2019c). Food losses occur along the food supply chain from harvest/slaughter/catch up to, but not including, the retail level, which includes restaurants. In contrast, food waste occur at the retail and consumption level (FAO, 2019c). Importantly, when considering the ways in which commercial kitchens can be made more efficient with respect to food resources, food that is uneaten by humans and which is then diverted to other economic uses, such as animal feed, is not regarded as quantitative food loss or waste. Similarly, those animal or plant parts that are inedible are also not considered food waste or loss.

While food waste is dealt with in several other chapters in this book (see Chapters 13 and 14), it is estimated that 670 million tonnes of food are lost or wasted in high-income countries, and 630 million tonnes in low- and middle-income countries (FAO, 2018a). This amounts to 1.3 billion tonnes or about a third of all edible foods. Figure 2.2 shows that food waste is created during production, handling and storage, processing, distribution and consumption. Depending on the region, most of the losses will occur on the side of the consumer or the producer. For example, 46%–61% of food losses and waste are a result of consumption practices in North America and Oceania, Europe and Industrialized Asia. In comparison, 28%–39% of losses occur during production in Latin America, South and Southeast Asia, as well as Sub-Saharan Africa (Searchinger et al., 2018). Notably, in terms of the share of food going to waste, North America and Oceania account for the greatest losses (42%), while as little as 15% is lost in Latin America.

Where does our food come from?

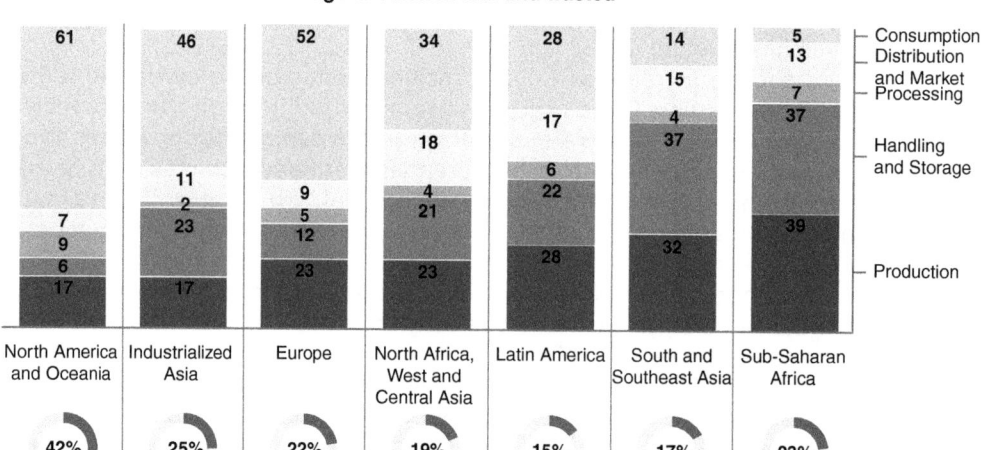

Figure 2.2 Food loss and waste by region and reason

The reasons for food loss and waste differ substantially depending on where in the world it is occurring. Each stage of the food system has specific issues it faces in reducing loss and waste. At the production/farm level, significant reasons include limited time for harvesting, climatic conditions, methods of harvesting and handling, and the marketing of produce to intermediaries and consumers, including the extent to which food, though completely edible, does not meet wholesaler or retailer standards for how it looks. For example, WRAP, the British waste prevention charity, estimated that in 2019, 3.6 m tonnes of edible food was lost on British farms alone, an amount ten times greater than the amount of food thrown away by UK retailers (Butler, 2019). These losses were only exacerbated as a result of COVID-19, for example, many locations in developed countries had too few people to help in harvesting because of restrictions on cross-border short-term work permits for agricultural workers (Aday & Aday, 2020; Bochtis et al., 2020; Seal, 2020).

Significant losses also occur in terms of storage conditions in the supply chain as well as the availability of transportation to get the food to market and to manufacturers and wholesalers, the latter being especially important for the restaurant sector. For storage, adequate cold storage is especially important in preventing food losses and reductions in the shelf life of products. At the wholesaler and retailer stage, food loss and waste is strongly related to shelf life, aesthetic standards in terms of colour, shape and size, and variability in demand (FAO, 2019c).

Other impacts on food systems that can potentially exacerbate food security include unsustainable agriculture that jeopardizes long-term food production, overuse of freshwater, climate change, oil prices, natural disasters as well as social conflicts, including forced migration and war. Not all of these aspects are currently considered in food security assessments. For example, the cost of oil is likely to affect trade, specifically in cereals, which countries in the Middle East and North Africa may not be able to import in the future (OECD & FAO, 2018). Climate policies may also have a significant effect on global trade if implemented at the scale necessary to prevent dangerous interference with the climate system (IPCC, 2014, 2018).

Assessments of food security also suffer from the lack of an inclusion of sudden disruptive effects in ecological systems. As an example, prolonged periods of drought in Europe in the summer of 2018 caused substantial forest fire risks, which destroyed 25,000 ha of forests in Sweden alone according to the government (Regeringen, 2019). As a governmental investigation outlined, forest fires were supported by very warm summer temperatures, in an analogue of future summers under scenarios of climate change (Regeringen, 2019). In Germany, the dry summer caused a 23% decline in the wheat harvest in comparison to the five-year average (Bundesministerium für Ernährung und Landwirtschaft (BLE), 2019). In France, an early warm period in March 2017 was followed by a cold spell in April, leading to a significant decline in grape yields, some 17% below the five-year average (Falstaff, 2017). These examples illustrate how weather extremes may influence yields in unprecedented ways. Lesk et al. (2016, p. 84) conclude, for the period 1964–2007, that droughts and extreme heat significantly reduced national cereal production by 9%–10%. This may increase under scenarios of climate change, and be difficult to forecast (Ben-Ari et al., 2018). Farmers are also facing new challenges in ecosystem health. For example, the role of pollinators – and their decline – has received much attention in recent years (Buchmann & Nabhan, 2012; Vanbergen & Initiative, 2013). Specifically, where conflicts and climate change impact food production simultaneously, this can lead to significant impacts (FAO, 2018a).

A global decline in biodiversity

Biodiversity is "the variety of life at genetic, species and ecosystem levels" (FAO, 2019b, p. xxxvii). Globally, a significant decline in biodiversity has been observed since the 1980s (Ehrlich & Ehrlich, 1981; Wilson & Peter, 1988; Wilson, 1992). It is estimated that there are over nine million types of plants, animals, protists and fungi (Cardinale et al., 2012), and it is increasingly understood that their diversity at genetic, species and ecosystem levels is closely linked to ecosystem productivity and ecosystem functioning (Daily, 1997; Cardinale et al., 2012; Hooper et al., 2012).

Biodiversity is also of central significance for agriculture. In its report *Biodiversity for Food and Agriculture* (FAO, 2019a, p. xxxvii), the FAO highlights that:

> Biodiversity for food and agriculture (BFA) is [...] the subset of biodiversity that contributes in one way or another to agriculture and food production. It includes the domesticated plants and animals raised in crop, livestock, forest and aquaculture systems, harvested forest and aquatic species, the wild relatives of domesticated species, other wild species harvested for food and other products, and what is known as "associated biodiversity", the vast range of organisms that live in and around food and agricultural production systems, sustaining them and contributing to their output.

The FAO (2019a) underlines that "agriculture" includes crop and livestock production, forestry, fisheries and aquaculture. Biodiversity makes production systems more resilient but is increasingly under pressure because of climate change, land use change, pollution, overharvesting and invasive species. This has caused a decline in biodiversity at all levels, i.e., genetic variety, species number and ecosystems. The FAO (2019a) also highlights that a third of fish stocks are overfished and a third of freshwater fish species are threatened. Species that contribute to ecosystem services, including pollinators, natural enemies of pests, soil organisms and wild food species are in decline, as are ecosystems delivering essential food and agriculture services, such as freshwater supplies, protection against hazards and provision of habitat for pollinators. Notably, humanity is dependent on a very small number of key species. While 6,000 plant species are cultivated for food, fewer than 200 make significant contributions to food production, with ten species accounting for half of the total aquaculture production, and nine plants representing 66% of all crop production. To maintain food security, it is of great relevance to maintain biodiversity and the ecosystem services it provides, such as healthy soils, pollinating, pest control and habitat provision (see Box 2.5 and FAO, 2019a).

Yet, biodiversity is declining rapidly. One area of conflict is the abundance of insects, with several studies now showing that insect biomass has been reduced significantly over recent decades (Hallmann et al., 2017; Sánchez-Bayo & Wyckhuys, 2019). Insects are crucial in ecosystem functioning, as they pollinate flowers, represent food for other species and contribute to nutrient cycling (Ollerton et al., 2011; Yang & Gratton, 2014). It is estimated that 80% of wild plants depend on insects for pollination (Ollerton et al., 2011), and an even higher share of cultivated plants (Williams, 1996). Fruits, vegetables, oilseeds, legumes and fodder are estimated to represent one-third of global food production, for example, and rely on pollination by honeybees (Richards, 2001; Buchmann & Nabhan, 2012). Pollination is now increasingly organized by commercial pollinators, at a considerable cost (Sumner & Boriss, 2006; Allsopp et al., 2008).

These insect populations disappear. One detailed study of the situation in Germany concluded, for example, that insect biomass had declined by 76% seasonally and by 82% in summer, over a period of 27 years (Hallmann et al., 2017). A global meta-review of 73 historical reports confirms that insect populations are in decline, suggesting that if rates of loss continue, 40% of the world insect species may face extinction until mid-century (Sánchez-Bayo & Wyckhuys, 2019). The authors highlight that affected insect groups include specialists that occupy particular ecological niches, as well as more common generalist species. The main drivers of insect loss include habitat loss, conversion to intensive agriculture and urbanization, pesticide and fertilizer use, pathogens and alien species, as well as climate change. In order to address this threat to global agriculture and productivity, far-reaching changes in production are necessary (Sánchez-Bayo & Wyckhuys, 2019).

> A rethinking of current agricultural practices, in particular a serious reduction in pesticide usage and its substitution with more sustainable, ecologically-based practices, is urgently needed to slow or reverse current trends, allow the recovery of declining insect populations and safeguard the vital ecosystem services they provide.
> (Sánchez-Bayo & Wyckhuys, 2019, p. 8)

As Sánchez-Bayo and Wyckhuys (2019) conclude, it is not only agriculture that is threatened by the loss of (insect) biodiversity, and agriculture is also in itself a major factor leading to the loss of biodiversity. There is thus a need to urgently return to more environmentally friendly agricultural practices to stop the decline in biodiversity, which is in stark contrast to current trends of agricultural intensification, as well as the need to further intensify production to meet the globally growing demand for food, as outlined by the FAO (2018a). This would suggest that significant change in the global food production system to support biodiversity can only be achieved in a situation where dietary habits change, i.e., where pressure to produce greater amounts of animal protein and higher-order foods declines.

Box 2.5 Reducing pesticide use in farming

A common myth, often promoted by pesticide companies, is that intensive use of pesticides is essential to growing food for increasing human populations. However, a report to the UN Human Rights Council (UNHRC) by the Special Rapporteur on the right to food (UNHRC, 2017) was severely critical of the corporations that manufacture pesticides, accusing them of the "systematic denial of harms" (p. 3), "aggressive, unethical marketing tactics" (p. 4), and heavy lobbying of governments which served to "obstructed reforms and paralysed global pesticide restrictions" (p. 18). According to Hilal Elver, the UN's special rapporteur on the right to food, the notion that pesticides are vital in protecting crops and ensuring sufficient food supplies

> is a myth … Using more pesticides is nothing to do with getting rid of hunger. According to the UN Food and Agriculture Organisation (FAO), we are able to feed 9 billion people today. Production is definitely increasing, but the problem is poverty, inequality and distribution.
>
> (quoted in Carrington, 2017)

The UNHRC (2017, para. 3–5) report concluded:

> Pesticides cause an array of harms. Runoff from treated crops frequently pollute the surrounding ecosystem and beyond, with unpredictable ecological consequences. Furthermore, reductions in pest populations upset the complex balance between predator and prey species in the food chain, thereby destabilizing the ecosystem. Pesticides can also decrease biodiversity of soils and contribute to nitrogen fixation, which can lead to large declines in crop yields, posing problems for food security.
>
> While scientific research confirms the adverse effects of pesticides, proving a definitive link between exposure and human diseases or conditions, or harm to the ecosystem presents a considerable challenge. This challenge has been exacerbated by a systematic denial, fuelled by the pesticide and agroindustry, of the magnitude of the damage inflicted by these chemicals, and aggressive, unethical marketing tactics remain unchallenged.
>
> Exposure to pesticides can have severe impacts on the enjoyment of human rights, in particular the right to adequate food, as well as the right to health. The right to food obligates States to implement protective measures and food safety requirements to ensure that food is safe, free from pesticides and qualitatively adequate. Furthermore, human rights standards require States to protect vulnerable groups, such as farm workers and agricultural communities, children and pregnant women from the impacts of pesticides.

> Arguments that the amount of pesticides currently in use could be greatly reduced without negative consequences for food supply, but with clear benefits for human, animal, plant and environmental health, are also supported by scientific research. Lechenet et al. (2017) examined the potential conflicts between pesticide use and productivity or profitability with data from 946 non-organic arable commercial farms in France with contrasting levels of pesticide use and different types of production. They were not able to detect any conflict between low pesticide use and either high productivity or high profitability in 77% of the farms. They estimated that total pesticide use could be reduced by 42% without any negative effects on both productivity and profitability in 59% of the farms they studied, which corresponded to an average reduction of 37%, 47% and 60% of herbicide, fungicide and insecticide use, respectively, and with the potential for pesticide reduction being higher in farms with high pesticide use than those with low use. Importantly, their results suggested that for insecticides, lower levels would result in increased production in 86% of farms and no farms at all would lose production.
>
> It is important to highlight that research was not conducted by people seeking to argue for chemical-free farming. According to Nicolas Munier-Jolain, at France's National Institute for Agricultural Research, and one of the team who conducted the study.
>
>> Our results are quite consistent with the [UNHRC, 2017] report. But [the research] does not mean pesticides are useless or inefficient … It's a big change, but not a revolution. If you want real reduction in pesticide use, give the farmers the information about how to replace them. This is absolutely not the case at the moment. A large proportion of advice is provided by organisations that are both selling the pesticides and collecting the crops. I am not sure the main concern of these organisations is to reduce the amount of pesticide used.
>>
>> (quoted in Carrington, 2017b)

Water use

Agriculture relies on high inputs of fertilizer, pesticides and water. Depending on the farming system, agriculture will mostly depend on rainfall, and farming systems in drier areas will require irrigation. As warmer climates are more suitable for plant growth, this can result in conflicts over water, which may not be a readily available resource. To distinguish the different types of water required for agriculture, green, blue and grey water can be differentiated (Box 2.6). In particular, blue water use is problematic, as it is sourced from surface water bodies or groundwater. Agriculture is highly water-intense and represents the most important area of human consumptive water use. This issue was first raised by Hoekstra (2003) in the discussion of "virtual water", i.e., the overall amount of water required to produce a given amount of agricultural output. More recent publications have adopted "embodied water" as terminology (e.g., Chen et al., 2018).

One estimate is that food production accounts for 66% of global water withdrawals and 84% of global water consumption (Hejazi et al., 2014). The FAO (2018a) suggests that the total annual water withdrawal for agriculture, municipalities and industries is more than 3,900 km^3, of which 70% are used for agriculture, mostly for irrigation. For the 16 major crops traded internationally, production required 810 km^3, including 65 km^3 of irrigation water and 745 km^3 of rainwater (Macdonald et al., 2015). As most crops are grown in comparably water-rich areas, this represents a major flow of water from water-rich to water-poor areas, as a result of the global trade in agricultural produce. As highlighted by Chen et al. (2018), developed economies including the USA and Japan, as well as large developing economies including China and India are drivers of freshwater use globally, with "significant net transfers [...] from resource-rich and less-developed economies to resource-poor and more-developed economies" (Chen et al., 2018, p. 931).

Figure 2.3 illustrates the amount of freshwater embodied in various crops. The amount will vary depending on climate, crop variety and agricultural practice (UNESCO, 2009), with for example wheat consuming 400–2,000 L per 1 kg, and meat 1,000–20,000 L per kg. On the basis of daily caloric requirements, an adult thus uses 2,000–5,000 L of embodied water per day, or about 1 L per kcal. Actual water requirements will depend on diet, as more plant-based diets (vegan) will have considerably lower water footprints than meat-based diets. Beverages can add considerable amounts of water. For example, the production of a litre of beer may require about 75 L of water; in other words, a person favouring to drink an alcoholic beverage may have a water requirement several orders of magnitude higher than someone drinking plain water.

While chocolate is the most water-intense product, at more than 17,000 L per kg, this does not necessarily translate into a significant environmental impact, as cocoa is often grown in areas with high levels of rainfall (green water), and a blue water share of only 1% (Chenoweth et al., 2014; see also Mekonnen & Hoekstra, 2010a, 2010b). In comparison, tomato production has a blue water component of 30% on global average (Chenoweth et al., 2014). Embodied water assessment should for this reason focus on

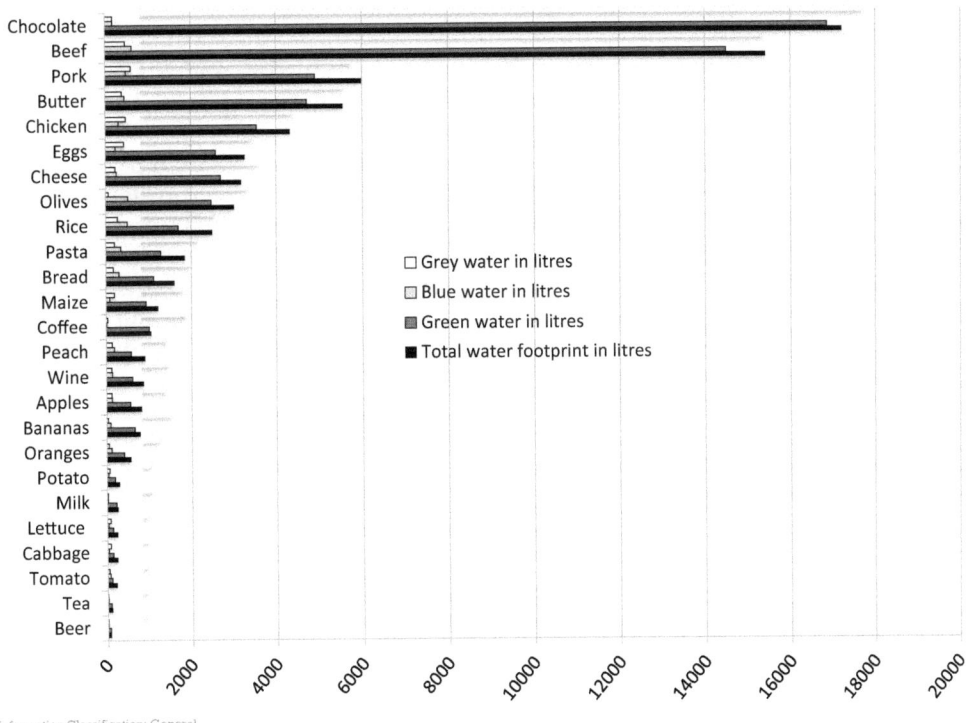

Figure 2.3 Water embodied in various foodstuffs

> **Box 2.6 Definitions of water required for agriculture and food production**
>
> - *Blue Water Footprint*: The amount of surface water and groundwater required (evaporated or used directly) to produce an item. For food, this refers mainly to crop irrigation.
> - *Green Water Footprint*: The amount of rainwater required (evaporated or used directly) to make an item. For food, this refers to dry farming where crops receive only rainwater.
> - *Grey Water Footprint*: The amount of freshwater required to dilute pollutants and make water pure enough to meet EPA water quality standards. For food, the water would have become polluted from agricultural runoff or leaching from the soil.
>
> Source: Grace Communications Foundation (Footprint) (2019)

problematic water requirements, which may in particular include blue water in areas with limited renewable water resources, and corresponding capacity to recharge aquifers. Apart from these considerations, it is also clear that meat and dairy production requires large amounts of water, as well as a relatively high share of blue water. Animals, and in particular cows drink large amounts of water, while also being fed with processed feed transported over large distances (Vanham et al., 2013a, 2013b).

Livestock diseases

Animal health has great importance for livestock production and is also linked to animal welfare, and human health. In the global production of animal protein, the control of animal diseases is of considerable economic importance, and past outbreaks of contagious diseases have led to considerable economic losses. An example is the 1996 bovine spongiform encephalopathy (BSE) outbreak in the UK and other countries, which necessitated the slaughter and disposal of 1.3 million animals under the UK's Over Thirty Months Scheme alone (Atkinson, 1999), and simultaneously had a severely negative impact on consumer confidence in beef products (Wales et al., 2006) as well as meat exports. Animal diseases can also have severe consequences for human health. In the case of BSE-infected cattle, Creutzfeldt-Jakob disease can be contracted by humans eating infected meats. More recently, outbreaks of Highly Pathogenic Avian Influenza have raised wider concerns over zoonoses (OECD, 2012), i.e., diseases that can affect animals and humans, and be transmitted between animals and humans. Considerable research is focused on the issue of vaccines and cures, with in particular antibiotics having received much attention because of implications for resistance developments in bacteria harmful to humans (Singer et al., 2003; Mathew et al., 2007).

The overall list of animal diseases is considerable. For example, Friedrich-Löffler-Institute in Germany lists a wide range of livestock and animal diseases (Table 2.5). These may not necessarily be fatal for animals but may make the animal protein derived from the livestock inedible or unmarketable.

The OECD (2012) discusses the economic implications of animal diseases, including loss of capital as a result of animal mortality, a reduction in marketable outputs and output quality, food loss, the cost of disease prevention and control, animal welfare impacts, trade restrictions, implications for tourism as well as human costs associated with disease. This underlines the need for production conditions that avoid disease

Table 2.5 Livestock disease
Source: Friedrich-Loeffler-Institut (FLI) (2019)

National Reference Laboratories for notifiable animal diseases	National Reference Laboratories for other reportable animal diseases	Other National Reference Laboratories for animal diseases
<ul><li>Monkeypox</li><li>African horse sickness</li><li>African swine fever (ASF)</li><li>American Foulbrood (NRL for bee diseases)</li><li>Equine infectious anaemia</li><li>Infectious salmon anaemia</li><li>Aujeszki's disease</li><li>Small hive beetle infestation (Aethina tumida)</li><li>Tropilaelaps infestation of honey bees</li><li>Dourine</li><li>Bluetongue disease</li><li>Bovine herpesvirus type 1 infection</li><li>Bovine viral diarrhoea</li><li>Bovine, porcine, ovine and caprine brucellosis</li><li>Ebola virus infection</li><li>Enzootic bovine leukosis</li><li>Epizootic haemorrhagic disease</li><li>Epizootic haematopoietic necrosis</li><li>Fowl plague</li><li>Infections with mollusc diseases (Bonamia spec., Marteilia refringens, Perkinsus marinus)</li><li>West-Nile-Virus</li><li>Infectious haematopoietic necrosis of salmonids</li><li>Ovine epididymitis</li><li>Lumpy-skin-disease</li><li>Bovine pleuropneumonia</li><li>Foot-and-mouth disease</li><li>Anthrax</li><li>Newcastle disease</li><li>Equine Encephalomyelitis</li><li>Sheep and goat pox</li><li>Blackleg</li><li>Rift Valley fever</li><li>Rinderpest</li></ul>	<ul><li>Contagious equine metritis</li><li>Campylobacteriosis</li><li>Chlamydiosis</li><li>Echinococcosis</li><li>Equine viral arteritis</li><li>Infectious laryngotracheitis of poultry</li><li>Maedi/Visna</li><li>Low pathogenic avian influenza</li><li>Paratuberculosis</li><li>Q Fever</li><li>Schmallenberg virus</li><li>Toxoplasmosis</li><li>Tularemia</li><li>Verotoxin-forming *E. coli*</li></ul>	<ul><li>Caprine arthritis and encephalitis</li><li>Hantavirus</li><li>Japanese encephalitis</li><li>Crustacean diseases</li><li>Crimean-Kongo Haemorrhagic fever</li><li>Mollusc diseases</li><li>NIPAH/Hendra virus infection</li><li>Tick-borne diseases</li></ul>

Table 2.5 continued

National Reference Laboratories for notifiable animal diseases	National Reference Laboratories for other reportable animal diseases	Other National Reference Laboratories for animal diseases
• Glanders • Bovine salmonellosis • Swine fever • Vesicular stomatitis • Taura syndrome • Rabies • Transmissible spongiform encephalopathies • Bovine trichomoniasis • Bovine tuberculosis • Swine vesicular disease • Bovine genital campylobacteriosis • Viral haemorrhagic septicaemia of salmonids • White spot disease of crustaceans • Yellowhead disease		

outbreaks. Yet, the need to contain diseases is far more urgent in industrial production, where density, faeces volumes, processed feeds and other factors contribute to the creation of environments in which bacteria and other organisms thrive.

Increases in livestock diseases are linked to various developments, including growing numbers of animals, industrialized breeding and climate change. Climate change is widely expected to exacerbate the problem of disease transmissions. For example, Vétérinaires sans Frontières Suisse (VSF) (2018) lists sudden livestock migrations as a result of human displacement, migration of birds or migration of wildlife as triggers for outbreaks. Such migrations can be caused by drought or flooding events. This highlights the need to better consider the implications of current and future change in the global food system, and the specific role of livestock breeding in the distribution and growth of disease.

An outlook: sustainable food systems

This chapter illustrated the considerable number of challenges global food production needs to master in the coming decades. The FAO (2017) summarizes these in ten challenges for the future of food and agriculture, illustrating the difficulty of maintaining and developing a food system that can provide ever-growing amounts of calories and nutrients, in a situation where environmental systems already are under serious pressure, while external threats increase (see Boxes 2.1, 2.5 and 2.7). Much evidence suggests that in particular the already poor will suffer from growing problems regarding food production. Scenarios integrating growth in food requirements and climate change highlight that in particular North Africa and countries in the Middle East will be among the most vulnerable. This also raises concerns regarding forced migration as a result of food insecurity (Afifi et al., 2014).

Yet, the complexity of global development trends may make it necessary to further refine and expand existing scenarios, which have put little emphasis on a number of issues that may gain importance in coming years. For example, food security assessments cannot adequately project short-term risks implied in climate change-related weather extremes that may cause transport disruptions or damage harvests. Other issues may emerge, such as the question of animal welfare.

To illustrate these examples, it may be argued that short-term effects of extreme weather events are currently not adequately recognized as a substantial challenge for food systems. Discussions of the food gap (Ranganathan, 2013; FAO, 2017) put little emphasis on this issue, for example, and even most modelling by the IPCC is focused on longer-term developments, i.e., scenarios to 2100 (e.g., IPCC, 2014). Yet, as the IPCC (2018) states in its most recent '1.5°C report', risks are now considered 'moderate to high' for extreme weather events, which represents an increase in the assessed level of risk compared to the IPCC's fourth assessment report (IPCC, 2014). Weather extremes can significantly affect harvests in the short term, with potentially severe consequences for local food availability (Lesk et al., 2016; Ben-Ari et al., 2018). Where such food shortages lead to food speculation, an issue raised by the World Development Movement (Jones, 2010) in its *Hunger Lottery Report*, this is likely to make poor families highly vulnerable to food price developments.

Animal welfare is not recognized as an SDG, though trends towards industrial meat production make this an increasingly important issue. Yet, animal welfare is unlikely a primary concern in a situation where global food production has to increase rapidly. Interrelationships between animal welfare and the SDGs have been discussed by the FAO (2018c), also because animal welfare organizations have repeatedly highlighted the need to integrate and link animal welfare to the SDGs (e.g., Cox, 2017). A conclusion may be that provisions of growing calorie numbers that also consider the SDGs in regard to climate change, wider environmental concerns and animal welfare can only be achieved in a situation where global diets become more plant-based.

In light of this, it seems clear that achieving the SDGs in the global food system will require enormous and far-reaching changes. Strategies are urgently needed, also in light of some apparent contradictions in the FAO's global challenges. For example, how can goals to significantly increase agricultural productivity year-on-year be aligned with reductions in the impacts of the global agro-industrial complex on ecosystems, species diversity and genetic diversity? The question will be how such divergent SDGs can be united in a common vision for a global sustainable food system. This book outlines the many ways in which chefs can make contributions to this enormous challenge on the basis of their daily decisions.

Box 2.7 FAO's global challenges facing food and agriculture

1. *Sustainably improving agricultural productivity to meet increasing demand*
   Demand for food will increase by an estimated 50% between 2012 and 2050, in a situation where the natural resource base is increasingly stressed, and where yield productivity gains have started to slow.
2. *Ensuring a sustainable natural resource base*
   Pressure is growing on agricultural land, water resources, forests, capture fisheries and biodiversity. An estimated 100 million ha of additional land for agriculture will be needed by 2050.

3 *Addressing climate change and intensification of natural hazards*
Climate change is expected to cause production losses and a decline in yield while contributing to the degradation of land, forests, water, fish stocks and other resources.

4 *Eradicating extreme poverty and reducing inequality*
High and rising inequality in income and access to resources are an underlying reason for hunger, specifically because poor people invest a significantly higher share of their budgets on food.

5 *Ending hunger and all forms of malnutrition*
Population growth will be concentrated in countries already facing food insecurity. This will increase challenges to provide food in sufficient quantity and quality at affordable prices.

6 *Making food systems more efficient, inclusive and resilient*
Growing reliance on global supply chains increases vulnerabilities, which include the high-calorie, but low-nutrient, content of many food items; the reduced access of small-scale producers and family farmers to viable markets; the high levels of food loss and waste; food safety problems; plant disease and animal health issues and the higher energy intensity and heavier ecological footprint associated with the lengthening of food chains.

7 *Improving income-earning opportunities in rural areas and addressing the root causes of migration*
Inequality in rural areas, with limited opportunities of decent work or access to social services leads to migration, mostly in Sub-Saharan Africa and South Asia.

8 *Building resilience to protracted crises, disasters and conflicts*
Violent conflict, natural hazards, food crises and the breakdown of local food systems, along with inadequate governance, represent a high vulnerability risk.

9 *Preventing transboundary and emerging agriculture and food system threats*
A growing number of outbreaks in transboundary animal and plant pests and diseases have been recorded, partially caused by climate change, and compounded by antimicrobial resistance.

10 *Addressing the need for a coherent and effective national and international governance*
Challenges facing global food production can only be addressed in integrated policies at national and international scales, requiring regulation, monitoring and accountability.

Source: FAO (2017)

Chapter 3

Climate-friendly food

Introduction: the climate change challenge

Climate change has turned into one of the world's most significant environmental challenges (IPCC, 2018). This is now generally acknowledged, along with the need to significantly reduce greenhouse gas emissions on a global scale and to limit global warming to a maximum of 2°C compared to pre-industrial times. Both Kyoto Protocol and Paris Agreement serve as international policy agreements towards this goal. The Kyoto Protocol was ratified in 1997, setting reduction targets for high-emitting countries known as Annex B parties under the principle of "common but differentiated responsibilities" (UNFCCC, 2018a). Emission reductions of 5% against 1990 levels were to be achieved during the first commitment period (2008–2012), and, under the 2012 Doha amendment, by 18% below 1990s levels in the period 2013–2020 (UNFCCC, 2018a). Under the Kyoto Protocol, countries emitting large amounts per person agreed to more significant emission cuts. In 2015, the Paris Agreement as a complementary framework for emission reductions became the first mitigation strategy to include virtually all countries in the world: of all the significant emitters, only the USA did not join this international effort to decarbonize economies. The Paris Agreement focuses on voluntary nationally determined contributions (the NDCs); which are national pledges to reduce emissions. High-emitting countries – on a per capita basis – are expected to make more significant contributions to mitigation and to implement "absolute economy-wide reduction targets" (UNFCCC, 2018b).

The challenge of reducing emissions to not exceed 2°C warming is enormous, also because very little had been done to decarbonize economies since the Kyoto Protocol was ratified in 1997. In virtually all economic sectors, emissions continued to grow. The IPCC (2018) now warns that human activities have already caused a 1.0°C increase in temperatures compared to pre-industrial levels and that warming is "likely to reach 1.5°C between 2030 and 2051 if it continues to increase at the current rate". This implies that current NDC pledges as submitted to the United Nations Framework Convention on Climate Change (UNFCCC) are insufficient to meet decarbonization goals, and that a mix of command-and-control, market-based and voluntary measures will be required to reduce emissions by 85% by 2050, compared to 2010 (IPCC, 2014). In absolute numbers, this means that greenhouse gas emissions from human activities have to remain below 1,000 Gt of carbon in total, of which two-thirds have already been emitted (IPCC, 2014). Food production is responsible for a significant share of CO_2, as well as emissions of nitrous oxide (N_2O) and methane (CH_4). Nitrous oxides and methane in particular are potent greenhouse gases, and food production is responsible for rapidly growing amounts of these gases being released in the atmosphere.

Net global emission pathways for CO_2 are illustrated in Figure 3.1. The figure shows observed monthly global mean surface temperatures, and the estimated anthropogenic warming range up to 2017. On the right-hand side, the likely range of modelled responses to various emission pathways indicates that unless very significant emission reductions are achieved, it is likely that temperatures will increase by 1.5°C compared to pre-industrial levels as soon as 2030–2050. Failure to reduce non-CO_2 emissions (such as N_2O and CH_4) considerably reduces the probability of limiting warming.

Under the more desirable 1.5°C maximum warming scenario, emissions have to steeply decline from 2020 onwards (Figure 3.2). The level of decarbonization needed to achieve this goal is equivalent to a decline from absolute emission levels by more

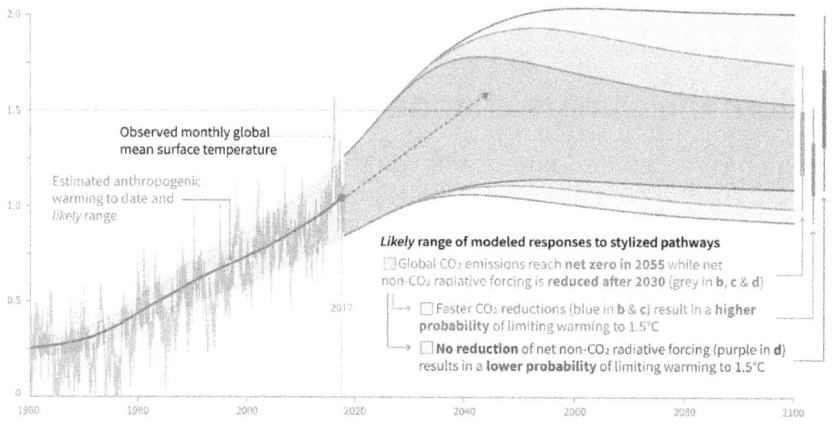

Figure 3.1 Global warming relative to 1850–1900, and pathways
Source: IPCC (2018)

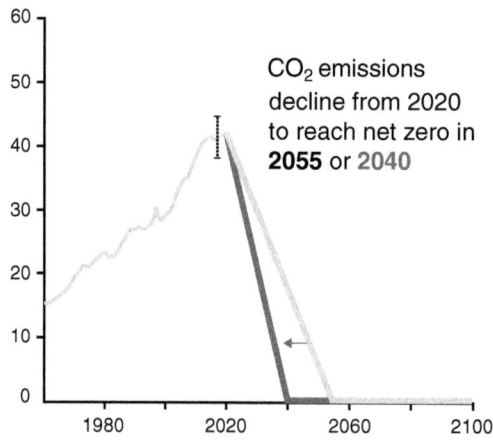

Figure 3.2 Emissions from different subsectors
Source: IPCC (2018)

than 5% per year. By 2040–2050, emissions would have to decline to net zero. Currently, the IPCC (2018) observes a warming trend that is at 0.2°C per decade due to past and ongoing emissions, with limited evidence that absolute emission levels are declining. As the International Energy Agency (IEA) (2019) reports:

> Global energy-related CO_2 emissions grew 1.7% in 2018 to reach a historic high of 33.1 Gt CO_2. It was the highest rate of growth since 2013, and 70% higher than the average increase since 2010. Last year's growth of 560 Mt was equivalent to the total emissions from international aviation.

The IEA (2019) also emphasizes that the growing use of renewable energy sources such as wind, sun, water or biomass already makes a significant contribution to the avoiding of emissions, equivalent to 215 Mt CO_2. Renewable energy expansion is led by China and Europe. Globally, the average carbon intensity of 1 kWh of electricity is now 475 g CO_2, 10% lower than in 2010. This highlights the great potential for restaurants to reduce emissions of greenhouse gases by purchases of 'green' energy (see also Box 3.1). While many countries have sought to reduce emissions, the USA grew in CO_2 emissions by 3.1% over 2017. As the IEA (2019) notes, the impact of weather conditions contributed to this trend, as cooling and heating needs were driven up by extreme weather. Such situations can be expected to become more relevant under scenarios of climate change.

The discussion shows that in order to stabilize the global climate, it will be necessary to significantly reduce emissions of greenhouse gases over very short periods of time. Furthermore, to stand a chance to reduce emissions in line with the 2.0°C warming stabilization objectives, decarbonization will have to become a priority throughout economic sectors. Depending on continent/country, emissions from different subsectors will have to make smaller or more substantial contributions to climate change. As illustrated in Figure 3.3 for the European Union, energy supply is the most relevant emissions subsector (29.3%), followed by transport (19.5%), industry (19%), residential and commercial (11.5%), agriculture (11.3%), waste management (3.2%), international aviation (3%) and international shipping (3%) (EEA, 2016). The food system is part of many of these subsectors, including all of agriculture, and significant parts of transportation, industry (storage and cooling, packaging, processing), aviation and shipping as well as waste management.

Worldwide, it is estimated that food production is responsible for 26% of emissions of greenhouse gases, or 13.7 Gt of CO_2-eq (Poore & Nemecek, 2018). Most of this (61%) is production-related, i.e., caused directly at the farm, with transportation, packaging, distribution and retail adding to overall food-related emissions (Poore & Nemecek, 2018). There is also a geographical concentration in energy use and emissions from agriculture, with China, India, Brazil and the USA emitting 50% of the overall total (FAO, 2018a). At the farm level, it is in particular beef and dairy production that have been linked to emissions of greenhouse gases. Depending on country, this contribution can be very significant. For example, an estimate for Austria is that beef and milk production alone accounts for 4.9% of the country's greenhouse gas emissions (Umweltbundesamt, 2018). Livestock is thus associated with a significant share of emissions from agriculture, though there can be significant differences between the production and consumption of animal protein. For example, the average supply of protein from animal sources is 60% in North America and Europe, more than 50% in Oceania and more than 40% in Latin America and the Caribbean. It is less than 30% in Asia, though there has been a rapid increase in recent years, and less than 15% in Africa (FAO, 2018a). This highlights the importance of understanding both production and consumption of foodstuffs with particularly significant implications for climate change.

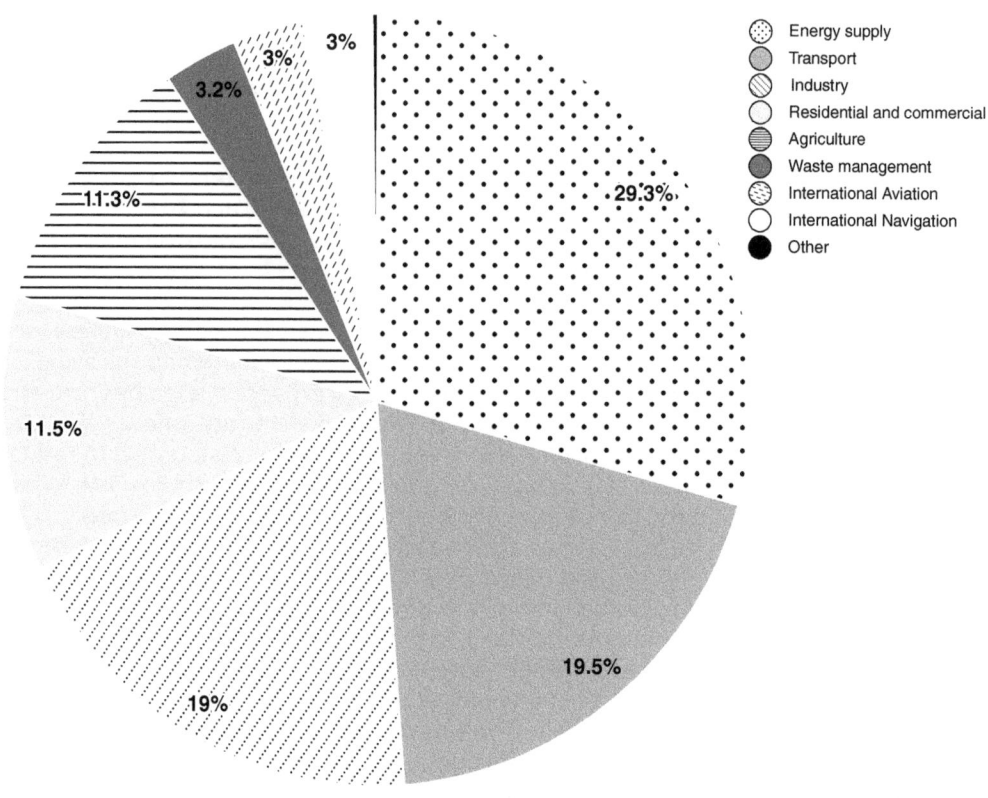

Figure 3.3 Emissions from different subsectors, European Union
Source: EEA (2016)

Animal protein production increases impacts on climate, land use and also has negative associated effects such as acidification, eutrophication and water use (Poore & Nemecek, 2018). Evidence suggests that the global food production system is currently developing in a direction that makes it more carbon-intense. As outlined in Chapter 2, urbanization and industrialization, market liberalization, growing incomes and changes in consumer attitudes have all contributed to changes in food consumption patterns (Kearney, 2010). These have resulted in a Westernization of food cultures, that is, an increased intake of meat, fat, processed foods, sugar and salt. All of these ultimately represent systemic changes facilitated by the global rise in supermarkets, year-around availability of foods, longer shelf lives and the growth of the global food agro-industry (Kearney, 2010).

Over the past 40 years, there has been a 1.4-fold increase in cattle, sheep and goat numbers, as well as a 1.6- and 3.7-fold growth in pig and poultry numbers (Smith et al., 2007). This resulted in year-on-year growth in emissions by about 0.9% in the 20 years up to 2010 (Kearney, 2010). This trend is not linear, however, with evidence that annual growth rates in emissions have increased since 2005 (Tubiello et al., 2013). There is concern that emissions will continue to grow. The World Resources Institute (WRI) (Searchinger et al., 2018) estimates that the 'mitigation gap', that is the likely difference between emissions from agriculture by 2050 (15 Gt CO_2-eq per year, including agriculture and land use change) and the target aligned with stabilizing global warming below 2°C (4 Gt CO_2-eq per year) will be a staggering 11 Gt CO_2-eq per year. Notably, limiting global warming to below 1.5°C will not only require holding agriculture-related emissions below 4 Gt CO_2-eq per year but will also demand reforesting "hundreds of millions of hectares of liberated agricultural land" (WRI, 2018).

To align the sector's development with the goal to stabilize the climate, Wollenberg et al. (2016) suggest that emissions from agriculture need to decline by about 1 Gt CO_2-eq per year to 2030. Up to this year, this would help the sector stay on track to limit warming to below 2°C. However, even in this very ambitious scenario, the sector's emissions would continue to grow to 6.15–7.78 Gt CO_2-eq per year because of the expansion of agriculture and land use change. This implies that far-reaching solutions have to be identified to reduce emissions from agriculture in line with planned steep mitigation trajectories. The WRI (Searchinger et al., 2018, pp. 10–11) suggests five major strategies to address this situation while also considering future land and food requirements. These strategies include:

1. *Reducing growth in demand for food and other agricultural products*
   This strategy relies on reducing food loss and waste; shifts to healthier and more sustainable diets; an avoidance of competition from bioenergy for food crops and land; a reduction in population growth.
2. *Increasing food production without agricultural land*
   This includes increased livestock and pasture productivity; improved crop breeding to boost yields; improved soil and water management; more frequent planting of existing croplands; adapting to climate change.
3. *Protecting and restoring natural ecosystems and limiting agricultural land-shifting*
   The suggestion is to link productivity gains with the protection of natural ecosystems; to limit inevitable cropland expansion to lands with low environmental value; to reforest abandoned, unproductive and liberated agricultural lands; to conserve and restore peatlands.
4. *Increasing fish supply*
   This strategy focuses on the improvement of wild fisheries management, increasing productivity and minimising the environmental impacts of aquaculture.
5. *Reducing greenhouse gas emissions from agricultural production*
   This last aspect is focused on the reduction of methane releases from ruminant animals; the reduction in emissions from manure and fertilizers; low-emissions rice management; increases in energy efficiency and a shift to non-fossil energy sources; the development of strategies to sequester more carbon in soils.

As has been outlined in preceding chapters, many of these strategies are contradictory, such as ambitions to increase productivity and to simultaneously reduce other environmental impacts such as biodiversity loss. Authors have thus called for the sustainable transformation of intensive agriculture (Rockström et al., 2017). As an example, Rockström et al. (2017) concluded that it would be necessary to:

- Plan and implement farm-level practices in the context of cross-scale interactions with catchments, biomes and the landscape as a whole. Maximize farm-level productivity by maximizing ecological functions, from moisture feedback to disease abatement, across scales.
- Integrate ecosystem-based strategies with practical farm practices, where natural capital (soil, biodiversity, nutrients, water) and multi-functional ecosystems are used as tools to develop productive and resilient farming systems.

- Develop system-based farming practices that integrate land, water, nutrient, livestock and crop management.
- Utilize crop varieties and livestock breeds with a high ratio of productivity to use of externally and internally derived inputs.
- Adopt circular approaches to managing natural resources (e.g., nutrient recycling) and mixing organic and inorganic sources of nutrients.
- Harness agro-ecological processes such as nutrient cycling, biological nitrogen fixation, allelopathy, predation and parasitism.
- Assist farmers in overcoming immediate sustainable intensification of agriculture adoption barriers and build incentives for their sustained adoption, rendering the ecological approach profitable in the long run.
- Build robust institutions of small farmers, led especially by women, which enable an equitable interface with both markets and government.

It may be argued that these are long-standing demands for the sustainable transformation of agriculture that have been voiced for decades. Yet, there is little evidence of change towards more sustainable practices and much evidence of developments towards a less sustainable agriculture. The real challenge is thus to identify and implement policies through which farms – and the global food corporations – will respect the sustainable development goals. It is noteworthy that the political side of the agricultural transformation, which arguably is the biggest barrier, is not discussed by the WRI (Searchinger et al., 2018), FAO (2018b, 2018c) or Rockström et al. (2017). While the international and supranational organizations concerned with agriculture and climate change have highlighted the problem and possible solutions, the more relevant question of how this can be translated into actual change remains insufficiently discussed.

A key insight into this context is that the transformation challenge will be significantly smaller if the overall amount of animal protein in the food system declines. For example, the WRI (Searchinger et al., 2018) concludes that limiting daily calories in animal protein halves the climate change food gap. All of this suggests that only a reversal in trends to consume growing amounts of animal protein, embedded in a range of other measures, may stand a chance to become aligned with global emission reduction trajectories. This requires a better understanding of the carbon intensity of different foodstuffs, or, in the context of restaurants, the "carbon foodprint" of menus (Gössling et al., 2011) and opportunities to market low-carbon choices.

Box 3.1 Dietary shifts to mitigate the climate crisis

Shifts towards low-carbon diets are integral to meeting climate change mitigation target. Kim et al. (2020) modelled the greenhouse gas (GHG) and water footprints of nine increasingly plant-forward diets, aligned with criteria for a healthy diet, specific to 140 countries. Vegan (exclusively plant-based) diets had the lowest per capita GHG footprints in 97% of the countries studied. Relative to vegan diets, those which were comprised of plant-based foods with modest amounts of low-food chain animals (i.e., forage fish, bivalve molluscs, insects) had comparably smaller GHG and water footprints. In 95% of the countries examined, diets that only include animal products for one meal per day were less GHG-intensive than lacto-ovo vegetarian diets (in which there are no terrestrial and aquatic meats); this is partly because of the GHG-intensity of dairy foods (Hedenus et al., 2014). The optimal choices among modelled diets varied between countries because of the different contributions of deforestation (e.g., forests being cut down and cleared for grazing and feed production) and highly intensive freshwater aquaculture (Kim et al., 2020). For example, deforestation accounted for 61% of the GHG footprint for Paraguay and over 10% of the footprint for 32 countries' baseline consumption patterns. This variation also highlights the importance of understanding the entire food system to understand the GHG impact of what sits on the restaurant plate (see Chapter 2).

Just as significantly, Kim et al. (2020) also modelled what would happen if all the 140 study countries adopted the *average* consumption pattern of high-income OECD countries. In this scenario, the per capita diet-related GHG and consumptive water footprints increased by an average of 135% and 47%, respectively. The countries with the most GHG-intensive baseline included those with the highest per capita intake of bovine meat (Argentina, Brazil, Australia); the most GHG-intensive bovine meat production (Paraguay, Chile) and the greatest contributions of deforestation to the GHG footprints of diets (Paraguay, Chile, Brazil) consumption. These findings highlight the impacts of increasing dairy and meat consumption and production for GHG emissions (Hedenus et al., 2014), and the importance of reducing animal-product intake in high consuming countries and developing viable diet transition strategies (Willett et al., 2019b).

The carbon intensity of diets

It has been long recognized that different foods vary significantly in their greenhouse gas intensity, measured per kg of food or per calorie (Carlsson-Kanyama, 1998). This can depend on a wide range of factors. For example, meats are generally more carbon intense because animals need significant input energy of plant calories (Pimentel & Pimentel, 2003). Table 3.1 shows that for lamb meat, and the ratio of energy input to protein output is 57:1, about 40:1 for beef or eggs; 14:1 for pork and dairy; 10:1 for turkey and 4:1 for chicken. Importantly, the production of eggs and dairy products also has a high ratio of energy input to protein output.

Animals, and in particular cows, also contribute to emissions of greenhouse gases through digestion, specifically methane (CH_4). For example, Ramírez-Restrepo et al. (2017) calculated lifetime emissions of cattle at about 72 kg CH_4, which is, in terms of

Table 3.1 Livestock ratio of energy input to protein output
Source: Pimentel and Pimentel (2003)

Livestock and animal products	Ratio of energy input to protein output (kcal)
Lamb	57:1
Beef cattle	40:1
Eggs	39:1
Swine	14:1
Dairy (milk)	14:1
Turkeys	10:1
Broilers	4:1

Climate-friendly food

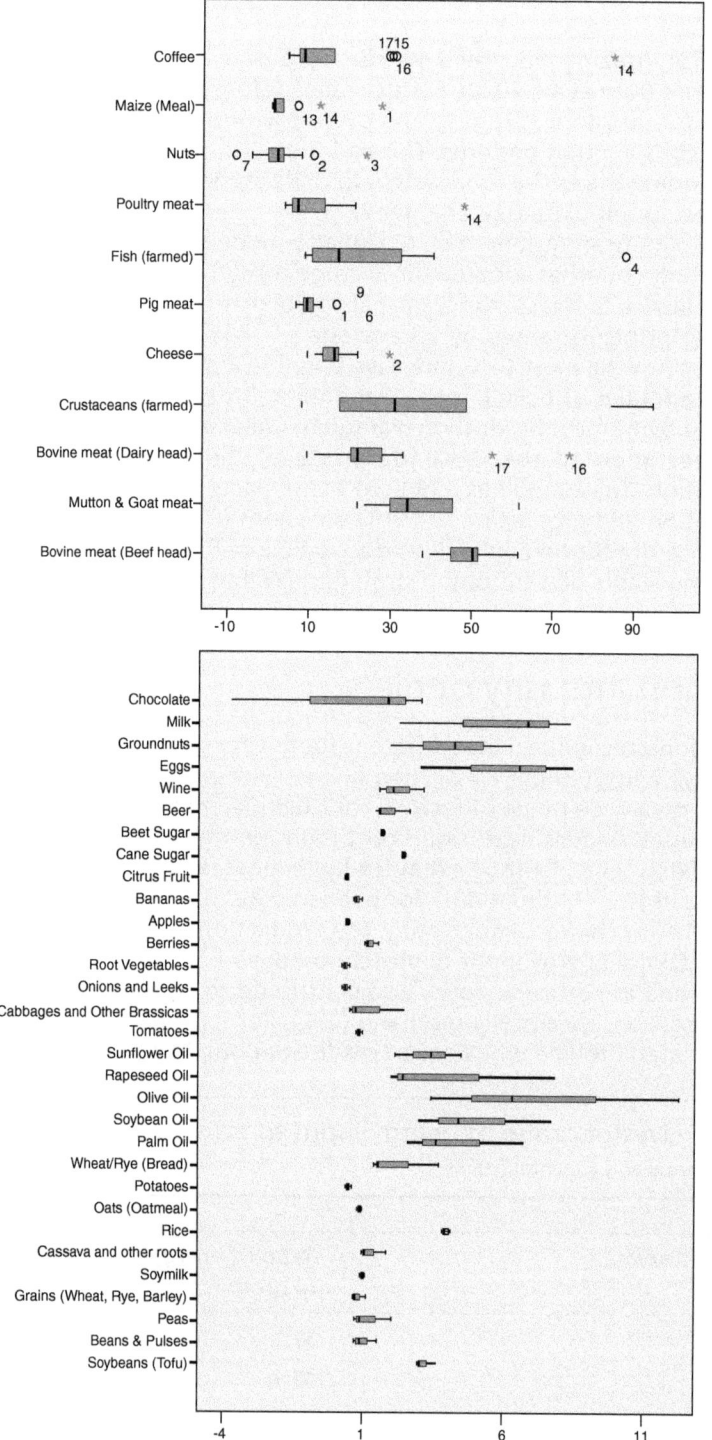

Figure 3.4 Emissions of greenhouse gases associated with food, kg CO_2-eq/kg

Boxplots show min-max values found in the studies assessed (end points), 10–90th percentile (centred bar) and median. Source: Poore and Nemecek (2018), Illustration: Hannes Antonschmidt global warming, equivalent to 1.7 t CO_2. Other factors that increase the carbon intensity of foodstuffs can be their seasonality with, in particular, production in heated greenhouses significantly increasing emissions (Gössling et al., 2011). Furthermore, fossil fuel inputs for production, transport, storage, packaging and retail all influence the carbon intensity of foodstuffs. Different food choices thus have a great impact on the overall contribution of the food system to climate change. Transport emissions, or 'food miles', are discussed in the final section of this chapter.

Figure 3.4 details emissions associated with the production of various foodstuffs (CO_2-eq per kg of produce; production only), based on a meta-study by Poore and Nemecek (2018). The figures indicate that the production of meats is very carbon-intense, and that there are considerable differences between meat. Beef is the most problematic, at a median value of approximately 50 kg CO_2-eq per kg. To illustrate this, a typical car in the European Union will emit about 120 g CO_2 per kilometre (EC, 2016). Eating a 200 g steak is consequently equivalent to one person driving 83 km in a car, an estimate not considering the energy needed to transport, distribute and prepare the steak. Other red meats, in particular sheep and pork, are also very carbon-intense, though this depends on farming practices. Figure 3.4 also highlights the carbon intensity of fish and in particular crustaceans produced in aquaculture. In comparison, fruits, beets, onions, root vegetables, tomatoes, cassava, oats, potatoes, beans or peas are all low carbon in comparison, at around 1 kg CO_2-eq per kg of produce. Nuts, milk, eggs and oils are approximately 5–7 times more carbon-intense.

Depending on diet, vastly different amounts of energy are required to feed one person. This is discussed in the following section both in relation to the global food system as well as individual diets.

Decarbonizing the food system

Greenhouse gas emissions are but one of the global food system's aspects of environmental concern, but a highly relevant one (Hall & Gössling, 2013). Reductions in emissions are theoretically possible throughout the food system, with its main components production, trade, food processing and retail; that is, mitigation can include supply-side and demand-side perspectives. This enables very different stakeholders to support decarbonization, though in a system largely managed on principles of cost-effectiveness, this is unlikely to be a priority for consumers and other stakeholders such as restaurants. Specifically, this calls for consideration of the role of transnational corporations, which function on principles of cost alone, and for whom even tiny profit gains can translate into significant economic value due to the large quantities of food purchased. This is equally true for restaurant chains. Here, only cost-inspired changes will represent meaningful arguments for change.

Supply-side reductions in emissions

Livestock breeding is the most relevant agricultural subsector in terms of emissions (FAO, 2013, 2018a). Within this subsector, it is beef (41%) and milk (19%) production that accounts for most emissions, followed by poultry meat (9%) and eggs (8%) (FAO, 2013). Main emission sources are feed production and processing (45%), enteric fermentation from ruminants (39%) and manure decomposition (10%). As outlined by the FAO (2013), a 30% decline in emissions could be achieved by adoption of best practice approaches to feeding practices, recovery and recycling of nutrients, energy savings and recycling along supply chains and better animal health management. In absolute numbers, the IPCC (2014) calculated a reduction potential of 7.2–11.0 Gt CO_2-eq per year for agriculture. However, this scenario requires very far-reaching supply and demand-side changes, which in turn would rely on very significant political interventions, as consumer behaviour alone is unlikely to sufficiently contribute to mitigation.

While agriculture's mitigation potential is thus potentially large, it should be clear that the vast number of farms makes it nearly impossible to introduce best practices worldwide, and within short timeframes. There is a notable absence of significant low-carbon policies for the agricultural sector (Fellmann et al., 2018). In consequence, relative efficiency gains are far lower than the observed and projected growth in livestock. Furthermore, more recent studies have outlined that there is significant competition for land, in which expanding livestock and biofuel sectors require growing areas of land, and also contribute to land use change while practically rendering impossible efforts to store growing amounts of CO_2 in afforestation schemes (van Vuuren et al., 2018). Overall, this suggests that while significant reductions in emissions are possible on the supply side, these are unlikely to be implemented globally on a best practice level, while an expansion of livestock breeding and biofuel production in particular is not compatible with the need to prevent further land use change in combination with global afforestation and reforestation efforts. If this assessment is accurate, it would have to be demand-side changes that have the greatest potential to reduce emissions from agriculture. This is not an insight shared by all authors, as for example Vieux et al. (2012) argued that it would be easier to reduce supply-side emissions. Yet, no specific roadmap has been provided by any author as to how this would be achieved, with a notable silence on the issue of agricultural politics.

Demand-side changes in diets to reduce emissions

The potential of various measures to reduce diet-related emissions has been discussed in a wide range of publications. On the most basic level, this has addressed the question of minimum food requirements under dietary recommendation scenarios. For example, Meier and Christen (2013) calculated that adjusting German diets to the recommendations of the German Commission on Diets (Deutsche Ernährungskommission) would reduce overall food consumption by 7%, and associated greenhouse gas emissions by 11%. This is also indirectly relevant for climate change, as secondary environmental benefits include a reduction in blue water requirements (−26%) and land use (−15%). In a similar study, Tom et al. (2016) calculated changes arising out of an adjustment of US food consumption to calorically balanced diets, which the authors concluded would yield a 9% reduction in energy, greenhouse gas emissions and blue water use.

Other studies have investigated the effects of adjusting consumption to more sustainable and healthier patterns for entire regions. For example, calculations for the EU suggest that halving meat, milk and egg consumption will cut greenhouse gas emissions by 40%, and area use by 25% (Westhoek et al., 2014). In a global assessment of changes to vegetarian diets, Poore and Nemecek (2018) calculate an opportunity to almost halve greenhouse gas emissions (−49%), corresponding to 5.5–7.4 Gt of CO_2-eq per year. The study also indicates that even though 80% of all farmlands are used for livestock, and this produces just 18% of global food calories (Poore & Nemecek, 2018). Overall, these findings would suggest that demand-side measures have a greater overall importance for reducing emissions: Unless diets change, it is unavoidable to constantly increase production, which represents a major barrier to decarbonization (see Box 3.2).

Box 3.2 The environmental value of vegetarian diets

A vegetarian diet has been increasingly positioned as a means to improve both public health and reduce human impact on the environment, for example, by reducing GHG emissions from livestock (Scarborough et al., 2014; Turner-McGrievy et al., 2016; Dinu et al., 2017; Willett et al., 2019b). Potential GHG emission reductions from the adoption of vegetarian or vegan dietary choices are estimated to be equivalent to a 50% reduction in transportation emissions (Berners-Lee et al., 2012). In the UK, Scarborough et al. (2014) estimate that daily food-related GHG emissions are 7.2 kg CO_2-eq for diets rich in meat and only 2.9 kg CO_2-eq for vegan diets. Increased plant-based diets may therefore have substantial environmental benefits and have become a focus in mitigating environmental change (Turner-McGrievy et al., 2016).

Plant-based options at fast-food restaurants that taste good might help get more people to commit to a planet-friendly diet (Byrne, 2021). According to Taylor Wolfram, a Chicago-based dietitian who specializes in veganism, fast-food businesses "are providing these offerings not only for vegans and vegetarians but for meat-eating customers who are interested in plant-based options as well" (quoted in Byrne, 2021). Wolfram comments that Burger King had a vegetarian burger on the menu for many years, but it didn't sell as well as the new 'beef like' alternatives. There is also substantial support for this observation, as in 2019, 95% of people in the USA who ordered vegan burgers when dining out are not vegetarians (Settembre, 2019). Some 228 million servings of plant-based burgers were purchased at quick-service restaurants in the USA in 2019, up 10% from 2018. And although beef burgers are still the most popular burger on menus, with 6.4 billion sold, growth has flattened (Settembre, 2019).

Among demand-side measures, various strategies can contribute to a reduction in emissions. For any intervention to be successful, it is important to understand food-emissions interrelationships. First of all, the higher the degree of industrialization and per capita wealth, the greater the amount of animal products consumed (Pradhan et al., 2013). As an example, a typical diet in France was found to be associated with about 4.2 kg CO_2-eq per day, though with considerable differences between individuals (Vieux et al., 2012). This amount represents a significant share of sustainable daily per capita emissions (Box 3.3). While Vieux et al. (2012) found a general relationship between energy intake and emissions, indicating that body mass and activity both will influence per capita energy requirements by more than a factor five, the study also confirmed that meat greatly influences the overall total (Vieux et al., 2012).

Pradhan et al. (2013) distinguish low, moderate, high and very high-calorie diets on the basis of systemically derived diets (Figure 3.5). Diets differ in regard to food components, energy content and associated emissions. Pradhan et al. (2013) note that low-energy diets with less than 2,100 kcal per capita and day contain more than 50% of cereals, or more than 70% of starchy roots, cereals and pulses. Animal protein consumption is negligible in both diets, which are most common in Africa and Asia. Diets with a moderate energy content are those with 2,100–2,400 kcal per capita per day, and typical in rice-based diets as prevalent in parts of Africa and Asia. High-calorie

Box 3.3 How much CO_2 is sustainable? And what contribution does a meal make?

Current levels of global emissions of greenhouse gases are unsustainable, and there is consensus that these need to decline quickly over the next two decades, by approximately 5% per year. With total global emissions of about 33 Gt CO_2 per year, and a world population of approximately 7.5 billion, per capita emissions are in the order of about 4.5 t CO_2 per year and person (World Bank, 2018). These need to be reduced by about 20% by 2025 (IPCC, 2014), that is, given continued population growth, less than 4 t CO_2 per capita and year. Divided by 365 days, this amounts to a sustainable 'budget' of about 10 kg CO_2 per person and day. Notably, this amount needs to cover food, housing, transportation and other consumption.

A sustainable budget of 10 kg CO_2 can be compared to the amount of energy needed to prepare a restaurant meal. As emphasized by Pradhan et al. (2013), food in high-calorie diets will cause emissions of about 5 kg CO_2 per day (considering only food production). This is already half of what can be considered sustainable. Restaurants add significantly to this amount as a result of their energy use. As an example, the energy needed in Austrian gastronomy has a cost of 5%–6% of turnover and corresponds to 5–10 kWh per meal served (Bayer et al., 2011). Most of this is used in the kitchen for cooking, heating, cooling and cleaning. Space heating adds to energy requirements. At average global emissions of about 0.475 kg CO_2 per kWh (IEA, 2019), food preparation will add up to 5 kg CO_2 per meal. This implies that for anyone in the European Union eating in a restaurant, daily emissions associated with food alone will already exceed the climatically sustainable threshold.

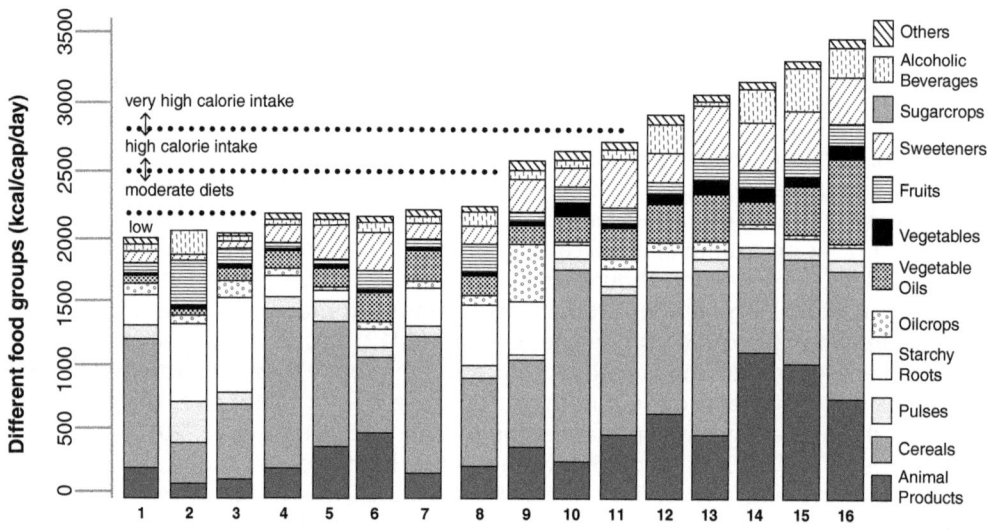

Figure 3.5 Dietary implications for climate change
Source: Pradhan et al. (2013)

diets (2,400–2,800 kcal per capita and day) are mostly found in the Caribbean and Pacific island states, as a result of a high fraction of fruits and oils. Very high-calorie diets are those with more than 2,800 kcal per capita and day, characterized by a high amount of meat and alcoholic beverages. These diets are also associated with the highest per capita emissions, ranging from 3.7 to 6.1 kg CO_2-eq per person and day. In comparison, low-energy diets are 3–5 times less emission-intense, at 1.43 kg CO_2-eq per person and day (Pradhan et al., 2013).

This illustrates the importance of diet changes on a personal level. Any reduction in meat consumption will greatly reduce emissions, as will a change from beef to other meats, and in particular white meat. The choice of in-season local vegetables will further reduce emissions with, in particular, vegetarian and vegan meals being considerably more climate-friendly than other diets. Importantly, Pradhan et al. (2013) calculated differences between dietary patterns for four diet groups, and individual choices can make even greater differences at both ends of the spectrum of food-associated emissions.

Climate-friendly diets in restaurants

Restaurants have many opportunities to influence dining patterns, following the general strategy of climate-friendly purchases, preparation and presentation (Gössling et al., 2011). The following sections discuss these strategies in the context of climate change; more general advice for the design of menus for healthier and sustainable food choices are discussed in Chapter 9.

Purchases

Options for restaurants to contribute to more climate-friendly food choices have been discussed from viewpoints including purchases, preparation and presentation (Gössling et al., 2011). Purchases are important because they influence food production patterns, often globally, and because they determine the carbon intensity of the menus offered. A key problem is that restaurants usually source their food purchases from wholesalers, and hence from global markets. Cost is the most relevant aspect in food order decisions, specifically for restaurants that represent chains. As an example, fast-food chains serving millions of meals per day will always seek to minimize the cost of foodstuff purchases, as even tiny cost reductions become important in terms of their overall implications for economic bottom-lines. This increases pressure on wholesalers to reduce prices, a pressure that is passed on to farmers to constantly reduce the cost of production.

However, the insight has grown in recent years that local farm purchases are not necessarily more expensive, though usually more time-intensive. They require additional management, as more separate orders have to be placed, and because menus have to be adjusted to the season, as not all foods are available throughout the year. In-season food purchases from local farms thus contribute to a decline in emissions because of reductions in transport distance (see also the following section), as well as orders of foodstuffs not produced with a high energy input, such as vegetables grown in heated greenhouses outside the season (Gössling et al., 2011).

Guests perceive local (and seasonal) food as significant added value, with studies showing that highlighting 'local' food items on buffets will increase the demand for these. If managed properly, local food can thus make a considerable contribution to making menus more attractive, and hence to improve guest experiences and overall satisfaction. Local food purchases increase economic opportunities for local farmers. To

> **Box 3.4   The carbon footprint of 'milk': is non-dairy better for the climate?**
>
> Dairy alternatives are increasingly popular as a result of food intolerance, animal welfare concerns or climate change considerations. It is increasingly understood that milk products are highly carbon-intense, and various alternatives have been developed in recent years that are currying favour with customers, including soy milk, almond milk and oat milk. In a study comparing dairy, almond and soy milk, Grant and Hicks (2018) concluded that almond milk, at a 3.85 kg CO_2-eq per L, is the least climate-friendly alternative, followed by soy milk (3.27 kg CO_2-eq per L) and dairy milk (2.75 kg CO_2-eq per L).
>
> However, the results of this study for the USA are heavily influenced by transport distances and electricity consumption at retail. Focusing on production only, both almond and soy milk are far superior to dairy milk, with a carbon footprint (cradle to gate) that is significantly lower for both almond and soy milk (Grant & Hicks, 2018). In their review of life cycle assessments of milk products, Grant and Hicks (2018) find a range of values from 0.37 to 3.18 kg CO_2-eq per kg of dairy milk, 0.34–0.44 kg CO_2-eq per kg/L of almond milk and 0.22–1.40 kg CO_2-eq per kg/L of soy milk. For almond milk it is, in particular, fertilizer production and irrigation (pumps using diesel) that contribute to emissions. This also indicates that production processes heavily influence outcomes, and that organic production characterized by low inputs of fertilizers, pesticides or irrigation is likely to require far less energy. Where transportation is minimized and where retail electricity requirements are reduced, soy and almond milk appear to have more favourable energy efficiencies. It needs to be noted, however, that all options are carbon-intense in the light of sustainable per capita per day emissions of about 10 kg CO_2 per day, notably covering all areas of consumption (Box 3.3).
>
> More limited information is available for oat and rice milk, which have recently emerged as substitutes for dairy milk. In a study of milk production on Swedish farms, Röös et al. (2016) concluded that, depending on scenario, oat milk caused 16%–41% lower direct greenhouse gas emissions than dairy milk.

purchase foodstuffs in season and directly from local farms can thus be a win-win situation for restaurants and the climate.

For many hotels, it may also be feasible to have their own kitchen garden for fresh herbs, another aspect much appreciated by guests as well as kitchen staff. In the context of climate change, it is also important for chefs to reduce the amounts of meat purchased, and to offer only small amounts of beef and cheese, as foodstuffs that are particularly high in emissions. Considering these suggestions for food purchases has great importance for the average carbon intensity of the menus offered.

Preparation

Various considerations become relevant when preparing meals, including the composition of menus, which may contain fewer meat-based dishes, and more vegetarian or even vegan options; a reduction in the amount of meat in relation to 'side dishes' and the complexity of cooking routines. This latter aspect relates to a wide range of issues from the use of frozen foodstuffs to the multiple heating of foods in complex cooking procedures. Avoiding food waste is as much part of preparation procedures as is the use of energy-efficient kitchen equipment. These aspects are discussed in greater detail in subsequent chapters.

Presentation

The presentation of foods in buffets or the marketing of individual dishes has great importance for food choices and can diminish the associated impact of food consumption patterns on climate change. In general terms, there is much evidence that attitudes towards sustainable business practices are positive, highlighting opportunities for restaurants to engage in and to communicate efforts to reduce emissions of greenhouse gases. A growing number of consumers are increasingly aware of the implications of energy consumption, and intent to positively contribute to climate change mitigation. For example, a 2017 Eurobarometer survey on climate change found that 74% of EU citizens consider climate change to be a "very serious problem" (EC, 2017, p. 5). The survey also shows that this percentage has increased continuously, even though there are regional variations, with North European countries perceiving climate change as a greater challenge than others. While 43% of residents in the EU think that national governments are responsible for tackling climate change, 38% believe that business and industry also have responsibility (multiple answers possible). Of importance in the context of this book, 41% of respondents also stated that to tackle climate change, they bought locally produced and seasonal food (EC, 2017).

These findings are closely connected to the understanding of the types of consumption that are more climatically problematic. This would for example include air travel (e.g., Cohen & Higham, 2011). The perceptions of the environmental implications of food choices are less clear, however, and there is evidence that, in particular, the consumption of meat is not associated with its 'true' climate impact, in that consumers still believe that meat is less significant for mitigation (Camilleri et al., 2019). Evidence would

---

Box 3.5 Beverages: should restaurants offer beer from the tap or in bottles?

Beverages are rarely discussed in terms of their energy requirements and associated emissions, even though they make a significant contribution to overall emissions from restaurant visits. In particular, single packaging is an issue for emissions. This can be illustrated on the basis of beer served from the tap in comparison to beer served in a bottle. Poore and Nemecek (2018, p. 990) highlighted this, showing that offering beer out of kegs implies an energy requirement of 0.02 kg CO_2-eq per litre of beer, while recycled bottles will increase emissions 15–40 times, to 0.3–0.75 kg CO_2-eq per litre of beer. Bottles that are not recycled and sent to landfill would entail even larger emissions, between 0.45 kg and 2.5 kg CO_2-eq (Poore & Nemecek, 2018, p. 990).

A detailed cradle-to-grave life cycle analysis of at home beer consumption in the UK found significant differences between the use of glass bottles (containing 85% recycled glass), steel and aluminium cans (Amienyo & Azapagic, 2016). The study found that packaging is on average 67% of the life cycle environmental impact, and a significant share of the overall total is a result of the production of packaging. This determines the carbon intensity of the different types of beer on offer, with steel cans (0.510 kg CO_2-eq per litre of beer) being superior to aluminium (0.574 kg CO_2-eq per litre) to glass bottles (0.842 kg CO_2-eq per litre). The study does not compare multiple-use glass bottles, or beer kegs, as used in restaurants. Both are likely to entail a lower carbon footprint. Overall, consumption of 4.5 billion litres of beer in the UK is estimated to have entailed a primary energy demand equivalent to 0.56% of UK primary energy consumption, and emissions of 2.16 Mt of CO_2-eq; this is 0.85% of UK emissions (Amienyo & Azapagic, 2016).

suggest, however, that this will change in the future, as the media is increasingly focusing on the implications of flying, driving and meat eating. For example, Germany saw significant debate on "Fliegen, Fahren, Fleisch essen" (flying, driving, eating meat) in early 2019 (Focus, 2019).

Given the growing awareness of climate change, convincing restaurant guests to choose vegetarian alternatives will become easier over time, and restaurants can contribute to increasing 'carbon literacy' by highlighting low-carbon choices (Shi et al., 2018). Guests can generally be approached in different ways. For example, staff can recommend more climatically sustainable menus as 'better' choices. This does not have to involve explicit, climate change-focused recommendations, however, as more climate-friendly foodstuffs often also have health benefits. As health can be associated with freshness and taste, all of which are highly important to people, there exist many opportunities to support climate-friendly decisions without mentioning climate change.

However, even where climate change is highlighted, this will positively influence menu choices. This was for instance tested in a Swiss university canteen that introduced a label in menus highlighting a "climate-friendly" option (Visschers & Siegrist, 2015). The authors found that sales of climate friendlier meals increased by 10%. Notably, the authors also found that sales increased over time, suggesting that customers learned to recognize the label as well as to favour food options with a lower impact. As with carbon labelling in more general food-contexts (Gadema & Oglethorpe, 2011; Hartikainen et al., 2014; Ekelund & Spendrup, 2016; Elofsson et al., 2016; Emberger-Klein & Menrad, 2018), research thus indicates that restaurant guests do perceive information on food item climate implications positively, and that they are willing to make pro-climate decisions (Filimonau et al., 2017a, 2017b).

Box 3.6 Animal or plant protein: is lab-grown meat or plant-based meat more climate friendly?

Cultured meat is created through

> exponential cell growth in bioreactors. In the first step a cell is extracted from a living animal, then the cell is fed with a media proliferate, and finally the resulting muscle and fat cells are structured in 3D scaffolding materials to meat. The result is meat which is identical to conventionally produced meat.
>
> (Kearney, 2019, p. 9)

According to the consultancy Kearny (2019), 46% of the worldwide harvest of soybeans, rice, maize, wheat and other produce, totalling 3.201 billion metric tonnes, is turned into animal feed. The authors suggest that the conversion rate of plant calories to cultured meat or vegan meat replacements is up to five times higher than for animal protein, implying that emissions of greenhouse gases for lab-grown meats would be far lower because of better energy utilization, and the avoidance of emissions associated with livestock breeding. In particular, methane (CH_4) is a potent greenhouse gas created by digestion. The consultancy claims that within 20 years, some 40% of all meat would be lab-grown. While this appears to represent a growth rate that is unreasonably steep, it is also notable that the Kearny report devotes little space to consumer preferences, which may be less favourable of lab-grown meats, as well as the question of the climatically even more important global transformation towards more vegetarian or vegan diets.

In the USA in 2019, approximately 18% of the adult population were trying to incorporate more plant-based foods into their diets, with 60% of US adults wanting more protein (Settembre, 2019). About 55% of Americans have expressed a willingness to consumer less red-meat in order to combat climate change, however, although there is clearly consumer interest in meat substitutes and plant-based fast food, the number of vegetarians in the USA remains at about 5%–6% (Byrne, 2021). Because they are generally low in saturated fat, high in fibre and nutrient dense plant-based diets are linked to a lower risk of heart disease and diabetes (see Chapter 8). But there is a difference between consuming an entire plant-based diet and single meal. These issues have been well described by Byrne (2021).

> Both Beyond and Impossible burgers contain 20 grams of protein per four ounces, while the same amount of 85 percent lean ground beef has 21 grams. The plant-based protein comes from a variety of sources—rice, pea, and mung bean protein in Beyond beef; soy and potato protein in Impossible beef. Since protein is important for both performance and general health, the fact that you can get just as much of it from plant-based beef as regular beef is a good thing.
>
> But there are downsides. Impossible beef contains the same amount of saturated fat as 85 percent lean ground beef: eight grams per four ounces. Beyond recently lowered its saturated fat content, but a serving still contains five grams. The Dietary Guidelines for Americans recommend limiting saturated fat to less than 10 percent of your total calorie intake, or about 22 grams per day for someone who eats around 2,000 calories. Too much saturated fat is associated with an increased risk of heart disease and stroke, regardless of whether it comes from plants or animals.
>
> (Byrne, 2021)

Consumer choice changes

The discussion indicates that it is very important to influence demand-side decision-making and to, in particular, increase carbon literacy as a precondition for more sustainable choices: only if consumers are aware of the implications of their food consumption will they be willing to adjust behaviour (Shi et al., 2018). Attitudes will then determine whether consumers actually adjust behaviour by favouring more climatically-friendly foods (Howell, 2018). It is primarily in this latter context that restaurants have great importance in making such choices attractive. Where carbon literacy can be increased, and where attitudes can be positively influenced, this may influence emissions not only in the context of food. Spill-over effects can, for instance, imply that consumers will also be more willing to transfer their environmentally friendly behaviour to other consumption areas, or to support green policies. These dimensions in emission reductions can be summarized as avoidance, shift, maximizing, contemplation and vote.

- *Avoidance* – to not consume specific items at all, such as beef or giant prawns, as these make comparably large contributions to climate change;
- *Shift* – to use products that are comparably less carbon intense, which could include a switch from red to white meats, for dairy to non-dairy products (milk, yoghurt);
- *Maximizing* – to use food products not only to the estimated due date, rather than to the point when they have become inedible;
- *Contemplation* – to induce spill-over effects; this is, to consider behavioural outcomes learned in the context of food even in other consumption domains;
- *Vote* – to empower political parties that advocate policies to reduce food waste or address other climatically unsustainable consumption or that increase pressure on businesses to decarbonize production.

Food miles

As the preceding chapters have outlined, the development of the global food system is driven by demand, specifically for animal protein, as well as market concentration, with large corporations operating in increasingly global markets seeking to constantly reduce unit costs. Cost is the most important single driver of the food system, and as various studies have shown, 'cost' is the most relevant factor for consumers when considering food purchases (Hartikainen et al., 2014; Emberger-Klein & Menrad, 2018). Cost pressure consequently drives the industrialization and globalization of food production, a process in which low transport cost is key. Only where this cost is negligible, it is even viable to consider international food imports by truck, ship or aircraft.

The amount of energy involved in food transportation is considerable. As an example, Germany will import vegetables and fruit by truck from France and Spain, as well as peas from Kenya and grapes from Brazil, by air (Gössling et al., 2011). In Europe, ships will bring fish caught in the Northern Atlantic, or tuna fish canned in Thailand. Imports and exports are often dependent on the season, which can result in reverse transport flows. As outlined in Chapter 2, New Zealand, the world's principal producer of kiwi fruits, is also an importer of green kiwis grown in Italy in January/February, when these are not available in the country.

Essentially, transportation opportunities are a function of cost. Trucks and ships can transport large volumes at a low cost, as the price of fuel is low if calculated per kilogram of produce. As an example, a 20-t truck driving from Spain to Germany may use 600 litres of fuel to arrive at its destination. This, however, translates into less than €0.04 per kg of produce at a cost of €1.20 per litre of diesel, an insignificant amount in comparison to the market price of, for example, oranges at about €2.00 per kg. Even if the truck drives back empty, the transport cost is low with regard to the fuel involved. This is equally true for air freight, given that kerosene is not taxed internationally, and will only cost a fraction of the fuel used for trucks, i.e., about €0.3 per litre. Even though the distances covered are usually larger, it is still economically viable to fly, for instance, grapes at their own weight in fuel: to fly 1 kg of grapes over a distance of about 4,000 km will require about 1 kg of fuel (Gössling et al., 2011). At a retail price of €5–8 per kg outside the season, the transport share of flying grapes from South Africa to Europe may remain feasible at less than 10% of the overall retail cost of grapes.

As a result, food is often transported over vast distances, with one recent estimate that 40% of all food is transported over borders (Poore & Nemecek, 2018). A study in

Table 3.2 Foodstuff energy intensity depending on transport mode
Source: Gössling et al. (2011)

Air international	0.725 kg CO_2/tkm
Marine international	0.015 kg CO_2/tkm
Rail	0.015 kg CO_2/tkm
Truck	0.190 kg CO_2/tkm

the UK concluded that 28% of all goods transported on UK roads represented agricultural and food produce (Pretty et al., 2005). Transportation requires large overall amounts of energy, and, depending on product, transport mode and distance, is also very energy-intense per kilogram of foodstuff. Even including storage at 1°C until spring, a study comparing German apples with apple imports from New Zealand, found that imports required a 27% higher energy use (Blanke & Burdick, 2005).

This also means that the relative share of emissions associated with transportation in food production is considerable. For instance, a study in the USA (Weber & Matthews, 2008) found that food was transported over long distances, i.e., 1,640 km for delivery and 6,760 km for the life cycle supply chain. Production accounted for 83% of the average US household's annual 8.1 t CO_2-eq footprint for food consumption. Transportation represented 11% of life cycle GHG emissions, and final delivery from producer to retail 4%. In other words, the 800 kg of CO_2-eq emitted annually for the transportation of food in the USA (10% of 8 t CO_2-eq) is equivalent to 80 days of sustainable emissions at 10 kg CO_2 per person and day. This also means that food consumption in the USA vastly exceeds annual sustainable emissions per capita (Box 3.4; Table 3.2).

As a general rule, organic food entails lower emissions during the production process, though a major problem is potentially associated with direct purchases at the farm. For example, a UK study concluded that end consumers driving a round-trip distance of more than 6.7 km in order to purchase organic vegetables implied that "carbon emissions are likely to be greater than the emissions from the system of cold storage, packing, transport to a regional hub and final transport to customer's doorstep used by large-scale vegetable box suppliers" (Coley et al., 2009, p. 150).

These examples illustrate the importance of food miles in overall emissions, and the need to reduce transport distances as well as the carbon intensity of the transport modes used. This again raises the question of fuel cost. In the context of air transport, tax exemptions have been discussed as a major reason for the continuous expansion of this transport mode. An estimate by Coady et al. (2017), considering air pollution, vehicle externalities, supply costs and general consumer taxes, puts the total value of fossil fuel subsidies at €4.6 trillion/year. A considerable share of this total is forwarded to airlines, shipping and trucking. Notably, oil price developments also determine the viability of trade with countries dependent on food calorie imports. This is essentially the case in all northern African countries, as well as the Gulf States. OECD and FAO (2018) suggest that in 2027, the price of cereal imports will increase by up to 14% due to changes in oil prices. For this reason, it is paramount that transport costs begin to reflect economic realities, as inefficient systems are more likely to collapse under new low-carbon regimes.

> **Box 3.7 Home food delivery systems**
>
> The emergence of information and communication technologies (ICT) has made it possible for consumers to use a growing number of apps. These also gain importance for deliveries from restaurants to customers who prefer to eat at home. While online platforms routing customer orders to restaurants have existed for some time, these are increasingly replaced by "new delivery players" (Hirschberg et al., 2016) that act as intermediaries between customers and restaurants. These players offer apps such as Foodora, Lieferando, Deliveroo or UberEats, and coordinate the purchasing of foods (the restaurant-based cooking service) with the delivery (the transport service), often on the basis of newly organized logistics networks. This opens up new markets even for restaurants that cannot organize delivery, in a market that is estimated to be worth €83 billion, or "one percent of the total food market and four percent of food sold through restaurants and fast-food chains" (Hirschberg et al., 2016). McKinsey & Company (Hirschberg et al., 2016) suggests that the market for new delivery services will be worth €20 billion by 2025, a trend only hastened by COVID-19 lockdowns and the growth of contactless purchasing.
>
> A key question in the context of this chapter is whether such emerging services increase or decrease emissions related to transportation. There is considerable potential for an increase in emissions if growing amounts of food are ordered online from restaurants, requiring fast delivery as they are freshly cooked. Where such services are organized by bicycle, as is often the case in European cities, emissions caused by transportation may be negligible; this is representing only some additional caloric energy needed by the cyclists to deliver the food. Where deliveries are organized by car, this will add significantly to emissions.

Conclusions

This chapter has examined the relationship between the food we eat and climate change. Importantly, it highlights how the GHG values of food on the restaurant table need to be understood in relation to the entire food system. Hence, this is why some meat and dairy products, and diets with a high amount of meat and dairy in them, have substantial impacts in terms of emissions. Therefore, sustainable food from a food services and restaurant perspective means considering not only the type of food but also where it comes from and how it was produced. And it is to some of these issues that we will now turn.

Chapter 4

Local foods

Introduction

"Local food" is, of course, not new. Prior to the development of industrialized food systems all fresh food had to be sourced locally and only dried, cured and/or smoked products could be transported over long distances. However, the use of local food has now become integral to our understanding of sustainable food services. Celebrity chefs promote local food that is "fresh", "local" and "in season" (Inwood et al., 2009). Better taste is often linked to seasonality (Chambers et al., 2007; Feldmann & Hamm, 2015; Zhang et al., 2020). The Slow Food movement and concepts like "eat your view" (Pollan, 2006) and the "100 mile diet" have also attracted considerable media and public interest (Rose et al., 2008; Smith & Mackinnon, 2009), together with the concept of 'local food heroes' – the local growers who supply such food (Khan & Prior, 2010; Ryder & Topalian, 2010; Roy et al., 2017). As a result, farmers' markets, food box delivery programmes, community supported agriculture and farm direct sales have grown in popularity since the late 1990s throughout much of the developed world (Hall & Gössling, 2016).

Local food systems are often regarded as a more sustainable alternative to globalized food systems (Gössling & Hall, 2013; Hall & Gössling, 2016). A refocusing on local food systems is typically regarded as a means of reengaging people with where their food comes from while simultaneously reducing the distance food is transported and enhancing contributions to local economies, including via the food services and hospitality sector (Hall & Gössling, 2013; Zhang et al., 2020). The use of local food by restaurants is not just a romantic gesture. Local or regional foods have considerable importance for resource use, climate change as well as local business economics. For many restaurants and consumers, local and regional foods are also associated with greater freshness and better taste, doing good for the local economy and reinforcing senses of place (Chen et al., 2021). Therefore, this chapter examines different notions of local food around the world, and how local food association can be used by restaurants to improve sales, better connections with the suppliers and customer loyalty. However, as the chapter discusses, local may not always be better, and the sustainable chef needs to have a better understanding of local foods in order to make informed decisions.

DOI: 10.4324/9781315187488-4

Defining the local

Although there is no consensus as to how to defining 'local' and exactly what constitutes a local food system (Hinrichs, 2003; Pearson et al., 2011b; Hall, 2013a), most definitions are "based on a general idea of where local food is coming from" (Dunne et al., 2011, p. 50). For example, King et al. (2010, p. 2):

> a local food product is defined as one that is raised, produced, and processed in the locality or region where the final product is marketed. This definition relies on the specification of a relevant 'locality or region' that may vary from place to place.

Local food systems have been variously described as 'face-to-face' agricultural markets (Hinrichs, 2000), local food networks (Jarosz, 2008), 'politically constructed boundaries' (Selfa & Qazi, 2005) and as 'alternative' food networks or systems (e.g., Jarosz, 2008; Mount, 2012; Thorsøe & Kjeldsen, 2016). The notion of 'local' therefore has a series of different meanings in the context of food that relate to the place and methods of production and exchange, the factors that drive consumer demand, the influence of producers in the food system and the regulatory and institutional structures that surround food supply (Sonnino & Marsden; 2006; Hall, 2013a). Not having a fixed definition contributes to the complexity and fluidity of the term (Roy, 2016), which can offer advantages in terms of potential inclusivity, but disadvantages with respect to different stakeholder perceptions of what is local. However, one means of better understanding the local is with respect to the different domains of 'local' proximity: geographical proximity, relational proximity, social, economic and environmental proximity, and value-added proximity (Eriksen, 2013; Roy, 2016; Roy et al., 2019a).

Local food as geographical proximity

Geographical proximity refers to "The explicit spatial/geographical locality, (e.g., area, community, place or geographical boundary) distance and/or radius (e.g., food miles), within which food is produced, retailed, consumed and/or distributed" (Eriksen, 2013, p. 51). However, "the local is not everywhere the same" (Allen et al., 2003, p. 63), "distances recognizable as 'local' are neither precise nor constant, but contextual" (Hinrichs & Allen, 2008, p. 342). For example, Morris and Buller (2003) differentiate between 'local' with respect to the regions within which products are produced, sold and consumed; and 'locality' specialty foods which are specifically branded and associated with place as a form of value-added product for export outside of the producing regions, e.g., products that have protected geographical designations (Goudis & Skuras, 2020; Sadílek, 2020). As noted above, the 100-mile diet is one distance-based approach to defining local (Rose et al., 2008), while distance is often used as a means of determining eligibility for farmers' markets (Hall, 2013a). In contrast, Blake et al. (2010) argue that any definition of local food

> in terms of miles is arbitrary and for some inadequate, as to achieve a healthy varied diet might be radius while consumers prefer a 100-mile radius that would give them greater variety in their food choices impossible given the climatic and physical characteristics of an area,
>
> (2010, p. 423)

which is an issue that clearly applies to high latitude and agriculturally marginal regions which may be characterized by high degrees of seasonality in food availability.

Local food as relational proximity

The notion of local food as relational proximity defines 'local' in terms of the business and market relations between actors and the reconnection of direct exchanges or shorter supply chains between producers and consumers (Cunningham, 2011; Mount, 2012; Duncan et al., 2021). "The direct relations between local actors (e.g., such as producers, distributors, retailers and consumers) reconnected through alternative production and distribution practices such as farmers markets, farm shops, cooperatives, box schemes, food networks" (Eriksen, 2013, p. 51), what is sometimes termed as "locavores" (Dunne et al., 2011). Relational proximity between producers and consumers is often presented as "immediate, personal and enacted in shared space" (Hinrichs, 2000, p. 295) and as creating "responsibility, communication, and care for each other and the land" (Kloppenburg et al., 2000, p. 184). As such, the development of face-to-face links between producers, consumers and others, such as restaurants, retailers and other foodservice providers, is regarded as a regenerative counterpoint to large scale, industrialized systems of food production and distribution (Hinrich, 2000; Duncan et al., 2021).

Local food as social, economic and environmental proximity

A local food system is a "collaborative effort to build more locally based, self-reliant food economies-one in which sustainable food production, processing, distribution, and consumption is integrated to enhance the economic, environmental and social health of a particular place" (Feenstra, 2002, p. 100). Local food systems explicitly link wider social, economic and environmental concerns with locality (Roy, 2016; Hedberg II & Zimmerer, 2020; Sellberg et al., 2020). As Feagan (2007, p. 23) noted, "being conscious of the constructed nature of the 'local,' 'community' and 'place' means seeing the importance of local social, cultural and ecological particularity in our everyday worlds". From this perspective, the local therefore becomes a way of enhancing sustainable regional development in an integrated manner.

Local food as intrinsic values of proximity

The values of proximity are the "different values (e.g., place of origin, traceability, authentic, freshness, quality, etc.) that different actors attribute to local food" (Eriksen, 2013, p. 51). Other values recognized in the local food literature, "typically include environmental sustainability, social justice, organic production, support of local and regional farmers, as well as eating seasonally" (Duram & Oberholtzer, 2010, p. 100), making visible those that feed us (Yamashita & Robinson, 2016); convenience and health (Blake et al., 2010); care, embeddedness and trust (DuPuis & Goodman, 2005; Roy et al., 2017); food literacy (Levkoe et al., 2020) and moral and ethical value of eating locally (Peterson, 2013; Navin, 2014; Ferguson & Thompson, 2021).

The various values of proximity identified in local foods are therefore closely related to values often identified with sustainable food systems overall with respect to social, economic and environmental dimensions of sustainability and the intersections between them (Gössling & Hall, 2013; see Chapters 1 and 2). Interestingly, Eriksen (2013) when highlighting the value of proximity across the various perspectives, borrows from Barham (2002, p. 350) who suggests, "there is one unifying characteristic that ties them all together. They all carry explicit messages about a product's value in registers that are usually considered to be non-market by economists". However, this picture is somewhat of an oversimplification given the way in which local foods have become commodified and promoted, often without a deeper analysis as to the extent to which they are more beneficial and sustainable (Schoolman, 2019) or their degree of localness (Schmitt et al., 2018). Indeed, Ferguson and Thompson (2021) argue that when faced with three options: buying local food, buying global (non-local) food and buying global food while also purchasing carbon offsets to mitigate the environmental impact of food transportation, the offsetting option is morally superior to the alternatives because it provides economic benefits to the poorest food workers while also mitigating transportation impacts.

Schmitt et al. (2018) also provided an interesting study by assessing the degree of localness of food value chains by applying five criteria, geographical distance, supply chain size, supply chain length, identity and governance, to two case studies from the Swiss cheese sector to quantify the level of "localness". They found that on average, the local cheese, L'Etivaz, obtained a degree of localness of 56% and the global one, Le Gruyère, 31%. There were only small differences in 'geographical distance' and 'supply chain length', but larger ones in 'supply chain size', 'identity' and 'governance', leading Schmitt et al. (2018, p. 573) to conclude, "that these cheeses hide a local–global hybridity, by promoting local attributes and values while being embedded in international markets". Nevertheless, despite claims with respect to the benefits of local food often not being sufficiently critically evaluated, local food systems are generally viewed as a solution to the negative externalities associated with the global industrialized food system (Roy, 2016; see also Chapter 2), especially with consumers increasingly demanding more information about the supply chain, "information about the food's origin and how it is handled and transported" (Bosona & Gebresenbet, 2011, p. 293) (see also Box 4.1).

Box 4.1 Grower definition of local food

Roy et al. (2019b) undertook a comparative analysis of farm-to-restaurant sales in New Zealand and Canada. As part of the study, growers were asked what local food meant to them. The definitions offered by the majority of respondents were based on geographical or political boundary lines (province or region), such as products 'grown' within the region or within a political boundary, rather than by a distance measure. In contrast, very few growers defined their 'local food' in terms of the mileage or distance they would travel to sell. The actual number of miles they would travel varied considerably, ranging from 90 in Christchurch, New Zealand, to a 100–210-mile radius from where they lived in Vancouver, Canada. A number of respondents in Christchurch defined local food according to political boundaries rather than by a distance measure. One respondent in Vancouver went even further to explain that he would prefer food to be grown closer, rather than simply within the geographical or political boundary lines or distance measures, and wanted it to be from as close as possible:

> For me, local means 'just up the road'. When I was in California, I bought strawberries from a surplus stand outside an enormous farm that supplies berries all over North America. I considered the roadside ones local (Vancouver respondent).
>
> (quoted in Roy et al., 2019b, p. 91)

Restaurants and local food: terroir cooking

Restaurants have not received as much attention as other parts of the culinary system, such as farmers' markets and artisan growers. However, they are an important element of the local food movement (Smith & Hall, 2003; Nummedal & Hall, 2006; Inwood et al., 2009; Severt et al., 2020). Restaurants can promote local food supply via their purchasing but just as importantly they can promote it via their menu and other marketing (Alfnes & Sharma, 2010; Roy et al., 2017). Restaurant purchasing of locally grown foods is therefore usually undertaken because of their perceived superior quality and freshness, to meet customer requests, to access unique products and to support local businesses (Reynolds-Allie & Fields, 2012; Roy, 2016). However, it should also be emphasized that ultimately foodservice and hospitality operations also respond strongly to consumer demands where since 2000 local foods have been a positive consumer trend (National Restaurant Association, 2018).

In one sense, the local food focus in many restaurants and foodservice providers is nothing new as it builds on traditional European, and especially French, focus on terroir and appellation, the geographical designation of where food comes from. Local food, by its definition, implies that its origin and the processes by which it is produced can be identified and, as a result is also linked to favourable perceptions of taste, quality and healthy and environmentally friendly production techniques (Buller & Morris, 2004). Nevertheless, the terroir tradition extends far beyond simply using local produce. "It [terroir] refers to the uniqueness of a place, one that gives food from a particular region its particular taste – meat, cheese, vegetables and fruit all taste differently in different regions", said Elizabeth Carter, editor of *Waitrose Good Food Guide*.

> But it is more than just soil and climate – it is the growing method and techniques, the application of habit and custom that defines the food. It's also about using old methods of preserving, fermentation, smoking, to preserve local, seasonal produce for the winter season.
>
> (Doward & Melli, 2016)

As Tresidder (2015) observed, the terroir restaurant can therefore be seen to differ itself from other restaurants by privileging the central relationship between food, culture, history and geographies to generate experience.

Raymond Blanc at Michelin starred Le Manoir aux Quat' Saisons, in Oxfordshire, which first opened in 1984, has been a long-time campaigner for terroir cooking and is regarded as being a major influence on modern British cooking and the re-emergence of artisan producers and farmers' markets. Visitors to the restaurant are free to wander around the gardens, where many of the ingredients for their meals are grown. One of the reasons for the restaurant garden was the lack of access to the ingredients he was seeking.

> ... I realised that *regional* cuisine no longer existed in Britain, so life would bear little resemblance to what I had known in France.
>
> In Britain, industrialization had largely squeezed the small home producer out of existence, bring the dreaded 'rationalization' and 'standardization' and eliminating consumer choice. This, of course, bred a most unhelpful attitude to consumers, chefs and anyone concerned with quality of produce, as I discovered to my cost. When I asked for anything that had not come off a conveyor belt, I was stared at in disbelief and considered a thorough nuisance. It was the start of many arguments.

Local foods

> In this cycle of apathy, I observed, the consumer accepts unquestioningly, so the producer never bothers to improve – and so it goes on. It was staggering to encounter such appalling ingredients for my culinary needs – and in a country which abounds in wonderful game, fish and meat.
>
> I had ambitious plans for changing the world of vegetables and this also proved to be a struggle.
>
> (Blanc, 1988b, p. 9)

Blanc's philosophy is clear in his cookbooks. For example, in the introduction to *Blanc Vite*, he states

> Good food starts with wholesome ingredients. Yet we remain complacent. Agriculture has become agrochemistry and, in order to get large yields, we have intensive farming that involves a large spectrum of chemicals damaging both nature and to ourselves at the end of the food chain.
>
> (Blanc, 1998a, p. 7)

Such criticisms are also reflected in the connection of regenerative farming to the development of alternative local food systems. Regenerative farming prioritizes soil health, biodiversity and ecological restoration, and forgoes most conventional industrial agriculture practices, including pesticides, synthetic fertilizers or feeding stock genetically modified crops and food. The perspective of such an approach was reflected in a comment on the growth in regenerative farming practices in the US, "If a farmer is not obsessed with the quality of his soil then he's merely a landowner" (quoted in Lampert, 2021).

Blanc, who was a president of the Sustainable Restaurant Association (SRA), became convinced of the importance of terroir growing up in France. According to Blanc:

> It's why I want to know as much detail as possible about every ingredient we serve to our guests, … By reconnecting people with their food, we create a population that will value what they eat, which in turn produces more fertile land, more prosperous farmers and a healthier nation that can enjoy the amazing food that is produced here in Great Britain. Food connects with everything – our landscape, our soil, our heritage, our health and the agriculture and industry of today is quite simply creating the society of tomorrow.
>
> (Raymond Blanc quoted in Doward & Melli, 2016)

Tom Tanner, spokesman for the SRA, acknowledged that terroir cooking asks hard questions of its practitioners. "There are challenges for some restaurants. In this country you have to think long and hard about how you are going to do stuff". However, the required response is to create relationships with suppliers, "They create a relationship with these people. They know how those farmers and fishermen are working, what techniques and farming methods they are using. They have faith in them, they invest their trust in the farmers" (in Doward & Melli, 2016; see also Chapter 7).

Shane Holland, executive chairman of Slow Food UK, which promotes sustainable food production, explained, some restaurants have no choice but to source their produce from further afield.

> One of the difficulties in the UK is that our food is quite industrial. We don't necessarily have very diverse agriculture in all areas. That can make it harder to source, depending on where you are. One of the reasons for the Sportsman

having such variety on its menu is that Seasalter has great meat, great fish, great seafood. It is more difficult to source that from a very, very small area. If you are trying to take meat from the local area, for example, that can be quite difficult because there is a shortage of abattoirs.

Box 4.2   The Sportsman

In 2016 the Sportsman was voted the restaurant of the year by a panel of industry experts for *Restaurant* magazine. Although it has been awarded a Michelin star, the restaurant was described by the Sportsman's own Twitter account as a "grotty rundown pub by the sea". As Granleese (2016) comments in reporting on the award, "It's not much better inside: old-school bar, mismatched wooden tables and chairs, simple blackboard menu. First-timers could be forgiven for heading back out to the car park and doublechecking the satnav".

The restaurant is located in Seasalter, just outside of the town of Whitstable, on the north-east coast of the county of Kent, England. The restaurant looks out over the flat landscape of the Thames estuary, a coastal marsh landscape that is often more associated with sheep grazing, cheap industrial land and caravan parks than fine dining. According to chef/patron Stephen Harris, who comes from the area:

> We're basically two restaurants in one: a pub with a dining room that also does a tasting menu. The tasting menu is all about terroirs, this area, but otherwise it's the standard starter, main and pud deal … I even make my own salt … but that's more a hookline, a romantic gesture to Kent and the sea.
>
> (quoted in Granleese, 2016)

According to *Restaurant* magazine's editor, Stefan Chomka:

> Stephen Harris once described the Sportsman as a 'grotty boozer by the sea'. But it's certainly way more than that. The former history teacher is one of a handful of UK chefs to practise genuine terroir cooking down in the Kent estuary.
>
> (quoted in Doward & Melli, 2016)

A review of the restaurant's tasting menu highlights these local qualities:

> So this is what was on the tasting menu: homemade pork scratchings; home-cured herring; three types of homemade bread, with the pub's own butter; two oyster amuse-bouches, one with apple foam and one with a granita of sea buckthorn, a startling jolt of citrus and a lovely surprise in midwinter. Mussel and bacon chowder with a garnish of ground bacon and chives, which was outstanding. Pintail duck, something I'd never eaten, was superb meat, beautifully cooked and rested, and came with the best bread sauce I've ever had. Home-cured ham: fantastic. Braised turbot with crab: running out of superlatives. Lamb breast poached, then breadcrumbed and fried (a French dish called Ste Menehould), served with mint sauce: genius idea. The rack and shoulder of the same lamb with cabbage and a fabulously deep,

resonant, unsticky meat sauce. Apple sorbet with popping candy. Iced cream cheese with breadcrumbs and pear: a sort of deconstructed-but-improved crumble. Delightful petits fours, including a tiny Gypsy tart – a Kentish speciality made with condensed milk. All this cost £55, which might not sound cheap, but I ate it three weeks ago and I'm still smiling when I think about it.

(Lancaster, 2011)

As noted elsewhere in this chapter, the concept of terroir is usually associated with wine. Yet Harris associates it with food overall:

It's just the idea of cooking what's around you. In Normandy, cooking uses lots of cream and apples; in Provence, it's olive oil and tomatoes. We just followed a similar idea but, obviously, Kent has a lot of food. It's very good for meat, shellfish, apples, pears, strawberries and raspberries.

(quoted in Doward & Melli, 2016)

To achieve this the restaurant grows most of its own vegetables and staff regularly forage on the Thames estuary mudflats to collect oysters and other items such as samphire and urchins. Lamb comes from a farm on the salt marshes which is visible from the restaurant carpark, while chickens also come from a nearby farm. Harris also makes his own butter, combining it with another local ingredient – seaweed. Salt is produced on the premises using local seawater (Doward & Melli, 2016).

Alexia Robinson, founder of Love British Food fortnight, explained.

The word local has been bastardised, … The classic example is the pub menu when you see a phrase like 'local lamb'. Nothing is more irritating; it's a meaningless expression. If this award gives local a more integral interpretation then that is to be hugely applauded.

Shane Holland, executive chairman of Slow Food UK, argued that some restaurants in Britain have no choice but to source their produce from further afield.

One of the difficulties in the UK is that our food is quite industrial. We don't necessarily have very diverse agriculture in all areas. That can make it harder to source, depending on where you are. One of the reasons for the Sportsman having such variety on its menu is that Seasalter has great meat, great fish, great seafood. It is more difficult to source that from a very, very small area. If you are trying to take meat from the local area, for example, that can be quite difficult because there is a shortage of abattoirs.

(quoted in Doward & Melli, 2016)

Stephen Harris has some sympathy with those comments but argued that in response to the problem chefs had to become more inventive with dealing with seasonality and local foods: "In the winter we have to look further afield, but there is so much good produce around here we can mainly use what is around".

> Importantly, the local becomes a very important part of the story and branding of the restaurant that helps differentiate in a crowded marketplace:
>
> > Terroir is about continuing a tradition, … We've maybe pushed it a bit further than the idea has been pushed before. I accept that making your own salt is a strange thing to do – but it's a kind of romantic idea. These days it's very fashionable to talk about the narrative behind the restaurant. When people come here they like the idea we even make our own salt. It's part of the story.
> >
> > (quoted in Doward & Melli, 2016)
>
> www.thesportsmanseasalter.co.uk

Local foods can clearly help restaurants to differentiate their products and add value (Alfnes & Sharma, 2010). The products produced by local food systems are frequently equated with notions of quality, freshness, health and superior flavour by both restaurants and their customers (Inwood et al. 2009; Roy et al., 2017), regardless of whether it is a restaurant that explicitly promotes its terroir as part of its positioning or not. Indeed, local food purchasing by restaurants is arguably good public relations, given that it can support local producers and the local economy, thereby reinforcing the economic and financial viability of local food networks (Schmit & Hadcock, 2012; Sharma et al., 2014). Nevertheless, a number of perceived barriers to restaurant purchase of local food have been identified including lack of knowledge; inconvenient ordering and delivery times; limited availability of products; variable costs, packaging and handling and inadequate distribution systems (Inwood et al. 2009; Roy et al., 2017). These issues are discussed further in Chapter 7.

Consumer demand for local food

The local food movement has long argued that it is reflecting consumer demand to "reconnect" consumers with the people and places that produce their food (Kneafsey et al., 2008; Hall & Gössling, 2013). However, Australian research (Birch et al., 2018), suggests that egoistic motivations may influence local food consumption decisions more strongly than altruistic ones. Much of the interest in local food has, perhaps somewhat paradoxically, been in the context of the local food of 'other places' in their role as tourist attractions (Sims, 2009). In this sense, local food is very much part of the notion of local food as a form of geographical proximity and authenticity (Rytkönen et al., 2018) and something that reinforces a sense of place (Chen et al., 2021). However, while tourist demand for the local is important for terroir restaurants it does not account for the wider desire of consumers to eat local in their own home environments and local restaurants. Therefore, other factors need to be taken into account.

The availability of local produce is a significant factor for restaurant customers. Lillywhite and Simonsen (2014) reported that for one-fifth of surveyed restaurant consumers, a restaurant's practice of 'buying locally' was the primary restaurant attribute of importance. A major factor that influences demand for local produce is the extent to which consumers are substantially alienated from contemporary food production in environmental, economic and social terms (Zepeda & Leviten-Reid, 2004;

Levidow & Psarikidou, 2011; Matacena & Corvo, 2020). In a study of over a thousand Californian consumers, Rainbolt et al. (2012) found that economic, environmental and social (fairness and responsibility) considerations are all important in purchasing local food, with the indication of 'local' being valued as of equal importance or even more important than 'organic', depending on the purchasing channel (see also Box 4.3). Economic considerations emerge in the notion of local food supporting local farmers and producers, including via farmers' markets (Hall, 2013), although there may be substantial differences between consumer segments (Weatherell et al., 2003; Selfa & Qazi, 2005; Denver et al., 2019) and belief systems (Zhang et al., 2020). For example, in Finland, Roininen et al. (2006) found that rural consumers consider local food as a way to support local production and create economic welfare while urban consumers linked local food consumption more to animal welfare, environment and health. Significantly, with respect to concepts such as food miles, both rural and urban consumers identified short transportation distances as a reason for local food preference. However, in a study of French consumers, Sirieix et al. (2008) found that "consumers are aware of distance and associated it with the complexities of food supply chains, but they do not take distance into account when they choose food products" (p. 511).

A range of motivations noted above were also identified in a German study of urban consumers (Zoll et al., 2018), that also included individual desire for high-quality food with respect to taste and freshness and health and more political and environmental consumerism motives, e.g., opposition to conventional agriculture and long-distance food transport. In terms of the role of relational proximity in local food, consumers were also found to often want to support a certain farmer and their philosophy and the community-building dimension of local food purchase (Zoll et al., 2018).

A survey of Australian consumers found that financially supporting local farmers (94%) and the local community (91%) were key factors, together with freshness (97%) in the purchase of regional fruit and vegetables (Godrich et al., 2020). The importance of freshness and taste has long been noted as a factor in local food research and is clearly of importance to restaurants and foodservice operators (Chambers et al., 2007; Hall, 2013; Roy, 2016). In a Norwegian study that used the lens of prosocial helping behaviour theory, Skallerud and Wien (2019) found that that empathic concern and social concern influence consumer attitude towards, and preference for, local food. Interestingly, they also observed that local patriotism influences the preference for local food even if consumers evaluate it as being of lower quality and less desirable than non-local food products, while even in a chain restaurant setting (Frash et al., 2015), patrons have been found willing to pay more for menu items made with local foods with social/community and freshness/taste motivations being the two strongest in terms of consumers' willingness to pay more for local foods in chain restaurants. Such local support may possibly even help overcome the extent to which the price of local food can be a barrier to purchase (Darby et al., 2008; Godrich et al., 2020).

Box 4.3 Short food supply chains and local food in the EU

There is substantial interest in local food in the EU. On average, 15% of EU farms sell more than half of their production directly to consumers (European Parliament, 2016). Nearly a quarter of Europeans consider "local or short supply chains" (24%) as an important characteristic of sustainable food and 47% as part of a sustainable diet, while half favour food choices that support the local economy (Eurobarometer, 2020).

A 2011 survey of 26,713 EU citizens revealed that 92% of respondents thought buying local agricultural products and foodstuffs beneficial and that the EU should promote their availability (Eurobarometer, 2011). People who agree that there are benefits to buying local products are more likely to argue that small farms need financial support because they play an important social role: 46% of those in this group endorse the social case for small farms, as opposed to 33% who say there are no benefits to buying local goods (Eurobarometer, 2011). In addition, many of those who support the idea of having labels to identify local products also support the social importance of small farms: 46% of people in this group do so compared with 38% who disagree that this kind of labelling would be useful (Eurobarometer, 2011).

The majority of respondents (55%) agreed that EU citizens should encourage local markets and distribution channels in all but five Member States: Italy, Malta, Austria, Poland and Portugal, with over half agreeing that there are consumer benefits to buying locally grown food from farms. Over half of the respondents also agreed that it would be beneficial to have labels identifying local products and these respondents were also more likely to recognize the benefits to consumers of buying local foods and to agree that the EU should help make local products more readily available and only 15% of respondents disagreed (Eurobarometer, 2011).

A 2012 Eurobarometer survey also showed that EU citizens strongly supported local food. Seventy-one percent of respondents said that the origin of food is important, with quality (96%) and price (91%) being the most important factors when buying local food. However, the Eurobarometer survey did find substantial differences between countries. More than half the respondents regard the geographical origin of food products as important, with the exception of the Netherlands (47%). Respondents in Greece (90%) and Italy (88%) mostly supported the idea that origin was important, with the level of support lower in the UK (52%) and Belgium (56%).

Local food as perceived by restaurants and chefs

Consumer interest is clearly a major driver in encouraging restaurants and foodservice providers to 'buy local'. However, this is a two-way process as many restaurants and chefs (see Box 4.2) are also seeking to generate customer interest in local products and food culture and will actively seek to promote it on the menu (Tellström et al., 2006). In their study in Ohio, Inwood et al. (2009) found that in their purchasing decisions restaurants were focused on taste and freshness, believing that local produce tasted superior to non-local produce, and less interested in production standards. Although issues of distribution and convenience were barriers to increased use, similar findings were also reflected in other research (Alonso & O'Neill, 2010; Sharma et al., 2014). Similarly, Tellström et al. (2006) identified obstacles related to distribution and delivery, availability and reliability of supply, ordering processes and time management issues in dealing with multiple suppliers, while the top four barriers listed by restaurants in New York in sourcing locally were: time constraints and inconvenience of dealing with multiple farmers; lack of confidence regarding product consistency; lack of confidence regarding products quality and availability of sufficient volumes of products (Schmit & Hadcock, 2012).

There is therefore significant variation in studies of local food purchasing by restaurants and foodservice providers that may reflect different food cultures and the historical development of supplier relationships in different locations (Roy et al., 2017). For example, in Curtis and Cowee (2009) study chef's preferences for purchasing locally produced foods in Nevada, 69% of chef respondents had never purchased from local producers. Of the respondents who did not make local purchases, 75% of those identified lack of necessary information about purchasing, inadequate availability and variety of products and lack of authority to choose suppliers as barriers. This last point highlights how many foodservice businesses that are part of chains and franchises are typically highly bureaucratic organizations that have little flexibility in local procurement with purchasing being conducted centrally so as to reduce costs as much as possible (Sharma et al., 2014).

Smaller, independent restaurants, therefore, tend to be the greatest supporters of local purchase, although seasonal factors in relation to product availability are still an important factor (Nummedal & Hall, 2006; Roy, 2016). Yet it is important to highlight that the use of local products may nevertheless still reflect 'global' menu items, such as pizza, kebabs or burgers, rather than high-end 'traditional' cuisine, or cuisine such as curry which has become part of a food culture as a result of migration (Akbar, 2021). For example, in Roy's (2016) study on restaurant use of local food, Chinese restaurants in Vancouver were one of the biggest users of local food as a proportion of all foodstuff buying. Indeed, as a result of food globalization, the relative number of restaurants that focus on terroir is much smaller, though much higher profile, than the providers of international cuisine, yet this latter group remain incredibly important with respect as local food users and potentially more sustainable restaurants.

Conclusions

This chapter has discussed the role of local food as part of the conceptualization of sustainable restaurants. As noted, the use of local food by restaurants can have significant benefits both for the business and for communities, local economies and the environment. Chefs and restaurants are also important opinion leaders in encouraging people to consume and purchase local foods (Inwood et al., 2009). However, as noted in the opening chapter, locally produced food is not automatically better for the environment than non-local food just because it is produced closer to the end customer (Ilbery & Maye, 2005; Hall & Gössling, 2013). Much depends on the metrics used. For example, is a locally produced food product that comes from energy and water-intensive, and high pesticide use farm production, better than the same product that has come from further away, but which was grown organically and with low energy levels? Indeed, distance alone is not a good indicator of overall environmental impact, as the impacts of producing a food item need to be considered together with the environmental and energy costs of transport (Wallgren, 2006; Saunders & Barber, 2008; Coley et al., 2011; Gössling & Hall, 2013). Using longitudinal data from the US Census of Agriculture to explore whether growth in local food systems is associated with decreased on-farm use of agricultural chemicals, Schoolman (2019) found that an increase in the strength of local food systems, measured as either the number of farms that market products directly to consumers, or as the total value of direct market products, has been broadly associated with a decrease in spending on agricultural chemicals in the USA as a whole. However, Schoolman (2019) concludes that the magnitude of the relationship between direct marketing to consumers and changes in agricultural chemical use has dwindled over time as well, to the point where it is not clear whether contemporary local food systems are still incentivizing farmers to reduce their use of pesticides.

A further issue is that while the focus of much media is on terroir restaurants and their significant role in influencing food trends, the reality is that they are usually in the minority. The reality is that every restaurant and foodservice provider, regardless of the cuisine they serve, should be encouraged to purchase locally wherever appropriate. However, there is also a further potential irony in the focus on the local and the relationship to terroir as, in recent years, with respect to labelling for example, while the French system of appellations is linked to terroir, it has also become tied to the global as intellectual property defined by the GATT and regulated by the WTO as a geographical indication (Barham, 2003), showing how the local and the global in the food system are deeply intricated and how the local is also an essential element in differentiating food from specific places in order to be able to sell it elsewhere. An important element of such labelling is that the origin of products is opened up to greater scrutiny thereby leading to increased transparency in the food chain and to the customer. Therefore, to understand the importance of the local in sustainable food it is also vital that we understand the global, and the way in which international benchmarking can provide valuable insights into what happens at the local.

Chapter 5

Organic food

Introduction

Organic food is an increasingly important part of sustainable restaurants and the sustainable kitchen. Being organic implies the use of food ingredients that are artificial spray and chemical-free, are not genetically modified or altered, and have been produced in as 'natural' a way as possible. Organic foods are purchased by consumers as they are perceived as being better for personal and planetary health than conventionally grown food (Pearson et al., 2011a; Hemmerling et al., 2015; Massey et al., 2018). Restaurants use organic foods for various reasons some of which are more geared towards profit rather than principle (Poulston & Yiu, 2011; Lu & Gursoy, 2017; Jeong & Jang, 2019). Nevertheless, restaurants and foodservice providers are critical elements in the promotion of greater consumption of organic food and therefore serve to leverage less intensive agricultural practices as well as new organic farming innovations. Together with farmer's markets, restaurants and their chefs are therefore at the forefront of encouraging more sustainable agricultural practices.

This chapter first discusses the definition of organic food, which is a key issue in its labelling and regulation, as well as the scale of organic agricultural production. It then goes on to review issues surrounding the costs of organic production and certification, before concluding with a discussion of organic food purchase.

Definitions and scale

Organic food production is associated with various environmental and social benefits, such as soil and plant health, nutritional quality and support of biodiversity; the latter also by omitting or minimizing the use of pesticides and industrial fertilizer (see Box 5.1). Organic agriculture improves soil quality by increasing carbon levels and organic matter content, which can help to improve water storage capacity and the slow release of nutrients (Karlen et al., 1990). Organic agriculture also has the potential to reduce the potential for plant disease (Reeve et al., 2016).

Implications for biodiversity have growing importance, given the observed decline in insects in many parts of the world (e.g., Hallmann et al., 2017). Various studies have highlighted that organic farming supports insect diversity because of restrictions in the

Box 5.1 Definitions of 'organic' agriculture

Definitions of organic food production were developed decades ago to better describe the basis and idea of this type of agriculture.

> Organic agriculture is a holistic production management system which promotes and enhances ecosystem health, including biological cycles and soil biological activity. Organic agriculture is based on minimising the use of external inputs, avoiding the use of synthetic fertilizers and pesticides. [...] methods are used to minimize pollution of air, soil and water. Organic food handlers, processors and retailers adhere to standards to maintain the integrity of organic agriculture products. The primary goal of organic agriculture is to optimize the health and productivity of interdependent communities of soil life, plants, animals and people.
>
> (FAO & WHO, 2001)

> Organic agriculture is a whole system approach based upon a set of processes resulting in a sustainable ecosystem, safe food, good nutrition, animal welfare and social justice. Organic production therefore is more than a system of production that includes or excludes certain inputs.
>
> (IFOAM, 2002)

The FAO (2002) added to these definitions an explanation in terms of related definitions:

> In contrast to food labelled as 'environmentally-friendly', 'green' or 'free-range', the label 'organic' denotes compliance with specific production and processing methods. Most synthetic pesticides and fertilizers, and all synthetic preservatives, genetically modified organisms, sewage sludge and irradiation are prohibited in all existing organic agriculture standards. Adherence to organic agriculture standards, including consumer protection against fraudulent practices, is ensured through inspection and certification. Most industrialized countries have regulations governing food labelled as 'organic'. Other terms also used are, depending on the language, 'biological' or 'ecological'.

In the United States, the Department of Agriculture (USDA), has set organic standards, which sets the rules and regulations for the production, handling, labelling and enforcement of all USDA organic products. In the USA,

> organic is a labeling term that indicates that the food or other agricultural product has been produced through approved methods. The organic standards describe the specific requirements that must be verified by a USDA-accredited certifying agent before products can be labeled USDA organic' (USDA, Agricultural Marketing Service.
>
> (USDA, AMS, n.d.)

use of agrochemicals and less intensive agricultural systems supporting insect habitats (Habel et al., 2019). This also supports other biodiversities such as bat populations, which rely on insect abundance (Wickramasinghe et al., 2004). Organic agriculture is also important with regard to climate change, as growing pressure on plants through weather extremes highlights the importance of creating more resilient food production systems. There are many definitions of organic food production, most of which emphasize that 'organic' comprises all production stages, and the need for change throughout the agroindustrial system (FAO, 2002).

Organic agriculture, along with consumer interest in organic foods, has grown continuously since the 1970s. In 2002, the Food and Agriculture Organisation (FAO, 2002) reported that:

> Global retail sales of certified organic products have increased to around $16 billion in 2000. In some national markets, a few organic products have obtained shares of 10 or even 15 percent. Organic sales represent a small share, between 1–2 percent, of global food and beverages [...].

The Research Institute of Organic Agriculture (FiBL) and the International Federation of Organic Agriculture Movements (IFOAM) suggest that by 2015, 179 countries provided data on organic agriculture, which now includes 50.9 million ha, or 1.1% of all agricultural lands (FiBL & IFOAM, 2019). This share has constantly grown, from 0.2% of all lands in 1999. Organic production was led by Australia: the country accounts for almost 45% of all organic production worldwide (22.7 million ha). Other countries with considerable shares of organic agriculture are Argentina, the USA, Spain, China, Italy, France, Uruguay, India and Germany. Figure 5.1, an update by FiBL (2019), shows that in Europe (including Russia), organic production is led by Spain, Italy, France and Germany. This distribution is slightly different if looking at the share of organic production in overall production, which is led by Austria (23.4%) before Estonia (19.6%) and Sweden (19.2%) (Eurostat, 2019).

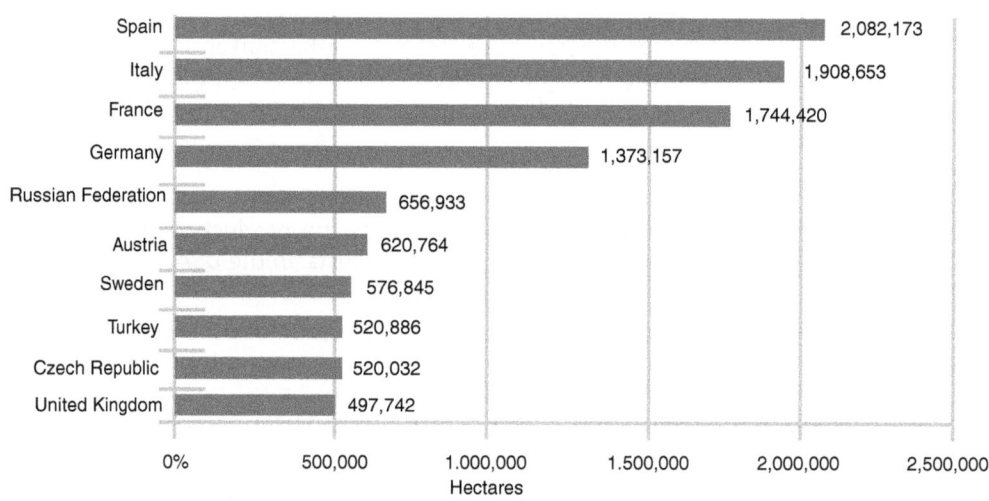

Figure 5.1 The ten European countries with the largest organic production

Most production is focused on cereals, followed by green fodders, oilseeds, dried pulses and vegetables. Of the permanent crops, it is coffee, olives, grapes, nuts and coca that cover the largest shares of land. Overall, there are some 2.4 million organic producers in the world. The economic value of the organic market is now estimated to be US$81.6 billion, almost half of this in the USA (48.7%), followed by Germany (11.6%) and France (7.5%). The highest per capita consumption of organic produce may be in Switzerland (Sahota, 2013).

As organic food production seeks to reduce environmental impacts in a situation where a growing world population requires more food, much attention has been paid to yields. Evidence suggests that organic yields are somewhat lower than conventional production. For example, Mäder et al. (2002) found in Central Europe that organic farming systems produced yields 20% lower, though input of fertilizer and energy was also considerably lower (34%–53%) and pesticide input by 97%. They concluded that soil fertility and higher biodiversity were likely to make organic farming systems less dependent on fertilizer. In another review, crop yield differences of between 2% and 60% were found (Lotter, 2003). More recent comparisons indicate that differences depend on system and site characteristics (Seufert et al., 2012; Ponisio et al., 2015), and Ponisio et al. (2015) concluded that organic yields were on average 19.2% lower than conventional yields. Seufert et al. (2012) conclude that for some crop types and growing conditions, organic production is almost equal to conventional agriculture, while for others, the gap is more significant. This was also confirmed by Ponisio et al. (2015), who

---

Box 5.2   Organic food sales boomed during COVID-19

Sales of organic food and drink increased substantially in the UK during COVID-19 lockdowns. Organic food and drink sales grew by 6.1%, almost double the 3.2% growth of non-organic food and drink products, in the year ending May 2020. It also reported an 18.7% increase in organic sales in the 12 weeks to the end of May, which included ten weeks of lockdown, compared with a 14.2% increase in non-organic equivalents (Smithers, 2020). Over the entire year, retailers and producers saw the organic market rise by 12.6% compared to 2019 (Soil Association, 2021). This was the category's highest growth level in 15 years with sales worth £2.79bn in 2020. Significantly, it was also the tenth consecutive year of growth in sales (White, 2021). Foodservice sales fell by 23.2% to £75.7m as a result of the pandemic's impact but retail sales and online and home delivery sales more than offset the temporary decline in sales in the hospitality and foodservice sector (White, 2021). Perhaps not surprisingly, consumer confidence in organic produce also continued to grow during the pandemic, with 41% of people agreeing that buying organically produced foods was good for sustainability at the start of 2020, a figure that increased to 50% by July by the time COVID-19 restrictions had affected consumers (White, 2021). According to Louisa Pharoah of the Soil Association,

> Organic farming is a whole system approach that nurtures the soil, biodiversity and our planet … The Covid-19 pandemic has meant more people appreciate where food comes from, and with the increased interest in growing veg in our gardens and home baking, there's never been a better time to talk to people about the benefits of organic farming.
>
> (quoted in Smithers, 2020)

emphasize that agricultural diversification practices including multi-cropping and crop-rotations can significantly reduce the gap in yields between organic and conventional systems.

While the case for organic agriculture is thus less favourable from a yield perspective, the situation is different from the viewpoint of environmental impacts, system resilience, economic viability and food quality (Reganold & Wachter, 2016). Studies show that organic production results in better soil conditions containing greater dry matter mass, and mycorrhizal associations. This is of great importance in drought situations, in which organic agriculture can outperform conventional systems (Lotter et al., 2003). There is also evidence that organic agriculture is more stable with regard to variability in year-to-year yields (Lotter, 2003), though this has been disputed more recently by Knapp and van der Heijden (2018). As detailed national studies show, organic farming systems may perform as conventional systems, with the former improving over time (Schrama et al., 2018). Given much evidence of lower yields in organic agriculture, environmental benefits have to be weighed against the need to feed a growing population, as outlined in Chapter 2. As the growing food gap is to a large degree dependent on future levels of meat consumption, this, however, is not a one-dimensional choice (see e.g., Joseph et al., 2019).

Organic food economics

Studies assessing the advantages and disadvantages of organic versus conventional food production have also discussed food quality, including the role of pesticide residues, heavy metal, mycotoxins, bacterial contamination or antibiotics. Generally, these studies have concluded that organic produce is better for human health as pesticide residue levels are lower, though there are no significant differences in heavy metals (except Cadmium, which is lower in organic foodstuffs), mycotoxins and bacteria (Gomiero, 2018). Reeve et al. (2016, p. 320) also suggested that fruits and vegetables grown organically contain more health-promoting phytochemicals, as a result of "greater plant stress, rhizosphere microbial communities, and/or lower available nitrogen".

As consumers are willing to pay premiums for foodstuffs perceived as healthier or more environmentally friendly, there is much evidence that organic agriculture is more profitable than conventional food production systems. Crowder and Reganold (2015) found, for example, that organic agriculture is 22%–35% more profitable than conventional agriculture. The authors concluded that to match the profitability of conventional agriculture, premiums have to be only in the range of 5%–7%, considering that organic yields are 10%–18% lower. Better profitability in organic agriculture is reflected in demand, with FiBL (2019) suggesting that the organic market in Europe saw a 10.9% growth in 2017, reaching a value of €10 billion in Germany alone. The Danes are now the highest spenders on organic foods, with €278 per person and year – this is more than eight times the European Union average.

While organic food production is more profitable, there is also a cost of food production imposed on society, specifically by conventional production (Pretty et al., 2005). This cost is related to the release of pesticides, nitrate, phosphate, eutrophication, greenhouse gas emissions, loss of biodiversity and health effects (Pretty et al., 2000). A considerable cost can also arise out of animal disease in industrialized food production and associated measures to contain the disease, culling of animals, feed bans, incineration and the removal of risk material. For instance, the cost of bovine spongiform encephalopathy in Germany is estimated to be in the order of €1.8–2.1 billion for the period 2000–2010 (Probst et al., 2013). This excludes the significant cost of decline in demand (Herrmann et al., 2002), and food security perceptions more generally.

In one detailed study of the environmental cost of farming in the UK, Pretty et al. (2005) concluded that food baskets are heavily subsidized, as environmental externalities are significant at £1.5 billion per year up to the farm gate. Notably, the authors estimate that more than £1.1 billion per year could be avoided if agriculture switched to organic production. As food is responsible for 28% of the goods transported on UK roads, externalities related to moving produce impose another £2.4 billion per year, plus another £1.3 billion per year for transportation from retail to home. Other subsidies amount to £2.9 billion per year. Together, these externalities represent an 11.8% subsidy to food consumption. Pretty et al. (2005) concluded that a switch to organic production would significantly reduce negative externalities, specifically for milk, eggs and different types of meat (Table 5.1).

Table 5.1 External costs to farm gate, UK (2000)
Source: Pretty et al. (2005)

Produce	External costs from conventional agriculture		Scenario: as if whole of UK was organic		Change in external cost from conventional to organic (%)
	Total external cost (million £ per year)	Unit external costs (per kg)	Total external cost (million £ per year)	Unit external costs (per kg)	
Cereals	378	1.72	71.1	0.32	−18.6
Potato	28	0.42	3.5	0.05	−11.9
Oil seed rape	50	3.54	9.7	0.69	−19.5
Sugar beet	21	0.22	3.7	0.04	−18.2
Fruit	5	1.44	0.8	0.25	−17.4
Vegetables	18	0.61	3.0	0.10	−16.4
Beef/veal	442	64.79	82.5	12.09	−18.7
Pork	127	12.81	37.6	3.79	−29.6
Poultry	88	5.68	29.4	1.91	−33.6
Mutton/lamb	158	43.57	59	16.3	−37.6
Milk	171	1.22	73.3	0.52	−42.6
Eggs	30	3.96	11.3	1.44	−36.4

Box 5.3 The cost of pesticide use

In 2016 Bourguet and Guillemaud conducted a review of the hidden and external costs of pesticide use. As they noted,

> Pesticides provide many benefits by killing agricultural and human pests. However, they also entail several types of costs, including internal costs due to the purchase and application of pesticides, and various other costs due to the impact of treatments on human health and the environment.
>
> (Bourguet & Guillemaud, 2016, p. 35)

In providing a comprehensive review of these costs and their evaluation, they identified four different categories of costs: regulatory costs, human health costs, environmental costs and defensive expenditures with those costs being either internal to the market, but hidden to the users, or external to the market and most often paid by a third party.

Regulatory costs were estimated at US$4 billion annually in the USA alone in the 2000s. However, Bourguet and Guillemaud (2016) argued that if all regulations were actually respected, these costs would have increased to US$22 billion. Health cost studies were generally found not to include fatal cases due to chronic exposure such as fatal outcomes of cancers (Andersson et al., 2014). If this had been done, Bourguet and Guillemaud (2016) suggest that it would have increased estimates of health costs by up to tenfold, e.g., from US$1.5 billion to US$15 billion in the USA in 2005.

The unintended impact of pesticide use on the environment is substantial (Fabricius, 2005; Geiger et al., 2010; Chopra et al., 2011; Mineau & Whiteside, 2013; Hallmann et al., 2014). Environmental costs were estimated as being of the order of being up to US$8 billion in the USA in 1992. Although the additional expenditures arising from defensive behaviour (Dickie, 2003) are little considered in the literature, they include at least the extra cost of the part of organic food consumption that is due to averting foodstuffs that are linked to pesticide use. Bourguet and Guillemaud (2016) estimate that this cost reached more than US$6.4 billion worldwide in 2012.

The review by Bourguet and Guillemaud (2016) highlights that the economic costs of pesticide use have undoubtedly been strongly underestimated in previous studies and are substantially ignored in relevant literature (Cooper & Dobson, 2007). They found that estimates of the overall hidden and external costs ranged from US$5.4 million in Niger in 1996 to US$13.6 billion in the USA in 1992. In undertaking a retrospective evaluation of benefit-cost ratios in various countries, Bourguet and Guillemaud (2016) identify a value of US$39.5 billion per year by the start of the 1990s, at which time the economic costs of pesticide use may have already outreached their benefits. In their conclusions, they emphasize that the key impact to be evaluated is the cost of illnesses and deaths triggered and favoured by chronic exposure to pesticides (Calvert et al., 2008; Cohn et al., 2015; Guyton et al., 2015; Soto & Sonnenschein, 2015), and find that "The benefit-cost ratio of pesticide use may have easily fallen below 1 if this cost had been taken into account" (Bourguet & Guillemaud, 2016, p. 35).

Differences in 'organic'

Statistics on organic produce do not usually contain classifications as to what differentiates 'organic' agriculture from conventional food systems. In this context, it is helpful to distinguish standards, labels and certifications. A *standard* refers to specific criteria or norms for produce that can also serve as benchmarks. *Labels* are the logos or stamps visually identifying a product's specific characteristics, helping consumers to identify foodstuffs with specific standards. *Certification* refers to a formal accreditation process, in which it is confirmed that the certified product meets a given set of (minimum) standards.

Table 5.2 German organic label criteria
Source: EC (2019)

Type	Characteristics
Organic I *soft criteria*	Based on EU regulation: • At least 95% of ingredients come from organic agriculture • Up to 0.9% genetically modified organisms possible • Partial organic production possible at farm • Restricted use of antibiotics and pesticides possible • Limitation of approved food additives (16% of conventional production)
Organic II *medium criteria*	As Organic I, but also: • 100% of ingredients come from organic agriculture • No genetically modified organisms (GMO)
Organic III *strict criteria*	As Organic I, but also: • 100% of ingredients come from organic agriculture • No genetically modified organisms (GMO) • No transport distances >200 km • Animal health and welfare considered, no antibiotics allowed • No pesticides allowed • Almost no food additives

It is generally possible to distinguish a wide range of approaches. Some of the criteria for organic produce are institutionalized, for instance by EU regulation, while other criteria are set by a wide range of certifying organizations (Tables 5.2 and 5.3). For example, the EC (2019) has set criteria for its EU-organic label that defines the standards for processed foods with several ingredients, the use of GMOs, the use of antibiotics and pesticides, as well as additives and other general farm rules. For instance, under its organic I category, farms may have mixed production of conventional and organic foodstuffs. Organic II and III are stricter standards in comparison.

Certifications are the most prominent information tools in the food sector, as they have significant influence on purchase intention as tools increasing trust (Nuttavuthisit & Thøgersen, 2017; see also Balogh et al., 2016; Tait et al., 2016). They exist in individual countries, regions or as globally represented labels. Ecolabel Index (2018), for example, lists 102 ecolabels for food products, restaurants, farms, vineyards and wineries, fisheries, businesses and retailers. The number of entities certified can range from a few ("Certified Australian Southern Rocklobster 'Clean Green' Program") to 10,000 producers ("Naturland"). Often, certifications address environment as well as social and animal welfare criteria ("Krav", Sweden). The largest certifications address fair working conditions (e.g., "Fairtrade"; "Fair Trade Certified"; "UTZ Certified"). The organizations behind the different labels can be not-for profit, for profit, industry associations or government (Ecolabel Index, 2018).

Table 5.3 sheds some light on organic certifications and the organizations behind the standards. A key characteristic of many standards is that they seek to go beyond legal production rules, which may often mean modest improvements over conventional

Table 5.3 Organic certifications

Organization/area	Short description
Council Regulation/State-Licensed 11.9 million ha total organic area in the EU (Eurostat, 2019)	In 2007, the European Council of Agricultural Ministers agreed on a new Council Regulation (Regulation 834/2007; EC, 2007) that sets out the principles, aims and basic rules for organic production, and defines how organic products are to be labelled. Several other labels have copied this standard. As an example, German 'Bio-Siegel' and French 'Agriculture Biologique' are both based on the EU-Eco-Regulation.
Organization of organic agriculture 140,000 ha, Switzerland (BioSuisse, 2016)	Bio Suisse Standards for the Production, Processing and Trade of 'Bud' Products defines standards for inspections and labelling in accordance with the EC (2007) Council Regulation 834/2007 and the Swiss Ordinance on Organic Farming (SR 910.18) (BioSuisse, 2015).
Public Corporation 637,805 ha, Austria (BMNT, 2019)	The AgrarMarkt Austria is explicitly called a quality label developed by the public corporation AMA Marketing for food products that fulfil the requirements of the Austrian Food Code, Edition IV, Chapter A8, and Council Regulation (EC) No. 834/2007. The certification exists in a colour version designating Austrian produce and a black and white version for produce from outside Austria (AMA, Marketing GesmbH, 2009).
Organic food association 170,000 ha, worldwide (Demeter, 2019)	Demeter is the label of a brand of biodynamic agriculture, with roots in anthroposophy. Biodynamic agriculture considers the farm as an organism characterized by closed nutrient loops. For instance, farmers cannot have more animals than can be fed with the fodder produced by the farm. A comprehensive verification process ensures strict compliance with the International Demeter Production and Processing Standards, as well as relevant organic regulations in the respective country where the food is produced (Demeter, 2016).
Organic food association, Germany 418,381 ha (Bioland, 2019)	Bioland is an association of organic farmers in Germany, with 7,700 members – including farmers, beekeepers and winegrowers. The organization also has 1,000 partners in associated businesses, such as bakeries, dairies, butchers and restaurants. Bioland seeks to integrate ecological, economic and social principles in an attempt to balance nature conservation goals and climate mitigation with sustainable jobs in rural areas on the basis of fair prices for organic produce (Bioland, 2019).
Organic-food association 440,000 ha, Germany (Naturland, 2019)	Naturland is an organic standard that goes beyond EU eco regulation, specifically with regard to genetic engineering, which is rejected by the organization. The organization applies its concept to foodstuffs sourced from around the world, i.e., including tropical and sub-tropical crops. For imported foodstuffs, there is also a fair-trade standard. The Naturland label involves 65,000 farmers, as well as fisheries and woodlands (Naturland, 2019).

Organization/area	Short description
State-licensed with federal regulation 2 million ha, USA (USDA, 2017)	The National Organic Program (NOP) is part of the United States Department of Agriculture's (USDA) Agricultural Marketing Service (AMS). The organization works as a public-private partnership and accredits companies that certify farms and businesses meeting the national organic standards. The standard foresees, for example, a minimum of 95% organic ingredients and no use of genetically modified organisms (AMS, 2019).
State-licensed organic certification system 984,486 ha, Canada (Canada Organic Trade Association, 2017)	Organic agriculture in Canada comprises some 5,000 organic operations, including 4,000 primary producers, 600 livestock operations and 1,500 processors, manufacturers and retailers certified with the label (Canada Organic Trade Association, 2017). The standards for Canadian organic produce are available from the Government of Canada (2018).
State-licensed organic certification system 35.6 million ha (FiBL & IFOAM, 2019)	The Australian Certified Organic standard denotes produce that is grown or processed without synthetic chemicals, fertilizers or genetically modified organisms. The standard is, according to its own description, "one of the most respected and rigorous standards in the world for organic production" (ACO Certification Ltd, 2019). Australia is experiencing a rapid growth in demand, and the country has, by a wide margin, the largest land area devoted to organic agriculture.

agriculture. Clearly, given consumers' willingness to pay premiums for organic produce, farmers can gain much by acquiring minimum certifications that in reality may mean little for the environment or social standards. Other labels may have strict criteria. Where different certifications exist in the same country – for instance, products in Germany may use EU-Eco-Regulation, or German versions BIO, Demeter, Bioland or Naturland – this is confusing for consumers who may not be able to distinguish certifications in terms of their implications for agriculture.

Figure 5.2 provides a global overview of organic agriculture by continent, showing that Australia is by far the largest producer in terms of land area, accounting for more than half of all organic agricultural lands in the world (ACO Certification Ltd, 2019; FiBL & IFOAM, 2019). However, in terms of value, Australia only accounts for some 3% of turnover (ACO Certification Ltd, 2019), with the global market for organic produce now reaching a value of €100 billion (FiBL & IFOAM, 2019). The second largest area for organic production can be found in Europe, followed by Latin America. As outlined earlier, Europe is the continent with the largest share of agricultural organic land.

Organic food

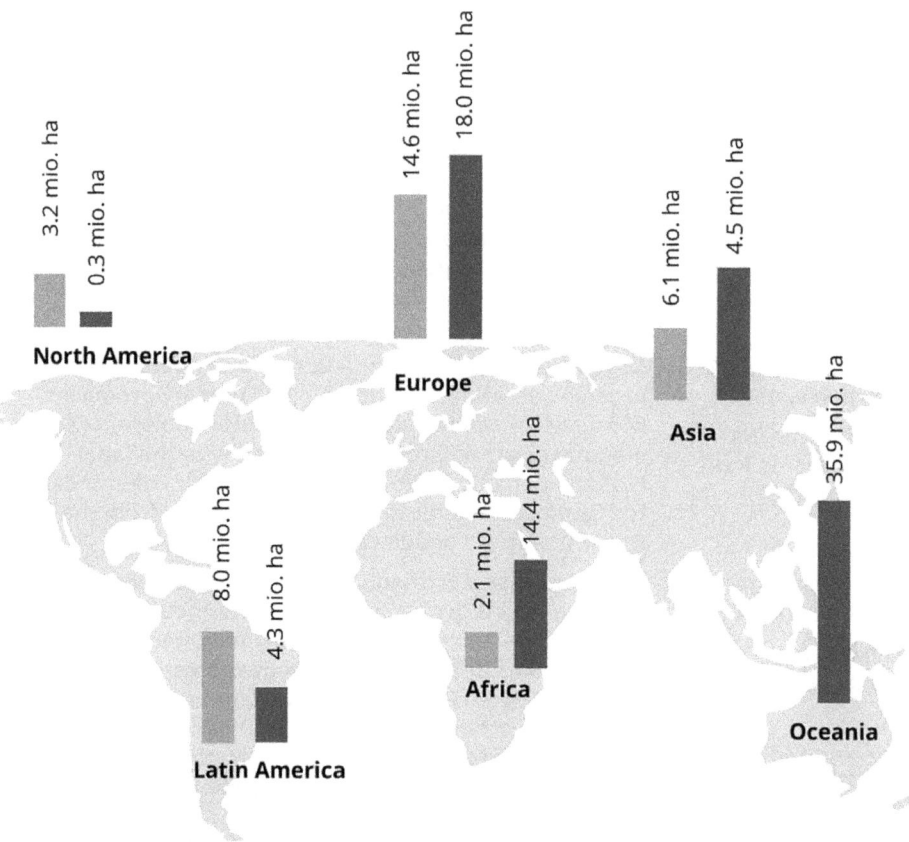

Agricultural land

Other areas (wild collection, beekeeping, aquaculture, forests, grazed non agricultural land)

Figure 5.2 Global overview of organic land area by continent

Box 5.4 Certified organic restaurants in the USA

Many restaurants use certified organic ingredients in their menu. However, in some countries, it is also possible to certify a restaurant as organic. In the USA, only a small number of restaurants have done so as it is a time-consuming process that has never gone mainstream but may become more popular given consumer interest in organic eating (Roth, 2016). After two years working with Oregon Tilth, an organization that certifies farms and other businesses, Restaurant Nora in Washington DC became the first certified organic restaurant in the USA in

1997, almost 20 years after first opening. Any US restaurant is allowed to put the word "organic" on the menu if it's using organic ingredients, as many do even if the restaurant is not certified. But in order to become fully certified restaurants not only have to source at least 95% certified organic ingredients for their menu, but also all cleaning products, storage, prep, sanitation and pest management, which falls under the guidelines.

The second certified organic restaurant was Tilth in Wallingford, Seattle, in 2006 run by chef Maria Hines. Two more organic certified restaurants were subsequently opened by her, but in 2019 she reduced her restaurant ownership to just Tilth and in October 2020, it closed following a 70% decline in patronage as a result of the COVID-19 pandemic (Vermillion, 2020). When interviewed about her environmental interests and commitments, Hines replied:

> Making the commitment to be certified organic—to me, that is political. You're saying no to GMOs, you're saying yes to proper farming practices, and you're saying that climate change does exist, and all of these things. You're saying that supporting the local economy is important and the way to go. You're saying that supporting your community, including your local farmers, and that all of the [restaurant] guests who participate in that movement of supporting organics means something.
>
> (quoted in Clement, 2019)

Roth (2016), suggests that, "Organic certification can be a business driver, but it can also be expensive and onerous". An illustration of this was the first certified organic restaurant in New York, GustOrganics, which opened in the West Village in 2008. Its owner Alberto Gonzales, found that it was almost impossible to operate his restaurant in the highly competitive dining market of New York. GustOrganics' food costs were high, it had problems with complying with both the New York City Department of Health and USDA regulations, and it was difficult to keep prices low enough to attract sufficient customers (Roth, 2016). Gonzales felt that he was probably undercapitalized when he opened the restaurant, but he also noted, "It's cheaper to do 50 or 75 percent organic than do 100 percent organic. It's very easy to be tempted to cut corners" (quoted in Roth, 2016). Indeed, Roth (2016) also suggests, "There may never be an overwhelming number of certified organic restaurants, fast food or otherwise; the barriers to entry are just too high".

Organic food purchases

Restaurant food choices are complex and embedded in a wide range of factors that come from the interaction between the consumer and the restaurant management and kitchen staff. Asioli et al. (2017) highlighted psychological, biological and physiological, situational and socio-cultural factors as well as intrinsic and extrinsic product characteristics as having relevance for organic food choices (Figure 5.3). In their review of 54 papers on consumer preferences for organic food, Asioli et al. (2017) confirmed that personal norms and ethical values, specifically with regard to environmental conservation and animal welfare, influence consumer choices. Among the extrinsic

Organic food

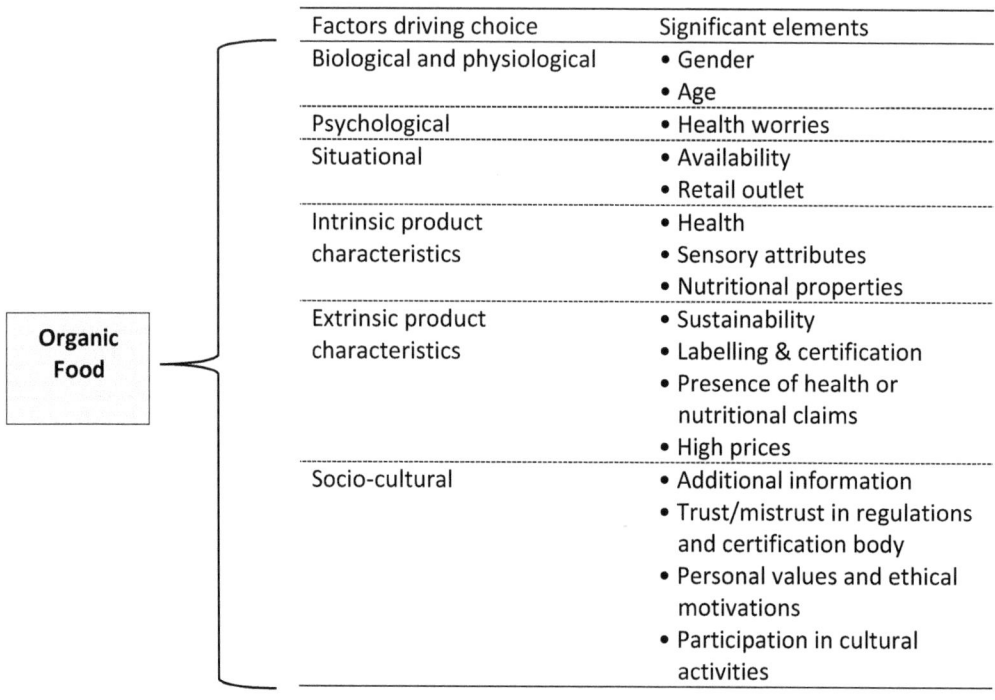

Figure 5.3 Complexity of organic food choices

product characteristics, this includes contributions to biodiversity, conservation and a lower energy use linked to emissions of greenhouse gases. Superior product quality is another important factor, as an intrinsic product characteristic. This includes nutritional value, health promoting effects and a general perception of organic produce being safer. Food safety concerns include, for example, the health implications of pesticides or genetically modified organisms. A different way of looking at these two motivational streams is thus in terms of personal benefits. For example, climate change is an issue concerning all humans, and personal efforts to reduce emissions represent altruistic behaviour. An individual choosing to live a low-carbon lifestyle is potentially reducing his options, to the advantage of society at large, profiting from mitigation. Health, on the other hand, is personal, and represents a tangible benefit. The health effects of food – its intrinsic product characteristics – are consequently far more likely to have relevance for consumers than extrinsic product characteristics. Purchase intentions can thus be assumed to be more strongly linked to personal benefits, and beliefs that organic produce is healthier, more nutritious, tastier or lower in calories (Williams & Hammitt, 2001; Yiridoe et al., 2005; Siegrist, 2008; Pino et al., 2012; Zagata, 2012; Lee et al., 2013; Asioli et al., 2014; Bryła, 2016; Hemmerling et al., 2016; Grzybowska-Brzezinska et al., 2017; Hasimu et al., 2017). Within the complexity of reasons for organic food choices, there is consequently a hierarchy in motivations. The interrelationships between food and health are also discussed in Chapter 8.

Labels are of importance in the context of organic foodstuff attractiveness, because they make organic produce more visible. Where organic food labels are seen as indicators of quality or better health characteristics, this can help to increase willingness to pay premiums or overcome negative price perceptions that are seen as a constraining

> **Box 5.5   The Swedish KRAV certification for restaurants**
>
> KRAV is an organization that develops organic standards in Sweden, which are promoted through a label. Swedish consumers are highly aware of the KRAV label, which is known to 98% of the adult population. KRAV includes criteria relating to the environment, animal welfare, good health and social responsibility, and is widely perceived as a quality label. To support and increase the use of organic produce in Swedish restaurants, KRAV introduced a three-tier label to highlight KRAV food services. The label indicates the share of organic produce in menus on the basis of stars. Restaurants certified with the one-star label use at least 25% organic produce, measured as the value of the share of KRAV, EU-organic or Marine Stewardship Council (MSC) in total purchases. Two stars indicate that at least 50% of the value represents organic foodstuffs, and three stars 90%. Apart from food purchases, restaurants are also held to purchase electricity from renewable sources and environmentally friendly cleaning detergents. There are about 1,400 KRAV-certified food services in Sweden, also including school kitchens and cafés (KRAV, 2019).

factor of organic food purchases by consumers (Hughner et al., 2007). However, a share of customers may also see organic labels as indicators of a higher cost that can become a deterrent to purchase intentions (Van Loo et al., 2014) as well as the capacity of restaurants to be able to carry organic product (see Box 5.4 for this problem in the US context). As a result, many restaurants only carry a limited inventory of organic produce. An important implication is here that depending on market, restaurants may or may not want to highlight organic food components in the menu. For instance, in the upper price segment, there is much evidence that organic produce will be perceived favourably, as a healthier, higher quality aspect of the food offered. As patrons in such restaurants are likely less focused on price, the inclusion of organic food components may even increase willingness to pay.

As discussed in Chapter 4, an important insight in this context is that 'local' produce is generally popular with customers, probably because they are associated with benefits to farmers and the local economy, short transport distances, fewer environmental impacts, quality, health, climate-friendliness and animal welfare (Carlsson et al., 2007; Darby et al., 2008; Liljenstolpe, 2011; Campbell et al., 2014; Niva et al., 2014; Feldmann & Hamm, 2015). 'Local' is probably also linked to a perceived understanding of production methods. These factors contribute to higher willingness to pay for food (Zanoli et al., 2013), and should thus be considered in the design of restaurant menus. Where restaurants do source local produce from farmers, this should also be communicated to guests.

Table 5.4 illustrates the cost of organic and Fairtrade in comparison to conventional produce, including some basic staples, popular processed foods, spices and beverages. The list illustrates that for many of these, organic production is considerably more expensive, though this is not necessarily mirroring higher production cost or lower yield, rather than the premiums customers are willing to pay. For example, organic cane sugar is 66% more expensive than conventionally produced sugar, and organic Fairtrade sugar 171%. As the Fairtrade cost is large a result of higher wages paid voluntarily to workers in the sugar industry, the price is an expression of the willingness of consumers to pay premiums in order to improve living conditions in poor countries. However, differences in the cost of items are not necessarily always one-sided. For instance, the

Table 5.4 Comparative cost of conventional, organic and Fairtrade produce, Germany

Source: Various websites (online shops), from Metro, Edeka24, GEPA, El Puente. Data for 2017

Product	Conventional (net, €/kg)	Organic (net, €/kg)	Organic & Fairtrade (net, €/kg)
Sugar (from cane)	2.32	3.86	6.29
Pasta	0.72	1.85	4.58
Rice	2.40	4.20	7.58
Quinoa	10.26	10.58	10.98
Chia seeds	10.98	12.93	25.71
Coconut milk	7.3 (L)	6.3 (L)	7.5 (L)
Honey	6.14	10.98	15.68
Nutella	3.01	8.23	11.98
Jam	6.76	6.73	12.62
Peanut butter	5.29	8.22	13.69
Raisins	9.69	8.41	11.96
Dates	9.38	11.68	16.87
Milk chocolate	10.2	12.1	14.9
Pepper (black)	14.99	43.93	40.93
Curry	10.98	51.21	25.79
Muscat nuts	57.45	112.54	42.80
Coffee	6.07	8.18	19.16
Espresso	7.47	16.58	22.95
Café crème	7.47	10.49	20.95
Black tea	52.5	34.5	73.8
Peppermint tea	29.7	53.3	87.9
Chamomile tea	44.5	49.7	99.7
Orange juice	0.83 (L)	2.42 (L)	1.99 (L)

comparison shows that depending on retailer, organic Fairtrade products can be cheaper than organic produce (orange juice), and that organic can be cheaper than conventional (coconut milk, jam, raisins, chocolate). For some products with high environmental impacts (Nutella), organic alternatives will be considerably more expensive, however. Overall, the list shows that it is meaningful for restaurants to compare different providers before ordering conventional foodstuffs: For many items, there may be a win-win situation in that the organic variety can be ordered at a lower price, yet be offered to customers at a price premium.

Box 5.6 Mainstreaming organic food in public kitchens and canteens

Sweden has seen a significant increase in debates on the environment in recent years, in which much focus has been placed on food production, consumption and waste and their interrelationship with climate change and other planetary boundaries. As a result, public campaigns have focused on reducing food waste volumes, and sought to increase the share of organic food consumed in communal kitchens (schools, universities, administrations). Sweden has a national goal to serve food in public kitchens that is 60% certified organic by 2030. Ecomatcentrum (2020) determined that in 2019, the share of organic food used in communities and the public sector amounted to 39%, up from less than 5% in 2005. In leading communities, up to 83% of all food is already organic.

Ecomatcentrum (2020) also highlights that there is a connection between organic and "climate smart" choices, a reduction in food waste and the share of vegetarian food served. More of the menus' protein should also be sourced from plants. Data shows that these goals are achieved simultaneously with organic choices, as decision-makers place greater emphasis on "appropriate" menu designs, both for reasons of awareness and available budgets. This is reflected in the very low-carbon content of the foods served, with values that in leading "organic" communities are as low as 1.7 kg CO_2-e per average kg of food purchased. Ecomatcentrum (2020) emphasizes that the cost of an organic plate is about €0.2 higher than a conventional plate. To balance the higher cost, kitchens have to be inventive to not exceed available budgets. Five strategies in particular have helped to reduce the average cost per dish served, in spite of the higher (and costlier) share of organic foodstuffs:

- To reduce the share of food going to waste;
- To reduce the share of animal protein;
- To increase the share of protein from grains, pulses and legumes;
- To introduce a veggie-day;
- To test and trial new recipes and meal plans.

The overview provided by Ecomatcentrum (2020) suggests that the introduction of organic food purchase quotas in communities on a voluntary, yet competitive, basis can make significant contributions to reducing negative environmental externalities related to food consumption. These changes also support healthier diets.

Conclusions

This chapter has highlighted some of the issues associated with organic foods. Although organic food and its promotion are extremely important for reducing the impacts of intensive agriculture, there are also differences in its definition and regulation between countries. Nevertheless, consumer demand and interest in organic food is continuing to grow as a result of concerns over the impacts of many modern farming practices on the environment and on personal health. These concerns have only expanded following the COVID-19 pandemic. Yet, despite the level of customer interest in organic foods, restaurants and foodservice providers often struggle to provide high percentages of organic produce in their menus as a result of the higher cost that many diners may be unwilling to pay. Therefore, as noted in the chapter, some restaurants limit the proportion of their menu which uses organic produce. However, this highlights the importance of having clear organic standards and labelling requirements so that those restaurants and foodservice operations that have high levels of organic produce are able to reap the benefits. Simultaneously, this may also help to remind the customer of the real cost of food in terms not only of the work in the kitchen and in service, but also the wider impacts of what we eat on society and the environment, a point taken up in Chapter 6 which integrates our understanding of sustainable foods.

Chapter 6

Sustainable foods

The importance of standards and certification

Introduction

Around the world, consumers are increasingly becoming concerned about what they eat, both in terms of the food itself, e.g., issues regarding the effects of food on personal health, nutrition and safety and the impacts of growing and transporting food to market, e.g., global environmental change, biodiversity loss, the climate crisis and waste in the environment, especially plastic (Hoogland et al., 2007; Lee & Yun, 2015; Massey et al., 2018). For example, in many countries, there are long-standing concerns over pesticides and hormones in food, antibiotics in meat, genetic modification and food irradiation (Hwang et al., 2006; Teisl et al., 2009; Zhou et al., 2016). Food safety refers to the quality of the food and production, distribution, marketing and consumption practices that prevent the contamination and deterioration of the food. The factors that affect food safety are concerns over the pesticides, hormones, additives and preservatives used in food production and processing and the improper handling of food during storage and consumption, e.g., having food stored at the wrong temperature (Prabhakar et al., 2010).

Chapters 2–5 highlighted some of the most important themes in addressing these concerns in the food system and in bringing sustainable food to the restaurant or caterer's table. However, while sustainable, organic, climate-friendly and local food are clearly significant how do the restaurant, food services provider and the consumer come to trust that what is on the plate is actually sustainable when they do not know the grower personally? Therefore, attention is increasingly given to the role of certification and labelling both to provide assurance to the consumer and to drive change down the food supply chain.

The importance of standards and certification

Food standards and certifications are implemented in the food market in order to help determine the safety and quality of food products, especially in long food chains in which there are no direct relationships between producers and consumers (Denny et al., 2016). One of the most significant aspects of the contemporary food governance system is that, in great part due to the internationalization of the food trade, there has been a shift from public to private food safety standards and from first-party certification to third-party certification as stakeholders have sought to develop more effective control over the food chain (Ibrahim, 2016). This is not to suggest that the importance of and implemented food standards has diminished, rather than to highlight that private government-regulated standards have become an important means of responding to changing and innovative food practices. Private standards have also become increasingly significant for product differentiation in markets that are driven by quality-based competition and that require a consistent food safety standard and quality attributes supported by branding and certification (Ibrahim, 2016). In some cases, private standards, e.g., Fair Trade or the Marine Stewardship Council (MSC), have also become adopted as international standards. Private standards, certification and labelling have also become increasingly important as a means to provide information to consumers regarding the sustainability attributes of a food product, e.g., animal welfare standards or organic status, in addition to the more generic labelling that is often required under consumer law, e.g., country of origin, calorie content, ingredients. However, given that private standards are ineffective and untrustworthy without an enforcement mechanism to encourage compliance along the food chain there is also the increasing use of third-party certification (TPC) that encourages stakeholders to use TPC in order to help implement and enforce the effectiveness of standards.

Certification is usually regarded as a quality assurance programme or scheme that is approved by a recognized accredited body (Albersmeier et al., 2009). The requirement to participate in a certification may be voluntary or mandatory. In the case of the latter that is usually a requirement of membership for a specific body or association, or to meet government requirements, for example with respect to advertising, export, food safety, nutrition and/or recognition of a particular status or quality (Kotsanopoulos & Arvanitoyannis, 2017; Santeramo et al., 2018; Manning et al., 2019). A key element of certification is that it is designed to generate trust in the food chain and products for consumers. This is a response to consumer uncertainty and what are known as Information asymmetries, and these occur when the processing of food products cannot be verified by the retailers or consumers of, for example, products that claim a particular level of or aspect of sustainability. Such products are considered as credence products (Sheldon, 2017). Such measures are regarded as extremely important in the case of sustainable food claims as sustainable products are characterized by credence qualities, associated with increased perceptions of risk, which can negatively influence consumers' purchase intentions (Brach et al., 2018). The more credible a food certification is seen therefore the greater is the reduction of uncertainty and perceived risk, e.g., in paying premium for a product that claims to be organic.

The traceability of food certification is also important for food products. Traceability means that it is possible to track back the product's origin and/or producers as well as the various elements of the supply chain given any issues with the food products safety and quality (Hatanaka et al., 2005). Traceability is significant both for confidence in the quality of a food certification, e.g., in the case of Fair Trade coffee (Raynolds, 2009), as well as for tracking any issues that may occur with a product (Hall, 2010). Certification also assists in developing product differentiation standards that act to develop compliance to such standards in supply chains (Henson & Humphrey, 2010; Touboulic et al., 2014). For example, in the case of the global organic agricultural market, Fouilleux and Loconto (2017) argue that certification, together with standard-setting and accreditation activities, act as a tripartite standards regime of governance that is inseparable from the market for certified organic product, i.e., they serve to mutually reinforce one another.

Private standards

The terms 'private standards' and 'voluntary standards' are interchangeable and reflect that they have been developed by private sector actors either alone or in cooperation with governments. According to Henson and Humphrey (2010), private standard certifications require the performance of five functions: standard setting, adoption, implementation, conformity and enforcement. Significantly, for private standards, there is no direct legal compulsion for compliance given that, unlike public standards, there is no legal or regulatory compulsion to ensure use. There is however an indirect regulatory requirement in many jurisdictions to ensure truth in advertising as well as copyright, brand and intellectual property protection which means that it is usually illegal to claim that a product has met a standard when it has not. Instead, with private standard compliance is usually achieved via market measures with respect to the value in implementing such standards, i.e., from a grower's perspective being able to sell your produce more effectively. As a result, "businesses use private standards ... strategically, whether it is to gain access to new markets, to coordinate their operations, to provide quality and safety assurance to their consumers, to complement their brands, or to define niche products and markets" (Hatanaka et al., 2005, p. 356). Private standards are therefore set by either a commercial or non-commercial entity that is usually connected to a non-government organization or industry organization and is adopted by private firms and organizations, e.g., individual growers or their collectives. Conformity is assessed by a private auditor and the standard is enforced by a private certification body (Henson & Humphrey, 2010).

Private standards have evolved and proliferated throughout the food system (Herzfeld et al., 2011; Fouilleux & Loconto, 2017). Henson and Humphrey (2010) argue that they have 'gone beyond' public regulations in two main ways. First, some private standards address issues beyond the limit of public regulations by developing standards that may provide more detail or are high than public standard, e.g., having stricter limits on pesticide residues than legally required in some jurisdictions and/or having a different range of pesticide requirements. Second, private standards may implement controls on products using criteria that are not subject to public regulations (Henson & Humphrey, 2010). For example, the Marine Stewardship Council (MSC) certification not only determines whether a fishery is 'sustainable' but also seeks to direct seafood consumers towards fisheries' products that are generated through sustainable practices (Gutiérrez et al., 2012; Agnew et al., 2014; Sampson et al., 2015). This example is also significant as it also highlights that one of the differences between private and public standards is that private standards tend to be more directed with respect to how outcomes are to be achieved. Nevertheless, Henson and Humphrey (2010, p. 1628) argue that there is

> a failure to recognise the diversity of private standards in terms of their institutional form, who develops and adopts these standards and why. In particular, there is a need to appreciate the close inter-relationships between public regulations and private standards and the continuing ways in which private standards evolve.

Box 6.1 Environmentally friendly food packaging

In order to reduce waste levels as well as impacts on the environment many restaurants and consumers are seeking to use environmentally friendly food packaging. B2B and end consumers play an important role in the market penetration of any environmentally friendly food packaging because it is they who decide whether or not to buy or use a particular product, e.g., as a doggy bag to take home from the restaurant. The use of environmentally friendly food packaging can also help reinforce the branding of any certification or the sustainability positioning of restaurants and foodservice operations.

Ketelsen et al. (2020) undertook a review of research on environmentally friendly food packaging and identified three main barriers to purchasing environmentally friendly packaging. First, consumers need guidance in recognizing environmentally friendly packaging, as although consumers primarily consider the packaging material and any ecolabels in their purchasing decision, they also consider other packaging design elements such as colours and pictures of 'nature' that can be misleading with respect to how environmentally friendly the packaging actually is. Second, consumers lack knowledge, in particular about new packaging materials such as bio-based packaging. Third, other product attributes such as price and product quality are more important to some consumers than environmentally friendly packaging. Nevertheless, there is often a significantly higher willingness on the part of consumers to purchase for environmentally friendly packaging and products with reduced packaging compared to products with standard packaging.

Third-party certification

The responsibility of a third-party certifier is to assess, evaluate and certify safety and quality claims by referring to a particular set of standards and compliance methods in a manner that provides assurance to stakeholders about the quality of the product (Hatanaka et al., 2005). Furthermore, in order to increase trust and legitimacy among consumers and stakeholders and potentially to limit liability, third-party certifiers also appeal to technical-scientific values such as independence, objectivity and transparency as part of the certification process. Usually, the process of obtaining third-party certification operates in the following way. First, a supplier applies to a particular third-party certifier for certification. Second, the third-party certifier conducts a pre-assessment and documentation review of a supplier's facilities and production operations. Third, the third-party certifier conducts field audits. Fourth, when conformity is verified, the third-party certifier issues a certification and allows the producer or supplier to label its products as certified. Typically, suppliers are responsible for meeting the costs of the audit.

Two general organizational forms of TPC usually apply – accredited or not accredited (Hatanaka & Busch, 2008). Accreditation is the process by which an authoritative organization gives formal recognition that a particular third-party certifier is competent to carry out specific tasks (Hatanaka et al., 2005). When not accredited, certification bodies may still issue a certificate and permit after compliance is verified in order to use its certification labels on and/or off their products. Where certifying bodies are accredited, they must gain approval from accreditation bodies as to when to provide certain TPC standards. From the reports made by the certification bodies, accreditation bodies then have the authority to decide whether or not to issue a certification to the suppliers. Prominent examples of accreditation bodies with respect to sustainable foods at the global level include the International Federation of Organic Agriculture Movements (IFOAM) (Box 6.2) and the Marine Stewardship Council (MSC).

Accreditation is a significant issue as one of the primary reasons given for the proliferation of TPC is its perceived character as independent and objective (Hatanaka

> **Box 6.2 IFOAM – Organics International**
>
> Formed in 1972 and now with members from over 120 countries and territories, the International Federation of Organic Agriculture Movements (IFOAM – Organics International) is the world's leading organic agriculture association. They defined organic agriculture as
>
> > A production system that sustains the health of soils, ecosystems, and people. It relies on ecological processes, biodiversity and cycles adapted to local conditions, rather than the use of inputs with adverse effects. Organic Agriculture combines tradition, innovation, and science to benefit the shared environment and promote fair relationships and good quality of life for all involved.
> >
> > (IFOAM – Organics International, 2021)
>
> With organic agriculture being based on four principles
>
> - Principle of Health – Organic agriculture should sustain and enhance the health of soil, plant, animal, human and planet as one and indivisible
> - Principle of Ecology – Organic agriculture should be based on living ecological systems and cycles, work with them, emulate them and help sustain them.
> - Principle of Fairness – Organic agriculture should build on relationships that ensure fairness with regard to the common environment and life opportunities.
> - Principle of Care – Organic agriculture should be managed in a precautionary and responsible manner to protect the health and well-being of current and future generations and the environment.
>
> (IFOAM – Organics International, 2021)

et al., 2005). In other words, it is the independence of third-party certifiers from other actors in the food system, namely buyers and sellers, which distinguishes TPC from first (audited by suppliers) or second-party certification (audited by retailers' paid technicians) (Tanner, 2000) because of the increased legitimacy it conveys to the process from the perspectives of a range of different actors (Miller & Bush, 2015). However, elsewhere Hatanaka and Busch (2008) argued that TPC typically exhibits organizational, but not operational independence.

> Thus, in contrast to the view of TPC as an objective governance mechanism, we argue that TPC is embedded in social, political and economic networks. This finding, … raises questions as to how TPC is structured and operates, who gets to decide the ways it is structured and operates, and the ways that TPC might differentially impact on actors in the food and agricultural sector.
>
> (Hatanaka & Busch, 2008, p. 73)

From the perspective of producers, restaurants and foodservice providers decisions over certification will typically be strongly influenced by consumer perceptions and the positioning of the business in the market. Certification is therefore a means to both establish trust with customers and promote business attributes (Nuttavuthisit & Thøgersen, 2017). However, as Ibrahim (2016, p. 32) observes,

> effective communication of certified status must be made in order to achieve successful value-added marketing. In other words, valued-added markets may be unsuccessful if the consumers are not aware of the existence and meaning of these commodities and also do not have a favourable attitude towards them.

In addition, although TPC products may be more acceptable to consumers the extent to which surveillance and market demands flow through to growers can nevertheless have unintended socio-economic effects. As Getz and Shreck (2006, p. 490) suggest,

> if the appeal of certified labels rests on the integrity of what the label represents to consumers, then such consumer movements would benefit from a more robust analysis of how certification intersects with and affects local spaces, cultures and communities at the point of production.

Therefore, an understanding of the relationship between certification and sustainability needs to be understood at all stages of the supply chain not just at the point as the product, and meal, is on the consumer's table. Growing organic, for example, also needs to meet the sustainability needs of the growers and the farm workers not just the end consumer. Nevertheless, the

> rapid proliferation of third-party certifiers globally and the breadth of standards that certification covers have produced a very complex set of institutional mechanisms that are difficult to categorize. For example, third-party certifiers verify supplier compliance of systems, processes, and products for both private and public standards that concern food safety (e.g., Codex standards), food quality (private retailer or processor standards), Good Agricultural Practices, Good Manufacturing Practices, and/or Good Management Practices (e.g., ISO 9000 standards), labor practices (e.g., SA 8000, … Fairtrade standards), environmental standards (e.g., ISO 14000 standards, Rainforest Alliance ECO-OK standards), and/or non-genetically modified materials.
>
> (Hatanaka et al., 2005, p. 357)

Organic and Fair Trade certification are widely considered as forms of sustainability certification (Getz & Shreck, 2006). However, as the following discussion indicates there are substantial challenges for some labels to gain acceptance and an overall issue of developing trust in the certification system.

The case of organic produce

As discussed in Chapter 5, organic food products are an output of an agricultural production system that sustains the health of soils, ecosystems and people by not using human-made chemical biocides or artificial fertilizers. However, the word 'organic' has been used in many different types of agricultural food products and can be applied and used in different ways in different jurisdictions (Aarset et al., 2004). In the USA and the EU, the certification processes are reasonably similar but there are differences in terms of standards and their interpretation. In the US, organic and non-organic crops are allowed to grow on the same production unit while in the EU they are not. According to Sawyer et al. (2008), if domestic organic standards reflect consumer tastes, and consumers have strong preferences for those standards, then harmonization to a common international standard may reduce the benefits consumers receive from organic products. They suggest that US organic policies tend to be supplier-driven while the EU policies appear more driven by consumer demands.

Food certification and labelling are particularly important for organic foods as a tool for signalling to consumers that a product is a certified organic product, especially as consumer perceptions of organic labelling schemes are subjective in nature and in many cases not based on objective knowledge (Janssen & Hamm, 2011, 2012a, 2012b). Depending on national food regulations and standards, organic foods can be labelled as organic products if they comply with the standards for organic production, processing, labelling and control (Janssen & Hamm, 2012b). The majority of organic imports are certified by international certification bodies based in Europe, the USA and Japan, which also highlights the demand for organic foods in these markets, although China is also becoming increasingly important given consumer response to food scares related to high levels of agrichemical residues (Xie et al., 2011, 2015).

Organic products, along with many other sustainable products, are credence products (Sheldon, 2017). That is while consumers believe that such products are better for them and/or the environment or community the specific valued characteristics of the product cannot be judged just by looking at it. Instead, there is reliance on a means of credible information, such as certification and labelling. Such certification provides reassurance regarding the quality and safety of products but may also act as a symbol of the wider sustainable agriculture system and healthy living, as well as the security of the supply chain (Midmore et al., 2011; Hemmerling et al., 2015). However, as the large number of different organic certifications shown in Chapter 5 illustrate, there is potential for the wide range of ecolabels to cause confusion in the market and erode consumer trust in sustainable products such as organic food (Nuttavuthisit & Thøgersen, 2017).

The sheer growth in sustainability labelling therefore raises issues of information asymmetries and uncertainty regarding product quality especially given large numbers of different brands and schemes, including those of imported products. Asymmetric information situations exist when consumers have a lack of information about the organic process, e.g., in the case of restaurants they are not able to rely on specific information from their suppliers and are instead reliant general information that may be available. Hence, it is difficult for them to assess organic food product attributes. As Ibrahim (2016) noted, this could then potentially negatively influence the development of demand for organic food products. As a result, certification and labelling are the main mechanisms of quality assurance to overcome information asymmetry issues (Liang, 2016). The role of certification and/or labelling in helping to ensure the credibility of organic food and other sustainability products as well as improve consumers' attitudes towards the food products is well described by Atkinson and Rosenthal (2014, p. 34):

> Consumers face an information deficit in which they must assess products and services based on incomplete, misleading, or otherwise imperfect information. In this asymmetric information environment, in which one side holds more or better information than the other, consumers rely on cues or signals as a means of evaluating product quality.

The implications of this are that organic food labels help transform the credence characteristics of products into search attributes, thereby allowing the consumer to better evaluate quality before purchasing the products.

As Ibrahim (2016) observes in some circumstances where certification or food labelling requirements and regulations are unclear, it is difficult for consumers to identify the authenticity of the organic products reducing the likelihood of purchase

(Atkinson & Rosenthal, 2014). Therefore, labelling and certification, including the information provided to consumers, is a major factor of the level of trust in a product. Regular organic consumers may feel more assured and confident when they see certification and labelling on organic food products. However, consumers generally consider organic products based on who certifies them and what was the process of certification the product went through (Hemmerling et al., 2015; Ibrahim, 2016). Nevertheless, in the case of organic foods there are at least broad international guidelines and international umbrella organizations, such as IFOAM – Organics International, to provide credibility to certification and labels. In the case of other food products and product characteristics that are associated with other aspects of sustainability, such recognition may be more difficult.

Sustainability certifications

The range of different food product attributes that fit notions of being sustainable, organic, eco or Fair Trade products is quite substantial. As the preceding chapters have highlighted, there are a number of dimensions of food that affect the sustainability of the food system and to which restaurants, food services and consumers wish to respond, particularly with respect to encouraging more environmentally friendly eating. However, while sustainability is encouraged in top-level government and UN documents and policies there is no single internationally accepted sustainable food guidelines available. In the same way, there is no single definition of what constitutes a sustainable restaurant. Therefore, the credibility of sustainably produced food products involves examining how trust in such products is created through independent monitoring and verification procedures (Sønderskov & Daugbjerg, 2011). Similarly, Daugbjerg et al. (2014) argue that ecolabels have an important role in promoting green consumption since most eco-labelled products are credence goods, implying that the valued process attributes they contain are not observable to the consumer even after purchase or consumption. Therefore, they argue that such labels will only work if the consumers know the production standards underpinning it and have trust in the label, an observation borne out in their study of Danish consumers.

As with organic labelling, sustainability attribute labelling and certification can increase consumer awareness, but the growth in the labelling and certification of eco or green food products has increased confusion among consumers and the risk of information overload. This situation has only been exacerbated by corporate efforts to mainstream sustainability in global product chains, by establishing their own product sustainability requirements that can also erode higher levels of product quality standardization by lowering the level of sustainability ambition (Chkanikova & Lehner, 2015). Co-branding between ecolabels and corporate brands may assist products being sold, although questions may still exist over the actual effects of such measures on sustainability (Chkanikova & Lehner, 2015). Nevertheless, it is very clear that better communication needs to be established between labels and certification schemes and the foodservice sector if trust in such labels is to be improved, although the development of certification schemes and recognition of their value can take time. For example, despite fair trade products being established in Western nations in the 1980s, in response to the trade inequalities existing between developed and developing nations, it required the establishment of the Fair Trade Labelling Organizations International (FLO) in 1997 (see www.fairtrade.net), which was charged with harmonizing the somewhat different fair trade standards and creating a single fair trade market to consistently develop and promote the brand and information about what Fair Trade means and generate a high level of acceptance (Hall, 2010; Box 6.3). According to Fair

> **Box 6.3 Fairtrade standards**
>
> - *Economic criteria* include the Fairtrade Minimum Price which aims to provide producers with a safety net against falling prices and allow long-term planning, along with a fixed Fairtrade Premium that provides farmers and workers with additional money to invest in improving the quality of their businesses and communities. Fairtrade also emphasizes long-term trading partnerships and requires buyers to provide pre-financing to producers who request it, opening access to capital to help stabilize their operations.
> - *Environmental criteria* emphasize ecologically and agriculturally sound practices, including responsible water and waste management, preserving biodiversity and soil fertility, and minimal use of pesticides and agrochemicals. Fairtrade prohibits the use of several hazardous materials and all genetically modified organisms (GMOs). Fairtrade does not require organic certification, but organic production is promoted and rewarded by higher Fairtrade Minimum Prices for organically grown products.
> - *Social criteria* for small-scale producers include requirements on democratic self-organization (typically in cooperatives), participatory decision-making, transparency, and non-discrimination (including gender equity). In plantation-type settings where hired labour is the norm, our standards require companies to operate with non-discriminatory employment practices, pay rates equal to or higher than the legal or regional minimum wages, freedom of association and collective bargaining rights for the workforce, safeguards for worker safety and health, and facilities to allow workers to manage the Fairtrade Premium. Forced labour and child labour are prohibited under the Fairtrade Standards.
>
> Source: Fairtrade International (2021)

Trade International (2021), for example, "the FAIRTRADE Mark [is] the most widely recognized ethical certification label globally".

For restaurants and food services Fair Trade certified products are primarily related to the use of chocolate, coffee and tea, which are primarily framed as sustainable products in relation to economic and social aspects of their production. In contrast, fish is a food product that is increasingly perceived as an environmental sustainability concern. The next section looks at the Marine Stewardship Council as a well-recognized sustainability standard body in this area.

Marine Stewardship Council (MSC)

The Marine Stewardship Council (MSC) is an independent non-profit organization and registered charity that sets a standard for sustainable wild fishing and allows the use of its label by accredited products and fisheries. The MSC is a good example of how sustainable food certification labelling has grown in parallel to the internationalization of fisheries exploitation and international trade as well as growth in public and industry concern over the sustainability of fish stocks, As Ponte (2012) pointed out, such market-based instruments of fishery governance are based on two widespread expectations: that complying with sustainability standards will lead to environmental benefits; and that certifications will not discriminate against specific social groups, countries or regions. However, Ponte (2012) went on to argue that the evidence of positive environmental impacts from MSC was not convincing over all the locations in which fisheries had been certified and suggested that as "an institutional solution to the global fishery crisis, the MSC seems to be better tuned to the creation of a market for 'sustainable fish' rather than 'sustainable fisheries'" (Ponte, 2012, p. 300). Interestingly, Bush and Oosterveer (2015) found that MSC fisheries employed labelling strategies to capture further market value from fishing practices that went beyond their initial conditions for MSC certification and sought further recognition for their activities through co-labelling with other bodies, including other international NGOs. They also noted that fisheries who could not meet MSC standards were utilizing other NGO and private sector-sponsored Fisheries Improvement Projects (FIPs) in order to provide an alternative route to international markets and to convince consumers of the sustainable attributes of their product. These issues are significant, in the case of Dolphin Safe and the Marine Stewardship Council certification schemes for tuna in the Pacific, for example, Miller and Bush (2015, p. 137) found that "despite substantially different levels of credibility within these networks, the application of an environmental standard is more connected to the authority of the standard setter than the credibility of the label".

Hadjimichael and Hegland (2016) analyzed three case studies of Marine Stewardship Council (MSC) certification: the Alaska Pollock Fishery, the Faroe Islands' Saithe Fishery and the Australian Northern Prawn Fishery and found that the incentives generated by market forces create a risk of certification schemes making questionable claims with respect to sustainability in order to increase and retain market shares. Such arguments have been made elsewhere. For example, Christian et al. (2013) reviewed objections to MSC status and the major concerns with certification as they relate to the MSC's three main principles of the sustainability of the target fish stock, low ecosystem impacts and effective, responsive management. Their analysis of the formal objections concluded that the MSC's principles for sustainable fishing were too lenient and discretionary, and their loose wording and existence of loopholes allowed for overly generous interpretation by third-party certifiers and adjudicators which, they argued, meant that the MSC label could be misleading for consumers and conservation funders (Christian et al., 2013).

Nevertheless, despite these concerns, the number of fisheries and consumer markets for MSC has continued to grow since the scheme was first introduced in 1996. As of 2019–2020, 17.4% of all wild marine catch (14.7 million tonnes) was engaged with the MSC with 18,735 different MSC labelled products on shelves with a sales value of over US$10 billion (MSC, 2020). Of the 17.4%, 15% was certified, 1.2% certified but suspended and 1.2% was in assessment. According to the MSC (2020, p. 12),

> An additional 8% of global marine wild catch came from fisheries working towards MSC certification (those in the In Transition to MSC program, Pathways Projects at stage 3 or 4, and fisheries improvement projects that have MSC certification as an explicit end goal). Altogether this represents over a quarter of the global marine wild catch.

Significantly, the number of countries in which MSC products were available had grown to 71 in 2019–2020 from the 36 countries in 2014, while 100 countries had MSC Chain of Custody which can be used for traceability (MSC, 2020).

The MSC has three different standards:

- The *MSC Fisheries Standard* is used to assess if a fishery is well managed and sustainable and assess whether fish stocks are sustainable, how environmental impacts are minimized and whether operations are well managed (see www.msc.org/standards-and-certification/fisheries-standard).

- The *MSC Chain of Custody Standard* is used to ensure that every company in an MSC product supply chain must have a valid Chain of Custody certificate. This is designed to ensure that MSC-certified products are traceable and separate from non-certified products (see www.msc.org/standards-and-certification/chain-of-custody-standard). The standard is reviewed every three years.
- The *Aquaculture Stewardship Council (ASC) and MSC Joint Standard* for environmentally sustainable and socially responsible seaweed production. Under the seaweed, standard operations must show that they actively minimize the impact of their seaweed operations on the surrounding environment. In addition, seaweed operations must be managed in a responsible manner so that they care for employee wellbeing and contribute to the local community (see www.asc-aqua.org/what-we-do/our-standards/seaweed-standard/). The Seaweed Standard also uses the existing MSC Chain of Custody Standard. As of the start of 2021, the ASC had 1,403 certified farms, 2,506 suppliers and 29,306 products overall, with four seaweed operations ASC-MSC jointly certified and two production units under assessment.

The MSC is the dominant international standard for sustainable fisheries. However, as discussed above, there are clear criticisms of its role and as to whether it has enabled sufficient reduction of the environmental impact of commercial fishing both directly with respect to standards and indirectly with respect to the influence of the market. For example, van Putten et al. (2020) examined seven MSC certified fisheries that operate in or from Western Australia with the intention of understanding why the fisheries sector participates in certification schemes on the supply side and the impacts and unintended benefits and costs of certification. They found that any positive economic impacts of certification were only realized in a small number of Western Australian MSC fisheries. They explained that this may be because only a small proportion of state-managed fisheries are sold with the MSC label and ex-vessel or consumer market price premiums are therefore usually not obtained. Positive impacts were instead primarily of a social or institutional nature. However, their interviewee's opinions were divided as to whether the combined non-monetary and monetary benefits of MSC certification outweighed the costs.

International fish stocks are under enormous stress. As noted in Chapter 2, a third of global fish stocks are overfished. While programmes such as MSC have clearly raised awareness of the pressures on fish stocks there are more demands being placed on them than ever before. As Cochrane (2021, p. 298) observes, "Globally, substantial problems remain in the status of stocks, threats to biodiversity, incidence of undesirable ecological impacts, economic inefficiencies, and poverty, food insecurity and marginalization of fishers and other dependents on fisheries, particularly small-scale fishers". Major issues still remain with governance and management regimes, especially in developing countries, while issues of conflict of interest still remain with programmes such as MSC and questions as to whether they are sufficient to address the damage being done to fish stock by overfishing. Nevertheless, in some instances, the market attractiveness of MSC and the promotion it can provide for certain fish species as being sustainable may help compensate for the failure of governments to better manage fisheries or even demarket some fish varieties where this would help their sustainability (Hall & Wood, 2021).

A 2016 survey by MSC of over 16,000 fish consumers in 21 countries found that 72% of respondents agree that in order to save the oceans, shoppers should only consume seafood from sustainable sources, although 75% of seafood consumers age 55+ agreed with the need to eat seafood only from sustainable sources compared with 67% of 18–34-year-olds (MSC, 2016). Overall, 62% said that they have more trust and confidence in brands that use ecolabels. More than half (54%) of seafood consumers say they are prepared to pay more for a certified sustainable seafood product. Those who have seen the blue MSC label place the value of the label at an average premium of 11% globally, although younger respondents (18–34) had 41% recall of seeing the blue MSC label, compared to 30% of older respondents (MSC, 2016).

Nevertheless, in the absence of governments insisting that fishing be undertaken sustainably and actively monitoring fish catch and operations consumers can face substantial challenges in selecting fish even if they do want to purchase sustainably. As Harvey (2019) notes,

> For shoppers looking to eat ethically, judging what fish meets that bill can be tricky, with a plethora of guidelines, coalitions and voluntary codes of practice, and labels that refer to sustainable farming or line-caught methods in place of standard nets.

Ruth Westcott, the campaign co-ordinator at the NGO Sustainable Fish Cities, advised:

> Don't be taken in by generic claims about fish being 'responsible' or 'sustainable', … Look for those on the Marine Conservation Society fish to eat list, or that carry a Marine Stewardship Council, or Aquaculture Stewardship Council (ASC), or the organic symbol.
>
> (quoted in Harvey, 2016)

Box 6.4   Certified sustainable wine

In many food cultures, wine is an integral part of the meal. However, while wine often has the image of being a natural product the reality is that in the majority of cases wine is produced through a highly industrialized process which, when viewed, can look more like a refining process. Furthermore, there is often substantial use of artificial fertilizer and biocides, as well as intensive irrigation, in the vineyard to produce grapes for wine production. Given the overall growth of consumer interest in more sustainable food products as well as the initiatives of some winegrowers, there has therefore been an increased number of initiatives to certify sustainable wine (Baird et al., 2020; Nave et al., 2021).

The longest running programme is that of the Lodi Winegrape Commission in California who started their sustainable winegrowing initiative in 1992. As part of its objectives the Lodi Winegrape Commission, seeks to "Identify and encourage implementation of environmentally benign and economically viable pest, weed, disease, and cultural strategies through the district-wide sustainable viticulture program" (Lodi Winegrape Commission, 2021). An analysis was conducted of 53 sustainable winegrowing programmes that were identified as operating from 2013 to 2015. Of the programmes 22 had a regional focus, and 30 programmes operated nationwide. ECO-PROWINE (http://ecoprowine.org/en/) was the only programme that was transnational in scope (six member countries of Italy, Spain, Portugal, Bulgaria, Greece and Austria). The USA had 15 regional programmes across seven states. Italy had at least 15 nationwide programmes in operation during the review period. The Sustainable Winegrowing New Zealand programme (www.nzwine.com/sustainability/sustainable-winegrowing-new-zealand/) was the only programme that was mandatory for members of the regional wine body (Baird et al., 2018).

There was substantial variation in the nature of the programmes. Out of the 53 programmes, 47 utilized self-assessment produces (88.8%) while four employed online self-assessment (7.5%). External audits were undertaken by 27 of the programmes (51%), with third-party certification offered by 26 of the sustainable winegrowing programmes (49%). Twenty-seven of the 53 programmes were privately funded, 16 featured a mixture of both public and private funding, with the remaining ten programmes being publicly funded. Curiously, given the potential promotion of sustainability values to consumers, only 39.6% of programmes were directly utilized in wine branding.

Details of the elements of each sustainable wine programme are given in Table 6.1. The most widely adopted environmental measures relate to water management, waste management, soil management and climate change and biodiversity. Just over half of programmes are organic while biosecurity is a very limited concern. With respect to socio-economic issues a large majority of the programmes have a strong community focus as well as engage in education and outreach. Labour law is only addressed in half of the programmes while migrant welfare, an important issue given the role of short-term migrant labour in harvesting or vine pruning (Baird et al., 2020), is only addressed in 17% of programmes.

Table 6.1 Components of sustainable wine certification programmes
Source: Hall et al. (2018)

Sustainability indicator	% of programmes using
Environmental issues	
Integrated pest management	71.6
Water management	92.5
Soil management	86.8
Waste management	88.7
Air quality	67.9
Energy efficiency	69.8
Biosecurity	1.9
Climate change mitigation or adaptation	86.8
Biodiversity	84.9
Low spray regime	73.6
Biodynamic	45.3
Organic	56.6
Socio-economic issues	
Labour law	52.8
Migrant workers	17.0
Community focus	90.6
Education and outreach	88.7
Health and safety	68.9
Training	75.5

Conclusions

This chapter has discussed the importance of certification and standards in sustainable food products and their labelling. This is an important issue as, even though local foods are an important consideration in sustainable food (see Chapter 4), the international nature of food supply means that there is a need for restaurant and foodservice operators to gain assurance on the quality and safety of the food they receive. A key role on certification and sustainability labels is to generate trust with consumers, whether businesses or end consumers. However, as noted in the chapter, the large number of labels does potentially create confusion in the market. Sustainability certification and labelling, along with the standards that go with them, are by no means perfect. There are issues with respect to implementation and penalties, industry influence, standards being too low, transparency and whether such measures improve sustainability along all stages of the food system rather than just being a marketing device. Nevertheless, despite criticisms, they remain better than nothing given the often government inaction with respect to food standards and their implementation and the influence of agri-business on government policies around the world. The role of standards also highlights the importance of procurement procedures and the development of trust with suppliers. These are maximized in local food suppliers and also with wholesalers. And it is to these relations and issues of procurement we will now turn to.

Chapter 7

Purchasing strategies and supply chains

Introduction

The food purchasing strategies of a restaurant or a foodservice operation are clearly a major component of its overall sustainability as they affect the characteristics of what is served to customers and what is wasted. The core principle of any food purchasing strategy is only to order as much as will be needed until the next purchase/delivery. By doing this, it means that there will be a high turnover of the food inventory so that it is fresh for customers and so that waste is reduced. Indeed, as noted in Chapter 1, appropriate purchasing lies at the heart of restaurant waste reduction programmes (Jungbluth et al., 2016; Sakaguchi et al., 2018; Dai et al., 2020; see Chapters 13 and 14 for a more detailed discussion on waste reduction).

Purchasing can be defined as obtaining from external sources all goods, services, capabilities and knowledge, which are necessary for running, maintaining and managing a food operation's primary and support activities in a manner that supports the operation's strategies and goals (after van Weele, 2002). However, sustainable purchasing is not just about considering waste levels, but it also means considering the impacts of what is being purchased in terms of how they were grown and how did they get from the farm to the restaurant kitchen (Baldwin et al., 2011). For example, in a study of the procurement options of the school catering services of the Italian city of Turin, Cerutti et al. (2018) found that the emissions of the average school meal resulted in 1.67 kg CO_2-eq per meal. The meal consisted of one starter (usually based on pasta, rice or soup), a main course for protein (e.g., meat, fish, omelette, cheese or protein-rich vegetables), a vegetable dish (fresh or cooked) and dessert (fruit, yogurt, sweets or fruit juice). From a life cycle analysis (LCA), Cerutti et al. (2018) identified that the production of food (including all agricultural practices and the production of all agricultural inputs such as fertilizers, pesticides, electricity, water management and machinery use) was responsible for about 78% of the greenhouse gas emissions. Food transport, including the transport of foods from where they were produced to local hubs and the transport of the food to the school canteens, accounted for 3% of emissions.

Changes in a menu, which would then be reflected in procurement policies, can therefore potentially have a substantial impact on the climate-friendly nature of the menu. As a result of conducting a LCA, Cerutti et al. (2018) identified two main means to reduce impacts from the agricultural phase of consumed foods: (I) the choice of foods from different production practices, in particular the substitution of conventional foods with organically produced food and (II) reducing meat consumption. Although

DOI: 10.4324/9781315187488-7

food logistics only account for a small proportion of emissions, it was suggested that procurement consider more local provisioning of food and improvements in local distribution. Their suggestions, with respect to making purchasing strategies more environmentally friendly, were supported by a study by Mistretta et al. (2019) on an Italian school catering service in terms of a wider range of environmental impacts. They reported that the food production phase was relevant to almost all of the assessed impact categories with all contributions to the categories being higher than 65%.

Despite the romantic image of early morning visits to farmers' markets and growers portrayed in food media and many cookbooks, the reality of commercial cooking is that most restaurants source their foodstuffs from wholesalers, while institutional food services purchasing is often directed by government policies on quality and price, while a substantial proportion of institutional food services is sub-contracted to commercial suppliers (Neto, 2020). However, in the case of the latter, government policies may have considerable impact on encouraging environmental purchasing (Lehtinen, 2012; Neto et al., 2016; Neto & Caldas, 2018).

This chapter examines the complexities of restaurant food purchases from producers, as well as the role of wholesalers in supplying restaurants and the valuable role they sometimes play in including smaller producers in the restaurant supply chain. In examining the purchase of local food by restaurants, Roy (2016, p. 45) concluded that:

> the general consensus of the reviewed research is that restaurant purchasing function is very important, but the criteria and procedures must be met and fulfilled in order to achieve the user (chefs) and supplier relationship to work. However, relatively little research has been done from restaurant and chef perspectives.

Despite this situation, this chapter highlights issues of continuity of supply, time investments, foodstuff cost, supplier relationships and food safety for restaurant purchasing as well as the importance of inventory management in terms of reducing costs, facilitating orders and reducing waste. The final section of the chapter discusses the importance of greening public procurement policies for institutional food services.

Restaurants and supply chain management

The very notion of a supply chain derives much of its logic from the fundamental principle of food chains. Information from the restaurant supply chain is essential to effective restaurant menu development and marketing, as information on a menu guides the customer through the food experience that is offered and its attributes, including where it comes from. The dishes on a menu often consist of many different ingredients that have been put together in a manner that is satisfying for the consumer at a quality and price point they are willing to pay. Furthermore, for most restaurants because they have a menu that is regularly offered to customers the ingredients need to be consistently provided for the period of time that an item is on the menu not only in terms of availability but also consistency with respect to price and quality. As a result of these factors, restaurants, therefore, place particular emphasis on reliability of supply, consistency, quality and price – all of which are tied to supply chain management. The search for increased sustainability, therefore, makes it even more important for restaurants and their customers to know where the food is from and how it was grown. Given the complexity of the food system and the extent to which food businesses have moved away from vertical integration strategies, i.e., growing their own, to concentrate on the core activity of cooking and serving food to satisfied customers, this therefore makes restaurant supply chain management and purchasing more important than ever.

The significance of supply chain management has been stimulated by the purchase of food from beyond the immediate surrounds of a restaurant. Whereas at one time a chef or restaurant manager would have personally known where the supply of their food came from, if they didn't grow it themselves, because of globalization food supply chains now span the world with increasing reliance being place on the intermediaries that get the food from the growers to the end market. For example, in a study of local food purchasing by central Iowa restaurants and institutions, Strohbehn and Gregoire (2003) identified that in food purchasing, the chefs' primary concerns were for product availability, quality and pricing. However, food purchasing also had to be efficient and effective in relation to the chef's other responsibilities. Therefore, in this case, sourcing menu ingredients locally rather than from wholesale suppliers was found to take up too much of chef's time. Indeed, as Chapter 4 highlighted, while locally grown food is now something that many restaurants are trying to reclaim there are issues in ensuring that there is an efficient and effective supply chain. Yet any restaurant or caterer that seeks to make their food offerings climate-friendly, sustainable or Fairtrade, needs to be confident of where their food is from.

A supply chain is defined as a system of suppliers, manufacturers, distributors, retailers and customers (both end consumer and business customers) where material, financial and information flows connect participants in both directions (Fiala, 2005). Supply chain management is a response to two main factors, "the management of outsources non-core activities and, given the diversity of consumer markets, the recognition of the synergistic value of collaboration, in terms of market access, information, technological developments and innovation" (Eastham, 2001, p. xviii). Supply chain management can, therefore, be defined as:

> Coordination and integration of all activities, in delivering a product from its initial primary source through to the consumer into a seamless process, thereby linking all partners in the chain internal and external to the organization. External linkages can be both horizontal and vertical.
>
> (Eastham, 2001, p. xviii)

However, while there are commonalities, there are significant differences between supply chains in a food service context and other products, the most important being that food supply chains are dealing with a perishable product often with a very limited lifespan in which it can be used. Highly perishable and potential hazardous products, i.e., if food goes off or it is something that a customer is allergic too, provide different challenges to foodservice operations in comparison to the supply chains of other industries (Murphy & Smith, 2009). Furthermore, Murphy and Smith (2009) argue that food service and hospitality operations emphasize supply chain management because of the quality issues and the need to accurately convey this information to their customers. Other differences relate to the importance of the origins and authenticity of a product and, in some cases where there are religious restrictions, to the need to ensure there is no contamination between restricted and non-restricted foods, for example, if dealing with halal or kosher foods (Ali et al., 2017; Hall & Prayag, 2020; Amalia et al., 2021).

In a food service and restaurant context, the benefits of appropriate supply chain management include improved coordination from supplier to customer; reduced lead times; greater productivity and efficiency; smaller inventories; increased delivery reliability; lower costs and assurance of product quality (Murphy & Smith, 2009; Roy, 2016; Cho et al., 2021). At restaurants, a properly managed supply chain also supports a restaurant's ability to identify, build and manage relationship with suppliers (Murphy & Smith, 2009).

Purchasing decisions

In independent restaurants, chefs have the primary responsibility for food purchasing decisions (Cho et al., 2019). In early Canadian research undertaken by Riegel and Haywood (1984), the most important purchasing criteria for chefs were timing and accuracy, with purchasing being integrated into daily kitchen responsibilities and routines. More recently, in a study of Australian chef purchase of seafood Lawley and Howieson (2015) found that the key purchase drivers were consistency of quality and supply. In contrast in corporate food organizations, such as fast-food franchise chains, purchasing decisions are primarily undertaken centrally so as to take advantage of the cost reductions available from national and regional purchasing contracts. As such, corporate purchasing is more geared towards commodity decisions involving high volume items. Price and guarantee of supply are the most frequently negotiated items in these contracts, which are strictly monitored for supplier adherence (Riegel & Reid, 1988; Patrucco et al., 2017; Bohunicky et al., 2019).

As noted above, restaurant purchasing behaviour does not follow a traditional demand-driven chain (Roy, 2016). Demand-driven purchasing is often associated with what is known as the "bullwhip effect", which occurs when organizations over order because they are fearful of limited supply (Tieman et al., 2020), while it can also often face low levels of required product availability as a result of seasonal conditions. In contrast, many perishable products, such as those that characterize food services, are supply-driven, as they cannot be stored indefinitely while awaiting customer orders. Roy (2016) noted that the local produce supply chain handles highly perishable produce with short shelf life that is characterized by seasonal production and local appreciation. Nevertheless, this can create problems as seasonal produce for a restaurant may not always be available with the result that chefs may be forced to seek non-local produce, often through the use of wholesalers.

Restaurant purchasing and procurement strategies require the development of supplier selection criteria in order to compare potential purchasing sources and to set clear product requirements. Supplier evaluation attributes fall into four main categories: reliability, competitive pricing, service support and technological capability (Katsikeas et al., 2004). Roy (2016) argued that hospitality studies apply similar criteria for supplier selection and buyer–supplier relationships. In her thesis on the catering sector in Iowa, Casselman (2010) identified guaranteed of quality products, product freshness, ability to deliver quantity needed or ordered, convenience in order process and guaranteed supply as the most important attributes for selecting suppliers. Less important supplier selection attributes were payment procedures, substitution availability, promotional allowances and suggestions for menu applications. Feinstein and Stefanelli (2017) identified five factors to be highly important to foodservice purchasers when selecting suppliers: ordering procedure and minimum order requirements, delivery schedule, credit terms and willingness to exchange price, free sample and return policy. Other factors identified as important by foodservice purchasers include use of technology, product variety, firm size and substitution availability (Roy, 2016).

The development of buyer–supplier relationships is an important part of procurement management process, especially for independent restaurants, given that kitchen and restaurant operations rely on efficient supplier(s) in order to function efficiently and profitably. Cho et al. (2021) focused on identifying the strategic criteria involved in selecting suppliers of restaurant products/services specific to casual dining, full service independent restaurants in the USA. Their results showed that 'product' and 'financial/technical' criteria had significant and positive effects upon operational benefits, while 'product' and 'service' had positive effects upon strategic benefits. When the sample was segmented into low and high supplier partnership groups, the positive effects of 'financial/technical' and 'cost/price' were significantly greater for the 'high' partnership group with respect to operational benefits. 'Product' and 'service' and their effects upon strategic benefits were greatest for the high partnership group. Interestingly, Murphy and Smith (2009) found that chefs appreciated personal relationships (regular contact) with their supplier through face-to-face meetings and menu tastings. However, the development of trust between chefs and their suppliers can take many years and can also take up considerable time. Therefore, given the time pressures on hospitality and foodservice operations, it is not surprising that much of the procurement undertaken by contemporary restaurants is done with wholesale distributors which can help consolidate purchasing.

Wholesale distributors

Foodservice operators generally do not obtain their products through self-distribution channels (a form of vertical integration in which food retail companies own and operate their own warehousing and distribution services) or manufacturer direct store delivery channels (defined as the delivery of merchandize from a manufacturer directly to a restaurant, bypassing warehouse facilities). Instead, for the majority of restaurants and foodservice providers products are delivered through the wholesale supply channel. In wholesale supply, channel products flow from manufacturers to distribution centres operated by wholesalers and then on to individual foodservice establishments. Within this distribution channel, wholesalers are therefore the conduit between food manufacturers and sometimes producers and foodservice operators (Roy et al., 2019a).

Wholesale distributors are food system intermediaries who arrange for the movement and transportation of food products and who generally have significantly higher capabilities than individual foodservice firms in terms of networks, delivery infrastructure and communication technologies, with the exception of the large chain restaurants or commercial catering suppliers, to access product markets (Crozet et al., 2013; Bernard et al., 2015). Wholesale distributors in the foodservice industry context can be classified as broadline, specialized and system wholesale distributors. Broadline wholesale distributors (e.g., Sysco and Gordon Food Services in Canada and the USA) offer one-stop shopping and carry a wide assortment of food and non-food products, focus on wholesale purchasing and have the goal of driving down prices to improve overall supply chain efficiency and profitability (Martinez, 2017). Specialized wholesale distributors (e.g., Costco) often serve niches that require specialized knowledge in product sourcing, handling or service and focus on specific product categories (e.g., dairy, fish, meat) or market segments (e.g., airlines) or maybe cash-and-carry establishments or warehouse clubs (Martinez, 2017). For example, as noted in Chapter 5, Costco is the largest purchaser of organic produce in the USA. System wholesale distributors serve a customer base that consists mostly of chain foodservice establishments with centralized purchasing and menu development (Martinez, 2017; Roy et al., 2019a).

Lawley and Howieson's (2015) study of seafood purchasing practices found that consistency of quality, supply and relationships with wholesalers were considered of greater importance by chefs, while price was not a major factor influencing choice. Similarly, Danenberg and Remaud (2010) also found that price was not a major factor in purchasing decisions but that the service offered by suppliers to chefs was considered the most important aspect of the supplier relationship followed by good quality products. Interestingly, chefs from Lawley and Howieson's (2015) study identified sustainability and branding as the least important factors influencing chef's choice of wholesalers to purchase from although chefs did not trust wholesalers in relation to sustainability issues. They also found that the majority of chefs who purchased from multiple wholesalers were not able to get everything from one wholesaler. Another reason for chefs using multiple wholesalers was that chefs suggested that they would increase their purchases from wholesalers if they were provided with better communication and information, and more consistency in terms of the quality, availability, size, packaging and labelling of the products.

Because of their role in the food system, wholesalers play a critical role in supply chain sustainability. Roy et al. (2019a, p. 4) argue in the case of local food purchase, "Like other intermediaries, wholesale foodservice distributors can play a beneficial role in the emergence and development of local food systems because of their reach beyond any direct interactions between farmers and end-consumers and farmers and restaurants" although some commentators urge caution. For example, Kirwan (2004, p. 398) argues there is "potential for the appropriation of the economic benefits associated with the embeddedness of production ... by dominant actors within the 'conventional' agrifood system, typified by the 'conventionalization' of organic food production". From the limited empirical work available, wholesale distributor's perceived benefits of purchasing local food are similar to those perceived by restaurants (see Chapter 4) and include: freshness, higher food quality products, nutritious and tasty products, convenience, cheaper prices, lower transportation costs, product availability, supporting local farmers, shorter shipping distances and supporting the local economy. Obstacles identified to wholesaler purchase of local food include: insufficient and/or inconsistent supply, short growing season, price, quality, liability and food safety issues, perceived lack of demand, processing and bidding requirements, lack of information and communication, timeliness in delivery and economic viability in local procurement (Roy, 2016; Roy et al., 2019a) (see Box 7.1).

Box 7.1 Barriers to local procurement by wholesale distributors

Roy et al. (2019a) reported on a study of local food procurement by wholesalers in Christchurch, New Zealand and Vancouver, Canada. The results of the study provide insights into the difficulties wholesalers can face in supporting sustainable food initiatives. In interviews with wholesale distributors, several diverse barriers were perceived as hindering them in procuring local food products. Inadequate volume/quantity of the products was regarded as the most challenging aspect of local procurement. In contrast, a respondent from Christchurch who was purchasing local food from local farmers as well as from local auction markets stated his satisfaction with the volume of local food products. However, he was frustrated that supermarket chains were purchasing larger volumes of local products directly from farmers, meaning that smaller wholesalers like his company face a potential shortage of local products at times.

> The biggest problem we are going to have with the supermarket that get growers to grow specifically for them like [Food company name] chicken, the growers grows chicken only for [Food company name]. That is also happening with produce too now. Some growers, they go straight to [Food company name] or [Food company name] and they just grow for these companies and it does not even go through the markets. The product goes straight from the growers to their big warehouses. So, supermarket picking up straight from growers and growers are not using the markets because

> supermarket uses so much volume. So we wholesalers particularly the smaller wholesalers are going to face problem about the products.
>
> (Christchurch respondent in Roy et al., 2019a, p. 13)
>
> The inability to provide consistent product quality was also a major reason for not increasing local sourcing:
>
> > the quality issue that is the main and hardest for us. Some cheese makers are trying to produce mass production cheese and the quality gets deteriorated and we won't buy their cheeses. We don't want that and it is a big reason, for us paramount is the quality of the cheese. If it is not good and if you are trying to meet the demand for everybody we do not buy that cheese.
> >
> > (Christchurch respondent in Roy et al., 2019a, p. 13)

Public foodservice procurement

As noted in Chapter 1, a substantial proportion of foodservice operations consists of institutional and non-profit catering, what is sometimes referred to as social food service (Table 7.1). Catering operations are also much more cost driven than independent restaurants and the larger companies that tender for institutional contracts, are similar to the larger fast-food corporations in terms of their business models with respect to cost minimization. The overall volume of meals served to public institutions is estimated

Table 7.1 Sectors and segments included in 'social food service'
Source: After Boyano et al. (2017)

Service	Elements
Business and industry (B&I)	Private companies, government employment, employees' restaurants, vocational training centres and workers' homes
Education	School canteens and kitchens, children's leisure centres, state primary and secondary schools, private schools, student canteens at universities and other kinds of high school
Healthcare	State hospitals, private clinics
Homes for the elderly	State homes, private homes
Other welfare homes	Homes for disabled adults, home for adults in difficulty, workers' centres, homes for disabled children, homes for children in difficulty, nursing homes and day centres for young children
Social leisure	Holiday camps, social tourism establishments, youth hostels, houses of youth and culture
Captive sector	Armed forces, fire stations, prisons, detention centres, homes for monitored education, religious communities

Table 7.2 Main environmental hotspots and causes from food procurement and catering services
Source: Neto et al. (2016); Boyano et al. (2017)

Product category	Environmental hotspot or potential improvement areas	Criteria
Food procurement		
Fish and seafood	• Depleting fish stocks • Production of feed for fish and the use of antifouling treatment in fish cages • Combustion of fossil fuels and the use of antifouling treatments in fishing vessels for wild caught species and equipment for aquaculture	Marine and aquaculture food products: • Avoid pressure on depleted fish stocks • Lower environmental impact of feed used in aquaculture
Meat Milk and cheese Eggs	• Land use and land use change (e.g., destruction of natural habitats, particularly forests and related CO_2 emissions associated to the production of feed, in particular soy) • Production and use of pesticides • Misuse of overuse of antimicrobials • Methane emissions from ruminants • Ammonia/nitrate emissions from rearing houses and manure storage • Water use and water pollution • Energy use (heating and cooling birdhouses) • Energy use in slaughtering	Organic production Animal welfare
Fruit and vegetables Bread and cereals	• Production and use of chemical fertilizers and pesticides • Soil degradation and potential run-off of excessive nitrogen in monoculture • Energy and water use for irrigation • Energy use when cultivating in greenhouses	Organic production • Lower eco-toxicity and lower global warming potential (GWP) • Containing more oxidants, less pesticides and heavy metals • Natural resources are expected to be better protected under organic production: air, biodiversity, soil and water

Product category	Environmental hotspot or potential improvement areas	Criteria
		Plant-based menus • Shifting away from meat • Weekly vegetarian day(s) • Plant-based sourced proteins
Oils and fats	• Land use and land use change (e.g., destruction of natural habitats, particularly forests and related CO_2 emissions) • Production and use of chemical fertilizers and pesticides • Energy use in farming • Methane release (anaerobic digestion of effluent in open pounds) • Disposal of waste in landfills lead to greenhouse gas emissions	Organic production Environmentally responsible fats • Better management systems used in the palm and soy oil production and extraction • Avoid deforestation • Use of fertilizers • Lower emissions in oil mills
Hot drinks	• Production and use of chemical fertilizers and pesticides • Drying of tea leaves • Energy use for water boiling	Organic production
Cold drinks	• Production and use of chemical fertilizers and pesticides • Energy and water use for irrigation • Energy use in the bottling process • Water use	Organic production
Transportation	• Long transport emissions	
Catering service		Competence of the tenderer • Prevention of food waste and other waste • Use of products and consumables with lower environmental impact • Energy use in catering services Chemical products and consumable goods • Use of lower environmental impact consumable goods, including: paper products, tableware, disposable items (such as cutlery) only for takeaway, rubbish bags and gloves, cleaning products (such as hand soaps, cleaning products and dishwasher detergents)
Operational support	• Lighting, HVAC, water use, supplies (cleaning, toilets and disposable products • Energy use and some cleaning products have a large impact on carcinogens, eco-toxicity and fossil fuels	

Table 7.2 continued

Product category	Environmental hotspot or potential improvement areas	Criteria
Food storage and food preparation	• Cook chill systems show a comparatively larger impact when compared to the cook-warm • Cook chill requires chill, cool storage and reheating. Cook warm is ready to eat. But since the cook chill system has less food waste than cook warm it has a lower impact in total (if including the effect of food waste)	• Energy and water consumption in kitchens • Use of energy-efficient kitchen equipment • Energy consumption and GWP of refrigerants (e.g., vending machines) • Use of energy efficient vending machines Environmental management measures and practices • Use of products and consumable goods with lower environmental impact • Water and energy use in catering services • Solid waste management Food and beverage waste prevention and food and beverage redistribution- Lower generation of food waste • Better food stock management, portion size of meals and adequacy to of meals consumer tastes Plant-based menus • Shifting away from meat • Weekly vegetarian day(s) • Plant-based sourced proteins
Waste management	• Production and disposal of organic waste • Use and disposal of packaging (e.g., landfill)	Other waste: prevention, sorting and disposal • Liquid and solid waste management
Transportation of catered food	• Long distances imply higher transport emissions	Food transportation • Lower combustion emissions from the vehicle fleet • Better planning of food transportation (raw and ready-prepared meals)
Processing of products by catering service	• Energy use in processing • Wastewater treatment • Energy and refrigerants used for cold storage	Energy and water consumption in kitchens

to be 55% of the total number of meals provided by catering companies in Europe (Neto, 2020). The most important sectors in Europe in terms of purchase volume and value that procure food and catering services are health/welfare (42.7% of the total meals served), education (31.4% of the total meals served) and business and industry (B&I) (17.8% of the total meals served). In 2008, the turnover of the EU contract catering industry was € 24.6 billion and employed around 600,000 people (Boyano et al., 2017). Self-operating public bodies and contract caterers on average share the food and catering market around 50/50, but there are substantial differences between EU Member States. For example, in Ireland, contract caterers account for 61.9% of the market, but in Sweden, they account for only 15% (Boyano et al., 2017).

Public foodservice procurement, including contracting out of catering services, are subject to government procurement policies. Because of the size of social food service procurement policies can therefore be an important tool for leveraging improvements with respect to sustainability throughout the entire food supply chain and, by virtue of their market share, can also influence private sector policies. For example, commercial companies that contract for public institutional catering are also likely to supply the private sector as well. The potential implications of such initiatives for sustainability are well illustrated by the development of EU food procurement and catering service criteria especially as, historically, the focus of corporate engagement by the catering sector in sustainability issues has been on energy savings, packaging reduction and food waste prevention rather than food purchasing (Boyano et al., 2017). Table 7.2 details the main environmental hotspots and improvement areas from procurement and criteria that can be developed.

Table 7.3 List of the environmental criteria in reviewed procurement schemes
Source: Adapted from Neto (2020)

Grouping	List of criteria taken from reviewed procurement schemes
Organic production	• Organic production
Aquaculture and marine products	• Aquaculture/marine products • List of recommended fish • Organic aquaculture
Integrated production	• Integrated production
Seasonal production	• Seasonal products
Palm oil	• Sustainable palm oil
Packaging	• Renewable raw materials • Avoid single unit/portion • Secondary and/or transport packaging to have a percentage of recycled content • Supplier take-back • No packaging of meals • Supplier to minimize • Pre-bottled water banned • Recyclable materials • No PVC • No polystyrene • Recycling facilities available

Table 7.3 continued

Grouping	List of criteria taken from reviewed procurement schemes
Transport	• Local/regional suppliers/ingredients – cutting food miles • Reduced per-vehicle emissions • Transport – reduce frequency of deliveries • Transport efficiency (unspecified)
Food service management	• Staff training in environmental aspects • EMS required or some aspects of an EMS • Cutlery, crockery reusable or made from renewable raw materials • Single-use material recyclable/biodegradable • Selective waste collection • Cleaning products • Catering equipment: energy efficient • Environmentally friendly paper products • Catering equipment (cooling) and vending machines: No ODS • Vending machines (energy use and design to reuse) • Maintenance plan: catering equipment and vending equipment • Waste management plan • Catering equipment: water efficient • Energy and water management/efficiency • Food waste prevention/minimization • Menu planning. A vegetarian offer per day • Catering equipment standards • Replacing parts for catering equipment and vending equipment • Reducing meat consumption • Carbon footprint measurement
Waste management (including food waste)	• Food waste collection and landfill diversion • Food waste: surpluses redistributed • Waste management (food and waste, oils and grease) and adequate transport and disposal

Neto (2020) investigated the sustainability criteria recommended to be used in European public acquisitions of food products and catering services. A total of 21 publicly available procurement schemes, from 11 European countries and used by several public authorities (e.g., countries, municipalities, schools) were analysed and reviewed for the type of single criteria used. Schemes cover not only purchases of food products but also catering services and kitchen and vending equipment. The results showed that about 30 different types of sustainability criteria were being used within procurement schemes. Environmental criteria were mostly used within the reviewed schemes (18 of the overall criteria reviewed are environmental related); ethical, social and health criteria were also covered within procurement guidelines (Table 7.3). Food ingredients used are very often a target area with a focus on the environmental aspects leading to reduced environmental impact from food and catering. The criteria mostly mentioned refer to organic production, seasonal and fresh produce, staff training, transportation and packaging, menu planning, waste management (including food waste), marine and aquaculture products and animal welfare. Ethical issues such as Fairtrade and health-related issues (e.g., food safety) are also significant (Neto & Caldas, 2018; Neto, 2020).

Conclusions

This chapter discussed the purchasing and procurement characteristics of foodservice operations. Different types of businesses and operations have different approaches to what they purchase, especially with respect to cost. Smaller independent restaurants tend to have much more of a focus on local foods while larger businesses engage in regional, national and even international contracting. Nevertheless, purchasing and procurement can have significant downstream effects on the supply chain because of restaurant and food operation needs. Arguably, one of the most significant areas here is institutional and social foodservice caterers because of the amount of food they purchase in bulk. The development of procurement guidelines by government at various levels can therefore have a great effect on both what is produced as well as what is consumed.

Chapter 8

Healthy and sustainable foods

Introduction

There is much debate about healthier diets in contemporary society. In industrialized countries, access to unhealthy foods has caused an obesity crisis, with estimates that there are in excess of 2.1 billion overweight or obese individuals in the world (in 2013) (Waterlander et al., 2018). Contrasting these figures, close to 850 million people are undernourished, prompting Waterlander et al. (2018, p. 124) to call for a comprehensive overhaul of the food system and "the way we grow, process, distribute and commercialize our food". While food is not a choice rather than a question of access or availability for a large share of humanity, unhealthy foods are ubiquitous and in high demand in industrialized countries. Some authors have highlighted that food choices are strongly influenced by marketing, and restaurants have been singled out as having important, yet often contradictory outcomes for food choices, in that they foster the consumption of foods that will lead to type 2 diabetes, heart diseases or cancer (Kang et al., 2015; Cohen, 2018). Opportunities to market healthier and sustainable foods are discussed in the following Chapter 9, while this chapter is concerned with the definition of 'healthier' foods, also drawing on previous chapters, to discuss 'healthier and sustainable' food choices.

It has become increasingly recognized that restaurants and other foodservice providers are integral to the provision of healthy and sustainable foods. This is because as increasing numbers of individuals and families consume a greater proportion of their calories away from home, the variety and quality of prepared restaurant menu items increasingly influence consumption patterns (Mikkelsen et al., 2007). As a result, restaurants as well as street vendors and fast-food outlets are an important, if not critical, element of the neighbourhood food environment in many parts of the world. Enabling people to access healthy foods in places where they live, learn, work or play is an essential public health priority. Growing attention is therefore being given to the foodscapes that surround people (see also Chapters 4 and 6) (Figure 8.1), especially as what people eat is very much determined by what is available in their food environment (Schettler et al., 2010; Garnett et al., 2015; Didinger & Thompson, 2020; Tonumaipe'a et al., 2021). Wansink (2010, p. 454) amusingly, yet accurately describes the situation, the provision of a healthier food environment enables a shift from "mindless eating to mindlessly eating better", sometimes also referred to as "health by stealth" (Hillier-Brown et al., 2017). As Mikkelsen (2011, p. 210) comments, "Along with shopping daily for food, meeting foods in different forms seems to create a 'landscape of foods'".

Healthy and sustainable foods

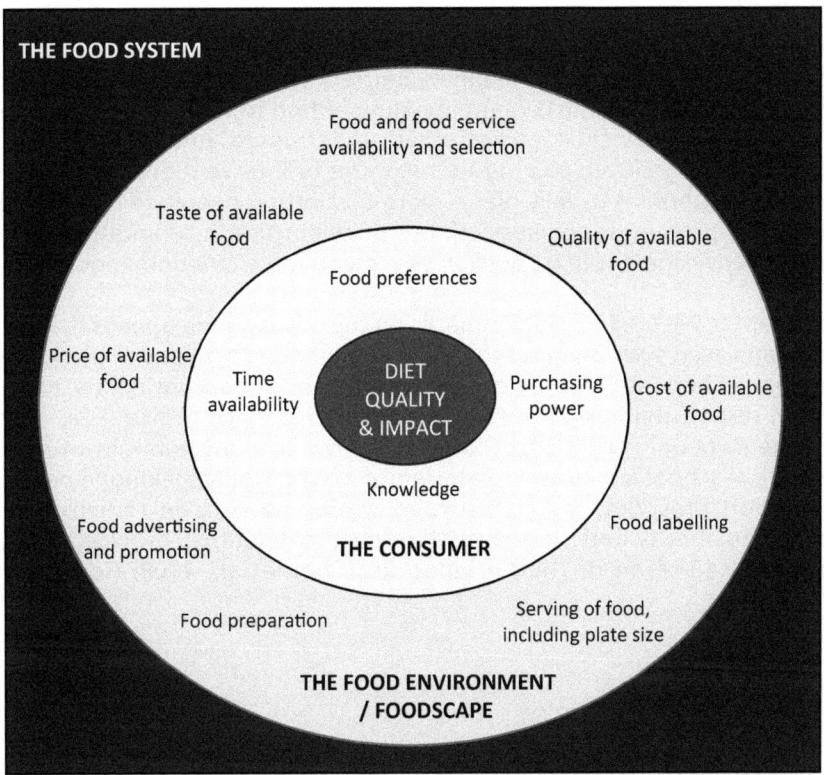

Figure 8.1 A healthy and sustainable food environment

The idea that food environments can be a powerful and independent determinant of food behaviour has been introduced through a number of health behaviour theories and most explicitly in the notion of obesogenicity.

In addition to the more commercial environments, eating outside the home also takes place in more 'captive' environments. Many governments and their agencies have implemented institutional food service as an integrated part of the public service provided in welfare systems including schools, kindergartens, institutions and worksites. Whereas institutional food service has traditionally been looked upon as a rather mundane and uncomplicated process of simply providing catering and food services to institutions, there is an increasing awareness and support of the idea that public food provision should play a much more active role in public health nutrition strategies.

(Mikkelsen, 2011, p. 201)

For example, Kirk et al. (2021) examined the barriers and facilitators to implementing provincial nutrition guidelines in recreation and sports facilities in three Canadian provinces. Recreation and sports facilities are a setting where people can be physically active. However, they found that the food environment in these settings that are ostensibly designed to encourage healthy behaviours do not reflect nutrition guidelines. Facilitators of good practice were found to be provincial or municipal expectations of guideline implementation, clear communication to staff around guideline directives and the presence of a champion within the community or facility who supported the implementation of nutrition guidelines. Barriers that were identified included an unhealthy food culture within community, competition from other food providers and issues within foodservice contracts that undermined healthy food provision. Nevertheless, it is significant to note that in terms of interventions to provide healthy eating choice emphasis is usually places more on alerting people to change behaviour (e.g., labelling, promotion, persuasion, use of celebrities in promotion) rather than changing the environment (e.g., portion size, menu reformulation, regulation) (Carins et al., 2021).

In this chapter, we are focusing primarily on the micro-foodscapes of the restaurant, institution and even such things as the plate and menu as a means of thinking healthy and sustainable food services. However, it is also important to consider the promotional and ethical responsibilities of restaurants and foodservice providers as part of the different media people experience. For example, while many public institutional food services, such as school and hospital catering, are increasingly seeking to be promoting healthier food lifestyles, many fast-food chains have been criticized for their contribution to obesity both directly with respect to what they provide and how they price as well as in terms of their promotions (Chou et al., 2008; Gortmaker et al., 2011).

Eating healthier

Which diets can be considered healthy and sustainable? Cook-Cottone et al. (2013) emphasize that healthy eating is about relationships of food, mind and body. This is an important insight, as there are many schools of thought as to what constitutes 'healthy' eating, with recommended diets including 'low-carb', 'keto', 'vegan', 'vegetarian', 'flexitarian', 'Mediterranean' (see also Chapter 6) as well as a wide range of specific diets designed to be nutritious, to promote specific health aspects, or to lead to weight loss (see e.g., US News, 2019). Definitions of 'healthy' vary accordingly, though there is a general consensus that it is important to avoid salt, fat, sugar; and to simultaneously exercise and control body weight (Kushi et al., 2012; Cook-Cottone et al., 2013).

In providing an outline for a generally healthy diet, the Harvard T. H. Chan School of Public Health (2019a, 2019b) suggests that vegetables and fruits should comprise half of the food eaten, and whole grains another 25%. Protein from fish, poultry, beans or nuts should make up the remainder. The T.H. Chan School also emphasizes the importance of bringing together human health and environmental sustainability, concluding that "it is important to adopt dietary patterns that are high in healthy plant-based foods and relatively low in red and processed meats" (Harvard T. H. Chan School of Public Health, 2019a), an issue that is discussed in more detail below.

Definitions of healthy food depend on viewpoint, which may be legal or dietary. For example, definitions may focus on legislated fat and salt content, or outcomes of diets in terms of disease (avoidance) (Box 8.1). An investigation into US consumer understandings of healthy diets found that there is complexity in perceptions of 'healthy', as consumers may consider animal origin, preservation and freshness/processing as well as nutrient and protein content (Lusk, 2019). Fat content in particular appears to influence perceptions of healthy negatively. Notably, foods labelled 'healthy' were interpreted by 40% of respondents to imply that they should be consumed in greater quantity.

> **Box 8.1 Definitions of healthy foods and diets**
>
> Any natural food popularly believed to promote or sustain good health, as by containing vital nutrients, being grown without the use of pesticides, or having a low sodium or fat content.
>
> (Dictionary.com, 2019)
>
> According to WHO [2018b], a healthy diet protects against malnutrition in all its forms, as well as non-communicable diseases (NCDs) such as diabetes, heart disease, stroke and cancer. It contains a balanced, diverse and appropriate selection of foods eaten over a period of time. In addition, a healthy diet ensures that a person's needs for macronutrients (proteins, fats and carbohydrates including dietary fibres) and essential micronutrients (vitamins and minerals) are met, specific to their gender, age, physical activity level and physiological state. Healthy diets include less than 30 percent of total energy intake from fats, with a shift in fat consumption away from saturated fats to unsaturated fats and the elimination of industrial trans fats; less than 10 percent of total energy intake from free sugars (preferably less than 5 percent); consumption of at least 400 g of fruits and vegetables per day; and not more than 5 g per day of salt (to be iodized). While the exact make-up of a healthy diet varies depending on individual characteristics, as well as cultural context, locally available foods and dietary customs, the basic principles of what constitutes a healthy diet are the same.
>
> (Food and Agriculture Organization of the United Nations (FAO), International Fund for Agricultural Development (IFAD), United Nations International Children's Emergency Fund (UNICEF), United Nations World Food Programme (WFP) and World Health Organisation (WHO), (2020), pp. xx–xxi)

Interrelationships of health and sustainability are increasingly acknowledged and have gained considerable importance in public debate. As Willett et al. (2019a, p. 1141) concluded:

> The scientific evidence today [...] robustly and conclusively shows that unhealthy diets are a major cause of premature death, at a scale that can explain approximately one fifth of premature deaths among adults globally each year.

Overweight and obesity

Overweight and obesity are defined as "abnormal or excessive fat accumulation that may impair health" (WHO, 2018a), and are usually assessed based on body mass index (BMI) calculations, i.e., a ratio of weight-for-height, where a person's weight is divided by the square of the person's height (kg/m^2). Being overweight in adults is defined as a BMI greater than or equal to 25, while obesity is a BMI greater than or equal to 30.

> **Box 8.2 Patterns of global obesity**
>
> - Worldwide obesity has nearly tripled since 1975.
> - In 2016, more than 1.9 billion adults, 18 years and older, were overweight. Of these, over 650 million were obese.
> - 39% of adults aged 18 years and over were overweight in 2016, and 13% were obese.
> - Most of the world's population live in countries where overweight and obesity kills more people than underweight.
> - 41 million children under the age of 5 were overweight or obese in 2016.
> - Over 340 million children and adolescents aged 5–19 were overweight or obese in 2016.
>
> Source: WHO (2018a)

Overweight and obesity are widespread phenomena. According to the World Health Organization (2018a), more than 1.9 billion adults are considered overweight, and of these, more than 650 million adults are obese (WHO, 2018a). Even higher figures have been presented by Waterlander et al. (2018). These suggest that at a minimum, 39% of the world's adult population are overweight, and 13% obese. In several countries, the situation is distinctive, as obesity has become a serious health concern and cost for the national economy. For instance, in the USA, 39.8% of adults and 20.6% of adolescents are classified as obese (data 2015–2016) (National Center for Health Statistics, U.S. Department of Health & Human Services, 2018).

Obesity levels have risen sharply and tripled since 1975 (WHO, 2018a). The number of obese adults increased from 100 million in 1975 to 671 million in 2016, and obesity is more common among women (WHO, 2018a). Considerable deviation from BMI 'normal' values is found in the USA, Australia, the Middle East, Europe, Mexico, Chile and Argentina (NCD Risk Factor Collaboration (NCDRISC), 2018). In stark contrast, being underweight is a serious health problem in India, with a prevalence of 22.7% among girls and 30.7% among boys.

Obesity is often a combination of lack of physical activity and poor diets, with regular consumption of fast foods, snacks, sweets, desserts and soft drinks in combination with large portion sizes increase the risk of becoming obese (Drewnowski & Darmon, 2005). As the WHO (2018a) emphasizes, "the fundamental cause of obesity and overweight is an energy imbalance between calories consumed and calories expended". Energy-dense foods high in fat are a primary concern, for which there may be different reasons, depending on the country. For example, Hadjikakou (2017, p. 119) found for Australia that the consumption of foods "not necessary for human health" amounted to 33%–39% of the overall food intake, with associated environmental impacts on water use, energy use, land use and greenhouse gas emissions.

In contrast to these findings, the WHO (2018a) suggests that healthy foods are not available for many poor families, while unhealthy food choices are supported by an absence of regulation. In North America, unhealthy food provisions have been linked to the food services industry, as highlighted by Chan et al. (2017, p. 6) "The restaurant industry is often targeted as a culprit in the obesity epidemic". Specifically, advertisements and food menus of fast-food chains support dietary choices unfavourable for human health, as they market foodstuffs high in salt, fats or sugar, and often in oversized portions (Robinson et al., 2007; Andreyeva et al., 2011; Jaworowska et al., 2013).

Education is a main inroad to healthier diets, as food preferences are learned. For this reason, Hawkes et al. (2015) suggest four principal mechanisms through which diets can be influenced, including (i) enabling environments for learning, (ii) the expression of healthy preferences, (iii) reassessing preferences at the point-of-purchase and (iv) stimulating a food-systems response. To understand relationships, Hawkes et al. (2015, p. 2410) explore school settings, economic instruments and nutrition labelling, finding that:

> effective food-policy actions are those that lead to positive changes to food, social, and information environments and the systems that underpin them. Effective food-policy actions are tailored to the preference, behavioural, socioeconomic, and demographic characteristics of the people they seek to support, are designed to work through the mechanisms through which they have greatest effect, and are implemented as part of a combination of mutually reinforcing actions.

These observations are highly relevant for restaurants, which may be seen as enabling environments for learning about food, both in direct ways (though information provided in menus or by staff) and in indirect ways (by developing an interest in food). Restaurants can support food preference expressions, and stimulate specific items at the point-of-purchase, i.e., the menu item choice.

Other findings of interest have been presented by Chan et al. (2017), who studied interrelationships of reward systems and behavioural choices. They distinguish immediate financial discounts and delayed behavioural rewards, suggesting that financial discounts paid to consumers will generate more immediate attention than behavioural rewards, which heighten attention to the future. Results of their experiments nevertheless support that behavioural rewards can encourage healthier food choices among individuals with less healthy eating habits (Chan et al., 2017). Such temporal perspectives in efforts to change behaviour are relevant, because indulgence in unhealthy foods is usually immediate, while preferences to maintain health represent longer-term goals. This was shown in a study by Milkman et al. (2010), who found that online grocery store purchases were healthier when delivery dates were in the far future (five days or later) than immediate (the following day). The implication for restaurants is that there will be a barrier for healthier (and generally more sustainable) menu choices in the immediate choice context of breakfast, lunch or dinner. In particular guests with lower levels of self-control will abandon potential longer-term health goals in favour of immediate rewards associated with an unhealthy food option. An important insight is thus that where choices can be influenced, for instance in the context of banquets where dinner choices have to be made prior to the event, there is a greater chance to sell healthier menu choices. However, the ways in which food choices can be influenced even in more spontaneous contexts are numerous and are discussed in detail in Chapter 9.

Box 8.3 Choose Health LA Restaurants Program

The Choose Health LA Restaurants Program is a partnership between the Los Angeles County Department of Public Health (DPH) and local retail restaurants to promote the availability of healthier menu options. To participate in this voluntary programme, restaurants must provide:

- smaller portion size options in addition to the existing menu items;
- drinking water, free of charge;
- healthier kids meals that include fruits and vegetables, healthy beverages and less fried foods (this is at select locations).

> Launched in September 2013, there are over 700 participating restaurant locations as of the beginning of 2021.
>
> Menus from all restaurants that had joined within one year of programme launch (n = 17 restaurant brands) were assessed (Gase et al., 2015). Participation in the programme resulted in restaurants making changes to their primary and children's menus. The majority of participating restaurants brands (12) made at least some changes to increase the availability of reduced-size portions and/or modify the items available on their children's menu (Gase et al., 2016a). It was also argued that the results of the intervention support restaurant compliance with programme criteria and menu improvements, even though they are voluntary, and therefore representing an important step towards implementing healthier food strategies in the food retail environment (Gase et al., 2016a, 2016b).
>
> www.choosehealthla.com/eat/restaurants/

Meat mass production and antimicrobial resistance

It is generally acknowledged that in particular red meat consumption is detrimental to health, with the Harvard T. H. Chan School of Public Health (Willett et al., 2019b) summarizing the results of three recent studies (Han et al., 2019; Vernooij et al., 2019; Zeraatkar et al., 2019) as reduced red or processed meat consumption as being associated with lower cancer mortality, type 2 diabetes and cardiovascular disease.

As the global production of meats increases – as does per capita consumption in many parts of the world (see Chapter 2) – meat production has direct health implications as well as indirect ones, such as production outcomes including antimicrobial resistance. Currently, there is much debate about the resistance of microbes, as available antibiotics have seen a significant decline in their effectiveness (Zaman et al., 2017). The emerging challenge of antimicrobial resistance (AMR), i.e., changes in the genetic setup of bacteria, fungi, viruses or parasites as a result of exposure to antimicrobial drugs, has been long known (e.g., Levy, 1982; Hawkey, 1998). Calls to address the issue have been repeated regularly (Carlet et al., 2011; Howard et al., 2013). The World Health Organization (WHO, 2018c) recently underlined the seriousness of antimicrobial resistance as one of the most relevant public health threats. As the organization emphasizes, antimicrobial resistance will increase health risks and the cost of health systems:

- Antimicrobial resistance threatens the effective prevention and treatment of an ever-increasing range of infections caused by bacteria, parasites, viruses and fungi.
- AMR is an increasingly serious threat to global public health that requires action across all government sectors and society.
- Without effective antibiotics, the success of major surgery and cancer chemotherapy would be compromised.
- The cost of health care for patients with resistant infections is higher than care for patients with non-resistant infections due to longer duration of illness, additional tests and use of more expensive drugs.
- In 2016, 490,000 people developed multi-drug resistant tuberculosis globally, and drug resistance is starting to complicate the fight against the human immunodeficiency virus (HIV) and malaria.

(WHO, 2018c)

While hospitals are widely considered key locations where resistances develop, industrial meat production is also seen as an important reservoir of antibiotic resistance and as conduits for zoonotic diseases to transfer to human populations. Resistant bacteria can also reach humans through food product chains (Witte, 1998). For instance, antibiotic resistance has been shown for *Listeria, Salmonella* or *Escherichia* species in meat products (Duffy et al., 1999; Yücel et al., 2005; Davis et al., 2018). AMR is a challenge for the food industry because some bacteria can survive in very different environments, easily reproduce and have severe health consequences. For example, *Listeria monocytogenes* is a foodborne microbe that can survive in environmental conditions including low temperature, low pH or high salt, making it possible for the organism to contaminate food products even after processing. The microbe causes various human illnesses, such as septicaemia, meningitis, meningoencephalitis or invasive infections in new-born and the elderly, along with serious complications during pregnancy with a fatality rate that can reach up to 20%–30% (Olaimat et al., 2018). Notably, the microbe has also been shown to be resistant to antibiotics including penicillin, ampicillin, tetracycline and gentamicin.

Food production continues to be a major area of use of antibiotics. Estimates suggest that half of all antimicrobial agents worldwide are used in industrial meat production (Wilcox, 1998), with up to 80% of total consumption of medically important antibiotics being consumed in the animal sector in some countries (WHO, 2017). The challenges of AMR have been understood decades ago, with the UK prohibiting the use of antibiotics as animal growth-promoting agents half a century ago, in 1970 (Van den Bogaard & Stobberingh, 1996). However, the struggle to limit their use in food systems continued over decades, as the large-scale production of animal protein had come to rely heavily on drugs, and was promoted by global drug manufacturers such as Bayer:

> In 1996, the FDA approved the use of fluoroquinolines in chickens and turkeys, primarily to prevent mortality associated with *Escherichia coli* infection. This inexplicable decision was reached despite strong opposition from the Centers for Disease Control (CDC), which cited the extraordinary value of these compounds in treating community- or hospital-acquired enteric infections in humans.
> (Falkow & Kennedy, 2001, p. 397)

In the late 1990s, countries including the UK, Denmark, Finland or Sweden had all eliminated the use of antibiotics as growth agents, and the European Union banned the use of antibiotics for growth promotion in 2006 (WHO, 2017). This was also a result of the World Health Organization advising against the practice and emphasizing that animals should not be treated with antibiotics used in human medicine (Falkow & Kennedy, 2001). Not all countries heeded the WHO's advice, however, as Falkow and Kennedy affirm (2001, p. 397) "the practice continues in the United States and many other nations". Even today, antibiotics are widely used, and only where animal protein production is organic, is it likely that animals are raised without these (Makary et al., 2018). This, again, is a matter of market shares, as for example less than 1% of US agriculture is organic (Makary et al., 2018).

Mass production of meat is the main problem in the context of AMR. Industrial-scale food production, in which large animal numbers are raised in crowded conditions and stables that cannot be adequately cleaned, microbes can develop, propagate and spread. This is particularly problematic where this includes resistant bacteria and genes that can spread to humans. As much as 20% of resistant infections in humans are linked to antibiotic use in agriculture (Makary et al., 2018). Documented routes of transfer from farms to humans include the use of manure as fertilizer, food animal transport, non-domesticated animals as well as agricultural workers (Silbergeld et al., 2008).

The issue of the transfer of diseases from farms and food production areas, such as fish and meat markets and abattoirs has only received further attention as a result of COVID-19 (Peters et al., 2020). Treating animals with the same class of antibiotics as humans can also result in cross resistances (Makary et al., 2018). In response, the WHO has called on farmers and food industry to stop using antibiotics to promote growth or to prevent disease in healthy animals, as a measure to prevent the spread of antibiotic resistance (WHO, 2017).

New ways of dealing with animal infectious diseases are now pursued, with attempts to replace antibiotics with for instance vaccines (Hoelzer et al., 2018). As underscored by Saad and Ahmed (2018, p. 9) "Antibiotics would not be necessary if animals were raised differently under good veterinary and husbandry practices that were less crowded and more sanitary". This is probably a key insight of relevance for this book, i.e., the fact that mass consumption of meats is instrumental in the antibiotics crisis. Consumer choices, including those made regarding organic meats or in favour of more vegetarian and vegan diets, have great importance for medical health challenges. This is equally true for the menus developed by restaurants, as well as the foodstuffs sourced, and hence the overall sustainability of the food system.

Food allergies

Food allergies have been primarily linked to milk, egg, soy, wheat, peanut, tree nuts, fish and shellfish (Ho et al., 2014). In a review of studies on plant food allergies, Zuidmeer et al. (2008) found allergy prevalence ranging from 0.1% to 4.3% for fruits and nuts, 0.1% to 1.4% for vegetables and <1% each for wheat, soy or sesame. Skin prick tests against wheat showed prevalences ranging as high as 3.6% and against soy as high as 2.9%, indicating that prevalence based on perception is lower than when tested for sensitization, i.e., part of the population is unaware of their allergies. Food allergy prevalence of more than 1%–2%, but less than 10% of the population have been confirmed in a meta-study by Chafen et al. (2010), and more recent reviews have concluded that food allergy prevalence is increasing (Sicherer & Sampson, 2018). Research also indicates that differences depend on age, with indications that food allergies may affect up to 15%–20% of infants (Ho et al., 2014) (see Box 8.4).

Causes for food allergies are linked to genetic, epigenetic and environmental risk factors (Sicherer & Sampson, 2018). These include sex (male sex in children), ethnicity (increased among Asian and black children) and genetics (familial associations, human leukocyte antigen, specific genes). Allergy risk factors can for instance be reduced by addressing hygiene (too clean environments), vitamin D insufficiency, lack of dietary fat (omega-3-polyunsaturated fatty acids) as well as antioxidants, more limited digestion of allergens, obesity or the timing and route of exposure to food (Sicherer & Sampson, 2018). Restaurants will not normally be able to influence the conditions leading to food allergies; hygienic conditions in kitchens, for example, are legislated. However, restaurants have important roles in offering menus that allow for food choices even for those suffering from several allergies. This is a considerable challenge, though restaurants have already adapted to this emerging issue, for instance by offering hot beverages using non-cow milk products.

It also deserves mentioning that allergies can be supported by changes in the physical environment. As highlighted by Reinmuth-Selzle et al. (2017), human environments have been undergoing significant changes over the past century, including an increase in ozone, nitrogen oxides, volatile organic compounds and particulate matter. These can "induce chemical modifications of allergens, increase oxidative stress in the human body, and skew the immune system toward allergic

> **Box 8.4   Restaurant staff and responses to food allergies**
>
> Lee and Sozen (2018) compare restaurant managerial staff and employees' attitudes towards food allergies, their food allergy knowledge and food allergy-related training. A total of 110 managerial staff and 229 restaurant employees participated in the study. The study found that most restaurants were willing to modify their recipes for customers with allergies. However, participants felt that it was the responsibility of customers to tell staff of their food allergy needs. Both managers and employees were able to identify certain symptoms of allergic reactions to food but lacked knowledge of allergen-handling. The managerial staff and employees had knowledge differences about how to respond to an allergic reaction and how to identify peanut derivatives on food labels. Overall, 70% of managerial staff indicated that they provided employee food allergy training but only 40% of employees indicated they had received such training. Managerial staff identified a lack of employee commitment and interest in allergen issues as barriers to training provision while employees felt that it was unnecessary. These findings are insightful as, in Canadian research, McAdams et al. (2018) found that restaurants that demonstrate a strong preparedness towards handling food allergy requests can deliver a better customer experience and increase customer loyalty.

reactions" (Reinmuth-Selzle et al., 2017, p. 4119). Air pollutants, in particular, are thought to "act as adjuvants and alter the immunogenicity of allergenic proteins, while climate change affects the atmospheric abundance and human exposure to bioaerosols and aeroallergens" (Reinmuth-Selzle et al., 2017, p. 4119). Even though interrelationships and interactions are not as yet fully understood, allergies are likely enhanced by air pollution and climate change. Notably, food transports contribute to both, again highlighting the importance of sourcing foodstuffs locally, and underlining the many interrelationships between healthy and sustainable foods. Chefs can make major contributions to resolving these issues by designing more local, organic or vegetarian/vegan menus.

Other health implications of food choices

There is now a vast body of literature on the implications of food choices on health. As outlined earlier, healthy diets help prevent malnutrition and a range of non-communicable diseases and conditions (WHO, 2018a). Optimal nutrition for young children will contribute to healthy growth and cognitive development while also reducing the risk of becoming overweight or obese or developing non-communicable diseases. However, many diets are characterized by high-energy foods, including in particular animal protein, fats, free sugars and salt/sodium. These can have negative consequences for health. For instance, overconsumption of sodium through salt can contribute to high blood pressure, increasing the risk of heart disease and stroke. Estimates are that every year, as many as 1.65 million deaths from cardiovascular causes are attributed to sodium intake above reference levels (Mozaffarian et al., 2014). Free sugars increase the risk of dental caries, a problem that is prevalent specifically in countries where dental services are unaffordable or unavailable to local populations, or where basic tooth hygiene is limited for economic reasons or because of social or economic marginalization (Yabao et al., 2005; Edelstein, 2006; Chi & Scott, 2019). High-calorie intakes can also lead to overweight and obesity (Ludwig et al., 2001). Free sugars also influence blood pressure, with evidence that lower sugar intake will reduce the risk for cardiovascular diseases (Ludwig et al., 2018). For this reason, recommendations by the World Health Organization (WHO) are to reduce the intake of free sugars to less than 10%, and preferably less than 5% of the total energy intake (Breda et al., 2019).

In contrast, consumption of healthier foodstuffs such as vegetables, dietary fibre included in whole grains, as well as fruit is often too low. To this end, the WHO (2018a) advises adults and children to consider the following guidelines.

For adults

- Fruit, vegetables, legumes (e.g., lentils and beans), nuts and whole grains (e.g., unprocessed maize, millet, oats, wheat and brown rice).
- At least 400 g (i.e., five portions) of fruit and vegetables per day, excluding potatoes, sweet potatoes, cassava and other starchy roots.
- Less than 10% of total energy intake from free sugars, which is equivalent to 50 g (or about 12 level teaspoons) for a person of healthy body weight consuming about 2000 calories per day, but ideally is less than 5% of total energy intake for additional health benefits. Free sugars are all sugars added to foods or drinks by the manufacturer, cook or consumer as well as sugars naturally present in honey, syrups, fruit juices and fruit juice concentrates.
- Less than 30% of total energy intake from fats. Unsaturated fats (found in fish, avocado and nuts, and in sunflower, soybean, canola and olive oils) are preferable to saturated fats (found in fatty meat, butter, palm and coconut oil, cream, cheese, ghee and lard) and *trans*-fats of all kinds, including both industrially produced *trans*-fats (found in baked and fried foods, and pre-packaged snacks and foods, such as frozen pizza, pies, cookies, biscuits, wafers and cooking oils and spreads) and ruminant *trans*-fats (found in meat and dairy foods from ruminant animals, such as cows, sheep, goats and camels). It is suggested that the intake of saturated fats be reduced to less than 10% of total energy intake and *trans*-fats to less than 1% of total energy intake. In particular, industrially produced *trans*-fats are not part of a healthy diet and should be avoided.
- Less than 5 g of salt (equivalent to about one teaspoon) per day. Salt should be iodized.

For infants and young children

- Infants should be breastfed exclusively during the first six months of life.
- Infants should be breastfed continuously until two years of age and beyond.
- From 6 months of age, breast milk should be complemented with a variety of adequate, safe and nutrient-dense foods. Salt and sugars should not be added to complementary foods.

To ensure healthy diets, the WHO (2018a) also provides cooking advice, both in terms of menu compositions as well as food preparation. While this advice may not always be practical for chefs to consider in menu compositions, various aspects reconfirm earlier recommendations. WHO (2018a) guidelines for consumers highlight the importance of various rules for fruit and vegetable, fat, salt and sugar consumption.

Fruits and vegetables:

- always including vegetables in meals;
- eating fresh fruit and raw vegetables as snacks;
- eating fresh fruit and vegetables that are in season; and
- eating a variety of fruit and vegetables.

Fats:

- reducing saturated fats to less than 10% of total energy intake;
- reducing *trans*-fats to less than 1% of total energy intake;
- replacing both saturated fats and *trans*-fats with unsaturated fats (monounsaturated fats and polyunsaturated fats);
- steaming or boiling instead of frying when cooking;
- replacing butter, lard and ghee with oils rich in polyunsaturated fats, such as soybean, canola (rapeseed), corn, safflower and sunflower oils;
- eating reduced-fat dairy foods and lean meats, or trimming visible fat from meat; and
- limiting the consumption of baked and fried foods, and pre-packaged snacks and foods (e.g., doughnuts, cakes, pies, cookies, biscuits and wafers) that contain industrially produced *trans*-fats.

Salt:

- limiting the amount of salt and high-sodium condiments (e.g., soy sauce, fish sauce and bouillon) when cooking and preparing foods;
- not having salt or high-sodium sauces on the table;
- limiting the consumption of salty snacks; and
- choosing products with lower sodium content.

Sugars:

- limiting the consumption of foods and drinks containing high amounts of sugars, such as sugary snacks, candies and sugar-sweetened beverages (i.e., all types of beverages containing free sugars – these include carbonated or non-carbonated soft drinks, fruit or vegetable juices and drinks, liquid and powder concentrates, flavoured water, energy and sports drinks, ready-to-drink tea, ready-to-drink coffee and flavoured milk drinks); and
- eating fresh fruit and raw vegetables as snacks instead of sugary snacks.

While it is evident that freshly picked vegetables provide additional health benefits as they contain more nutrients and vitamins (Serafini et al., 2002; Vallejo et al., 2003), interest in such foods grows when these are purchased from farmers markets, i.e., locally (see Chapter 9). This is because such markets provide direct linkages between producers and consumers, increasing the interest in food, and specifically vegetables and fruits (Sage, 2003). To purchase foodstuffs directly from farmers and to communicate this to customers should thus be a central strategy for restaurants seeking to market healthier and more sustainable food choices.

> **Box 8.5 Labelling unhealthy foods: examples from Chile and Ecuador**
>
> The Chile Ministry of Health implemented a law in 2015 that regulates nutritional information of food products, and their labelling regarding energy (calories), sodium, sugar and saturated fat (USDA Foreign Agricultural Service, 2015). The law focuses on food products favoured by children to address obesity resulting out of unhealthy diets.
>
> Limits for the content of energy are 275 kcal/100 g for foods, and 400 mg/100 g for sodium, 10 g/100 g for total sugar and 4 g/100 g for saturated fat. Equivalent values for liquid foods are 70 kcal/100 ml for energy, 100 mg/100 ml for sodium, 5 g/100 ml for total sugar and 3 g/100 ml for saturated fat. Foods that exceed the limits are required to use black stop signs, indicating foods high in salt, sugar, energy or saturated fat, with one stop sign for each of the nutrients in excess. The law also states that:
>
> - The product shall not be sold, marketed, promoted or advertised within establishments of preschool, primary or high school education.
> - The product shall not be advertised on media or means of communication that target children under 14 years old, such as posters, printed materials, point of sale or textbooks, nor in television, radio, internet, magazines or in advertising space during or close to the latter, when the capture audience is greater than or equal to 20% of children under 14 years of age.
> - The product shall not be given freely to children under 14 years old nor can they use commercial hooks directed to that public such as toys, accessories, stickers or other similar incentives.
>
> Similar legislation was passed by the Government of Ecuador in 2014, requiring processed foods to carry a traffic light label indicating sugar, fat and salt levels. The label has to be placed on a white or grey background and must be proportional in size to the package. The bars, which can be red, yellow or green, indicate high, medium or low levels of fat, sugar or salt. Research shows that the label is easily understood by consumers and that it has a modest effect on consumer choices (Freire et al., 2017). More important is perhaps that companies have started to reduce levels of added fat, sugar or salt, in order to increase their label rating.

Towards healthy and sustainable food

Previous sections and chapters have described interrelationships of human health and global environmental change, and the need to adjust global diets in a way that resolves the multiple conflicts involved in the contemporary food system. For large parts of the global population, this will mean to increase energy levels and nutrition of the food consumed, while for many developed countries, diets have to be adjusted to lower environmental impacts and to reduce negative health impacts.

Box 8.6 The WHO recommendations for healthy diets

- Healthy dietary practices start early in life – breastfeeding fosters healthy growth and improves cognitive development, and may have longer-term health benefits such as reducing the risk of becoming overweight or obese and developing NCDs later in life.
- Energy intake (calories) should be in balance with energy expenditure. To avoid unhealthy weight gain, total fat should not exceed 30% of total energy intake. Intake of saturated fats should be less than 10% of total energy intake, and intake of trans-fats less than 1% of total energy intake, with a shift in fat consumption away from saturated fats and trans-fats to unsaturated fats, and towards the goal of eliminating industrially produced trans-fats.
- Limiting intake of free sugars to less than 10% of total energy intake is part of a healthy diet. A further reduction to less than 5% of total energy intake is suggested for additional health benefits.
- Keeping salt intake to less than 5 g per day (equivalent to sodium intake of less than 2 g per day) helps to prevent hypertension, and reduces the risk of heart disease and stroke in the adult population.

Source: WHO (2018b)

In a meta-study, this challenge was addressed by a Lancet Commission (Willett et al. 2019b). Based on a number of assumptions, such as a daily energy intake of 2,500 calories per adult and balanced diets, the Commission investigated diets that simultaneously minimize planetary change including climate change, biodiversity loss, freshwater use, interference with the global nitrogen and phosphorus cycles, and land-system change. To feed a population of 10 billion people by 2050, the Commission concludes that a healthy reference diet would have to largely consist of vegetables, fruits, whole grains, legumes, nuts and unsaturated oils. Protein sources including seafood and poultry would be limited, while very little red meat, processed meat, added sugar, refined grains and starchy vegetables would be consumed. This planetary diet would limit consumption of many food items and include a redistribution of food at a global scale. By 2050, the reduction in red meats would be 50% compared to current levels – notably with a world population some 2.5 billion larger than today – while consumption in vegetables, fruits, legumes and nuts would double. Health effects of dietary changes would be substantial, with an estimated reduction in premature deaths by 10.8–11.6 million per year.

One of the greatest issues in achieving a healthy diet is its cost and affordability. FAO et al. (2020) highlight that healthy diets cost 60% more than diets that only meet the requirements for essential nutrients and cost almost five times as much as diets that meet only the dietary energy needs obtained via a starchy staple (Table 8.1). This means that the cost of a healthy diet is considerably higher than the international poverty line (US$ 1.90 purchasing power parity (PPP) per day). An important conclusion with respect to dietary provision and its intersection with the global food system (see Chapter 2) is that the cost of a diet therefore "increases incrementally as the diet quality increases – from a basic energy sufficient diet to a nutrient adequate diet and then to a healthy diet including more diversified and desirable food groups – across all regions and

Table 8.1 Cost of a healthy diet per person per day (US$ equivalents)

Source: Adapted from WHO et al. (2020)

Diet	Description	World	Africa	Asia	Latin America and the Caribbean	Oceania	North America and Europe	Low-income countries	Lower middle-income countries	Upper middle-income countries	High-income countries
Energy efficient (starchy staple)	Provides adequate calories for energy balance for work each day. This is achieved using only the basic starchy staple for a given country (e.g., maize, wheat or rice only).	0.79	0.73	0.88	1.06	0.55	0.54	0.70	0.88	0.87	0.71
Nutrient adequate	Not only provides adequate calories, but also relevant nutrient intake values of macro- and micro-nutrients through a balanced mix of carbohydrates, protein, fat, essential vitamins and minerals.	2.33	2.15	2.18	2.83	2.07	2.29	1.98	2.40	2.52	2.31

Diet	Description	World	Africa	Asia	Latin America and the Caribbean	Oceania	North America and Europe	Low-income countries	Lower middle-income countries	Upper middle-income countries	High-income countries
Healthy	Provides adequate calories and nutrients, but also includes a more diverse intake of foods from several different food groups. It is intended to meet all nutrient intake requirements and to help prevent malnutrition, including diet-related non-communicable diseases.	3.75	3.87	3.97	3.98	3.06	3.21	3.82	3.98	3.95	3.43

Healthy and sustainable foods

country income groups globally" (FAO et al., 2020, p. 65). At the global level, a healthy diet is on average affordable, as the cost represents approximately 95% of average food expenditures per capita per day. However, as Table 8.1 highlights there are considerable variations in affordability around the world. Overall, this means that more than three billion people on the planet cannot afford a healthy diet (FAO et al., 2020).

Table 8.2 Planetary diet focused on health, 2,500 kcal/day
Source: Willett et al. (2019b)

Food category	Macronutrient intake (possible range), g/day	Caloric intake, kcal/day
Whole grains Rice, wheat, corn	232 (0%–60% of energy)	811
Tubers or starchy vegetables Potatoes and cassava	50 (0–100)	39
Vegetables All vegetables Dark green vegetables Red and orange vegetables Other vegetables	300 (200–600) 100 100 100	23 30 25
Fruits All fruit	200 (100–300)	126
Dairy foods Whole milk or derivative equivalents (e.g., cheese)	250 (0–500)	153
Protein sources Beef and lamb Pork Chicken and other poultry Eggs Fish Legumes Dry beans, lentils and peas Soy foods Peanuts Tree nuts	7 (0–14) 7 (0–14) 29 (0–58) 13 (0–25) 28 (0–100) 50 (0–100) 25 (0–50) 25 (0–75) 25	15 15 62 19 40 172 112 142 149
Added fats Palm oil Unsaturated oils Dairy fats (included in milk) Lard or tallow	6.8 (0–6.8) 40 (20–80) 0 5 (0–5)	60 354 0 36
Added sugars All sweeteners	31 (0–31)	120

The challenge of achieving the objective of a planetary diet is illustrated in Table 8.2. While for virtually anyone in the developing world, the outlined diet would represent a vast improvement to current diets, the opposite is likely true for perceptions in the industrialized world, where McDonald's US$1 burger meals are readily available, and where per capita consumption of meats and other high protein sources is high and would have to decline, in some cases dramatically. This is specifically relevant for the hospitality sector, where per person food consumption can be high. For example, a study in a four-star hotel in Greece revealed per person per day consumption of 385 g of meats (115 g of this pork, 66 g beef and 84 g chicken), along with 95 g of fish and 44 g of seafood (Gössling et al., 2015). This can be compared to 7 g of beef, 7 g of pork, 29 g of chicken and 28 g of fish per capita and day recommended in the planetary diet. The hotel's consumption of meats and fish is about eight times higher than the planetary diet, indicating the importance of food consumption in leisure contexts, and the specific role of restaurants in developing entirely different menus.

As this chapter has highlighted the world faces a considerable health and environmental problem in relation to what we eat. As the FAO et al. (2020, p. 93) concluded,

> If current food consumption patterns continue, diet-related health costs linked to non-communicable diseases and their mortality are projected to exceed USD 1.3 trillion per year by 2030. On the other hand, shifting to healthy diets would lead to an estimated reduction of up to 97 percent in direct and indirect health costs, thus creating significant savings that could be invested now to lower the cost of nutritious foods.

However, a healthy diet is also important to the planet. As noted in Chapter 6, the diet-related social cost of GHG emissions is projected to exceed US$1.7 trillion per year by 2030, while the adoption of healthy diets that include sustainability considerations would reduce the social cost of GHG emissions by an estimated 41%–74% in 2030 enabling both healthier individuals and a healthier environment. The restaurant and food services sector clearly has a substantial role it can play in such initiatives by what it places on the menu and how it is promoted.

Given that individuals are influenced by the places in which they select, purchase and consume food, food services can inform customers on food choices and influence less motivated consumers by structuring the eating environment to assist and encourage healthier eating. Unfortunately, evidence suggests that most voluntary, population-level healthy eating schemes that have aimed to inform consumers have had little effect on consumer choice (Ellison et al., 2013; Hillier-Brown et al., 2017; Carin et al., 2021). Foodservice businesses and operations have engaged with programmes that move beyond information provision to modify options, foods or service practices. However, as Carin et al. (2021, p. 21) concluded, "the voluntary actions taken by businesses may need to extend further to substantially shape the food environment to achieve a health benefit". Similarly, Hillier-Brown (2017, p. 18) found that their results suggest that,

> it is the level of intrusiveness of an intervention, rather than the type of policy function, that determines the impact of the intervention. More 'intrusive' interventions (e.g. restrict choice and manipulate price) appear more effective than less intrusive interventions that simply include providing information and enabling choice (e.g. calorie labelling law).

How menu marketing, changes in portion sizes and the presentation of specific foods can support healthy and sustainable diet choices is discussed in the following chapter.

Chapter 9

Menu marketing, portions and presentation

Introduction: intervening with food choices

Consumer food choices, eating behaviour and food waste patterns have received much attention from public health and sustainable agriculture advocates because consumer decisions have great importance for reducing calorie intake, the selection of healthier foodstuffs and the environmental implications of the food system (e.g., Hawkes et al., 2015; Vaitkeviciute et al., 2015; Bucher et al., 2016; Mirosa et al., 2016). They also influence the development of the food system more generally, as much of the overconsumption and wastage of food takes place in industrialized countries, where food and animal feed are imported from developing countries. Consumption patterns thus also influence trade flows in food (see Chapter 2).

Figure 9.1 illustrates where food is purchased/consumed, and where choices can be influenced. Consumers may purchase foods in very different contexts, including supermarkets and farmers markets, special interest stores (bakeries, butchers, delicatessen) as well as fast-food chains, restaurants, hotels, on the street or through

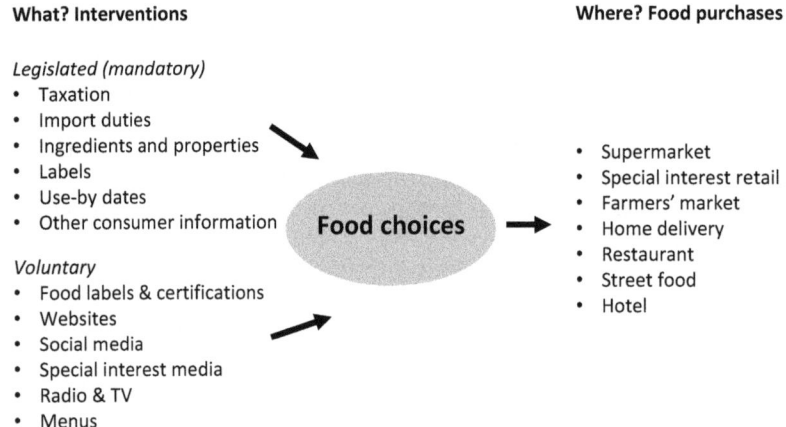

Figure 9.1 Where food is purchased/consumed and where choices can be influenced

home deliveries. Food is a consumer item that is affected by legislation, i.e., standards for preservation, storage, hygiene, preparation (food services), or the food properties themselves, for instance in terms of their salt, sugar or fat content. International food standards are published in the Codex Alimentarius by the Food and Agriculture Organization (FAO) and the World Health Organization (WHO) (2019). All of these set global and national frameworks for the trade and sales of foodstuffs.

As a result, for many food items, legislation is specific and standard-setting, representing a command-and-control approach defining the product or its use. This can also include legislation that is country-specific, and more flexible. For example, in Sweden, restaurants may use foodstuffs for cooking even after their official use-by dates have been passed (Livsmedelsverket, 2019), i.e., chefs are allowed to make decisions regarding food products' edibility based on taste or smell, in an effort to reduce food waste (see Chapters 13 and 14). The consumption of specific foods can also be regulated by market-based measures, such as taxes or duties increasing the cost of consumption. As an example, significant sugar taxes exist in a wide range of countries, such as Mexico (Colchero et al., 2016) or the UK (Jones, 2016). Some consumer information tools may be mandatory for producers, in the sense that they have to be used, and voluntary for consumers, who can choose to ignore or consider the information that has been provided. An example are labels indicating a product's healthiness regarding salt, sugar and fat content, which are legislated in for example Ecuador or Chile (see Chapter 8).

Food choices can also be influenced by a variety of voluntary soft-policy interventions. Labels can inform about nutrient content to affect decision-making, but they can also communicate a wide range of other food properties, which may include aspects as diverse as regional or organic production, or whether the food has been produced in a way that is more animal-friendly, GMO-free, low-carbon or low-carb. Another way of influencing consumers includes websites, radio, TV and other media that address consumers on the basis of their specific food interests. As discussed in the following sections, there now exists a great variety of such information channels reaching out to vast consumer numbers. Finally, restaurants have many of the most tangible opportunities to influence consumers, because they can edit choices, recommend or highlight specific dishes. As these are connected to food experiences, restaurants have a key role in consumer decision-making, yet one that needs to be balanced with expectations. These opportunities are described in greater detail in the following sections.

Consumer decision-making

The effectiveness of interventions to inspire and affect consumer food choices will depend on the design (e.g., the form of presentation), the character of the information (e.g., the knowledge type or appeal) as well as the more general consumer context in which they are presented (e.g., supermarket purchases or eating out). Evidence suggests that different groups in society will be more or less inclined to make decisions supportive of healthier and more sustainable food systems, and for a considerable share of consumers, cost will always be the most important or even the only relevant parameter (Hoek et al., 2017a; Luís et al., 2018). For this reason, it is paramount to understand the general frameworks within which consumer decision-making can be influenced.

So far, there is not much evidence of significant changes towards healthier *and* more sustainable diets at the scale required to meet the objectives of planetary and people health (Gose et al., 2016; see Chapter 8). On the contrary, evaluations of information campaigns and food certifications show that these have had limited effects on food decisions (Roberto et al., 2012b; Crockett et al., 2014; Wong et al., 2014; Fuerst et al.,

2015; Spanos et al., 2015), with evidence that while health has considerable importance for consumers, the environment does not (Hoek et al., 2017b). Societal change is always a slow process as new trends have to develop and become a mainstream interest before they turn into cultural norms. For this reason, interventions need to be optimized to support sustainable food choices. Some insights in this regard have been presented by van der Linden (2014), who highlights – in the context of climate change – that appeal designs as well as informational content both have importance for the effectiveness of information tools. As van der Linden (2014) affirms, attempts to influence consumer decision-making have for a long period of time been based on cognitive-analytical approaches, which presuppose that knowledge changes attitudes and that new attitudes will lead to behavioural change. Campaigns have also used affective-experiential approaches, sometimes based on negative emotional appeals and guilt messaging. Such morally charged appeal designs have perhaps been the least successful in altering consumer decisions, which is why more recent information campaigns use social-normative approaches, with longer-term goals of promoting social and moral norm change (van der Linden, 2014).

Social-normative campaigns are better aligned with insights that persuasive appeal designs need to overcome psychological barriers (van der Linden, 2014). This can be best achieved by considering three aspects: first, by providing factual, procedural and effectiveness knowledge, i.e., 'What is the problem?', 'How can it be addressed?' and 'Which difference will this make?'. These three knowledge dimensions help consumers assess the implications of their decisions; yet, it is rare for labels or certifications to actually provide this information (Gössling & Buckley, 2016). Second, it is important for information tools to appeal to behaviour that is commonly approved and morally right, as well as in line with majority expectations. Humans like to believe to be part of a majority – which also explains the power of social norms in guiding behaviour (Hall, 2014). A third aspect may be added, i.e., that highlighting tangible aspects of sustainable food choices, such as health benefits, is likely to significantly improve their appeal. Where personal advantages are involved in a behaviour, this will vastly increase the attractiveness of specific choices.

Box 9.1   A win-win in the revision of a children's menu

An estimated 32% of US children aged 2–19 are overweight or obese (Ogden et al., 2014). At the same time, approximately one-third of American children eat fast food on any given day with a typical restaurant children's menu including "high-calorie foods like pizza, macaroni and cheese, and chicken nuggets, served with a side of salty French fries and a sugary drink like soda or lemonade" (Anzman-Frasca et al., 2016, p. 3). And, among these consumers, one-third of their daily calories come from fast food (Shonkoff et al., 2018). Therefore, there are increasing efforts to encourage the adoption of healthier children's menus.

In 2012, the Silver Diner, a regional restaurant chain located mainly in the Baltimore-Washington, DC, metropolitan area, revised its children's menu to offer healthier items. The new menu included significantly more menu options that met nutrition standards, and all children's entrées were automatically paired with healthy side dishes such as strawberries, mixed vegetables and side salads. The restaurant removed French fries and sugary soft drinks from the children's menu, although those items could be substituted at no additional charge. Researchers examined the outcomes of the menu changes including changes in children's orders as well as restaurant revenues (Table 9.1).

Table 9.1 Results of changes in a children's menu

Source: Anzman-Frasca et al. (2016)

Item	Before menu changes (%)	Shortly after menu changes (%)	One year later (%)	Two years later (%)
Healthy children's entrées ordered	3.1	45.7	44.6	43.0
Healthy children's side dishes ordered	38.4	74.1	76.1	74.8
French fries ordered	57.0	22.0	20.2	21.4
Soda ordered	34.7	29.7	25.3	24.1

The result of the menu change was a win-win for customers, the restaurant chain and healthy eating goals: orders of healthier food items increased, and restaurant revenue also continued to grow. After the menu changes, almost half of children's entrées ordered were from the healthier children's meal options, compared to only 3% of children's entrées ordered before the changes. The proportion of children's meal orders that included at least one healthy side also increased substantially (Anzman-Frasca et al., 2015). Strawberries were the most popular healthy side dish, accounting for 63% of the side dishes served with children's entrées after the menu was changed. Milk and juice orders also increased after the menu changes, and soda orders decreased (Anzman-Frasca et al., 2015, 2016). Significantly, these changes were sustained over the following two years. An important business result of the menu change was that

> including more healthy options on the kids' menu did not hurt overall restaurant revenue and may have even supported continued growth. Total annual revenue across all Silver Diner restaurant locations grew by 5.3% from 2013 to 2014, exceeding the average revenue growth in leading family dining chains for the same period.
> (Anzman-Frasca et al., 2016, p. 3)

In more general terms, there is now much evidence that attitudes towards sustainable business practices are positive, and that a growing number of consumers are intent to positively contribute to the environment (e.g., Eurobarometer, 2012). It is less clear whether implications of food consumption are as yet fully internalized by consumers, however. For example, the consumption of meat is not associated with its 'true' climate impact, as highlighted by Camilleri et al. (2019), and assessments of the effectiveness of certifications on food packaging have concluded that these initiate limited changes in consumer preferences (Cecchini & Warin, 2016). However, informational campaigns *do* affect choices, and giving more thought to their design and normative appeal content could help increase their effectiveness in the future. As Cook et al. (1998, p. 164) affirm, consumers do have knowledge on food, though this will vary, along with perspectives on the importance of sustainability, and corresponding outcomes for food choices:

> far from being ignorant about the origins of foods, consumers actually have wide-ranging, if socially differentiated, knowledges. Childhood memories, experiences of travel, the booming media coverage of food issues, even geography lessons at school … In consequence, to portray consumers as ignorant about the origins of the foods they eat – even keeping as an honourable exception small groups of super-knowledgeable ethical shoppers, vegetarians and health "freaks" – is grossly simplistic.

This offers many opportunities to influence food choices, though it also suggests that where preferences for certain products (e.g., strawberries outside the season) exist, and where sacrificing such opportunities are considered self-denial (Stoll-Kleemann et al., 2001), it will be more difficult to address choices. To strengthen tangible aspects of food choices can in such situations improve their appeal. To stay with the example of strawberries, it may be enough to underline that seasonal, regional fruits are fresher and thus tastier, as even indirect cues will influence behaviour. For example, studies in restaurants have shown that menus providing nutritional information will stimulate sales of low-fat dishes (Albright et al., 1990). Likewise, descriptive food names make food items characterized in this way more attractive (Wansink et al., 2001), while images have been shown to have a positive effect on consumer attitudes (Hou et al., 2017). Such images also serve as cues, with research showing, for example, that to include illustrative reference to the sea is sufficient to increase fish choices in restaurants (Guénguen & Jacob, 2012).

These examples underscore the importance of tailoring information, and to highlight personal benefits. 'Healthier' or 'local', for example, will often be more sustainable choices that also represent more tangible benefits to the individual (Röös & Tjärnemo, 2011; Feucht & Zander, 2018). The design of more sustainable menus should rely on greater direct or indirect emphasis on personal benefits to increase the appeal of such food choices to customers. If this is combined with recommendations by staff focused on tangible benefits or the local origin of foodstuffs, this will affect choices very directly. These insights for menu design also underline the wider importance of restaurant communication strategies, which are often limited to a simple presentation of the different dishes. Before these are discussed in greater detail, the chapter turns to information tools and their relevance for consumers.

Box 9.2 The importance of taste in the provision of healthy eating alternatives

An online survey was administered in the USA by Nielsen via their Harris Poll Online to a national panel of 711 parents and their 8- to 12-year-old children that examined children's likelihood of ordering particular side dishes; receptivity to healthier side dishes and beverages; changes in receptivity to healthier side dishes and parent awareness (Shonkoff et al., 2018). A majority of children said they were likely to order a meal with a vegetable (60%), fruit (78%) or French fry (93%) side dish. Sixty-eight percent of children were receptive to receiving a fruit or vegetable side dish instead of French fries; or milk, water or flavoured water instead of soda (81%) with their restaurant children's meal. The most common reason given was liking/taste (Shonkoff et al., 2018).

Another study by Anzman-Frasca et al. (2017) of parents and children at quick and full-service restaurants examined parent/child perspectives on child meal selection and toy incentives. A total of 63% of children in the study ordered from the children's menu, of which 8% ordered healthier children's meals. Half of the parents reported that children determined their own food orders. Taste was the most common reason for children's meal choices (72%), followed by nutrition (41%) and habit (21%); cost was a minor consideration (3%). Of the children who responded, 95% stated that their meal tasted 'yummy' (Anzman-Frasca et al., 2017). Interestingly, restaurant managers interviewed as part of the study perceived that dining out was often viewed as a special occasion by parents so they were more lenient in children's menu choice which may be an important factor for consideration in family-oriented restaurants (Anzman-Frasca et al., 2017).

The studies highlight an extremely important point in restaurant food interventions to encourage healthier and sustainable eating. Intervention approaches that do not address food and menu appeal and/or the familiarity of meal options may not be successful. In other words, campaigns that only provide nutrition information, for example, will not work. A fundamental premise of healthy and sustainable restaurant and foodservice meals therefore is that the food has to taste good as well.

Information tools

Food labels and certifications are probably the most widespread tools to influence consumer decision-making. For example, Chapter 5 presented labels for organic foods, which are now available in a large number of countries. The omnipresence of such labels, as well as many recent developments such as the growing interest in vegetarian or vegan diets, supports trends for consumers to become more aware of the health and environmental implications of their food choices. Food certifications thus have an important role in fostering systemic change in the food system, in that they contribute to 'food literacy', i.e., in particular nutrition knowledge and interest in wider aspects of the food system with relevance for health (Perry et al., 2017). Notably, food labels will also increase literacy with regard to climate change, environment or animal welfare, i.e., aspects not usually included in definitions of food literacy (Vidgen & Gallegos, 2014; Perry et al., 2017; Truman et al., 2017). As outlined in previous chapters, certifications can focus on specific food types, organic production, fair trade or health aspects and be regional, national or global in geographical scope.

Certifications are the most common information tools, of which Ecolabel Index (2018) lists 102 that are currently used to highlight specific food product or restaurant characteristics. Ideally, certifications will not only influence decisions in specific purchasing contexts but also address a wider range of dimensions underlying more sustainable consumer food choices. These dimensions include *avoidance*, i.e., an understanding that some foodstuffs should not be chosen at all. This will be mostly relevant for certifications emphasizing that a product is not healthy to consume. For example, black labels for unhealthy foods as introduced in Chile may have such an effect on consumers. In the future, carbon labels (Box 9.1) may prevent a share of consumers from purchasing food that is carbon intense. Secondly, certifications may support *shifts* in consumer decisions in favour of more sustainable food choices, including, for example, seasonal or regional produce. Ideally, consumer information tools in the food sector would have two additional effects, i.e., *spill-over effects* to other areas of consumption, where insights learned in the context of food choices would also be applied; as well as the *voting for policies* that advance more sustainable food agendas.

As food choices are everyday choices more strongly characterized by habit, there is a considerable potential for certifications and other information tools to inform behavioural change. These would work towards three interrelated goals, i.e., to:

- *Inform* about product characteristics, and hence to empower consumers to consider their actions.
- *Inspire* sustainable and healthy choices, i.e., to convince consumers that these are qualitatively better choices.
- *Increase* knowledge about sustainability challenges, i.e., to contribute to an understanding of the consequences of consumption.

Certifications and labels

Table 9.2 shows different food certifications and their consumer relevance, based on discussions in the preceding chapters and sections. It can be assumed that health aspects will always rank highest for the individual and that certifications referring to nutritional value or calorie content will have the greatest relevance for consumer choices. 'Local' and regional foodstuffs will also be relevant, as tangible benefits are implied in such choices. This is likely true for hormone-, GMO- and antibiotic-free foodstuffs as well. Healthy or local food choices will be attractive for a rather large range of customers, even though nutrition facts, which are readily available on most food products, appear to be considered less often when purchases are made. In restaurants, this information is not readily available, unless highlighted in menus. Organic, vegetarian and climate-friendly choices would seem to be less relevant to customers, even though awareness appears to be increasing, which is likely to have repercussions for markets as well.

A related issue is how customers are informed about product characteristics. Some information is displayed in ways that is difficult for consumers to ignore. As an example, the traffic light label indicating sugar, fat and salt levels in Ecuador (see Chapter 8) must be displayed in a way that is proportional to package size (Freire et al., 2017), while nutrition facts may often be printed on the backside, and in fine print. In a meta-review

Table 9.2 Types of food-related certifications and consumer-relevance

Aspect	Example	Customer relevance	Market
Health (sugar, fat, salt)	Health star rating	High	Large
Low calorie	Nutrition facts	Medium to high	Medium
Local/regional	Producer information	Medium to high	Large
Hormone/GMO/Antibiotics	"Raised without"	Medium to high	Medium to large
Organic	USDA Organic	Medium	Small
Vegetarian	EU V-label	Low to high	Small to medium
Vegan	EU V-label	Low to high	Small
Climate-friendly	UK Carbon Trust	Low	Small to medium

of certifications, Cecchini and Warin (2016) concluded that traffic light (colour) schemes are indeed the most effective labelling schemes, i.e., twice as effective as other food labels or "Guideline Daily Amounts" information in affecting food choices (Table 9.3). Traffic light certifications were found to increase the number of people selecting

Table 9.3 Overview of studies on food labelling and their outcomes

Source: Based on Cecchini and Warin (2016), updated

Type of food labelling system studied	Population studied	Authors' conclusions	Author, year
i Simple 'healthy choice' tick; ii Multiple traffic light label; iii Monochrome Guideline Daily Amount label; iv Coloured Guideline Daily Amount label; v 'No label'.	420 adults in Hamburg, Germany	Traffic lights are the most efficient in stimulating change. Yet, they are unlikely to significantly influence food choices.	Borgmeier & Westenhoefer, 2009
i Green low-fat label; ii Red high-fat label; iii No label.	287 participants in London cinema	No major effects of nutritional labels on food choices.	Crockett et al., 2014
Smart Choices front-of-package nutrition label	216 US consumers	Labels increase knowledge but have limited impact on behaviour.	Roberto et al., 2012a
Seven front-of-pack labelling schemes (traffic light; percentage daily intake; star rating approach)	4,357 grocery shoppers in Australia	Labels have potential to support healthier choices.	Watson et al., 2014
i No label; ii Traffic light; iii Traffic light protein/fibre; iv Facts up front; v Facts up front and nutrients.	703 US consumers	Traffic lights approach performs best.	Roberto et al., 2012a
Serving size labels	104 female undergraduate students in Australia	Clear influence on portion size choices.	Spanos et al., 2015
Cholesterol-lowering claims on food	1,017 consumers of plant sterols, 1,002 consumers of oat fibre	Nutrition-related claims elicited more positive responses than taste control claims.	Wong et al., 2014
Emoticons and colours on food labels	955 consumers, representative of the UK	Nutritional labels had no effect on choice of snacks.	Vasiljevic et al., 2015

healthier options by 29.4% while other food labels yielded an increase of 14.7% and Guideline Daily Amount information by 11.9%. Traffic light schemes appeal intuitively, but they can also include additional information that is more comprehensive, contributing to awareness regarding food characteristics, and advancing food literacy.

Carbon labels

Carbon labels are a specific type of label that can be expected to be more frequently displayed on products in the future (Liu et al., 2016). Carbon labels inform about the CO_2 or greenhouse content of a product, though there are also carbon neutral labels, suggesting that emissions associated with the foodstuff have been offset. Carbon labels were first introduced by supermarket chains such as Tesco in the UK or Walmart in Chile but later retracted. This may have been owed to a lack of impact on shifting demand (Hornibrook et al., 2015) or because the labels confused consumers (Gadema & Oglethorpe, 2011; Hartikainen et al., 2014). Yet, rather than abandon the idea of carbon labelling food products, Gadema and Oglethorpe (2011, p. 815) suggest that it was necessary to establish: "effective linkages between food policy and food market actors to drive a targeted and coherent carbon labeling policy". To date, studies suggest that the effect of carbon labels on food purchasing decisions has remained limited (Gadema & Oglethorpe, 2011; Hartikainen et al., 2014; Emberger-Klein & Menrad, 2018). It needs to be noted, however, that there is an evolution from awareness building to knowledge generation to attitude change and behavioural change. It may thus be possible that supermarkets gave up on carbon labels too early, i.e., before consumers managed to develop an understanding of carbon implications, notably within a wider social norm of an individual's responsibility to act.

There currently exist various carbon labels for food, of which the most widely established appears to be the Carbon Trust food label in the UK. Various food certifications also consider greenhouse gas emissions as part of the aspects assessed under a given label. Carbon labels now exist in Canada, Korea, Japan, France, the USA and Taiwan, with evidence that the understanding of labels grows over time (Li et al., 2017). For example, Vanclay et al. (2011) tested carbon labelling of groceries in Australia. Using green (low), yellow (medium) and black (high) carbon footprint symbols on food items, they could show that sales of "black" items ("bad" in terms of climate change) declined by 4% during the first month, and 6% during the second month of the study period, while sales of "green" products increased by 2% in the first, and 4% in the second month. The authors concluded that there may be a learning effect involved. This was also found by Visschers and Siegrist (2015), who tested the effect of a "climate-friendly choice" label on menus. Research suggests that restaurant guests do perceive information on food item carbon content positively (Filimonau et al., 2017a), even though less positively than "local" labels (Feucht & Zander, 2018).

The more limited acceptance of carbon labels may be explained by the complexity of global warming, i.e., a phenomenon that is more abstract, and in a situation where purchases of low-carbon foodstuffs will entail less tangible personal benefits than for "local" or "organic" certifications (Gadema & Oglethorpe, 2011; Röös & Tjärnemo, 2011; Upham et al., 2011; Hartikainen et al., 2014). It has also been suggested that "local" is associated with benefits to farmers and the local economy, shorter transport distances, fewer environmental impacts as well as quality and health (Darby et al., 2008; Campbell et al., 2014; Feldmann & Hamm, 2015). Several of these aspects represent personal benefits, which can also be indirect. For example, shorter transport distances may imply a sense of control where the food is coming from, and under which conditions it is produced.

A key question in the context of food certifications is whether the many different aspects covered can be combined. For example, it has been concluded that "local" claims can be meaningfully combined with "more climate-friendly" because short transport distances can go along with lower emissions (see, however, Coley et al., 2009). The benefit is that products with lower carbon emissions would become more attractive for consumers primarily interested in local foods. This has been proposed by Onozaka and McFadden (2011) and could be explored in greater detail for other foods, as well as restaurant menus in order to increase the attractiveness of low-carbon diets. Another potential avenue to increasing carbon literacy and interest in low-carbon foods is to connect these to health issues.

Online information tools

Finally, websites, social media, special interest print and online media, TV shows as well as online information distributed by governmental and non-governmental organizations all have key roles in creating greater attention for sustainable and healthy foods (Table 9.3). Often, these information tools explicitly seek to educate the public, advocating for healthier, more sustainable food choices, but they also support trends indirectly, by highlighting health benefits, recommending recipes or entertainment in food shows.

Examples in Table 9.4 illustrate the wide range of initiatives to reduce meat consumption, to increase the attractiveness of vegetarian or vegan food choices and to

Table 9.4 Examples of media supporting meat-free food choices

Type of medium	Focus	Example
Website	Reducing meat consumption	whyeatlessmeat.com
App	Directory of vegetarian and vegan restaurants Calculations of protein intake Vegetarian recipes Barcode-based identification of vegan products Vegetarian cooking advice	Happy Cow Veg Protein III Veggie weekend Is it vegan? How to cook everything vegetarian?
Blog	Plant-based cooking blog	Oh she glows
Social media	Facebook – vegetarian diets Instagram – veg food photographs Twitter – vegetarian information	The Vegetarian Society #vegetarian @VegTimes
Special interest digital media	Lifestyle magazine	Veggie
Special interest print media	Lifestyle magazine	Vegan Food & Living
YouTube channel	Indian (vegetarian) cooking	Tarla Dalal
Radio podcast	Fitness	No meat athlete radio
Non-governmental organization	Healthy diets to prevent obesity	American Heart Association
Governmental organization	Healthier diets	Better Health Channel, Victoria State Government, Australia

support more active lifestyles. The great number of such initiatives that can be found online also bears evidence of wider societal change: many food choices that would have stood out years ago as representing niche lifestyles now represent mainstream consumer tastes. This is also evidenced by a growing number of restaurants offering or even specializing in vegetarian or vegan menus. Interest in such diets has clearly turned into a social norm, and in many countries, restaurants will now regularly offer meat-free alternatives.

Choice-editing

Restaurants have very important roles in "choice-editing"; this is to not offer specific foodstuffs or dishes because they involve significant environmental impacts, contributions to climate change or because they raise animal welfare concerns or have impacts working against the Sustainable Development Goals (see Chapter 2). Options for choice-editing were for example raised in the context of unhealthy diets and fast food, with Allder (2008) suggesting that takeaway restaurants play a more central role in menu content, including nutrition information on menus. As Allder (2008, p. 8) emphasized:

> If we are going to beat the rise of obesity and its attendant health problems, takeaway restaurants must be part of the solution. Alongside the nutrition information and signposting, we want to see more options on their menus with lower saturated fat, salt and sugar content, and less salt, saturated fat and sugar in their existing products. This kind of 'choice-editing' takes the burden for responsible choices off the consumer, by eliminating some of the opportunities to make less healthy choices and by making healthier choices the norm.

Here, choice-editing is understood as not using specific foodstuffs in menu designs at all. A list of 'problematic' foods is outlined in Table 9.5. Examples include foods that lead to large-scale environmental damage, such as giant prawns (see also Box 9.4), species that are endangered or red-listed, highly carbon-intensive or raising animal welfare concerns. The list in Table 9.4 is provisional, in the sense that more foodstuffs need to be considered problematic in a 'healthy and sustainable' context, such as all red meats.

Many restaurants seem to believe that specific foodstuffs need to be offered in order to provide attractive menus. For some restaurants specializing in unsustainable foods, this is a highly problematic situation. For example, a European steakhouse specializing in South American meat is unlikely to improve its environmental performance

Table 9.5 Examples of foodstuffs that should be choice-edited

Food item	Reason
Giant prawns	Farmed in converted mangrove forests, highly carbon-intense storage and transport (Henriksson et al., 2018)
Cod, halibut, tuna, ...	Threatened species (for a full list see Greenpeace, 2019)
Beef	Climate-incompatible methane emissions (Willett et al., 2019b)
Foie gras	Animal welfare concerns, force-feeding (Buller & Cesar, 2007)
Veal, battery birds	Industrial production without animal welfare concern (Harrison, 2013)

> **Box 9.3 Scandic choice-editing of giant prawns**
>
> Giant prawns imported from tropical countries have been linked to mangrove destruction, land seizures and violence against locals (Martinez-Alier, 2002). Prawn farming now occupies vast tracts of land, with global farmed shrimp production reaching close to 4 million tonnes in 2018 (FAO, 2019b). Most prawns are produced in developing countries including India, Ecuador, Viet Nam, Indonesia, Burma, Thailand, Malaysia, Brazil, Nicaragua and Honduras; the major import nations are the USA, Japan, the European Union, China, Republic of Korea, Australia and New Zealand (FAO, 2019b).
>
> Scandic Hotels decided in 2006 to no longer serve giant prawns in its restaurants. Before the decision, some 100,000 kg of prawns were served annually. According to management, removing prawns from menus did not have any negative effect on sales: Prawn dishes belonged to the high-priced choices, but prawns were also costly to purchase. Different fish dishes were offered as substitutes. In an effort to be fully transparent about the decision, the chain even decided to set up posters informing customers that prawns had been removed from menus for environmental reasons. This strengthened the Scandic brand and its sustainability-based brand: the media reporting on the initiative was estimated to have a $150,000 marketing value for the chain. Customer reactions were very positive – no negative reactions were reported (Gössling, 2010).

significantly by choice-editing: the very product is unsustainable due to its focus on beef. It is generally acknowledged that beef and soy production are key drivers of deforestation in the Amazon for example (Nepstad et al., 2006). However, for most restaurants, there are many options for choice-editing foods, as the removal of problematic foods from restaurant menus will usually go unnoticed by customers. With growing awareness of problematic foods, choice-editing may even be a strategy pre-empting critical consumer perspectives, voiced, for example, in restaurant evaluations. For an example of a chain removing giant prawns from their menus, see Box 9.3.

Insights for menu design

While much research on food interventions has focused on consumer views, less is known about the perspectives of restaurant managers. Filimonau and Krivcoca (2017) found in their study of manager views in "casual dining restaurants" in Bournemouth, UK that food and service quality, in the context of value for money considerations, were considered the most relevant aspects for diners. Managers however acknowledged that food "quality" included personal health and environment, with a tendency for healthier food preferences. Yet, managers were sceptical towards suggestions to "overload" menus with information, and they did not believe that carbon content information would influence choices. A notable exception was a reference to "local" foodstuffs, an aspect seen as a driver of choices. Managers even believed that the use of "local" produce would allow them to charge premiums.

Filimonau et al. (2017a) then tested in a field experiment how a menu providing information on carbon content, nutrition and calorie values, as well as the country of origin of foodstuffs would influence customer perceptions. Diners saw the provision of such information as generally useful, with evidence that the provenance of the foodstuffs involved in dishes caused surprise, as many foods had travelled around the

> **Box 9.4 Reinventing fast food: Max Burgers**
>
> The Swedish food chain Max Burgers opened in 1968 and had grown to 120 restaurants and an annual turnover of €220 million by 2018 (Max Burgers, 2019). The chain sticks out from other fast-food chains because of its focus on health and climate change in all of its marketing. This included "the world's first bike-in" franchise in Gotland, a lacto-ovo menu, low-fat cooking practices and ambitions to become "climate positive". In 2008, Max Burgers was the first restaurant to indicate the carbon content of different burger choices, while the company also sought to offset emissions by tree planting. In 2016, the chain introduced a new menu with a greater number of non-meat options, and a goal to sell 50% non-red meat burgers by 2022 (Max Burgers, 2019).
>
> While "offsetting" emissions through tree planting is a questionable strategy (Gössling et al., 2007), Max Burgers also puts a major focus on reducing emissions, for example sourcing most vegetables during the season, and all meats (and most vegetables) from Swedish farms. Fish purchases are eco-certified (Max Burgers, 2019). These decisions helped to establish a low-carbon CO_2 baseline for all products offered and were combined with a communication strategy seeking to influence customer choices by offering a range of vegan, vegetarian and low-carbon burger choices. In 2008, the chain originally displayed CO_2 estimates for each burger. This approach was later replaced with labels indicating vegetarian, vegan and low-carbon choices.
>
> Max Burgers reports that their food choice is a success. As studies have concluded that carbon labels on restaurant menus do not work (Babakhani et al., 2020), the discrepancy has to be explained with one of several factors: this includes consumer cultures, which may vary between Swedish and consumers in other countries; or the design of the labels used by Babakhani et al. (2020), which also do not consider the three dimensions of successful appeal design identified by van der Linden (2014), i.e., factual, procedural and effectiveness knowledge.

world – diners were generally unaware of how global food sourcing had become. Filimonau et al. (2017a) concluded that carbon content did not represent an aspect of major importance for customers, though consumers like to be informed about the origin of foodstuffs, nutritional and calorific values (see also Pulkkinen et al., 2016). This again confirms that it is more prudent to approach diners indirectly to support more sustainable choices, i.e., by highlighting "local" attributes in menus. Furthermore, sustainable choices will also often be healthier choices that can be singled out by prominent listings in menus, or labels underlining nutritional benefits. This is of particular relevance for restaurant managers, who may often ponder the benefits of organic produce in relation to their cost (Poulston & Yiu, 2011).

Menu marketing strategies have been discussed by Wansink and Love (2014), who suggest "engineering strategies" based on shifting attention, enhancing taste expectations and increasing perceptions of value. The overall goal is to sell healthier foodstuffs that also offer greater profit margins to restaurants (Wansink & Love, 2014). A starting point for shifting attention is the insight that customers often lean towards specific choices, which makes it necessary to highlight alternatives. To use the terminology of 'house specials' or 'favourites' helps suggest that such items are popular, representing a consumption norm. It is also possible to offer less favourable dishes – from a health/environment point of view – at a specifically high price, to make alternatives stand out as more reasonably priced. A potential risk of this latter strategy is that this might encourage a specific type of customer to focus on such dishes, i.e., those seeking to show that they are not impressed by high prices or even buying items because of their high price (Bagwell & Bernheim, 1996). According to Wansink and Love (2014), taste expectations can be enhanced by the use of sensory, geographic, nostalgic or brand names. Descriptions of the taste, smell or texture of foodstuffs raise taste expectations, as do associations of a geographic area with food. Nostalgic names will be associated with tradition, family or national origin, which are all related to basic human needs for stability, sociality and place. The recommendation of brand names is more problematic, as large corporations are a key determinant of unsustainable agricultural systems (see Chapter 2). Finally, the perception of value can be increased through various strategies, such as not to list prices in one column to prevent customers to base their decisions on direct price comparison (Wansink & Love, 2014). However, the argument may be turned around, as direct price-comparison options may also be a valid strategy to increase the sales of vegetarian dishes at lower prices.

Wansink and Love (2014) recommend to avoid having 'healthy' menu sections, and to rather market-specific dishes as 'light and fresh', or to use descriptive titles to increase attractiveness, such as 'succulent Italian seafood fillet' rather than 'seafood salad'. They also suggest to place healthy items in menu corners, where they draw more attention, and to have a 'house favourites' section in which the healthier items are listed first. To further guide attention towards specific dishes, logos, icons, recommendations or photos may be used. Design techniques (bolding, colouring) can be used to further highlight choices. These insights can inspire strategic menu architecture, with co-benefits of increasing margins, as well as the overall price-setting deemed acceptable by customers (Frash et al., 2015).

Box 9.5 Promoting healthy eating in the African American community

Obesity represents a major public health epidemic among the US African American community. African American (AA) adults have the highest age-adjusted prevalence rate for obesity (47.8%) than all other ethnic groups in the USA (Ogden et al., 2014), with the rate continuing to grow in the southern states. African Americans also tend to eat less vegetables and fruit and more fast food than other groups. African American food consumption is also affected by their foodscapes, with AA communities tending "to have more fast food restaurants but fewer supermarkets and stores selling healthy foods than White neighborhoods" (Crimarco et al., 2020, p. 169). One of the barriers that has been identified in AA adoption of a healthier diet is the perception that eating healthier means foregoing "soul food" in their cultural identity. Soul food describes the particular foodways that developed from the slave origins of AAs. As Hughes (1997, p. 274) comments, "soul food is an expression of the central core of Black culture". Although soul food is noted for its use of vegetables, e.g., black-eyed peas, okra, collard, kale, mustard greens, turnips), yams, sweet potatoes, it also utilizes substantial amounts of fried food, especially fried chicken, and pork. Nevertheless, in recent years a growing health-conscious movement in the AA community has prompted a number of vegan soul food restaurants that provide completely plant-based (i.e., no meat, diary or animal products), soul food dishes to open up throughout the US South.

> In Crimarco et al.'s (2020) study of vegan soul food restaurants several themes emerged from the interviews with restaurant owners as to how restaurant owners of vegan soul food restaurants view their roles as promoters of health in their community and the strategies that they use to make plant-based diets more appealing to AA adults:
>
> - Providing greater physical and economic access to vegan meals;
> - Educating the customer about vegan diets and healthy eating;
> - Emphasizing high-quality ingredients and good taste;
> - Changing cooking and lifestyle habits, not only by exposure to vegan food but also by offering cooking classes;
> - The importance of eating plant-based foods for ethical reasons or as a revolutionary act, not only with respect to animal and environmental welfare but also for being 'woke' to the interests of the AA community.
>
> The findings of Crimarco et al.'s (2020) research are significant not only because of their relevance to the AA community but also because they reinforce World Health Organization recommendations that, as part of the wider food environment, restaurants are important place-based intervention sites for strategies and promotions that improve healthy eating behaviours (Vandevijvere et al., 2015).

Conclusions

Figure 9.2 develops a five-step methodology towards the design of healthy and sustainable menus. This approach places most responsibility on restaurants. Chefs and management make a series of decisions that will narrow down the choices of the customer, to then guide decision-making towards 'desirable' dishes. As a first step, this involves the choice-editing of foodstuffs (Table 9.5). 'Problematic' species, foods that are climatically problematic, as well as raising concerns for animal welfare will be removed from menus. In a second step, the number of dishes offered is limited. This is important if predominantly fresh produce is to be used for cooking (health), and freezer storage capacity is reduced (energy and greenhouse gas emissions). Restaurants should also avoid buffet offers, as these have been found to incur more food waste (see Chapters 13 and 14). A third step includes the composition of dishes with a focus on local, fresh produce, limited amounts of animal protein (less than 25% of the overall food offered), as well as a choice of vegetarian and vegan alternatives. Step four focuses on the menu design, i.e., the way in which dishes are offered. Menus should place vegetarian and vegan alternatives prominently, and highlight those mostly based on local foodstuffs. This may be achieved on the basis of a small 'local' label or more detailed information; ideally, this could even include the names of the farm from where a specific food item is sourced. While the focus on 'local' should be a priority, chefs should seek to also use organic produce, which can be indirectly marketed as a quality signifier. For example, reference to the farm at which a certain foodstuff has been produced may outline that the farm is 'organic certified', if this applies. Finally, recommendations can have significant influence on choices. For this, service staff can be trained to recommend healthier and more sustainable choices based on tangible benefits to diners, i.e., attributes such as 'tasty', 'fresh' or 'local':.

Step 1: Choice-editing
Do not use unhealthy or unsustainable foodstuffs

Step 2: Menu set-up
Limit the number of dishes to those that can be prepared with fresh foodstuffs
Avoid forms of high-waste offers, such as buffets

Step 3: Dish composition
Use local, fresh produce
Include animal protein only as side dish
Offer range of vegetarian and vegan alternatives

Step 4: Menu design
Refer prominently to vegetarian and vegan dishes
Highlight dishes mostly composed of local foodstuffs
Provide information on origin of foodstuffs

Step 5: Recommendations
Have service-staff recommend specifically healthy and sustainable dishes
Underscore these choices' tangible benefits: healthy, tasty, fresh, local

Figure 9.2 Five steps in the design of healthy and sustainable menus

The general design of menus leads to secondary considerations. For example, there is much evidence that the way food is presented and served also influences the amount of food consumed. Key elements in reducing overconsumption thus include portion sizes, bundled meals and impulse marketing strategies, for which some researchers have called for standards and regulation (Cohen, 2018) – also because there is an overall trend in some countries and restaurant types to offer larger portion sizes (Zlatevska et al., 2014). Research has also shown that there are complexities, as restaurant customers have been shown to choose less healthy – high calorie – side dishes including drinks and desserts when menu choices are claimed to be healthy (Chandon & Wansink, 2007).

These issues can be addressed in different ways. For instance, restaurants should always consider whether they want to offer standard soft drinks, or one of the many alternatives, such as sugar-reduced sodas or fruit juices. Restaurants can also consider the portion sizes offered, which should be adjusted to optimum portion sizes that do not generate food waste (see Chapters 13 and 14). Where it is difficult to determine such standards, it is possible to offer different portion sizes to suit different appetites. This is specifically important for children, who are often offered a choice of unhealthy and unsustainable dishes catering to "child tastes" – a policy that does not encourage taste development by children while also treating them as disinterested in "advanced" food choices. Parents will be less inclined to purchase a regular, healthy meal for children where this incurs the full cost of a standard menu option. As the examples highlight, there are many opportunities for restaurants to work towards menu marketing and presentation that foster sustainable food choices.

Chapter 10

Making the most of your food; nose-to-tail and leaf-to-root eating, and packaging

Introduction

Efficient food preparation is one of the most important strategies for reducing food waste and for reducing unnecessary purchasing. The chapter discusses the importance of using the whole animal, including fish, and of getting the most out of fruit and vegetable purchases. Often these measures reflect the training at culinary school, but which are often forgotten to be applied in kitchen routines. Practices include promoting nose-to-tail eating and, in some cases, introducing new items to the menu, or even such basic measures as making your own soups and stock. Ironically, as will be discussed, this can mean relearning old skills and recipes. However, such measures also tie closely to interest in local foods (see Chapter 4), the importance of naturalness for consumers, and reducing waste (see Chapters 13 and 14). This chapter discusses some of the dimensions of 'leaf-to-root' and 'top-to-tail' eating before looking at consumer perceptions. The chapter will then briefly discuss some of the issues associated with efficient food packaging before concluding.

Empathy for food

One of the most important ways to increase efficiency in resource use and also to reduce the amount of waste that is produced in the restaurant is to use more of the animal or vegetable that is being cooked. For example, cooking the whole potato rather than peeling reduces food wastage and is also more healthy and nutritious at the same time. This approach to food by chefs and cooks is often referred to as 'leaf-to-root' or 'top-to-tail' eating and is often presented as being a somewhat innovative kitchen and menu development (Finney, 2019). Although this supposed 'innovation' is somewhat ironic given that the more 'holistic' use of food was, and arguably still is, a mark of societies and communities that did not have large food surpluses or economic surpluses with which to purchase food. Indeed, maximizing the ingredients available to you is also a hallmark of seasonal cooking and the use of local foods (see Chapter 4). The shift away from such eating styles is also strongly related to the 'modernization' of food chains and the emphasis by supermarkets and similar retailers to the standardization of the food that is eaten and the social construction of what good food should look like via food advertising and promotion. The effects of such purchasing power down

Box 10.1 Hugh's *War on Waste*

In the first programme of Hugh Fearnley-Whittingstall's *War on Waste* BBC documentary series, Hugh visiting a parsnip farm in Norfolk in the east of England that supplies the Morrisons supermarkets, the fourth largest chain of supermarkets in the UK. The programme highlighted how produce is subjected to stringent aesthetic restrictions. When processing parsnips for inclusion in the supermarket's two products, smaller pre-packed and larger loose parsnips, those considered too short or 'too wonky' were discarded. It was pointed out to viewers that although discarded produce can be used as animal feed or soup ingredients, the amount of produce at the farm destined for disposal in a single week amounted to around 20 tonnes, enough to fill, the programme found, around 280 shopping trolleys. Tristram Stuart, creator of food waste campaign Feedback, said on the programme

> You'd have to be an expert or a machine to tell the difference between rejected parsnips and the parsnips that end up on supermarket shelves. Their policies are causing hidden mountains of food waste ... across the country. ... We've proved that the public will buy so-called cosmetically imperfect fruit and vegetables. In 2012, 300,000 tonnes of ugly, cosmetically imperfect fruit and vegetables were sold. There was a really bad harvest, we lost 40 per cent of the potatoes in this country and ... just put into our supermarkets those ugly potatoes that previously would have been rejected. No one even noticed. Potato sales stayed the same, no one got more complaints. The bottom line is those potato standards are far too strict and they need to be relaxed. To cause waste on this scale is criminal, it's unspeakable in fact.
>
> (quoted in Perchard, 2015)

the supply chain affects not only what consumers can purchase on the supermarket shelves and what farmers can sell easily, but also, over time, what consumers come to regard as attractive and 'good food' (Bunn et al., 1990; Creusen & Schoormans, 2005; Jaeger et al., 2018).

The negative reaction to the standardization of food products and the consequent homogenization of appearance and taste has come from several sources. Most important of these, arguably, has simply been the enormous amount of waste that has arisen from perfectly edible food not being used (Aschemann-Witzel et al., 2015; see also Chapters 13 and 14). This has been the subject of a number of food waste campaigns, with some lead by chefs (Ankeny et al., 2019). For example, Hugh Fearnley-Whittingstall of the River Cottage restaurant and television series hosted a series of BBC documentary programmes on the war on waste which highlighted the impact of cosmetic standards on farmers and the amount of food thrown out by restaurants, especially fast-food operations, and by consumers at home (Box 10.1). As Ying (2018) argues, "If chefs as a group decide that sustainable food is better food, consumers will follow", especially if such chefs have a high profile on television and other media.

A second major factor in encouraging more efficient eating and food preparation is the ethics of eating (Rothgerber, 2015; Hyland, 2017; Kemper, 2020). Danish chef Rene Redzepi, co-owner of the Michelin-starred restaurant Noma in Copenhagen and famous for the promotion of Nordic cuisine focused on localism had an extended stay in Australia (Redzepi, 2016), in which he offered a purely vegetarian menu featuring foraged native ingredients. However, this was followed by a meat-based menu including teal, moose leg, reindeer tongue and wild duck brain. Ankeny and Bray (2019) suggest that these changes make clear that Redzepi's options for ethical eating are not limited to plants and that it is also important to utilize available, and especially neglected, resources in novel ways. While, of course, some vegetarians and vegans may argue that eating any meat is unethical, those people that do eat meat would argue that if they are going to do so then it should be undertaken with concern for both animal welfare and letting as little of the animal go to waste as possible. Such conscientious omnivorism, also sometimes referred to as flexitarianism, which is those people who are reducing their meat consumption, means that for such people the consumption of meat or fish is appropriate only when it satisfies certain ethical standards. Such ethical consumers have been found to evaluate animals less favourably, meat more favourably and were lower in idealism, misanthropy and in-group identification than vegans and vegetarians. Nevertheless, as may be expected, the perceived differences between conscientious omnivores and vegans and vegetarians on the acceptability of killing animals for food were mediated by beliefs about animals and meat (Rothgerber, 2015). Haile (2013) sought to develop an argument for virtuous meat consumption from both an ethical and theological perspective. She noted,

> Those who take the question of eating meat seriously from both an ethical and theological perspective usually do so in order to either oppose eating meat as totally unethical or to defend a vegetarian way of life as more morally sound than an omnivorous way of life.
>
> (Haile, 2013, p. 83)

Working within the Roman Catholic tradition, Haile attempted to provide a moral defence of an omnivorous way of life by following the principles of virtue ethics in seeking "to do justice to the living majesty, nobility, and beauty of the good" (Romano Guardini quoted in Haile, 2013, p. 84). Therefore, in order to do justice to the animal or vegetable that is being consumed, it is appropriate to eat as sustainably, as wholly and as ethically as possible. Hermannsdóttir et al. (2016) describe this as 'empathy for food'.

The third major response for more efficient eating is from the chef community. 'Modern' food preferences have implied that many parts of an animal are not used for human consumption. Meat and meat-like products are one of those areas whereby food preferences, dislikes and controversies appear exacerbated compared with other food types, with a range of factors influencing why certain items are eaten or avoided (Holm & Møhl, 2000). For instance, it is increasingly uncommon in Western society to eat feet, intestines, organs or blood, all of which are edible in principle. As food choices are to a large degree an outcome of learned behaviours that can also be 'unlearned', some restaurants have in recent years sought to change their approach of using more animal parts, including uncommon cuts or organs that would otherwise be used to produce processed foods (such as sausages) or animal feed. One of the first to discuss this was Fergus Henderson, an extremely influential London chef who in 1999 published *Nose to Tail Eating: A Kind of British Cooking*, republished in the USA in 2004 as *The Whole Beast* (Rayner, 2021). The book makes the point that only a few parts of an animal cannot be eaten (such as skin, fur or claws), and provides advice and recipes for anyone interested in eating more than just a few selected cuts such as steak or filet (Henderson, 1999, 2004; also see Henderson & Gellatly, 2007 which includes a pudding section). According to Henderson:

> Nose to tail eating means it would be disingenuous to the animal not to make the most out of the whole beast; there is a set of delights, textural and flavoursome, which lie beyond the fillet.
>
> (Henderson, 1999, n.p.)

Significantly, Henderson's description of nose-to-tail eating highlights that it is not just an ethical decision but also very much focused on taste, and especially the taste of dishes which were once a regular part of people's diets and restaurant fare. Using all of the animal is therefore very much a part of traditional cooking and foodways. Philpot (2007), in a discussion of Henderson's (2004) book, illustrates the changes that have taken place in modern food production with the example of chicken. In 1962 in the USA, 83% of broilers were marketed whole, 15% in cuts and 2% were 'further processed', for instance as chicken nuggets. Some 40 years later, 50% were 'further processed', 42% were sold in cuts and 8% as whole birds. The development mirrors the growth of fast-food outlets, ready-made foods and a general interest in specific cuts, such as chicken breasts. He also outlines that in the USA, the number of chickens slaughtered increased three-fold between 1969 and 1992, indicating that cheap meat availability and changing customer preferences have led to a significant increase in production.

A number of restaurants have started to explore markets for nose-to-tail gastronomy. For example, Fergus Henderson's St. John restaurant in London which opened in 1994, or Herz und Niere in Berlin, have specialized in offering changing menus that may include black pudding, beef lung, pig kidney, auroch's heart, chip ladle liver, lamb brain or a terrine of udder (from the menu of Herz and Niere). Notably, the chefs have won numerous awards with their menus, including 15 points in the 2020 Gault Millau (see www.herzundniere.berlin). The focus on taste and traditional dishes in nose-to-tail eating is well reflected in chef Anthony Boudain's introduction to the 2004 edition of Henderson's book:

> It is ... a reminder – and a respectful one at that – of what is good about food – about the essential, nearly forgotten elements of a great meal, a homage, an honouring of the foodstuffs we eat, a refutation of nothing more than waste and disregard. If Nose to Tail makes a statement, it's that nearly every part of nearly everything we eat can be delicious in the hands of a patient and talented cook – something most good cooks and most French and Italian mothers have known for centuries. It honours the past at least as much as it points to a brave new future.
>
> (Boudain, 2004, n.p.)

If Fergus Henderson changed the way that many chefs and restaurants thought about meat, then Josh Niland from Australia has taken a similar approach to fish. Niland is the chef owner of a 34-seat restaurant, Saint Peter, and a shop, Fish Butchery, in Sydney, Australia. He is also the author of *The Whole Fish Cookbook* (Niland, 2019). In being compared to Henderson, Niland's response is very informative:

> I think the same thing could have been said for Fergus 25 years ago, ... I'm sure back then there were plenty of avant-garde chefs taking the centre of the circle out of a fillet of beef and putting it with 12 different mushrooms and celebrating that in all its glory. Then Fergus comes along and unapologetically puts an oxtail on a plate with a fork in it, or a pipe of bone marrow with some toast next to it. It's not a middle finger to the system, but it's definitely, 'Don't forget there's all

of this as well...' Because if an animal gets killed, if a fish gets killed, you have to commit yourself to using the whole thing, ... It's simple, basic logic.

(quoted in Lewis, 2019)

According to Niland (2019, p. 9), "Our entire way of thinking about how we process fish needs to be overhauled, with far more consideration given to the elements of the fish that would traditionally be considered 'waste'". In the UK, for example, it is estimated that only 43% of fish and shellfish caught in the UK is eaten by humans; the bones, head and offal are either tossed away or ground into fishmeal. For cod and haddock, two of the most popular fish, fillets make up just 50% of their whole weight (Finney, 2019). At Saint Peter and the Fish Butchery, Niland aims to use 90% in some form (Lewis, 2019). His philosophy with fish "is to minimise waste and maximise flavour". This is done primarily with whole fish cookery and dry ageing.

> Buying and cooking only fish fillets is not only creatively limiting but also neglects the majority of the fish – a shame, both from an ethical and sustainable point of view. Using the whole fish shows a great amount of respect for what is a globally depleting commodity.
>
> (Niland, 2019, p. 10)

Dry ageing means keeping fish in a low-temperature, low-moisture environment so as to enhance its flavour profile and maintain it in premium condition for longer (around 20 days seems to be the maximum). Niland, along with some other fish chefs, believes that any contact with water should be minimized, partly this is for taste as it is much harder to get the skin on a wet fish to crisp, and also for longevity as wet fish may have more bacteria and spoil more quickly (Lewis, 2019). According to Niland:

> I feel like the fish shop that has fillets of fish draped over ice is just the most ludicrous thing ever, ... I don't get it. I don't understand why someone is standing with a fire hose and re-spritzes the fish to make it look wet, because somehow that makes it feel more like its fresh and it's out of the water. It's absurd.
>
> [For the home cook] Just take the fish out of the plastic, out of the paper, and put it on a cake rack in your refrigerator, ... Let the fan blow over it for a bit, so the skin dries out and when it comes time for cooking, whether you are baking, roasting, pan-frying, you'll find the skin is just far more pleasant to cook with rather than just being really wet. And you'll find your fish won't have nearly as much odour.
>
> (quoted in Lewis, 2019)

The impact of chefs such as Henderson and Niland on approaches to eating is significant as they highlight a way to improve the efficiency of food preparation in the kitchen and influence what consumers are willing to accept and pay for. However, one of the most important observations comes from Nathan Outlaw, a high profile British fish chef who regards Niland as a 'game changer' and commented, "Josh has basically taken all the old ways of fish prep and cookery and thrown the bad ones out the window and turned what remains on its head" (quoted in Lewis, 2019). This is important because it highlights that many of the attitudes of chefs towards using meat, fruit and vegetables most efficiently stem from how chefs and kitchen staff are trained, i.e., if one has not received the training with respect to using more of the animal and reducing waste it is very hard to suddenly do so.

> **Box 10.2   Using more of the fish**
>
> In many countries using the many different parts of a fish in addition to the fillet is a normal part of cuisine, and of chef's training. In Iceland, fish stomachs are stuffed with cod's liver (Finney, 2019). According to Niland, people in Spain, Scandinavia and Asian and African countries eat fish "livers, eyeballs and sperm all the time, … but, for me, the question was: how can I get people like my mum to enjoy them?" (quoted in Finney, 2019). For the waste minimization, maximum flavour techniques are not taught in culinary schools in Britain and in many other countries. Instead, the many British chefs who are practising such measures tend to be self-taught and from cultures that encourage more whole fish eating. For example, Finney (2019) gives the example of longstanding chef Jeremy Lee, of Quo Vadis restaurant in London:
>
>> [Lee] has vivid memories of his first trips to Spain. "Smoked cod roe on hot buttered toast was something we adored, growing up [in Scotland], but it wasn't until I visited Catalonia and Basque country that I saw cod tripe, hake throat and curious bits and bobs baked with potato and salsa verde." A later trip around Norway's fjords introduced him to "poached pieces of cod's liver and roe with boiled potatoes" – and he was struck by the simplicity of the dish, which required only basic equipment. This Scandi speciality demonstrated just how easy it is to create something "fruity and delightful" from fish offal, an ease Lee emulates in Quo Vadis's fish pate (which mixes the smoked livers and hearts of herring with the meat itself) and hearty, bones-and-bits-based veloutés …
>>
>> "There needs to be more demand," Lee agrees. "My local fishmonger, Fin & Flounder, has always been very amenable. I just need to call them … Generally, the fishmonger throws the bones and trimmings away, but I take them off his hands because it's treasure, and it's free."
>>
>> (Finney, 2019)
>
> Finney (2019) also liked the sound of 'tongue in cheek' ravioli suggested by Adam Handling of the Frog restaurants for the name as much as the zero-waste mentality. "Fish tongue, throat and cheeks are delicious. You don't have to do much to make them taste good", he says, of an approach to fish that is as much about "commercial sense" as it is about "saving the planet. … My staff value the ingredients, but they also value every penny going in and out of the kitchen" (Adam Handling, quoted in Finney, 2019).
>
> https://www.saintpeter.com.au
> www.quovadissoho.co.uk/restaurant/
> www.frogbyadamhandling.com

Using the whole beast versus reconstitution

As suggested above, one of the issues in using the whole beast, fish or, in some cases, even the whole vegetable, may require a change in some consumers perceptions of what is, and what is not, appropriate to eat, especially foods such as offal (McWilliams, 2017). Decisions about what food is desirable or not, are "closely bound to a people's history and their geographic origin and evolve in relation to lifestyle, tradition, and education" (Ramos-Elorduy, 1997, p. 249). Ruby and Heine (2012), for example, suggest that repugnance towards offal is more likely in it is in individualistic cultures such as Europe and North America. Culture is obviously important for the consumption of different cuts of meat, including how it is prepared and cooked, but fundamental to many contemporary consumers is also its sensory appeal. According to Tucker (2014, p. 169), "The sensory appeal (or alternately the element of 'disgust') of meat has been ranked as one of the most important determinants of meat desirability and of avoidance". Studies of sensory appeal have shown significant differences between countries or market segments with respect to the importance of sensory appeal. Prescott et al.'s (2002) cross-cultural comparison of Japanese, Taiwanese, Malaysian and New Zealand consumers found that New Zealanders were much more concerned with the sensory appeal of food above anything else (including the price, convenience and health implications). Gender can also play a significant difference. For example, in Western countries, the consumption of red meat, and steak, in particular, is portrayed as a sign of masculinity (Nath, 2011), while Tobler et al. (2011) found that women are more willing than men to consider environmental reasons for reducing the amount of meat in their diet.

Tucker (2014) ran a series of focus groups in New Zealand on the issue of meat reduction practices including the adoption of nose-to-tail eating: "Whether and what participants would consume in terms of products that come under the nose-to-tail eating practice, and why or why not" (p. 172). When participants were asked about their views of nose-to-tail eating, it was found that they were overwhelmingly positive (75.4% of participants) about the practice as something that could be taken up across the country. No significant relationship between gender and position towards nose-to-tail eating was found but older participants tended to have a more positive view. The majority view for all income categories other than the highest income bracket was positive overall, while those participants who had a family relationship to farming were also positive (Tucker, 2014). "Sensory appeal was both the main reason put forward for why this practice was seen positively, but also why it was seen negatively" (Tucker, 2014, p. 172).

> The main reason for expressing positive views toward nose-to- tail eating were based on sensory appeal, in particular the taste of specific foods as stated by these individuals: "Sheep face – I eat regularly as a roast; trotters, boil-up... chicken feet – gorgeous!" (39f); "Pig's cheeks are beautiful, really nice. Chickens feet – didn't mind them, they're actually quite nice – chewy – they're funny things" (20f); and "it sounds really gross, but my favourite part of the fish head is actually the eyeballs because it's got all the flavour and you're sucking [on them] and you're like 'oh, it's so nice'" (47f). ... Second to this were reasons based on an 'ethic' of utilising (and therefore) eating the entire animal. Typical of the kind of responses here was: "At least they use every bit of the creature. I feel that nose-to-tail eating is honouring the animal by using every little bit" (24f); and "If you don't use all parts of the animal it's a waste and quite disrespectful to the animal" (29f). [The bracketed code refers to a random number allotted to the individual participant, and the letter (f or m) refers to the gender of the participant: m = male; f = female.]
>
> (Tucker, 2014, pp. 172–173)

In a more recent study, Bearth et al. (2021) report on a survey of Swiss consumers' willingness to engage with animal by-products. They found that expectations regarding the sensory qualities of animal by-products are essential for consumer acceptance (see also Henchion & McCarthy, 2019). Bearth et al. (2021) suggest barriers for consumers to engage with animal by-products revolve around negative expectations of the sensory qualities. Therefore, disgust could be tackled by increasing familiarity and enhancing visibility and availability, for example by serving as an appetizer or amuse-bouche in restaurants. Culinary-based drivers, frequent childhood experiences with animal by-products and social norms were observed by Bearth et al. (2021) to be the most relevant for consumers' willingness to engage with animal by-products and therefore provide opportunities for their incorporation into the promotion of traditional local cuisines (Henchion & McCarthy, 2019). Finally, Bearth et al. (2021) found that the provision of information had no impact on the willingness of consumers to engage with animal by-products and neither did value-based drivers, such as reducing food waste or encouraging sustainable food consumption. Instead, they concluded that their research supports "the notion that changes need to be implemented in a longer term by changing current habits and installing new dietary and culinary habits" (Bearth et al., 2021, p. 4).

Consumer preferences and perceptions have changed along with these developments. For example, Nitzko and Spiller (2019) showed that German consumers found the efficient use of plants on the basis of 'leaf-to-root' principles more acceptable than the efficient use of animals. The 'leaf-to-root' principle refers to

> the holistic utilization of agricultural plants; i.e. not only the 'first cuts' (the parts of plants that are usually consumed) [that] are used for human nutrition but also those parts which are otherwise thrown away (the so-called 'second cuts', e.g. peel, roots, leaves, stems and stalks').
>
> (Nitzko & Spiller, 2019, p. 2)

Non-standard 'misfit' or 'ugly' fruits and vegetables are also significant for restaurants because of their potential to be used in dishes where their appearance is not an issue, and where otherwise they might not have a culinary end use. Similarly, as noted above, discarded animal parts such as offal, skins or heads of fish are often rich in nutrients and taste, and there are options to mechanically separate and reconstitute meats. Nevertheless, there are potential differences in terms of how the previously discarded parts are presented to customers and used in dishes depending on the orientation of the consumer.

Those people who are aware of the connection between the flesh they consume and the living animal, and as such are more accepting or even encouraging of eating items that others may consider more repulsive possess, possess what is known as a zoophagan logic (Tucker, 2014). These are the consumers who are attracted to the style of restaurant characterized by the cooking of Fergus Henderson and chefs like him. However, preference to completely disassociate the body part to be eaten from the animal it came from (Ruby & Heine, 2012) is very much part of a logic by which, the more like an animal a food item 'looks', the less appealing it will be to some. This is known as a sarcophagan logic (Tucker, 2014). This is not just specialist academic speak, as consideration of such an approach may be a way to encourage some people to eat more of the whole beast, e.g., making pate, sausages and meat spreads, that otherwise would not countenance such a change. Non-standard fruits/vegetables and 'leaf-to-root' eating were evaluated more positively in Nitzo and Spiller's (2019) study, than the more efficient use of animal-based foods. Fruits and vegetables are generally characterized by a healthy and positive image.

Although Nitzo and Spiller (2019) highlight ongoing efforts to derive natural flavourings, dietary fibres or enzymes out of formerly discarded by-products, it is noticeable that consumers favoured more 'natural' products. If the options of the more efficient use of plant-based and animal-based foods are considered separately, that the options of using products in their natural form, e.g., non-standard fruits and vegetables, 'leaf-to-root' and 'nose-to-tail')

> were evaluated more positively in comparison to those options which subjected the by-products to some form of processing (reconstituted meat, mechanically separated meat, and valuable substances from plant-based by-products). These results indicate a strong preference for naturalness in food, for low levels of processing and for the absence of additives.
>
> (Nitzo & Spiller, 2019, p. 14)

This desire for naturalness is something that has been identified in other studies (Román et al., 2017; NRA, 2018) and it is also strongly connected to wider concerns over the sustainability of food. Importantly, improvements in the efficiency of what is used from fruit, vegetables, meat and fish depend very much on what goes in the restaurant or foodservice kitchen and how it is presented to customers. This requires knowledge on the part of chefs and the kitchen brigade as well as effective menu marketing to promote a positive sensory experience to the customer.

Efficient packaging

In terms of improved efficiency in the kitchen, an increasingly important issue is the use of packaging of foods for customers. The issue has long been significant for fast-food restaurants but it has become a broader issue given the growth in pick up and take away foods (see Chapters 3 and 12), especially following the impact of COVID-19 and the need of many restaurants to adopt new business models that had a greater emphasis on the meal being eaten outside of the restaurant (Held, 2020). This meant that single-use plastic bags for example had a dramatic resurgence in use in many countries because of health concerns and, as Held (2020) commented, "throwing something away that came from outside the home and was touched by unknown hands simply feels safer".

COVID-19 clearly had a significant number of initiatives to reduce plastic waste in the hospitality and food services sector. For example, in January 2020, Berkeley, California put in place a new rule requiring all cafés and restaurants to start charging 25 cents for disposable cups. The cups, in addition to lids, utensils and straws, must also be certified compostable. In addition, if it were not for the pandemic eateries that offer on-site dining would have been required to serve customers using reusable plates, cups and cutlery in the summer of 2020 (Wozniacka, 2020).

The plastic conundrum highlights the issues of plastics in the food services sector (see Chapter 1 for a discussion on the impacts of plastic on the environment and human health). Long regarded as integral to the fast-food and café sector for takeaways, even independent restaurants were using them to encourage customers to take their leftover food home in doggy bags so as to reduce food waste. So what is best?

Unfortunately, life cycle assessments of many compostable containers suggest that they are not necessarily better than plastics in terms of environmental benefits. For example, compostable food serviceware made from plants such as corn, sugar cane and bamboo is sometimes referred to as 'biodegradable', but it must be processed at specialized industrial facilities. In Oregon in the USA, all of the state's compost manufacturing facilities said in 2019 that they would not accept compostable products because of contamination,

> as consumers often throw in non-compostable lookalike items into their bins. Removing this trash increases the use of water, energy and other resources and

> **Box 10.3   Disrupting the 'to-go culture'**
>
> For Here Please is an Oakland-based non-profit associated with MudLab zero-waste café and grocery store in Oakland, California, that helps cafés and restaurants reduce single-use plastics. In 2019, they helped convert Perch Coffeehouse into the first disposable-free cafe in Oakland. The café offers a 25-cent discount to customers who bring their own mug and charges a small fee for renting out a reusable cup.
>
> Nossa Familia Coffee in Portland, Oregon, started a Zero Waste coffee shop in 2018 where all customers are charged 25 cents for a disposable to-go cup and given 25 cent discount for bringing their own cup. According to the company the move significantly shifted coffee drinkers' behaviour. The use of a 'to-go' cup was cut in half, from 66% to 31% with 17% of their customers bringing their own cup. In 2019, Nossa Familia introduced the surcharge in all its Portland cafés.
>
> MudLab: https://mudlaboak.com
> Nossa Familia Coffee: www.nossacoffee.com

> drives up operating costs ... [while] some compostable packaging designed to hold up to wet or and greasy food contains highly toxic 'forever chemicals' called PFAS.
> (Wozniacka, 2020)

Unless they are of an appropriate composition 'compostables' may therefore negatively affect the composting process in some location's waste management, create more trash and potentially continue consumer adoption of single-use items. This means that they are detracting from the most environmentally beneficial practices which are reducing and reusing (Wozniacka, 2020).

From a life cycle perspective therefore the best packaging outcome needs to be derived from an evaluation of the raw materials used, the manufacturing process, the transportation system and what happens to the waste. In many ways therefore, the supposed compostability of some items may therefore be just an excuse to continue with single-use items when other options may be available. For example, GO Box, a Portland and San Francisco-based company, provides a reusable takeout container service, offering those who purchase takeout a sturdy plastic reusable container to eliminate the need for single-use clamshells containers. The reusable containers are checked out from vendors via an app and then dropped off at designated locations. At the end of their lives, the plastic reusable containers are recycled (Wozniacka, 2020). It is even conceivable for example, that such containers could even be provided to customers as part of loyalty programmes. Reusable containers also have resource inputs into making them but by encouraging customers to reduce and reuse overall resource use and waste can be reduced.

Conclusions

This chapter has focused on efficiency as a means of reducing material use and waste in restaurants and food services. It has noted the way in which seeking to use the whole plant or animal can provide substantial contributions to sustainability with the biggest barrier often being people's perceptions of what was previously regarded as waste. Clearly, more efficient use of plants and animals has a strong ethical dimension, but most importantly they have to please the customer on the plate and have strong sensory appeal as well as be marketed on the menu appropriately. This is an educational challenge above all else, as chefs and foodservice operations need to learn how to make use of more animal and vegetable parts so as to make them appealing. Such an approach to restaurant sustainability is actually not particularly novel or innovative but means understanding the way that many traditional and local foods were prepared, and providing them on the menu in a modern context, especially with respect to their perceived naturalness and other values.

Chapter 11

Efficient restaurants and kitchens

Introduction

Restaurants are among the most energy-intensive types of commercial buildings. Because of their long hours of operation, specialized equipment and levels of consumer demand, US restaurants have been estimated to consume, by area, nearly three times the energy of the average commercial building (Sustainable Foodservice Consulting, 2016c). In the UK, estimates have been even higher. Mudie et al. (2016, p. 66) suggest that:

> Commercial kitchens are some of the most profligate users of gas, water and electricity in the UK. As a result, they can leave a large carbon footprint, with relevant benchmarks (in kWh/m²) exceeding ten times the energy benchmarks of the majority of commercial premises (i.e. offices, retail premises, etc.).

The largest portion of energy use is consumed by cooking and food preparation, followed closely by heating, ventilation and cooling (HVAC). A breakdown of the average energy use at foodservice operations is shown in Table 11.1. Yet one of the difficulties in examining different evaluations and studies of efficient restaurants and kitchens is that the scale and boundaries of any evaluation, i.e., what is included and what is left out, and the metrics being used are often different, while significant differences also occur between foodservice operations in different countries and in offering various food styles. For example, using energy use data from the USA, the UK Carbon Trust (2008) and the Chartered Institute of Building Services Engineers (CIBSE) and Catering for a Sustainable Future Group (CSFG) (2009) estimated that the total energy use of Britain's catering industry was in excess of 21,600 million kWh per year with 50% of this originating from non-commercial catering operations (e.g., hospitals, schools and other institutions), 20% from hotel and guest house kitchens and the remaining 30% from commercial kitchens (e.g., restaurants, public houses, cafes) (Mudie et al., 2013), although later research suggested found that consumption was almost double the previous sector estimates of 6,480 million kWh per year, leading to recommendations of the use of normalized performance indicators, such as kitchen size (e.g., m²) and kWh per x amount of turnover (Mudie et al., 2013; Mudie & Vadhati, 2017). Mudie (2016) also noted that many of the benchmarks used in the UK with respect to energy benchmarking in commercial kitchens had not been updated since the 1980s, while Mudie et al. (2016, p. 76) also highlighting that, 'current catering appliance design does not lend itself well to energy-thrift behaviour. Appliances are often not insulated and without appropriate controls'. However, EU ecodesign and building directives will undoubtedly help encourage improved appliance design and use.

Nevertheless, there is general awareness that kitchen appliances have become vastly more efficient in recent years, and kitchens can save very significant amounts of water and energy by choosing the right appliances as well as innovations including plumbing fixtures, water heating, air conditioning, refrigeration and cold rooms or induction cooking. Energy and water consumption are also closely associated with cost, making these issues increasingly central to sustainable restaurant management (Box 11.1 highlights the emphasis put on the cost dimensions of adopting efficiency measures by Pacific Gas & Electric in its identification of ten ways foodservice operations can become more efficient). This, together with the following chapter, provides a breakdown of some of the technological measures that can be taken to provide a more efficient and sustainable commercial kitchen and restaurant, especially with respect to energy. The following chapter will look specifically at the application of smart technologies.

Table 11.1 Average energy use in US foodservice operations and full-service restaurant

Source: Sustainable Foodservice Consulting (2016c); Full-service restaurant: U.S. Environmental Protection Agency Energy Star program NRA (2016)

Foodservice operations		Full-service restaurant	
Function	%	Function	%
Food preparation	24.4	Food preparation	35
Heating	16.6	HVAC	28
Refrigeration	16.4	Refrigeration	6
Sanitation	15.7	Sanitation	18
Lighting	9.6	Lighting	13
Cooking	6.8		
Ventilation	5.6		
Computers	0.5		
Office equipment	0.5		
Other	3.7		

Box 11.1 Pacific Gas & Electric (PGE): ten ways foodservice businesses can become more energy efficient

Pacific Gas & Electric (PGE) is California's leading electricity utility which as a result of both state initiatives and the effects of recent droughts in California has become a leading actor in encouraging energy and water efficiency in the state.

1 *Use energy-efficient fryers, griddles and ovens.* Energy-efficient fryers can save restaurant owners $100–$450 annually (depending on whether it is an electric

or gas model) and they also increase productivity, making the cooking process more efficient because they offer shorter cook times and higher pound-per-hour production rates. Commercial griddles that have earned ENERGY STAR certification are about 10% more efficient than older models.

2. *Use high-efficiency convection ovens.* Convection ovens offer many opportunities for foodservice business owners to switch to more energy-efficient restaurant equipment. ENERGY STAR-certified gas ovens are almost 50% more efficient than standard versions. Certified electric convection ovens are also more efficient than standard models, and they idle at lower rates.

3. *Use more efficient ice machines.* Bigger models are almost always more energy-efficient and they can provide twice the capacity while halving the energy cost per weight of ice.

4. *Heat restaurant water with high-efficiency electric, gas and solar storage condensing water heaters.* Full-service restaurants can reduce their annual energy usage by an average of 1,740 therms annually and save more than $1,500 a year by switching to an efficiency-certified commercial water heater. High-efficiency storage condensing water heaters use a multi-pass heat exchanger to extract a large amount of energy from the combustion process. This process condenses exhaust gases, thus streamlining the water-heating process.

5. *Switch to low-flow pre-rinse spray valves.* Replacing standard pre-rinse spray valves at the dishwashing station with more efficient low-flow versions can reduce energy usage by 25%–60% as well as water usage. Efficient spray valves are just as effective at clearing food from dishes.

6. *Replace old refrigerator lighting with less energy-intensive LED case lighting.* Advancements in light-emitting diode (LED) bulb technology make it ideal for installation in refrigerated food and beverage cases. Refrigerated LED lighting for restaurants operates much better in low temperatures than standard bulb models, turning on and off instantly, even in sub-zero temperatures. LED refrigerated case lighting also gives off less heat than other bulbs, leading to reduced cooling loads in the refrigeration unit.

7. *Reduce wasted walk-in refrigerator energy with strip curtains and automatic door closers.* Adding strip curtains and automatic door closers to walk-in refrigerators is among the easiest and most affordable energy-efficient options available to foodservice businesses. Combined, strip curtains and automatic door closers can reduce air infiltration by 75%.

8. *Use electronically commutated motors (ECM) and fan controllers in a restaurant's fan system.* Most standard model indoor restaurant fan systems operate at a constant speed. ECMs and other modern fan controllers are pieces of energy-efficient restaurant equipment that optimize fan energy usage by adapting it to changing needs throughout the day. Fan controllers can reduce fan energy consumption in foodservice businesses by up to two-thirds.

9. *Implement smart defrost controls and coil cleaning practices to lower costs.* On-demand defrost control effectively optimizes the duration of defrost cycles than timed defrost, leading to much less wasted energy. Defrost controls and monthly cleaning of cooling coils, which helps to ensure proper heat transfer and airflow, can reduce operational costs by 25% or more and help to prevent early compressor failure.

10. *Replace older bulbs with energy-efficient T8 fluorescent and LED.* T8 fluorescent lighting for restaurants is an incredibly simple way to reduce energy

> consumption. These replacement light bulbs can easily be substituted for older, less efficient fluorescent bulbs. Low-wattage T8 fluorescent bulbs are up to 25% more efficient than older fluorescent models, and they can be swapped quickly. They can also be used in any number of spaces within a restaurant, including overhead lighting in the dining room, back-of-the-house storage areas and nearly anywhere in the kitchen. Restaurant signage also presents optimal places to implement LED lighting, as many of those signs can be easily switched to LED. LEDs offer longer lifespans, lower energy consumption and higher quality light than older bulb models.
>
> Source: Modified from Shah (n.d.)

Energy and water contributions from restaurant operations and kitchens

Environmentally friendly and green kitchens and restaurants have the potential to make a substantial contribution to sustainability, attract and retain customers (DiPietro et al., 2013) and, from the perspective of many restaurant and foodservice operation owners and managers, reduce costs while maintaining menu quality. Even though their energy use is considerable, in some circumstances, such as with a large number of covers, commercial kitchens may be more efficient than household kitchens in preparing food if calculated on a per-meal basis (Carlsson-Kanyama et al., 2003). However, an important starting point in seeking to increase the efficiency of restaurant and foodservice operations is understanding the different contributions of various parts of the business and the kitchen.

Mudie et al. (2016) analyzed 14 sites in England that belonged to a large chain of UK gastro-pubs (comprising almost 200 premises), all offering the same food menu with common items including burgers, pies, sausages, hot sandwiches and casseroles. All 14 sites had a 'typical' range of appliances although there were differences between them. "While there is a general template setup for the pubs (laid down by the central office), the layouts, makes, models and capacities and number of the appliances differ substantially between the sites" (Mudie et al., 2016, p. 67). Staff were not aware of any monitoring so as to ensure that behaviours did not change.

Whole building electricity and gas consumption was monitored for one year at one site to represent a case study of the gastro-pub's annual energy usage. This was undertaken so as to take into account seasonal changes in consumer behaviour (e.g., holiday seasons) and appliance use (e.g., heating in winter and air conditioning in summer). The whole building study site's hot water was only used in cleaning operations and the toilet facilities; tap hot water was generally not used for cooking operations and warewashing appliances were cold fill. The results of the analysis of annual energy consumption are detailed by business (physical area) (Table 11.2) and end functions (Table 11.3). Mudie et al.'s (2016) results clearly show that the kitchen is by far the largest user of energy in the restaurant and that, in terms of end function, the cooking of food and the storage of food together represents the largest energy-using activities accounting for almost 75% of the building's annual use. However, before looking specifically at kitchen efficiency the chapter will discuss some of the elements surrounding the need for efficient buildings.

Table 11.2 Annual energy consumption in gastro-pub by business (physical) area
Source: Mudie et al. (2016)

Area	Description	%
Kitchen	Air handling, lighting, cooking equipment, refrigeration, hot storage, warewashing	63
Restaurant	Air handling, lighting, sundry sockets (vacuum, etc.), gas central heating, hot water	16
Cellar	Air handling, beverage cooling, beverage pumps	5
Bar	Glass washing, lighting, bottle fridges, ice machine, coffee machine	10
Other		6

Table 11.3 Annual energy consumption in gastro-pub by end function
Source: Mudie et al. (2016)

Area	Description	%
Warewashing	Dish, cutlery and glass washers	4
Freezers and fridges	All walk-in, stand-alone and under-counter refrigeration and freezing units, ice machines and cellar beverage chillers	28
Cooking	All appliances utilized to prepare meals and store hot food, coffee machine	42
Lighting	All external and internal lighting	10
Air handling and hot water	All air handling including ventilation, gas central heating, air conditioning (restaurant and bar), cellar cooling	13
Other	Sundry sockets used ad hoc (e.g., vacuuming), building alarms, hand driers, beverage pump, office computer	3

An efficient building

The starting point for an efficient restaurant and kitchen is an efficient building. Overall, buildings account for more than a third of the world's total energy consumption. Ideally, new buildings can be designed as net-zero/near-zero energy buildings (NZEB/nZEB) which feature efficient containment systems (the thermal quality of the envelope of a building: walls, roofs, floors, windows), HVAC (Heating, ventilation and air conditioning) systems and equipment. NZEB represents a zero balance in terms of energy demand and supply, on a given time frame (usually one year), while an nZEB building produces 'slightly less' energy than the energy it needs to assure comfortable conditions and indoor air quality (Cunha & Oliveira, 2020). However, the definition of 'slightly less' varies according to the building context, such as the climatic conditions. Furthermore, in the European context, different countries have different indicators. For example, in most countries, the main nZEB indicator is the annual specific primary energy consumption ($kWh_{PE}/(m^2 \cdot year)$). Some member states have chosen to relate the nZEB level to their best energy certification category (i.e., A++ class), while other countries have selected the equivalent CO_2 emissions as the main indicator or are using CO_2 emissions as complementary information in addition to the primary energy indicator. Significantly, a large number of EU states have also defined a minimum contribution from renewable energy sources. Apart from showing the importance of regulation in encouraging greater building efficiency the EU situation also highlights the wide range of measures that can be applied in seeking to achieve the same goal (D'Agostino & Mazzarella, 2019).

Vujnović and Dović (2021) estimated that achieving nZEB standards for a new hotel building in Croatia was feasible with a payback period of 16 years at current costings and they found that the most cost-optimal source of heating for a new nZEB hotel was an air-to-water heat pump coupled with a gas boiler and that forced ventilation resulted in lower cooling demand, but greater delivered energy than that with fan coils. However, the vast majority of commercial restaurant and foodservice operations are in already existing buildings that would need to be retrofitted to meet nZEB standards. The hospitality and foodservice sector represents a substantial challenge in terms of retrofitting to nZEB standards due to the hosting elements of the business which means customer comfort, care and services are a top priority. Furthermore, any retrofit solution should ideally allow implementation while the business is in operating and with minimal disruptions to customers and staff (Salem et al., 2020) and, perhaps most importantly from a business perspective, be economically viable. From an economic perspective the three main barriers to the retrofitting of commercial buildings are:

- stakeholders may only look at short-term profitability;
- there is inconsistent data about profitability; and
- budgetary constraints.

In addition, if no refurbishment need exists, replacement of an element of a building only for energy-saving reasons is most probably unfeasible from a business perspective (Heljo & Vihola, 2012 in Holopainen et al., 2016). A retrofitted commercial nZEB building typically incorporates high levels of insulation, double or triple glazing (depending on local climate), an efficient boiler or ground source heat pump (GSHP) and a renewable solar energy system, while the five most common criteria in the selection of technologies for high energy performant buildings are investment cost, performance, operational cost, life cycle cost and user-friendliness and maintenance (ZEBRA2020, 2016).

Box 11.2 Energy performance and cost analysis for the nZEB retrofit of a typical UK hotel

Salem et al. (2020) conducted an energy performance analysis to identify the primary energy consumption (PEC) level, post-retrofit, which could represent the cost-optimal level for a UK nZEB hotel. They compared four different types of retrofit with respect to insulation and glazing, lighting, HVAC/DHW (Domestic hot water) and renewable/microgeneration systems. Total energy consumption considers heating, cooling, auxiliary, lighting, DHW, equipment (such as kitchen equipment) and displaced electricity (where applicable). The carbon emission calculations take into consideration building systems, air/plan side HVAC control(s), building envelope elements (insulation, glazing), lighting/daylighting interactions, energy consumption, business schedule, fuel type, ventilation, DHW. Finally, the PEC is the amount of primary energy consumed in order to meet the building's energy demand (heating, cooling, DHW, lighting and auxiliaries) and is also the net of any electrical energy displaced, where applicable. They found that there were often substantial differences in the global costs of different retrofit packages with several not meeting nZEB standards. "This highlights the importance of selecting a variety of [energy efficiency measures] that meet the building's energy demand, rather than focussing on one retrofit aspect and working around that" (Salem et al., 2020). They found a significant 30% gap between the cost-optimal solution and the nZEB target.

> However, considering the fact that the cost-optimal solution offered a reduction of 52% and 45% in primary energy consumption and global costs in comparison to the baseline scenario it can be said that it is still a viable option in terms of reducing the energy consumption but not fully meeting the nZEB standard. Therefore, the cost-optimal solution offered a considerable reduction in both energy and costs. It may be that with the current level and price of EEMs available, finding a balance between the energy and cost benefits is one of the best options to carrying out energy retrofits and as such technologies become widespread in use, it is always possible to carry out further, albeit minor, retrofits in the future to fully meet the required standard.
>
> (Salem et al., 2020)

As they noted, buildings need to be understood as a system in seeking to reduce energy use, prioritizing one aspect of retrofitting and neglecting another leads to an 'incomplete' retrofit that either fails to lower the energy demand of a building or improve overall energy efficiency. Nevertheless, from the perspective of both the business and reducing energy consumption and emissions even small changes in the type of efficiency measure selected can help reduce global costs. All buildings, at certain points in their lifecourse, require refurbishment. "These points should, therefore, be seen as opportunities for improvement rather than replacement. In this manner the nZEB standard may also be achieved over stages rather than at once" (Salem et al., 2020).

Box 11.3 How do you get restaurants excited about efficiency?

Jeffrey Clark from the US National Restaurant Association (NRA) raises the very important point as to why restaurants tend to not care about energy or water. According to Clark (2015), energy and water are an afterthought for most restaurants because utility costs were a relatively small component of operating costs and profitability. Using 2010 NRA figures he showed that food and beverage sales and salaries and wages were almost ten times the cost of utilities and were therefore the focus of most managers (Table 11.4). He argued that just communicating in terms of the number of watts saved was not going to be of interest instead restaurant players had to be engaged "by communicating attention grabbing and memorable ideas" (Clark, 2015) by:

- highlighting losses from inaction, rather than savings from action/changed behaviour;
- leverage association – it's more persuasive to align with things that people like (e.g., food);
- appeal to self-interest and identity;
- avoid negative descriptive norms (common behaviours that are undesirable; e.g., 75% of people leave lights on when not at home). For example, by pointing out that it takes three glasses of water to serve one glass on the table (one for ice, one to wash up and the water itself).

Instead, Clark (2015) therefore advocated:

- Working with the five senses:
    - See pilot lights get turned down.
    - Feel the cold air leaking out of the open refrigerator.

- Explain the "why" better:
    - Especially for chefs! They are used to talking about taste, smell, and tooth feel; not electrons.

- Work towards market mechanisms to change behaviour – fats, oils, greases as an example because there is a market for biofuel.
- Using a personal touch.

Table 11.4 Top restaurant operating costs and profitability
Source: NRA in Clark 2015

Cost category	Family dining (under $15) (%)	Casual dining ($15–$25) (%)	Fine dining ($25 and up) (%)	All limited service (%)
Food and Beverage Sales	32.2	31.8	31.9	31.9
Salaries and Wages	33.7	33.2	33.7	29.4
Restaurant Occupancy	4.9	5.1	6.1	7.7
Utility Costs	3.6	3.4	3.5	3.0
Pre-Tax Profit Margin	3.0	3.5	1.8	5.9

Note: NRA family and casual dining definitions have changed since 2010 (e.g., family dining went from $15 to $10 per person).

Lighting

Lighting represents approximately 9%–13% of a restaurant's energy bill. Depending on location and food serviced type and is one of the simplest and most cost-effective areas in which to reduce energy consumption and save money in a foodservice establishment (Sustainable Foodservice Consulting, 2016a). As of 2017, nearly eight in ten US restaurant operators were using energy-efficient equipment to light their operations, including compact fluorescent light bulbs (CFL) and light-emitting diode (LED) lighting (NRA, 2018). Incandescent bulbs are much less energy efficient than other types of lighting sources and are being phased out in many countries. The luminous efficiency of an incandescent bulb is about 2%–5% which means they are wasting about 95% of the input energy, most of which is being converted into heat. Incandescent bulbs also have a short-rated life of 750–1,000 hours compared to the 50,000 hours lifetime of an LED bulb (Cho et al., 2014). Nevertheless, there are some restaurant situations in which they are still sometimes used. Cheaper LEDs may be unsuitable in some hot kitchen areas, while they do not have as much dimming capability as an incandescent bulb or be compatible with all dimming units. However, in the case of the latter dimming units and light fittings can be changed as part of refurbishments (Sustainable Foodservice Consulting, 2016a).

Compact fluorescent lamps (CFL) are a more energy-efficient lighting source as they use 50%–80% less energy than incandescent light bulbs and last up to ten times longer. Their downside from an environmental perspective is that they contain a small amount of mercury which therefore requires specific recycling procedures while, from a lighting perspective, they take a number of minutes to meet maximum luminosity. Energy Star provides a light savings calculator that estimates annual savings using LEDs. Each 60 W equivalent LED bulb running 12 hours a day is estimated by Energy Star to save about $22 a year in energy costs (Sustainable Foodservice Consulting, 2016a). In the Canadian context, Cho et al. (2014) identified a number of benefits from adopting LED as part of a pub refurbishment which demonstrated significant economic benefits from adopting LED which would be magnified given the number of bulbs used in foodservice properties (Table 11.5).

Table 11.5 Economic impacts of the adoption of different forms of lighting for a Vancouver pub
Source: Cho et al. (2014)

	LED	CFL	Incandescent
Light bulb projected lifespan	50,000 hours	10,000 hours	1,200 hours
Watts per bulb (equiv. 60 watts)	10	14	60
Cost per bulb	$35.95	$3.95	$1.25
KWh of electricity used over 50,000 hours	500	700	3,000
Cost of electricity (@ 0.10 per KWh)	$50	$70	$300
Bulbs needed for 50 k hours of use	1	5	42
Equivalent 50 k hours bulb expense	$35.95	$19.75	$52.50
Total cost for 50 k hours	$85.75	$89.75	$352.50

> **Box 11.4 Energy efficiency websites**
>
> Energy Star (commercial buildings): www.energystar.gov/buildings
> Energy Star (products): www.energystar.gov
> Consortium for Energy Efficiency (CEE) Directory of Efficient Equipment: www.ceedirectory.org

Heating, ventilation and cooling (HVAC)

Depending on the location space heating and air conditioning can make up about 25% of a restaurant's energy bill, the largest energy cost next to cooking (Sustainable Foodservice Consulting, 2016b). Air quality and temperatures are a significant issue in restaurants and in their kitchens (Luengas et al., 2015). Different types of cooking produce different chemicals and particulate matter (Yun-Chun et al., 2015; Gysel et al., 2018). Atmospheric particulate matter, also called aerosol, can be divided into the total suspended particles (TSP), and particulates of different sizes: particulate matter (PM_{10}), fine particulate matter ($PM_{2.5}$), submicron particles ($PM_{1.0}$) and ultrafine particles ($PM_{0.1}$), with the finer the matter the more harmful to human health (Zhang et al., 2017). In a comparative study of a traditional student canteen and open-style cafeteria, Zhang et al. (2017) found that particle concentration decreases with increasing distance from the cooking source. In a traditional student canteen, in which the cooking area is separate from the serving area, fewer large diameter particles can disperse and the small particles occupy a larger proportion. The concentrations varied little with distance in the traditional cafeteria design because there was a glass panel in front of the food sale window and the kitchen was enclosed. In contrast, in the case of the open-style cafeteria, the particle concentration was much higher than in the traditional canteen, and the mass concentration of PM_{10} substantially exceeded recommended levels because the exposed cooking produces more particulate matter that was able to escape in the dining area.

Indoor charcoal cooking in restaurants can be extremely attractive for customers to observe but can also create significant issues with air quality. Taner et al. (2013) collected particulate matter from 14 restaurants that cooked with charcoal in Kocaeli in Turkey. The total hazard quotient (total HQ) identified for $PM_{2.5}$ was a little over four times greater than the acceptable limit. The excess lifetime cancer risk (total ELCR) for PM2.5 was also higher than the acceptable limit. Among all of the carcinogenic elements present in PM2.5, the cancer risks resulting from chromium and arsenic exposure were the highest, which is a potentially significant issue for those who work in such restaurants (Taner et al., 2013).

Heat recovery is a means of becoming more efficient in energy use in hospitality and foodservice businesses using heat resources that already exist in the restaurant (Wang et al., 2017). For example, Alkhamis et al. (1998) reported on the use of a coil heat exchanger to recover waste heat from the exhaust gas stream from ovens in a university canteen, which was then employed to heat water for washing dishes and cleaning floors. More than 60% of the heat from the kitchen furnace could be recovered and was a 'highly economical' device.

Commercial kitchens are a major user of water (see below), for example, Schestak et al. (2020) examined the potential for heat recovery from commercial kitchens' drain water and conducted a life cycle analysis of the costs and benefits of producing and installing a heat recovery system for a restaurant case study and the entire UK foodservice sector. An LCA was used to determine the various impacts of heat recovery systems that were made from different materials in a heat exchanger in the shape of a concentric double-walled pipe, pipework and fittings. The design option with the smallest environmental footprint combined a heat exchanger made out of polypropylene-graphite (PP-GR) with polyethylene pipework, exhibiting 80%–99% less environmental impact compared with components made out of (35% recycled) copper (Schestak et al., 2020). In comparing the environmental impacts of two different heat recovery set-ups with energy savings, it was found that a PP-GR based system would pay back all LCA burdens of the assessed environmental impact categories, within two years, while payback times for the copper-based system vary depending on the replaced energy source and could exceed the ten-year operational lifetime of the system. When looking at typical flow rates in UK food outlets, it was found that net environmental savings can be realized above a threshold water consumption of 555 L/day, using current technology. Extrapolation of the results to the UK foodservice sector indicated that there was an annual greenhouse gas emission mitigation potential of about 500 Gg CO_2 equivalent if such measures were adopted (Schestak et al., 2020).

An alternative approach to heat recovery was utilized by Wang et al. (2020) who sought to recover heat from the abundant waste heat that is generated by kitchens in the cooking process and is usually directly discharged to the outside environment along with the exhaust air. Wang et al. (2020) examined a water-heating and dish-drying system based on heat recovery from the exhaust air of a commercial kitchen and studied the influence of terminal functions, cooking methods, exhaust air modes and drying items, on operating performance of a heat recovery system. The results indicated that the heat transfer rates of water heating and dish drying were 7.17 kW and 0.40 kW respectively, accounting for 95% and 5% of the total heat transfer of the system.

Kitchen appliances

In a typical commercial kitchen, the stove and oven are operational throughout the entire hours of foodservice. As a result, energy consumption is only marginally affected by trade volume. For example, Mudie et al. (2016) observed there is increased energy consumption over the weekend when more people are eating out. However, there was a 152% reduction in meal output on a Monday compared with a Saturday in the gastro-pubs she was studying, consumption only decreased by 20%. Mudie et al. (2016) argued that this was primarily due to operator behaviour. However, they did also note a significant variation in the kWh per meal 'efficiency ratio' between the sites, ranging from 1.52 kWh/meal per week efficiency at the most efficient kitchen) to 3.32 kWh/meal per week at the least efficient kitchen. It was also found that kitchens rarely reduced the energy consumption of appliances during the mid-afternoon lull in cooking volume. Table 11.6 shows the average monitored kitchen consumption composition (%) of different appliances. The total average refrigerated storage electricity usage was 41% of the kitchen total, with the remaining 59% attributed to cooking appliances.

Table 11.6 Average monitored kitchen consumption composition (%) of different appliances
Source: Mudie et al. (2016)

Appliance	Contribution to energy consumption %
Walk-in fridge	5
Walk-in freezer	13
Grill	12
Steamer	4
Heat lamps	7
Bain marie	9
Fryers	13
Combi-ovens	12
Other cooking appliances	2
Other refrigeration	23

Refrigeration

Refrigeration is one of the major items of energy consumption in foodservice operations although there is still substantial capacity to improve uptake of energy-efficient appliances. For example, in the USA in 2017 not quite half of restaurant operators had Energy Star-rated refrigerators (NRA, 2018) (see Table 11.7). A key element in ensuring good energy control, as well as food safety, is to ensure that appliances are regularly maintained and services. In their UK study, Mudie et al. (2016) reported that the conditions of the refrigerating appliances in the gastro-pubs they were studying were poor, with half of the units (including walk-ins) having some kind of fault or developing problem. Post-maintenance usage of a walk-in freezer in a kitchen during the study showed a 45% reduction in electricity use. The most common fault was incorrect temperatures being displayed, with the digitally displayed temperature not always being the actual monitored temperature of the refrigerator, which corresponds to electricity wastage as well as concerns over food perishing, leading to increased waste (see Chapters 13 and 14), and food quality and safety. Interestingly, they reported

> a barrier to the implementation of planned, preventative maintenance (PPM) contracts in multi-site operators ... is their prohibitive cost. Yearly PPM servicing is likely to yield substantial overall savings in its first year as equipment is brought to a suitable condition. However, the further benefit in future years is reduced compared with the yearly cost of maintenance contracts. Performing maintenance 'in house' within the kitchen operators may be cheaper; however, it will require substantial initial training and increased payrolls for the operator. This would need to be balanced against potential electricity savings.
>
> (Mudie et al., 2016, pp. 69–70)

Kitchen layout is also important in maximizing energy efficiency. Having refrigeration appliances in close proximity to a heat source (e.g., a grill or stove) may increase

Table 11.7 Proportion of Energy Star-rated appliance type in US restaurant operations

Source: NRA (2018)

Energy Star-rated appliance type	All restaurants (%)	By segment		By ownership	
		Table service (%)	Limited service (%)	Independent (%)	Chain/ Franchisee (%)
Refrigerator	46	48	44	52	42
Freezer	41	43	40	46	38
Icemaker	41	43	38	44	39
Dishwasher	25	37	13	32	19
Fryer	22	29	14	27	18

electricity consumption by up to 30% (Mudie et al., 2016). However, this is a situation that illustrates the issue of reconciling sustainability practices with cooking practices.

> When questioned regarding the motivations for the locations of fridges in close proximity to heat sources, kitchen operators were far more concerned with the kitchen layout with regards to the physical work flow requirements of chefs during cooking, for example, all appliances required for dessert production in one area, all appliances for preparation of meats in another area, regardless of the potential cost savings in placing refrigeration away from grills and ovens.
>
> (Mudie et al., 2016, p. 70)

Cooking equipment

Grills and ovens contribute a relatively constant load to restaurant kitchens' energy use. However, a major factor in their relative energy efficiency is their management in relation to demand. As Mudie and Vadhati (2017, p. 214) note, "The physical principles of cooking are overridden by the manner in which the appliances are used by the staff". For example, in Mudie et al.'s (2016) study of UK gastro-pubs the variation in electricity consumption from grill use ranged from 49 kWh in the worst property subject to "poor, (but typical) operator behaviour. The appliance was switched to maximum where it remained until the end of service" (p. 70), to 14 kWh in the best property; a 71% saving compared with the typical operation owing to appropriate behavioural management alone. In the case of the latter, the grill was managed much more appropriately from an energy conservation perspective; with the temperature being reduced when the grill was not in operation. This meant that the second kitchen consistently served more meals at lower electricity usage when compared with the first, with the only considerable difference was with respect to the operators' behaviour in using the appliance (Mudie et al., 2016). Such findings highlight the importance of restaurants having firing/ starting up and powering/shutting down schedules which can keep ovens and grillers ready to use at the appropriate time. Such measures can also be managed by energy management systems (see Chapter 12).

Cooking equipment user behaviour can therefore be classified into different strategies:

1 Equipment left at normal operating settings throughout a shift (default);
2 Unused equipment turned off or onto stand-by mode during prolonged quiet periods;
3 Energy use minimized by turning appliances off at every reasonable opportunity (this is synonymous with appliances that use cooking activity sensors).

The differences between strategies in terms of energy use is substantial. In a comparison of their impact in a UK commercial kitchen, Mudie and Vadhati (2017) found that in some cases, such as gas hob usage, savings of 91%–99% are calculated from improved operator behaviour. In terms of the overall kitchen, energy consumption savings of 29.36% for behavioural strategy 2 were identified, compared with strategy 1. This represents actual savings of 71,041 kWh, 21,087 kg CO_2-eq and £4,031 per year. Energy consumption savings of 46.24% using behavioural strategy 3, represented actual savings of 111,892 kWh, 35,486 kg CO_2-eq and £7,034 per year. Potentially, with improved staff training a fourth 'bespoke' strategy between strategies 2 and 3 could be undertaken. Importantly, such findings also highlight the extent to which operational costs are much more significant than the purchase costs of appliances. Indeed, as Mudie and Vadhati (2017, p. 216) concluded,

> This over-specification is particularly pertinent when considering appliances with high 'idle' cooking energies (and those without cooking activity sensors), such as the salamander grill, gas oven and gas hob. These appliances use close to maximum power input regardless of food throughput, unless chefs practice appropriate energy minimizing behavior.

Water

Hospitality businesses and foodservice operations account for nearly 15% of commercial/institutional water use in the USA (NRA, 2018). Deng and Burnett (2002) report that 22% of water use in a luxury hotel in Hong Kong occurred in the kitchen while following a study of Hilton and Scandic hotels, Bohdanowicz and Martinac (2007) suggest an average water use for dining guests of between 35 L and 45 L per cover. Styles et al. (2015) report that water use in a mid-range hotel with a small restaurant serving breakfast to all guests plus meals to conference and à-la-carte guests numbering less half the number of overnight guests, equated to approximately 20 L per guest-night. Water consumption in the food catering and hospitality sector is mainly reported as that used for food preparation, and employee and customer water use. In the case of food preparation activities, they include washing and preparing food; washing food preparation areas and equipment; cooking; food waste disposal channels and dishwashers/glasswashers (WRAP, 2013b). However, there is a scarcity of good data on water use across different restaurant types and cuisines and the different ways in which water use is regulated and charged for (Gössling et al., 2015; Styles et al., 2015) (see Box 11.5).

The majority of water used in restaurants in the USA is taken up in the kitchen and dishwashing (Table 11.8). Water-saving equipment has not become as widely adopted in restaurants as energy saving equipment (Table 11.9), although some US states, such as California, have mandated the use of some water-saving technologies as a result of drought (Gloede, 2015). Twenty-seven percent of restaurant operators use low-flow faucet aerators in their hand sinks. Costing about $3 each these devices can reduce

Box 11.5 Water usage and costs for casual dining restaurants in Kansas

VanSchenkhof (2011) investigated the water usage and costs for casual dining restaurants (CDRs) in Kansas, USA. Results indicated that an average of 1,766 gallons (1 gallon = 3.785 L) of water were used each day per restaurant, 12.79 per gallons per day for each seat, 68 gallons per employee and 0.73 gallons per interior square foot. Significant demographics that impacted water consumption were season (summer being the highest), population, menu (those with a wider range of options), type of ownership (franchise and corporate CDR's expended significantly more water than independent operators), water source (surface water), irrigation (i.e., watering greenspace outside the restaurant) and days open (those open seven days a week). No significant differences in water use were found between restaurants that reported using water reduction equipment versus those that did not. Whether or not a manager could or accurately recall the previous month's water expenses also had no significant differences in water consumption. For water costs, CDRs paid an average of $6.54 per 1,000 gallons of water consumed and had mean annual expenses of $5,026 on revenues of $2,554,254 which was the equivalent of a water cost percent of 0.42%. However, the study also noted tremendous variability in water expenses, annual revenues and demographic variables. According to VanSchenkhof (2011, p. 149),

> There is variability because no two CDR's are the same with differences in footprint, revenues, water expenses, and likely differences from management, policies, and procedures. This inconsistency suggests that water expense percentage may become an effective internal efficiency measure which may lead to more efficient water consumption.

Table 11.8 Example of average end use of water in US restaurants
Source: NRA (2018); see also Gloede (2015)

Use	%
Kitchen/dishwashing	52
Domestic/restroom	31
Other	12
Landscaping	4
Cooling & Heating	1

hot-water use at a hand sink by 60%, with just one faucet aerator at a hand sink potentially saving 9,000 gallons (almost 41,000 L) of hot water per year (NRA, 2018). As a result, the adoption of such measures leads to water as well as energy savings. As a result of using aerators Shari's Café and Pies in the USA reduced their water costs by 7%–10% reduction, while Arby's Restaurant Group, Inc., another restaurant chain reduced water consumption from 2011 through 2013 at company-owned restaurants by more than 75 million gallons of water (115 Olympic-sized pools) (Gloede, 2015).

Opportunities for reduction of water use in the food services sector are similar to those in other commercial and institutional facilities, especially in the hotel sector. For

Efficient restaurants and kitchens

Table 11.9 Proportion of US restaurant operators, by type of operation, use water-saving equipment

Source: NRA (2018)

Equipment	All restaurants (%)	By segment		By ownership	
		Table service (%)	Limited service (%)	Independent (%)	Chain/ Franchisee (%)
Low-flush toilets	44	48	40	51	39
Faucet aerators	27	31	24	27	28
High-efficiency pre-rinse spray valves	26	28	24	26	25
Tankless water heater	24	21	26	18	29
Motion-activated toilets or faucets	21	24	18	16	25
Waterless urinals	11	12%	0	12	10

example, the Environment Agency (2012, in Amaris et al., 2015) reported significant water reduction in six hotels by an average of 25% per day per guest thanks to the use of effective water-saving measures. These included the use of push taps and trigger hose spray taps, infra-red controlled spray and push taps, infra-red controlled waterless urinals and lower volume toilet cisterns.

Potential water reduction measures in the kitchen include:

- Use infra-red controlled push taps and trigger-operated spray head hoses for washing food products;
- Operate only fully loaded dish/glass washers. Filling the racks will make the dishwasher more efficient with the water it is already using. Use the rinse-hold setting on the dishwasher, if it has one, rather than rinsing dishes under the tap;
- Dry peel instead of wet peeling (in case of some legumes, vegetables and fruits);
- Wash food products and utensils in a bowl rather than under running water;
- Immediate reporting of leaking washers or taps by staff, followed by repair;
- Scrape plates before placing in the dishwasher so that the economy settings on dishwashers can be used;
- Sweep or wipe floor/benches rather than using a hose tap;
- Equipment and water control accessories should be regularly maintained and services;
- Upgrade high water consuming equipment to more efficient models so that all appliances are water efficient;
- Don't thaw food under running water;
- Train staff to turn it off. Water or water-using equipment is often left flowing or operating when not needed. Saving water can be as simple as turning down a valve or turning off a switch or tap;

- Garbage disposal units use about 6 L of water per day. Put suitable scraps into a composter rather than down the sink;
- When washing dishes by hand, don't rinse them under running water. If there are two sinks, fill the second one with rinsing water. If there is only one sink, stack washed dishes in a dish rack and rinse them with a pan of water;
- If waiting for hot water to come through the tap, catch the water and use it to water plants, rinse dishes or wash fruits and vegetables;
- Make sure the hot-water system is not set too high. Adding cold water to cool very hot water is wasteful (Amaris et al., 2015; Water Supplies Department, 2016; Living Water Smart, n.d.).

Table 11.10 KPIs and technical details of best practice in small-medium sized, or larger, commercial kitchens
Source: Styles et al. (2015)

Aspect	Indicators of best practice
Monitoring	Kitchen water consumption is monitored separately and recorded at least once per month[a]
Dish washing	Waste grinders not used Pre-rinse spray valves are fitted with trigger operation and have a maximum flow rate of ≤6 L/min New stationary (under-counter or hood type) dishwashers have rated water consumption ≤3 L per rack Tunnel dishwashers are installed with heat recovery and heat pump Dishwashers are connected to hot-water supply, or to a dedicated [renewable energy supplied] boiler in the case of tunnel washers New conveyor dishwashers have rated water consumption of ≤2 L per rack equivalent Dishwasher racks are filled before loading into the dishwasher
Food preparation	Sink taps are installed with foot pedal or sensor operation and have maximum flow rate ≤12 L/min Steam cookers consume ≤8 L water per hour of operation Thawing under running water is avoided
Cleaning	The use of hoses to wash floors is avoided (mops or "water brooms" used instead) Cleaning agents do not contain the following: alkylphenolethoxylates (APEO) and alkylphenol derivatives (APD), dialkyl dimethyl ammonium chloride (DADMAC), linear alkylbenzene sulphonates (LAS), reactive chlorine compounds (exemption if required by authorities for hygiene reasons[a] At least 70% of the purchase volume of chemical cleaning products (excluding oven cleaners) for dish washing and cleaning are ecolabelled[a]

[a] Nordic Ecolabelling criteria.

Efficient restaurants and kitchens

Most water-saving recommendations in restaurants are aimed at the kitchen. However, in Hong Kong, the best practice guidelines for water conservation in catering and hospitality also include guidelines for dining area operations and wait staff:

- Serve/refill water only upon customers' request;
- Provide self-service drinking water station for customers;
- Provide basic dining utensils and serve extra utensils only upon customers' request;
- Replace bone plates and dining utensils only upon customers' request;
- Use powder cleaning agent to clean carpet instead of water or steam;
- Display water-saving notices to raise customers' awareness on water conservation (Water Supplies Department, 2016, p. 13).

Styles et al. (2015) also note a number of water savings that can be made from the adoption of good kitchen practices but, importantly, the extent to which they become cost savings for businesses will depend on the jurisdiction and how restaurants are charged for the water they consume. Clearly, the more water costs a restaurant the more likely it is that they will reduce consumption where possible. Styles et al. (2015) suggested a series of key performance indicators and best practices for commercial kitchens which provide useful benchmarks for the development of a water management system in restaurant kitchens (Table 11.10).

Box 11.6   Behavioural measures with staff and management to encourage better water use

Education and awareness

- Raising staff awareness is a cost-effective and sustainable way to save water at your business or workplace. Behavioural changes are the cheapest to fix – they're free! So be sure to focus on these.
- Install reminder signs in your kitchen and bathroom areas to remind staff and customers to use water wisely.
- Display water smart posters in kitchens, staff rooms and toilets.
- Reduce water wastage by regularly checking and fixing leaks in taps, toilet cisterns, pipes and appliance hoses.

Get management on board

- Having senior managers on board will enable you to investigate, propose and implement water efficiency measures.
- Top-Down/Bottom-Up Approach – the water-saving message should be consistent across the organization.
- Start water-saving practices from the site's senior management levels.

Get staff on board

- Spread the word – let everyone know about this – get staff involved in the program.
- Talk to staff about your water-savings initiatives. Include water-saving policies and procedures in staff induction.

- Encourage staff to contribute to water-saving ideas. They may already have great ideas about how to save water and this may be their chance to make them happen.
- Discuss water efficiency at team meetings and keep staff up to date on how the site is tracking against its goals water use figures.
- Urge employees to report leaks and other issues.
- Provide incentives, for example, you could consider adding water conservation targets to staff performance reviews.

Set a target

- What is your workplace goal? Setting a goal can help to focus attention on what needs to be done and how to achieve it.
- Identify 'water efficiency champions' and celebrate their achievements.

Source: Living Water Smart (n.d.)

Box 11.7 Kempinski Hotel Corvinus, Budapest

The Kempinski Hotel Corvinus in Budapest, Hungary, serves an average of 400–600 hot meals a day in its restaurants. Prior to changing its dishwashing technology, pot washing in the kitchen was done using a 3-bowl sink system, which meant manual soaking of utensils, scrubbing, rinsing and then sanitizing in a chemical dip. The water tap was left flowing resulting in wet, slippery floors and the need to constantly mop the floor. This setup was time-consuming and uses massive amounts of water (2,408 L of water a day), energy (to heat the water) and chemicals. The hotel also had difficulty in finding suitable kitchen staff.

The hotel installed a front-loading pot washer that suits operations ranging from 400 up to 3,000 meals per day, which enables the kitchen porters to return the pots and pans to the chefs at a faster rate. For example, four pieces of GN 2/1 (650 × 530 mm², 4.5 L capacity) can be washed and sanitized in two to six minutes, depending on wash cycle. Water and electricity consumption went down by 60.1% in the pot-washing area, with less demand for labour (Table 11.11).

Table 11.11 Change in pot washing per annum following installation of new dishwashing technology

	Before	After
Water consumption	878,970 L	350,400 L
Cost	Ft 468,052	Ft 186,588
Water savings		60.1%
Energy consumption	30,617 kWh	12,206 kWh
Cost	Ft 1,071,611	Ft 427,196
Energy savings		60.1%

Conclusions

This chapter has discussed some of the measures that lead to the creation of an efficient restaurant and kitchen. Although the kitchen is clearly a major driver in energy and water use and conservation, the condition of the overall building is also clearly important. New builds have a clear advantage over refurbishments with respect to efficiency although there are a number of measures businesses can take. Refurbishments are also an opportunity to upgrade equipment. It is also clear that for many restaurants the main driver in adopting new efficient appliances and technologies is the perceived cost relative to returns. However, there is clear evidence of positive returns with respect to electricity costs. More research needs to be undertaken on water efficiencies, although the direct relationship between energy use and water use in many areas suggests that there should be substantial benefits, although a key driver is the cost of the water to the restaurant. While this chapter has primarily focused on the hardware of restaurant efficiency the next chapter will briefly discuss the software that can potentially integrate the different elements of a restaurant to promote greater efficiency.

Box 11. 8   Water-saving websites

US Environmental Protection Authority, Water Sense: www.epa.gov/watersense/commercial-buildings
Waterwise: www.waterwise.org.uk
Smart Approved Watermark: www.smartwatermark.org/news/articles/smart-watermark-launched-europe/
Smart Water (New Zealand): www.smartwater.org.nz/being-water-smart/water-smart-tips/
Water Rating (Australia): www.waterrating.gov.au/choose

Chapter 12

The intelligent kitchen

Using management systems to promote sustainability

Introduction

One of the distinguishing factors of the contemporary restaurant and commercial kitchen environment is the impact of smart technology and the Internet of things, by which there is greater connectivity between appliances, people, systems and products (Mercan et al., 2020). The hyperconnectivity inherent in such technology brings together the capacity to integrate a range of different elements which provides data not only to improve levels of customer satisfaction (Kim & Ham, 2006), but to improve sustainability by reducing food waste and energy and water consumption.

The use of smart technologies, such as cloud-based apps for food ordering, has been hastened by COVID-19 as customers and foodservice operations sought to reduce human contact and social distance. However, it is important to recognize that the adoption of smart kitchen and restaurant technologies that can monitor orders and inventory, as well as energy and water consumption provide new ways of ensuring a more efficient kitchen in terms of both resources and costs. Such measures have become part of, what DeMicco et al. (2014) described as, 'The eco-restaurant of the future'. The previous chapter discussed the various environmental dimensions of kitchen appliances and building design. This chapter looks at the way in which different management systems can be used by managers and staff to improve their understanding of how individual appliances and efficiency initiatives can be integrated. This chapter, therefore, discusses how new technologies and systems can be used in the kitchen with respect to promoting sustainability. The interrelationships of these issues in terms of human resources, strategies and technologies, are also noted. Two types of systems are discussed: restaurant management systems (RMS), including connectivity to food apps, and comprehensive energy management (CEM)/energy management systems (EMS) which, as will be discussed, cover much more than just energy (Figure 12.1). The chapter discusses their importance and how ultimately the creation of an intelligent kitchen is to do with the commitment of staff, managers and owners, far more than the focus on technology alone.

Restaurant management systems

A restaurant management system (RMS) is a type of point-of-sale (POS) software that has been specifically designed for restaurants, bars, cafés, food trucks, cloud (dark,

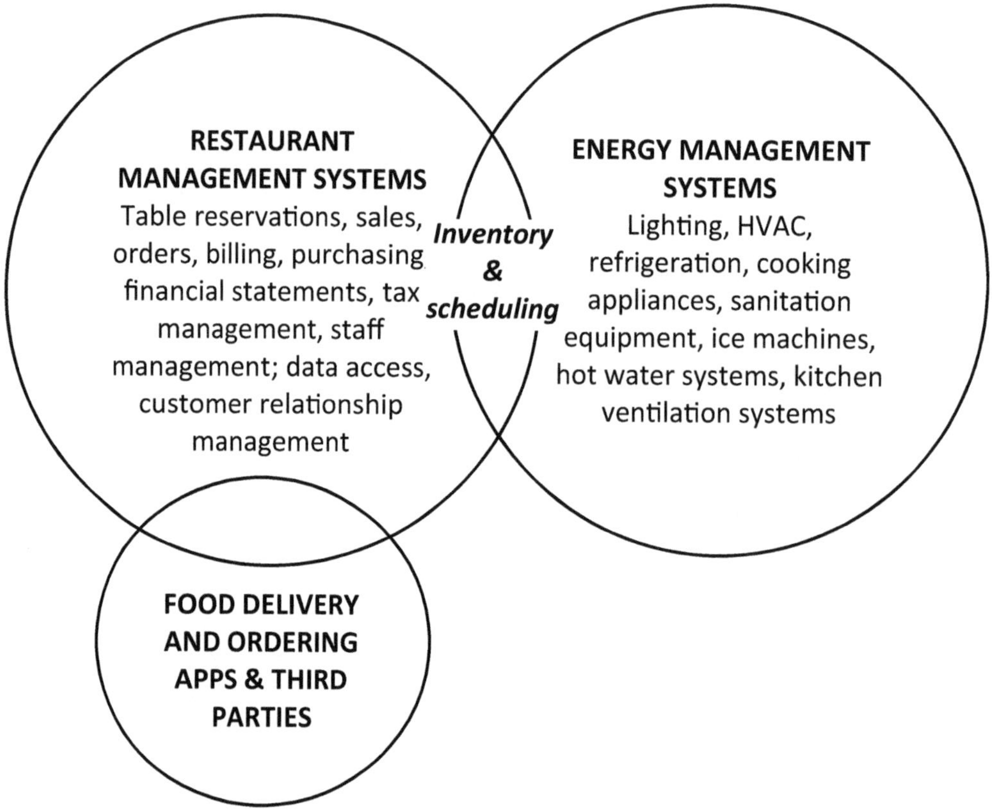

The intelligent kitchen

Figure 12.1 Interrelationships between systems in the development of sustainable restaurant management systems

RESTAURANT MANAGEMENT SYSTEMS
Table reservations, sales, orders, billing, purchasing, financial statements, tax management, staff management; data access, customer relationship management

ENERGY MANAGEMENT SYSTEMS
Lighting, HVAC, refrigeration, cooking appliances, sanitation equipment, ice machines, hot water systems, kitchen ventilation systems

Inventory & scheduling

FOOD DELIVERY AND ORDERING APPS & THIRD PARTIES

virtual and ghost) kitchens, food delivery services and others foodservice operations, as well as providing point-of-sale management it also includes inventory and staff management. For example, "ingredient-level inventory updates, the ability for waitstaff to send orders directly from the table to the kitchen, split billing and kitchen displays" (Kuligowski, 2020). Increasingly, they also enable:

- tracking of table reservations, sales, orders and billing whether in the restaurant and/or online, and connecting restaurant sales to inventory so as to make purchasing more efficient;
- viewing accurate, real-time financial statements;
- managing staff schedules;
- data access; and
- customer relationship management (CRM) tools, such as mailing lists or rewards programmes, e.g., frequent purchase rewards.

RMS are either bought or leased by restaurants from providers (Heart & Pliskin, 2002), with decisions as to which strategy to adopt dependent on initial costs and capacity to upgrade (Heart et al., 2007). From a sustainability perspective, the most important type of RMS is a so-called end-to-end system that allows substantial inventory control by enabling a manager to see the relationship between what is being ordered from the menu and what is stocked in the kitchen. Being able to see this relationship means that items can be ordered in so that they are appropriate to levels of demand thereby reducing food wastage (see Chapters 13 and 14 for more detail on food waste). The end-to-end system is therefore much more comprehensive than a standard POS system which just connects the orders taken by waitstaff, to the kitchen and to customer billing. Nevertheless, it creates pressures in the kitchen in terms of food preparation and the creativity of kitchen staff as to work most effectively it needs to be run with standardized recipes. In addition, as with any system, purchase of RMS raises issues over software and hardware compatibility especially in terms of being able to run on different devices, integration with third-party systems, e.g., reservation, pick-up or dining out systems. For example, this includes apps developed specifically for individual restaurants or chains as well as third-party food ordering apps such as FoodPanda (www.foodpanda.com) (East Asia, Pakistan, Bangladesh, Romania and Bulgaria); Deliveroo (https://deliveroo.co.uk) (most popular app in Europe); Swiggy (www.swiggy.com) (India), Zomato (www.zomato.com) (Europe, North America, Gulf States, India, Sri Lanka, East Asia, Australia, New Zealand, South Africa, Brazil, Chile) and Uber Eats (www.ubereats.com), available in many countries including Brazil, Japan, Mexico, India and the USA.

Food delivery apps that tie into RMS are becoming popular for several reasons:

- For consumers, the menu is visible and easily accessible within the app.
- For consumers who are concerned about eating in crowded spaces for health reasons, the apps provide an opportunity for low or no contact dining.
- They offer ordering options for delivery or takeaway, which should be integrated into the restaurants own inventory management.
- They offer real-time in-app delivery tracking.
- Restaurants can use geo-location notifications to connect with customers.

Integrating delivery/off-premise dining into the restaurant management system

Even prior to COVID-19 off-premise dining was increasing as a result of the growing use of apps. The NRA (2019) argues that this is a result of customer need for convenience which they found was "driving increased off premises usage across all formats takeout, drive thru and delivery" (p. 2). From the results of a survey of a nationally representative sample of foodservice consumers who order delivery, takeout or drive-through at least once every two to three months, undertaken in April 2019, the NRA (2019) found that 18–34-year-old consumers were more likely to engage in off-premise dining that those aged 35 and older. Overall, 92% of survey participants stated that they used drive-through at least once a month (29% higher than a year previously), 90% having take-out (29% higher than a year previously), 79% restaurant delivery and 53% third-party delivery. Although in-person orders, either by phone (59%) or walk-in (51%) continued (22% used a kiosk to place orders), use of online technology was becoming more widespread, with 79% of respondents saying they had placed orders using a restaurant's website or app in the past year. In terms of delivered food, 91% of consumers had placed orders via a restaurant's app or website within the past year, 60% had used a third-party delivery service with 11% using a voice assistant and 8% text (NRA, 2019).

Off-premise sales are also regarded as beneficial by foodservice operators (Table 12.1), with 74% of business respondents investing in off-premise programmes, "operators say making these options available generates additional sales for their business, brings in new customers that would have sought out other restaurants,

Table 12.1 Off-premise options in US restaurants
Source: National sample of 400 restaurant operators (170 limited service and 230 full service) who offer delivery, takeout or drive-through in NRA (2019)

Off-premise options	Percent of operators
Regular takeout (customers enter the restaurant to pick up the orders themselves)	99
Delivery provided by a third-party service	66
Delivery provided by own restaurant staff	55
Catering	46
Grab-and-go	30
Curbside pick-up	24
Drive-through	20
Food trucks	14

Table 12.2 Gap between consumer demand and availability
Source: NRA (2019)

Item	Consumer's undertaking (%)	Operators offering (%)
Delivery orders via restaurant website	65	45
Delivery orders via restaurant app	43	18
Receptive to ordering via virtual assistant if available (e.g., Amazon Alexa)	31	12

increases profitability of their operation and increases check averages" (NRA, 2019, p. 3). However, there is a significant gap between consumer demand and the capacity of restaurants to provide off-premise options (Table 12.2). The growth in off-premise sales has therefore created new challenges for operators which highlight the need for effective restaurant management systems as it has created difficulties in planning and forecasting food prep and staffing, while the growth in sales also means that the types of food packaging used need to be considered. The latter being a clear issue with respect to waste. Significantly, in terms of adoption issues and the gap between consumer demand and availability, the NRA (2019, p. 6), reported,

> Once an operator has decided to invest in technology, it can be difficult to identify which solution is best-suited for the operation and difficult to seamlessly deploy that new technology and train the staff on proper use. Of those operators using new technology to support off-premises orders, over one out of ten have experienced challenges.

Table 12.3 US restaurant consumer likeliness of using, if available
Source: NRA (2019)

Technology	%
Vehicles with built in heating trays to keep food warm	69
Autonomous delivery	41
Food cooked while en route	36

The environmental implications of the growth of food delivery services are still relatively unknown with much depending on the delivery mode, e.g., bicycle versus motorbike versus car. However, the growth in the use of apps and web-based ordering has led to the emergence of a new kind of restaurant kitchen, variously referred to as a 'cloud kitchen', 'virtual kitchen' or 'virtual restaurant' which has no seating or takeaway counter but takes orders online that then get picked up and delivered by the allocated fleet (Limetray, 2019). Proponents of the adoption of cloud technology (Restaurants Canada, 2019; Te, 2019), often claim environmental benefits from adopting such technologies without providing detailed analyses. While the sentiments of, for example, Restaurants Canada (2019) with respect to the adoption of smart technology are laudable:

> Tomorrow's smart cities will want, or demand through regulation, that smart 'connected' restaurants (and other businesses, too) monitor and manage their resources to minimize their impact on the community. Therefore, in most every way that matters, a smarter restaurant is essentially a more sustainable one, from its measurably reduced environmental footprint to its ability to quickly respond to unexpected yet necessary changes.

The actual reality needs to be evaluated with the situation becoming even more problematic with the implications of emerging food delivery technologies for sustainability (Table 12.3).

Box 12.1 Features to look for in restaurant management systems

When determining which restaurant management system to use, Kuligowski (2020) recommends looking for the following five features:

1. *Sales and tax tracking*. The RMS should track all sales data, such as top menu items, busiest selling times, best-performing staff and profits, to help make business decisions. The software should also provide detailed records for tax reporting purposes. Financial information regarding menu items is especially important with respect to ordering and the relative return on purchasing decisions.
2. *Order management*. Restaurant staff should be able to easily manage tables, reservations, billing and menu items through the RMS. Managers should also

be able to control refunds, voids and comps and view order statuses as well as, if relevant, pre-authorize credit cards to open bar tabs.
3 *Inventory management*. Knowing exactly how much product that is on hand helps determine when and how much to reorder from vendors and therefore reduce waste levels in the restaurant.
4 *Reporting and customer data*. RMS can potentially track and filter sales and customer data to enable better relationship marketing. This could include direct marketing of seasonal menu information, for example, or other information such as waste reduction incentives, such as promoting the availability of doggy bags.
5 *Marketing, gift cards and reward programs*. RMS can provide marketing tools such as promotions, gift cards and loyalty or rewards programs, e.g., a free cup of coffee or other giveaway for each ten Fair Trade coffee purchases.

Source: After Kuligowski (2020)

Energy Management Systems

A Comprehensive Energy Management (CEM)/Energy Management System (EMS) programme measures every watt of energy used in an operation, then implements sustainability programme and/or updates equipment and facilities to ensure they are running as efficiently as possible (Sustainable Foodservice, 2016c). It is a computerized platform that allows operators to control and monitor energy-using equipment within a building. CEM/EMS typically control a building's lighting and heating ventilation and air conditioning (HVAC) systems (excluding kitchen exhaust hoods). Significantly for restaurant and foodservice operations, the scope of CEM/EMS can be extended to include refrigeration, cooking appliances, sanitation equipment, ice machines, hot water systems and kitchen ventilation systems. In some cases, CEM/EMS have been integrated with demand-controlled kitchen ventilation (DCKV) systems. As such the 'energy' in CEM/EMS is something of a misnomer as they offer a potentially comprehensive building and operations management tool, with some restaurant end users finding reduction in energy consumption to be a positive by-product of the systems other functions (Cornelius et al., 2014; Fisher, 2015; Capehart & Brambley, 2020).

The primary features offered with most EMSs are equipment monitoring, scheduling, controls and alarms for HVAC and lighting systems that may reduce unnecessary energy expenditures and identify equipment malfunctions (Figure 12.2). Select CEM/EMS providers offer advanced energy-saving features as well as peak demand management and load-shifting measures (Cornelius et al., 2014). Table 12.4 details the software and hardware components that can be available as part of CEM/EMS packages.

The first step of any CEM/EMS is to measure and record energy use so that the effectiveness of measures can be documented. However, effective measurement requires the use of appropriate metrics and the application of relevant tools to collect data to develop datasets that are relevant to management. Increasingly, such data is being gathered by comprehensive software programmes. For example, Energy Star in the USA is a software programme that helps benchmark resource costs, find effective facility improvements, compare multiple facilities and track progress with respect to energy, water, waste and GHG emissions. The software is free and available online (www.energystar.gov/buildings/benchmark). According to Energy Star (n.d.), nearly

The intelligent kitchen

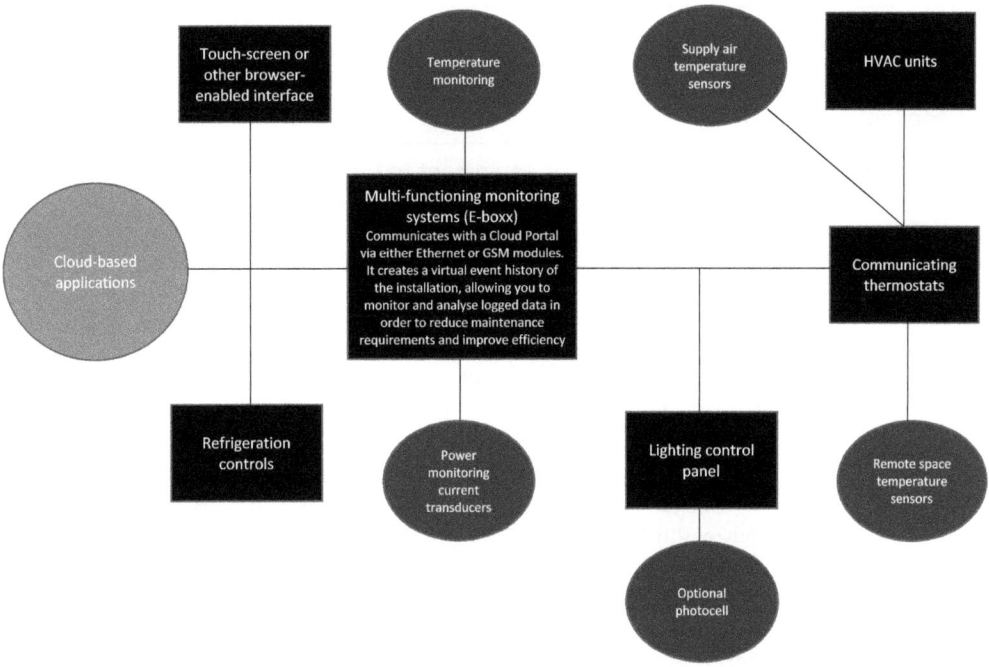

Figure 12.2 Potential EMS system architecture for a restaurant

Table 12.4 Potential components of EMS packages
Source: Cornelius et al. (2014); Fisher (2015)

Component	Description
Software	
Dashboard	The dashboard is the central access point for operators to view monitoring data and control equipment. Dashboards usually feature a schematic of the installed EMS equipment, a list of logged data points, configurable schedules and equipment controls.
Equipment monitoring	Serves as a data logging platform for all of the connected sensors.
Equipment control	The most common type of automated control is equipment on/off scheduling, e.g., lighting, exhaust fans, HVAC unoccupied mode and cooking equipment.
Alarms	Are configured to alert operators when monitored equipment is operating abnormally, or if a programmed threshold is reached that requires action (such as when internal temperatures of refrigeration rise above safe levels for a period of time).
Anomaly detection	Some EMS include adaptive logic which can detect equipment anomalies based on normal usage patterns which can identify malfunctioning equipment.

Table 12.4 continued

Component	Description
Advanced energy-saving logic	Improves control of equipment to reduce energy expenditure. Examples of this include, but are not limited to: Demand control ventilation Lighting dimming Smart defrost Economizer control Water heater output temperature control and setback Recirculation pump control Booster heater night-time shut off Load shifting, e.g., ice machine
Demand response	Some EMS systems can shift load off of utility peak usage periods. For larger cold storage units, EMS can pre-cool walk-in freezers to allow units to "coast" through peak hours. Ice machines may be load-shifted to produce at night and store throughout the day.
Building peak demand management	Integrated features to reduce building peak demand charges for restaurants. Such strategies include preventing simultaneous condenser cycling between multiple rooftop units.
Multiple communication protocols	Some EMS accept multiple communication protocols to widen the range of accepted equipment. Incompatible protocols are a barrier for integrating EMS with existing equipment and systems.
Hardware	
Thermostat	Thermostatic setpoints as well as unoccupied mode scheduling may be controlled through the thermostat or through the online dashboard.
Control panel	The control panel is a touchscreen access point to the online dashboard. While the dashboard may also be accessed through mobile devices and online, the in-store control panel offers managers on-site oversight.
Module boxes	Sensors and actuators connect to voltage and pulse channels on central module boxes. Each module box features multiple channels and can interface with a number of sensors and actuators. These modules can be connected through hardware or by wireless to the EMS and may be used to monitor and control all desired points. Most EMS have designated modules for lighting control and equipment monitoring and control.
Sensors	Nearly any sensor can be integrated with an EMS provided that the pulse or voltage output may be read by the monitoring module. Common monitored values with EMS products include temperature, humidity, energy usage, water flow, walk-in door status and economizer position.
Actuators	Equipment may be controlled remotely through actuators (a device that makes a mechanism or system move or operate), e.g., relays connected to the HVAC and lighting circuits.
Wireless modem	Wireless modems that connect components of the EMS as well as communicate with the main dashboard.

25% of US commercial building space is already actively benchmarking in Portfolio Manager, making it the industry-leading benchmarking tool and it is also used as a national benchmarking tool in Canada.

However, while programmes like Portfolio Manager are useful at the property level they may not provide detailed enough information for many restaurant operations, especially when trying to encourage staff behaviour in real time. Therefore, a more detailed and useful option is to use an interval data collection system that connects to electric, gas and water meters and track energy and water use at set, time-stamped intervals (usually every 30 minutes) or via continuous tracking. In some countries, such systems are available from energy and water utilities or via third parties. These systems are very useful in that you can see energy and water use change throughout the day in relation to staff and customer activity and that information can then be used to change practices, start-up times or track down energy and water use problems (Sustainable Foodservice, 2016c). Nevertheless, to be effective CEM/EMS have to be integrated into the day-to-day operations of any restaurant:

> With or without a tracking system, a CEM program looks at everything from equipment types and placement to thermostat settings, employee habits and ways to avoid peak load costs. For example, if your operation can make it through working hours without making additional ice it may be an effective solution to set the icemaker to run overnight to decrease load charges.
>
> One of the simplest methods for reducing energy use is creating an energy checklist that schedules start-up and shutdown times for lighting and equipment so they are turned on only when needed, turned down during slow periods and turned off when not needed. There are literally thousands of ways to reduce energy, but no one CEM solution for all organizations.
>
> (Sustainable Foodservice, 2016c)

Furthermore, a difficulty for many restaurant operations is being able to select the CEM/EMS that best fits their needs and is a cost-effective investment. This is a challenge as there are a range of options available. In reviewing the use of EMS by foodservice operations in California, Cornelius et al. (2014, pp. 1, 2) concluded:

> there is a wide diversity among products and features offered by EMS vendors. The core hardware capabilities of all systems observed were comparable; however, the individual software-driven features offered between products varied significantly. While a majority of systems focus on control and monitoring of HVAC and lighting, select providers offer additional areas of focus including DCKV integration, smart defrost, and other advanced energy saving features. EMS products were found not to be "out-of-the-box" solutions for foodservice and require extensive installation and commissioning at each site.
>
> The results of this study showed that energy savings of the EMS depend greatly upon the pre-existing equipment conditions, scheduling, and commissioning. Based on the field site analyses, market research, and surveys conducted in this study, EMS was found to be a viable tool for equipment maintenance and diagnostics. However, it was limited in respect to energy saving and load-shifting capabilities ...

Industry adoption of CEM/EMS has been limited with quick-service chain restaurants (QSRs) being the area in which they have been most widely used. In the case of the application of DCKV to water conservation, Fisher (2015) reported savings of the order of 31.8%–67.9% and monetary savings of a minimum of $800 per unit over a year. However, a barrier for many restaurants is the cost. Cornelius et al. (2014, p. 5) note:

> Both EMS and DCKV systems individually exhibit installed costs that typically range from $10,000 to $30,000 depending on the size of the restaurant and the complexity of the system configuration. This economic barrier, along with the uncertainty with respect to actual energy savings, has kept these systems from becoming standard practice in restaurant design.

Other financial barriers include unknown payback period, ongoing service fees, cost of data analysis. In addition, there are a range of operational (behavioural and scheduling procedural change, installation and commissioning, technology adoption) and technical barriers (foodservice building conditions, hardware reliability, proprietary communication protocols, security) to utilizing CEM/EMS.

As noted in Chapter 11, as of 2017 79% of US restaurant operators used CFL or LED lighting. However, the proportion using programmable HVAC technologies was less (Table 12.5). The proportions are interesting as using programmable lighting systems can also lead to considerable efficiency gains. Similarly, start-up/shut-down schedules can also be programmed and monitored so as to avoid wasteful idling.

Smart technologies can also be used in other areas of the kitchen such as monitoring and managing waste and connecting such data to ordering as well as storage control. In the case of food waste management, just over half of all US restaurants use a computer spreadsheet by only a quarter were using food waste-specific software or app, even though three-quarters of restaurants were monitoring their waste daily (Table 12.6). The advantages of using food waste apps are dealt with in more detail in Chapter 14. However, as noted above, they are ideally integrated with the wider restaurant management and energy systems.

Table 12.5 Proportion of restaurant operators, by type of operation, who report they use efficient lighting, programmable thermostats or start-up, shut-down schedules

Source: NRA (2018)

Technology	All restaurants (%)	By segment		By ownership	
		Table service (%)	Limited service (%)	Independent (%)	Chain/ Franchisee (%)
CFL or LED lighting	79	82	76	79	79
Programmable HVAC thermostats	61	62	60	58	63
Start-up, shut-down schedules	63	68	58	58	67

Table 12.6 Use of food waste-specific software

Technology	All restaurants (%)	By segment		By ownership	
		Table service (%)	Limited service (%)	Independent (%)	Chain/ Franchisee (%)
Method of tracking food waste					
Manually (pen and paper)	57	65	51	76	48
On a computer spreadsheet or chart	51	41	59	38	57
Via food waste-specific software or smartphone app	26	24	27	7	35
Frequency of waste monitoring					
Daily	74	58	84	66	76
Weekly	21	31	13	22	21
Monthly	4	7	1	7	3
Quarterly	1	1	1	3	0

Conclusions

This chapter has provided a brief overview of the management systems that are increasingly being used in restaurants and foodservice kitchens. It has focused on the two main systems, restaurant management systems (RMS), which are an adapted form of POS systems applied to food services, and which are inherently focused on sales; and comprehensive energy management (CEM)/energy management systems (EMS) which, despite their name, act as building management systems. The intersection between the two systems is with respect to their role in scheduling and inventory management. In addition to these two systems, the growth in off-premise dining, which has been reinforced by COVID-19 restrictions and concerns over contagion, has led to the need to integrate third-party food ordering and delivery apps in with the RMS.

While the adoption of RMS and EMS clearly has benefits in terms of the efficiency of restaurant operations, the impacts of food ordering and delivery apps on sustainability have yet to be fully evaluated. Although such apps can be connected to RMS and inventory management the growth of online orders raises significant staff issues. Indeed, the growth of the Internet of things and the capacity for automation may create significant pressure on employment in the sector as well as flow-on effects of standardization in various parts of the food chain. Nevertheless, in the short term at least, the greater use of appropriate software and apps does have the potential to make restaurants and foodservice operations much more efficient, a point taken up in more detail in the next two chapters that examine food waste issues.

Chapter 13

Minimizing waste
Technology and management

Introduction

Food waste is a global problem and is high on the international agenda, as it is interlinked with several of the United Nations' Sustainable Development Goals (SDGs) (UN, 2017). FAO et al. (2013) estimate that worldwide, some 1.3 billion tonnes of food are lost or wasted annually, and the UN has called to "by 2030, halve per capita global food waste at the retail and consumer levels and reduce food losses along production and supply chains, including post-harvest losses" (UN, 2017). Food waste is generated during different stages of the food supply chain, i.e., production at the farm, post-harvest handling and storage, processing and packaging, distribution (wholesale/retail), preparation, presentation and consumption (Figure 13.1) (Box 13.1 provides examples of significant definitions of food loss and waste (FLW)). Notably, a significant share of food is also lost because of forms of industrial production (Box 13.2; see also Chapter 2).

> **Box 13.1 Definitions related to FLW**
>
> There is no single internationally accepted definition of what constitutes FLW, which can make comparisons between different countries and legal jurisdictions, as well as different restaurants and studies very difficult (Priestley, 2016). A commonly used definition in the EU and the UK is that of the FUSIONS (Food Use for Social Innovation by Optimising Waste Prevention Strategies) project which ran during 2012–2016 and which sought to establish harmonization in food waste monitoring in the EU. The FUSIONS definition was
>
> > any food, and inedible parts of food, removed from the food supply chain to be recovered or disposed (including composted, crops ploughed in/not harvested, anaerobic digestion, bio-energy production, co-generation, incineration, disposal to sewer, landfill or discarded to sea).
>
> > (FUSIONS, 2016, p. 24)
>
> This does not include "food or inedible parts of food removed from the food supply chain sent to animal feed or used for the production of bio-based material/biochemical processing. In addition, packaging is not included in the food waste

definition" (FUSIONS, 2016, p. 25). Distinguishing between food loss and food waste is extremely important, "as the types of interventions that can affect consumer behaviour (food demand) are different from those that encourage suppliers to reduce food losses (food supply)" (FAO, 2019c, p. 5). Two widely used definitions of FLW are from the FAO (2019c):

> Food loss is the decrease in the quantity or quality of food resulting from decisions and actions by food suppliers in the chain, excluding retail, food service providers and consumers.
>
> Food waste is the decrease in the quantity or quality of food resulting from decisions and actions by retailers, food services and consumers.
>
> (FAO, 2019c, p. 5)

The World Resources Institute (WRI) developed an FLW standard in order to better inventory food waste and loss (see www.flwprotocol.org). The inventory is flexible in allowing users to choose which particular scope is most appropriate for their FLW inventory as users need to "choose whether to quantify both food and associated inedible parts removed from the food supply chain, only food, or only associated inedible parts" (WRI, 2016, p. 2). Under the inventory food and inedible parts are defined:

> *Food*: Any substance—whether processed, semi-processed, or raw—that is intended for human consumption. "Food" includes drink, and any substance that has been used in the manufacture, preparation, or treatment of food. "Food" also includes material that has spoiled and is therefore no longer fit for human consumption. It does not include cosmetics, tobacco, or substances used only as drugs. It does not include processing agents used along the food supply chain, for example, water to clean or cook raw materials in factories or at home.
>
> *Inedible parts*: Components associated with a food that, in a particular food supply chain, are not intended to be consumed by humans. Examples of inedible parts associated with food could include bones, rinds, and pits/stones. "Inedible parts" do not include packaging. What is considered inedible varies among users (e.g., chicken feet are consumed in some food supply chains but not others), changes over time, and is influenced by a range of variables including culture, socio-economic factors, availability, price, technological advances, international trade, and geography.
>
> (WRI, 2016, p. 2)

The inventory then goes on to identify the various possible destinations of unconsumed food and inedible parts: animal feed, bio-material/processing, codigestion/anaerobic digestion, composting/aerobic process, controlled combustion, land application, landfill, not harvested/ploughed-in, refuse/discards/litter, sewer/wastewater treatment. The materials included (e.g., food only, inedible parts only or both), together with the destinations, are then combined with the timeframe and boundary of analysis (e.g., the food category, life-cycle stage, geography and organization) to provide a basis for inventory (WRI, 2016). With respect to the measurement of FLW the FAO definitions of quantitative and qualitative FLW are:

> *Quantitative food loss and waste* (also referred to as physical food loss and waste) is the decrease in the mass of food destined for human consumption as it is removed from the food supply chain.
> *Qualitative food loss and waste* refers to the decrease in food attributes that reduces its value in terms of intended use.
>
> (FAO, 2019c, p. 5)
>
> Quantitative FLW are therefore the physical decrease in food mass resulting from decisions and actions by retailers, food services and consumers as food passes along the food supply and value chain.
>
> Qualitative FLW refer to declines in food attributes that reduce the value of food in terms of its intended use, e.g., declines in nutritional value and/or the economic value of food because of reductions in quality, which may also result in unsafe food. Qualitative food loss results from decisions and actions by food suppliers in the chain, while qualitative food waste results from actions by retailers, food services and consumers (FAO, 2019c).

Box 13.2 Industrial food production and contamination-related losses in the USA

The industrial production of meat entails enormous losses, as illustrated by examples of food recalls. For instance, Simmons Prepared Foods, a corporation producing chicken for restaurants, schools, hospitals and distributors in the USA, had to recall more than two million pounds of chicken because of contamination with metal. According to *USA Today* (Tyko, 2019), the United States Department of Agriculture (USDA) had classified the contamination as a Class I recall, defined as a "health hazard situation where there is a reasonable probability that the use of the product will cause serious, adverse health consequences or death".

The total amount of meat wasted in the USA is much higher. The USDA suggests that of the inspected poultry in March 2019, 0.24% of the live weight, and 0.87% of the post-mortem weight were condemned (USDA, 2019). While relative shares would appear small, total numbers are significant, also shedding light on the vast animal numbers slaughtered in the USA. Condemned poultry amounted to 47 million pounds in March 2019, equivalent to more than seven million chickens in just one month. Condemned foods have to be disposed of, as they cannot be used for human consumption. While industrial production thus presupposes food losses, it is ironically the larger firms that are better equipped to weather meat and poultry recalls (Pozo & Schroeder, 2016), illustrating that in industrial production, food losses are anticipated, and planned for as an operational cost.

While a number of global estimates have been presented on food waste, it is less clear whether these are reliable, and whether these adequately consider the different parts of the food supply chain (Parfitt et al., 2010). For instance, Lundqvist et al. (2008) estimated that about 50% of all food is lost before it is even bought by the consumer. Yet, even losses on the consumer side are significant, and authors have concluded that food waste can be reduced along the entire food chain, and by both producers and consumers (Cinzia, 2017). To date, very little is done in most countries to avoid food losses, or to re-use discarded food. For example, in the USA, 75% of all food waste goes to landfill

(United States Environmental Protection Agency (EPA), 2019). Likewise, in the European Union, it was expected that food waste would more than double over the period 2010–2020 as a result of population growth and rising disposable income (EC, 2010).

Food loss is also a relative category that does not distinguish the nutritional value and calorie content of different foodstuffs: letting a kg of tomatoes go to waste is not identical to losing a kg of pork because the production of animal protein is associated with greater emissions of greenhouse gases, antibiotics use, nutrient discharge and the requirement of larger amounts of water, energy and land. Food waste should consequently be discussed from quantitative and qualitative viewpoints. There is also an ethical aspect, as animals are often raised and slaughtered under conditions that ignore animal welfare. Bearing in mind these distinctions, food waste has implications for the amount of all edible materials intended for human consumption that is discarded, lost, degraded or contaminated (FAO, 1981), with a view to the energy value of the food lost (Smil, 2004), as well as its implications for animal welfare, greenhouse gas emissions or land requirements. The general consensus is that food waste has to be avoided throughout the food supply chain (Parfitt et al., 2010), and especially with regard to animal protein. However, as well as being something that is regarded as important with respect to the environment and sustainability, it is also increasingly seen as just being good business sense.

There are different assessments regarding food losses, which take into consideration some or all aspects of the food system value chain. For instance, Gustavsson et al. (2011) suggested in an assessment for the FAO that worldwide, some 317 Mt of cereals, 245 Mt of roots and tubers, 43 Mt of oilseeds and pulses, 492 Mt of fruit & vegetables, 61 Mt of meat, 17 Mt of fish and seafood, and 120 Mt of milk and eggs are wasted annually. In low-income countries, with warm and humid climates, rodents, parasites and fungi are responsible for most losses, i.e., for reasons largely equivalent to the lack of or inadequacy of storage facilities. To reduce food losses, Gustavsson et al. (2011) suggest focusing on the early supply chain, i.e., to improve poor infrastructure and transportation, and to address the lack of refrigeration.

In developed countries, food losses mostly occur late in the supply chain, often because of aesthetic aspects, as the colour, shape or cleanliness of foods determines their marketability (Gustavsson et al., 2011). Even though this is not mentioned by the authors, there are also norm considerations, i.e., the size, weight or shape of produce. Other reasons for food losses include transport, and, in retail, poor temperature management (too cold/too warm). In kitchens, the main reasons for food losses are the limited attention paid to waste issues, as well as food safety legislation, forbidding, for example, the re-use of specific food items (Gustavsson et al., 2011). In this context, much attention has been paid to best-before dates, which have relevance mostly in households, though depending on country, restaurants may also be held to consider best-before dates.

As this introduction outlines, food waste reductions need to be achieved along the entire supply chain. There is also a strong case to be made for food waste reductions in

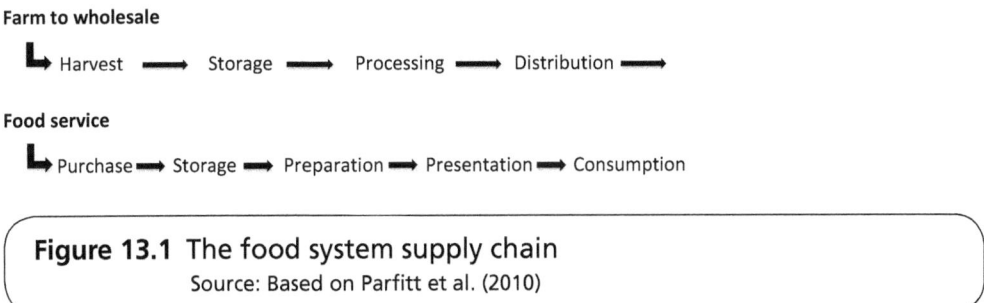

Figure 13.1 The food system supply chain
Source: Based on Parfitt et al. (2010)

restaurants, where much food is lost as a result of suboptimal purchasing, storage and preparation procedures (United Against Waste, 2015). Avoiding food losses can also be based on an avoidance hierarchy as shown in Figure 13.2: Prevention of food waste is more important than re-use (human consumption), which again is better than recycling (animal feed), other recovery (e.g., compost, energy) and disposal. In this context, it is useful to distinguish between avoidable, partially avoidable and unavoidable food waste. The WRAP report (Quested & Johnson, 2009, p. 4) describes these as "food and drink thrown away that was, at some point prior to disposal, edible (e.g. slice of bread, apples, meat)" (*avoidable food waste*); "food and drink that some people eat and others do not (e.g. bread crusts), or that can be eaten when a food is prepared in one way but not in another (e.g. potato skins)" (*possibly avoidable food waste*) and "waste arising from food or drink preparation that is not, and has not been, edible under normal circumstances (e.g. meat bones, eggshells, pineapple skin, tea bags)" (*unavoidable food waste*).

Marthinsen et al. (2012) underline that it is also important to distinguish between different types of food services. These include (a) *hotels, restaurants and cafés* that often operate under similar conditions, i.e., catering to a market of continuously changing customers, including a share of international business or leisure travellers; (b) *canteens and catering*, i.e., foodservice provisions for employees in companies or guests partaking in events and (c) *the public and private sector*, including schools, hospitals, nursing homes or administrations. Various related service sectors may be included in food waste avoidance strategies because they are usually overlooked, yet important in terms of the types of food served, or the share of food that goes to waste. Table 13.1 outlines the operational and waste characteristics of different foodservice organizations which provides some of the indications of the corresponding amount of food waste per week and some of the issues businesses face in being able to reduce waste. Marthinsen et al. (2012) also mention fuel stations with their focus on meat-based fast foods catering to specific takeaway markets; shops selling fast food; retail chains such as supermarkets offering takeaway foods and retailers with food offers such as IKEA's restaurants. All of these food services compete with restaurants, cafés and canteens, and usually on the basis of foods focused on animal protein, sourced at very low prices.

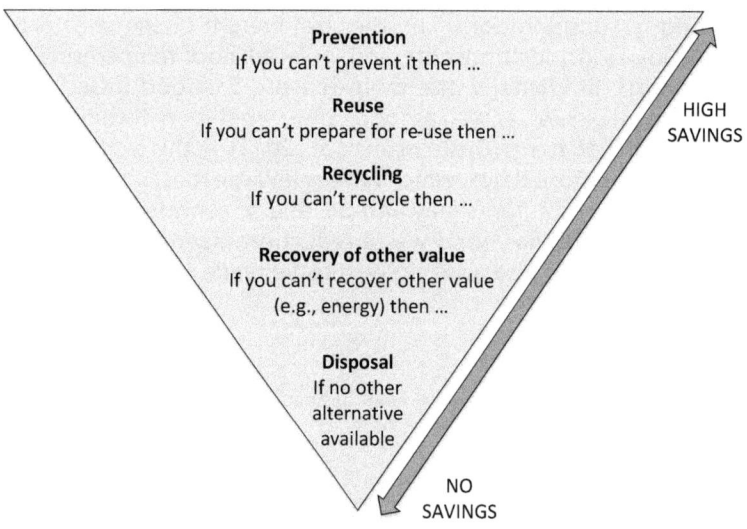

Figure 13.2 Food waste prevention hierarchy
Source: Based on Papargyropoulou et al. (2014)

Table 13.1 Operational and waste characteristics of different foodservice businesses

Source: After Resource Efficient Scotland (2017)

Type of food service	Style of food	Trading hours	Space for waste	Staff	Waste levels	Estimated weekly food waste
Café	Food prepared to order, mainly snacks and sandwiches	Six-day trading equivalent to 20 full covers per day/120 covers per week	Limited space for waste treatment Limited equipment budget	Low staff levels	Relatively low food waste from customers	Approx. 40–60 kg per week
Hotel	Full meal service including buffet breakfast as well as lunch and dinner Regular catered functions for up to 500 guests, average two per week	Seven-day trading, equivalent to 260 full covers per day/1,820 covers per week	Space available for waste storage and treatment	Staff available for food waste responsibilities as part of wider duties	Relatively high levels of food waste from buffet and function trade	Approx. 750–900 kg per week
Institutional canteen	All day buffet style food service Significant amounts of pre-prepared food at peak meal times	Five-day trading, equivalent to 120 full covers per day/600 covers per week	Kitchen and outside space available for food waste treatment and storage	Some staff time available for food waste responsibilities as part of wider duties	Relatively high volumes of food waste from servery format	Approx. 300–500 kg per week

Table 13.2 Catalysts and barriers to food waste avoidance

Source: Marthinsen et al. (2012)

Food waste avoidance catalysts	• High media and guest attention to the issue of avoidable food waste
	• Concrete customer demands for improvements and environmental standards
	• Long-term strategies and commitments made by the larger operators to different certifications, eco labels, green key, etc.
	• Smaller operates will follow the leaders based on best practice work within the sector
	• Reducing avoidable food waste often gives a reduction in costs
Food waste avoidance barriers	• There are still some conflicts of interest between the two ambitions: food safety vs avoidable food waste prevention. It is thus a need to join forces and build bridges between two important goals for society. Still it is regarded too easy to discard edible food!
	• Discarding food is relatively cheap and thus not an important factor to reduce avoidable food waste compared to the potential extra revenues by selling more food available

A key question for the food service is why it should engage in waste avoidance. Previous chapters in this book have outlined reasons ranging from involving staff, to customer expectations, to business economics (Martinez-Sanchez et al., 2016; see also Table 13.2). United Against Waste (2018) calculated, for example, that hotels, restaurants and canteen kitchens in Austria produced 185,000 t of food waste, with a value of €380 million. The economic loss for restaurants is significant. A study of two restaurants in Switzerland concluded, for example, that 7.7%–10.7% of all food purchases were wasted, primarily because of too large portion sizes. The authors found that 78%–92% of this could be avoided, amounting to 10.5–16.5 tonnes of edible food per year, with an economic value of approximately US$85,000 per year and restaurant (Betz et al., 2015). For restaurants, strategies to avoid food waste can thus be profitably combined with economic considerations.

In a study of the hospitality sector in the Nordic countries, Marthinsen et al. (2012) found that many businesses were already certified or eco-labelled, prioritized waste sorting, sought to reduce avoidable food waste and relied on action plans to avoid food losses. There was also a low interest in governmental instruments other than informational campaigns. Businesses reported that they focused on targets, routines for portion size, education of staff, awareness campaigns and menu planning to reduce food waste levels. Yet, Marthinsen et al. (2012) concluded that of the 680,000 tonnes of food waste generated by the hospitality sector in Finland, Sweden, Norway and Denmark, 456,000 tonnes represent avoidable waste.

Avoiding waste in hospitality: an overview

An overview of strategies to reduce food waste in hospitality services is provided in Figure 13.3. The figure is an overview of intervention stages, as discussed in subsequent sections as well as in Chapter 14 (Minimizing waste: behaviour), and shows that waste avoidance strategies can focus on three stages, which are here described as pre-kitchen, kitchen & service as well as post-kitchen. Within each of these stages, there exist different options to address food waste through planning, management, technology, services and policies. Combined, these have a considerable potential for foodservice providers to reduce food waste to insignificant quantities.

Pre-kitchen stages include demand forecasting, procurement, stock management and menu design. *Demand forecasting* has great relevance for procurement and

	Pre-kitchen			
Stage	*Demand forecasting*	*Procurement*	*Stock management*	*Menu design*
Measure	- Inhouse statistics - Use of apps	- Delivery times - Producer purchases - Apps	- Shelf-live balance - Seasonal produce - Produce with short best-by dates - Apps	- Low-CO_2 - Re-use - Seasonal - Vegetable-based - A la carte - Apps
Training	M, C, K	M, C, K	M, C, K	M, C

⬇

	Kitchen & service			
Stage	*Planning & technology*	*Cooking*	*Recommendations*	*Plating*
Measure	- Demand response - Kitchen equipment	- Routines - Dish complexity	- Vegetarian options - Daily specials - Portion size	- Portion size - Plate presentation
Training	M, C, K	C, K	C, K, S	C, K

⬇

	Post-kitchen			
Stage	*Leftovers*	*Overproduction*	*After services*	
Measure	- Food containers	- Last-minute sales - Staff meals - Food bank donations	- Energy recovery	
Training	S	K	K	

M: Management; C: Chefs; K: Kitchen staff; S: Service staff

Figure 13.3 Overview of options for food waste avoidance management
Source: Based on Filimonau and De Coteau (2019)

production, as food services should seek to neither overstock nor overproduce. For many restaurant types, demand will depend on factors that are not necessarily considered in daily planning routines, such as local events, bank holidays or specific weather conditions. Yet, these can have great relevance for customer turnout, but they are difficult to consider in advance. For example, reliable weather forecasts are only available for about a week, and specific weather conditions in a location may deviate from more general forecasts. Yet, the difference in turnout between a sunny and a rainy day can be significant. For this reason, in-house statistics can help to supplement "gut feeling" on expected demand, and apps will help to guide decisions based on earlier demand. To optimize demand forecasting requires management, chefs and kitchen staff to cooperate. Where the problem is advanced with the help of technology or statistics, this may also require staff training.

Procurement refers to orders of produce, which means that managers and chefs have to balance the amount of in particular fresh produce with delivery times (see also Chapter 7). This is even more complicated where fresh produce is sourced directly from farmers. Apps can help staff to organize procurement procedures, for instance by keeping track of available foodstuffs. They also require training of management, chefs and kitchen staff. *Stock management* can help to balance products with shorter and longer shelf lives, and to include a significant share of fresh, seasonal produce. Best-before dates and the amount of food available can be tracked via apps. For larger restaurants, this also opens up interesting opportunities to source produce with short shelf lives from wholesalers, with a view to reducing waste higher up in the food value chain, and at a very reasonable cost. For instance, a wholesaler overstocking of tomatoes can theoretically sell these to a restaurant turning these into a tomato-based soup, salad or side-dish, which can also be offered as a daily special. New apps can facilitate such transactions. Finally, *menu design* is of importance with regard to shorter and longer perspectives, i.e., to plan attractive menus in advance, often covering an entire week if daily changing courses are offered, and also with a view to including foodstuffs that need to be used because they approach best-before dates. Menu design should consider a wide range of aspects: The menus offered should include foodstuffs low in CO_2, i.e., seasonal, local produce and limited amounts of meats and other forms of animal protein. Where this is necessary and feasible, overproduction from previous days should be re-used. A la carte serving is generally preferable to buffets. Again, apps can be used to minimize waste. Training comprises in particular managers and chefs, i.e., those in charge of menu design and planning.

The stage 'kitchen & service' offers to reduce food waste during planning, through the introduction of innovative technology, with regard to cooking routines, recommendations made to guests and plating. More specifically, all kitchens should be equipped with state-of-the-art *technology* to reduce energy use. As an example, induction-based cooking is vastly more energy-efficient than gas or conventional cooking (see Chapter 12). This is also true for refrigeration and freezing. New technologies help avoid food losses, which may, for instance, occur because of broken cold chains: New technologies will automatically indicate a broken cold chain. In recent years, a wide range of new technologies have also become available that help avoiding, reusing and recycling food waste. For instance, best-before dates can be recorded and chefs be informed about foodstuffs that need to be used, while order control applications can automatically consider the existing storage to avoid overstocking.

Planning includes the assessment of demand for specific dishes to avoid overproduction, as well as the content and composition of dishes with regard to meat to side-dish ratios, or the number of vegetarian and vegan dishes available. Planning may be considered an issue for management, chefs and kitchen staff. *Cooking* refers to routines that conserve energy and reduce waste. For example, frozen products should not be thawed under running warm water. Peels and other preparation-related food waste should be kept to a minimum, and some of the waste may be re-used (bones for broth, for example). Training on these issues is mostly required for chefs and kitchen staff. *Recommendations* are very important to increase the share of vegetarian choices; to support sales of daily specials that cannot be stored or contain foodstuffs with short best-before dates as well as with regard to portion size, where restaurants may offer different options adjusted to appetites. Apart from chefs and kitchen staff, recommendations are a field that requires the training of service staff. Finally, *plating* can also refer to portion size where these are standardized, i.e., to only offer the amount of food guests will likely eat, as well as to present foods in a way that makes plates seem full and attractive. Training is mostly relevant for chefs and kitchen staff.

The post-kitchen food waste avoidance stage is concerned with leftovers, overproduction and after services. For example, customers may not have eaten all of the food served, even in a situation where portion sizes are already adjusted to average appetites. In such situations, patrons can be offered food containers to take home *leftovers*. As leftovers are a sensitive issue, service staff have to be trained to suggest food containers sensibly. *Overproduction* refers to production that remains uneaten, for which there may be different reasons. Chefs may have wrongly guessed popular choices or customer numbers. Overproduction does not have to be discarded, however, as it can be sold in last-minute sales to customers who will fetch, though not eat the food at the restaurant. Overproduction may also be offered to staff, or food banks. There are now many apps available to organize such transactions. This requires training, in particular, kitchen staff. Finally, *after services* refers to all foods that cannot be used for human consumption. Usually, this is food waste that would have to be disposed, though there are now many options to at least recover the energy contained in the food waste, by using the waste for biogas production (Box 13.3). Fats and oils may be recovered for similar purposes. Other organic waste may be composted. Table 13.2 provides an overview of the different stages. The following sections discuss opportunities in greater detail, as they pertain to technology and management, while Chapter 14 focuses on the role of staff and consumer behaviour in minimizing waste.

Box 13.3 Monklands Hospital, Airdrie, Scotland

Monklands, a district general hospital with a 24-hour accident and emergency department and 521 inpatient beds, was used as a case study by the Scottish Government's Resource Efficient Scotland programme to illustrate the way in which institutional food providers can better manage waste. Between 300 kg and 400 kg of food waste is collected daily by the hospital in a vacuum processor system. It was then transported into an adjacent vacuum waste storage tank for collection by a tanker. At Monklands, the waste slurry was collected weekly and recycled into biogas for generating electricity at a nearby anaerobic digestion

> plant, although it can also be used for fertilizer. According to the hospital's Catering Services Manager, Peter King,
>
>> There are a lot of waste handling systems out there … This one ticked a lot of boxes including savings on water and electricity, reduced carbon footprint and a rebate from the water board because we are no longer putting food waste down the drains. We also get duty of care paperwork from the waste processor. We are a hospital and we have to watch what we do with our food waste. We did look at alternatives but chose this system because it is hygienic, fully sealed and includes the tank housing, which has its own heating, lighting and odour control.
>>
>> Source: Resource Efficient Scotland (2017)

Understanding food waste in food services

A considerable number of reports from mostly European organizations have analyzed sources of food waste. In an Austrian study, United Against Waste (2018) found that plate leftovers constituted the most significant source of food waste in canteen kitchens (Figure 13.4). In accommodation and restaurants, preparation losses accounted for most

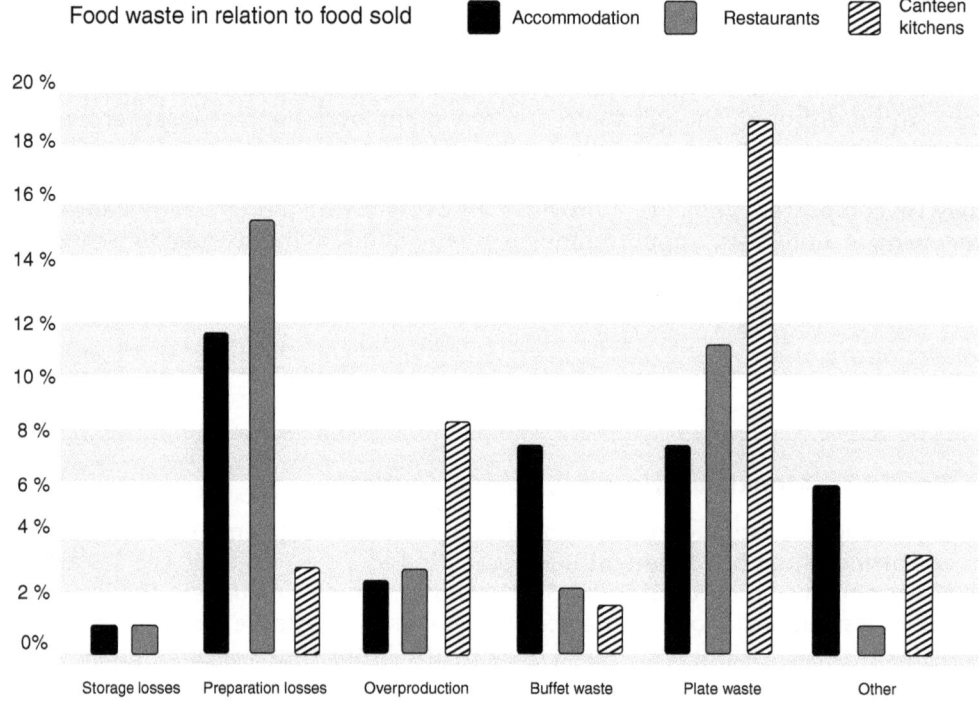

Figure 13.4 Food waste as share of food purchases
Source: Based on United Against Waste (2018)

of the food waste. This comparison indicates that canteen kitchens prepare food more efficiently, though the portion sizes served are too large. Other reasons for food waste include overproduction, a problem mostly for canteen kitchens as well as buffet leftovers as a significant source of waste in accommodation. These figures suggest that there is an important difference between accommodation, restaurants and canteen kitchens in terms of the efficiency with which food is prepared, offered and eaten. Strategies to reduce food waste should thus be developed individually for each of these food subsectors.

As 5%–45% of all food go to waste, figures raise the question as to whether restaurants and other food providers cook more efficiently than people at home. While no direct comparisons appear to exist, data on food consumption in some hotels seems to suggest that the volumes consumed in holiday contexts are significantly higher than at home (Gössling & Peeters, 2015). There is also a qualitative implication, as the food wasted in restaurants includes a high share of meat and fish (15%), while in accommodation, it is milk products (10%) that represent a significant share of losses (United Against Waste, 2018). Meat, fish and milk products are higher-order foods that have greater environmental implications than, for instance, vegetables or salads. United Against Waste (2018) also points at a high share of beverages going to waste, accounting for 36% of food waste in accommodation, and 12% in restaurants. This situation may be different in other service sectors, such as fuel stations offering takeaway food (Box 13.4).

An aspect of food waste that is not often discussed is wastewater. Restaurant wastewater contains organic, suspended solids, oil and grease. Large quantities of wastewater are also produced on cruise ships, where sewage and other wastewater are not usually treated separately (Box 13.5). Wastewater is also important in restaurants because oil and grease can coat wastewater pipes and subsequently clog these, which is a problem specifically in developing countries where oil and grease traps may not be legislated or available (Singh et al., 2014). Notably, wastewater can also contain detergents or chemicals used to clean rooms or to wash laundry. Where wastewater

---

Box 13.4 Food losses in fuel stations

Fuel stations in many countries have sought to increase sales of food, as a result of the small profit margins on fuel sales, as well as to make fuel stations more attractive to 'consumers-on-the-go' (Azimont & Araujo, 2010). Apart from products with longer shelf lives, such as beverages, candy or crisps, fuel stations often offer takeaway food choices, which are usually focused on meats (hot dogs or hamburgers). As Marthinsen et al. (2012) outline, fuel stations can have important roles in food sales, with data for Norway indicating that close to 3% of all meats distributed in the country are bought by fuel stations and fast-food stalls. More recently, some fuel stations have also started to carry a range of products with short shelf lives, such as bread and pastry, or hot food such as wraps, sushi or salads. Often, consumer interest in these foods has remained low, and anecdotal evidence suggests that a large share of these foods is discarded (Zeit Online, 2020). Yet, the system is maintained for fear of competing fuel stations appearing to offer a better service, or because of hopes for customers to develop a taste for fuel station food. While no studies exist as yet on the phenomenon, newspaper reports have indicated that a major share of the food on offer is lost (Zeit Online, 2020).

> **Box 13.5 Food waste management on cruise ships**
>
> Cruise ship kitchens cater to several thousand passengers and staff, i.e., they provide food to the equivalent of a small city. Significant pollution has been linked to nutrient loads from food waste (Wilewska-Bien et al., 2016). As an example of the scale of food waste generation, Cruise line Costa reports food waste amounting to 216 g per meal (Costa Cruises, 2018). Multiplied with the 54 million meals prepared per year on the costa fleet, the overall total amount of food waste is close to 12,000 tonnes per year. Notably, a study of three board restaurants showed that the crew produced more waste per person and meal than cruise passengers (Futouris, 2019). The study also revealed that more than half of all food waste was overproduction-related, and hence avoidable. Plate waste made up another 18% of the food waste – also avoidable – while production waste, which may be only partially avoidable, accounted for 29%. Only 2% of food was lost as a result of storage or exceeded best-before dates (Futouris, 2019).
>
> Cruise ships also produce significant amounts of wastewater, at around 200 L per passenger per day; it is not clear which share is produced by kitchens, however (Costa Cruises, 2018). As cruise lines are increasingly aware of the issue of food waste, they have recently sought to reduce volumes. For example, Costa Cruises (2018) engages in a 4GOODFOOD campaign to reduce food waste, by training crew members and a "taste don't waste" campaign directed at guests. Yet, Costa's data indicates that for every meal eaten, half a meal (216 g per person) goes to waste. Cruise ships sometimes burn food waste to reduce their volume as storage capacity is limited, a process that requires significant amounts of diesel.
>
> On a smaller scale, food waste problems are also relevant for ferries. An example is Viking Line, a smaller ferry service operating in the North and Baltic Seas, which reports having recycled the equivalent of 1,500 tonnes of used oils in 2017 (Viking Line, 2019). The ferry line reports that a share of waste is burned or disposed of, indicating that the ferry and cruise industries still have a long way to go in avoiding food waste to levels that can be considered sustainable.

remains untreated, it can have detrimental environmental impacts. Singh et al. (2014) recommend that hotels and restaurants have oil and grease traps, as well as settling tanks and potentially even septic tanks, where treatment plants are unavailable.

Stages in the avoidance of food waste

As individual studies of food waste show (Duursma et al., 2016), there can be great differences in daily waste levels, depending on the amount of food prepared, actual demand, as well as food components. Duursma et al. (2016) found, for example, that the food going to waste varied for individual components between 0.8% and 78% on a daily basis, and between 6.9% and 21.7% when considering longer-term averages. The study illustrates the importance of planning and backup plans to recover foods not sold. The authors also conclude that measurement procedures are in itself a strategy to reduce food waste, as they increase staff awareness. They note that even if chefs manage to save a few hundred grams of food per day, this will accumulate to hundreds of kilos per year, with corresponding economic savings.

Measuring and evaluating food waste

To reduce the share of food waste, various measures have been suggested. All start with building awareness, for which food waste measurement is a valuable introductory strategy. Where staff is involved, and where reduction targets are set – possibly in combination with incentives for staff if goals are met – this will usually have the effect of reducing waste on the basis of awareness-building alone (Marthinsen et al., 2012; United Against Waste, 2018).

Planning and preparation

Preparation-related food waste is responsible for 45% of overall totals in restaurants, and 31% in accommodation (United Against Waste, 2018). This is because peels and other food parts considered not servable are usually discarded, even though they can be used for various purposes, including soups, sauces, puree or to increase tastiness. To minimize the amount of discarded food it is thus necessary to educate chefs on options to use food remains such as peels and to collect items in separated boxes. Where this is part of running a restaurant or the education of chefs, it will put menu planning high on the agenda for food waste reduction. Marthinsen et al. (2012) report, for example, that for a majority of chefs in Nordic countries, purchasing routines and menu planning are the most important strategies for restaurants to reduce food waste. Planning production, for instance with regard to bank holidays or expected weather conditions, is also key in avoiding food losses. The latter can also involve cooking on demand, for instance for breakfast, where specific foods such as eggs and bacon may only be fried on request. Notably, overproduction is an issue that accounts for 8%–9% of food waste in restaurants and accommodation (United Against Waste, 2018). This can be a result of specific components or side-dishes remaining unused because of a lack of demand or erroneous planning. For some foodstuffs, such as soups, weather conditions may have great influence on demand. Overproduction may often be discarded, even though it may be stored for later consumption, be re-used or given away to staff or charity. Three strategies, in particular, can help minimize food waste related to overproduction, i.e., to (a) limit the pre-preparation of foods to the number of portions that are guaranteed to be sold; (b) re-use leftovers in new dishes where this is feasible and (c) offer unsold dishes to staff as a free bonus or give these to charity. Surprise menus may also be a suitable option to use food remains (Box 13.6).

Stocking food

A share of food is lost because of purchasing and stocking routines. Marthinsen et al. (2012) report that in most hotels and restaurants, there is a target of a ten-day rotation of stocks, based on first-in, first-out principles. Where such routines are followed, food rarely expires by date, and Marthinsen et al. (2012) conclude that food losses as a result of best-before dates being passed are not a significant issue in the hospitality sector in the Nordic Countries. This is also confirmed for other sectors, such as cruises (Futouris, 2019).

Buffet management

Buffets are a major source of food waste, though they are often an important element of the hotel experience, and thus difficult to abandon. Alternatives, such as individually ordered breakfasts, are also costlier to arrange, as they require more preparation time and service. As outlined by United Against Waste (2018), buffet waste can amount to

> **Box 13.6 Food remains as surprise menu**
>
> In many restaurants, a mixture of dishes remains unused, specifically in small family businesses that keep closed one day in the week. Instead of discarding the food, restaurant Steirereck am Pogusch in Austria invented "Restl-Essen", the food remains in the evening (United Against Waste, 2018). As the restaurant keeps closed on Monday, as is still practiced in many central European restaurants, the Sunday evening offer is a reasonably priced three-course surprise menu for €10. As reported by the restaurant, the usually slow Sunday evening has become widely popular, allowing the restaurant to sell remaining foods while also increasing turnover. The example also illustrates the importance of understanding guest preferences, as the success of the surprise menu was not expected. Dialogue with guests, also with regard to portion size, is thus an important part of avoiding food loss (Marthinsen et al., 2012).

21% of food losses in accommodation and 7% in restaurants. This indicates that restaurants are more efficient in offering buffets. Several observations are relevant with regard to food waste minimization. First of all, most countries have legislation prohibiting the re-use of food that has been on buffet display. There is also an expectation by guests to be presented with a wide range of offers, as buffets often contain more than 150 food components (Gössling, 2010). Even when guests arrive late for the buffet, they expect to be served the same components as earlier guests, which means that a share of food will always represent leftovers. Decorations will also often be disposed after buffets have been closed. Various management options can help reducing buffet waste:

- Offer smaller unit sizes and more frequent refills.
- Use smaller and flatter bowls and plates to offer foods.
- Inform about food content to avoid guests taking food they do not like.
- Highlight foodstuffs with lower environmental impacts to encourage their use.
- Do not use food as decoration.
- Offer drinks out of machines.
- Offer remaining food on buffets to staff as a free breakfast/lunch/dinner.

Other strategies to reduce food waste

There are many other strategies to avoid food waste, also considering food types. For instance, a strawberry flown to Austria from Egypt will have a high carbon footprint for transportation. If this strawberry goes to waste, the impact is significantly greater than losing a strawberry grown in Austria. Kitchen staff should thus be aware of seasons and purchase foodstuffs with a view to minimizing energy use for transportation, storage and refrigeration (Tables 13.3a and 13.3b).

There are also several other options to reduce food waste through management, which will always be based on an educated and motivated staff. For any business with an interest to reduce food waste, staff training and motivation is thus a valuable and necessary investment. United Against Waste (2018) also highlights that communication processes have great relevance for waste avoidance, i.e., discussions between service and kitchen to understand guest expectations and food waste amounts. Therefore, the training and education of staff is an important part of the behavioural changes surrounding waste management (see Chapter 14).

Table 13.3a Seasonal calendar for fruit in Northern Italy

Source: Futouris (2018)

Fruits	January	February	March	April	May	June	July	August	September	October	November	December
Apple	X					X	X	X	X	X	X	X
Apricot					X	X	X	X				
Blackberry							X	X	X			
Blueberry							X	X	X			
Cherry					X	X	X					
Chestnut									X	X		
Fig						X	X	X	X			
Grape									X	X	X	
Kaki									X	X		
Melon						X	X	X	X			
Peach					X	X	X	X	X			
Pear						X	X	X	X	X	X	X
Plum						X	X	X	X			
Raspberry						X	X	X	X			
Redcurrant								X	X			
Watermelon					X	X	X	X				
Strawberry				X	X	X						

Table 13.3b Seasonal calendar for fruit in Canterbury, New Zealand

Source: Seasonal calendar for fruits grown on Michael Hall's farming property, Tai Tapu, Canterbury, New Zealand

Fruits	January	February	March	April	May	June	July	August	September	October	November	December
Almond			X	X								
Apple	X	X	X	X	X							X
Apricot	X	X										
Blackberry			X	X								
Blackcurrant	X										X	X
Cherry											X	X
Chestnut				X	X							
Chilean Guava				X								
Feijoa					X	X						
Fig		X	X	X	X							
Grape			X	X								
Grapefruit	X							X	X	X	X	X
Hazelnut			X	X				X	X			
Lemon	X	X	X	X	X	X	X	X	X	X	X	X
Mandarin	X	X	X						X	X	X	X

Fruits	January	February	March	April	May	June	July	August	September	October	November	December
Medlar					X	X						
Melon			X	X								
Nashi		X	X									
Orange	X	X					X	X	X	X	X	X
Peach		X	X	X								
Peachcot			X	X								
Pear	X	X	X	X								X
Persimmon				X	X							
Plum	X	X	X									X
Raspberry	X										X	X
Redcurrant											X	X
Strawberry	X	X	X	X							X	X
Walnut			X	X								

Technology to avoid food waste

Various technologies exist to manage stored food and to control best-before dates. These can help avoid food losses, as there is a constant control of the amounts of food available. Planning tools can also be used to reduce the carbon content of menus, or to donate leftovers to food banks (Table 13.4). As highlighted by Davies and Legg (2018), food sharing initiatives have grown in many parts of the world and are increasingly facilitated by apps and websites.

While many of these websites and apps help avoid food waste, it deserves to be mentioned that many more are designed to increase the efficiency of restaurants and to cater to growing guest expectations. For example, phone charging stations or guest WIFI zones are considered important in some restaurant types, while in others, loyalty and reward programs are implemented to increase the share of returning guests. Restaurants face a cost of technology solutions as diverse as wait list management, staffing, reservations, inventory management, payments, marketing or tablet point of service platforms. Given the low profitability of many restaurants, this also means that restaurants seek to cut the cost of foodstuffs. An alternative may be to reduce waste amounts, i.e., to use technology to realize corresponding savings. A number of examples are outlined in the following.

Tracking waste

Technical solutions include apps that track, record and analyze waste. For instance, Winnow is a technical installation including a camera and scales that can detect and weigh the food waste type thrown away. It is connected to software that analyzes the food waste to determine food types, amounts and value, as well as the time and date. This helps restaurants to understand plate waste or overproduction and provides a basis for menu planning, as well as the adjustment of portion sizes (Winnowsolutions.com). The program automatically increases awareness of food waste, and educates staff directly (learning about the application, its functioning and purpose) as well as indirectly (learning how food waste can be avoided through different measures).

Table 13.4 Examples of websites and apps reducing food waste

- Schoox.com – App-based employee education
- Best Before – App providing an overview of best-by dates
- Fridge Pal – App creating food inventory and shopping lists
- United Against Waste – Website tool to assess economic value of 'saved' food
- Spoiler Alert – B2B trading of excess food through discount sales or donations
- Matsmart.se – Website offering excess production, foods about to expire, seasonal foods or food in old packaging at 20%–90% below retail price
- Eaternity.org – Website helping restaurants to assess the carbon content of their menus
- Gocopia.com – App helping restaurants to assess food waste and make donations
- RescuingLeftoverCuisin – Website organizing food donations
- MealConnect – Website organizing food donations

E-water

Electrolyzed water is an option to avoid other forms of chemical sanitizers, which are detrimental to human health, more environmentally harmful, costly, inefficient, affecting food quality or difficult to remove in treatment plants (Rahman et al., 2016). Electrolyzed water is tap water that may contain HOCl (for use as sanitizer) or NaOH (for use as cleaner), both of which can be produced through electrolyzing salt (NaCl) dissolved in water. HOCl acts as a microbial agent that penetrates the membrane of viruses, bacteria, fungi and spores, and damages membrane, DNA and enzyme activity within very short periods of time of less than 20 seconds. Electrolyzed water has been shown to efficiently eliminate microorganisms, though it is environmentally harmless and does not negatively affect human health. Rahman et al. (2016) conclude that electrolyzed water has great potential in food industries to reduce impacts. Other applications, such as stabilized aqueous ozone – ozone made from oxygen and enriched and solved in water – can also be used for cleaning purposes to eliminate viruses, bacteria or fungi. Ozone dissolved in water converts back to water and oxygen and is now offered as a cleaning solution by companies such as Tersano.com.

Cold chains

Various innovations are currently developed by universities, starts-ups and the food sector. Intelligent food packaging is expected to control storage times and temperature. Broken cooling chains are the main reason for the loss of food and can be constantly controlled by intelligent packaging. Warning systems that inform about food that is about to expire are another option to make sure no produce is lost, as they allow chefs to design a daily menu to use the food, or to donate the item to a food bank. Such applications are offered by companies such as Whywaste.com.

Excess food

Portals such as Foodloopz.se help trading in excess food. Sometimes, food producers, retailers or others may have specific types of excess food that cannot be sold quick enough through conventional market channels. This may also include foodstuffs that are difficult to sell due to their shape or size. Restaurants and hotels with buffets can prepare and use comparably large volumes of such produce, specifically food types with short shelf lives, such as certain vegetables, fruits or fish. This offers new opportunities for purchasing food that would otherwise go to waste, and to enrich buffets or to design daily specials on the basis of very reasonably priced produce.

Excess production that has not been sold can be offered through app to customers willing to buy lunch or dinner at competitive prices. For example, the Swedish app Karma.life is used by 7,500 companies including hotels, restaurants, cafés, supermarkets and retailers, and has 1.1 million users. The app registers and offers unsold food to customers coming to pick it up at the foodservice provider. According to the app, this has reduced food waste by 50%–80% and generated an additional average revenue of €30,000–€40,000 per year and business. As a side effect, many customers are known to also buy other products at normal prices when picking up their food. A similar app is offered by Resqclub.com or Toogoodtogo.co.uk.

A growing number of start-ups focus on the use of produce not considered suitable for sale because of concerns regarding its shape or look, overproduction or waste side products. ReFed.com, an organization that tracks developments in the food waste industry, suggests that there are many new businesses and non-profit outfits that transform food. For example, fruit and vegetables can be used to produce juices (e.g., organizations such as Rescued.se; WrtmInWtr.com) or fruit snacks. Barnana.com transforms bruised, overripe or imperfect bananas into dehydrated banana snacks. Regrained.com uses grains from beer brewing to create bars rich in protein, fibre and nutrients. A growing number of new solutions to avoiding food waste by transforming raw materials into healthy products with longer shelf lives seem to come into existence every year.

Box 13.7   Waste distribution charities

Many restaurants and foodservice businesses donate their food surplus and sometimes their time to food waste distribution charities and it is an important part of the role that restaurants can play in their communities (see Chapter 15). Such charities arguably only became even more important as a result of the economic impacts of COVID-19. Prior to the pandemic, the UK national network of 18 independent food distribution charities Fareshare (https://fareshare.org.uk) was usually delivering enough food to make one meal a week through its network of charities, but as of July 2020 delivering enough for two million. According to Seal (2020), "In the first week of lockdown, the charity saw a short-lived crash in its normal supermarket fresh food surpluses but was almost overwhelmed by catering industry donations – a 1,500% increase on last April".

Another waste-food redistribution charity, City Harvest (www.cityharvest.org.uk), which provides food support to over 300 organizations in London also doubled its usual output. In this case, because of COVID-19 business restrictions to their normal customers, hotel and catering kitchens were loaned by Crystal Palace football club, the Savoy hotel, a Mayfair private members' club and Wimbledon's All England Lawn Tennis Club to create 1.4m meals by July 2020 (Seal, 2020). According to Chef Lauren Everet who works at the Soup Kitchen (https://soupkitchenlondon.org/#section-aboutus), a resource for the homeless, elderly, lonely and vulnerable on Tottenham Court Road in London, which is supplied by City Harvest.

> We've seen the young, 18–21-year-olds, and many pension-age guests. We've seen people who obviously haven't been sleeping rough very long, and some who look as if they're on the cusp of homelessness. We had 161 people in recently, which was a new record for us, but we fed them all. There is a small percentage of people who are what we call 'food poor': they may afford accommodation, but cannot afford bills, transport and food. We've given them a food parcel to take home that lasts a week to 10 days.
>
> (quoted in Seal, 2020)

Lack of available cool storage facilities during COVID-19 also meant that some restaurant foods were donated to food charities because they were unable to be used. The food redistribution charity REfUSE (https://refusedurham.org.uk), in Chester-le-Street in County Durham, England, operates a 'Pay As You Feel' community cafe and restaurant in Chester-le-Street, a private catering brand Conscious Kitchen and a Waste-Not Box delivery scheme, along with its education and partnership programmes. According to Mim Skinner from REfUSE, "Our staples are usually milk and bread. Now we are getting high levels of luxury products – manchego, mozzarella and parmesan – and only a few tins of beans. This morning we got 300 pheasant breasts meant for restaurants" (quoted in Seal, 2020). Nevertheless, according to food waste campaigner Tristam Stuart (www.tristramstuart.co.uk) who collects food for the food waste charities Feedback (https://feedbackglobal.org) and Food for All (https://foodforalluk.com), "Redistribution should never be regarded as the solution to poverty or hunger, and it certainly isn't a viable solution to food waste. … At best, redistribution organisations are sticking plasters with big notices on them saying, 'We need to restructure the food system'" (quoted in Seal, 2020).

Unavoidable food waste

Depending on the production stage and the type of food waste produced, different options exist to optimally use harvest residuals, food processing residues, unsalable food or pre- and post-cooking kitchen waste, including leftovers, expired food or plate waste (Xu et al., 2018). Post-harvest residuals, which may include fruits, vegetables or fish, can be converted into animal feed, or be used for biodiesel or methane production on the basis of anaerobic digestion. Food processing residues, including peels, slaughterhouse waste, cheese whey or brewery waste, can be donated, or be used as animal feed, for biofuel or methane production, or be turned into compost.

Most relevant for restaurants are unsalable foods as well as pre- and post-cooking kitchen waste. Unsalable foods can be turned into animal feed or be used for methane production, as well as compost. Pre- and post-cooking kitchen wastes can be donated or be used for methane production. Recyclable cooking oils can constitute a large share of food waste, and be re-used for different purposes such as biofuel production, as their energy content is high. Xu et al. (2018) outline that anaerobic digestion to generate biogas is not currently a major part of food waste re-use, as there are many challenges regarding the technical process of methane production. Yet, they conclude that anaerobic digestion may become a more frequently used technique for energy recovery from food waste in the future. This will also be a question of national policies, as for instance China and South Korea have built food waste-to-biogas sectors, along with waste management systems to decrease food waste volumes (de Clercq et al., 2017). This, however, may often be a question of national policies. For instance, Marthinsen et al. (2012) outlined for the Nordic countries that many hotels already separated kitchen waste for use in compost or biogas.

Generally, food waste should never go to landfill. There are many options to turn it into energy or compost with the help of grinders and digestors. For example, Grind2Energy is a food waste grinder that can produce a slurry that can go to biogas utilities using anaerobic digestion to produce methane. Solutions to reduce food waste that needs to be disposed of, for instance in landfill sites where composting or biogas options do not exist, also include bio-digesters that reduce the quantity of food waste by separating water from food waste through microbial digestion (e.g., see feedtheorca.com; waste2-0.com).

> **Box 13.8 FAO food loss and waste database**
>
> Sustainable Development Goal Indicator 12.3 states "By 2030, to halve per capita global food waste at the retail and consumer levels and reduce food losses along production and supply chains, including post-harvest losses" (FAO, 2019c, p. xi) In order to help chart the relative success in achieving the goal the FAO provide an online database on food loss and its causes. The database contains data and information from openly accessible reports and studies that measure FLW across a wide range of different food products, different stages of the supply and value chain, from different geographical areas and countries and for different time periods. The data is open to public use and can be queried, downloaded and plotted in an interactive and structured way. The database suggests that an estimated 17% of food that was available to consumers (approximately 931 million metric tonnes (1.03 billion tonnes)), was wasted in homes, retail outlets and restaurants in 2019.
>
> www.fao.org/platform-food-loss-waste/flw-data/en/

This chapter has outlined some of the mechanisms that are available to reduce waste in restaurants and other foodservice businesses. However, reductions in waste are not just technological but also require changes in the behaviour of staff and, potentially, customers, and these issues are discussed in more depth in the next chapter.

Chapter 14

Minimizing waste
Behaviour

Introduction

The previous chapter examined issues of food waste more from a technical perspective. However, technologies do not effectively deal with food waste if managed in isolation. The behavioural side of waste reduction and management is therefore critical. In this chapter, we discuss the behavioural dimension of minimizing waste in the context of the consumer as well as restaurant and business staff and how their shifts in behaviour can help reduce waste and promote a shift to more sustainable restaurants. This is because the extent of food waste generation in foodservice operations is not only a response to over-purchasing, serving styles and timing, and the type of food served but also the degree of involvement and interest of the restaurant staff and the guests (Pirani & Arafat, 2016; Dhir et al., 2020). The first part of the chapter discusses consumer behaviour and the second the behaviour of restaurant staff. Several case studies also illustrate the way in which interventions that manage the intersection of the two can have significant benefits for customers, restaurants and the environment.

Food waste as a behavioural problem

Food waste is a global problem, though one that is framed by cultural, personal, political, geographic and economic drivers (Thyberg & Tonjes, 2016). For example, as outlined in Chapters 2 and 13, food loss can result from infrastructural shortcomings, such as inappropriate or non-existing storage capacity, the lack of access to refrigeration or broken cold chains. In some industrialized countries, food waste is encouraged by the comparatively low cost of food, or the disposal cost of food waste (Marthinsen et al., 2012). More generally, Thyberg and Tonjes (2016) suggest that, at a macro-scale, it is the modernization of food systems, represented by industrialization, economic growth, urbanization and globalization that is the main driver of food losses (Table 14.1). This hints at the importance of cultural and social norms in discussions of food waste.

Thyberg and Tonjes (2016) discuss cultural norms and individual behaviour as two major barriers to food waste avoidance. For example, depending on food culture, there are considerable differences regarding the foodstuffs considered edible or inedible. Even though this is not explicitly acknowledged by the authors, the question as to what foods are "edible" is learned (Rozin et al., 1986), and will, to a considerable degree, depend on the scarcity or abundance of food as well as religious and cultural mores

Table 14.1 Modernization's effects on food systems
Source: Thyberg and Tonjes (2016)

Factor	Description	Effect on food systems
Industrialization	Transition from food production and preparation at home to large-scale operations and factories	Increases distancing of people from food production and preparation
Increases food preparation outside the home
May reduce food costs
Contributes to abundance and variety of food
Economic growth	Increase in disposable income	Increases diet diversification; particularly a transition away from traditional food
May cause reductions in disposable income spent on food
Urbanization	Population shift from rural to urban areas which requires the extension of food supply systems to feed urban populations	Increases diet diversification
Increases distancing of people from food production
Globalization	Shift from local to global food sources; transition of dietary patterns away from traditional ways towards global trends	Increases diet diversification away from local foods
Increases distancing of people from food production

(Filimonau et al., 2020; Filimonau & Ermolaev, 2021). Societies in which food availability is limited tend to be less wasteful, as evident from statistics on food waste. The Food and Agriculture Organization (FAO) (2011) suggests that *production-to-retail* losses are typically around 160–180 kg per person per year in world regions including North America, Europe or Oceania. They are significantly lower in South and Southeast Asia, where they are around 115 kg per capita and year, and in Latin America, where they are higher at close to 200 kg per capita and year. However, *consumer food waste* amounts to a few kg per year in Sub-Saharan Africa and is in excess of 100 kg per capita and year in North America and Oceania (Figure 14.1). People living in extreme poverty will typically produce zero food waste. Survival may even force such people to scavenge discarded food, in both developed and developing countries (Black, 2007; Gössling & Schumacher, 2012), and in many developing countries scavenging, also for food, is a form of work in the informal economy (Nas & Jaffe, 2004).

The wastefulness of different cultures, and, indeed, 'waste cultures' are embedded in social norms and views of food. For example, there is evidence that cultures that have a strong appreciation for food waste less, as they place emphasis on moderation and quality. Rozin (2005) mentions France as an example of such a country, where it is also more common to eat very different parts of animals. In comparison, the USA has been discussed as a country where emphasis is placed on abundance and quantity (Bloom,

2010), and where food waste, for instance as plate waste, is considered 'normal'. This points at different social and moral norms, over which consumers may or may not feel guilty to waste food (Stancu et al., 2016). Food waste generation may also be related to habits and emotions (Russell et al., 2017), while leaving food on the plate may also

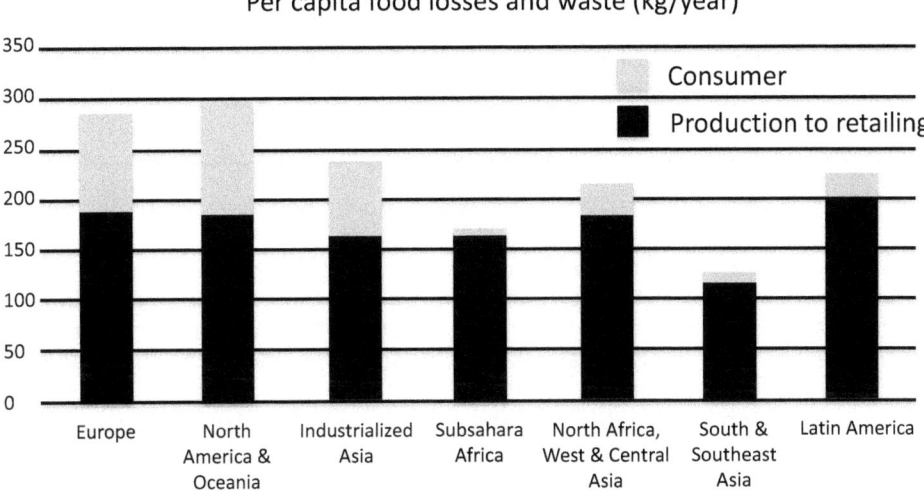

Figure 14.1 Per capita food losses in different world regions
Source: Based on FAO (2011)

Box 14.1   Saudi Arabian and Indian attitudes towards leftover food

As this book has highlighted, attitudes towards food and waste are learned and need to be understood within the socio-cultural and economic context. However, the majority of the literature is based on studies undertaken in Western countries or does not engage with minority populations and their foodways. Yet different cultural and religious beliefs may serve as significant constraints in changing behaviours and encouraging food waste reduction. For example, in a study of the dietary beliefs and practices of Asian Indian immigrants in the USA, Mukherjea et al. (2013) found that respondents criticized the refrigeration and reheating of meal leftovers. Many participants in the study believed that food stored in refrigerators and freezers led to negative health consequences. Food that was cooked and then reheated the following day was considered bad for health. Furthermore, a number of respondents emphasized that leftovers are uncommon in India because any remaining food would be given to domestic servants or, if people are unable to afford hired help, they most probably would not be "burdened" with extra food (Mukherjea et al., 2013).

> The way that notions of food waste are primarily framed by social norms and hedonistic influences is also the major focus of Aleshaiwi and Harries (2020) study of the attitudes of Saudi women to leftovers. Four main reasons for the classification of leftover food as unwanted were identified. First, food touched by others, such as plate leftovers, is perceived as unclean as it fosters feelings of disgust. Second, in contrast, clean leftovers tend to be seen as less desirable for hedonistic reasons because they do not provide the same sensory experience as eating fresh food. Third, the rejection of leftovers might be related to the implications of rising levels of affluence for their attractiveness. Finally, food may become unwanted as a result of social norms regarding eating home-cooked food outside the home.

be connected to issues of gender, although this is also framed by the cultural context (Collison & Colwill, 1987; Sebbane & Costa, 2018; Dhir et al., 2020).

Another significant factor in behavioural aspects of food waste is that different generations can have substantially different attitudes to food, dining and notions of waste (Brombach, 2017; Halkier, 2017; Dhir et al., 2020). Furthermore, attitudes may also be transferred between generations, particularly from parents to their children (Renzaho et al., 2012). For example, Venn et al. (2017) undertook a study of the food and grocery shopping behaviours of baby boomers who are often portrayed as engaging in excessive levels of consumption that run counter to notions of sustainable living and to inter-generational wellbeing. They found that the shopping practices of these men and women were primarily influenced by two factors: (a) parental values and upbringing leading to the reification of thrift and frugality as virtues, alongside aspirations for self-actualization, which served to reinforce some good food waste reduction practices and (b) the influence of household context and roles on consumption choices. However, in the case of the latter this also meant that bulk buying, cooking and freezing of food was often conducted without also paying attention to food waste issues. Furthermore, attitudes to food waste between generations can also vary when eating out, e.g., is it appropriate to bring leftovers home or not? Table 14.2 details some of the inter-generational differences with respect to food and consumption. Importantly, because of their life experiences different generations will have different attitudes with respect to what is considered as food waste and how it is treated. This insight can also be helpful in the development of promotion and communication campaigns that seek to change food behaviours and attitudes towards waste.

Other cultural and personal factors that can determine food waste volumes include the amount of food purchased, an aspect that is related to shopping frequency (Pearson et al., 2013). Where people shop small amounts frequently, food waste is less likely than in situations of overstocking. Even though not discussed by Pearson et al. (2013), this would also point at the importance of regular access. For instance, in industrialized countries, rural populations may have to travel far to the next supermarket and buy correspondingly larger amounts of food. Age has also been found to be linked to food waste, as younger people waste more than older people. In Europe, this aspect has been linked to food shortages after WW II and awareness of the value of food among elderly citizens (Quested et al., 2013), though similar results were also found in other countries (Hamilton et al., 2005). People planting, harvesting, gathering or hunting part or all of their own food may also be more aware of the value of food, specifically it guarantees their survival (Ingold, 2000). In Western countries, household size also predicts food waste, as larger households waste less per capita than smaller households, though households with children waste more than households without children.

Table 14.2 Generations characteristics with respect to food and consumption

Source: Renzaho et al. (2012); Rhodes et al. (2016); Visser et al. (2016); Brombach (2017); Nielsen (2017); Francis & Hoefel (2018)

Generation (when born)	Estimated % of global population 2017	Life-defining events	Behavioural traits	Consumption technologies	Food consumption characteristics/meals	Food values	Primary communication media	Attitude towards technology
Traditionalists (silent/maturists) ≈1900–1945	9	• World War I and II • Great Depression • Fascism	• Loyalty • Hard work • Discipline • Value authority • Conservative	• Radio	• Regular meals • Usually only with family • Only seasonal and regional food • Extremely careful with respect to wasting food • Special dishes on the holiday	• Home cooking is a female chore • Table manners important • Children had to be quiet at the table • Male (husband's) preferences are cooked • Food is a gift	• Formal letter	• Largely disengaged
Baby Boomers ≈1946–1964	24	• Cold War • Authoritarianism • Women's rights • Civil rights movements	• Responsibility • Idealistic • Collectivist • Work-centric	• Fridge becomes standard • Vinyl and movies • Cookbooks • Recipes in newspapers and on the radio	• Regular meals • Seldom out of house, sometimes in restaurants, mainly traditional foods • Food is rarely wasted • Some convenience food • Cooked lunch	• Home cooking mainly female chore • Table manners important • Male (husband's) preferences are cooked • Food is a gift	• Telephone	• Early IT adaptors
Generation X ≈1965–1980	20	• Capitalism • Vietnam War • Mutually Assured Destruction • Anti-apartheid movement • Palestinian Liberation Movement	• Efficiency • Individualist • Materialistic • Competitive • Self-reliance • Flexible	• Brands and cars • Vinyl and cassette • Luxury articles • Cookbooks • Cooking programmes on television	• Most of the time regular meals • Often out of home eating • 'International' cooking now undertaken or eaten out • Convenience food • Some food waste • Either cooked lunch or cooked dinner instead	• Sometimes male (husband) cooks • Health and wholesome food is important • Table manners less important • Food is not self-evident	• Telephone	• Digital immigrants

Table 14.2 continued

Generation (when born)	Estimated % of global population 2017	Life-defining events	Behavioural traits	Consumption technologies	Food consumption characteristics/meals	Food values	Primary communication media	Attitude towards technology
Generation Y/ Millennials ≈1981–1992	22	• Globalization • Thatcherism and Reaganism • Technology and Internet Emergence • Terrorism • End of Cold War	• Sociable • More confident • Less independent • Technologically comfortable • Family-centric	• Labelling systems • CDs • Microwaves common • Personal computers • Cookbooks • Cooking shows as part of lifestyle television • Specialist food magazines	• Some regular meals, sometimes on the go, often with friends • Eating is substantially value driven • International recipes at home and in restaurant • Substantial food waste • Emergence of sustainability concern	• Males cook as well, although females still cook more • Eating has become represented as part of lifestyle • Food is important as part of lifestyle • Resourcefulness framed in terms of sustainability	• Telephone • Email	• Digital natives
Generation Z ≈1995–2010	26	Post-Great Recession Neoliberalism Global warming Digital Natives Mobility Social Networking	Poor communication skills Always connected Multi-taskers Realistic	Downloads Mobile phones Specialist cooking and lifestyle channels Cookbooks explicitly connected to other media and celebrity chefs Dishwashers standard	Used to ordering in and dining out Often eats alone; less regular meals; eats whenever Increased attention to social, economic and sustainable production of food, including reducing food waste	Males and females both cook; although less people know how to cook Food is important as part of sustainable lifestyle and cosmopolitanism Importance of recycling	Text message or social media Hand-held communication devices	Technoholics (entirely dependent IT)

Interrelationships with income seem unclear, as studies have not found that higher income households regularly waste more (Thyberg & Tonjes, 2016).

Overall, there is much evidence that food waste generation at the household level is to a significant degree embedded in culture, attitudes, awareness and routines (Graham-Rowe et al., 2014; Thyberg & Tonjes, 2016; Filimonau et al., 2020). These results also have relevance for gastronomy, because norms exist regarding consideration as to what is 'normal' to do in kitchens, for instance in terms of food use routines, as well as staff behaviour that may often represent 'at home' perspectives on food waste. For example, food waste generation varies by region, purpose, the type of consumer and restaurant size. Private dining appears to generate less per cover waste than dinner between friends or a business banquet; tourists produce more per cover waste than residents and the larger the restaurants, the greater the waste (Wang et al., 2017). In the UK hospitality and foodservice sector, 40% of food that is wasted is carbohydrates, including potato, bread, pasta and rice (WRAP, 2013a), with the average cost of food waste per meal being the highest for the restaurant subsector and lowest for staff catering (WRAP, 2013a).

A range of studies have shown that food waste reductions can be achieved on the basis of interventions. Food waste can be reduced by the promotion and use of fresh, local and quality food; standardization and limitation of menu items; knowledge and experience in kitchen and menu processes and restrictions to plate size (Tatáno et al., 2017). Other strategies used to reduce the environmental impacts of food wastage include use of composting technologies, encouraging consumers to take leftover foods home and diversion of food to welfare programs (Sakaguchi et al., 2018). Government or institutional campaigns to reduce food waste can also lead to changes in food service and consumer waste reduction behaviours as well as beliefs with respect to waste (Priestley, 2016; Filimonau et al., 2020) (see Box 14.2). In a review of 17 studies, Reynolds et al. (2014) found that interventions based on information, technology innovation, policies, system

---

Box 14.2 The Guardians of Grub

The UK's first food waste action week took place from 1 to 7 March 2021. WRAP, the organization behind the scheme, says reaching citizens of all ages with this message is essential for creating lasting change and reaching the UN Sustainable Development Goal of halving food waste around the world by 2030. Television chef Nadiya Hussain, who fronted the campaign, said:

> Wasting food is a major contributor to climate change. And it isn't just the leftovers on our plate to consider but the many resources that go into producing our food, like water and land. If we each make small changes, we'd dramatically reduce the amount of food that ends up in the bin.
>
> (quoted in Sherwood, 2021)

The 2021 campaign focused both on home food waste as well as the hospitality sector.

The WRAP campaign that focuses on the hospitality sector is known as the Guardians of Grub. The campaign highlights that of the 1.1 million tonnes of food thrown away by the Hospitality and Food Service industry in the UK every year at a cost of £3.2 billion (equivalent to about 18% of the food purchased), 75% of the food wasted could have been eaten. The campaign run in conjunction with the industry provides operational resources, saving calculator, campaign guide, case studies and a short online course.

Guardians of Grub: https://guardiansofgrub.com

change or practice change can lead to a significant decline in food/plate waste – up to 57% in hospitality contexts. Several of the findings receive further discussion below.

Plate size

One of the most central insights in the literature on restaurant practices to avoid food waste concerns plate or bowl size, with evidence that smaller plates reduce the amount of food taken from buffets, the amount that is actually eaten as well as the volumes of plate waste. This was first studied in an experiment involving French fries, in which the standard size of fries in paper bags was subsequently reduced, leading to a significant reduction in the consumption of French fries per diner as well as plate waste (Freedman & Brochado, 2010). Kallbekken and Saelen (2013) studied plate size reductions vis-à-vis social cues in hotels in Norway, which both proved to be effective, leading to a 20% decline in food waste. Related findings were presented by Wansink and van Ittersum (2013) who found in experiments in the USA that visual norms and plate size had significant effects on waste in self-service contexts. They found that the larger the provided bowls, the more customers would overfill, and the larger the plates, the more food would be taken. Diners choosing larger plates served themselves 52% more, consumed 45% more and wasted 135% more than users of smaller plates. Plate size consequently influenced the overall amount taken, the amount actually eaten as well as the amount wasted. In a related study in the USA, plate disposability was found to also affect buffet food waste volumes, with permanent plates leading to a 51% reduction in plate waste compared to disposable plates (Williamson et al., 2016).

Plate waste reductions can also be achieved through other interventions directed at consumer behaviour, such as awareness campaigns or policy changes. These latter strategies may be more relevant in cafeterias and canteens, where they can involve children or students. For example, students who participated in the weighing of plate waste in a US university cafeteria reduced food waste levels by 15% (Whitehair et al., 2013). In another study, students at a Dutch university were asked to consider their appetite when ordering their ready meal. Students were informed about food waste and offered the choice of a reduced portion size. Even though the smaller portion size was not cheaper, orders of smaller portions increased and plate waste declined (Jagau & Vyrastekova, 2017). As Richter (2017) postulates, food waste behaviour is driven by the understanding of the problem. She distinguishes guilty food wasters, unwitting food wasters and careless food wasters, referring to the degree of awareness and behaviour. Any reduction in food waste based on behaviour will require an awareness of the problem as well as ideally, an understanding of how one's own actions can help reduce the problem (van der Linden, 2014).

Policy changes can also affect waste behaviour. For instance, experiments with changes in school dietary guidelines were found to result in vegetable waste reduction by 15%–28% (Cohen et al., 2014; Schwartz et al., 2015), as vegetables represented a less appreciated meal component that remained particularly often uneaten. In another study, education about food waste also had the effect of a 33% waste reduction from main dishes (Martins et al., 2016). All studies illustrate that awareness and effectiveness knowledge (how to reduce food waste) have important repercussions for food waste. In their review of these studies, Reynolds et al. (2014) conclude that the most efficient intervention is downsizing plate or bowl sizes. This measure can be applied to buffet

Minimizing waste: behaviour

> **Box 14.3 Reducing plate waste**
>
> Apart from larger plates resulting in overload and plate waste at buffets, plate waste is also a problem when dishes are chosen from menus. The reasons for plate waste were reported by United against Waste (2018) to include oversized standard portions; unpopular or oversized side dishes and beverages offered in jugs or pots. The amount of food wasted can be reduced dramatically by a number of simple measures, with the added bonus of economic savings on food purchases and disposal. To achieve food waste reductions, food services should:
>
> - measure and analyze food waste and its components;
> - be variable with side dishes, let guests choose what they want;
> - make portion sizes variable, or reduce portion sizes;
> - offer smaller portions with an option of a free second serving;
> - take-home options for uneaten food can be offered proactively;
> - offer beverages on the basis of refills.

choices, as well as in menus by offering variable portion sizes. Reducing plate size is also an inexpensive and simple measure that does not interfere with guest expectations, as patrons can go for refills (in buffet contexts), or order an additional course in a la carte contexts.

Buffets are one of the largest sources of food waste in hotels with much of the wasted food in traditional buffet settings being high-value foods such as meats. Close (2018) argued that relatively simple behavioural solutions could substantially reduce the amount of buffet waste. He noted that non-waste aware approaches keep food on the buffet fully stocked until the last minute of service and does not adjust for leftovers, meaning that substantial amounts of bacon, sausage and eggs then get thrown away at the end of the breakfast serving. Instead, hotels should shift certain items from buffet service to à la carte cooking near the end of mealtimes in order to reduce waste without negatively impacting the customer experience. In addition, he argues that it is appropriate repurposes leftovers into other items such as "doggy bags" for guests who

> **Box 14.4 "Clean dish, clean conscience!"**
>
> The "Clean dish, clean conscience!" initiative was a food waste reduction campaign trailed at the School of Agriculture canteen, University of Lisbon, in Portugal. The initiative was a simple and inexpensive education campaign undertaken to raise awareness of the need to reduce plate waste, by establishing the connection between food waste and personal behaviour in the mind of students and canteen staff.
>
> In the first stage plate waste from canteen users was measured over a ten-day period. After this period, a waste consumption index and per capita waste consumption were calculated to evaluate the level of satisfaction of the consumer and the related concern about food wastage. This was classified as 'Bad' and it

> was concluded that canteen customers did not have strong convictions about avoiding food waste.
>
> During the second stage of the project a communication and education campaign was implemented with plate waste being monitored for a further 16 days to assess its effectiveness. The campaign's approach was basic and consisted of displaying simple and affordable informative posters in strategic areas of the canteen with simple messages reminding people not to take food they knew they would not eat. This initiative alone led to a mean reduction in the waste consumption index of approximately 15%. A parallel action to encourage the separation of organic and inorganic waste was also implemented, which had an active participation rate of over 70% of canteen users.
>
> The initiative achieved its objective of reducing plate waste simply by raising awareness of the food waste issue in the institution's canteen and also suggesting actions regarding "how-to" reduce waste. A key component of reducing waste in institutional foodservice environments is therefore just making users aware of food waste issues and why they matter. Importantly, the strategy was only effective with the collaboration of the canteen staff.
>
> Source: Lagorio et al. (2018); Pinto et al. (2018)

arrive after service hours or incorporate them into other dishes. Importantly with respect to changing behaviours and expectations, Close (2018) suggests that hotels should make customers aware of their efforts to reduce food waste and why they are doing so, also thereby encouraging customers by example not to waste food.

Food containers

Take-home food containers for leftovers, also known as doggy bags, are increasingly common in restaurants. However, as will be discussed, they also represent a form of behavioural barrier to reducing food waste. The idea is that taking home leftovers reduces food waste, provided the food is actually eaten later on. Food containers also come at a cost of other garbage, specifically when these are made of aluminium: there is evidence that designs of food containers often ignore the issue of material input (see Bozzola et al., 2017). Food services should thus seek to adjust portion sizes before they consider offering food containers to take home leftovers. It is also currently unknown how much of the food taken home is actually eaten, or if a share is also discarded. Yet, experiments show that knowledge of being able to take home uneaten food reduces the amount of food eaten (Zuraikat et al., 2018).

Food containers are now available in different forms and sizes, and they can be made from recycled or biodegradable materials. To take home food as an offer will not be an option for all foodservice types, as in particular upscale restaurants will not usually have a cultural norm that acknowledges waste generation. This also highlights one of the main barriers to 'take home norms', as conflicting emotions may exist in the context of food waste. As Sirieix et al. (2017) highlight, personal norms would be supportive of waste avoidance, and hence encourage the use of food containers. Yet, food waste may also create feelings of shame of not having eaten all food, which may make it more difficult to acknowledge the problem and to ask for food containers. Mirosa et al. (2018) also identify other factors that act as barriers to food container use, such as convenience (not going home directly after the meal) as well as social stigma (concerns what others may think). They also identified quality, health and food safety, as well as taste concerns as issues with importance for disinterest in food containers; cost savings, on the other hand, were a highly relevant motivation for food container use.

These findings suggest that food services need to more proactively inform about the availability of food containers where this is necessary. An indirect indication, such as a small note in a menu, is probably more suitable for this purpose than to ask guests directly, as guests may feel embarrassed and obliged to take home the uneaten food but discard it later on. Currently, it is uncommon in restaurants in many countries to offer food containers, and equally uncommon for customers to ask for these (Mirosa et al., 2018).

As this discussion highlights, take-home containers are a question of restaurant food culture. Principato et al. (2018) found that almost a third of restaurant managers in a study of restaurants in Northern Italy claimed to have never heard about containers to take home leftovers, and many stated to not be interested in offering such an innovation because the food would not have the same quality when eaten later. They also believed that customers were not interested in food containers. Principato et al. (2018) concluded that it was important for managers to understand food waste reduction as a cost saving strategy. Importantly, in their study, restaurants with meat-based menus showed a tendency to waste more than other restaurants, again highlighting the issue of specific food cultures and norms.

Bags and containers to take home uneaten food are now available in all designs, including compostable plastic containers, as well as bags and containers made from recycled paper (also compostable paper), from palm leaves, glucose from milled corn, wood pulp or sugarcane (see websites: Biologischverpacken.de; Mrtakeoutbags.com; Vegware.com). In many regions and countries, the use of food containers to take home leftovers is actively promoted, sometimes in national campaigns, to encourage guests

---

Box 14.5 Which nudges work best in reducing food waste?

Nudging is a term used to describe the reconfiguring of the 'choice architecture' of consumers to encourage beneficial decision-making by organizing the context, process and environment in which individuals make consumption decisions and, in so doing, exploiting people's 'cognitive biases' to manipulate choice (Kallbekken & Sælen, 2013; Stöckli et al., 2018). The approach has been very influential in considering environmental behavioural change with one report to the UK government suggesting 'approaches based on "changing contexts" – the environment within which we make decisions and respond to cues – have the potential to bring about significant changes in behaviour at relatively low cost' (Dolan et al., 2010, p. 8) and which provided a checklist to consider when seeking to nudge consumers:

1. *Messenger*: We are heavily influenced by who communicates information.
2. *Incentives*: Our responses to incentives are shaped by predictable mental shortcuts such as strongly avoiding losses.
3. *Norms*: We are strongly influenced by what others do.
4. *Defaults*: We 'go with the flow' of pre-set options.
5. *Salience*: Our attention is drawn to what is novel and seems relevant to us.
6. *Priming*: Our acts are often influenced by sub-conscious cues.
7. *Affect*: Our emotional associations can powerfully shape our actions.

8 *Commitments*: We seek to be consistent with our public promises and reciprocate acts.
9 *Ego*: We act in ways that make us feel better about ourselves.

A key insight of such an approach in the foodservice context is that people do not act as isolated individuals, and instead food consumption and behaviours are socially situated and are often deeply embedded with habits and norms being significant. As discussed at the beginning of this chapter, food consumption is a multilayered phenomenon that is full of meaning including its role as a signifier of identity, cultural and social affiliations and relationships. In foodservice operations, nudges and other behavioural interventions have been found to reduce food waste at buffets (Chen & Jai, 2018; Dolnicar et al., 2020), reducing plate size (Tatáno et al., 2017; and as discussed above) as well as a la carte interventions such as removing side plates (Camilleri-Fenech et al., 2020). Social cues include using offering to pack leftovers for customers (Hamerman et al., 2018), posters (Kallbekken & Sælen, 2013) or having prompt/information cards on the diners' table (Stöckli et al., 2018).

The effectiveness of nudging is different for different types of establishments and contexts (Dhir et al., 2020). For example, reduced plate size was identified as being more effective than social cues given through posters in a study of hotel restaurants, leading to a waste reduction of approximately 20% and no negative implications for customer satisfaction (Kallbekken & Sælen, 2013). Using agent-based simulation for all-you-can-eat foodservice operations to examine food waste minimization while maintaining service quality (i.e., low wait-time, unsatisfied-hunger and walk-out percentages), Ravandi and Jovanovic (2019) found that reducing plate size from large to small decreases plate waste by up to 30%. However, and reflecting the importance of measurement in the assessment of food waste interventions, total waste as the sum of food surplus and plate waste was lower with large plates.

Box 14.6 Does being vegetarian reduce food waste? The case of Korean restaurant diners

In South Korea, people usually eat out at restaurants approximately 14 times per month and spend 300,000 Korean Won (KRW) per person (US$1 was equivalent to KRW 1,147) each month on dining out (Ministry of Agriculture, Food and Rural Affairs, 2018). However, the average Korean throws out 930 g of rubbish each day, 40% of which is food waste which is more than 130 kg of per capita food waste a year. This is a higher level of food waste per capita by consumers in Europe and North America which is estimated at 95–115 kg a year (Jackson, 2018) and is also translated into substantial levels of food waste when eating out. The main reason for food waste in foodservice in Korea is the selection of primarily vegetable-based side dishes, known as banchan, the most famous of which is kimchi, that accompanies most restaurant meals without extra charge (Jackson, 2018).

Kim et al. (2020) used an extended value-attitude behaviour (VAB) theoretical model to examine is being vegetarian, or having other eating characteristics, influenced waste reduction behaviours in Korean restaurants. VAB theory is based on the notion that the influence of values on specific behaviour is mediated by attitudes towards the behaviour, meaning that in a specific situation "the influence should theoretically flow from abstract values to midrange attitudes to specific behaviors" (Homer & Kahle, 1988, p. 638). Value refers to a type of social cognition that functions to facilitate adaptation to one's environment (Homer & Kahle, 1988). Attitude means an individual's consistent tendency to respond favourably or unfavourably towards an object in question (Vaske & Donnelly, 1999). Behaviour describes the volitional control of the individual and, as a result, the most direct predictor of a behaviour is intention to engage in that behaviour (Homer & Kahle, 1988; Vaske & Donnelly, 1999). Such insights are important as they can help identify better ways to communicate with restaurant customers about waste reduction behaviour. In Korea, vegetarians including vegans and flexitarians account for approximately 20% of the total population (10 million people) (Korea Vegetarian & Vegan Association, 2019). In Kim et al.'s (2020) study, three types of vegetarians are included: vegetarians who do not eat the products or by-products of animal and fish slaughter, such as meat and fish; vegans who do not eat any animal products, such as meat, fish, eggs, milk, cheese or honey and flexitarians who are vegans, but occasionally eat by meat when unable to get vegetable food.

Increasing numbers of Koreans are embracing environmentally friendly eating and organic foods and reducing their intake of animal-based foods for reasons including health, animal welfare and protecting the environment (Han, H. et al., 2019; Lee, 2019). Vegetarianism and veganism are an important part of this market reorientation (Han, H. et al., 2019). Due to the growing number of environmentally friendly eaters in Korea, the new term "vegenomic" which combines vegetable and economic, has emerged, and the related market is steadily growing with the number of vegan restaurants and bakeries more than doubling between 2014 and 2019, to more than 300 (Korea Vegetarian & Vegan Association, 2019).

In terms of food-related behaviours, Sims (1978) suggests that vegetarians' values, attitudes, beliefs and behaviours are more likely to address food-related ethical, religious and health values than those of non-vegetarians. With respect to animal welfare issues Preylo and Arikawa (2008) identified gender differences between vegetarians and non-vegetarian males with respect to human-directed empathy and attitudes towards animals although there are no differences between non-vegetarian and vegetarian women. Vegetarian attitudes towards the importance of health, product information, novelty, ecological products, social relationships and social events are regarded as being more positive than non-vegetarians, whereas non-vegetarians are less occupied by health issues than vegetarians (Hoek et al., 2004). With regard to healthy dietary behaviours, vegetarians score higher than non-vegetarians in terms of food pyramid guidelines and lifestyle indices among Americans and Canadians (Le et al., 2018).

Kim et al. (2020) undertook an online panel survey of 370 Koreans of which 258 were non-vegetarians, 107 were vegetarians and five vegans. Females made up 53.1% of the non-vegetarian respondents and 58.0% of the vegetarians respectively. The majority of respondents attended a university and/or higher: non-vegetarians (70.9%) and vegetarians (73.2%). Subjects earned a monthly family income of KRW four million and over, with non-vegetarian's income (61.2%) higher than that of vegetarians (56.3%). All subjects from both groups dined out once a month or more. More than a third of the non-vegetarian sample dined out for family gatherings (37.2%), and more than a third of the vegetarian sample dined out for social gatherings (38.3%). The majority of subjects spent 10,000–50,000 KRW per person for eating out on average (non-vegetarians: 84.1%, vegetarians: 88.4%) and participated in waste reduction at work (non-vegetarians: 58.8%, vegetarians: 75.9%) as well as at home (non-vegetarians: 65.1%, vegetarians: 82.1%). More non-vegetarians had recently dined at environmentally neutral restaurants (74.4%) and casual/family full-service restaurants (76.7%), than vegetarians, while vegetarians had recently dined at environmentally friendly restaurants (63.4%) and casual/family full-service restaurants (56.2%).

Based on the results, and perhaps unsurprisingly, the perceived value of sustainability has the highest significant effect on attitudes, implying that if a diner perceives high value of sustainability, the diner has a better attitude towards waste reduction while eating out. In addition, sustainability values significantly influence social norms among restaurant consumers. The results also suggest that sustainable eating behaviour is mostly affected by each individual's beliefs on a specific action. Eating style has a significant effect on sustainable eating out behaviour in restaurants. In other words, being vegetarian does mean stronger attitudes towards waste reduction and environmentally friendly eating out behaviours. The study concluded that the strong linkages between extended VAB constructs provide opportunities and challenges for restaurants to reduce waste, save resources and recycling, resulting in reduced operation costs.

The findings also suggest that restaurants could develop marketing and communication strategies to better promote waste reduction strategies. Although such measures are often utilized in an accommodation context, e.g., promoting towel reuse and limiting how often rooms are cleaned, they are far less utilized in restaurants and catering. Nevertheless, waste reduction practices can be promoted as beneficial and legitimate behaviours with initiatives, such as offering customers containers for leftovers, being regarded as culturally acceptable behaviours even in Asian contexts (Kim et al., 2020).

to take home leftovers (Bozzola et al., 2017; Mirosa et al., 2018). An important finding by Mirosa et al. (2018) is that guests favour specific types of containers, with Styrofoam being the least popular option – perhaps because of environmental considerations. Where bags and containers are offered, the environmental implications of plastic, Styrofoam or aluminium packaging should be considered, and such take-home options be avoided.

Staff training and education

To involve staff in waste management is a challenge, specifically in food cultures that have so far placed limited interest in reducing the amount of food that is discarded – for instance, Hall et al. (2009) highlighted that food waste volumes have dramatically increased in the USA since the 1970s. However, the financial impacts of municipal charging for waste disposal on restaurants and foodservice operations as well as recognition that there are substantial direct savings to be made that can improve profitability means that foodservice businesses are increasingly interested in educating staff on waste reduction practices and changing behaviours. A summary of the average

Table 14.3 Estimated average cost of food being wasted in the UK hospitality and foodservice sector (HaFS)

Source: WRAP (2013a)

Subsector	Total food waste (000 tonnes)	Total food waste cost per tonne (thousand tonnes) (£/tonne)	Total cost (£ million)	Average cost per meal (£/meal)	Average cost of avoidable food waste (£/tonne)	Average cost of total food waste (£/tonne)
Restaurants	199	3,500	682	0.97	4,800	3,500
Pubs	173	2,100	357	0.41	2,900	2,100
Education	123	2,100	250	0.22	2,500	2,100
Healthcare	121	1,900	230	0.22	2,400	1,900
Hotels	79	4,000	318	0.52	6,300	4,000
Quick Service Restaurants	76	3,500	277	0.14	4,500	3,500
Services	68	1,700	112	0.43	2,000	1,700
Leisure	60	4,000	241	0.46	5,800	4,000
Staff catering	21	2,200	44	0.05	3,000	2,200
UK HaFS total	920	2,800	2,511			
UK HaFS average				0.38	3,700	2,800

costs of food waste for the hospitality and food services sector in the UK is shown in Table 14.3.

Staff training is therefore an essential part of food waste prevention strategies. For example, Duursma et al. (2016) noted that routines to assess waste (weighing portions, reducing portion sizes or calculating the impact of waste) already had a significant impact on kitchen routines, as chefs reused a greater share of food, seeking to minimize wastage. Changes in kitchen practices should therefore lead to behavioural change. However, it is important to recognize that changed staff behaviour needs to include everyone involved in food service and not just the kitchen staff, as important as they are. For example, waitstaff can actively encourage diners to take their leftovers home rather than have any feelings of embarrassment in doing so (Hamerman et al., 2018).

A key issue in staff training and education is where does the instigation for new initiatives come from? Government and industry associations play a significant role here by the regulations that are put in place for food waste and the costs that are associated with it. Such measures therefore provide a financial encouragement to owners and management to be more proactive in their actions. Filimonau et al. (2020), for example, highlight the importance of this in the Chinese context where food waste habits have long been engrained in Chinese food culture where, in a study of senior restaurant managers on food waste, they suggest the need for free-to-attend specialist training to restaurant managers and staff on how to mitigate food waste occurring in kitchens.

In addition, they highlight the importance of public campaigns that focus on food waste in order to generate awareness.

Personal beliefs and values of restaurant managers and foodservice staff also play a major role in the adoption of food waste practices (Principato et al., 2018). Perhaps not surprisingly, managers and staff that assign high importance to the environment are more likely to save food from going to waste (Heikkilä et al., 2016; Martin-Rios et al., 2018). Nevertheless, the role of the overall food environment and especially regulatory requirements that affect cost will usually be the most important factor in adoption of practices (Filimonau & De Coteau, 2019).

Educational measures should be based on three types of knowledge, i.e., factual, procedural and effectiveness knowledge (van der Linden, 2014). These knowledge dimensions include a problem description; a 'solution' in terms of the measures through which the issue can be addressed and information regarding the difference this will make in terms of 'saved' food or reduced environmental impact. To base education on knowledge dimensions consequently helps staff to engage in food waste avoidance, though it also means that restaurants have to develop this knowledge by measuring and monitoring waste amounts to define the problem (and to measure progress). Alternatively, restaurants may hire external help. There are many consultancies

---

Box 14.7 Overview of steps in strategic food waste (avoidance) management

Strategic food waste management requires data regarding the amounts and quality of food going to waste, ideally over time. Based on this data, restaurants and food services can discuss strategies to minimize waste volumes. For this reason, it is advisable to set out with the development of a waste reduction strategy grounded in a measuring and monitoring approach. The distinction of food waste fractions is necessary to define areas where food is lost, and how each of these might be addressed on the basis of the food waste prevention hierarchy (Figure 13.2).

Step 1

Separate food waste into categories and note the amounts lost

- For spoilt produce (storage)
- Waste from preparation and production
- Overproduction
- Plate waste
- Buffets

Step 2

Plan menus that reduce waste

- Fewer components reduce waste.
- A lower dish variety increases control.
- Develop an understanding of guest numbers and preferences.
- Waste of perishable produce can be avoided by using it in several dishes.
- The number of items with longer shelf-life can be increased.
- Apps can aid in food management, specifically when used in recipe management.

> **Step 3**
>
> Prevent food spoilage
>
> - Purchasing procedures are based on continuous stock control.
> - Foodstuffs are delivered freshly with high quality foodstuffs increasing shelf-life.
> - Stock control is based on first-in, first out management.
> - Vacuum packaging, marinating and other methods can increase shelf-life.
> - Dish-of-the-day and similar approaches can help marketing dishes based on produce approaching its use-by date.
>
> **Step 4**
>
> Reducing food waste on buffets and plates.
>
> - Discuss whether you can avoid buffets.
> - Offer limited quantities in small portions, refill if necessary.
> - Use flat plates for display of food items.
> - Label ingredients to help customers avoid tastes they may not like.
> - Offer small portion sizes, specifically of meat, fish or milk products.
> - Offer different portion sizes, and work out optimums.
> - Proactively offer paper-based containers to take home leftovers.

specializing in food waste reductions or sustainable management practices more generally. This is potentially costlier, but likely meaningful from a business economics viewpoint, as the amount of food saved will improve the economic bottom line.

To increase staff interest, restaurant management can engage in various strategies. For example, willingness to support food waste reduction strategies can be improved by highlighting that avoiding food waste is a moral obligation, commonly approved by experts and society, and in line with majority expectations. To make this more tangible, restaurant management may also share the profits of avoided waste with staff, as an economic bonus (Marthinsen et al., 2012), for example, as part of annual or seasonal bonuses.

Conclusions

This chapter has examined the behavioural dimension of food waste. Apart from the role of the modern food system in influencing food waste behaviour it has also noted the importance of different food cultures, including kitchen cultures, as well as gender and inter-generational differences, all of which are significant not just as aspects of consumption but also because they indicate a basis for trying to influence food waste practices as a result of interventions which can range from education and communication campaigns by wait staff through to influencing waste behaviour by changing the physical environment of dining, such as changing plate size or other elements of what is on the table.

The chapter also highlights that restaurant and foodservice staff are critical influences on guest behaviour, and that they also need to be brought into food waste programmes in order to make them effective. As a result, education and communication campaigns need to be direct at the industry as well so as to encourage waste behavioural change.

Chapter 15

The restaurant in the community

Introduction

Restaurants take their origins from two different sources: first, in providing food for paying customers from the wealthier members of society and second, in the provision of hospitality to guests, often travellers, with such provision often being given for free or for a donation. This tension in the nature of restaurant hospitality remains through to the present day. While some privileged people save labour time by eating at restaurants, others rely on food banks, catering services for the less privileged or go hungry. Nevertheless, many restaurants and foodservice operations do see themselves as part of a local community in terms of both the place in which they are located as well as the foodservice and restaurant community. At its most basic the notion of community may just mean the local economic community from which food is purchased, however, more often than not, there is a wider sense of social and economic community in terms of the location in which a restaurant is embedded, with its regular customers, suppliers and neighbouring establishments. Importantly, such notions of community can also be significant contributors to sustainability and being able to withstand change, at both the individual and business level, as well as in the community itself.

Restaurants and the chefs and cooks who work within them can therefore take an active role in encouraging improved sustainable behaviours in their community. Examples can include community-based gardens, cooking events, charity work, encouraging sustainable forms of eating as well as different forms of community-based activism. There are a wide range of ways in which chefs and restaurants can help causes whether by donations, sponsorship or by time. Many of these measures are undertaken to assist the less advantaged in society. For example, in July of 2018, Chef Ravinder Bhogal's restaurant Jikoni, in London's Marylebone, was serving 'community lunches', priced at £12, with £1 being donated to the Marylebone Food Cycle and the Felix Project (Rayner, 2018). However, COVID-19 has arguably forced a further, deeper, reconsideration of the role of the restaurants and foodservice providers in the community especially with respect to what the food system will shift to post-COVID and has also raised questions about the role of food security in community resilience (Collicutt, 2009; Blake, 2019). As Nunn (2020) comments,

> most kitchens are likely to return to their regular routine, just with a bit more outdoor seating and perspex partitions, gracefully pivoting back from their newfound social commitments. But there is still hope that some restaurants will cling to this renewed focus on community in a post-coronavirus landscape.

The most basic form of community participation for restaurants may include their involvement in local festivals, encouragement of local producers and contribution to regional and local food promotion. Thinking of the restaurant as being part of the community can also help foster social and economic aspects of sustainability. Many chefs and restaurants go further and advocate for the role of food services as part of encouraging greater food justice with respect to changing the food system. In response to increasing obesity, diabetes and food-related contributions to climate and environmental change (Freudenberg et al., 2011). Arguably, the notion of a sustainable restaurant and food system includes both ecological protection and social justice by definition. However, food justice is arguably a stronger interpretation of the social dimensions of food than what many actors in the food system would envisage, given that food justice represents "a transformation of the current food system, including but not limited to eliminating disparities and inequities" (Gottlieb & Joshi, 2010, p. ix). Interestingly, such notions are not new or limited to recent interest in the transition to more sustainable food systems. In times of economic crisis, community food hubs have long provided vital lifelines to communities in the form of canteens (Nunn, 2020). For example, in the UK, during the Second World War, the Minister for Food, Lord Woolton, developed plans for local government run 'communal feeding centres' to supply hot food for those unable to afford to eat at restaurants, although the name was deemed unacceptable because of the potential association with communism. British Prime Minister Winston Churchill instead gave them the name 'British Restaurants' and by 1941 they were feeding over half a million people per day. Nunn (2020) also suggests that they introduced the British working class to the idea of dining out and presaged the democratization of restaurants in the 1950s and 1960s.

In the late 1960s, in California, the Black Panthers organized to provide free school breakfasts for impoverished children, with the programme eventually expanding to 23 cities and 20,000 children (Collier, 2015). This was one of the first organized free breakfast programmes in the USA and highlighted some of the racial and economic food inequities that existed then (and continue to exist). As Nunn (2020) observes,

> The legacy of these projects, whether grudging or revolutionary, was not so much in how many mouths they fed, but in the conversations they started over access to food. Six years after the Panthers scheme, the government finally introduced free school breakfasts.

Several chapters have already highlighted the ways in which restaurants and foodservice operations are active in their communities in various ways. Chapter 4 focused on the connections between restaurants and their suppliers as part of local food networks with, as both this chapter and Chapter 7 on purchasing strategies highlighted; these networks being social as well as economic, with the role of trust being critical for long-term restaurant-supplier relationships (Roy et al., 2017, 2019a, 2019b). Chapter 8 noted the importance of healthy food and the restaurant as a vehicle to promoting healthier eating. Such measures may become part of community-based restaurant health campaigns in which restaurants cooperate with health agencies and, sometimes, local authorities in seeking to promote healthier food options or ways of eating (Valdivia Espino et al., 2015; Lindberg et al., 2018; Carins et al., 2021). Food waste (see Chapter 14) also has an important community dimension as leftover food can be contributed to food banks and other initiatives, some of which are discussed here. For example, in the USA, approximately one in five restaurants who participated in a NRA survey donated edible leftovers to charities, while the main reason for not donating was concern over liability or food safety (NRA, 2018). Significantly, in the same research it was reported that 50% of consumers consider the donation of leftover foods as an important factor in restaurant selection (NRA, 2018).

This chapter therefore further illustrates some of the ways in which restaurants and chefs act to involve themselves in the community, create conversations and contribute to changing the nature of the food system in order to make it more sustainable, not just with respect to the environment, but also in relation to the socio-economic dimensions of sustainability and food justice. It first discusses initiatives to reduce stigma and reduce waste before examining broader issues of food justice and helping the disadvantaged as well as community owned establishments.

Reducing stigma

In November 2017, Casey House in Toronto, Canada's first and only standalone hospital for people living with HIV/Aids, opened June's, a pop-up restaurant that was the world's first eatery in which all of the kitchen staff were HIV positive. Fourteen people staffed the kitchen and Toronto chef Matt Basile designed a menu and helped with training. The purpose of the pop-up was to challenge the stigma and myths surrounding HIV/AIDS given that a poll had suggested that only half of Canadians would knowingly share or eat food prepared by someone who is HIV positive. According to Joanne Simons of Casey House,

> There were a lot of questions about what happens if somebody cuts themselves in the kitchen and they're HIV positive, ... We manage that like anybody would in a kitchen: you make sure you provide first aid, you clean up the area, you throw away whatever has been touched by the blood and you clean the surfaces. We would do that regardless of whether you have HIV or not – that's just common sense. ... There's absolutely no risk that somebody can contract HIV from sharing a meal, ... HIV doesn't live well out of the body for any length of time and through the cooking the virus dies.
>
> (quoted in Kassam, 2017)

A similar, though more permanent, type of scheme is that of Universo Santi (http://universosanti.com), a restaurant in the southern Spanish city of Jerez, in which all the staff are disabled. The 20 staff, whose ages range from 22 to 62, were recruited from an original list of 1,500. To qualify, applicants had to be unemployed and have more than 35% disability. The head of human resources, for example, has cerebral palsy (Burgen, 2019). Some of Spain's top chefs, among them Martín Berasategui, Joan Roca and Ángel León, have contributed recipes and their time as guest chefs at the restaurant the name of which commemorates Santi Santamaria, chef at the Michelin three-star Can Fabes in Catalonia until his sudden death of a heart attack in Singapore in 2011. However, as Antonio Vila, the president of the Fundación Universo Accesible, a not-for-profit organization dedicated to helping people with disabilities join the mainstream workforce, states,

> People don't come here because the staff are disabled but because it's the best restaurant in the area. Whatever reason they came for, the talking is about the food. I always wanted to show what people with disabilities, given the right training, were capable of, ... They were not represented in the world of haute cuisine.
>
> (quoted in Burgen, 2019)

Universo Santi is arguably the most high-end such initiative but others do exist although some have struggled as a result of the impact of COVID-19 on hospitality operations. La Fourchette de Collserola in Barcelona, Spain (https://lafourchettedecollserola.com), is a restaurant offering Mediterranean cuisine staffed by 20 people with a range of physical and mental disabilities. Brownies & Downies (www.browniesanddownies.nl) is a Dutch café franchise run by people with Down's syndrome and other disabilities that has also opened in Belgium and South Africa (Burgen, 2019). Another similar project was the One Eighty Restaurant in Portadown, Northern Ireland, which was a social enterprise project established in 2011 and provided work experience and training for 16- to 22-year-olds with learning difficulties to work in hospitality. Unfortunately, like many restaurants, the project had to close during COVID-19, which also highlights the financial fragility of such initiatives (Portadown Times, 2020).

Waste campaigns

As noted earlier in the book, more than 900 million tonnes of food is thrown away every year. Wasted food is responsible for approximately 8%–10% of greenhouse gas emissions, so if food waste was a country, it would be the third-biggest emitter of greenhouse gases on the planet. Chefs have played a substantial role in community-based initiatives and actions to reduce waste. British TV cook Nadiya Hussain is working with WRAP and offering tips and leftovers recipes via Instagram and Italian restaurateur Massimo Bottura, chef patron of Modena eatery Osteria Francescana, which has three Michelin stars, has been appointed UNEP goodwill ambassador "in the fight against food waste and loss". Throughout the lockdown in Italy, his family produced an online cooking show called Kitchen Quarantine, encouraging people to "see the invisible potential" in every ingredient (Gill, 2021). Bottura is also extremely active in trying to help connect waste campaigns to helping the disadvantaged in society (Box 15.1). According to Bottura in his introduction to his book *Bread is Gold*,

> The good thing is that everyone can participate [in reducing food waste around the world]. A recipe after all is a solution to a problem. Choose to be part of the solution by cooking and sharing a meal around a table. It might be the most revolutionary thing you do all day.
>
> (Bottura & Friends, 2017, p. 9)

Box 15.1 Food for Soul

The not-for-profit organization Food for Soul was founded in 2016 by the Italian chef Massimo Bottura with the aim of encouraging chefs, artists, designers and food suppliers, to collaborate in building and sustaining community-based projects (Bottura & Friends, 2017). As of early 2021, there were four main projects: Refettorio Felix in London, Refettorio Ambrosiano in Milan, Refettorio Gastromotiva in Rio de Janeiro and Refettorio in Paris.

In 2016, Massimo Bottura was voted the number one chef in the world with his three Michelin-starred restaurant, Osteria Francescana, in the northern Italian city of Modena being regarded as one of the finest in the world. However, he regards his greatest achievement as Food for Soul, his project to feed the poor and cut food waste. According to Bottura, "the role of the chef is much more than the sum of his recipes [and] the principle of Food for Soul is inclusiveness … but also a kind of joy at life" (Adams, 2017).

The first site for Food for Soul was Refettorio Ambrosiano in Greco, an outer suburb of Milan, in Italy. Refettorio began as a pop-up concept for the 2015 Milan World Expo. The original plan was to create a kitchen at Milan's central railway station, in which chefs would be invited to cook for the city's homeless, including refugees, using food deemed unsuitable for sale in supermarkets, in order to make a statement about waste and taste. A refettorio is the place where monks and nuns came together to share meals with the word coming from the Latin *reficere*, which means to rebuild and restore (Bottura & Friends, 2017). Through the Catholic charity Caritas Amrosiana, the biggest Catholic charity organization in Milan, Bottura's idea reached the Vatican and, as a result, Pope Francis suggested a more sustainable gesture of locating Refettorio in one of the poor quarters on the city's periphery.

Subsequently, the parish priest of Greco, Don Giuliano, suggested a derelict church hall and theatre next to his church as a venue and thus the location of Refettorio Ambrosiano was chosen. Although the setting is very different from Osteria, Bottura believes the two places are linked by a commitment to quality. Bottura's restaurant in Modena has 52 staff producing food for 28 guests at lunch and dinner. At Refettorio Ambrosiano, volunteer chefs from some of Milan's top restaurants and around the world donate their time to cook for about a hundred homeless people each sitting. The chefs are assisted by local volunteers and food is donated by a supermarket and is whatever is close to its sell-by date or is misshapen or damaged but still edible. According to Bottura:

> The knowledge, creativity and know-how of professional chefs was essential to prove that salvaged food, overripe or bruised and beyond expiration dates, as well as scraps and trimmings that otherwise would be thrown away, were not only edible, but even delicious.
>
> The Refettorio Ambrosiano opened its doors on May 28, 2015, and thanks to the sustained work of Caritas Ambrosiana, continues to serve guests five days a week. We put words aside and took action. We learned that limitations inspire creativity. When putting food on the table is a challenge, miracles happen in the kitchen. We were enlightened by the genious of necessity. We brought dignity back to the table by changing the dynamics of the dining room and serving unexpected food to the most vulnerable. I wanted our guests to feel welcomed. I remember the very first nights at the Refettorio, when the guests barely spoke to each other. In a matter of weeks, guests and volunteers and chefs were joking around. The meal became a celebration. Most important, we gave food a voice, gave waste a place, and nourished a community. We confirmed what we had only imagined: that a meal can unite, revive and renew. And during it all, we were reminded that cooking is an act of love.
>
> (Bottura & Friends, 2017, p. 8)

A sense of the meal and setting is conveyed by Adams (2017):

> Bottura heads straight for the kitchen for a quick appraisal of tonight's menu – aubergine and courgette with mozzarella and parmesan, a cannelloni (the chefs are just rolling the pasta), raspberry ice cream (from a mountain of glorious slightly overripe fruit that has just been delivered). After a brief exclamatory tasting he whistle-stops me around the room's art

work, the last supper mural on the wall, the 14 oak refectory tables, each one created by a different celebrated Italian designer, in a spirit of one-upmanship.

Interestingly, when the project was first announced local people protested believing that the initiative would encourage addicts and refugees to congregate in the town square. However, when the locals saw the commitment of architects, artists and chefs to transform the site, many opponents changed their opinion of the project with a number now acting as volunteers. According to Adams (2017) Bottura

> didn't want to create a utilitarian soup kitchen. He wanted a place where people whose lives were all about being shut out could have at least one hour in a day when they could "enjoy the pleasure of a beautiful meal in a beautiful place". To begin with, Bottura says, Refettorio's "customers" – who are invited as part of a social programme for three months at a time – were suspicious. "People didn't even look in your eyes. They came in, ate in 20 minutes and left immediately." However, after a month they understood that Bottura and his team were not going away. "We knew we were being accepted when they started complaining," he says, with a smile. "No more soup! We want pasta!'"

Refettorio Felix at St. Cuthbert's Centre is a collaboration with Chef Massimo Bottura's non-profit organization Food for Soul and the Felix Project, a food waste charity, that opened in London in 2017. The St. Cuthbert's Centre is a 30-year-old charity. One of the reasons Bottura wanted to open in London, was "the perception that Britain has become somewhere that wants to close its doors to the homeless, to refugees" (Adams, 2017). The centre seeks to provide:

> Physical, emotional and social care
> Hospitality and inclusion
> Compassion and practical support
> A renewed sense of purpose
> Sustainability of practices and services

www.refettoriofelix.com/about-us/

The centre is a drop-in and therapeutic centre for vulnerable and socially isolated people including those from refugee communities. The centre's guests are often homeless and dealing with mental illness and/or substance misuse when they come to the centre. Every weekday the centre with its chef volunteers offers an extremely high quality three-course lunch made entirely from surplus food together with services including therapeutic counselling, stimulating courses, free laundry and showers and creative workshops.

Food for Soul: www.foodforsoul.it
Refettorio Felix at St. Cuthbert's Centre: www.refettoriofelix.com

During COVID-19, in which restaurants had to close down or change how they provided food to customers because of the need for social distancing, many restaurants also provided services to health workers and/or the disadvantaged. For example, Le Bab, a kebab restaurant in London's Covent Garden, reopened its kitchens to run as a not-for-profit organization called the London Restaurant Co-operative, enabling chefs and waiters to keep working. They were producing one vegan and non-vegan dish a day, for local delivery. Menus were posted daily and dishes cost £7. For each £4 tip on top of the order, a meal was delivered to University College Hospital, or the St Martin's in the Fields homelessness charity. Wilson's in Bristol, UK, set up a GoFundMe page to enable them to cook food for National Health Service (NHS) workers. Chef Tom Kerridge adapted by expanding the butchery part of his Marlow pub, the Butcher's Tap (www.thebutcherstapandgrill.co.uk), into a shop selling a mixture of dry goods, home bread-making kits and ready meals. The latter were made available at 50% off for all NHS workers along with free local delivery (Rayner, 2020).

Helping the disadvantaged and highlighting political and social issues

Charities and trusts are important organizations for involving chefs in community projects. For example, in April 2018 London Chef Imad Alarnab, himself a refugee, ran a pop-up supper club Choose Love Syrian Kitchen, in conjunction with the charity Help for Refugees, to directly fund Hope Hospital, a paediatric facility and the only hospital in northern Aleppo, serving 250,000 people (Khomami, 2018; Samadder, 2018). As of early 2021 he had raised more than £200,000 for Choose Love, which supports refugees and displaced people across Europe (Iqbal, 2021). Such was the success of his efforts that through crowdfunding he raised the funds to open a 60 seat restaurant Imad's Syrian Kitchen (www.imadssyriankitchen.co.uk) on Carnaby Street in Soho, London, in May 2021, and he has pledged a pound from every bill to be donated to Choose Love (Iqbal, 2021).

An award-winning charity in France and the UK is the Refugee Community Kitchen (refugeecommunitykitchen.com) which began in December 2015. In their first four years, the charity has served nearly 2.3 million mainly plant-based meals to refugees in France and to the homeless in the UK, through the help of 20,000 volunteers (Lewis, 2019b). Part of the charity's ethos is that the people they serve should have agency over their meals, which should be culturally appropriate. As a result, a condiments table is a key part of their offering: there is hummus, sumac, onions, za'atar, pickles and salt with which people can garnish their food (Lewis, 2019b). According to Sam Jones, one of the founders,

> We were tapping into a collective consciousness that loads of people were tapping into: we're rich and we're privileged as a society and individuals, we can see suffering and we feel powerless and not represented by our governments. And actually it's close enough, we can do something.
>
> (quoted in Lewis, 2019b)

Another act of community activism by chefs was the November 2016 Cook for Syria campaign led by Chef Angela Hartnett and an anonymous food blogger and critic known as Clerkenwell Boy (www.instagram.com/clerkenwellboyec1/?hl=en, https://linktr.ee/ClerkenwellBoy) which raised money for UNICEF UK's Children of Syria fund. The first event of the campaign was a £150 a head charity dinner in London, at which six leading chefs, Angela Hartnett, Fergus Henderson, José Pizarro, Nuno Mendes, Sami

Tamimi and Yotam Ottolenghi, cooked their own signature dishes with a Middle Eastern twist. Scores of restaurants also put Syrian-inspired recipes on to the menus especially to support the campaign and donated some of the cost (McVeigh, 2016).

Arguably one of the more radical and confronting exercises undertaken by a chef with respect to highlighting issues of disadvantage in a community was that of Chef Tunde Wey in New Orleans in 2018. Chef Wey conducted an experiment in February 2018 to see if customers would pay different prices depending on their colour. Black people could pay $12 and White people would be asked to pay $30 for their pre-fixed Nigerian food box lunch. The median net income for white families in New Orleans is more than $63,000, while for black families, it is just below $26,000. Wey's $18 food price gap was intended to approximate this earnings gap. According to Wey,

> First I introduce the facts and as a white person, you are now an antagonist in this framework, ... But I offer you an easy out. You can pay $12 or you can pay $30. What are you going to do?
>
> (quoted in Lartey, 2018)

Nearly 80% of white customers agreed to pay the inflated price for the box lunch, although white patrons who decided to pay the $30 were more likely to be female: 91% of white women did so compared with just 55% of men. Nevertheless, the point of the experiment was not to redistribute wealth but to start a conversation. According to Wey, "This isn't going to change the racial wealth disparities in the city, ... It was meant to show, in principle, what the burden of cost looks like for people who have less resources" (quoted in Lartey, 2018).

Improving school food

Another example of chef work in the community is the charity Chefs in Schools (see Box 15.2) which since 2018 has been working in the UK to show that, with the guidance of an expert chef, schools can provide fresh, nutritious, creative meals for a similar price, or less, than contract caterers. They currently serve more than 11,000 pupils in 35 schools across greater London and, in collaboration with the LEAP Foundation, built and run The Hackney School of Food which is a community garden and cookery school, set in the grounds of a primary school (see www.hackneyschooloffood.com).

Cumming (2020) wrote of the experiences of Chefs in School in trying to change how food meals are tackled in schools with the case of Woodmansterne School in Lambeth, south London and the work of Head chefs Jake Taylor and Sam Riches. Teachers were sceptical about the new food regime as were the existing catering team, who were suddenly being told the food they had served for decades was no longer appropriate, and they would have to learn new skills. According to Taylor,

> There was resistance, ... I'm 30 and Sam's 29, so at first the staff were a bit like, 'Who are these kids coming in and trying to mess with the programme?' I think we've done alright, but I don't really know. You have to earn those levels of trust and respect.
>
> (quoted in Cumming, 2020)

One of their first acts was to put the wages up from minimum to living wage. This meant that the price of a meal rose to £2.30, mostly to accommodate the increased staff wages. The ingredient cost is only 60 p per meal. They also had to negotiate with their new customers, 700 primary and secondary pupils used to a diet of pizza, chips, chicken wings and beige carbohydrate. According to Taylor, "We'd done lots of mass catering, so the volume wasn't the issue … It was more the brutality of the kids. They tell you exactly how they feel" (quoted in Cumming, 2020).

> ### Box 15.2   Chefs in School
>
> While writing the School Food Plan with a colleague, Henry Dimbleby (a governor at his children's state primary, Gayhurst Community School in Hackney, London, and now chair of Chefs in Schools, Henry co-authored the 2013 School Food Plan and also co-founded Leon Restaurants and the Sustainable Restaurant Association) posted a tweet asking whether anyone would be interested in taking over the school kitchen. Nicole Pisani, then head chef at the acclaimed Soho restaurant Nopi, part of the Ottolenghi group of restaurants, decided to apply and was offered the job by the school's head, Louise Nichols (now Executive Headteacher of the Leap Federation of Schools in Hackney). According to Pisani,
>
>> Like a lot of chefs, I came to a point where I needed something else, physically and mentally, … I looked at the school job and thought, 'Brilliant – I'll work Monday to Friday, and school holidays, and they're never going to call me on a Saturday.'
>>
>> (quoted in Cumming, 2020; see also Chapter 16 on wellbeing in the restaurant kitchen)
>
> Since arriving at Gayhurst, Pisani retrained the school cooks using the restaurant brigade system. They cook everything from scratch and bake bread daily. She also took charge of the cooking curriculum, teaching the children to butcher whole chickens and cook over fire pits in the playground. According to Pisani,
>
>> It's more expensive to hire a chef, but you are buying skills of budgeting, reducing waste and cooking tougher pieces of meat, … Lots of restaurant cooking is about taking something you can buy cheaply and making it taste glamorously expensive. Buying bread to feed 400 kids cost £140. When we made it from scratch, including the labour cost, it was £40.
>>
>> (quoted in Cumming, 2020)
>
> This work became the model for Chefs in Schools who now work to help other schools in the UK completely transform the standards of school food and food education and work in different areas of deprivation in the UK.
>
> During the COVID-19 Summer of 2020, Chefs in Schools created a box scheme, half produce and half ready-made meals, with the idea that a box would feed a family for a week. The boxes were available to parents whose children are eligible for free school meals. Chefs in Schools also provided hampers to families that schools knew needed support but were not eligible for free meals supported by the UK government. Between 27 April and 27 August 2020, they served more than 327,000 meals from five hubs, using food from restaurants Wahaca and Hawksmoor and food waste charities such as The Felix Project, as well as their regular suppliers (Cumming, 2020).
>
> www.chefsinschools.org.uk

Box 15.3 Mainstreaming organic food in public kitchens and canteens

Sweden has seen a significant increase in debates on the environment in recent years, in which much focus has been placed on food production, consumption and waste and their interrelationship with climate change and other planetary boundaries. As a result, public campaigns have focused on reducing food waste volumes, and sought to increase the share of organic food consumed in communal kitchens (schools, universities, administrations). Sweden has a national goal to serve food in public kitchens that is 60% certified organic by 2030. Ekomatcentrum (2020) determined that in 2019, the share of organic food used in communities and the public sector amounted to 39%, up from less than 5% in 2005. In leading communities, up to 83% of all food is already organic.

Ecomatcentrum (2020) also highlights that there is a connection between organic and "climate smart" choices, a reduction in food waste and the share of vegetarian food served. More of the menus' protein should also be sourced from plants. Data shows that these goals are achieved simultaneously with organic choices, as decision-makers place greater emphasis on "appropriate" menu designs, both for reasons of awareness and available budgets. This is reflected in the very low carbon content of the foods served, with values that in leading "organic" communities are as low as 1.7 kg CO_2-eq per average kg of food purchased. Ecomatcentrum (2020) emphasizes that the cost of an organic plate is about €0.2 higher than a conventional plate. To balance the higher cost, kitchens have to be inventive to not exceed available budgets. Five strategies in particular have helped to reduce the average cost per dish served, in spite of the higher (and costlier) share of organic foodstuffs:

- to reduce the share of food going to waste;
- to reduce the share of animal protein;
- to increase the share of protein from grains, pulses and legumes;
- to introduce a veggie-day;
- to test and trial new recipes and meal plans.

The overview provided by Ecomatcentrum (2020) suggests that the introduction of organic food purchase quotas in communities on a voluntary, yet competitive, basis can make significant contributions to reducing negative environmental externalities related to food consumption. These changes also support healthier diets.

Communities saving their drinking and eating places

Public houses are often centre of community life in the UK, especially in small rural villages but also in other areas. However, because of high taxes (a third of the cost of a pub pint is made up of taxes), and the actions of the large breweries and competition from restaurant and other chains, many traditional public houses have been forced to close because of their low levels of profit, particular as their real estate value may be higher if they were converted to apartments or other uses (Morris, 2018). Significantly, the British experience is not isolated, as similar concerns have been expressed about the future of bistros in France. A bistro is an eatery that is open from morning to night, serves moderately prices local French foods and has an active bar. Around 1990, bistros represented about half of all restaurants in Paris, as of 2018 that figure had dropped to 14% (Song, 2018). Bistro culture in France, like pub culture in the UK, is therefore under substantial threat.

In 2015, one real estate agent told the *Guardian* that selling a pub in north London as a potential residential site could attract a price of up to one million pounds, while selling it as a trading pub would attract up to £450,000 (Osborne, 2016). In March 2018. the Campaign for Real Ale (CAMRA), the largest single-issue consumer group in the UK, claimed that 18 British pubs were being closed every week (Morris, 2018). In response, many communities have bought their own local public houses, with the act of purchasing and, often, restoration, often playing a significant part in community building (Carter, 2017; Morris, 2018). For example, in 2017 a small north Yorkshire village pub, The George & Dragon in Hudswell, which was saved by its local community after going bankrupt during the recession in 2008 was named the best in the UK by CAMRA.

When The George & Dragon closed in 2008, it left the village with no other facilities for residents apart from a village hall. Within two years, the community had formed the Hudswell Community Pub group and raised £220,000 to buy the public house back. The pub now provides a hub for community life, with a library and a convenience shop selling milk, eggs and newspapers. It also offers community allotments and free Internet access for patrons. According to Paul Ainsworth, CAMRA's coordinator for pub of the year finalist, "The George & Dragon is a great example of how a pub has been resurrected as a true community asset", while James Alcock, general manager at the Plunkett Foundation, which provided support and funding for the venture, said:

> Community-owned pubs such as the George & Dragon are an exceptional example of how a community can succeed in running an enterprise. Within a short space of time, a community has rallied together in order to save a vital village resource and have now been rewarded for all their hard work.
>
> (quoted in Smithers, 2017)

The 2019 Pub of the Year winner, The Wonston Arms, near Sutton Scotney in Hampshire, had a similar story. Left derelict for several years, the local community had sought to raise the funds to purchase the property but fell short of the required funds. However, a regular at the pub left his career in marketing to take over the freehold, but nevertheless worked closely with the community. As a result, the Wonston Arms is also at the heart of fundraising for the local area. It has generated in excess of £25,000 from the pub community and every month, and it hosts a pop-up cafe, which has raised more than £7,000 for local charitable causes (Marsh, 2019).

The UK initiatives are made possible by the *2011 Localism Act*, which allows communities to apply to their local council to have a building listed as an "asset of community value". If the owner of a listed asset, such as a public house, wants to sell a listed asset, a moratorium period is then triggered during which it cannot be sold. The purpose of this period is to give community groups time to develop a proposal and raise the necessary funds to bid for the property (Marsh & Morris, 2018).

The biggest community buy-back in the UK was that of The Packhorse in the village of South Stoke, just south of Bath. In 2012, the pub was shut and earmarked for housing. According to villager Jenny John,

> It was a terrible blow … Our sense of community suffered. There's a church and village hall but not everyone goes to those. The Packhorse was the only place where everyone went, where you got to meet your neighbours regularly. The loss to the village was huge.
>
> (quoted in Morris, 2018)

In response 450 shareholders joined together to put in more than £1m to purchase and refurbish the pub, along with many hours of work by volunteers. The project leader, Dom Moorhouse, stated,

> It evolved into the biggest community pub buy-back project in British history, ... I think people got stuck in because they wanted to save a beautiful old building, but also because they did not want to lose a place of social connection ... We've proved to local communities across the country what is possible and we'd love to see similar successes elsewhere. It's been hard work but worth the effort. It's brought together so many people across the generations.
>
> (quoted in Morris, 2018)

Food justice and food services

As has been noted several times in this book, while there is an obesity epidemic in much of the developed world, there is simultaneously immense food insecurity on a global scale, and enormous gaps between the food haves and have nots within country with substantial food poverty existing in otherwise wealthy countries (Friel et al., 2006; Taylor-Robinson et al., 2013; Cooper et al., 2014; May et al., 2019; Power et al., 2020; Strong, 2021). For example, in the UK, the Trussell Trust network, which covers around 60% of food banks, reported an increase in three-day food parcels provided from 61,000 in 2010/2011 to 1,583,000 in 2018/2019, while 8%–10% of households were regarded as food insecure in 2016–2018 and around 11% of children lived in food insecure households in 2016 (Sosenko et al., 2019). Such a situation raises serious questions and the structure of the food system and its social sustainability. Restaurants and community-based catering may have a significant role to play in this area. According to Nunn (2020), "Not only should access to healthy, nutritious food be a universal right, but social eating can be a solution for those reliant on mutual aid networks, whether they are elderly, disabled, vulnerable or simply lonely".

An example of such an initiative is the National Food Service (NFS) (www.nationalfoodservice.uk) in the UK. The National Food Service campaign started in Sheffield in 2018. The founding initiatives are from northern UK cities facing significant cuts in welfare services but which have active communities that seek to tackle issues such as food waste, food poverty or social isolation. The NFS aims to create free-at-point-of-use social eating hubs that are run by local communities. As a result of COVID-19 restrictions branches had to switch to a takeaway and delivery model and have convinced local restaurants to join the scheme. According to Nunn (2020) some restaurants are now planning to make it a permanent feature of their business model by not just supplying surplus food to NFS branches, but also transforming their lunch services into contribute-what-you-can social eating spaces, subsidized with the profits they make from their dinner service. Advantages of the NFS community-based approach is that it gives those being served food more involvement in ensuring that meals are appropriate in terms of culture, nutrition and dietary requirements, plus it also avoids the stigma and sense of shame that food banks have (Strong, 2021). According to Carys Kettlety, co-founder of Bristol NFS, the way the system works means there is "no segregation between rich and poor, working and non-working, deserving and undeserving" (quoted in Nunn, 2020).

Nunn (2020) suggests that the 'elephant in the room' with respect to food insecurity is the role of government as, in many countries in which austerity measures have reduced government funding and disparities between rich and poor have widened, government have seemingly withdrawn substantial support for food welfare measures.

Interestingly, a US initiative which used a food system approach shows a way in which to help improve food welfare outcomes while also supporting restaurants and farms.

In April 2020, when the city of Phoenix in Arizona received federal *Cares Act* relief to assist with the impact of COVID-19, the City Council allocated $951,000 to help not only the jobless who needed food but also the farmers who needed buyers and the chefs and cooks who needed work as a result of restaurant restrictions and lack of custom. The resulting programme, Feed Phoenix, provided positive benefits to local businesses as well as tens of thousands of meals between July and December 2020, and was so successful that it was extended into spring 2021. The programme, run by the non-profit Local First Arizona, restored links in the local food supply chain by connecting farms with restaurants and caterers. Local First purchased produce from farms, then paid restaurants and caterers to prepare meals and deliver them to distribution points such as food banks and refugee housing where customers could take them at no cost. Feed Phoenix disbursed meals through nearly 30 distribution points and the programme coordinated deliveries to three to eight distribution centre a day, with 50–500 meals available at each, depending on the caterer or restaurant's capacity and the distribution centre. According to Rosanne Albright, the city council's environmental programs coordinator, these funds could have simply been disbursed to food banks, but stakeholders hoped "to shore up our food system, to help people get back to work, to help our farmers, and to recognize grassroots organizations doing this work" (quoted in Malloy, 2020). Kimber Lanning, the founder and executive director of Local First Arizona, "The city could have awarded one very large contract to one very large company to just prepare all of those meals, … Instead, we decided to create a program to touch as many businesses as possible" (quoted in Malloy, 2020). As a result, the project helped to keep 16 farms and nearly all of the 45 participating restaurants and caterers financially afloat during the pandemic. According to Malloy (2020), participants were saying that even when the programme ends, its effect will persist, through the new distribution channels and business partnerships it has created. As Rosanne Albright observed, "What is going to be left behind is a stronger community food network" (quoted in Malloy, 2020). The Phoenix project highlights the potential role that government support can play in enabling a food system that is socio-economically sustainable. As Nunn (2020) concluded,

> many food justice projects already exist – from community kitchens and food-buying co-operatives, to communal food-growing in gardens and farms. Each one is already tailored to the needs of its community – all they would need is more chefs and volunteers, as well as local authority funding.

Conclusions

This chapter has highlighted some of the ways in which restaurants and foodservice operators contribute to their communities in both a narrow sense and in a wider context of food system change. As noted in the introduction to the chapter, social justice is an important driver for some of the initiatives undertaken with respect to disadvantaged groups, such as those facing food insecurity, as well as ensuring that schoolchildren receive decent school meals. However, it is important to recognize that these initiatives go beyond reducing food waste to rethinking the wider food system and how it can be made more sustainable, points which we will return to in the final chapter.

Chapter 16

Conclusions and futures
Expanding the restaurants and foodservice sustainability menu

Introduction

Chefs and restaurants have become increasingly recognized as playing a major role in influencing what people eat and the overall nature of their food consumption. This is particularly the case of so-called celebrity chefs and the role of food media; however, there are also a variety of organizations, for example sustainable restaurant associations and the Slow Food movement, that are influencing how people eat and engage in the wider conversation on the implications of what we eat and the nature of the wider food system. As René Redzepi, chef patron of the award-winning Noma restaurant in Copenhagen, states:

> Chefs have a new opportunity – and perhaps even an obligation – to inform the public about what is good to eat, and why. But we ourselves need to learn much more about issues that are critical to our world: culinary history, native flora, the relationship between food and food supply systems, sustainability and the social significance of how we eat. There is no conflict between a better meal and a better world.
>
> (Redzepi, 2011)

Chefs, restaurants and foodservice operations are therefore at the forefront of sustainability and are increasingly important actors in encouraging sustainable food consumption and production. However, as this book has highlighted there are numerous challenges in developing a more sustainable kitchen and restaurant including the basic problem of which sustainability factors should be included (see Chapter 1) and how do you find a balance between them. This chapter concludes the book by highlighting some of the challenges that chefs and restaurants face in developing sustainable strategies and the wider issues facing the development of sustainable culinary systems.

Developing sustainable culinary systems

Cuisine is shaped by "a distinctive set of basic food, flavour principles, preparation techniques, rules of consumption, and a supply infrastructure for getting food from field to fork" (Belasco, 2008, p. 34). The components of cuisine can therefore be understood in terms of the foods which are used and where they come from; how it is prepared in terms of techniques and technologies and the waste that is generated and where it goes; how it is presented included the desired flavours; how it should be consumed and the environment where it is consumed. All of these ingredients, together with hospitality – how we welcome guests to sit down and eat – are of crucial importance to understanding the sustainability of restaurants and foodservice operations. Nevertheless, given the enormous strains on the sustainability of the contemporary food system, e.g., in terms of resource use, environmental change and biodiversity loss, land use change, the climate crisis, waste and environmental and human health there is a need to improving the recipe of the culinary food-service and restaurant component of the food system – as what goes into any recipe determines what comes out (Hall, 2020).

The dominant focus in considering cuisine and hospitality in education and research has long been how the various elements of cuisine can best be commoditized and converted from a collective good to a commercial product. Many texts on professional cooking and foodservice operations, for example, contain little information on waste management strategies and sustainability with notions of efficiency being limited to narrow financial interpretations of portion size. This situation also misses the potential win-win scenario that exists with having a more efficient operation as, in many restaurants, realization of the economic benefits of adopting energy and water efficient approaches and waste reduction strategies has been the primary entrée to sustainability (see Chapters 13 and 14). The commercialization of hospitality is, of course, nothing new and is part of the broader changes in society marked by the advance of capitalism and shifts in social and economic practices so that food is increasingly prepared, eaten or taken out as a commercial transaction (Warde & Martens, 1998; Burnett, 2004; Ketter, 2019; Hall & Prayag, 2020). In short, food along with hospitality and travel has become industrialized. Undoubtedly, those who do not like cooking may be grateful for this and the social and economic shifts that have given rise to the restaurant, café, fast-food takeaway, home or room delivery and pre-prepared meals, are welcomed by many. However, such changes are also extremely uneven and while the economic and social structures of industrialized food globalization benefit some, even to the point of mass obesity (Hall, 2018; Jaacks et al., 2019; see also Chapter 8), there remain many who are food insecure, if not outright starving (Food and Agriculture Organization of the United Nations (FAO), International Fund for Agricultural Development (IFAD), United Nations International Children's Emergency Fund (UNICEF), United Nations World Food Programme (WFP) and World Health Organization (WHO), 2020). For example, in Chapter 15 we noted that an estimated 10% of people in the UK are food insecure; in the USA during the COVID-19 pandemic in the week before Christmas 2020, the food insecure figure was close to 25% (Lakhani, 2021). Moreover, the US figures are uneven between different ethnic groups. Hunger, defined as not having enough to eat sometimes or often during the previous week, was reported to be between 19% and 29% of Black households with children over the course of the pandemic compared to 7%–14% of white American families. Latino families experienced the second highest rates of hunger, ranging from 16% to 25% nationally (Lakhani, 2021).

> **Box 16.1 Mark Bittman on the true costs of our cheap food and the American diet**
>
> One of the most damning statistics is that close to 50% of the food that's available [in the USA] is in the form of ultra processed food. So ultra processed food is what I call junk food. What many of us call junk food. And it means food that contains non-food ingredients; food that your grandmother, great grandmother, maybe at this point wouldn't have recognized as food.
>
> Food that you can't cook yourself. Food that you don't find in your own kitchen in the normal course of cooking and eating. A food that didn't exist before the 20th century. …
>
> It's important to recognize that because ultra processed food is cheap and it's fast and it's widely available; people without time and without money, are more likely to buy that kind of food. But everybody eats junk food. And it also poisons the environment for everybody.
>
> The answer is to increase the availability and affordability of real food. It's not let's make better personal choices, because they go back to that statistic. And that's why I think it's so important that you can only buy, you can only eat what there is. Since actually no one is growing food, we're all on the market. And if the market is 50% junk food, that's what people are eating.
>
> (Mark Bittman quoted in Milman, 2021)
>
> Bittman is a journalist (formerly for the *New York Times*), television presenter, food writer, and author of 30 books, including the bestselling *How to Cook Everything* (Bittman, 1998) and has been the recipient of International Association of Culinary Professionals, Julia Child, and James Beard awards for his food writing.
>
> www.markbittman.com

Expanding the menu

How we define things is of importance. As to how we frame a problem or issue will determine the answers we get or even search for. In the case of sustainable restaurants and foodservice operations, it is not sufficient to look just at what happens on the guests' table, as important as that is, but to understand what happens over the life course of the restaurant and in relation to the wider food system. As noted in Chapter 1, such a question is vital as the greatest environmental impact of a restaurant or foodservice operation lies in what it procures (Baldwin et al., 2011). The sheer size of the extent of food purchase by the hospitality and restaurant sector means that it has an enormous impact on the food supply chain, food production and, consequently, land use. Critical questions then arise: Is it local? How was it produced? What assurances exist as to its production and packaging? How has production for restaurants and food services influenced the local and global food system? Did small producers benefit? To really appreciate the relationship between food and eating out we need to look beyond the restaurant table. The menu for restaurant and foodservice operations therefore needs to change.

Fundamental to any improved appreciation of the contribution of restaurants and foodservice operations to sustainability is to understand them within the wider context of the food system and the visitor economy not just in terms of customer relations, as important as that is. Without an appreciation of that larger context and the web of economic, social and environmental relations that are involved we can never really understand what the contribution of restaurants and food services to sustainability actually is. In a world in which food (in)security and obesity are a major challenge; insect numbers including pollinating species such as bees have collapsed; rainforest is cut down to produce palm oil or graze more cattle; wild fisheries stocks are in decline or have collapsed and global heating poses an existential threat to many communities and species, what the customer ate – or not in the case of the food insecure – becomes a critical issue for any kind of food and hospitality business that wishes to be regarded as sustainable (Hall, 2020).

Undoubtedly, hospitality and restaurant businesses can help sustain traditional food practices and help promote the growing of heirloom and heritage varieties of fruit and vegetables as well as animal stock, as well as appropriate foraging (Hall, 2013b, 2016), but it can also lead to their loss as well. The ubiquitous farmed salmon of many a global hotel chain's breakfast buffet is based on feeding the farmed salmon fishmeal produced from other fish species with about 5 kg of fish or more required to produce a kilogram of salmon (Bavington, 2011). And then it has to be shipped of course producing further emissions. Embracing the local can be one response to this situation but how then does that affect other aspects of local food security, i.e., cost and availability, and what is the willingness to pay more to support local and seasonal food as well as to consume differently? Do some foodservice operations therefore complement local food systems or change them in an unsustainable manner? This is something which national and regional fast-food franchise operations have often been identified of doing (Morland & Evanson, 2009; Baker & Friel, 2016; Baker et al., 2020). Therefore, greater consideration needs to be given to the design of food systems and the role of restaurants and foodservice organizations within them (Hall, 2020).

Recommendations for producers and retailers of local food in appealing to more "mindful" consumers suggest that focused marketing and communication strategies, clearer branding and labelling of produce and training of service staff can influence food purchasing and consumption behaviours (Birch et al., 2018). However, training and education is an issue for the wider foodservice community. The training and education of the next generation of chefs, cooks, kitchen and restaurant staff needs to enable them to not only manage the changes that are taking place with respect to sustainable food, including waste reduction and consumer health, but also the greater use of fruit and vegetables and also meat substitutes such as insects, which are widely eaten in many cultures but tend to have a 'yuck' factor in Western cooking, new vegetable-based meat substitutes and the use of in-vitro meats. As noted several times in this book (i.e., see Chapters 8 and 10), along with more ethical forms of consumption, health is a key driver for reducing meat consumption. If restaurant and foodservice operations are to encourage meat reduction it also means that they need to address consumer concerns about iron and protein inadequacies in a meat-reduced diet and tackle a lack of knowledge around being able to prepare vegetarian meals that maximize sensory appeal and are tasty, i.e., what to cook and how (Schösler et al., 2012; Tucker, 2014). In addition, there is also a simple fact that there are many people who appreciate meat, and for these people it is essential that the restaurants and foodservice businesses be more efficient with their use of animals and fish and use more of what is on the animal (see Chapter 10).

> **Box 16.2 The influence of chefs on sustainability**
>
> There are limitations to what restaurants can change, of course. Of all the things we eat, commodity-raised beef is the single largest contributor to climate change, owing mostly to poor manure-disposal techniques. High-end restaurants can turn to more sustainable choices (grass-fed and "carbon-ranched" cattle are better alternatives) but as long as diners want $1 cheeseburgers, feedlot cows will continue to fart and poop our planet warmer. Plus, in the grand scheme of things, the restaurant industry makes up only a small part of the food system, which accounts for somewhere around a third of the world's greenhouse gases. Even if we recruited a thousand restaurants to go carbon-neutral, it wouldn't change the trajectory of the climate.
>
> But this is where the frivolous side of food is important. Food is not simply a commodity – it's a cultural undertaking. In fact, it's pop culture. People admire chefs and covet restaurants. If chefs as a group decide that sustainable food is better food, consumers will follow. Twenty-five years ago, organic produce meant very little to most people. Thanks largely to the work of chefs, organic is now a widely held value.
>
> (Ying, 2018)
>
> Chris Ying, former editor of *Lucky Peach* and founder of a non-profit organisation called ZeroFoodprint, which helps restaurants understand and reduce their climate impact.
>
> www.zerofoodprint.org

Reducing the amount of meat that people consume is regarded as a potentially major contribution to reducing greenhouse gas (GHG) emissions, to conserving biodiversity and to improving health. Avoiding meat and dairy products is the single biggest way an individual can reduce their environmental impact together with reducing travel by jet aircraft (Marsh, 2021).

Poore and Nemecek (2018) showed that the global area occupied by farmland use could be reduced by more than 75%, an area equivalent to the USA, China, European Union and Australia combined, and it could still feed the world if meat and dairy production ceased to exist. Domesticated livestock has a huge environmental and land use footprint providing 18% of calories on 83% of farmland (Carrington, 2018) (Table 16.1). Converting grass into meat is a lot like converting coal or oil into electricity as it comes with an immense cost in emissions. For beef originating from beef herds, the highest-impact 25% of producers account for 56% of the beef herd's GHG emissions and 61% of its land use (an estimated 1.3 billion metric tonnes of CO_2-eq and 950 million ha of land, primarily pasture) (Poore & Nemecek, 2018). This sort of impact illustrates why beef production results in up to 105 kg of GHG per 100 g of protein, while tofu produces less than 3.5 kg of GHG for the same amount of protein (Poore & Nemecek, 2018).

There is a range of different estimates as to the impact of a vegan diet on emissions. In a UK study from 2012, the expected reduction in GHG emissions was 0.45 tonnes CO_2-eq/person/year, about 3% of the then total, giving a reduction across the UK population of 27.8 million tonnes/year (Alston et al., 2012), while a more recent study from Argentina suggests that a vegan diet would reduce emissions per person by

Table 16.1 Contribution of farmed animal products at global scale
Source: Poore and Nemecek (2018)

Category	Contribution (%)
Calories	18
Protein	37
Freshwater withdrawals	33
Air pollution	56
Water pollution	57
Greenhouse gas emissions	58
Land use	83

20%–30%. The latter perhaps is not surprising given that the GHG emissions of the current Argentinian diet are very high (5.48 ± 1.71 kg CO_2-eq/person/day), with beef production contributing to 71% of emissions (Arrieta & Gonzalez, 2018). These figures highlight the differences that exist between countries, depending on their foodways, as well as the different types of analyses that can be conducted. However, regardless, it is clear that dietary changes can help in making a sustainable transition (Poore & Nemecek, 2018; Marsh, 2021).

It is unlikely that people will give up eating meat or dairy altogether, even if substantial taxes were imposed. In addition, some forms of sustainable farming and horticulture, such as permaculture and regenerative agriculture, often integrate livestock into low carbon farming practices, while some biodiversity conservation also relies on limited use of livestock to graze weeds, spread seeds and create a patchwork of micro-habitats (Biró et al., 2019). However, traditional organic farming practices with animals produce a lower surplus of meat to go to market. Therefore, a critical role in any food transition is for chefs and restaurants to influence consumer behaviour by what they provide on the table, the menu marketing of dishes and, perhaps most importantly, ensuring that it provides an outstanding sensory experience. The taste, smell and look of a meal is potentially a major influence in encouraging people to eat differently if it continues to satisfy them. However, in so doing it is also vital that the restaurants and the people who work in them also look after their own wellbeing.

Staff health and wellbeing

Kitchen work is hard work. The hours are long and unsociable, especially in restaurants, and it is also mentally and physically intense. You are standing on your feet for hours, often undertaking careful knife work and having to be exact in cooking times and presentation. For high-end restaurants, there is pressure on attaining and retaining Michelin stars or other accolades. However, the pressure is substantial no matter what the type of restaurant or café you work in as meals or a drink has to be out in a given time to an appropriate standard. Perhaps not surprisingly, the mental health of the kitchen is something that needs greater consideration in framing the social dimensions of the sustainable restaurant. For example, in 2017 Unite, the UK's largest union, conducted a survey of professional chefs in London and the impact of their working conditions upon them. Forty-four percent of those surveyed regularly worked between 48 and 60 hours a week, with it now being standard practice for employers to include an automatic 'opt-out' of the 48-hour a week rule under the Working Time Regulations in workers' contracts although the clause is often hidden, with workers unaware that they have opted-out of this protection (Unite Legal Services, 2021). Seventy-nine percent said they'd had an accident or a near miss through fatigue. More than a quarter were drinking to get through their shift and 56% were taking painkillers, while 51% said they suffered from depression due to overwork (Unite Legal Services, 2021). Given these figures it should not be surprising that chefs are nearly twice as likely to be addicted to alcohol and drugs as the wider population and 9% more vulnerable to suicide (Adams, 2019). However, perhaps because of its culture, "the hospitality industry in particular has been slow to talk about [mental health issues at work]" (Emma Mamo, head of workplace wellbeing at the mental health charity Mind, quoted in Rayner, 2017). Similarly, Adams (2019) suggests:

> Some of these statistics have been fuelled by a working culture which, through the 1990s and 2000s fetishised extreme pressure and made the kitchen seem like a war zone. The suicide of Anthony Bourdain last year, the chef who did so much to create that high-adrenaline charge around cooking, provoked a lot of soul-searching. ... One result has been a generational shift, even among alpha-males who run kitchens.

Box 16.3 The professional kitchen is not a TV set

Despite the supposed glamour of celebrity chefs on television the restaurant and foodservice kitchen is hard work. The primary health issue for chefs is "overwork and exhaustion coupled with a salaried pay check that does not reflect the number of hours you put in" (Chef Kevin Reynolds in Rayner, 2017). Chefs are often contracted for 45 hours a week but often end up working at least ten more hours than this with no extra pay. Alternatively, it will be managed over a month, so that they end up doing 90 hours one week, and just 20 the next. According to veteran chef Brian Mcelderry part of the problem is catering colleges and courses because there is an imperative to pass students whether they have reached an appropriate level or not as a result of the students paying fees: "The pressure is just getting worse, ... They're passing kids out of college who aren't qualified and then they end up in kitchens and they can't cope" (quoted in Rayner, 2017). To make matters worse many restaurants are still difficult environments in which to work (Lewis, 2018), occupational stress and health issues are widespread (Kim et al., 2013) and pay levels may be poor and not reach liveable wage levels, especially in larger cities (Hunt, 2016). In the USA, the restaurant sector is the lowest paying employer: seven of the 11 lowest paying jobs and the two absolute lowest paying jobs in the USA are restaurant jobs (Jayaraman, 2014; Coplen, 2018). As Jeremy King of the Wolseley, the Delauney and Brasserie Zedel restaurants describes it: "The hierarchical system, the dependence on fear rather than encouragement, has meant that for too long it was an incredibly harsh environment" (quoted in Rayner, 2017). This situation is very well described by Jay Rayner:

> As the evidence stacks up, one thought becomes unavoidable: the restaurant business model is dysfunctional. Customers regularly complain about the

cost of restaurant meals, as if chefs and restaurateurs are involved in some filthy "get rich quick" project. And yet, to make the economics stack up, cooks are required to work ludicrous hours which, due to chef shortages and rent rises, are only getting longer. Kevin Reynolds describes how he has seen deskilling in the kitchen over time. "The skilled senior members of the brigade left and were never replaced with a similar skill levels."

One of the great truisms of thinking about the sustainability of restaurants and food services is the need to pay the real cost of food. Here, this is not just to do with resource inputs and waste and efficient kitchens but also about the wellbeing of kitchen, wait and cleaning staff. All of the people who help get the meal onto the plate and look after the restaurant space in which it is prepared and eaten. As Rayner (2017) says,

> The problem is that so much of this takes place not in front of the diners but closed away behind the kitchen door. As diners we may complain about the cost of our restaurant meals. We may wish it were otherwise. But the reality is that, far too often, it's not us who are paying too high a price. It's the people who are doing the cooking.

In her study of labour in restaurants and food services in Oregon, Coplen (2019) observed that although conscious consumers use sustainability-branded restaurants and grocery stores to 'vote with their forks' for environmental sustainability and vibrant local economies, many of the workers in these industries face the same poverty wages, discrimination and exploitative labour practices that plague the sector overall. As she states in the title of her thesis "Poverty wages are not fresh, local, or sustainable" (Coplen, 2019). How then should the sector respond?

Reduce the number of services. One option may be to reduce the number of services that a restaurant is open for in order to improve their staff's quality of life. Rayner (2017) suggests that these tend to be very high-end restaurants, such as Sat Bains in Nottingham, where the economic model makes it possible. However, Chef Bains admitted it was not necessarily an entirely altruistic measure but one undertaken to attract and retain the best staff when there is a chef shortage and a three-day weekend is a way to do that.

Better career and personnel management. Have an internal reward and incentive scheme to assist in career management and well as develop better management skills of individuals in the kitchen and their work lives. Rayner provides the interesting example of Jeremy King who employs over 200 cooks in his many kitchens. King had recently refurbished the kitchens at the Colbert restaurant on Sloane Square in London and his restaurants also employ older cooks and more women in order to improve the work atmosphere. In addition, his restaurants introduced new shifts from just after 9 am until around 3 pm in order to enable parents to drop their children off at school, prep for and then cook some of the lunch service, before leaving for the school pick-up run. According to King,

> Kitchens are noisy, hot stressful places [there are UK laws covering cold in the workplace but none about heat stress] … We've replaced all the gas

stoves with induction which immediately reduces heat and noise ... If any of my staff hear me swear I have to pay them £5. ... All-male environments are very harsh. Women in kitchens are a simple way to destress them.

(quoted in Rayner, 2017)

Work time regulations. Related to the above an obvious measure in those countries that have work time regulations, is for such regulations to be followed by employers. For example, in the UK, Unite is calling on the restaurant sector to end 'the work until you drop', long hours' culture by encouraging employers to fully comply with the Working Time Regulations, including the right to 11 hours rest a day and one day off a week, as well as dropping the automatic 48-hour week opt-out clauses in workers' contracts (Unite Legal Services, 2021).

Living wage. A key issue is also ensuring that staff receive a living wage. However, in some jurisdictions, restaurant associations and lobby groups have actively campaigned against such measures and opposed staff being able to join unions (Walmsley et al., 2019), even though such improvements may have positive implications for businesses in terms of an expression of care for employees, the basis for a high quality service business model, a marker of corporate social responsibility and worker retention (Douglas et al., 2020; Werner, 2021).

Unfortunately, as Rayner (2017) concludes, "It all sounds very encouraging, but these initiatives may be the exception, not the rule".

The wellbeing of the sector

Clearly, a sustainable restaurant and foodservice sector needs to be financially viable. The COVID-19 experience has pushed many restaurants to the limit and, in many cases, over it. Some restaurants have adapted by developing new income streams and adapting their business operations. One of the main ways that business adapted and changed during COVID-19 was to make even greater use of online ordering and delivery apps so as to meet social distancing requirements and reduce contact. It is likely that the impact of these changes will be long-term and create new dining and ordering practices that will have substantial implications for the restaurant and foodservice operation sector, and independent restaurants in particular. For example, Shenker (2021) suggests, "The takeaway service may have felt like a lifeline during lockdown, but its ambitious vision will dramatically change the way we eat".

Four major impacts of these changes can be recognized. First, the commission for ordering, pick-up and delivery is substantial and cuts into a restaurant's margins. Second, the companies that provide apps and pick-up and delivery services gain information on restaurant customers that can be used in the development of their own operations or contracted 'dark kitchens', places where meals are prepared entirely for delivery. Third, delivery apps aggregate restaurants in an area and arguably create new forms of competition while the ranking of restaurants in such systems is often opaque. Finally, many restaurants are concerned about "something more intangible: a fear that as many of us become accustomed to selecting lunch or dinner through a smartphone, our relationship to food itself, and the social context that surrounds it, is shifting" (Shenker, 2021).

Conclusions and futures

> **Box 16.4 Alternative food delivery platforms**
>
> Although online platforms such as Just Eat, Uber Eats or Deliveroo dominate delivery food app business, in recent years there has been an emergence of an array of grassroots alternatives to these platforms, from regional courier collectives to online services that allow small restaurants to market delivery options directly to customers. For example, York collective in the UK (https://yorkcollective.co.uk) is an example of a cycle courier collective for both food and retail. An international federation of such organizations, Coopcycle, has also been developed (https://coopcycle.org/en/federation/). Another example is that FoodeBikes, an eco-friendly delivery service in London (www.foodebikes.co.uk). According to the co-developer of the platform Henal Chotai, one of the proprietors of Red Cup Cafe in Harrow, north-west London, the public appetite for platforms that do a better job of supporting independent restaurants is growing fast:
>
>> Independent restaurants in this country are on their knees right now, but at the same time the value of what we bring to society – the importance of real, human hospitality, the places where you go and form happy memories – has been magnified, … We're battered and bruised, but we're ready to fight for our futures. So I beg everyone, when you can: go out and visit your local small restaurant, find a way of buying from them directly. We've been here for our local communities and we need our local communities to help us – and the country at large – get back on our feet.
>>
>> (Henai Chotai, quoted in Shenker, 2021)

There is clearly a danger to the uberization of the restaurant scene. From an environmental perspective, the points raised in this book with respect to food services apply no matter what the nature of the restaurant or food service is. However, there are also enormous social benefits of the coming together in physical spaces to share food and culture, which are integral to notions of hospitality and defining a restaurant experience. Such places are arguably also those that are potentially more likely to provide living wages to their employees and be more engaged with their communities and local suppliers.

Conclusions: changing the menu

This book has sought to provide insights into how the restaurant and foodservice sector, the business within it, their kitchens and their staff can contribute to sustainability. By going through the various stages of the production process from fork to farm it has highlighted not only the various sustainability challenges that are faced but also some of the solutions. Significantly, many responses can actually add to the bottom-line of a sector undergoing a significant financial challenge.

There is no single silver bullet for climate or environmental change, or for sustainability overall. Instead, there is a need to combine different potential responses. For example, as was noted in the introductory chapter, the decision as to whether conventionally farmed local food is better than organic food from outside the district or not, is one that needs to be assessed on a range of different criteria that will often be different depending on where a restaurant is located. Nevertheless, these are questions that more chefs, cooks and businesses, as well as educators, need to become more aware of. Engaging in such conversations is an important first step, but in order to 'save the planet' it will require restaurants to change their practices with respect to the resources they use, especially with procurement, while people will need to change the way they eat. This will mean that, quite literally, many restaurants will need to change their menu. However, chefs and cooks are the best placed to make this possible with their creativity and understanding of food providing a basis to still encourage people to eat out and enjoy the food experience. Sustainability is often portrayed as something that is 'boring', 'dry' and full of denial for indulgence and pleasure, perhaps something that is seemingly the opposite of eating out – or ordering in. Yet nothing could be further from the truth. Many of the world's greatest chefs and restaurateurs have sought to make their food more sustainable without sacrificing the pleasure of eating and the enjoyment of good hospitality. This is now something that the sector as a whole and those that work within it need to adopt so that we can have our cake and eat it too, both now and in the future.

References

Aarset, B., Beckmann, S., Bigne, E., Beveridge, M., Bjorndal, T., Bunting, J., McDonagh, P., Mariojouls, C., Muir, J., Prothero, A., Reisch, L., Smith, A., Tveteras, R., & Young, J. (2004). The European consumers' understanding and perceptions of the 'organic' food regime: The case of aquaculture. *British Food Journal*, *106*(2), 93–105.

ACO Certification Ltd. (2019). *Australian certified organic.* https://www.aco.net.au/Pages/Operators/ACOStandards.aspx

Adams, T. (2017). Massimo Bottura and his global movement to feed the hungry. *The Observer*, 21 May. https://www.theguardian.com/lifeandstyle/2017/may/21/massimo-bottura-feed-the-hungry-food-for-soul

Adams, T. (2019). Alcohol and chefs: A real kitchen nightmare. *The Observer*, 14 July. https://www.theguardian.com/society/2019/jul/14/alcohol-chefs-real-kitchen-nightmare

Aday, S., & Aday, M. S. (2020). Impact of COVID-19 on the food supply chain. *Food Quality and Safety*, *4*(4), 167–180.

Afifi, T., Liwenga, E., & Kwezi, L. (2014). Rainfall-induced crop failure, food insecurity and out-migration in Same-Kilimanjaro, Tanzania. *Climate and Development*, *6*(1), 53–60.

Agence France-Presse. (2021). Michelin awards star to vegan restaurant for the first time in France. *The Guardian*, 19 January. https://www.theguardian.com/world/2021/jan/19/michelin-awards-star-to-vegan-restaurant-for-the-first-time-in-france

Agnew, D. J., Gutiérrez, N. L., Stern-Pirlot, A., & Hoggarth, D. D. (2014). The MSC experience: Developing an operational certification standard and a market incentive to improve fishery sustainability. *ICES Journal of Marine Science*, *71*(2), 216–225.

Agricultural Marketing Service, U.S. Department of Agriculture (AMS). (2019). *National organic program.* https://www.ams.usda.gov/about-ams/programs-offices/national-organic-program

Akbar, A. (2021). From kala bhuna to shatkora curry – let's all get a taste for Bangladesh. *The Observer*, 21 March. https://www.theguardian.com/world/2021/mar/21/from-kala-bhuna-to-shatkora-curry-lets-all-get-a-taste-for-bangladesh

Albersmeier, F., Schulze, H., Jahn, G., & Spiller, A. (2009). The reliability of third-party certification in the food chain: From checklists to risk-oriented auditing. *Food Control*, *20*(10), 927–935.

Albright, C. L., Flora, J. A., & Fortmann, S. P. (1990). Restaurant menu labeling: Impact of nutrition information on entree sales and patron attitudes. *Health Education Quarterly*, *17*(2), 157–167.

Aleshaiwi, A., & Harries, T. (2020). A step in the journey to food waste: How and why mealtime surpluses become unwanted. *Appetite*, *158*, 105040.

Alfnes, F., & Sharma, A. (2010). Locally produced food in restaurants: Are the customers willing to pay a premium and why? *International Journal of Revenue Management*, *4*(3–4), 238–258.

Ali, M. H., Tan, K. H., & Ismail, M. D. (2017). A supply chain integrity framework for halal food. *British Food Journal*, *119*(1), 20–38.

Alkhamis, T. M. Alhusein, M. A., & Kablan, M. M. (1998). Utilization of waste heat from the kitchen furnace of an enclosed campus. *Energy Conversion and Management*, *39*(10), 1113–1119.

Allder, J. (2008). UK takeaway health: How takeaway restaurants can affect your chances of a healthy diet [pdf]. *National Consumer Council.* https://www.communityfoodandhealth.org.uk/wp-content/uploads/2008/09/takeaway-health.pdf

References

Allen, P., FitzSimmons, M., Goodman, M., & Warner, K. (2003). Shifting plates in the agrifood landscape: The tectonics of alternative food initiatives in California. *Journal of Rural Studies*, *19*(1), 61–75.

Allsopp, M. H., de Lange, W. J., & Veldtman, R. (2008). Valuing insect pollination services with cost of replacement. *PLOS ONE*, *3*(9), e3128. doi:10.1371/journal.pone.0003128.

Alonso, A. D., & O'Neill, M. (2010). Small hospitality enterprises and local produce: A case study. *British Food Journal*, *112*(11), 1175–1189.

Alston, L., Smith, J. N., & Powles, J. W. (2012). Impact of a reduced red and processed meat dietary pattern on disease risks and greenhouse gas emissions in the UK: A modelling study. *BMJ Open*, *2*(5), e001072.

AMA Marketing GesmbH. (2009). *We love organic* [pdf]. http://shop.ama-marketing.at/fileadmin/downloads/webshop/Broschueren/Download_BIO_Herstellerverzeichnis_English.pdf

Amalia, P., Handayani, N., Apriza, M., & Kusrini, E. (2021). Risk analysis in halal fast food supply chain restaurant using risk map method. *International Journal of Mechanical Engineering Technologies and Applications*, *2*(1), 61–66.

Amaris, C., Santos, T. O., Gowreesunker, B. L., Tassou, S. A., & Kolokotroni, M. (2015). Environmental impacts, energy and emissions reductions from food catering in the UK. In *29th EFFOST International Conference Proceedings* (pp. 569–574). Athens.

Amienyo, D., & Azapagic, A. (2016). Life cycle environmental impacts and costs of beer production and consumption in the UK. *The International Journal of Life Cycle Assessment*, *21*(4), 492–509.

Andersson, H., Tago, D., & Treich, N. (2014). *Pesticides and health: A review of evidence on health effects, valuation of risks, and benefit-cost analysis*. Institut d'Économie Industrielle (IDEI).

Andreyeva, T., Kelly, I. R., & Harris, J. L. (2011). Exposure to food advertising on television: Associations with children's fast food and soft drink consumption and obesity. *Economics & Human Biology*, *9*(3), 221–233.

Anheuser-Busch Inbev. (2016). *Annual report 2016*. https://www.ab-inbev.com/content/dam/universaltemplate/ab-inbev/investors/reports-and-filings/annual-and-hy-reports/2017/03/AB%20InBev%20Annual%20Report%202016%20-%20Financial%20report.pdf

Ankeny, R. A., & Bray, H. J. (2019). Red meat and imported wine: Why ethical eating often stops at the restaurant door. *The Conversation*, 8 January. https://theconversation.com/red-meat-and-imported-wine-why-ethical-eating-often-stops-at-the-restaurant-door-106926

Ankeny, R. A., Phillipov, M., & Bray, H. J. (2019). Celebrity chefs and new meat consumption norms: Seeking questions, not answers. *M/C Journal*, *22*(2). doi:10.5204/mcj.1514.

Anzman-Frasca, S., Angstrom, H., Lynskey, V., & Economos, C. (2016). Beyond chicken fingers and French fries: New evidence in favor of healthier kids' menus. *The Global Fruit & Veg Newsletter*, *12*(July/August), 3.

Anzman-Frasca, S., Folta, S. C., Glenn, M. E., Jones-Mueller, A., Lynskey, V. M., Patel, A. A., Tsi, L., & Lopez, N. V. (2017). Healthier children's meals in restaurants: An exploratory study to inform approaches that are acceptable across stakeholders. *Journal of Nutrition Education and Behavior*, *49*(4), 285–295.

Anzman-Frasca, S., Mueller, M. P., Sliwa, S., Dolan, P. R., Harelick, L., Roberts, S. B., Washburn, K., & Economos, C. D. (2015). Changes in children's meal orders following healthy menu modifications at a regional US restaurant chain. *Obesity*, *23*(5), 1055–1062.

Arrieta, E. M., & Gonzalez, A. D. (2018). Impact of current, National Dietary Guidelines and alternative diets on greenhouse gas emissions in Argentina. *Food Policy*, *79*, 58–66.

Aschemann-Witzel, J., de Hooge, I., Amani, P., Bech-Larsen, T., & Oostindjer, M. (2015). Consumer-related food waste: Causes and potential for action. *Sustainability*, *7*, 6457–6477.

Asioli, D., Aschemann-Witzel, J., Caputo, V., Vecchio, R., Annunziata, A., Næs, T., & Varela, P. (2017). Making sense of the "clean label" trends: A review of consumer food choice behavior and discussion of industry implications. *Food Research International*, *99*, 58–71.

Asioli, D., Canavari, M., Pignatti, E., Obermowe, T., Sidali, K. L., Vogt, C., & Spiller, A. (2014). Sensory experiences and expectations of Italian and German organic consumers. *Journal of International Food & Agribusiness Marketing*, *26*(1), 13–27.

Atkinson, L., & Rosenthal, S. (2014). Signaling the green sell: The influence of eco-label source, argument specificity, and product involvement on consumer trust. *Journal of Advertising*, *43*(1), 33–45.

Atkinson, N. (1999). *The impact of BSE on the UK economy.* Report of Ministry of Agriculture, Fisheries and Food.

Auta, H. S., Emenike, C. U., & Fauziah, S. H. (2017). Distribution and importance of microplastics in the marine environment: A review of the sources, fate, effects, and potential solutions. *Environment International, 102,* 165–176.

Azimont, F., & Araujo, L. (2010). The making of a petrol station and the "on-the-move consumer": Classification devices and the shaping of markets. *Industrial Marketing Management, 39*(6), 1010–1018.

Babakhani, N., Lee, A., & Dolnicar, S. (2020). Carbon labels on restaurant menus: Do people pay attention to them? *Journal of Sustainable Tourism, 28*(1), 51–68.

Bagwell, L. S., & Bernheim, B. D. (1996). Veblen effects in a theory of conspicuous consumption. *The American Economic Review, 86*(3), 349–373.

Bahnson, F., & Wirzba, N. (2012). *Making peace with the land: God's call to reconcile with creation.* InterVarsity Press.

Bailey, A. (2020). The chipping market state of play. *Agriculture and Horticulture Development Board (AHDB),* 7 May. Retrieved from https://ahdb.org.uk/news/the-chipping-market-state-of-play

Baird, T., Hall, C. M., & Castka, P. (2018). New Zealand winegrowers attitudes and behaviours towards wine tourism and sustainable winegrowing. *Sustainability, 10*(3), Art. 797.

Baird, T., Hall, C. M., Castka, P., & Ramkissoon, H. (2020). Migrant workers' rights, social justice and sustainability in Australian and New Zealand wineries: A comparative context. In S. L. Forbes, T. De Silva & A. Gilinsky Jr. (Eds.), *Social sustainability in the global wine industry* (pp. 107–118). Palgrave Pivot.

Baker, P., & Friel, S. (2016). Food systems transformations, ultra-processed food markets and the nutrition transition in Asia. *Globalization and Health, 12*(1), 1–15.

Baker, P., Machado, P., Santos, T., Sievert, K., Backholer, K., Hadjikakou, M., Russell, C., Huse, O., Bell, C., Scrinis, G., Worsley, A., Friel, S., & Lawrence, M. (2020). Ultra--processed foods and the nutrition transition: Global, regional and national trends, food systems transformations and political economy drivers. *Obesity Reviews, 21*(12), e13126.

Baldwin, C., Wilberforce, N., & Kapur, A. (2011). Restaurant and food service life cycle assessment and development of a sustainability standard. *The International Journal of Life Cycle Assessment, 16*(1), 40–49.

Balogh, P., Békési, D., Gorton, M., Popp, J., & Lengyel, P. (2016). Consumer willingness to pay for traditional food products. *Food Policy, 61,* 176–184.

Barham, E. (2002). Towards a theory of values-based labeling. *Agriculture & Human Values, 19,* 349–360.

Barham, E. (2003). Translating terroir: The global challenge of French AOC labeling. *Journal of Rural Studies, 19*(1), 127–138.

Bavington, D. (2011). *Managed annihilation: An unnatural history of the Newfoundland cod collapse.* UBC Press.

Bayer, G., Sturm, T., & Hinterseer, S. (2011). *Kennzahlen zum Energieverbrauch in Dienstleistungsgebäuden.* ÖGUT [pdf]. https://www.oegut.at/downloads/pdf/e_kennzahlen-ev-dlg_zb.pdf

BBC. (2020). Coronavirus: Belgians urged to eat more chips by lockdown-hit potato growers. *BBC News,* 27 April. https://www.bbc.com/news/world-europe-52439934

BBC. (2021). Epicurious: US food website ditches beef in new recipes over environment. *BBC News,* 28 April. https://www.bbc.com/news/world-us-canada-56902869

Bearth, A., Khunnutchanart, K., Gasser, O., & Hasler, N. (2021). The whole beast: Consumers' perceptions of and willingness-to-eat animal by-products. *Food Quality and Preference, 89,* 104–144.

Belasco, W. (2008). *Food: The key concepts.* Berg.

Ben-Ari, T., Boé, J., Ciais, P., Lecerf, R., Van der Velde, M., & Makowski, D. (2018). Causes and implications of the unforeseen 2016 extreme yield loss in the breadbasket of France. *Nature Communications, 9*(1), 1627.

Benvenuti, L., De Santis, A., Santesarti, F., & Tocca, L. (2016). An optimal plan for food consumption with minimal environmental impact: The case of school lunch menus. *Journal of Cleaner Production, 129,* 704–713.

References

Bernard, A. B., Grazzi, M., & Tomasi, C. (2015). Intermediaries in international trade: Products and destinations. *Review of Economics and Statistics, 97*(4), 916–920.

Berne Declaration (BD) & EcoNexus. (2013). *Agropoly. A handful of corporations control world food production* [pdf]. https://www.publiceye.ch/fileadmin/doc/Saatgut/2014_PublicEye_Themenheft_1_EN_Agropoly.pdf

Berners-Lee, M., Hoolohan, C., Cammack, H., & Hewitt, C. N. (2012). The relative greenhouse gas impacts of realistic dietary choices. *Energy Policy, 43*, 184–190.

Betz, A., Buchli, J., Göbel, C., & Müller, C. (2015). Food waste in the Swiss food service industry – Magnitude and potential for reduction. *Waste Management, 35*, 218–226.

Bioland. (2019). *About Bioland.* https://www.bioland.de/ueber-uns/about-bioland.html

BioSuisse. (2015). *Standards for the production, processing and marketing of 'bud' products* [pdf]. https://www.bio-suisse.ch/media/VundH/Regelwerk/EN/rl_2015_e_gesamt_web_02.07.2015.pdf

BioSuisse. (2016). *Bio in Zahlen* [pdf]. https://www.bio-suisse.ch/media/Ueberuns/Medien/BioInZahlen/JMK2017/DE/bio_in_zahlen_2016.pdf

Birch, D., Memery, J., & Kanakaratne, M. D. S. (2018). The mindful consumer: Balancing egoistic and altruistic motivations to purchase local food. *Journal of Retailing and Consumer Services, 40*, 221–228.

Biró, M., Molnár, Z., Babai, D., Dénes, A., Fehér, A., Barta, S., Sáfiáng, L., Szabadosh, K., Kišh, A., Demeter, L., & Öllerer, K. (2019). Reviewing historical traditional knowledge for innovative conservation management: A re-evaluation of wetland grazing. *Science of the Total Environment, 666*, 1114–1125.

Bittman, M. (1998). *How to cook everything*. John Wiley & Sons.

Black, R. (2007). Eating garbage: Socially marginal food provisioning practices. In J. MacClancy, J. Henry & H. Macbeth (Eds.), *Consuming the inedible: Neglected dimensions of food choice* (pp. 141–149). Berghan Books.

Blake, M. K. (2019). More than just food: Food insecurity and resilient place making through community self-organising. *Sustainability, 11*(10), Art. 2942.

Blake, M. K., Mellor, J., & Crane, L. (2010). Buying local food: Shopping practices, place, and consumption networks in defining food as local. *Annals of the Association of American Geographers, 100*(2), 409–426.

Blanc, R. (1998a). *Blanc vite. Fast, fresh food from Raymond Blanc*. Headline.

Blanc, R. (1988b). *Recipes from Le Manoir aux Quat'Saisons*. Guild Publishing.

Blanca-Alcubilla, G., Bala, A., Hermira, J. I., De-Castro, N., Chavarri, R., Perales, R., & Fullana-i-Palmer, P. (2018). Tackling international airline catering waste management: Life zero cabin waste project. State of the art and first steps. *Detritus, 3*(September), 159–166.

Blanke, M., & Burdick, B. (2005). Food (miles) for thought-energy balance for locally-grown versus imported apple fruit. *Environmental Science and Pollution Research, 12*(3), 125–127.

Bloom, J. (2010). *American wasteland*. Da Capo Press.

Bochtis, D., Benos, L., Lampridi, M., Marinoudi, V., Pearson, S., & Sørensen, C. G. (2020). Agricultural workforce crisis in light of the COVID-19 pandemic. *Sustainability, 12*(19), 8212.

Bohdanowicz, P., & Martinac, I. (2007). Determinants and benchmarking of resource consumption in hotels–Case study of Hilton International and Scandic in Europe. *Energy and Buildings, 39*, 82–95.

Bohunicky, M., Desmarais, A. A., & Entz, M. (2019). Self-operated vs. corporate contract: A study of food procurement at two universities in Manitoba. *Canadian Food Studies/La Revue canadienne des études sur l'alimentation, 6*(1), 43–74.

Borgmeier, I., & Westenhoefer, J. (2009). Impact of different food label formats on healthiness evaluation and food choice of consumers: A randomized-controlled study. *BMC Public Health, 9*(1), Art. 184.

Bosona, T. G., & Gebresenbet, G. (2011). Cluster building and logistics network integration of local food supply chain. *Biosystems Engineering, 108*(4), 293–302.

Bottura, M., & Friends. (2017). *Bread is gold: Extraordinary meals with ordinary ingredients*. Phaidon.

Boudain, A. (2004). Introduction. In F. Henderson, *Nose to tail eating: A kind of British cooking*. Bloomsbury.

References

Bourguet, D., & Guillemaud, T. (2016). The hidden and external costs of pesticide use. In E. Lichtfouse (Ed.), *Sustainable agriculture reviews* (pp. 35–120). Springer.

Boyano, A., Espinosa, N., Rodriguez, R., Neto, B., & Wolf, O. (2017). *Revision of the EU GPP criteria for food procurement and catering services*, 3rd technical report, JRC Science Hub.

Bozzola, M., Dal Palù, D., & De Giorgi, C. (2017). Design for leftovers. From food waste to social responsibility. *The Design Journal, 20*(sup1), S1692–S1704.

Brach, S., Walsh, G., & Shaw, D. (2018). Sustainable consumption and third-party certification labels: Consumers' perceptions and reactions. *European Management Journal, 36*(2), 254–265.

Breda, J., Jewell, J., & Keller, A. (2019). The importance of the World Health Organization sugar guidelines for dental health and obesity prevention. *Caries Research, 53*(2), 149–152.

Brombach, C. (2017). Meals and eating practices within a multi-generational approach: A qualitative insight study. *International Journal of Clinical Nutrition & Dietetics, 3*(122), 1–6.

Browne, M. A., Niven, S. J., Galloway, T. S., Rowland, S. J., & Thompson, R. C. (2013). Microplastic moves pollutants and additives to worms, reducing functions linked to health and biodiversity. *Current Biology, 23*(23), 2388–2392.

Bryła, P. (2016). Organic food consumption in Poland: Motives and barriers. *Appetite, 105*, 737–746.

Bucher, T., Collins, C., Rollo, M. E., McCaffrey, T. A., De Vlieger, N., Van der Bend, D., ... & Perez-Cueto, F. J. (2016). Nudging consumers towards healthier choices: A systematic review of positional influences on food choice. *British Journal of Nutrition, 115*(12), 2252–2263.

Buchmann, S. L., & Nabhan, G. P. (2012). *The forgotten pollinators*. Island Press.

Buller, H., & Cesar, C. (2007). Eating well, eating fare: Farm animal welfare in France. *International Journal of Sociology of Food and Agriculture, 15*(3), 45–58.

Buller, H., & Morris, C. (2004). Growing goods: The market, the state, and sustainable food production. *Environment and Planning A, 36*(6), 1065–1084.

Bundesministerium für Ernährung und Landwirtschaft (BLE). (2019). *Erste europäische Getreidemarkt-Analyse liegt vor [First European wheat market analysis is available]*. https://www.ble.de/SharedDocs/Pressemitteilungen/DE/2019/190425_Getreidemarkt.html;jsessionid=CC8300D0BF836F0DE5FAAB75A734DB5B.2_cid325

Bundesministerium Nachhaltigkeit und Tourismus (BMNT). (2019). *Trend zu biologischer Landwirtschaft hält an* [Organic agriculture trend continues]. BMNT.

Bunn, D., Feenstra, G. W., Lynch, L., & Sommer, R. (1990). Consumer acceptance of cosmetically imperfect produce. *Journal of Consumer Affairs, 24*, 268–279.

Bureau Européen des Unions de Consommateurs (BEUC). (2020). *One bite at a time: Consumers and the transition to sustainable food. Analysis of a survey of European consumers on attitudes towards sustainable food*. BEUC.

Burgen, S. (2019). 'It has transformed my life': The restaurant where all staff have a disability. *The Guardian*, 10 June. https://www.theguardian.com/world/2019/jun/10/universo-santi-spanish-restaurant-disabilities-jerez

Burnett, J. (2004). *England eats out: A social history of eating out in England from 1830 to the present*. Pearson.

Bush, S. R., & Oosterveer, P. (2015). Vertically differentiating environmental standards: The case of the Marine Stewardship Council. *Sustainability, 7*(2), 1861–1883.

Butler, S. (2019). More than £1bn of food wasted before reaching supermarkets – study. *The Guardian*, 15 July. https://www.theguardian.com/environment/2019/jul/25/food-waste-farms-before-reaching-supermarkets-wrap-study

Butler, S. (2020). The global coffee market has had a rollercoaster year amid Covid crisis. *The Guardian*, 4 September. https://www.theguardian.com/business/2020/sep/04/the-global-coffee-market-has-had-a-rollercoaster-year-amid-covid-crisis

Byrne, C. (2021). Is fast food healthier when it's plant-based? Alternatives to animal products aren't necessarily better for you. *Outside*, 3 February. https://www.outsideonline.com/2421586/health-food-isnt-medicine

Calvert, G. M., Karnik, J., Mehler, L., Beckman, J., Morrissey, B., Sievert, J., Barrett, R., Lackovic, M., Mabee, L, Schwartz, A., Mitchell, Y., & Moraga-McHaley, S. (2008). Acute pesticide poisoning among agricultural workers in the United States, 1998–2005. *American Journal of Industrial Medicine, 51*, 883–898.

Camilleri, A., Larrick, R. P., Hossain, S., & Echeverri, D. (2019). Consumers underestimate the emissions associated with food but are aided by labels. *Nature Climate Change, 9*, 53–58.

Camilleri-Fenech, M., i Sola, J. O., Farreny, R., & Durany, X. G. (2020). A snapshot of solid waste generation in the hospitality industry. The case of a five-star hotel on the island of Malta. *Sustainable Production and Consumption, 21*, 104–119.

Campbell, J., DiPietro, R. B., & Remar, D. (2014). Local foods in a university setting: Price consciousness, product involvement, price/quality inference and consumer's willingness-to-pay. *International Journal of Hospitality Management, 42*, 39–49.

Canada Organic Trade Association. (2017). *Organic agriculture in Canada: By the numbers* [pdf]. Retrieved from https://www.ota.com/sites/default/files/Org_Ag_Canada_overview_17.03.03-FINAL.pdf

Capehart, B. L., & Brambley, M. R. (Eds.). (2020). *Automated diagnostics and analytics for buildings*. Routledge.

Carbon Trust. (2008). *Food preparation and catering: Increase carbon savings without compromising on quality, CTV035*. Carbon Trust.

Cardinale, B. J., Duffy, J. E., Gonzalez, A., Hooper, D. U., Perrings, C., Venail, P., … Naem, S. (2012). Biodiversity loss and its impact on humanity. *Nature, 486*(7401), 59–67.

Carino, S., Porter, J., Malekpour, S., & Collins, J. (2020). Environmental sustainability of hospital foodservices across the food supply chain: A systematic review. *Journal of the Academy of Nutrition and Dietetics, 120*(5), 825–873.

Carins, J., Pang, B., Willmott, T., Knox, K., Storr, R., Robertson, D., Rundle-Thiele, S., & Pettigrew, S. (2021). Creating supportive eating places: A systematic review of food service initiatives. *Health Promotion International*, doi:10.1093/heapro/daaa155.

Carlet, J., Collignon, P., Goldmann, D., Goossens, H., Gyssens, I. C., Harbarth, S., … Richtmann, R. (2011). Society's failure to protect a precious resource: antibiotics. *The Lancet, 378*(9788), 369–371.

Carlsson, F., Frykblom, P., & Lagerkvist, C. J. (2007). Consumer willingness to pay for farm animal welfare: Mobile abattoirs versus transportation to slaughter. *European Review of Agriculture Economics, 34*(3), 321–344.

Carlsson-Kanyama, A. (1998). Climate change and dietary choices—How can emissions of greenhouse gases from food consumption be reduced? *Food Policy, 23*(3–4), 277–293.

Carlsson-Kanyama, A., Ekström, M. P., & Shanahan, H. (2003). Food and life cycle energy inputs: Consequences of diet and ways to increase efficiency. *Ecological Economics, 44*(2), 293–307.

Carrington, D. (2017). UN experts denounce 'myth' pesticides are necessary to feed the world. *The Guardian*, 7 March. https://www.theguardian.com/environment/2017/mar/07/un-experts-denounce-myth-pesticides-are-necessary-to-feed-the-world

Carrington, D. (2018). Avoiding meat and dairy is 'single biggest way' to reduce your impact on Earth. *The Guardian*, 31 May. https://www.theguardian.com/environment/2018/may/31/avoiding-meat-and-dairy-is-single-biggest-way-to-reduce-your-impact-on-earth

Carter, W. (2017). We saved our ailing local pub – now it's the heart of the community. *The Guardian*, 7 April. https://www.theguardian.com/voluntary-sector-network/2017/apr/07/community-pubs-month-camra-brighton-the-bevy

Casselman, A. (2010). *Local foods movement in the Iowa catering industry*. Graduate Theses and Dissertations, 11493. Iowa State University.

Cecchini, M., & Warin, L. (2016). Impact of food labelling systems on food choices and eating behaviours: A systematic review and meta-analysis of randomized studies. *Obesity Reviews, 17*(3), 201–210.

Center for International Environmental Law (CIEL). (2019). *Plastic & health: The hidden costs of a plastic planet*. CIEL.

Cerutti, A. K., Ardente, F., Contu, S., Donno, D., & Beccaro, G. L. (2018). Modelling, assessing, and ranking public procurement options for a climate-friendly catering service. *The International Journal of Life Cycle Assessment, 23*(1), 95–115.

Chafen, J. J. S., Newberry, S. J., Riedl, M. A., Bravata, D. M., Maglione, M., Suttorp, M. J., … Shekelle, P. G. (2010). Diagnosing and managing common food allergies: A systematic review. *JAMA, 303*(18), 1848–1856.

References

Chambers, S., Lobb, A., Butler, L., Harvey, K., & Traill, W. B. (2007). Local, national and imported foods: A qualitative study. *Appetite*, *49*(1), 208–213.

Chan, E. K., Kwortnik, R., & Wansink, B. (2017). McHealthy: How marketing incentives influence healthy food choices. *Cornell Hospitality Quarterly*, *58*(1), 6–22.

Chandon, P., & Wansink, B. (2007). The biasing health halos of fast-food restaurant health claims: Lower calorie estimates and higher side-dish consumption intentions. *Journal of Consumer Research*, *34*(3), 301–314.

Charlebois, S., Creedy, A., & von Massow, M. (2015). "Back of house" – focused study on food waste in fine dining: The case of Delish restaurants. *International Journal of Culture, Tourism and Hospitality Research*, *9*(3), 278–291.

Chen, B., Han, M. Y., Peng, K., Zhou, S. L., Shao, L., Wu, X. F., ... Chen, G. Q. (2018). Global land-water nexus: Agricultural land and freshwater use embodied in worldwide supply chains. *Science of the Total Environment*, *613–614*, 931–943.

Chen, C. J. R. (2008). *College and university dining service administrators' intention to adopt sustainable practices: An application of the theory of planned behavior* (Doctoral dissertation). Iowa State University, Iowa, ProQuest Dissertations Publishing, 2008. 3379179.

Chen, C. J. R., Gregoire, M. B., Arendt, S., & Shelley, M. C. (2011). College and university dining services administrators' intention to adopt sustainable practices: Results from US institutions. *International Journal of Sustainability in Higher Education*, *12*(2), 145–162.

Chen, H. S., & Jai, T. -M. (2018). Waste less, enjoy more: Forming a messaging campaign and reducing food waste in restaurants. *Journal of Quality Assurance in Hospitality and Tourism*, *19*(4), 495–520.

Chen, N. C., Hall, C. M., & Prayag, G. (2021). *Sense of place and place attachment in tourism*. Routledge.

Chenoweth, J., Hadjikakou, M., & Zoumides, C. (2014). Quantifying the human impact on water resources: A critical review of the water footprint concept. *Hydrology and Earth System Sciences*, *18*(6), 2325–2342.

Chi, D. L., & Scott, J. M. (2019). Added sugar and dental caries in children: A scientific update and future steps. *Dental Clinics*, *63*(1), 17–33.

Chkanikova, O., & Lehner, M. (2015). Private eco-brands and green market development: towards new forms of sustainability governance in the food retailing. *Journal of Cleaner Production*, *107*, 74–84.

Cho, A., Hurd, E., Gogna, A., Ma, F., & Zhou, M. (2014). *Sustainable Pub: Energy*, UBC Social Ecological Economic Development Studies (SEEDS) Student Report, University of British Columbia.

Cho, M., Bonn, M. A., Giunipero, L., & Divers, J. (2019). Restaurant purchasing skills and the impacts upon strategic purchasing and performance: The roles of supplier integration. *International Journal of Hospitality Management*, *78*, 293–303.

Cho, M., Bonn, M. A., Giunipero, L., & Jaggi, J. S. (2021). Supplier selection and partnerships: Effects upon restaurant operational and strategic benefits and performance. *International Journal of Hospitality Management*, *94*, 102781.

Choi, I., Kim, W. G., & Yoon, J. (2017). Energy intake from commercially-prepared meals by food source in Korean adults: Analysis of the 2001 and 2011 Korea national health and nutrition examination surveys. *Nutrition Research and Practice*, *11*, 155–163.

Chopra, A. K., Sharma, M. K., & Chamoli, S. (2011). Bioaccumulation of organochlorine pesticides in aquatic system—An overview. *Environmental Monitoring and Assessment*, *173*, 905–916.

Chou, S. -Y., Rashad, I., & Grossman, M. (2008). Fast-food restaurant advertising on television and its influence on childhood obesity. *Journal of Law and Economics*, *51*, 599–618.

Christian, C., Ainley, D., Bailey, M., Dayton, P., Hocevar, J., LeVine, M., Nikoloyuk, J., Nouvian, C., Velarde, E., Werner, R., & Jacquet, J. (2013). A review of formal objections to Marine Stewardship Council fisheries certifications. *Biological Conservation*, *161*, 10–17.

Cinner, J. E., Adger, W. N., Allison, E. H., Barnes, M. L., Brown, K., Cohen, P. J., ... & Marshall, N. A. (2018). Building adaptive capacity to climate change in tropical coastal communities. *Nature Climate Change*, *8*(2), 117–123.

References

Cinzia. M. (2017). A focus on the state of the art of food waste/losses issue and suggestions for future research. *Waste Management, 68,* 557–570.

Cirillo, T., Fasano, E., Castaldi, E., Montuori, P., & Cocchieri, R. A. (2011). Children's exposure to Di(2-ethylhexyl)phthalate and dibutylphthalate plasticizers from school meals. *Journal of Agricultural and Food Chemistry, 59*(19), 10532–10538.

Clark, J. (2015). Making energy efficiency make cents. In Better Buildings, US Department of Energy, *Reducing energy consumption in restaurants and kitchens.* https://betterbuildingssolutioncenter.energy.gov/sites/default/files/Wednesday%20-%20Reducing%20Energy%20Consumption%20in%20Restaurants%20and%20Kitchens_%20Turning%20Down%20the%20Heat%20on%20Energy%20Bills.pdf

Clement, B. J. (2019). Seattle star chef Maria Hines on the radical decision to run just one restaurant. *The Seattle Times,* 27 March. https://www.seattletimes.com/life/food-drink/seattle-star-chef-maria-hines-on-the-radical-decision-to-run-just-one-restaurant/

Close, A. (2018). *Rethinking the Buffet: 3 Things hotels can do now to reduce food waste,* April 9, 2018. https://flwprotocol.org/rethinking-buffet-3-things-hotels-can-now-reduce-food-waste/

Coady, D., Parry, I., Sears, L., & Shang, B. (2017). How large are global fossil fuel subsidies? *World Development, 91,* 11–27.

Cochrane, K. L. (2021). Reconciling sustainability, economic efficiency and equity in marine fisheries: Has there been progress in the last 20 years? *Fish and Fisheries, 22*(2), 298–323.

Cohen, D. A. (2018). Food for thought: How dietitians can help people make healthy food choices. *Nutrition Today, 53*(1), 13–17.

Cohen, J. F., Richardson, S., Parker, E., Catalano, P. J., & Rimm, E. B. (2014). Impact of the new US Department of Agriculture school meal standards on food selection, consumption, and waste. *American Journal of Preventive Medicine, 46*(4), 388–394.

Cohen, S. A., & Higham, J. E. S. (2011). Eyes wide shut? UK consumer perceptions on aviation climate impacts and travel decisions to New Zealand. *Current Issues in Tourism, 14*(4), 323–335.

Cohn, B. A., La Merrill, M., Krigbaum, N. Y., Yeh, G., Park, J. S., Zimmermann, L., & Cirillo, P. M. (2015). DDT exposure in utero and breast cancer. *The Journal of Clinical Endocrinology & Metabolism, 100*(8), 2865–2872.

Colchero, M. A., Popkin, B. M., Rivera, J. A., & Ng, S. W. (2016). Beverage purchases from stores in Mexico under the excise tax on sugar sweetened beverages: Observational study. *BMJ, 352,* h6704.

Coley, D., Howard, M., & Winter, M. (2009). Local food, food miles and carbon emissions: A comparison of farm shop and mass distribution approaches. *Food Policy, 34*(2), 150–155.

Coley, D., Howard, M., & Winter, M. (2011). Food miles: Time for a re-think? *British Food Journal, 113*(7), 919–934.

Collicutt, J. (2009). Community resilience: The future of business continuity. *Journal of Business Continuity & Emergency Planning, 3*(2), 145–152.

Collier, A. K. (2015). The Black Panthers: Revolutionaries, free breakfast pioneers. *National Geographic,* 5 November. https://www.nationalgeographic.com/culture/article/the-black-panthers-revolutionaries-free-breakfast-pioneers

Collier, P., & Dercon, S. (2014). African agriculture in 50 years: Smallholders in a rapidly changing world? *World Development, 63,* 92–101.

Collison, R., & Colwill, J. S. (1987). Food waste in public houses and restaurants and customer attitudes. *International Journal of Hospitality Management, 6*(3), 163–167.

Cook, I., Crang, P., & Thorpe, M. (1998). Biographies and geographies: Consumer understandings of the origins of foods. *British Food Journal, 100*(3), 162–167.

Cook-Cottone, C. P., Tribole, E., & Tylka, T. L. (2013). *Healthy eating in schools: Evidence-based interventions to help kids thrive.* American Psychological Association.

Cooper, J., & Dobson, H. (2007). The benefits of pesticides to mankind and the environment. *Crop Protection, 26,* 1337–1348.

Cooper, N., Purcell, S., & Jackson, R. (2014). *Below the breadline: The relentless rise of food poverty in Britain.* Oxfam GB, Church Action on Poverty and The Trussell Trust.

Coplen, A. K. (2018). The labor between farm and table: Cultivating an urban political ecology of agrifood for the 21st century. *Geography Compass, 12*(5), e12370.

Coplen, A. K. R. (2019). *"Poverty wages are not fresh, local, or sustainable": Building worker power by organizing around (re) production in Portland's "sustainable" food industry*. Ph.D. in Urban Studies. Portland State University. doi:10.15760/etd.6968.

Corbyn, Z. (2021). Interview. Shanna Swan: 'Most couples may have to use assisted reproduction by 2045'. *The Observer*, 28 March. https://www.theguardian.com/society/2021/mar/28/shanna-swan-fertility-reproduction-count-down

Cornelius, A., Fisher, D., Frantz, E., & Karas, A. (2014). *Energy Management Systems (EMS) and Demand-controlled Kitchen Ventilation (DCKV) energy savings in restaurants*. ET ProjectNumber: ET13PGE815, Pacific Gas and Electric Company. https://www.etcc-ca.com/sites/default/files/reports/et13pge8151_dcvandemsreport_final.pdf

Costa Cruises. (2018). *Sustainability report 2018*. Costa Crociere Group.

Cox, J. (2017). Sustainable development goals and animal issues: Preparing for the UN's high level political forum. *World Animal Net*, 10 May. http://worldanimal.net/world-animal-net-blog/item/439-sustainable-development-goals-and-animal-issues-preparing-for-the-un-s-high-level-political-forum

Creusen, M. E. H., & Schoormans, J. P. L. (2005). The different roles of product appearance in consumer choice. *Journal of Product Innovation and Management*, 22, 63–81.

Crimarco, A., Turner-McGrievy, G. M., Botchway, M., Macauda, M., Adams, S. A., Blake, C. E., & Younginer, N. (2020). "We're not meat shamers. We're plant pushers.": How owners of local vegan soul food restaurants promote healthy eating in the African American community. *Journal of Black Studies*, 51(2), 168–193.

Crippa, M., Solazzo, E., Guizzardi, D., Monforti-Ferrario, F., Tubiello, F. N., & Leip, A. (2021). Food systems are responsible for a third of global anthropogenic GHG emissions. *Nature Food*, 2(3), 198–209.

Crockett, R. A., Jebb, S. A., Hankins, M., & Marteau, T. M. (2014). The impact of nutritional labels and socioeconomic status on energy intake. An experimental field study. *Appetite*, 81, 12–19.

Crowder, D. W., & Reganold, J. P. (2015). Financial competitiveness of organic agriculture on a global scale. *Proceedings of the National Academy of Sciences*, 112(24), 7611–7616.

Crozet, M., Lalanne, G., & Poncet, S. (2013). Wholesalers in international trade. *European Economic Review*, 58, 1–17.

Cui, Y., Cacciolatti, L., Woock, P., Liu, Y., & Zhang, X. (2016). A qualitative exploratory investigation on the purchase intention of consumers affected by long-term negative advertising: A case from the Chinese milk sector. *Economia Agro-Alimentare*, 20, 263–282.

Cumming, E. (2020). The restaurant chefs transforming school meals. *The Observer*, 20 September. https://www.theguardian.com/education/2020/sep/20/the-restaurant-chefs-transforming-school-meals-lockdown-coronavirus-challenges

Cunha, F. O., & Oliveira, A. C. (2020). Benchmarking for realistic nZEB hotel buildings. *Journal of Building Engineering*, 30, Art. 101298.

Cunningham, E. (2011). Where can I find resources on the local food movement? *Journal of the American Dietetic Association*, 111(7), 1094–1094.

Curtis, K. R., & Cowee, M. W. (2009). Direct marketing local food to chefs: Chef preferences and perceived obstacles. *Journal of Food Distribution Research*, 40(2), 26–36.

D'Agostino, D., & Mazzarella, L. (2019). What is a nearly zero energy building? Overview, implementation and comparison of definitions. *Journal of Building Engineering*, 21, 200–212.

Dai, T., Yang, Y., Lee, R., Fleischer, A. S., & Wemhoff, A. P. (2020). Life cycle environmental impacts of food away from home and mitigation strategies—A review. *Journal of Environmental Management*, 265, Art. 110471.

Daily, G. C. (Ed.) (1997). *Nature's services. Societal dependence on natural ecosystems*. Island Press.

Danenberg, N., & Remaud, H. (2010). *Barriers and drivers of the SA food service sector's purchase of seafood*. Paper presented at the Seafood Directions Conference, Melbourne, Australia.

Darby, K., Batte, M. T., Ernst, S., & Roe, B. (2008). Decomposing local: A conjoint analysis of locally produced foods. *American Journal of Agricultural Economics*, 90(2), 476–486.

Daugbjerg, C., Smed, S., Andersen, L. M., & Schvartzman, Y. (2014). Improving eco-labelling as an environmental policy instrument: Knowledge, trust and organic consumption. *Journal of Environmental Policy & Planning*, 16(4), 559–575.

References

Davies, A. R., & Legg, R. (2018). Fare sharing: Interrogating the nexus of ICT, urban food sharing, and sustainability. *Food, Culture & Society, 21*(2), 233–254.

Davis, G. S., Waits, K., Nordstrom, L., Grande, H., Weaver, B., Papp, K., … Price, L. B. (2018). Antibiotic-resistant *Escherichia coli* from retail poultry meat with different antibiotic use claims. *BMC Microbiology, 18*(1), 174.

De Clercq, D., Wen, Z., Gottfried, O., Schmidt, F., & Fei, F. (2017). A review of global strategies promoting the conversion of food waste to bioenergy via anaerobic digestion. *Renewable and Sustainable Energy Reviews, 79*, 204–221.

de Laurentiis, V., Hunt, D. V. L., Lee, S. E., & Rogers, C. D. F. (2019). EATS: A life cycle-based decision support tool for local authorities and school caterers. *International Journal of Life Cycle Assessment, 24*, 1222–1238.

Deloitte. (2021). *Global powers of retailing 2021* [pdf]. https://www2.deloitte.com/content/dam/Deloitte/global/Documents/Consumer-Business/gx-global-power-retailing-2021.pdf

Demeter. (2016). *Steiner's impulse for agriculture* [pdf]. https://www.demeter.net/sites/default/files/public/pdf/di_steinersimpulse.pdf

Demeter. (2019). *Biodynamic Federation – Demeter-International e.V.* https://www.demeter.de/organisation/demeter-international

DeMicco, F., Seferis, J., Bao, Y., & Scholz, M. E. (2014). The eco-restaurant of the future: A case study. *Journal of Foodservice Business Research, 17*(4), 363–368.

Deng, S. M., & Burnett, J. (2002). Water use in hotels in Hong Kong. *Hospitality Management, 21*, 57–66.

Denny, R. C., Worosz, M. R., & Wilson, N. L. (2016). The importance of governance levels in alternative food networks: The case of red meat inspection rules. *Rural Sociology, 81*(4), 601–634.

Denver, S., Jensen, J. D., Olsen, S. B., & Christensen, T. (2019). Consumer preferences for 'Localness' and organic food production. *Journal of Food Products Marketing, 25*(6), 668–689.

Dhir, A., Talwar, S., Kaur, P., & Malibari, A. (2020). Food waste in hospitality and food services: A systematic literature review and framework development approach. *Journal of Cleaner Production, 270*, Art. 122861.

Dickie, M. (2003). Defensive behavior and damage cost methods. In P. A. Champ, K. J. Boyle & T. C. Brown (Eds.), *A primer on nonmarket valuation* (pp. 395–444). Springer.

Dictionary.com (2019). *Health food.* https://www.dictionary.com/browse/health-food

Didinger, C., & Thompson, H. (2020). Motivating pulse-centric eating patterns to benefit human and environmental well-being. *Nutrients, 12*(11), Art. 3500.

Dinu, M., Abbate, R., Gensini, G. F., Casini, A., & Sofi, F. (2017). Vegetarian, vegan diets and multiple health outcomes: A systematic review with meta-analysis of observational studies. *Critical Reviews in Food Science and Nutrition, 57*(17), 3640–3649.

DiPietro, R. B., Cao, Y., & Partlow, C. (2013). Green practices in upscale foodservice operations. *International Journal of Contemporary Hospitality Management, 25*(5), 779–796.

Dolan, P., Hallsworth, M., Halpern, D., King, D., & Vlaev, I. (2010). *MINDSPACE: Influencing behaviour through public policy.* Cabinet Office and Institute for Government.

Dolnicar, S., Juvan, E., Grün, B. (2020). Reducing the plate waste of families at hotel buffets—A quasi-experimental field study. *Tourism Management, 80*, Art. 104103.

Douglas, J., Williamson, D., & Harris, C. (2020). Dirty deeds, done dirt cheap: Creating 'hospitable wages' through the living wage movement. *Hospitality & Society, 10*(1), 3–22.

Doward, J., & Melli, M. (2016). Seaweed, salt and soil: How 'terroir' cooking put local flavour on the plate. *The Observer*, 3 July. https://www.theguardian.com/lifeandstyle/2016/jul/02/terroir-food-local-sportsman-pub

Drewnowski, A., & Darmon, N. (2005). The economics of obesity: Dietary energy density and energy cost. *The American Journal of Clinical Nutrition, 82*(1), 265S–273S.

Duffy, G., Cloak, O. M., O'Sullivan, M. G., Guillet, A., Sheridan, J. J., Blair, I. S., & McDowell, D. A. (1999). The incidence and antibiotic resistance profiles of *Salmonella* spp. on Irish retail meat products. *Food Microbiology, 16*(6), 623–631.

Duncan, J., Carolan, M., & Wiskerke, J. S. (Eds.). (2021). *Routledge handbook of sustainable and regenerative food systems.* Routledge.

Dunne, J. B., Chambers, K. J., Giombolini, K. J., & Schlegel, S. A. (2011). What does 'local' mean in the grocery store? Multiplicity in food retailers' perspectives on sourcing and marketing local foods. *Renewable Agriculture and Food Systems, 26*(1), 46–59.

DuPuis, E. M., & Goodman, D. (2005). Should we go home to eat? Toward a reflexive politics of localism. *Journal of Rural Studies, 21*(3), 359–371.

Duram, L., & Oberholtzer, L. (2010). A geographic approach to place and natural resource use in local food systems. *Renewable Agriculture and Food Systems, 25*(2), 99–108.

Duursma, G., Vrenegoor, F., & Kobus, S. (2016). Food waste reduction at Restaurant De Pleats: Small steps for mankind. *Research in Hospitality Management, 6*(1), 95–100.

Eastham, J. (2001). Preface. In J. Eastham, L. Sharples & S. Ball (Eds.), *Food supply chain management: Issues for the hospitality and retail sectors* (pp. xvii–xx). Butterworth-Heinemann.

Ecolabel Index. (2018). *Homepage*. Retrieved from http://www.ecolabelindex.com

Ecomatcentrum. (2020). *Ekomatcentrum marknadsrapport. Ekologiskt i offentlig sektor 2020* [Organic food center market report. Organic in the public sector] [pdf]. http://ekomatcentrum.se/wp-content/uploads/2020/10/Rapport-Marknadsrapport-EMC-2020.pdf

Edelstein, B. L. (2006). The dental caries pandemic and disparities problem. *BMC Oral Health, 6*, S2. doi:10.1186/1472-6831-6-S1-S2.

Eerkes-Medrano, D., Thompson, R. C., & Aldridge, D. C. (2015). Microplastics in freshwater systems: A review of the emerging threats, identification of knowledge gaps and prioritisation of research needs. *Water Research, 75*, 63–82.

Ehrlich, P., & Ehrlich, A. (1981). *Extinction*. Ballantine Books.

Ekelund, L., & Spendrup, S. (2016). Climate labelling and the importance of increased vegetable consumption. *Acta Hortic., 1132*, 191–198.

Ellison, B., Lusk, J. L., & Davis, D. (2013). Looking at the label and beyond: The effects of calorie labels, health consciousness, and demographics on caloric intake in restaurants. *International Journal of Behavioral Nutrition and Physical Activity, 10*(1), 21.

El-Mobaidh, A. M., Razek Taha, M. A., & Lassheen, N. K. (2006). Classification of in-flight catering wastes in Egypt air flights and its potential as energy source (chemical approach). *Waste Management, 26*(6), 587–591.

Elofsson, K., Bengtsson, N., Matsdotter, E., & Arntyr, J. (2016). The impact of climate information on milk demand: Evidence from a field experiment. *Food Policy, 58*, 14–23.

Emberger-Klein, A., & Menrad, K. (2018). The effect of information provision on supermarket consumers' use of and preferences for carbon labels in Germany. *Journal of Cleaner Production, 172*, 253–263.

Energy Star. (n.d.). *Benchmark your building using ENERGY STAR® Portfolio Manager®*. Retrieved from https://www.energystar.gov/buildings/benchmark

Environment agency. (2012). *Saving water in hotels and guest houses, UK*. Environment Agency.

Eriksen, S. N. (2013). Defining local food: Constructing a new taxonomy–three domains of proximity. *Acta Agriculturae Scandinavica, Section B–Soil & Plant Science, 63*(sup1), 47–55.

Eurobarometer. (2011). *The common agriculture policy*. Special Eurobarometer 368. Directorate-General for Communication.

Eurobarometer. (2012). *European attitudes towards food security, food quality and the countryside*, Special Eurobarometer 389. http://ec.europa.eu/agriculture/survey/2012/389_en.pdf

Eurobarometer. (2020). *Making our food fit for the future – Citizens' expectations*. Special Barometer 505.

European Commission (EC). (2007). *Council Regulation (EC) No 834/2007* [pdf]. https://eur-lex.europa.eu/LexUriServ/LexUriServ.do?uri=OJ:L:2007:189:0001:0023:EN:PDF

European Commission (EC). (2010). *Preparatory study on food waste across EU 27* [pdf]. https://ec.europa.eu/environment/eussd/pdf/bio_foodwaste_report.pdf. Accessed 14 February 2020.

European Commission (EC). (2016). *Reducing CO_2 emissions from passenger cars*. http://ec.europa.eu/clima/policies/transport/vehicles/cars/index_en.htm

European Commission (EC). (2017). *Special Eurobarometer 459. Climate change* [pdf]. https://ec.europa.eu/clima/sites/clima/files/support/docs/report_2017_en.pdf

European Commission (EC). (2018). *Statistical Factsheet. European Union* [pdf]. https://ec.europa.eu/agriculture/sites/agriculture/files/statistics/factsheets/pdf/eu_en.pdf

European Commission (EC). (2019). *Organics at a glance*. https://ec.europa.eu/info/food-farming-fisheries/farming/organic-farming/organics-glance#legislation

European Environment Agency (EEA). (2016). *Sectoral greenhouse gas emissions by IPCC sector*. https://www.eea.europa.eu/data-and-maps/daviz/change-of-co2-eq-emissions-2#tab-chart_4

References

European Food Safety Authority (EFSA). (2016). Presence of microplastics and nanoplastics in food, with particular focus on seafood. *EFSA Journal*, *14*(6), Art. 4501.

European Parliament. (2016). *Short food supply chains and local food systems in the EU*. Briefing Paper, September. https://www.europarl.europa.eu/RegData/etudes/BRIE/2016/586650/EPRS_BRI(2016)586650_EN.pdf

Eurostat. (2019). *Organic farming statistics*. https://ec.europa.eu/eurostat/statistics-explained/index.php?title=Organic_farming_statistics

Fabricius, K. E. (2005). Effects of terrestrial runoff on the ecology of corals and coral reefs: Review and synthesis. *Marine Pollution Bulletin*, *50*, 125–146.

Fair Trade International. (2021). *How Fairtrade differs from other labels*. https://www.fairtrade.net/about/how-fairtrade-differs

Falkow, S., & Kennedy, D. (2001). Antibiotics, animals, and people – again! *Science*, *291*(5503), 397. doi:10.1126/science.1058907.

Falstaff. (2017). *Frankreich: Schlechteste Weinernte seit 1945*. [France: Worst grape yield since 1945]. https://www.falstaff.at/nd/frankreich-schlechteste-weinernte-seit-1945/

Feagan, R. (2007). The place of food: Mapping out the local in local food systems. *Progress in Human Geography*, *31*(1), 23–42.

Feenstra, G. (2002). Creating space for sustainable food systems: Lessons from the field. *Agriculture and Human Values*, *19*(2), 99–106.

Feinstein, A. H., & Stefanelli, J. M. (2017). *Purchasing: Selection and procurement for the hospitality industry* (9th ed.). John Wiley & Sons.

Feldmann, C., & Hamm, U. (2015). Consumers' perceptions and preferences for local food: A review. *Food Quality and Preference*, *40*(Part A), 152–164.

Fellmann, T., Witzke, P., Weiss, F., Van Doorslaer, B., Drabik, D., Huck, I., Salputra, G., Jansson, T., & Leip, A. (2018). Major challenges of integrating agriculture into climate change mitigation policy frameworks. *Mitigation and Adaptation Strategies for Global Change*, *23*(3), 451–468.

Ferguson, B., & Thompson, C. (2021). Why buy local? *Journal of Applied Philosophy*, *38*(1), 104–120.

Feucht, Y., & Zander, K. (2018). Consumers' preferences for carbon labels and the underlying reasoning. A mixed methods approach in 6 European countries. *Journal of Cleaner Production*, *178*, 740–748.

Fiala, P. (2005). Information sharing in supply chains. *Omega*, *33*(5), 419–423.

Filimonau, V., & De Coteau, D. A. (2019). Food waste management in hospitality operations: A critical review. *Tourism Management*, *71*, 234–245.

Filimonau, V., & Ermolaev, V. A. (2021). The sleeping giant? Food waste in the foodservice sector of Russia. *Journal of Cleaner Production*, *297*, 126705.

Filimonau, V., & Krivcova, M. (2017). Restaurant menu design and more responsible consumer food choice: An exploratory study of managerial perceptions. *Journal of Cleaner Production*, *143*, 516–527.

Filimonau, V., Lemmer, C., Marshall, D., & Bejjani, G. (2017a). 'Nudging' as an architect of more responsible consumer choice in food service provision: The role of restaurant menu design. *Journal of Cleaner Production*, *144*, 161–170.

Filimonau, V., Lemmer, C., Marshall, D., & Bejjani, G. (2017b). Restaurant menu re-design as a facilitator of more responsible consumer choice: An exploratory and preliminary study. *Journal of Hospitality and Tourism Management*, *33*, 73–81.

Filimonau, V., & Magklaropoulou, A. (2020). Exploring the viability of a new 'pay-as-you-use' energy management model in budget hotels. *International Journal of Hospitality Management*, *89*, Art. 102538.

Filimonau, V., & Sulyok, J. (2021). 'Bin it and forget it!': The challenges of food waste management in restaurants of a mid-sized Hungarian city. *Tourism Management Perspectives*, *37*, 100759.

Filimonau, V., Zhang, H., & Wang, L. E. (2020). Food waste management in Shanghai full-service restaurants: A senior managers' perspective. *Journal of Cleaner Production*, *258*, Art. 120975.

Finney, C. (2019). Fin-to-gill eating: How to cook fish without discarding a thing. *The Guardian*, 26 September. https://www.theguardian.com/food/2019/sep/26/fin-to-gill-eating-cook-sustainably-heads-organs-bones

Fisher, D. (2015). Integrating DCKV with EMS: A field-study perspective. In Better Buildings, US Department of Energy, Reducing energy consumption in restaurants and kitchens. https://

betterbuildingssolutioncenter.energy.gov/sites/default/files/Wednesday%20-%20 Reducing%20Energy%20Consumption%20in%20Restaurants%20and%20Kitchens_%20 Turning%20Down%20the%20Heat%20on%20Energy%20Bills.pdf

Focus. (2019). Ich mag Fleisch. Ich fliege gern. Ich fahre Auto. 40 Ideen, wie Sie trotzdem klimafreundlicher leben können. [I enjoy meat. I like to fly. I drive a car. 40 ideas to live more climate friendly], *Focus Magazin* 24, 8 June. Retrieved from https://www.focus.de/magazin/archiv/rubriken-titel-ich-mag-fleisch-ich-fliege-gern-ich-fahre-auto_id_10804184.html

Food and Agriculture Organization (FAO). (1981). *Food loss prevention in perishable crops. FAO Agricultural Service Bulletin, no. 43*, FAO Statistics Division.

Food and Agriculture Organization (FAO). (2002). *Organic agriculture, environment and food security*. FAO.

Food and Agriculture Organization (FAO). (2011). *Save food: Global Initiative on food loss and waste reduction.* http://www.fao.org/save-food/resources/keyfindings/en/

Food and Agriculture Organization (FAO). (2013). *Tackling climate change through livestock.* http://www.fao.org/ag/againfo/resources/en/publications/tackling_climate_change/index.htm

Food and Agriculture Organization (FAO). (2017). *The future of food and agriculture. Trends and challenges* [pdf]. http://www.fao.org/3/a-i6583e.pdf

Food and Agriculture Organization (FAO). (2018a). *World food and agriculture – statistical pocketbook 2018.* http://www.fao.org/publications/card/en/c/CA1796EN

Food and Agriculture Organization (FAO). (2018b). *The state of world fisheries and aquaculture* [pdf]. http://www.fao.org/3/I9540EN/i9540en.pdf

Food and Agriculture Organization (FAO). (2018c). *Transforming the livestock sector through the Sustainable Development Goals* [pdf]. http://www.fao.org/3/CA1201EN/ca1201en.pdf

Food and Agriculture Organization (FAO). (2019a). *The state of the world's biodiversity for food and agriculture: FAO Commission on Genetic Resources for Food and Agriculture* [pdf]. http://www.fao.org/3/CA3129EN/CA3129EN.pdf

Food and Agriculture Organization (FAO). (2019b). *An estimated 3 million tonnes of shrimp entered the international trade in 2018.* http://www.fao.org/in-action/globefish/market-reports/resource-detail/en/c/1199292/

Food and Agriculture Organization (FAO). (2019c). *The state of food and agriculture 2019. Moving forward on food loss and waste reduction*. FAO.

Food and Agriculture Organization of the United Nations (FAO). (2016). *The state of food and agriculture 2016. Climate change, agriculture and food security*. FAO.

Food and Agriculture Organization of the United Nations (FAO), International Fund for Agricultural Development (IFAD), & United Nations World Food Programme (WFP). (2013). *The state of food insecurity in the world 2013: The multiple dimensions of food security.* FAO.

Food and Agriculture Organization of the United Nations (FAO), International Fund for Agricultural Development (IFAD), United Nations International Children's Emergency Fund (UNICEF), United Nations World Food Programme (WFP), & World Health Organisation (WHO). (2020). *The state of food security and nutrition in the world 2020. Transforming food systems for affordable healthy diets*. FAO. doi:10.4060/ca9692en.

Food and Agriculture Organization (FAO) & World Health Organization (WHO). (2001). *Codex Aimentarius Commission. Guidelines for the production, processing, labelling and marketing of organically produced foods*. FAO/WHO.

Food and Agriculture Organization (FAO) & World Health Organization (WHO). (2019). *Codex Alimentarius: International food standards.* Retrieved from http://www.fao.org/fao-who-codexalimentarius/en/

Fouilleux, E., & Loconto, A. (2017). Voluntary standards, certification, and accreditation in the global organic agriculture field: a tripartite model of techno-politics. *Agriculture and Human Values*, 34(1), 1–14.

Francis, T., & Hoefel, F. (2018). *True Gen': Generation Z and its implications for companies.* McKinsey & Company. https://www.mckinsey.com/industries/consumer-packaged-goods/our-insights/true-gen-generation-z-and-its-implications-for-companies

Frash, Jr, R. E., DiPietro, R., & Smith, W. (2015). Pay more for McLocal? Examining motivators for willingness to pay for local food in a chain restaurant setting. *Journal of Hospitality Marketing & Management*, 24(4), 411–434.

References

Freedman, M. R., & Brochado, C. (2010). Reducing portion size reduces food intake and plate waste. *Obesity, 18*(9), 1864–1866.

Freire, W. B., Waters, W. F., Rivas-Mariño, G., Nguyen, T., & Rivas, P. (2017). A qualitative study of consumer perceptions and use of traffic light food labelling in Ecuador. *Public Health Nutrition, 20*(5), 805–813.

Fresán, U., Martínez-Gonzalez, M. A., Sabaté, J., & Bes-Rastrollo, M. (2018). The Mediterranean diet, an environmentally friendly option: Evidence from the Seguimiento Universidad de Navarra (SUN) cohort. *Public Health Nutrition, 21*(8), 1573–1582.

Freudenberg, N., McDonough, J., & Tsui, E. (2011). Can a food justice movement improve nutrition and health? A case study of the emerging food movement in New York City. *Journal of Urban Health, 88*(4), Art. 623.

Friedrich-Loeffler-Institut (FLI). (2019). *List of animal diseases.* https://www.fli.de/en/services/national-reference-laboratories/list-of-animal-diseases/

Friel, S., Walsh, O., & McCarthy, D. (2006). The irony of a rich country: Issues of financial access to and availability of healthy food in the Republic of Ireland. *Journal of Epidemiology & Community Health, 60*(12), 1013–1019.

Fuerst, F., McAllister, P., Nanda, A., & Wyatt, P. (2015). Does energy efficiency matter to home-buyers? An investigation of EPC ratings and transaction prices in England. *Energy Economics, 48*, 145–156.

Fuller, F., Huang, J., Ma, H., & Rozelle, S. (2006). Got milk? The rapid rise of China's dairy sector and its future prospects. *Food Policy, 31*(3), 201–215.

FUSIONS (Food Use for Social Innovation by Optimising Waste Prevention Strategies). (2016). *Recommendations and guidelines for a common European food waste policy framework*, WP3 –T3.4, Deliverable D3.5 for The European Commission, FP7-Coordination and Support Action (Contract No 311972). doi:10.18174/392296.

Futouris. (2018). *The Futouris sustainable food manual.* https://www.modul.ac.at/uploads/files/user_upload/Futouris_Sustainable_Food_Manual.pdf. Accessed 29 February 2020.

Futouris. (2019). *Reduction of food waste on cruise ships.* https://www.futouris.org/en/projects/reduction-of-food-waste-on-cruise-ships/

Gadema, Z., & Oglethorpe, D. (2011). The use and usefulness of carbon labelling food: A policy perspective from a survey of UK supermarket shoppers. *Food Policy, 36*(6), 815–822.

Garnett, T., Mathewson, S., Angelides, P., & Borthwick, F. (2015). *Policies and actions to shift eating patterns: What works. A review of the evidence of the effectiveness of interventions aimed at shifting diets in more sustainable and healthy directions.* Food Climate Research Network.

Gase, L. N., Kaur, M., Dunning, L., Montes, C., & Kuo, T. (2015). What menu changes do restaurants make after joining a voluntary restaurant recognition program? *Appetite, 89*, 131–135.

Gase, L. N., Montes, C., & Kuo, T. (2016a). Choose Health LA Restaurants: A voluntary restaurant recognition program. *The Global F&V Newsletter, 12*(July/August), 2.

Gase, L. N., Montes, C., Robles, B., Tyree, R., & Kuo, T. (2016b). Media outlet and consumer reactions to promotional activities of the Choose Health LA Restaurants program in Los Angeles County. *Journal of Public Health Management and Practice, 22*(3), 231–244.

Geiger, F., de Snoo, G. R., Berendse, F., Guerrero, I., Morales, M. B., Onate, J. J., Eggers, S., Pärt, T., Bommarco, R., Bengtsson, L., Clement, L. W., Weisser, W. W., Olszewski, A., Ceryngier, P., Hawro, V., Inchausti, P., Fischer, C., Flohre, A., Thies, C., & Tscharntke, T. (2010). Persistent negative effects of pesticides on biodiversity and biological control potential on European farmland. *Basic and Applied Ecology, 11*(2), 97–105.

Getz, C., & Shreck, A. (2006). What organic and Fair Trade labels do not tell us: Towards a place-based understanding of certification. *International Journal of Consumer Studies, 30*(5), 490–501.

Geueke, B., Wagner, C. C., & Muncke, J. (2014). Food contact substances and chemicals of concern: A comparison of inventories. *Food Additives & Contaminants: Part A, 31*(8), 1438–1450.

Geyer, R., Jambeck, J. R., & Law, K. L. (2017). Production, use, and fate of all plastics ever made. *Science Advances, 3*(7), e1700782.

Gill, V. (2021). Food waste: Amount thrown away totals 900 million tonnes. *BBC News.* Retrieved from https://www.bbc.com/news/science-environment-56271385

Gloede, K. (2015). Three comprehensive strategies to reduce water consumption. *The Architect Magazine*, 12 May. https://www.architectmagazine.com/technology/three-comprehensive-strategies-to-reduce-water-consumption_o

Godrich, S., Kent, K., Murray, S., Auckland, S., Lo, J., Blekkenhorst, L., Penrose, B., & Devine, A. (2020). Australian consumer perceptions of regionally grown fruits and vegetables: Importance, enablers, and barriers. *International Journal of Environmental Research and Public Health, 17*(1), Art. 63.

Gomiero, T. (2018). Food quality assessment in organic vs. conventional agricultural produce: Findings and issues. *Applied Soil Ecology, 123*, 714–728.

Gortmaker, S. L., Swinburn, B. A., Levy, D., Carter, R., Mabry, P. L., Finegood, D. T., Huang, T., Marsh, T., & Moodie, M. L. (2011). Changing the future of obesity: Science, policy, and action. *The Lancet, 378*(9793), 838–847.

Gose, M., Krems, C., Heuer, T., & Hoffmann, I. (2016). Trends in food consumption and nutrient intake in Germany between 2006 and 2012: Results of the German National Nutrition Monitoring (NEMONIT). *British Journal of Nutrition, 115*(8), 1498–1507.

Gössling, S. (2010). *Carbon management in tourism: Mitigating the impacts on climate change.* Routledge.

Gössling, S., Broderick, J., Upham, P., Ceron, J. P., Dubois, G., Peeters, P., & Strasdas, W. (2007). Voluntary carbon offsetting schemes for aviation: Efficiency, credibility and sustainable tourism. *Journal of Sustainable Tourism, 15*(3), 223–248.

Gössling, S., & Buckley, R. (2016). Carbon labels in tourism: Persuasive communication? *Journal of Cleaner Production, 111*, 358–369.

Gössling, S., Garrod, B., Aall, C., Hille, J., & Peeters, P. (2011). Food management in tourism. Reducing tourism's carbon 'foodprint'. *Tourism Management, 32*(3), 534–543.

Gössling, S., & Hall, C. M. (2013). Sustainable culinary systems: An introduction. In C. M. Hall & S. Gössling (Eds.), *Sustainable culinary systems: Local foods, innovation, and tourism & hospitality* (pp. 3–44). Routledge.

Gössling, S., Hall, C. M., & Scott, D. (2015). *Tourism and water*. Channel View Publications.

Gössling, S., & Peeters, P. (2015). Assessing tourism's global environmental impact 1900–2050. *Journal of Sustainable Tourism, 23*(5), 639-659.

Gössling, S., & Schumacher, K. P. (2012). Conceptualizing the survival sector in Madagascar. *Antipode, 44*(2), 321–342.

Gottlieb, R., & Joshi, A. (2010). *Food justice*. MIT Press.

Goudis, A., & Skuras, D. (2020). Consumers' awareness of the EU's protected designations of origin logo. *British Food Journal, 123*(13), 1–18.

Government of Canada. (2018). *Organic production systems. General principles and management standards* [pdf]. http://publications.gc.ca/collections/collection_2018/ongc-cgsb/P29-32-310-2018-eng.pdf

Grace Communications Foundation (Foodprint). (2019). *The water footprint of food*. https://foodprint.org/issues/the-water-footprint-of-food/#easy-footnote-bottom-1-1286

Graeub, B. E., Chappell, M. J., Wittman, H., Ledermann, S., Kerr, R. B., & Gemmill-Herren, B. (2016). The state of family farms in the world. *World Development, 87*, 1–15.

Graham-Rowe, E., Jessop, D. C., & Sparks, P. (2014). Identifying motivations and barriers to minimising household food waste. *Resources, Conservation and Recycling, 84*, 15–23.

GRAIN. (2016). *The global farmland grab in 2016: How big, how bad?* https://www.grain.org/article/entries/5492-the-global-farmland-grab-in-2016-how-big-how-bad

Granleese, B. (2016). How a 'grotty rundown pub' became the UK's best restaurant. *The Guardian*, 28 June. https://www.theguardian.com/lifeandstyle/shortcuts/2016/jun/28/grotty-pub-uk-best-restaurant-sportsman-kent-menu

Grant, C. A., & Hicks, A. L. (2018). Comparative life cycle assessment of milk and plant-based alternatives. *Environmental Engineering Science, 35*(11), 1235–1247.

Granuldisk. (n.d.). *Kempinski Hotel Corvinus*, Budapest. https://www.granuldisk.com/cases/kempinski-hotel-corvinus-budapest/

Gray, A. (2016). Which countries spend the most on food? This map will show you. *World Economic Forum*, 7 December. https://www.weforum.org/agenda/2016/12/this-map-shows-how-much-each-country-spends-on-food/

Gray, S., Orme, J., Pitt, H., & Jones, M. (2017). Food for Life: evaluation of the impact of the Hospital Food Programme in England using a case study approach. *JRSM Open, 8*(10), doi:10.1177/2054270417712703.

Greenpeace. (2019). *Red list fish*. https://www.greenpeace.org/usa/oceans/sustainable-seafood/red-list-fish/

References

Grob, K., Biedermann, M., Scherbaum, E., Roth, M., & Rieger, K. (2006). Food contamination with organic materials in perspective: Packaging materials as the largest and least controlled source? A view focusing on the European situation. *Critical Reviews in Food Science and Nutrition, 46*(7), 529–535.

Grzybowska-Brzezinska, M., Grzywinska-Rapca, M., Zuchowski, I., & Borawski, P. (2017). Organic food attributes determining consumer choices. *European Research Studies Journal, 20*(2A), 164–176.

Guéguen, N. & Jacob, C. (2012). The effect of menu labels associated with affect, tradition and patriotism on sales. *Food Quality and Preference, 23*(1), 86–88.

Gustavsson, J., Cederberg, C., Sonesson, U., Van Otterdijk, R., & Meybeck, A. (2011). *Global food losses and food waste*. FAO.

Gutiérrez, N. L., Valencia, S. R., Branch, T. A., Agnew, D. J., Baum, J. K., Bianchi, P. L., Cornejo-Donoso, J., Costello, C., Defeo, O., Essington, T. E., Hilborn, R., Hoggarth, D. D., Larsen, A. E., Ninnes, C., Sainsbury, K., Selden, R. L., Sistla, S., Smith, A. D. M., Stern-Pirlot, A., Teck, S. J., Thorson, J. T., & Williams, N. E. (2012). Eco-label conveys reliable information on fish stock health to seafood consumers. *PLOS ONE, 7*(8), e43765.

Guyton, K. Z., Loomis, D., Grosse, Y., El Ghissassi, F., Benbrahim-Tallaa, L., Guha, N., Scoccianti, C., Mattock, H., & Straif, K. (2015). Carcinogenicity of tetrachlorvinphos, parathion, malathion, diazinon, and glyphosate. *Lancet Oncology, 16*, 490–491.

Gysel, N., Welch, W. A., Chen, C. L., Dixit, P., Cocker III, D. R., & Karavalakis, G. (2018). Particulate matter emissions and gaseous air toxic pollutants from commercial meat cooking operations. *Journal of Environmental Sciences, 65*, 162–170.

Habel, J. C., Samways, M. J., & Schmitt, T. (2019). Mitigating the precipitous decline of terrestrial European insects: Requirements for a new strategy. *Biodiversity and Conservation, 28*(6), 1343–1360.

Hadjikakou, M. (2017). Trimming the excess: Environmental impacts of discretionary food consumption in Australia. *Ecological Economics, 131*, 119–128.

Hadjimichael, M., & Hegland, T. J. (2016). Really sustainable? Inherent risks of eco-labeling in fisheries. *Fisheries Research, 174*, 129–135.

Haile, B. K. (2013). Virtuous meat consumption: A virtue ethics defense of an omnivorous way of life. *Logos: A Journal of Catholic Thought and Culture, 16*(1), 83–100.

Halkier, B. (2017). Normalising convenience food? The expectable and acceptable places of convenient food in everyday life among young Danes. *Food, Culture & Society, 20*(1), 133–151.

Hall, C. M. (2010). Blending coffee and fair trade hospitality. In L. Joliffe (Ed.), *Coffee culture, destinations and tourism* (pp. 159–171). Channelview.

Hall, C. M. (2013a). The local in farmers' markets in New Zealand. In C. M. Hall & S. Gössling (Eds.), *Sustainable culinary systems: Local foods, innovation, tourism and hospitality* (pp. 99–121). Routledge.

Hall, C. M. (2013b). Why forage when you don't have to? Personal and cultural meaning in recreational foraging: A New Zealand study. *Journal of Heritage Tourism, 8*(2–3), 224–233.

Hall, C. M. (2014). *Tourism and social marketing*. Routledge.

Hall, C. M. (2016). Heirloom products in heritage places: Farmers markets, local food, and food diversity. In D. Timothy (Ed.), *Heritage cuisines: Traditions, identities and tourism* (pp. 88–103). Routledge.

Hall, C. M. (2020). Improving the recipe for culinary and food tourism? The need for a new menu. *Tourism Recreation Research, 45*(2), 284–287.

Hall, C. M., Baird, T., Gillespie, A., Gössling, S., & Roy, H. (2018). Healthy eating for a healthy planet? Issues in developing sustainable restaurants. Presented at Tomorrow's Food Travel Conference, 8–10 October 2018, Centre for Tourism, University of Gothenburg, Sweden.

Hall, C. M., & Gössling, S. (Eds.) (2013). *Sustainable culinary systems: Local foods, innovation, tourism and hospitality*. Routledge.

Hall, C. M., & Gössling, S. (Eds.) (2016). *Food tourism and regional development: Networks, products and trajectories*. Routledge.

Hall, C. M., & Prayag, G. (Eds.) (2020). *The Routledge handbook of halal hospitality and Islamic tourism*. Routledge.

Hall, C. M., & Wood, K. J. (2021). Demarketing tourism for sustainability: Degrowing tourism or moving the deckchairs on the Titanic? *Sustainability*, *13*(3), 1585.

Hall, D. (2010). Food with a visible face: Traceability and the public promotion of private governance in the Japanese food system. *Geoforum*, *41*(5), 826–835.

Hall, K. D. (2018). Did the food environment cause the obesity epidemic? *Obesity*, *26*(1), 11–13.

Hall, K. D., Guo, J., Dore, M., & Chow, C. C. (2009). The progressive increase of food waste in America and its environmental impact. *PLOS ONE*, *4*(11), e7940. doi:10.1371/journal.pone.0007940.

Hallmann, C. A., Foppen, R. P., van Turnhout, C. A., de Kroon, H., & Jongejans, E. (2014). Declines in insectivorous birds are associated with high neonicotinoid concentrations. *Nature*, *511*, 341–343.

Hallmann, C. A., Sorg, M., Jongejans, E., Siepel, H., Hofland, N., Schwan, H., … Goulson, D. (2017). More than 75 percent decline over 27 years in total flying insect biomass in protected areas. *PLOS ONE*, *12*(10), e0185809. doi:10.1371/journal.pone.0185809.

Hamerman, E. J. Rudell, F., & Martins, C. M. (2018). Factors that predict taking restaurant leftovers: Strategies for reducing food waste. *Journal of Consumer Behaviour*, *17*(1), 94–104.

Hamilton, C., Denniss, R., & Baker, D. (2005). *Wasteful consumption in Australia*. The Australia Institute.

Han, H., Hwang, J., Lee, M. J., & Kim, J. (2019). Word-of-mouth, buying, and sacrifice intentions for eco-cruises: Exploring the function of norm activation and value-attitude-behavior. *Tourism Management*, *70*, 430–443.

Han, M. A., Zeraatkar, D., Guyatt, G. H., Vernooij, R. W., El Dib, R., Zhang, Y., … Lopes, L. C. (2019). Reduction of red and processed meat intake and cancer mortality and incidence. *Annals of Internal Medicine*, *171*, 711–720.

Harrison, R. (2013). *Animal machines*. CABI.

Hartikainen, H., Roininen, T., Katajajuuri, J. M., & Pulkkinen, H. (2014). Finnish consumer perceptions of carbon footprints and carbon labelling of food products. *Journal of Cleaner Production*, *73*, 285–293.

Harvard T. H. Chan School of Public Health. (2019a). *Healthy eating plate*. https://www.hsph.harvard.edu/nutritionsource/healthy-eating-plate/

Harvard T. H. Chan School of Public Health. (2019b). *New "guidelines" say continue red meat consumption habits, but recommendations contradict evidence*. https://www.hsph.harvard.edu/nutritionsource/2019/09/30/flawed-guidelines-red-processed-meat/

Harvey, F. (2019). How can shoppers make sense of sustainable fish labels? *The Guardian*, 2 October. https://www.theguardian.com/environment/2019/oct/02/how-can-shoppers-make-sense-of-sustainable-fish-labels

Harvey, M., McMeekin, A., & Warde, A. (2004) Conclusion: Quality and processes of qualification. In M. Harvey, A. McMeekin & A. Warde (Eds.), *Qualities of food* (pp. 192–207). Manchester University Press.

Hasimu, H., Marchesini, S., & Canavari, M. (2017). A concept mapping study on organic food consumers in Shanghai, China. *Appetite*, *108*, 191–202.

Hatanaka, M., Bain, C., & Busch, L. (2005). Third-party certification in the global agrifood system. *Food Policy*, *30*(3), 354–369.

Hatanaka, M., & Busch, L. (2008). Third-party certification in the global agrifood system: An objective or socially mediated governance mechanism? *Sociologia Ruralis*, *48*(1), 73–91.

Hawkes, C., Smith, T. G., Jewell, J., Wardle, J., Hammond, R. A., Friel, S., Thow, A. M. & Kain, J. (2015). Smart food policies for obesity prevention. *The Lancet*, *385*(9985), 2410–2421.

Hawkey, P. M. (1998). Action against antibiotic resistance: No time to lose. *The Lancet*, *351*(9112), 1298–1299.

Hays, J., & Shonkoff, S. B. C. (2016). Toward an understanding of the environmental and public health impacts of unconventional natural gas development: A categorical assessment of the peer-reviewed scientific literature, 2009–2015. *PLOS ONE*, *11*(4), e0154164.

Heart, T., & Pliskin, N. (2002). Renting restaurant applications from application service providers. *International Journal of Hospitality Information Technology*, *2*(2), 45–61.

Heart, T., Pliskin, N., & Curley, K. F. (2007). Remote application services as means for aligning business and IT. *International Journal of Electronic Business*, *5*(2), 176–187.

References

Hedberg II, R. C., & Zimmerer, K. S. (2020). What's the market got to do with it? Social-ecological embeddedness and environmental practices in a local food system initiative. *Geoforum, 110*, 35–45.

Hedenus, F., Wirsenius, S., Johansson, D. J. A. (2014). The importance of reduced meat and dairy consumption for meeting stringent climate change targets. *Climatic Change, 124*, 79–91.

Heikkilä, L., Reinikainen, A., Katajajuuri, J., Silvennoinen, K., & Hartikainen, H. (2016). Elements affecting food waste in the food service sector. *Waste Management, 56*, 446–453.

Hejazi, M., Edmonds, J., Clarke, L., Kyle, P., Davies, E., Chaturvedi, V., … Moss, R. (2014). Long-term global water projections using six socioeconomic scenarios in an integrated assessment modeling framework. *Technological Forecasting and Social Change, 81*, 205–226.

Held, L. (2020). How the pandemic is creating a plastic boom. *Civil Eats*, 28 April.

Heljo, J., & Vihola, J. (2012). Energiansäästömahdollisuudet rakennuskannan korjaustoiminnassa. Tampereen teknillinen yliopisto. Rakennustekniikan laitos. Rakennustuotanto-ja talous. Raportti 8. http://www.tut.fi/ee/Materiaali/Epat/EPAT_loppuraportti.pdf

Hemmerling, S., Asioli, D., & Spiller, A. (2016). Core organic taste: Preferences for naturalness-related sensory attributes of organic food among European consumers. *Journal of Food Products Marketing, 22*(7), 824–850.

Hemmerling, S., Hamm, U., & Spiller, A. (2015). Consumption behaviour regarding organic food from a marketing perspective—A literature review. *Organic Agriculture, 5*(4), 277–313.

Henchion, M., & McCarthy, M. (2019). Facilitators and barriers for foods containing meat coproducts. In C. M. Galanakis (Ed.), *Sustainable meat production and processing* (pp. 237–250). Academic Press.

Henderson, F. (1999). *Nose to tail eating: A kind of British cooking*. Bloomsbury.

Henderson, F. (2004). *The whole beast*. HarperCollins.

Henderson, F., & Gellatly, J. P. (2007). *Beyond nose to tail: A kind of British cooking: Part II*. Bloomsbury.

Henriksson, P. J., Jarvio, N., Jonell, M., Guinée, J. B., & Troell, M. (2018). The devil is in the details: The carbon footprint of a shrimp. *Frontiers in Ecology and the Environment, 16*, 2. doi:10.1002/fee.1748.

Henson, S., & Humphrey, J. (2010). Understanding the complexities of private standards in global agri-food chains as they impact developing countries. *The Journal of Development Studies, 46*(9), 1628–1646.

Hermannsdóttir, H. S., Dawes, C., Gideonsen, H., & De Moor, E. (2016). Designing with empathy: Implications for food design. In P. Lloyd & E. Bohemia (Eds.), Future focused thinking – DRS International Conference 2016, 27–30 June, Brighton, United Kingdom. doi:10.21606/drs.2016.520.

Herrmann, R., Thompson, S. R., & Krischik-Bautz, S. (2002). Bovine spongiform encephalopathy and generic promotion of beef: An analysis for "quality from Bavaria". *Agribusiness, 18*(3), 369–385.

Herzfeld, T., Drescher, L. S., & Grebitus, C. (2011). Cross-national adoption of private food quality standards. *Food Policy, 36*(3), 401–411.

Higgins-Desbiolles, F., Moskwa, E., & Wijesinghe, G. (2019). How sustainable is sustainable hospitality research? A review of sustainable restaurant literature from 1991 to 2015. *Current Issues in Tourism, 22*(13), 1551–1580.

Higgins-Desbiolles, F., & Wijesinghe, G. (2019). The critical capacities of restaurants as facilitators for transformations to sustainability. *Journal of Sustainable Tourism, 27*(7), 1080–1105.

Hillier-Brown, F. C., Summerbell, C. D., Moore, H. J., Routen, A., Lake, A. A., Adams, J., White, M., Araujo-Soares, V., Abraham, C., Adamson, A. J., & Brown, T. J. (2017). The impact of interventions to promote healthier ready-to-eat meals (to eat in, to take away or to be delivered) sold by specific food outlets open to the general public: A systematic review. *Obesity Reviews, 18*(2), 227–246.

Hinrichs, C. C. (2000). Embeddedness and local food systems: Notes on two types of direct agricultural market. *Journal of Rural Studies, 16*(3), 295–303.

Hinrichs, C. C. (2003). The practice and politics of food system localization. *Journal of Rural Studies, 19*(1), 33–45.

Hinrichs, C. C., & Allen, P. (2008). Selective patronage and social justice: Local food consumer campaigns in historical context. *Journal of Agricultural and Environmental Ethics, 21*(4), 329–352.

Hirschberg, C., Rajko, A., Schumacher, T., & Wrulich, M. (2016). The changing market for food delivery. *McKinsey & Company*, 9 November. Retrieved from https://www.mckinsey.com/industries/high-tech/our-insights/the-changing-market-for-food-delivery

Ho, M. H. K., Wong, W. H. S., & Chang, C. (2014). Clinical spectrum of food allergies: A comprehensive review. *Clinical Reviews in Allergy & Immunology, 46*, 225–240.

Hoek, A. C., Luning, P. A., Stafleu, A., & De Graaf, C. (2004). Food-related lifestyle and health attitudes of Dutch vegetarians, non-vegetarian consumers of meat substitutes, and meat consumers. *Appetite, 42*(3), 265–272.

Hoek, A. C., Pearson, D., James, S. W., Lawrence, M. A., & Friel, S. (2017a). Healthy and environmentally sustainable food choices: Consumer responses to point-of-purchase actions. *Food Quality and Preference, 58*, 94–106.

Hoek, A. C., Pearson, D., James, S. W., Lawrence, M. A., & Friel, S. (2017b). Shrinking the food-print: A qualitative study into consumer perceptions, experiences and attitudes towards healthy and environmentally friendly food behaviours. *Appetite, 108*, 117–131.

Hoekstra, A. Y. (Ed.) (2003). *Virtual water trade. Proceedings of the international expert meeting on virtual water trade. IHE, 12–13 December* [pdf]. https://waterfootprint.org/media/downloads/Report12.pdf

Hoelzer, K., Bielke, L., Blake, D. P., Cox, E., Cutting, S. M., Devriendt, B., Erlacher-Vindel, E., Goossens, E., Karaca, K., Lemiere, S., & Metzner, M. (2018). Vaccines as alternatives to antibiotics for food producing animals. Part 2: New approaches and potential solutions. *Veterinary Research, 49*, 70. doi:10.1186/s13567-018-0561-7.

Holbrook, E. (2013). Dining on deception: The rising risk of food fraud and what is being done about it. *Risk Management, 60*(4), 28–32.

Holm, L., & Møhl, M. (2000). The role of meat in everyday food culture. An analysis of an interview study in Copenhagen. *Appetite, 34*(3), 277–283.

Holopainen, R., Milandru, A., Ahvenniemi, H., & Häkkinen, T. (2016). Feasibility studies of energy retrofits–Case studies of nearly zero-energy building renovation. *Energy Procedia, 96*, 146–157.

Homer, P. M., & Kahle, L. R. (1988). A structural equation test of the value-attitude-behavior hierarchy. *Journal of Personality and Social Psychology, 54*(4), 638–646.

Hoogland, C. T., de Boer, J., & Boersema, J. J. (2007). Food and sustainability: Do consumers recognize, understand and value on-package information on production standards? *Appetite, 49*(1), 47–57.

Hooper, D. U., Adair, E. C., Cardinale, B. J., Byrnes, J. E., Hungate, B. A., Matulich, K. L., Gonzalez, A., Duffy, J. E., Gamfeldt, L., & O'Connor, M. I. (2012). A global synthesis reveals biodiversity loss as a major driver of ecosystem change. *Nature, 486*(7401), 105–108.

Hornibrook, S., May, C., & Fearne, A. (2015). Sustainable development and the consumer: Exploring the role of carbon labelling in retail supply chains. *Business Strategy and the Environment, 24*(4), 266–276.

Hou, Y., Yang, W., & Sun, Y. (2017). Do pictures help? The effects of pictures and food names on menu evaluations. *International Journal of Hospitality Management, 60*, 94–103.

Howard, S. J., Catchpole, M., Watson, J., & Davies, S. C. (2013). Antibiotic resistance: Global response needed. *The Lancet Infectious Diseases, 13*(12), 1001–1003.

Howell, R. A. (2018). Carbon management at the household level: A definition of carbon literacy and three mechanisms that increase it. *Carbon Management, 9*(1), 25–35.

Huang, E., Gregoire, M. B., Tangney, C., & Stone, M. K. (2011). Sustainability in hospital foodservice. *Journal of Foodservice Business Research, 14*, 241–255.

Hughes, M. H. (1997). Soul. Black women and food. In C. Counihan & P. van Esterik (Eds.), *Food and culture: A reader* (pp. 272–280). Routledge.

Hughner, R. S., McDonagh, P., Prothero, A., Shultz, C. J., & Stanton, J. (2007). Who are organic food consumers? A compilation and review of why people purchase organic food. *Journal of Consumer Behaviour, 6*(2–3), 94–110.

Humm, D. (2021). Eleven Madison Park. https://www.elevenmadisonpark.com

Hunt, K. P. (2016). #LivingOffTips: Reframing food system labor through tipped workers' narratives of subminimum wage exploitation. *The Journal of Agriculture, Food Systems, and Community Development, 6*(2), 165–177.

Hwang, Y. J., Roe, B. E., & Teisl, M. F. (2006). Does price signal quality? Strategic implications of price as a signal of quality for the case of genetically modified food. *International Food and Agribusiness Management Review, 9*, 93–114.

References

Hyland, S. (2017). Eco eating. *Food Australia*, *69*(4), 38–39.

Ibrahim, M. A. (2016). *Understanding Malaysian food retailers' perception of and attitude towards organic certification*. PhD thesis, University of Canterbury.

Ilbery, B., & Maye, D. (2005). Alternative (shorter) food supply chains and specialist livestock products in the Scottish–English borders. *Environment and Planning A*, *37*(5), 823–844.

Imhof, H. K., Laforsch, C., Wiesheu, A. C., Schmid, J., Anger, P. M., Niessner, R., & Ivleva, N. P. (2016). Pigments and plastic in limnetic ecosystems: A qualitative and quantitative study on microparticles of different size classes. *Water Research*, *98*, 64–74.

Ingold, T. (2000). *The perception of the environment: Essays on livelihood, dwelling and skill*. Routledge.

Intergovernmental Panel on Climate Change (IPCC). (2014). Summary for policymakers. In O. Edenhofer, R. Pichs-Madruga, Y. Sokona, E. Farahani, S. Kadner, K. Seyboth, A. Adler, I. Baum, S. Brunner, P. Eickemeier, B. Kriemann, J. Savolainen, S. Schlömer, C. von Stechow, T. Zwickel & J. C. Minx (Eds.), *Climate Change 2014: Mitigation of Climate Change. Contribution of Working Group III to the Fifth Assessment Report of the Intergovernmental Panel on Climate Change* (pp. 1–30). Cambridge University Press.

Intergovernmental Panel on Climate Change (IPCC). (2018). *Special report: Global warming of 1.5°C*. http://www.ipcc.ch/report/sr15/

International Energy Agency (IEA). (2019). *Global energy & CO_2 status report*. https://www.iea.org/geco/emissions/

International Federation of Organic Agriculture Movements (IFOAM). (2002). *International Federation of Organic Agriculture Movements 2nd draft 2002 basic standards for organic production and processing*. IFOAM.

International Federation of Organic Agriculture Movements (IFOAM – Organics International) (2021). IFOAM – Organics International. Retrieved from https://www.ifoam.bio

International Land Coalition (ILC). (2020). *Uneven ground. Land inequality at the heart of unequal societies. Research findings from the land inequality initiative synthesis report*. International Land Coalition Secretariat.

Inwood, S. M., Sharp, J. S., Moore, R. H., & Stinner, D. H. (2009). Restaurants, chefs and local foods: Insights drawn from application of a diffusion of innovation framework. *Agriculture and Human Values*, *26*(3), 177–191.

Iqbal, N. (2021). I fled Syria with just £12 … now I have my own restaurant in Soho. *The Guardian*, 16 May. https://www.theguardian.com/food/2021/may/16/i-fled-syria-with-just-12-now-i-have-my-own-restaurant-in-soho

Jaacks, L. M., Vandevijvere, S., Pan, A., McGowan, C. J., Wallace, C., Imamura, F., … Ezzati, M. (2019). The obesity transition: Stages of the global epidemic. *The Lancet Diabetes & Endocrinology*, *7*(3), 231–240.

Jackson, B. (2018). *Don't waste that banchan: Where South Korea's food waste goes*. https://www.koreaexpose.com/banchan-south-korea-food-waste/

Jaeger, S. R., Machín, L., Aschemann-Witzel, J., Antúnez, L., Harker, F. R., & Ares, G. (2018). Buy, eat or discard? A case study with apples to explore fruit quality perception and food waste. *Food Quality and Preference*, *69*, 10–20.

Jagau, H. L., & Vyrastekova, J. (2017). Behavioral approach to food waste: An experiment. *British Food Journal*, *119*(4), 882–894.

Jang, Y. J. (2016). *Top managers' environmental values, leadership, and stakeholder engagement in promoting environmental sustainability in the restaurant*. PhD. Dissertation. Iowa State University, Graduate Theses and Dissertations 15940. https://lib.dr.iastate.edu/etd/15940

Jang, Y. J., Kim, W. G., & Lee, H. Y. (2015). Coffee shop consumers' emotional attachment and loyalty to green stores: The moderating role of green consciousness. *International Journal of Hospitality Management*, *44*, 146–156.

Janssen, M., & Hamm, U. (2011). Consumer perception of different organic certification schemes in five European countries. *Organic Agriculture*, *1*(1), 31–43.

Janssen, M., & Hamm, U. (2012a). Product labelling in the market for organic food: Consumer preferences and willingness-to-pay for different organic certification logos. *Food Quality and Preference*, *25*(1), 9–22.

Janssen, M., & Hamm, U. (2012b). The mandatory EU logo for organic food: Consumer perceptions. *British Food Journal*, *114*(3), 335–352.

Jarosz, L. (2008). The city in the country: Growing alternative food networks in metropolitan areas. *Journal of Rural Studies*, *24*(3), 231–244.

Jaworowska, A., Blackham, T., Davies, I. G., & Stevenson, L. (2013). Nutritional challenges and health implications of takeaway and fast food. *Nutrition Reviews*, *71*(5), 310–318.

Jayaraman, S. (2014). Feeding America: Immigrants in the restaurant industry and throughout the food system take action for change. *Social Research: An International Quarterly*, *81*(2), 347–358.

Jeong, E., & Jang, S. S. (2019). Price premiums for organic menus at restaurants: What is an acceptable level? *International Journal of Hospitality Management*, *77*, 117–127.

Jones, C. M. (2016). The UK sugar tax—A healthy start? *British Dental Journal*, *221*(2), 59–60.

Jones, T. (2010). The great hunger lottery. How banking speculation causes food crises [pdf]. *World Development Movement*, July. https://www.globaljustice.org.uk/sites/default/files/files/resources/hunger_lottery_report_6.10.pdf

Jonsson, A., & Foss, N. J. (2011). International expansion through flexible replication: Learning from the internationalization experience of IKEA. *Journal of International Business Studies*, *42*(9), 1079–1102.

Joseph, S., Peters, I., & Friedrich, H. (2019). Can regional organic agriculture feed the regional community? A case study for Hamburg and North Germany. *Ecological Economics*, *164*, 106342. doi:10.1016/j.ecolecon.2019.05.022.

Jung-a, S., Oliver, C., & Burgis, T. (2008). Daewoo to cultivate Madagascar land for free. *Financial Times*, 20 November. https://www.ft.com/content/6e894c6a-b65c-11dd-89dd-0000779fd18c

Jungbluth, N., Keller, R., & König, A. (2016). ONE TWO WE—Life cycle management in canteens together with suppliers, customers and guests. *The International Journal of Life Cycle Assessment*, *21*(5), 646–653.

Kaljonen, M., Peltola, T., Salo, M., & Furman, E. (2019). Attentive, speculative experimental research for sustainability transitions: An exploration in sustainable eating. *Journal of Cleaner Production*, *206*, 365–373.

Kallbekken, S., & Sælen, H. (2013). 'Nudging' hotel guests to reduce food waste as a win–win environmental measure. *Economics Letters*, *119*(3), 325–327.

Kang, J., Jun, J., & Arendt, S. W. (2015). Understanding customers' health food choices at casual dining restaurants: Using the value-attitude-behaviour model. *International Journal of Hospitality Management*, *48*, 12–21.

Kang, J. W., & Namkung, Y. (2018). The effect of corporate social responsibility on brand equity and the moderating role of ethical consumerism: The case of Starbucks. *Journal of Hospitality & Tourism Research*, *42*(7), 1130–1151.

Karlen, D. L., Erbach, D. C., Kaspar, T. C., Colvin, T. S., Berry, E. C., & Timmons, D. R. (1990). Soil tilth: A review of past perceptions and future needs. *Soil Science Society of America Journal*, *54*(1), 153–161.

Kassam, A. (2017). The restaurant kitchen where everyone has HIV: 'We want to challenge stigma'. *The Guardian*, 8 November. https://www.theguardian.com/world/2017/nov/08/canada-toronto-restaurant-hiv-aids-kitchen-staff-stigma

Katsikeas, C. S., Paparoidamis, N. G., & Katsikea, E. (2004). Supply source selection criteria: The impact of supplier performance on distributor performance. *Industrial Marketing Management*, *33*(8), 755–764.

Kearney, A. T. (2019). *How will cultured meat and meat alternatives disrupt the agricultural and food industry?* Retrieved from https://www.atkearney.com/documents/20152/2795757/How+Will+Cultured+Meat+and+Meat+Alternatives+Disrupt+the+Agricultural+and+Food+Industry.pdf/06ec385b-63a1-71d2-c081-51c07ab88ad1?t=1559860712714

Kearney, J. (2010). Food consumption trends and drivers. *Philosophical Transactions of the Royal Society of London B: Biological Sciences*, *365*(1554), 2793–2807.

Kemper, J. A. (2020). Motivations, barriers, and strategies for meat reduction at different family lifecycle stages. *Appetite*, *150*, 104644.

Ketelsen, M., Janssen, M., & Hamm, U. (2020). Consumers' response to environmentally-friendly food packaging: A systematic review. *Journal of Cleaner Production*, *254*, 120123.

Ketter, E. (2019). Eating with EatWith: Analysing tourism-sharing economy consumers. *Current Issues in Tourism*, *22*(9), 1062–1075.

References

Kevany, S. (2020). Millions of farm animals culled as US food supply chain chokes up. *The Guardian*, 29 April. https://www.theguardian.com/environment/2020/apr/29/millions-of-farm-animals-culled-as-us-food-supply-chain-chokes-up-coronavirus

Khan, F., & Prior, C. (2010). Evaluating the urban consumer with regard to sourcing local food: A Heart of England study. *International Journal of Consumer Studies*, 34(2), 161–168.

Khomami, N. (2018). How Syrian refugee chef's London kitchen is helping Aleppo hospital. *The Guardian*, 29 April. https://www.theguardian.com/world/2018/apr/29/how-syrian-refugee-chefs-london-kitchen-is-helping-aleppo-hospital

Kim, B. F., Santo, R. E., Scatterday, A. P., Fry, J. P., Synk, C. M., Cebron, S. R., Mekonnen, M. M., Hoekstra, A. Y., de Pee, S., Bloem, M. W., Neff, R. A., & Nachman, K. E. (2020). Country-specific dietary shifts to mitigate climate and water crises. *Global Environmental Change*, 62, 101926.

Kim, H., Jayaraman, S., Landsbergis, P., Markowitz, S., Kim, S., & Dropkin, J. (2013). Perceived discrimination from management and musculoskeletal symptoms among New York City restaurant workers. *International Journal of Occupational and Environmental Health*, 19(3), 196–206.

Kim, M. J., & Hall, C. M. (2020). Can sustainable restaurant practices enhance customer loyalty? The roles of value theory and environmental concerns. *Journal of Hospitality and Tourism Management*, 43, 127–138.

Kim, M. J., Hall, C. M., & Kim, D. (2020). Predicting environmentally friendly eating out behavior by value-attitude-behavior theory: Does being vegetarian reduce food waste? *Journal of Sustainable Tourism*, 28(6), 797–815.

Kim, W. G., & Ham, S. (2006). The impact of information technology implementation on service quality in the hotel industry. *Information Technology in Hospitality*, 4(4), 143–151.

King, R. P., Hand, M. S., Digiacomo, G., Clancy, K., Gómez, M. I., Hardesty, S. D., Lev, L., & Mclaughlin, E. W. (2010). *Comparing the structure, size, and performance of local and mainstream food supply chains*. United States Department of Agriculture, Economic Research Service.

Kirk, S. F. L., Olstad, D. L., McIsaac, J. D., Prowse, R. J. L., Caswell, S., Hanning, R., Raine, K. D., Mâsse, L. C., & Naylor, P. J. (2021). Appetite for change? Facilitators and barriers to nutrition guideline implementation in Canadian recreational facilities. *Health Promotion International*. doi:10.1093/heapro/daab017.

Kirwan, J. (2004). Alternative strategies in the UK agro-food system: Interrogating the alterity of farmers' markets. *Sociologia Ruralis*, 44(4), 395–415.

Kloppenburg, Jr, J., Lezberg, S., De Master, K., Stevenson, G., & Hendrickson, J. (2000). Tasting food, tasting sustainability: Defining the attributes of an alternative food system with competent, ordinary people. *Human Organization*, 59(2), 177–186.

Knapp, S., & van der Heijden, M. G. (2018). A global meta-analysis of yield stability in organic and conservation agriculture. *Nature Communications*, 9(1), Art. 3632. doi:10.1038/s41467-018-05956-1.

Kneafsey, M., Cox, R., Holloway, L., Dowler, E., Venn, L., & Tuomainen, H. (2008). *Reconnecting consumers, producers and food: Exploring alternatives*. Bloomsbury Publishing.

Kónya, H. E., & Gergely, O. (2016). The food we eat…. *Acta Universitatis Sapientiae, Social Analysis*, 6(2), 5–20.

Korea Vegetarian & Vegan Association. (2019). About 20% of the total population are vegetarians. http://www.kvva.or.kr/notice/news.php?ptype=view&idx=1231&page=1&code=news

Kotsanopoulos, K. V., & Arvanitoyannis, I. S. (2017). The role of auditing, food safety, and food quality standards in the food industry: A review. *Comprehensive Reviews in Food Science and Food Safety*, 16(5), 760–775.

KRAV. (2019). *KRAV-märkt restaurang*. https://www.krav.se/om-krav/krav-markningen/krav-markt-restaurang/

Kuligowski, K. (2020). Small business guide to a restaurant management system. *Business.com*, 17 July. https://www.business.com/articles/restaurant-management-system-guide/

Kushi, L. H., Doyle, C., McCullough, M., Rock, C. L., Demark-Wahnefried, W., Bandera, E. V., Gapstur, S., Patel, A. V., Andrews, K., & Gansler, T. (2012). American Cancer Society guidelines on nutrition and physical activity for cancer prevention: Reducing the risk of cancer with healthy food choices and physical activity. *CA: A Cancer Journal for Clinicians*, 62(1), 30–67.

Lagorio, A., Pinto, R., & Golini, R. (2018). Food waste reduction in school canteens: Evidence from an Italian case. *Journal of Cleaner Production*, *199*, 77–84.

Lakhani, N. (2021). One in four faced food insecurity in America's year of hunger, investigation shows. *The Guardian*, 14 April. https://www.theguardian.com/environment/2021/apr/14/americas-year-of-hunger-how-children-and-people-of-color-suffered-most?CMP=series_embed_box

Lampert, N. (2021). Colorado's 'rebel' farmers – 'I'd like to see industrial farming go extinct'. *The Guardian*, 8 May. https://www.theguardian.com/environment/2021/may/08/colorado-regenerative-farming-cedar-springs

Lancaster, J. (2011). Restaurant review: The Sportsman, Seasalter, Kent. *The Guardian*, 26 February. https://www.theguardian.com/lifeandstyle/2011/feb/26/the-sportsman-seasalter-restaurant-review

Lartey, J. (2018). Should white people pay more for lunch? New Orleans chef tests social experiment. *The Guardian*, 18 March. https://www.theguardian.com/us-news/2018/mar/18/new-orleans-chef-food-experiment-black-white-pay-more

Lawley, M., & Howieson, J. (2015). What chefs want when buying Australian seafood. *Journal of Food Products Marketing*, *21*(1), 1–11.

Le, L. T., Sabaté, J., Singh, P. N., & Jaceldo-Siegl, K. (2018). The design, development and evaluation of the vegetarian lifestyle index on dietary patterns among vegetarians and non-vegetarians. *Nutrients*, *10*(5), 542–527.

Lechenet, M., Dessaint, F., Py, G., Makowski, D., & Munier-Jolain, N. (2017). Reducing pesticide use while preserving crop productivity and profitability on arable farms. *Nature Plants*, *3*, Art. 17008.

Lee, H. J. (2019). Does consumption of organic foods contribute to Korean consumers' subjective well-being? *Sustainability*, *11*(19), Art. 5496.

Lee, H. J., & Yun, Z. S. (2015). Consumers' perceptions of organic food attributes and cognitive and affective attitudes as determinants of their purchase intentions toward organic food. *Food Quality and Preference*, 39, 259–267.

Lee, W. J., Shimizu, M., Kniffin, K. M., & Wansink, B. (2013). You taste what you see: Do organic labels bias taste perceptions? *Food Quality and Preference*, *29*(1), 33–39.

Lee, Y. M., & Sozen, E. (2018). Who knows more about food allergies – restaurant managerial staff or employees? *British Food Journal*, *120*(4), 876–890.

Lehtinen, U. (2012). Sustainability and local food procurement: A case study of Finnish public catering. *British Food Journal*, *114*(8), 1053–1071.

Lesk, C., Rowhani, P., & Ramankutty, N. (2016). Influence of extreme weather disasters on global crop production. *Nature*, *529*(7584), 84–87.

Levidow, L., & Psarikidou, K. (2011). Food relocalization for environmental sustainability in Cumbria. *Sustainability*, *3*(4), 692–719.

Levkoe, C. Z., Knezevic, I., Appavoo, D., Moraes, A., & Scott, S. (2020). Serving up food studies online: Teaching about "food from somewhere" from nowhere. *Food, Culture & Society*, *23*(3), 434–453.

Levy, S. B. (1982). Microbial resistance to antibiotics. An evolving and persistent problem. *Lancet*, *2*, 83–88.

Lewis, T. (2018). The great British chef shortage: why eating out is under threat. *The Observer*, 18 March. https://www.theguardian.com/business/2018/mar/18/great-british-chef-shortage-eating-out-under-threat-brexit

Lewis, T. (2019a). Josh Niland: Meet the chef pioneering the 'nose to tail' of fish. *The Observer*, 17 November. https://www.theguardian.com/food/2019/nov/17/josh-niland-whole-fish-cookbook-pioneer-chef-nose-to-tail-fish

Lewis, T. (2019b). OFM Awards 2019: Outstanding achievement – Refugee Community Kitchen. *The Observer*, 20 October. https://www.theguardian.com/food/2019/oct/20/ofm-awards-2019-outstanding-achievement-refugee-community-kitchen

Li, Q., Long, R., & Chen, H. (2017). Empirical study of the willingness of consumers to purchase low-carbon products by considering carbon labels: A case study. *Journal of Cleaner Production*, *161*, 1237–1250.

References

Liang, R.-D. (2016). Predicting intentions to purchase organic food: The moderating effects of organic food prices. *British Food Journal*, *118*(1), 183–199.

Liljenstolpe, C. (2011). Demand for value-added pork in Sweden: A latent class model approach. *Agribusiness*, *27*(2), 129–146.

Lillywhite, J. M., & Simonsen, J. E. (2014). Consumer preferences for locally produced food ingredient sourcing in restaurants. *Journal of Food Products Marketing*, *20*(3), 308–324.

Limetray. (2019). Cloud kitchen — What is it? *Limetray*, 18 July. Retrieved from https://medium.com/@LimeTrayTech/cloud-kitchen-what-is-it-d2dfdecdd7e

Lindberg, R., Sidebottom, A. C., McCool, B., Pereira, R. F., Sillah, A., & Boucher, J. L. (2018). Changing the restaurant food environment to improve cardiovascular health in a rural community: Implementation and evaluation of the Heart of New Ulm restaurant programme. *Public Health Nutrition*, *21*(5), 992–1001.

Liu, T., Wang, Q., & Su, B. (2016). A review of carbon labeling: Standards, implementation, and impact. *Renewable and Sustainable Energy Reviews*, *53*, 68–79.

Living Water Smart. (n.d.). *10 tips to help you save water in the kitchen at your business*. https://www.livingwatersmart.com.au/articles/10-tips-help-you-save-water-kitchen-your-business

Livsmedelsverket. (2019). *Vad betyder datummärkningen?* https://www.livsmedelsverket.se/matvanor-halsa--miljo/miljo/ta-hand-om-maten-minska-svinnet/vad-betyder-datummarkningen

Lodi Winegrape Commission. (2021). *Lodi Winegrape Commission*. https://www.lodiwine.com/Lodi-Winegrape-Commission

Lotter, D. W. (2003). Organic agriculture. *Journal of Sustainable Agriculture*, *21*(4), 59–128.

Lotter, D. W., Seidel, R., & Liebhardt, W. (2003). The performance of organic and conventional cropping systems in an extreme climate year. *American Journal of Alternative Agriculture*, *18*(3), 146–154.

Lowder, S. K., Skoet, J., & Raney, T. (2016). The number, size, and distribution of farms, smallholder farms, and family farms worldwide. *World Development*, *87*, 16–29.

Lu, L., & Gursoy, D. (2017). Does offering an organic food menu help restaurants excel in competition? An examination of diners' decision-making. *International Journal of Hospitality Management*, *63*, 72–81.

Ludwig, D. S., Hu, F. B., Tappy, L., & Brand-Miller, J. (2018). Dietary carbohydrates: Role of quality and quantity in chronic disease. *BMJ*, *361*, k2340. doi:10.1136/bmj.k2340.

Ludwig, D. S., Peterson, K. E., & Gortmaker, S. L. (2001). Relation between consumption of sugar-sweetened drinks and childhood obesity: A prospective, observational analysis. *The Lancet*, *357*(9255), 505–508.

Luengas, A., Barona, A., Hort, C., Gallastegui, G., Platel, V., & Elias, A. (2015). A review of indoor air treatment technologies. *Reviews in Environmental Science and Bio/Technology*, *14*(3), 499–522.

Luís, S., Vauclair, C. M. & Lima, M. L. (2018). Raising awareness of climate change causes? Cross-national evidence for the normalization of societal risk perception of climate change. *Environmental Science & Policy*, 80, 74–81.

Lundqvist, J., de Fraiture, C., & Molden, D. (2008). Saving water: From field to fork—curbing losses and wastage in the food chain. *SIWI Policy Brief*. SIWI.

Lusk, J. L. (2019). Consumer beliefs about healthy foods and diets. *PLOS ONE*, *14*(10), e0223098. doi:10.1371/journal.pone.0223098.

MacDonald, G. K., Brauman, K. A., Sun, S., Carlson, K. M., Cassidy, E. S., Gerber, J. S., & West, P. C. (2015). Rethinking agricultural trade relationships in an era of globalization. *BioScience*, *65*(3), 275–289.

Mäder, P., Fliessbach, A., Dubois, D., Gunst, L., Fried, P., & Niggli, U. (2002). Soil fertility and biodiversity in organic farming. *Science*, *296*(5573), 1694–1697.

Makary, M. A., Kaczmarski, K., & Nachman, K. (2018). A call for doctors to recommend antibiotic-free foods: Agricultural antibiotics and the public health crisis of antimicrobial resistance. *The Journal of Antibiotics*, *71*, 685–687.

Malloy, C. (2020). Phoenix didn't just feed the hungry. It saved farms and restaurants. *Bloomberg CityLab*, 18 December.

Manning, L., Luning, P. A., & Wallace, C. A. (2019). The evolution and cultural framing of food safety management systems—Where from and where next? *Comprehensive Reviews in Food Science and Food Safety*, *18*(6), 1770–1792.

Marine Stewardship Council (MSC). (2016). *Seafood consumers put sustainability before price and brand*. MSC. https://www.msc.org/docs/default-source/default-document-library/about-the-msc/msc-consumer-survey-2016-infographic-seafood-consumers-put-sustainability-before-price-and-brand.pdf

Marine Stewardship Council (MSC). (2020). *Celebrating and supporting sustainable fisheries. The Marine Stewardship Council Annual Report 2019–2020*. MSC.

Marsh, S. (2019). Hampshire pub left derelict four years ago named best in UK. *The Guardian*, 28 February. https://www.theguardian.com/lifeandstyle/2019/feb/28/hampshire-pub-wonston-arms-camra-pub-of-the-year

Marsh, S. (2021). Going vegan: can switching to a plant-based diet really save the planet? *The Guardian*, 25 April. https://www.theguardian.com/lifeandstyle/2021/apr/25/going-vegan-can-switching-to-a-plant-based-diet-really-save-the-planet

Marsh, S., & Morris, S. (2018). Pub saved by locals serves first pint after reopening. *The Guardian*, 18 March. https://www.theguardian.com/uk-news/2018/mar/18/pub-saved-by-locals-serves-first-pint-after-reopening

Marthinsen, J., Sundt, P., Kaysen, O., & Kirkevaag, K. (2012). *Prevention of food waste in restaurants, hotels, canteens and catering*. Nordic Council of Ministers.

Martin-Rios, C., Demen-Meier, C., Gössling, S., & Cornuz, C. (2018). Food waste management innovations in the foodservice industry. *Waste Management*, *79*, 196–206.

Martinez, S. (2017). *Wholesaling*. United States Department of Agriculture, Economic Research Service.

Martinez-Alier, J. (2002). *The environmentalism of the poor: A study of ecological conflicts and valuation*. Edward Elgar.

Martinez-Sanchez, V., Tonini, D., Møller, F. & Astrup, T. F. (2016). Life-cycle costing of food waste management in Denmark: Importance of indirect effects. *Environmental Science & Technology*, *50*(8), 4513–4523.

Martins, M. L., Rodrigues, S. S., Cunha, L. M., & Rocha, A. (2016). Strategies to reduce plate waste in primary schools–experimental evaluation. *Public Health Nutrition*, *19*(8), 1517–1525.

Massey, M., O'Cass, A., & Otahal, P. (2018). A meta-analytic study of the factors driving the purchase of organic food. *Appetite*, *125*, 418–427.

Matacena, R., & Corvo, P. (2020). Practices of food sovereignty in Italy and England: Short food supply chains and the promise of de-commodification. *Sociologia Ruralis*, *60*(2), 414–437.

Matei, A. (2020). Laugh if you want, but the 'McPlant' burger is a step to a greener world. *The Guardian*, 18 November. https://www.theguardian.com/commentisfree/2020/nov/18/laugh-if-you-want-but-the-mcplant-burger-is-a-step-to-a-greener-world

Mathew, A. G., Cissell, R., & Liamthong, S. (2007). Antibiotic resistance in bacteria associated with food animals: A United States perspective of livestock production. *Foodborne Pathogens and Disease*, *4*(2), 115–133.

Mato, Y., Isobe, T., Takada, H., Kanehiro, H., Ohtake, C., & Kaminuma, T. (2001). Plastic resin pellets as a transport medium for toxic chemicals in the marine environment. *Environmental Science & Technology*, *35*(2), 318–324.

Max Burgers. (2019). *Hållbarhetsrapport [Sustainability report]*. www.maxburgers.com

May, J., Williams, A., Cloke, P., & Cherry, L. (2019). Welfare convergence, bureaucracy, and moral distancing at the food bank. *Antipode*, *51*(4), 1251–1275.

McAdams, B., Deng, A., & MacLaurin, T. (2018). Food allergy knowledge, attitudes, and resources of restaurant employees. *British Food Journal*, *120*(11), 2681–2694.

McCabe, M. S. (2017). Eating for the environment: The potential of dietary guidelines to achieve better human and environmental health outcomes. *Environmental Law*, *47*, 741–763.

McGrath, M. (2018a). World's largest food and beverage companies 2018: Anheuser-Busch, Nestlé and Pepsi top the list. *Forbes*, 6 June. https://www.forbes.com/sites/maggiemcgrath/2018/06/06/worlds-largest-food-and-beverage-companies-2018-anheuser-busch-nestle-and-pepsi-top-the-list/#755536be1b08

References

McGrath, M. (2018b). The largest restaurant companies in the world 2018: McDonald's and Starbucks at top of food chain. *Forbes*, 6 June. https://www.forbes.com/sites/maggiemcgrath/2018/06/06/the-largest-restaurant-companies-in-the-world-2018-mcdonalds-and-starbucks-at-top-of-food-chain/#510bc51d6fd1

McVeigh, T. (2016). Top chefs and Instagram star show solidarity with Syria – in the kitchen. *The Observer*, 15 October. https://www.theguardian.com/lifeandstyle/2016/oct/15/cook-for-syria-top-chefs-join-clerkenwell-boy

McWilliams, M. (Ed.). (2017). *Offal: Rejected and reclaimed food. Proceedings of the Oxford Symposium on Food and Cookery 2016*. Prospect Books.

Meier, T., & Christen, O. (2013) Environmental impacts of dietary recommendations and dietary styles: Germany as an example. *Environmental Science & Technology, 47*(2), 877–888.

Mekonnen, M., & Hoekstra, A. (2010a). *The green, blue and grey water footprint of crops and derived crop products. Vol. 2: Appendices. Value of water. Research report series No. 47*. UNESCO-IHE Institute for Water Education.

Mekonnen, M., & Hoekstra, A. (2010b). *The green, blue and grey water footprint of farm animals and animal products. Vol. I: Main report. Value of water. Research report series No. 48*. UNESCO-IHE Institute for Water Education.

Menzie, W. D., Soto-Viruet, Y., Bermúdez-Lugo, O., Mobbs, P. M., Perez, A. A., Taib, M. & Wacaster, S. (2013). Review of selected global mineral industries in 2011 and an outlook to 2017 [pdf]. *United States Geological Survey (USGS)*. https://pubs.usgs.gov/of/2013/1091/OFR2013-1091.pdf

Mercan, S., Cain, L., Akkaya, K., Cebe, M., Uluagac, S., Alonso, M., & Cobanoglu, C. (2020). Improving the service industry with hyper-connectivity: IoT in hospitality. *International Journal of Contemporary Hospitality Management, 33*(1), 243–262.

Midmore, P., Francois, M., & Ness, M. (2011). Trans-European comparison of motivations and attitudes of occasional consumers of organic products. *NJAS – Wageningen Journal of Life Sciences, 58*(3–4), 73–78.

Mikkelsen, B. E. (2011). Images of foodscapes: Introduction to foodscape studies and their application in the study of healthy eating out-of-home environments. *Perspectives in Public Health, 131*(5), 209–216.

Mikkelsen, L., Erickson, C., & Nestle, M. (2007). Creating healthy food environments and preventing chronic disease. In L. Cohen, S. Chehimi & V. Chavez (Eds.), *Prevention is primary: Strategies for well-being* (pp. 287–296). Jossey-Bass Wiley.

Milkman, K. L., Rogers, T., & Bazerman, M. H. (2010). I'll have the ice cream soon and the vegetables later: A study of online grocery purchases and order lead time. *Marketing Letters, 21*, 17–35.

Miller, A. M., & Bush, S. R. (2015). Authority without credibility? Competition and conflict between ecolabels in tuna fisheries. *Journal of Cleaner Production, 107*, 137–145.

Milman, O. (2021). Mark Bittman's warning: the true costs of our cheap food and the American diet. *The Guardian*, 25 April, https://www.theguardian.com/environment/2021/apr/25/our-unequal-earth-mark-bittman-cheap-food-american-diet

Mineau, P., & Whiteside, M. (2013). Pesticide acute toxicity is a better correlate of US grassland bird declines than agricultural intensification. *PLOS ONE, 8*, e57457.

Ministry of Agriculture, Food and Rural Affairs. (2018). *Trend of eating out in 2019*. Retrieved from http://www.mafra.go.kr

Mirosa, M., Liu, Y., & Mirosa, R. (2018). Consumers' behaviors and attitudes toward doggy bags: Identifying barriers and benefits to promoting behavior change. *Journal of Food Products Marketing, 24*(5), 563–590.

Mirosa, M., Munro, H., Mangan-Walker, E., & Pearson, D. (2016). Reducing waste of food left on plates: Interventions based on means-end chain analysis of customers in foodservice sector. *British Food Journal, 118*(9), 2326–2343.

Mistretta, M., Caputo, P., Cellura, M., & Cusenza, M. A. (2019). Energy and environmental life cycle assessment of an institutional catering service: An Italian case study. *Science of the Total Environment, 657*, 1150–1160.

Morland, K. B., & Evenson, K. R. (2009). Obesity prevalence and the local food environment. *Health & Place, 15*(2), 491–495.

Morris, C., & Buller, H. (2003). The local food sector: A preliminary assessment of its form and impact in Gloucestershire. *British Food Journal, 105*(8), 559–566.

Morris, S. (2018). More and more pubs are closing every day: Here's how we saved ours. *The Guardian*, 18 March. https://www.theguardian.com/commentisfree/2018/mar/18/closing-pub-packhorse-reopens-south-stoke-somerset-campaign

Mount, P. (2012). Growing local food: Scale and local food systems governance. *Agriculture and Human Values*, 29(1), 107–121.

Mozaffarian, D., Fahimi, S., Singh, G. M., Micha, R., Khatibzadeh, S., Engell, R. E., Lim, S., Danaei, G., Ezzati, M., & Powles, J. (2014). Global sodium consumption and death from cardiovascular causes. *New England Journal of Medicine*, 371(7), 624–634.

Mudie, S. (2016). Energy benchmarking in UK commercial kitchens. *Building Services Engineering Research and Technology*, 37(2), 205–219.

Mudie, S., Essah, E. A., Grandison, A., & Felgate, R. (2016). Electricity use in the commercial kitchen. *International Journal of Low-Carbon Technologies*, 11, 66–74.

Mudie, S., Essah, E., Grandison, A., & Felgate, R. (2013). Benchmarking energy use in licensed restaurants and pubs. In *CIBSE Technical Symposium*, 11–12 April 2013, Liverpool John Moores University, Liverpool.

Mudie, S., & Vadhati, M. (2017). Low energy catering strategy: Insights from a novel carbon-energy calculator. *Energy Procedia*, 123, 212–219.

Mukherjea, A., Underwood, K. C., Stewart, A. L., Ivey, S. L., & Kanaya, A. M. (2013). Asian Indian views on diet and health in the United States: Importance of understanding cultural and social factors to address disparities. *Family & Community Health*, 36(4), Art. 311.

Muncke, J., Backhaus, T., Geueke, B., Maffini, M. V., Martin, O.V., Myers, J. P., Soto, A. M., Trasande, L., Trier, X., & Scheringer, M. (2017). Scientific challenges in the risk assessment of food contact materials. *Environmental Health Perspectives*, 125(9), Art. 095001.

Murphy, J., & Smith, S. (2009). Chefs and suppliers: An exploratory look at supply chain issues in an upscale restaurant alliance. *International Journal of Hospitality Management*, 28(2), 212–220.

Namkung, Y., & Jang, S. (2013). Effects of restaurant green practices on brand equity formation: Do green practices really matter? *International Journal of Hospitality Management*, 33, 85–95.

Nas, P. J., & Jaffe, R. (2004). Informal waste management. *Environment, Development and Sustainability*, 6(3), 337–353.

Nath, J. (2011). Gendered fare? A qualitative investigation of alternative food and masculinities. *Journal of Sociology*, 47(3), 261–278.

National Center for Health Statistics, U.S. Department of Health & Human Services. (2018). *Obesity and overweight*. http://www.cdc.gov/nchs/fastats/obesity-overweight.htm

National Restaurant Association (NRA). (2018). *The state of restaurant sustainability 2018*. NRA.

National Restaurant Association (NRA). (2019). *Harnessing technology to drive off premises sales*. NRA.

Naturland. (2019). *Naturland international*. https://www.naturland.de/de/naturland/naturland-international.html

Nave, A., do Paço, A., & Duarte, P. (2021). A systematic literature review on sustainability in the wine tourism industry: Insights and perspectives. *International Journal of Wine Business Research*. doi:10.1108/IJWBR-09-2020-0046.

Navin, M. C. (2014). Local food and international ethics. *Journal of Agricultural and Environmental Ethics*, 27(3), 349–368.

NCD Risk Factor Collaboration (NCDRISC). (2018). *Body mass index*. http://www.ncdrisc.org/bmi-mean-map.html

Nepstad, D. C., Stickler, C. M., & Almeida, O. T. (2006). Globalization of the Amazon soy and beef industries: Opportunities for conservation. *Conservation Biology*, 20(6), 1595–1603.

Nestlé. (2019). *Dairy*. https://www.nestle.com/csv/raw-materials/dairy

Neto, B. (2020). Analysis of sustainability criteria from European public procurement schemes for foodservices. *Science of the Total Environment*, 704, 135300.

Neto, B., & Caldas, M. G. (2018). The use of green criteria in the public procurement of food products and catering services: A review of EU schemes. *Environment, Development and Sustainability*, 20(5), 1905–1933.

References

Neto, B., Rodríguez Quintero, R., Wolf, O., Sjögren, P., Lee, P., & Eatherley, D. (2016). *Revision of European green public procurement criteria for food and catering services*. Preliminary report (draft) working document. JCR.

Nielson. (2017). *The Nielsen total audience report*. https://www.nielsen.com/us/en/insights/report/2017/the-nielsen-total-audience-report-q1-2017/#

Niland, J. (2019). *The whole fish cookbook: New ways to cook, eat and think*. Hardie Grant Books.

Nitzko, S., & Spiller, A. (2019). Comparing "leaf-to-root", "nose-to-tail" and other efficient food utilization options from a consumer perspective. *Sustainability, 11*(17), 4779.

Niva, M., Mäkelä, J., Kahma, N., & Kjærnes, U. (2014). Eating sustainably? Practices and background factors of ecological food consumption in four Nordic countries. *Journal of Consumer Policy, 37*, 465–484.

Norwegian Seafood Council. (2017). *Seafood exports worth NOK 91.6 billion in 2016*. https://en.seafood.no/news-and-media/news-archive/seafood-exports-worth-nok-91.6-billion-in-2016/

Nummedal, M., & Hall, C. M. (2006). Local food in tourism: An investigation of the New Zealand South Island's bed and breakfast sector's use and perception of local food. *Tourism Review International, 9*(4), 365–378.

Nunn, J. (2020). What if restaurants continued to feed local communities after lockdown lifts? *The Guardian*, 6 June. https://www.theguardian.com/commentisfree/2020/jun/06/restaurants-communities-lockdown-business-good-food

Nuttavuthisit, K., & Thøgersen, J. (2017). The importance of consumer trust for the emergence of a market for green products: The case of organic food. *Journal of Business Ethics, 140*(2), 323–337.

Ogata, Y., Takada, H., Mizukawa, K., Hirai, H., Iwasa, S., Endo, S., Mato, Y., Saha, M., Okuda, K., Nakashima, A., & Murakami, M. (2009). International Pellet Watch: Global monitoring of persistent organic pollutants (POPs) in coastal waters. 1. Initial phase data on PCBs, DDTs, and HCHs. *Marine Pollution Bulletin, 58*(10), 1437–1446.

Ogden, C. L., Carroll, M. D., Kit, B. K., & Flegal, K. M. (2014), Prevalence of childhood and adult obesity in the United States, 2011–2012. *JAMA, 311*(8), 806–814.

Okrent, A. M., Elitzak, H., Park, T., & Rehkamp, S. (2018). *Measuring the value of the US food system: Revisions to the food expenditure series*. Economic Research Service Technical Bulletin Number 1948. US Department of Agriculture.

Olaimat, A. N., Al-Holy, M. A., Shahbaz, H. M., Al-Nabulsi, A. A., Abu Ghoush, M. H., Osaili, T. M., … Holley, R. A. (2018). Emergence of antibiotic resistance in *Listeria monocytogenes* isolated from food products: A comprehensive review. *Comprehensive Reviews in Food Science and Food Safety, 17*(5), 1277–1292.

Ollerton, J., Winfree, R., & Tarrant, S. (2011). How many flowering plants are pollinated by animals? *Oikos, 120*(3), 321–326.

Onozaka, Y., & McFadden, D. T. (2011). Does local labeling complement or compete with other sustainable labels? A conjoint analysis of direct and joint values for fresh produce claim. *American Journal of Agricultural Economics, 93*(3), 693–706.

Organisation for Economic Co-operation and Development (OECD). (2012). *Livestock diseases: Prevention, control and compensation schemes*. doi:10.1787/9789264178762-en

Organisation for Economic Co-operation and Development (OECD) & Food and Agriculture Organization (FAO). (2018). *Agricultural outlook 2018–2027*. OECD & FAO.

Osborne, H. (2016). Councils should protect pubs from developers, says Camra. *The Guardian*, 17 August. https://www.theguardian.com/money/2016/aug/17/london-council-protects-historic-pubs-conversion-wandsworth

Papargyropoulou, E., Lozano, R., Steinberger, J. K., Wright, N., & bin Ujang, Z. (2014). The food waste hierarchy as a framework for the management of food surplus and food waste. *Journal of Cleaner Production, 76*, 106–115.

Papargyropoulou, E., Wright, N., Lozano, R., Steinberger, J., Padfield, R., & Ujang, Z. (2016). Conceptual framework for the study of food waste generation and prevention in the hospitality sector. *Waste Management, 49*, 326–336.

Parfitt, J., Barthel, M., & Macnaughton, S. (2010). Food waste within food supply chains: Quantification and potential for change to 2050. *Philosophical Transactions of the Royal Society of London B: Biological Sciences, 365*(1554), 3065–3081.

Park, J., & Kim, H. J. (2014). Environmental proactivity of hotel operations: Antecedents and the moderating effect of ownership type. *International Journal of Hospitality Management, 37*, 1–10.

Park, J., Kim, H. J., & McCleary, K. W. (2014). The impact of top management's environmental attitudes on hotel companies' environmental management. *Journal of Hospitality & Tourism Research, 38*, 95–115.

Patrucco, A. S., Luzzini, D., & Ronchi, S. (2017). Achieving innovation through supplier collaboration: The role of the purchasing interface. *Business Process Management Journal, 23*(6), 1270–1289.

Payne, A. (2020). The UK is set to have at least 95,000 tonnes of unwanted potatoes after the coronavirus lockdown closed fish and chip shops. *Business Insider*, 14 May. https://www.businessinsider.com.au/coronavirus-potato-farmers-face-supply-crisis-after-fish-and-chip-shops-close-2020-5?_ga=2.3810800.1945485555.1614949730-1800150389.1614949730&r=US&IR=T

Pearson, D., Henryks, J., & Jones, H. (2011a). Organic food: What we know (and do not know) about consumers. *Renewable Agriculture and Food Systems, 26*(2), 171–177.

Pearson, D., Henryks, J., Trott, A., Jones, P., Parker, G., Dumaresq, D., & Dyball, R. (2011b). Local food: Understanding consumer motivations in innovative retail formats. *British Food Journal, 113*(7), 886–899.

Pearson, D., Minehan, M., & Wakefield-Rann, R. (2013). Food waste in Australian households: Why does it occur? *Australasian-Pacific Journal of Regional Food Studies, 3*, 118–132.

Perchard, E. (2015). TV chef wages 'war on waste'. *Resource. Sharing Knowledge to Promote Waste as a Resource*, 3 November. https://resource.co/article/tv-chef-wages-'war-waste'-10592

Perry, E. A., Thomas, H., Samra, H. R., Edmonstone, S., Davidson, L., Faulkner, A., … Kirkpatrick, S. I. (2017). Identifying attributes of food literacy: A scoping review. *Public Health Nutrition, 20*(13), 2406–2415.

Peters, A., Vetter, P., Guitart, C., Lotfinejad, N., & Pittet, D. (2020). Understanding the emerging coronavirus: What it means for health security and infection prevention. *Journal of Hospital Infection, 104*(4), 440–448.

Peterson, G. R. (2013). Is eating locally a moral obligation? *Journal of Agricultural and Environmental Ethics, 26*(2), 421–437.

Philpot, T. (2007). Flesh and bone: Toward a whole-beast meat-eating ethos. *Gastronomica, 7*(2), 106–109.

Pimentel, D., & Pimentel, M. (2003). Sustainability of meat-based and plant-based diets and the environment. *The American Journal of Clinical Nutrition, 78*(3), 660S–663S.

Pino, G., Peluso, A. M., & Guido, G. (2012). Determinants of regular and occasional consumers' intentions to buy organic food. *Journal of Consumer Affairs, 46*(1), 157–169.

Pinto, R. S., dos Santos Pinto, R. M., Melo, F. F. S., Campos, S. S., & Cordovil, C. M. D. S. (2018). A simple awareness campaign to promote food waste reduction in a University canteen. *Waste Management, 76*, 28–38.

Pirani, S. I., & Arafat, H. A. (2016). Reduction of food waste generation in the hospitality industry. *Journal of Cleaner Production, 132*, 129–145.

Pollan, M. (2006). *The omnivore's dilemma: A natural history of four meals*. Penguin Press.

Ponisio, L. C., M'Gonigle, L. K., Mace, K. C., Palomino, J., de Valpine, P., & Kremen, C. (2015). Diversification practices reduce organic to conventional yield gap. *Proceedings of the Royal Society B: Biological Sciences, 282*(1799). doi:10.1098/rspb.2014.1396.

Ponte, S. (2012). The Marine Stewardship Council (MSC) and the making of a market for 'sustainable fish'. *Journal of Agrarian Change, 12*(2–3), 300–315.

Poore, J., & Nemecek, T. (2018). Reducing food's environmental impacts through producers and consumers. *Science, 360*, 987–992.

Portadown Times. (2020). Restaurant which provides employment for young people with special needs closes its doors. *Portadown Times*, 5 August. https://www.portadowntimes.co.uk/news/people/restaurant-which-provides-employment-young-people-special-needs-closes-its-doors-2933909

Poulston, J., & Yiu, A. Y. K. (2011). Profit or principles: Why do restaurants serve organic food? *International Journal of Hospitality Management, 30*(1), 184–191.

Power, M., Doherty, B., Pybus, K., & Pickett, K. (2020). How COVID-19 has exposed inequalities in the UK food system: The case of UK food and poverty. *Emerald Open Research, 2*, Art. 11, doi:10.35241/emeraldopenres.13539.2.

References

Pozo, V. F., & Schroeder, T. C. (2016). Evaluating the costs of meat and poultry recalls to food firms using stock returns. *Food Policy, 59*, 66–77.

Prabhakar, S. V. R. K., Sano, D., & Srivastava, N. (2010). Food safety in the Asia-Pacific region: Current status, policy perspectives, and a way forward. In *Sustainable consumption and production in the Asia-Pacific region: Effective responses in a resource constrained world*, IGES White Paper III (pp. 215–238). Institute for Global Environmental Strategies.

Pradhan, P., Reusser, D. E., & Kropp, J. P. (2013). Embodied greenhouse gas emissions in diets. *PLOS ONE, 8*(5), e62228. doi:10.1371/journal.pone.0062228.

Prescott, J., Young, O., O'Neill, L., Yau, N. J. N., & Stevens, R. (2002). Motives for food choice: A comparison of consumers from Japan, Taiwan, Malaysia and New Zealand. *Food Quality and Preference, 13*, 489–495.

Pretty, J. N., Ball, A. S., Lang, T., & Morison, J. I. (2005). Farm costs and food miles: An assessment of the full cost of the UK weekly food basket. *Food Policy, 30*(1), 1–19.

Pretty, J. N., Brett, C., Gee, D., Hine, R., Mason, C. F., Morison, J. I. L., Raven, H., Rayment, M., & van der Bijl, G. (2000). An assessment of the total external costs of UK agriculture. *Agricultural Systems, 65*(2), 113–136.

Preylo, B. D., & Arikawa, H. (2008). Comparison of vegetarians and non-vegetarians on pet attitude and empathy. *Anthrozoös, 21*(4), 387–395.

Priestley, S. (2016). *Food waste*. House of Commons Library briefing paper CBP07552. House of Commons.

Principato, L., Pratesi, C. A., & Secondi, L. (2018). Towards zero waste: An exploratory study on restaurant managers. *International Journal of Hospitality Management, 74*, 130–137.

Probst, C., Gethmann, J. M., Heuser, R., Niemann, H., & Conraths, F. J. (2013). Direct costs of bovine spongiform encephalopathy control measures in Germany. *Zoonoses and Public Health, 60*(8), 577–595.

Pulkkinen, H., Roininen, T., Katajajuuri, J. M., & Järvinen, M. (2016). Development of a climate choice meal concept for restaurants based on carbon footprinting. *The International Journal of Life Cycle Assessment, 21*(5), 621–630.

Quested, T., & Johnson, H. (2009). Household food and drink waste in the UK. *WRAP* [pdf]. Retrieved from https://wrap.org.uk/resources/report/household-food-and-drink-waste-uk-2009

Quested, T. E., Marsh, E., Stunell, D., & Parry, A. D. (2013). Spaghetti soup: The complex world of food waste behaviours. *Resources, Conservation and Recycling, 79*, 43–51.

Raab, C., Baloglu, S., & Chen, Y. (2018). Restaurant managers' adoption of sustainable practices: An application of institutional theory and theory of planned behavior. *Journal of Foodservice Business Research, 21*(2), 154–171.

Rahman, S. M. E., Khan, I., & Oh, D. H. (2016). Electrolyzed water as a novel sanitizer in the food industry: Current trends and future perspectives. *Comprehensive Reviews in Food Science and Food Safety, 15*(3), 471–490.

Rainbolt, G. N., Onozaka, Y., & McFadden, D. T. (2012). Consumer motivations and buying behavior: The case of the local food system movement. *Journal of Food Products Marketing, 18*(5), 385–396.

Ramírez-Restrepo, C. A., Van Tien, D., Le Duc, N., Herrero, M., Le Dinh, P., Van, D. D., Hoa, S. L. T., Chi, C. V., Solano-Patiño, C., Lerner, A. M., & Searchinger, T. D. (2017). Estimation of methane emissions from local and crossbreed beef cattle in Daklak province of Vietnam. *Asian-Australasian Journal of Animal Sciences, 30*(7), 1054–1060.

Ramos-Elorduy, J. (1997). Insects. A sustainable food source? *Ecology of Food and Nutrition, 36*(2–4), 247–276.

Ranganathan, J. (2013). The global food challenge explained in 18 graphics. *World Resources Institute (WRI)*, 3 December. https://www.wri.org/blog/2013/12/global-food-challenge-explained-18-graphics

Ravandi, B., & Jovanovic, N. (2019). Impact of plate size on food waste: Agent-based simulation of food consumption. *Resource Conservation and Recycling, 149*, 550–565.

Rayner, J. (2017). Is being a chef bad for your mental health? *The Observer*, 26 November. https://www.theguardian.com/society/2017/nov/26/chefs-mental-health-depression

Rayner, J. (2018). Holborn Dining Room: 'Its pork pie is a bold expression of pig' – restaurant review. *The Guardian*, 15 July. https://www.theguardian.com/lifeandstyle/2018/jul/15/holborn-dining-room-its-pork-pie-is-a-bold-expression-of-pig-restaurant-review

Rayner, J. (2020). Haenyeo, Brooklyn: 'An evolved take on the Korean repertoire', *The Guardian*, 29 March. https://www.theguardian.com/food/2020/mar/29/jay-rayner-restaurant-review-haenyeo-brooklyn-jenny-kwak-union-street-cafe-red-rooster

Rayner, J. (2021). Fergus Henderson's 'whole animal' recipes inspired chefs on both sides of the Atlantic. *The Guardian*, 28 February. https://www.theguardian.com/food/2021/feb/28/jay-rayner-on-restaurants-fergus-hendersons-inspirational-whole-animal-eating

Raynolds, L. T. (2009). Mainstreaming fair trade coffee: From partnership to traceability. *World Development*, 37(6), 1083–1093.

Redzepi, R. (2011). René Redzepi: 'What we eat matters: There's no conflict between a better meal and a better world'. *The Observer*, 14 August. https://www.theguardian.com/lifeandstyle/2011/aug/14/rene-redzepi-chefs-better-food

Redzepi, R. (2016). Redzepi on Redzepi: The Noma Australia exit interview. *Gourmet Traveller*. 30 March. https://www.gourmettraveller.com.au/news/restaurant-news/redzepi-on-redzepi-the-noma-australia-exit-interview-3702

Reeve, J. R., Hoagland, L. A., Villalba, J. J., Carr, P. M., Atucha, A., Cambardella, C., Davis, D. R., & Delate, K. (2016). Organic farming, soil health, and food quality: Considering possible links. *Advances in Agronomy*, 137, 319–367.

Reganold, J. P., & Wachter, J. M. (2016). Organic agriculture in the twenty-first century. *Nature Plants*, 2(2), 15221. doi:10.1038/nplants.2015.221.

Regeringen. (2019). *Skogsbränderna sommaren 2018 [Forest fires summer 2018]*. SOU 2019:7 [pdf]. https://www.regeringen.se/4906d2/contentassets/8a43cbc3286c4eb39be8b347ce78da16/skogsbranderna-sommaren-2018-sou-2019-7.pdf

Reinmuth-Selzle, K., Kampf, C. J., Lucas, K., Lang-Yona, N., Fröhlich-Nowoisky, J., Shiraiwa, M., Lakey, P. S., Lai, S., Liu, F., Kunert, A. T., & Ziegler, K. (2017). Air pollution and climate change effects on allergies in the anthropocene: Abundance, interaction, and modification of allergens and adjuvants. *Environmental Science & Technology*, 51(8), 4119–4141.

Renzaho, A. M., McCabe, M., & Swinburn, B. (2012). Intergenerational differences in food, physical activity, and body size perceptions among African migrants. *Qualitative Health Research*, 22(6), 740–754.

Research Institute of Organic Agriculture (FiBL). (2019). *Organic agriculture worldwide: Key results from the FiBL survey on organic agriculture worldwide 2019*. http://orgprints.org/35383/3/FiBL-2019-Regions-2017.pdf

Research Institute of Organic Agriculture (FiBL) and IFOAM – Organics International. (2019). *FiBl and IFOAM the world of organic agriculture. Statistics & emerging trends 2019*. IFAOM.

Resource Efficient Scotland. (2017). *Managing food waste in the hospitality and food service industry*. Resource Efficient Scotland.

Restaurants Canada. (2019). Smart cities, smarter restaurants: Future-proof your operations. 18 April. https://blog.restaurantscanada.org/index.php/2019/04/18/smart-cities-smarter-restaurants-future-proof-your-operations/

Restuccia, D., Spizzirri, U. G., Parisi, O. I., Cirillo, G., Curcio, M., Lemma, F., Puoci, F., Vinci, G., & Picci, N. (2010). New EU regulation aspects and global market of active and intelligent packaging for food industry applications. *Food Control*, 21(11), 1425–1435.

Reynolds, C. J., Mavrakis, V., Davison, S., Høj, S. B., Vlaholias, E., Sharp, A., … Boland, J. (2014). Estimating informal household food waste in developed countries: The case of Australia. *Waste Management & Research*, 32(12), 1254–1258.

Reynolds-Allie, K., & Fields, D. (2012). A comparative analysis of Alabama restaurants: Local vs non-local food purchase. *Journal of Food Distribution Research*, 43(1), 65–74.

Rhodes, K., Chan, F., Prichard, I., Coveney, J., Ward, P., & Wilson, C. (2016). Intergenerational transmission of dietary behaviours: A qualitative study of Anglo-Australian, Chinese–Australian and Italian–Australian three-generation families. *Appetite*, 103, 309–317.

Richards, A. J. (2001). Does low biodiversity resulting from modern agricultural practice affect crop pollination and yield? *Annals of Botany*, 88(2), 165–172.

References

Richter, B. (2017). Knowledge and perception of food waste among German consumers. *Journal of Cleaner Production, 166*, 641–648.

Riegel, C. D., & Haywood, K. M. (1984). Purchasing attitudes & behavior in Canadian foodservice firms. *Hospitality Education and Research Journal, 9*(1), 72–82.

Riegel, C. D., & Reid, R. D. (1988). Food-service purchasing: Corporate practices. *Cornell Hotel and Restaurant Administration Quarterly, 29*(1), 24–29.

Roberto, C. A., Bragg, M. A., Schwartz, M. B., Seamans, M. J., Musicus, A., Novak, N., & Brownell, K. D. (2012a). Facts up front versus traffic light food labels: A randomized controlled trial. *American Journal of Preventive Medicine, 43*(2), 134–141.

Roberto, C. A., Shivaram, M., Martinez, O., Boles, C., Harris, J. L., & Brownell, K. D. (2012b). The smart choices front-of-package nutrition label: Influence on perceptions and intake of cereal. *Appetite, 58*(2), 651–657.

Robinson, J., & Bennett, E. L. (Eds.). (2000). *Hunting for sustainability in tropical forests*. Columbia University Press.

Robinson, T. N., Borzekowski, D. L., Matheson, D. M., & Kraemer, H. C. (2007). Effects of fast food branding on young children's taste preferences. *Archives of Pediatrics & Adolescent Medicine, 161*(8), 792–797.

Rochman, C. M., Tahir, A., Williams, S. L., Baxa, D. V., Lam, R., Miller, J. T., Teh, F. C., Werorilangi, S., & Teh, S. J. (2015). Anthropogenic debris in seafood: Plastic debris and fibers from textiles in fish and bivalves sold for human consumption. *Scientific Reports, 5*(1), 1–10.

Rockström, J., Williams, J., Daily, G., Noble, A., Matthews, N., Gordon, L., Wetterstrand, H., DeClerck, F., Shah, M., Steduto, P., & de Fraiture, C. (2017). Sustainable intensification of agriculture for human prosperity and global sustainability. *Ambio, 46*(1), 4–17.

Roininen, K., Arvola, A., & Lähteenmäki, L. (2006). Exploring consumers' perceptions of local food with two different qualitative techniques: Laddering and word association. *Food Quality and Preference, 17*(1), 20–30.

Román, S., Sánchez-Siles, L. M., & Siegrist, M. (2017). The importance of food naturalness for consumers: Results of a systematic review. *Trends in Food Science & Technology, 67*, 44–57.

Röös, E., Patel, M., & Spångberg, J. (2016). Producing oat drink or cow's milk on a Swedish farm— Environmental impacts considering the service of grazing, the opportunity cost of land and the demand for beef and protein. *Agricultural Systems, 142*, 23–32.

Röös, E., & Tjärnemo, H. (2011). Challenges of carbon labelling of food products: A consumer research perspective. *British Food Journal, 113*(8), 982–996.

Rose, N., Serrano, E., Hosig, K., Haas, C., Reaves, D., & Nickols-Richardson, S. M. (2008). The 100-mile diet: A community approach to promote sustainable food systems impacts dietary quality. *Journal of Hunger & Environmental Nutrition, 3*(2–3), 270–285.

Roth, A. (2016). Why organic restaurant certification matters. *Civil Eats*, 18 April. https://civileats.com/2016/04/18/why-organic-restaurant-certification-matters/

Rothgerber, H. (2015). Underlying differences between conscientious omnivores and vegetarians in the evaluation of meat and animals. *Appetite, 87*, 251–258.

Roy, H. (2016). *The role of local food in restaurants: A comparison between restaurants and chefs in Vancouver, Canada and Christchurch, New Zealand*. Ph.D. Dissertation. University of Canterbury, New Zealand.

Roy, H., Hall, C. M., & Ballantine, P. W. (2017). Trust in local food networks: The role of trust among tourism stakeholders and their impacts in purchasing decisions. *Journal of Destination Marketing & Management, 6*(4), 309–317.

Roy, H., Hall, C. M., & Ballantine, P. W. (2019a). Connecting local food to foodservice businesses: An exploratory qualitative study on wholesale distributors' perceived benefits and challenges. *Journal of Foodservice Business Research, 22*(3), 261–285.

Roy, H., Hall, C. M., & Ballantine, P. W. (2019b). Supply chain analysis of farm-to-restaurant sales: A comparative study in Vancouver and Christchurch. In J. Byrom & D. Medway (Eds.), *Case studies in food retailing and distribution* (pp. 87–104). Woodhead Publishing.

Royal Association of British Dairy Farmers (RABDF). (2020a). *Q & A: Getting to grips with the impactofCovid19onmilksupplyissues*.https://www.rabdf.co.uk/latest-news/2020/4/8/q-amp-a-getting-to-grips-with-the-impact-of-covid19-on-milk-supply-issues?rq=pour

Royal Association of British Dairy Farmers (RABDF). (2020b). *Further detail needed on dairy hardship funds as some farmers could lose out*. https://www.rabdf.co.uk/latest-news/2020/6/4/further-detail-needed-on-dairy-hardship-funds-as-some-farmers-could-lose-out?rq=April%202020

Rozin, P. (2005). The meaning of food in our lives: A cross-cultural perspective on eating and well-being. *Journal of Nutrition Education and Behavior, 37*, S107–S112.

Rozin, P., Fallon, A., & Augustoni-Ziskind, M. (1986). The child's conception of food: The development of categories of acceptable and rejected substances. *Journal of Nutrition Education, 18*(2), 75–81.

Ruby, M. B., & Heine, S. J. (2012). Too close to home: Factors predicting meat avoidance. *Appetite, 59*, 47–52.

Ruhlman, M. (2017). *Grocery: The buying and selling of food in America*. Abrams.

Russell, S. V., Young, C. W., Unsworth, K. L., & Robinson, C. (2017). Bringing habits and emotions into food waste behaviour. *Resources, Conservation and Recycling, 125*, 107–114.

Ryder, T., & Topalian, C. (2010). *Edible: A celebration of local foods*. John Wiley & Sons.

Rytkönen, P., Bonow, M., Girard, C., & Tunón, H. (2018). Bringing the consumer back in—The motives, perceptions, and values behind consumers and rural tourists' decision to buy local and localized artisan food—A Swedish example. *Agriculture, 8*(4), Art. 58.

Saad, M. M. E. D., & Ahmed, M. B. M. (2018). Necessary usage of antibiotics in animals. In S. Savic (Ed.) *Antibiotic use in animals* (pp. 9–23). InTechOpen, doi:10.5772/intechopen.71257.

Sadílek, T. (2020). Utilization of food quality labels included in the European Union quality schemes. *International Journal on Food System Dynamics, 11*(1), 72–83.

Sage, C. (2003). Social embeddedness and relations of regard: Alternative 'good food' networks in south-west Ireland. *Journal of Rural Studies, 19*(1), 47–60.

Sahota, A. (2013). The global market for organic food and drink. In H. Willer, J. Lernoud & L. Kilcher (Eds.), *The world of organic agriculture. Statistics and emerging trends 2013. FiBL-IFOAM Report* (pp. 132–137). Research Institute of Organic Agriculture (FiBL) and International Federation of Organic Agriculture Movements (IFOAM).

Sakaguchi, L., Pak, N., & Potts, M. D. (2018). Tackling the issue of food waste in restaurants: Options for measurement method, reduction and behavioral change. *Journal of Cleaner Production, 180*, 430–436.

Salem, R., Bahadori-Jahromia, A., Mylon, A., Godfrey, P., & Cook, D. (2020). Energy performance and cost analysis for the nZEB retrofit of a typical UK hotel. *Journal of Building Engineering, 31*, Art. 101403.

Samadder, R. (2018). Eat a falafel, save a life – have I found the only pop-up that deserves to stay popped up? *The Guardian*, 8 April. https://www.theguardian.com/commentisfree/2018/apr/08/eat-a-falafel-save-a-life-have-i-found-the-only-pop-up-that-deserves-to-stay-popped-up

Sampson, G. S., Sanchirico, J. N., Roheim, C. A., Bush, S. R., Taylor, J. E., Allison, E. H., Anderson, J. L., Ban, N. C., Fujita, R., Jupiter, S., & Wilson, J. R. (2015). Secure sustainable seafood from developing countries. *Science, 348*(6234), 504–506.

Sánchez-Bayo, F., & Wyckhuys, K. A. (2019). Worldwide decline of the entomofauna: A review of its drivers. *Biological Conservation, 232*, 8–27.

Santeramo, F. G., Carlucci, D., De Devitiis, B., Seccia, A., Stasi, A., Viscecchia, R., & Nardone, G. (2018). Emerging trends in European food, diets and food industry. *Food Research International, 104*, 39–47.

Saunders, C., & Barber, A. (2008). Carbon footprints, life cycle analysis, food miles: Global trade trends and market issues. *Political Science, 60*(1), 73–88.

Sawyer, E. N., Kerr, W. A., & Hobbs, J. E. (2008). Consumer preferences and the international harmonization of organic standards. *Food Policy, 33*(6), 607–615.

Saxe, H., Jensen, J. D., Bølling Laugesen, S. M., & Bredie, W. L. P. (2019). Environmental impact of meal service catering for dependent senior citizens in Danish municipalities. *International Journal of Life Cycle Assessment, 24*, 654–666.

Scarborough, P., Appleby, P. N., Mizdrak, A., Briggs, A. D. M., Travis, R. C., Bradbury, K. E., & Key, T. J. (2014). Dietary greenhouse gas emissions of meat-eaters, fish-eaters, vegetarians and vegans in the UK. *Climatic Change, 125*(2), 179–192.

Schaider, L. A., Balan, S. A., Blum, A., Andrews, D. Q., Strynar, M. J., Dickinson, M. E., Lunderberg, D. M., Lang, J. R., & Peaslee, G. F. (2017). Fluorinated compounds in U.S. fast food packaging. *Environmental Science and Technology Letters, 4*(3), 105–111.

Schestak, I., Spriet, J., Styles, D., & Williams, A. P. (2020). Emissions down the drain: Balancing life cycle energy and greenhouse gas savings with resource use for heat recovery from kitchen drains. *Journal of Environmental Management, 271*, Art. 110988.

References

Schettler, T., Gottlieb, M., & Sirois, E. (2010). The food environment: Changing 50 years of growing an inflammatory diet. *Public Policy and Aging Report, 20*(3), 9–15.

Schmit, T. M., & Hadcock, S. E. (2012). Assessing barriers to expansion of farm-to-chef sales: A case study from upstate New York. *Journal of Food Research, 1*(1), 117–125.

Schmitt, E., Dominique, B., & Six, J. (2018). Assessing the degree of localness of food value chains. *Agroecology and Sustainable Food Systems, 42*(5), 573–598.

Schoolman, E. D. (2019). Do direct market farms use fewer agricultural chemicals? Evidence from the US Census of Agriculture. *Renewable Agriculture and Food Systems, 34*(5), 415–429.

Schösler, H., de Boer, J., & Boersema, J. J. (2012). Can we cut out the meat of the dish? Constructing consumer-oriented pathways towards meat substitution. *Appetite, 58*, 39–47.

Schrama, M., De Haan, J. J., Kroonen, M., Verstegen, H., & Van der Putten, W. H. (2018). Crop yield gap and stability in organic and conventional farming systems. *Agriculture, Ecosystems & Environment, 256*, 123–130.

Schwartz, M. B., Henderson, K. E., Read, M., Danna, N., & Ickovics, J. R. (2015). New school meal regulations increase fruit consumption and do not increase total plate waste. *Childhood Obesity, 11*(3), 242–247.

Seal, R. (2020). Reality bites: how the pandemic changed the way we eat. *The Guardian*, 4 July. https://www.theguardian.com/environment/2020/jul/04/reality-bites-how-the-pandemic-changed-the-way-we-eat

Searchinger, T., Waite, R., Hanson, C., & Ranganathan, J. (2018). Creating a sustainable food future: A menu of solutions to feed nearly 10 billion people by 2050. *World Resources Institute (WRI)*, July. https://www.wri.org/our-work/project/world-resources-report/world-resources-report-creating-sustainable-food-future

Sebbane, M., & Costa, S. (2018). Food leftovers in workplace cafeterias: An exploratory analysis of stated behavior and actual behavior. *Resource. Conservation and Recycling, 136*, 88–94.

Selfa, T., & Qazi, J. (2005). Place, taste, or face-to-face? Understanding producer–consumer networks in local food systems in Washington State. *Agriculture and Human Values, 22*(4), 451–464.

Sellberg, M. M., Norström, A. V., Peterson, G. D., & Gordon, L. J. (2020). Using local initiatives to envision sustainable and resilient food systems in the Stockholm city-region. *Global Food Security, 24*, 100334.

Serafini, M., Bugianesi, R., Salucci, M., Azzini, E., Raguzzini, A., & Maiani, G. (2002). Effect of acute ingestion of fresh and stored lettuce (*Lactuca sativa*) on plasma total antioxidant capacity and antioxidant levels in human subjects. *British Journal of Nutrition, 88*(6), 615–623.

Settembre, J. (2019). Good news for Beyond Meat? 95% of people who order vegan burgers when dining out aren't even vegetarians. *MarketWatch*, 6 August. https://www.marketwatch.com/story/more-meat-eaters-are-ordering-plant-based-burgers-when-dining-out-2019-07-17

Seufert, V., Ramankutty, N., & Foley, J. A. (2012). Comparing the yields of organic and conventional agriculture. *Nature, 485*(7397), 229–232.

Severt, K., Shin, Y. H., Chen, H. S., & DiPietro, R. B. (2020). Measuring the relationships between corporate social responsibility, perceived quality, price fairness, satisfaction, and conative loyalty in the context of local food restaurants. *International Journal of Hospitality & Tourism Administration*. doi:10.1080/15256480.2020.1842836.

Shah, P. (n.d.). 10 ways food service businesses can become more energy efficient, Pacific Gas & Electric. https://www.pge.com/en/mybusiness/save/smbblog/article/10-ways-food-service-businesses-can-become-more-energy-efficient.page?redirect=yes

Sharma, A., Moon, J., & Strohbehn, C. (2014). Restaurant's decision to purchase local foods: Influence of value chain activities. *International Journal of Hospitality Management, 39*, 130–143.

Sheldon, I. M. (2017). Certification mechanisms for credence attributes of foods: Does it matter who provides diagnosis? *Annual Review of Resource Economics, 9*, 33–51.

Shenker, J. (2021). 'They're stealing our customers and we've had enough': Is Deliveroo killing restaurant culture? *The Guardian*, 25 April. https://www.theguardian.com/global-development/2021/apr/25/deliveroo-tech-delivery-restaurant-service-dark-kitchens

Sherwood, H. (2021). Millions sign up to anti-food-waste apps to share their unused produce. *The Observer*, 21 March. https://www.theguardian.com/environment/2021/mar/21/millions-sign-up-to-anti-food-waste-apps-to-share-their-unused-produce

Shi, J., Visschers, V. H., Bumann, N., & Siegrist, M. (2018). Consumers' climate-impact estimations of different food products. *Journal of Cleaner Production, 172*, 1646–1653.

Shonkoff, E. T., Anzman-Frasca, S., Lynskey, V. M., Chan, G., Glenn, M. E., & Economos, C. D. (2018). Child and parent perspectives on healthier side dishes and beverages in restaurant kids' meals: Results from a national survey in the United States. *BMC Public Health, 18*(1), 1–10.

Sicherer, S. H., & Sampson, H. A. (2018). Food allergy: A review and update on epidemiology, pathogenesis, diagnosis, prevention, and management. *Journal of Allergy and Clinical Immunology, 141*(1), 41–58.

Siegrist, M. (2008). Factors influencing public acceptance of innovative food technologies and products. *Trends in Food Science & Technology, 19*(11), 603–608.

Silbergeld, E. K., Graham, J., & Price, L. B. (2008). Industrial food animal production, antimicrobial resistance, and human health. *Annual Review of Public Health, 29*, 151–169.

Silvennoinen, K., Heikkilä, L., Katajajuuri, J.-M., & Reinikainen, A. (2015). Food waste volume and origin: Case studies in the Finnish food service sector. *Waste Management, 46*, 140–145.

Sims, L. S. (1978). Food-related value-orientations, attitudes, and beliefs of vegetarians and non-vegetarians. *Ecology of Food and Nutrition, 7*(1), 23–35.

Sims, R. (2009). Food, place and authenticity: Local food and the sustainable tourism experience. *Journal of Sustainable Tourism, 17*(3), 321–336.

Singer, R. S., Finch, R., Wegener, H. C., Bywater, R., Walters, J., & Lipsitch, M. (2003). Antibiotic resistance—The interplay between antibiotic use in animals and human beings. *The Lancet Infectious Diseases, 3*(1), 47–51.

Singh, S. K., Kaushik, V., Soni, S., & Lamba, N. (2014). Waste management in restaurants: A review. *International Journal of Emerging Engineering Research and Technology, 2*(2), 14–24.

Sirieix, L., Grolleau, G., & Schaer, B. (2008). Do consumers care about food miles? An empirical analysis in France. *International Journal of Consumer Studies, 32*(5), 508–515.

Sirieix, L., Lála, J., & Kocmanová, K. (2017). Understanding the antecedents of consumers' attitudes towards doggy bags in restaurants: Concern about food waste, culture, norms and emotions. *Journal of Retailing and Consumer Services, 34*, 153–158.

Skallerud, K., & Wien, A. H. (2019). Preference for local food as a matter of helping behaviour: Insights from Norway. *Journal of Rural Studies, 67*, 79–88.

Smil, V. (2004). Improving efficiency and reducing waste in our food system. *Environmental Sciences, 1*(1), 17–26.

Smith, A., & Hall, C. M. (2003). Restaurants and local food in New Zealand. In C. M. Hall, L. Sharples, R. Mitchell, N. Macionis & B. Cambourne (Eds.), *Food tourism around the world* (pp. 249–267). Butterworth-Heinemann.

Smith, A., & MacKinnon, J. B. (2009). *The 100-mile diet: A year of local eating*. Vintage Canada.

Smith, P., Martino, D., Cai, Z., Gwary, D., Janzen, H., Kumar, P., … Sirotenko, O. (2007). Agriculture. In B. Metz, O. R. Davidson, P. R. Bosch, R. Dave & L. A. Meyer (Eds.), *Climate Change 2007: Mitigation. Contribution of Working Group III to the Fourth Assessment Report of the Intergovernmental Panel on Climate Change*. Cambridge University Press.

Smithers, R. (2017). Cheers! Pub saved by its customers rated best in the UK. *The Guardian*, 3 March. https://www.theguardian.com/lifeandstyle/2017/mar/03/cheers-pub-saved-by-its-customers-rated-best-in-the-uk

Smithers, R. (2020). UK organic food and drink sales boom during lockdown. *The Guardian*, 3 September. https://www.theguardian.com/environment/2020/sep/03/uk-organic-food-and-drink-sales-boom-during-lockdown

Soil Association. (2021). *The case for organic has never been stronger: Retailers and producers have seen the organic market rise by 12.6% compared to 2019*, 11 February. https://www.soilassociation.org/news/2021/february/11/time-to-support-organic/

Sønderskov, K. M., & Daugbjerg, C. (2011). The state and consumer confidence in eco-labeling: organic labeling in Denmark, Sweden, The United Kingdom and The United States. *Agriculture and Human Values, 28*(4), 507–517.

Song, V. (2018). Is the iconic Parisian bistro dying? *BBC Travel*, 10 July.

Sonnino, R., & Marsden, T. (2006). Beyond the divide: Rethinking relationships between alternative and conventional food networks in Europe. *Journal of Economic Geography, 6*(2), 181–199.

References

Sosenko, F., Littlewood, M., Bramley, G., Fitzpatrick, S., Blenkinsopp, J., & Wood, J. (2019). *State of hunger: A study of poverty and food insecurity in the UK*. Trussell Trust.

Soto, A. M., & Sonnenschein, C. (2015). DDT, endocrine disruption and breast cancer. *Nature Reviews Endocrinology, 11*(9), 507–508.

Souza, T. N., & Louzada, M. L. (2020). The association between types of restaurants and the consumption of ultra-processed food. *European Journal of Public Health*, 30 (Supplement 5), Art. ckaa166–254.

Spanos, S., Kenda, A. S., & Vartanian, L. R. (2015). Can serving-size labels reduce the portion-size effect? A pilot study. *Eating Behaviors, 16*, 40–42.

Stancu, V., Haugaard, P., & Lähteenmäki, L. (2016). Determinants of consumer food waste behaviour: Two routes to food waste. *Appetite, 96*, 7–17.

Stöckli, S., Dorn, M., & Liechti, S. (2018). Normative prompts reduce consumer food waste in restaurants. *Waste Management, 77*, 532–536.

Stoll-Kleemann, S., O'Riordan, T., & Jaeger, C. C. (2001). The psychology of denial concerning climate mitigation measures: Evidence from Swiss focus groups. *Global Environmental Change, 11*(2), 107–117.

Strohbehn, C. H., & Gregoire, M. B. (2003). Case studies of local food purchasing by central Iowa restaurants and institutions. *Foodservice Research International, 14*(1), 53–64.

Strong, S. (2021). Towards a geographical account of shame: Foodbanks, austerity, and the spaces of austere affective governmentality. *Transactions of the Institute of British Geographers, 46*(1), 73–86.

Styles, D., Schoenberger, H., & Galvez-Martos, J. L. (2015). Water management in the European hospitality sector: Best practice, performance benchmarks and improvement potential. *Tourism Management, 46*, 187–202.

Sumner, D. A., & Boriss, H. (2006). Bee-conomics and the leap in pollination fees. *Agricultural and Resource Economics Update, 9*(3), 9–11.

Sung, K. K., Tao, C. W. W., & Slevitch, L. (2020). Restaurant chain's corporate social responsibility messages on social networking sites: The role of social distance. *International Journal of Hospitality Management, 85*, 102429.

Sustainable Foodservice Consulting. (2016a). *Energy efficient lighting*. https://www.sustainablefoodservice.com/cat/lighting.htm

Sustainable Foodservice Consulting. (2016b). *Heating, ventilation and air conditioning*. https://www.sustainablefoodservice.com/cat/hvac.htm

Sustainable Foodservice Consulting. (2016c). *Energy conservation*. http://www.sustainablefoodservice.com/cat/energy-efficiency.htm

Sustainable Restaurant Association. (2021). *Our work*. https://thesra.org/our-aims/

Svenska Yle. (2014). *Norsk lax med blåvita vingar*. https://svenska.yle.fi/artikel/2014/01/06/norsk-lax-med-blavita-vingar

Swan, S. H., & Colino, S. (2021). *Count down: How our modern world is threatening sperm counts, altering male and female reproductive development, and imperiling the future of the human race*. Simon & Schuster.

Swinnen, J. F. (2009). The growth of agricultural protection in Europe in the 19th and 20th centuries. *World Economy, 32*(11), 1499–1537.

Tait, P., Saunders, C., Guenther, M., & Rutherford, P. (2016). Emerging versus developed economy consumer willingness to pay for environmentally sustainable food production: A choice experiment approach comparing Indian, Chinese and United Kingdom lamb consumers. *Journal of Cleaner Production, 124*, 65–72.

Tamarkin, D., & Hoffmann, M. (2021). The planet on the plate: Why Epicurious left beef behind. *Epicurious*, 26 April. https://www.epicurious.com/expert-advice/why-epicurious-left-beef-behind-article?

Taner, S., Pekey, B., & Pekey, H. (2013). Fine particulate matter in the indoor air of barbeque restaurants: Elemental compositions, sources and health risks. *Science of the Total Environment, 454*, 79–87.

Tanner, B. (2000). Independent assessment by third-party certification bodies. *Food Control, 11*, 415–417.

Tatáno, F., Caramiello, C., Paolini, T., & Tripolone, L. (2017). Generation and collection of restaurant waste: Characterization and evaluation at a case study in Italy. *Waste Management, 61*, 423–442.

Taylor, M. (2020). Global food industry on course to drive rapid habitat loss – research. *The Guardian*, 2 December. https://www.theguardian.com/environment/2020/dec/21/global-food-industry-to-drive-rapid-habitat-loss-research

Taylor-Robinson, D., Rougeaux, E., Harrison, D., Whitehead, M., Barr, B., & Pearce, A. (2013). The rise of food poverty in the UK. *BMJ*, *347*, f7157.

Te, S. (2019). Sustainability in modern restaurants: The great, hidden by-product of cloud technology. *Xe*, *19*, 104–105.

Teisl, M. F., Fein, S. B., & Levy, A. S. (2009). Information effects on consumer attitudes toward three food technologies: Organic production, biotechnology, and irradiation. *Food Quality and Preference*, *20*(8), 586–596.

Tellström, R., Gustafsson, I. B., & Mossberg, L. (2006). Consuming heritage: The use of local food culture in branding. *Place Branding*, *2*(2), 130–143.

Thamagasorn, M., & Pharino, C. (2019). An analysis of food waste from a flight catering business for sustainable food waste management: A case study of halal food production process. *Journal of Cleaner Production*, *228*, 845–855.

The Chartered Institute of Building Services Engineers (CIBSE) and Catering for a Sustainable Future Group (CSFG). (2009). *TM50—energy efficiency in commercial kitchens*. CIBSE.

The Grocer. (2021). Plastic and the pandemic: Consumer priorities in a changing world. *The Grocer*, 29 March.

Thorsøe, M., & Kjeldsen, C. (2016). The constitution of trust: Function, configuration and generation of trust in alternative food networks. *Sociologia Ruralis*, *56*(2), 157–175.

Thyberg, K. L., & Tonjes, D. J. (2016). Drivers of food waste and their implications for sustainable policy development. *Resources, Conservation and Recycling*, *106*, 110–123.

Tieman, M., Zakaria, Z., Sulaiman, A., & Ramli, S. Q. (2020). Halal procurement strategy in the food industry: A focus group discussion. *International Journal of Islamic Marketing and Branding*, *5*(3), 167–180.

Tobler, C., Visschers, H. M., & Siegrist, M. (2011). Eating green. Consumers' willingness to adopt ecological food consumption behaviors. *Appetite*, *57*, 674–682.

Tom, M. S., Fischbeck, P. S., & Hendrickson, C. T. (2016). Energy use, blue water footprint, and greenhouse gas emissions for current food consumption patterns and dietary recommendations in the US. *Environment Systems and Decisions*, *36*(1), 92–103.

Tonumaipe'a, D., Cammock, R., & Conn, C. (2021). Food havens not swamps: A strength-based approach to sustainable food environments. *Health Promotion International*. doi:10.1093/heapro/daab021.

Touboulic, A., Chicksand, D., & Walker, H. (2014). Managing imbalanced supply chain relationships for sustainability: A power perspective. *Decision Sciences*, *45*(4), 577–619.

Tremblay, S., Lucotte, M., Revéret, J. P., Davidson, R., Mertens, F., Passos, C. J. S., & Romana, C. A. (2015). Agroforestry systems as a profitable alternative to slash and burn practices in small-scale agriculture of the Brazilian Amazon. *Agroforestry Systems*, *89*(2), 193–204.

Tresidder, R. (2015). Eating ants: Understanding the terroir restaurant as a form of destination tourism. *Journal of Tourism and Cultural Change*, *13*(4), 344–360.

Trier, X., Granby, K., & Christensen, J. H. (2011). Polyfluorinated surfactants (PFS) in paper and board coatings for food packaging. *Environmental Science and Pollution Research*, *18*(7), 1108–1120.

Truman, E., Lane, D., & Elliott, C. (2017). Defining food literacy: A scoping review. *Appetite*, *116*, 365–371.

Tubiello, F. N., Salvatore, M., Rossi, S., Ferrara, A., Fitton, N., & Smith, P. (2013). The FAOSTAT database of greenhouse gas emissions from agriculture. *Environmental Research Letters*, *8*(1), 015009.

Tucker, C. A. (2014). The significance of sensory appeal for reduced meat consumption. *Appetite*, *81*, 168–179.

Turner-McGrievy, G. M., Leach, A. M., Wilcox, S., & Frongillo, E. A. (2016). Differences in environmental impact and food expenditures of four different plant-based diets and an omnivorous diet: Results of a randomized, controlled intervention. *Journal of Hunger & Environmental Nutrition*, *11*(3), 382–395.

Tyko, K. (2019). Chicken recall: More than 2 million pounds recalled, may be contaminated with metal. *USA Today*, 6 November. https://eu.usatoday.com/story/money/food/2019/11/06/2-million-pounds-chicken-recalled/2512022001/

References

Umweltbundesamt. (2018). *Emissionskennzahlen Datenbasis 2016 [Emission data]*. Vienna: Environment Agency Austria. http://www.Environment Agency Austria.at/fileadmin/site/umweltthemen/verkehr/1_verkehrsmittel/EKZ_Pkm_Tkm_Verkehrsmittel.pdf

Unite Legal Services. (2021). Two-thirds of London chefs believe long hours' culture is harming their health, Unite survey reveals. *News*, 12 February. https://www.unitelegalservices.org/news-stories/two-thirds-of-london-chefs-believe-long-hours-culture-is-harming-their-health-unite-survey-reveals

United Against Waste. (2015). *Avoidance of food waste in catering, accommodation and commercial kitchens. Final report* [pdf]. https://united-against-waste.at/wp-content/uploads/2015/05/Endbericht_UAW_ABF_tatwort_final_ARA.pdf?eb6772

United Against Waste. (2018). *Avoid food waste, save costs & protect the environment. Brochure savings tips & service offers for gastronomy and hotel business* [pdf]. https://united-against-waste.at/wp-content/uploads/2015/05/UAW_Gastro_LR.pdf?fa6be0

United Nations (UN). (2017). *Sustainable development goals.* https://sustainabledevelopment.un.org/?menu=1300

United Nations Educational, Scientific and Cultural Organization (UNESCO). (2009). *United Nations world water development report 3. Water in a changing World.* UNESCO. http://www.unesco.org/new/en/natural-sciences/environment/water/wwap/wwdr/wwdr3-2009/

United Nations Framework Convention on Climate Change (UNFCCC). (2018a). *What is the Kyoto Protocol?* https://unfccc.int/process-and-meetings/the-kyoto-protocol/what-is-the-kyoto-protocol/what-is-the-kyoto-protocol

United Nations Framework Convention on Climate Change (UNFCCC). (2018b). *What is the Paris Agreement?* https://unfccc.int/process-and-meetings/the-paris-agreement/what-is-the-paris-agreement

United Nations Human Rights Council (UNHRC). (2017). *Report of the Special Rapporteur on the right to food*, Human Rights Council, Thirty-fourth session 27 February–24 March 2017, United Nations General Assembly, 24 January, A/HRC/34/48. https://documents-dds-ny.un.org/doc/UNDOC/GEN/G17/017/85/PDF/G1701785.pdf?OpenElement

United States Department of Agriculture (USDA). (2017). *Certified organic survey. 2016 summary* [pdf]. https://downloads.usda.library.cornell.edu/usda-esmis/files/zg64tk92g/70795b52w/4m90dz33q/OrganicProduction-09-20-2017_correction.pdf

United States Department of Agriculture (USDA). (2019). *Poultry slaughter* [pdf]. https://downloads.usda.library.cornell.edu/usda-esmis/files/3197xm04j/n009w967m/2v23w3090/psla0419.pdf

United States Department of Agriculture (USDA), Agricultural Marketing Service (USDA, AMS). (n.d.). Organic. https://www.ams.usda.gov/grades-standards/organic-standards

United States Department of Agriculture (USDA) Foreign Agricultural Service. (2015). *Chile's new nutritional labelling law* [pdf]. Retrieved from https://www.fas.usda.gov/data/chile-chiles-new-nutritional-labeling-law

United States Environmental Protection Agency (EPA). (2019). *Advancing sustainable materials management: 2017 fact sheet* [pdf]. https://www.epa.gov/sites/production/files/2019-11/documents/2017_facts_and_figures_fact_sheet_final.pdf

Upham, P., Dendler, L., & Bleda, M. (2011). Carbon labelling of grocery products: Public perceptions and potential emissions reductions. *Journal of Cleaner Production, 19*(4), 348–355.

US News. (2019). *Best diets overall.* https://health.usnews.com/best-diet/best-diets-overall

Vaitkeviciute, R., Ball, L. E., & Harris, N. (2015). The relationship between food literacy and dietary intake in adolescents: A systematic review. *Public Health Nutrition, 18*(4), 649–658.

Valdivia Espino, J. N., Guerrero, N., Rhoads, N., Simon, N., Escaron A. L., Meinen A., Javier Nieto, F., & Martinez-Donate, A. P. (2015). Community-based restaurant interventions to promote healthy eating: A systematic review. *Preventing Chronic Disease, 12*, 140455.

Vallejo, F., Tomás-Barberán, F., & García-Viguera, C. (2003). Health-promoting compounds in broccoli as influenced by refrigerated transport and retail sale period. *Journal of Agricultural and Food Chemistry, 51*(10), 3029–3034.

Van den Bogaard, A. E., & Stobberingh, E. E. (1996). Time to ban all antibiotics as animal growth-promoting agents? *The Lancet, 348*(9027), Art. 619. https://doi.org/10.1016/S0140-6736(05)64838-6

van der Linden, S. (2014). Towards a new model for communicating climate change. In S. A. Cohen, J. E. S. Higham, P. Peeters & S. Gössling (Eds.), *Understanding and governing sustainable tourism mobility: Psychological and behavioural approaches* (pp. 243–277). Routledge.

van Dooren, C., & Aiking, H. (2016). Defining a nutritionally healthy, environmentally friendly, and culturally acceptable low lands diet. *The International Journal of Life Cycle Assessment*, *21*(5), 688–700.

Van Loo, E., Caputo, V., Nayga, R., & Verbeke, W. (2014). Consumers' valuation of sustainability labels on meat. *Food Policy*, *49*(Part 1), 137–150.

Van Putten, I., Longo, C., Arton, A., Watson, M., Anderson, C.M., Himes-Cornell, A., Obregón, C., Robinson, L., & Van Steveninck, T. (2020). Shifting focus: The impacts of sustainable seafood certification. *PLOS ONE*, *15*(5), p.e0233237.

van Vuuren, D.P., Stehfest, E., Gernaat, D. E., Berg, M., Bijl, D. L., Boer, H. S., Daioglou, V., Doelman, J. C., Edelenbosch, O. Y., Harmsen, M., & Hof, A. F. (2018). Alternative pathways to the 1.5 C target reduce the need for negative emission technologies. *Nature Climate Change*, *8*(5), 391–397.

Vanbergen, A. J., & Initiative, T. I. P. (2013). Threats to an ecosystem service: Pressures on pollinators. *Frontiers in Ecology and the Environment*, *11*(5), 251–259.

van Weele, A. (2002). *Purchasing and supply chain management: Analysis, planning and practice*. Thomson Learning.

Vanclay, J. K., Shortiss, J., Auselbrook, S., Gillespie, A. M., Howell, B. C., Johanni, R., Maher, M. J., Mitchell, K. M., Stewart, M. D., & Yates, J. (2011). Customer response to carbon labelling of groceries. *Journal of Consumer Policy*, *34*, 153–160.

Vandevijvere, S., Dominick, C., Devi, A., & Swinburn, B. (2015). International network for food and obesity/non-communicable diseases research, monitoring and action support. The healthy food environment policy index: Findings of an expert panel in New Zealand. *Bulletin of the World Health Organization*, *93*(5), 294–302.

Vanham, D., Hoekstra, A. Y., & Bidoglio, G. (2013a). Potential water saving through changes in European diets. *Environment International*, *61*, 45–56.

Vanham, D., Mekonnen, M. M., & Hoekstra, A. Y. (2013b). The water footprint of the EU for different diets. *Ecological Indicators*, *32*, 1–8.

Vanhonacker, F., Van Loo, E. J., Gellynck, X., & Verbeke, W. (2013). Flemish consumer attitudes towards more sustainable food choices. *Appetite*, *62*, 7–16.

VanSchenkhof, M. (2011). An investigation of water usage in casual dining restaurants in Kansas (Doctoral dissertation, Kansas State University).

Vasiljevic, M., Pechey, R., & Marteau, T. M. (2015). Making food labels social: The impact of colour of nutritional labels and injunctive norms on perceptions and choice of snack foods. *Appetite*, *91*, 56–63.

Vaske, J. J., & Donnelly, M. P. (1999). A value-attitude-behavior model predicting wildland preservation voting intentions. *Society and Natural Resources*, *12*(6), 523–537.

Venn, S., Burningham, K., Christie, I., & Jackson, T. (2017). Consumption junkies or sustainable consumers: Considering the grocery shopping practices of those transitioning to retirement. *Ageing & Society*, *37*(1), 14–38.

Vermillion, A. (2020). Maria Hines will close tilth this month. *Seattle Met*, 22 October. https://www.seattlemet.com/eat-and-drink/2020/10/maria-hines-will-close-tilth-seattle-this-month

Vernooij, R. W., Zeraatkar, D., Han, M. A., El Dib, R., Zworth, M., Milio, K., ... Swierz, M. J. (2019). Patterns of red and processed meat consumption and risk for cardiometabolic and cancer outcomes: A systematic review and meta-analysis of cohort studies. *Annals of Internal Medicine*, *171*(10), 732–741.

Vétérinaires sans Frontières Suisse (VSF). (2018). *Livestock diseases. Surveillance & early warning systems guidelines handbook*. VSF.

Vidergar, P., Perc, M., & Lukman, R. K. (2020). A survey of the life cycle assessment of food supply chains. *Journal of Cleaner Production*, *286*, 125506.

Vidgen, H. A., & Gallegos, D. (2014). Defining food literacy and its components. *Appetite*, *76*, 50–59.

Vieux, F., Darmon, N., Touazi, D., & Soler, L. G. (2012). Greenhouse gas emissions of self-selected individual diets in France: Changing the diet structure or consuming less? *Ecological Economics*, *75*, 91–101.

References

Viking Line. (2019). *No discharges into the sea*. https://www.vikingline.com/en/environment/emissions-and-waste/no-discharges-into-the-sea/

Visschers, V. H., & Siegrist, M. (2015). Does better for the environment mean less tasty? Offering more climate-friendly meals is good for the environment and customer satisfaction. *Appetite, 95*, 475–483.

Visser, S. S., Hutter, I., & Haisma, H. (2016). Building a framework for theory-based ethnographies for studying intergenerational family food practices. *Appetite, 97*, 49–57.

Vujnović, N., & Dović, D. (2021). Cost-optimal energy performance calculations of a new nZEB hotel building using dynamic simulations and optimization algorithms. *Journal of Building Engineering, 39*, Art. 102272

Wales, C., Harvey, M., & Warde, A. (2006). Recuperating from BSE: The shifting UK institutional basis for trust in food. *Appetite, 47*(2), 187–195.

Wallgren, C. (2006). Local or global food markets: A comparison of energy use for transport. *Local Environment, 11*(2), 233–251.

Walmsley, A., Partington, S., Armstrong, R., & Goodwin, H. (2019). Reactions to the national living wage in hospitality. *Employee Relations, 41*(1), 253–268.

Wang, K., Li, N., Peng, J., Wang, X., Wang, C., & Wang, M. (2017). A highly efficient solution for thermal compensation of ground-coupled heat pump systems and waste heat recovery of kitchen exhaust air. *Energy and Buildings, 138*, 499–513.

Wang, L.-E., Liu, G., Liu, X., Liu, Y., Gao, J., Zhou, B., … Cheng, S. (2017). The weight of unfinished plate: A survey based characterization of restaurant food waste in Chinese cities. *Waste Management, 66*, 3–12.

Wang, Y., Shen, C., Sun, P., Li, C., & Zhang, C. (2020). Utilization of waste heat from commercial kitchen exhaust for water heating and dish drying. *Journal of Building Engineering, 32*, Art. 101788.

Wansink, B. (2010). From mindless eating to mindlessly eating better. *Physiology & Behavior, 100*(5), 454–463.

Wansink, B., & Love, K. (2014). Slim by design: Menu strategies for promoting high-margin, healthy foods. *International Journal of Hospitality Management, 42*, 137–143.

Wansink, B., Painter, J. M. & Van Ittersum, K. (2001). Descriptive menu labels' effect on sales. *Cornell Hotel Restaurant and Administration Quarterly, 42*, 68–72.

Wansink, B., & Van Ittersum, K. (2013). Portion size me: Plate-size induced consumption norms and win-win solutions for reducing food intake and waste. *Journal of Experimental Psychology: Applied, 19*(4), 320–332.

Warde, A., & Martens, L. (1998). Eating out and the commercialisation of mental life. *British Food Journal, 100*(3), 147–153.

Water Supplies Department. (2016). *Best practice guidelines for water usage in catering industry*, https://www.waterconservation.gov.hk/filemanager/en/content_31/Catering_BPG-e.pdf

Waterlander, W. E., Mhurchu, C. N., Eyles, H., Vandevijvere, S., Cleghorn, C., Scarborough, P., … Seidell, J. (2018). Food futures: Developing effective food systems interventions to improve public health nutrition. *Agricultural Systems, 160*, 124–131.

Watson, W. L., Kelly, B., Hector, D., Hughes, C., King, L., Crawford, J., … Chapman, K. (2014). Can front-of-pack labelling schemes guide healthier food choices? Australian shoppers' responses to seven labelling formats. *Appetite, 72*, 90–97.

Weatherell, C., Tregear, A., & Allinson, J. (2003). In search of the concerned consumer: UK public perceptions of food, farming and buying local. *Journal of Rural Studies, 19*(2), 233–244.

Weber, C. L., & Matthews, H. S. (2008). Food-miles and the relative climate impacts of food choices in the United States. *Environmental Science & Technology, 42*(10), 3508–3513.

Weis, T. (2007). *The global food economy: The battle for the future of farming*. Zed Books.

Werner, A. (2021). Why do managers of small and medium-sized businesses seek voluntary living wage accreditation? – An exploration of choice rationales, *European Journal of Work and Organizational Psychology*. doi:10.1080/1359432X.2021.1908417.

Westhoek, H., Lesschen, J. P., Rood, T., Wagner, S., De Marco, A., Murphy-Bokern, D., Leip, A., van Grinsven, H., Sutton, M. A., & Oenema, O. (2014). Food choices, health and environment: Effects of cutting Europe's meat and dairy intake. *Global Environmental Change, 26*, 196–205.

White, K. (2021). Organic sales hit 15-year high as locked-down shoppers flock to category. *The Grocer*, 10 February. https://www.thegrocer.co.uk/sourcing/organic-sales-hit-15-year-high-as-locked-down-shoppers-flock-to-category/652996.article

White, M. J., Muhidin, S., Andrzejewski, C., Tagoe, E., Knight, R., & Reed, H. (2008). Urbanization and fertility: An event-history analysis of coastal Ghana. *Demography*, *45*(4), 803–816.

Whitehair, K. J., Shanklin, C. W., & Brannon, L. A. (2013). Written messages improve edible food waste behaviors in a university dining facility. *Journal of the Academy of Nutrition and Dietetics*, *113*(1), 63–69.

Wickramasinghe, L. P., Harris, S., Jones, G., & Vaughan Jennings, N. (2004). Abundance and species richness of nocturnal insects on organic and conventional farms: Effects of agricultural intensification on bat foraging. *Conservation Biology*, *18*(5), 1283–1292.

Wilcox, M. H. (1998). Antibiotic use and abuse. *The Lancet*, *352*(9134), 1152. doi:10.1016/S0140-6736(05)79803-2.

Wilewska-Bien, M., Granhag, L., & Andersson, K. (2016). The nutrient load from food waste generated onboard ships in the Baltic Sea. *Marine Pollution Bulletin*, *105*(1), 359–366.

Williams, D. R., Clark, M., Buchanan, G. M., Ficetola, G. F., Rondinini, C., & Tilman, D. (2021). Proactive conservation to prevent habitat losses to agricultural expansion. *Nature Sustainability*, *4*, 314–322.

Willett, W., Rockström, J., & Loken, B. (2019a). The EAT–Lancet Commission: A flawed approach? - Authors' reply. *The Lancet*, *394*(10204), 1141–1142.

Willett, W., Rockström, J., Loken, B., Springmann, M., Lang, T., Vermeulen, S., … Jonell, M. (2019b). Food in the Anthropocene: the EAT–Lancet Commission on healthy diets from sustainable food systems. *The Lancet*, *393*(10170), 447–492.

Williams, I. H. (1996). Aspects of bee diversity and crop pollination in the European Union. In A. Matheson, S. L. Buchmann, C. O'Toole, P. Westrich & I. H. Williams (Eds.), *The conservation of bees* (pp. 63–80). New York: Academic Press.

Williams, P. R., & Hammitt, J. K. (2001). Perceived risks of conventional and organic produce: Pesticides, pathogens, and natural toxins. *Risk Analysis*, *21*(2), 319–330.

Williamson, S., Block, L. G., & Keller, P. A. (2016). Of waste and waists: The effect of plate material on food consumption and waste. *Journal of the Association for Consumer Research*, *1*(1), 147–160.

Wilson, E. O. (1992). *The diversity of life*. Harvard University Press.

Wilson, E. O., & Peter, F. M. (Eds.) (1988). *Biodiversity*. National Academy Press.

Witte, W. (1998). Medical consequences of antibiotic use in agriculture. *Science*, *279*(5353), 996–997.

Wollenberg, E., Richards, M., Smith, P., Havlík, P., Obersteiner, M., Tubiello, F. N., Herold, M., Gerber, P., Carter, S., Reisinger, A., & Van Vuuren, D. P. (2016). Reducing emissions from agriculture to meet the 2 C target. *Global Change Biology*, *22*(12), 3859–3864.

Wong, C. L., Mendoza, J., Henson, S. J., Qi, Y., Lou, W., & L'abbé, M. R. (2014). Consumer attitudes and understanding of cholesterol-lowering claims on food: Randomize mock-package experiments with plant sterol and oat fibre claims. *European Journal of Clinical Nutrition*, *68*(8), 946–952.

World Bank. (2018). *CO_2 emissions (metric tons per capita)*. https://data.worldbank.org/indicator/EN.ATM.CO2E.PC

World Health Organization (WHO). (2017). *Stop using antibiotics in healthy animals to prevent the spread of antibiotic resistance*. https://www.who.int/news-room/detail/07-11-2017-stop-using-antibiotics-in-healthy-animals-to-prevent-the-spread-of-antibiotic-resistance

World Health Organization (WHO). (2018a). *Obesity and overweight*. https://www.who.int/en/news-room/fact-sheets/detail/obesity-and-overweight

World Health Organization (WHO). (2018b). *Healthy diet*. https://www.who.int/news-room/fact-sheets/detail/healthy-diet

World Health Organization (WHO). (2018c). *Antimicrobial resistance*. https://www.who.int/news-room/fact-sheets/detail/antimicrobial-resistance

World Resources Institute (WRI). (2016). *Food loss and waste accounting and reporting standard, executive summary*. WRI. https://www.flwprotocol.org/wp-content/uploads/2019/03/FLW_Standard_Exec_Summary.pdf

References

World Resources Institute (WRI). (2018). *Executive Summary (Synthesis)*. https://research.wri.org/wrr-food/executive-summary-synthesis

Wozniacka, G. (2020). Plastic to-go containers are bad, but the alternatives might not be much better. *GreenBiz*, 5 February.

WRAP. (2013a). *Overview of waste in the UK hospitality and food service sector*. WRAP.

WRAP. (2013b). *Water usage in the UK food and drink industry, Summary report*. WRAP.

WRAP. (2020). *UK progress against Courtauld 2025 targets and UN Sustainable Development Goal 12.3*. WRAP. https://wrap.org.uk/sites/default/files/2020-11/WRAP-Progress_against_Courtauld_2025_targets_and_UN_SDG_123.pdf

Xie, B., Tingyou, L., & Yi, Q. (2011). Organic certification and the market: Organic exports from and imports to China. *British Food Journal*, *113*(10), 1200–1216.

Xie, B., Wang, L., Yang, H., Wang, Y., & Zhang, M. (2015). Consumer perceptions and attitudes of organic food products in Eastern China. *British Food Journal*, *117*(3), 1105–1121.

Xu, F., Li, Y., Ge, X., Yang, L., & Li, Y. (2018). Anaerobic digestion of food waste: Challenges and opportunities. *Bioresource Technology*, *247*, 1047–1058.

Yabao, R. N., Duante, C. A., Velandria, F. V., Lucas, M., Kassu, A., Nakamori, M., & Yamamoto, S. (2005). Prevalence of dental caries and sugar consumption among 6–12-y-old schoolchildren in La Trinidad, Benguet, Philippines. *European Journal of Clinical Nutrition*, *59*(12), 1429–1438.

Yamashita, L., & Robinson, D. (2016). Making visible the people who feed us: Educating for critical food literacy through multicultural texts. *Journal of Agriculture, Food Systems, and Community Development*, *6*(2), 269–281.

Yang, L. H., & Gratton, C. (2014). Insects as drivers of ecosystem processes. *Current Opinion in Insect Science*, *2*, 26–32.

Ying, C. (2018). I left my serious job for the frivolous food industry: But chefs can bring change to the table. *The Guardian*, 11 March. https://www.theguardian.com/lifeandstyle/2018/mar/12/i-left-my-serious-job-for-the-frivolous-food-industry-but-chefs-can-bring-change-to-the-table

Yiridoe, E. K., Bonti-Ankomah, S., & Martin, R. C. (2005). Comparison of consumer perceptions and preference toward organic versus conventionally produced foods: A review and update of the literature. *Renewable Agriculture and Food Systems*, *20*(4), 193–205.

Yücel, N., Cıtak, S., & Önder, M. (2005). Prevalence and antibiotic resistance of listeria species in meat products in Ankara, Turkey. *Food Microbiology*, *22*(2–3), 241–245.

Yun-Chun, L., Shu, M., Ho, S. S. H., Wang, C., Cao, J. J., Wang, G. H., Wang, X. X., Wang, K., & Zhao, X. Q. (2015). Characteristics of PM2: 5 emitted from different cooking activities in China. *Atmospheric Research*, *166*, 83–91.

Zagata, L. (2012). Consumers' beliefs and behavioural intentions towards organic food. Evidence from the Czech Republic. *Appetite*, *59*(1), 81–89.

Zaman, S. B., Hussain, M. A., Nye, R., Mehta, V., Mamun, K. T., & Hossain, N. (2017). A review on antibiotic resistance: Alarm bells are ringing. *Cureus*, *9*(6): e1403. doi:10.7759/cureus.1403.

Zanoli, R., Scarpa, R., Napolitano, F., Piasentier, E., Naspetti, S., & Bruschi, V. (2013). Organic label as an identifier of environmentally related quality: A consumer choice experiment on beef in Italy. *Renewable Agriculture and Food Systems*, *28*(1), 70–79.

ZEBRA2020. (2016). Nearly zero energy building strategy 2020—strategies for a nearly zero-energy building market transition in the European Union. http://zebra2020.eu/website/wp-content/uploads/2014/08/ZEBRA2020_Strategies-for-nZEB_07_LQ_single-pages-1.pdf

Zeit Online. (2020). *Aral. Die Wegwerf-AG*. https://www.zeit.de/2020/06/aral-tankstelle-paechter-rewe-to-go-lebensmittel-wegwerfen

Zepeda, L., & Leviten-Reid, C. (2004). Consumers' views on local food. *Journal of Food Distribution Research*, *35*(3), 1–6.

Zeraatkar, D., Han, M. A., Guyatt, G. H., Vernooij, R. W., El Dib, R., Cheung, K., … Rabassa, M. (2019). Red and processed meat consumption and risk for all-cause mortality and cardiometabolic outcomes. *Annals of Internal Medicine*, *171*(10), 703–710.

Zhang, D., Jin, X., Yang, J., Du, X., & Yang, Y. (2017). Experimental study of inhalable particle concentration distribution in typical university canteens. *Journal of Building Engineering*, *14*, 81–88.

Zhang, T., Grunert, K. G., & Zhou, Y. (2020). A values–beliefs–attitude model of local food consumption: An empirical study in China and Denmark. *Food Quality and Preference*, *83*, Art. 103916.

Zhou, G., Hu, W., & Huang, W. (2016). Are consumers willing to pay more for sustainable products? A study of eco-labeled tuna steak. *Sustainability*, *8*(5), 494.

Zlatevska, N., Dubelaar, C., & Holden, S. S. (2014). Sizing up the effect of portion size on consumption: A meta-analytic review. *Journal of Marketing*, *78*(3), 140–154.

Zoll, F., Specht, K., Opitz, I., Siebert, R., Piorr, A., & Zasada, I. (2018). Individual choice or collective action? Exploring consumer motives for participating in alternative food networks. *International Journal of Consumer Studies*, *42*(1), 101–110.

Zuidmeer, L., Goldhahn, K., Rona, R. J., Gislason, D., Madsen, C., Summers, C., Sodergren, E., Dahlstrom, J., Lindner, T., Sigurdardottir, S. T., & McBride, D. (2008). The prevalence of plant food allergies: A systematic review. *Journal of Allergy and Clinical Immunology*, *121*(5), 1210–1218.

Zuraikat, F. M., Roe, L. S., Smethers, A. D., & Rolls, B. J. (2018). Doggy bags and downsizing: Packaging uneaten food to go after a meal attenuates the portion size effect in women. *Appetite*, *129*, 162–170.

Index

Africa 44, 46, 55, 235
agri-business 120; as part of culinary system 40
agricultural chemicals 88
agriculture 3, 19–26, 31, 33–43, 88, 95, 113, 141, 268; biodiversity loss 47–50; community supported agriculture 77; corporate agribusiness 36–43; in culinary system 40; disease 52–54; emissions 59–66; FAO global challenges 55–56; food security 19, 44–50, 55, 94; future 54–56; local 82–86; organic agriculture 90–100, 111; water use 50–52; see also food production
Agriculture and Horticulture Development Board (AHDB) 42
air conditioning 26, 180, 182–183, 188–189
air quality 9, 18, 119, 184, 188
Alarnab, Imad 256
Aldi 37
alkylphenol derivatives (APD) 195
alkylphenolethoxylates (APEO) 195
allergies 142–145; restaurant response to 143
alternative distribution channels see alternative food networks; local food systems
alternative food networks 78; see also local food systems
alternative food systems 78; see also local food systems
aluminium 39
animal welfare 21, 55, 86, 103, 128, 157, 162, 166, 170, 223, 245; certification 97, 103, 133; choice editing 162; and climate change 55; and dairy alternatives 70; and livestock disease 52; in meat purchasing 15, 17; and organic agriculture 86, 101
antibiotics 94, 107, 213; antimicrobial resistance 140–142; and organic certification 97
antimicrobial resistance 140–142
appellation 81, 89
apples 75, 84, 214, 225, 226; emissions 64; water footprint 51
apricots 225, 226

aquaculture 32, 33–34, 47, 61, 63; and biodiversity 47–48; carbon intensity 65; certification 128, 131; as part of culinary system 40; see also MSC, seafood
Aquaculture Stewardship Council 118
Arab cuisine 235
Argentina 63
Australia 33, 63, 159; 163, 170–171, 201, 267; carbon labelling 160; emissions 63; food security 44; MSC fisheries 117; obesity 138; organic production 92, 99; retailers 36, 37; Western Australia 117
authenticity 123; and local food 85; organic food 113; see also certification

Bains, Sat 270
Bananas 230; emissions 64; water footprint 51
Bangladesh 201
battery farming 162
beef 27, 67, 151; choice editing 162–163, 266; costs 95; global consumption 44; greenhouse gas emissions 4, 7, 59, 63, 64, 65, 267, 268; offal 171; planetary diet 150; substitution 27, 67, 69, 73; water footprint 51
beer 41; consumer confidence 52; disease 52; emissions 64, 71; market concentration 38; packaging 71; waste 71, 230; water footprint 51
Belgium 87
Beyond beef 73
biocides 112, 118; as part of culinary system 40; see also pesticides
biodiversity 47–50, 55, 90, 117, 119, 128, 267; conservation 268; ecosystem strategies 61, 268; environmentally friendly eating 3, 21, 30, 107, 147, 267; fair trade 115; loss 47–48, 61, 264; organic production 93, 94, 95, 111; regenerative farming 82
biodynamic farming 119
biofuel 21, 33, 66, 186; from waste 231
biosecurity 119
Bittman, Mark 265; and the American diet 265
Black Panthers 251

Index

Blanc, Raymond 81–82
Bottura, Massimo 253–255; waste campaigns 253
Boudain, Anthony 171
branding 22, 23, 85, 114, 125, 266; certification 110; and green growth approaches to culinary systems 22, 23; private standards 108; wine 119
Brazil 33, 39, 44, 59, 63, 74, 163, 201
bread 83, 128, 258; emissions 64; packaging 7; waste 128, 214, 221, 231, 239; water footprint 51
British Hospitality Association 41
Brownies & Downies 253
Bulgaria 201
Burma 163
The Butcher's Tap 256
butter 83, 84; health 144, 145

cabbage 83; water footprint 51
calories 45, 62, 55, 72–73, 102, 134, 267; carbon intensity 63; food gap 44; food security 44; health 144, 147–149, 154; international trade 32; labelling 146; lost and wasted by region and reason 46; obesity 138
Campaign for Real Ale (CAMRA) 260
Canada 4, 16, 32, 37, 44; consumption of meat and milk 44; carbon labels 160; energy benchmarking 207; local food 80; organic production 99; restaurant technology 203; wholesalers 125, 126
carbon emissions *see* emissions
carbon footprint 4, 132, 220; commercial kitchens 179; food waste 3; labelling 160; of milk 70; transport 224; *see also* climate change; emissions
carbon intensity 59, 62; decarbonizing the food system 65–70; of diets 63–65, 71; of menus 70; transport 75; *see also* climate change; emissions
carbon neutral 160; *see also* emissions
carbon offsets 80
carrots 7
catering 3, 16, 124, 202; greenhouse gas emissions 25; energy use in UK 179; environmental impact 121–122, 128; environmental interest 10, 15, 130–132; health 135–136, 167; packaging 42; procurement 127–132; school 121–122; sectoral characteristics 1–2; waste 4, 7, 43, 196, 220, 230; *see also* food service sector
cattle 52; biodiversity loss 266; disease 52; emissions 63; increase in global numbers 33, 34, 60; *see also* beef
celebrity chef 77, 238, 263, 269
Center for International Environmental Law (CIEL) 7, 9
Centers for Disease Control (CDC) 141

certification 107–120, 157–160; carbon 160; consumer decision-making 153, 157; credibility 108; food literacy 157; local 159–160; MSC 115–118; organic 96, 98–99, 103, 111, 114, 158; traceability 108; *see also* branding; labeling; trademarks
cheese 43, 70, 81, 84, 121, 127, 128, 154; Cornish Blue 43; emissions 64; health 144; L'Etivaz 80; Le Gruyère 80; local 80, 81; planetary diet 150; Swiss 80; vegans 245; waste 231; water footprint 51
Chefs in Schools 257–258
cherries 225, 227
chicken 151; carbon intensity 63; changes in production 171, 212; contamination 212; feet 174, 211; global numbers 33, 34; nuggets 154, 171; planetary 150; procurement 126; soul food 165; water footprint 51, wings 258
Chile 63
China 3, 32, 41, 51, 164, 267; consumption of meat and milk 44, 45; emissions 59; food production 33; organic production 92, 113; renewable energy 59; waste management 231
chocolate 104; cost 104; emissions 64; fair trade 115; organic 104; water footprint 51
choice editing 162–163, 166, 167; Scandic 163
Choose Love 256
circular economy 15, 25, 62
circular ecosystem 28, 62
City Harvest 230
cleaning 195
climate change 26, 42, 56, 57–63; adaptation 119; carbon intensity of diets 63–65; decarbonizing the food system 65–76; dietary implications 68; impacts 44–48, 54; mitigation 57, 60–62, 65–66, 71, 98, 102, 119, 189; and weather extremes 55; *see also* emissions
cloud technology 203
cod 162
Codex Alimentarius 153
coffee 41–42, 145, 183, 204; cost to consumer 93; emissions 64; environmental impacts 39; fair trade 104, 108, 115; market concentration 39; organic 104; prices 42; production 93; shops 33, 41, 43, 177; waste 177; water footprint 51
Colbert Restaurant 270
cold rooms 180
collaboration 123, 255, 257; risk factor 138; waste reduction 242
commodity chains *see* food chains; food systems
community food systems *see* local food systems
community supported agriculture 77
compact fluorescent lamps (CFL) 187, 208

competitiveness 101, 105, 124, 229, 237, 259; restaurant strategies 15, 36
Comprehensive Energy Management (CEM) 199, 204, 207–208
Concentrated Animal Feeding Operations (feedlots) 267
consumerism 9; environmental 86
cookbooks 82, 122; generational use of 237–238
cooking 70, 166, 168, 254, 265; education 264; emissions 68; energy use 179–183, 188–192, 200, 204, 217; environmental impact 26; health 7, 144, 145, 252, 268; household 24, 237; insects 266; offal 171, 175; as part of culinary system 40; restaurant 76, 122, 153, 164, 175, 218–219, 237, 241, 268, 270; school 258; seasonal 168; social media 161; sustainable 27, 28, 172; terroir 81–85; waste 231, 236, 253
Coopcycle 272
Cornish Cheese Company 43
corporations 32, 34, 36–41; dominance of food system 32, 49, 62, 65, 185; as drivers of food consumption 32; emissions 74; marketing 45; role in diet 34
Costa Cruises 222
Costco 37, 125
COVID-19 9, 42, 43, 46, 143, 230, 250, 262, 271; and food insecurity 264; and food supply chain 41; home food delivery systems 76, 199, 201–203, 261, 271; impact on restaurants 28–29, 230, 253, 255, 258, 261, 271; organic sales 93; packaging 176; waste 176
cuisine 88, 252, 264; local 88–89, 169; Mediterranean 253; Nordic 169–170; regional 81; sustainable 264; vegetable-based 28–29
cuisine tourism *see* food tourism
culinary education 168, 173, 263
culinary networks, *see* networks
culinary systems 16, 81; sustainable 16, 19, 263–268
culinary tourism *see* food tourism
Czech Republic 92

dairy 43, 45, 74, 125, 144; alternatives 70, 74; emissions 3, 59, 62–64; environmental impact 267; health 145, 267; livestock numbers 33; Planetary diet 150; water footprint 52; *see also* butter; cheese; milk
dates 104; cost 104
dates of food 254; best before 213, 217–219, 222, 223, 228; delivery 139; use-by 152, 153
Delish 4, 20
Deliveroo 76, 201, 272
Denmark 141; antibiotics for livestock 141; Copenhagen 169, 263; waste 216
di-n-butylphthalate (DBP) 7

di(2-ethylhexyl)phthalate (DEHP) 7
dialkyl dimethyl ammonium chloride (DADMAC) 195
diet 62–63, 65–70; American 265; change 32, 62–63; cost of 148; and emissions 62–65, 66–67, 70, 138, 151, 267–268; and health 134–140, 100-mile diet 77, 78, 80; local 77–80; Low Lands 9; Mediterranean 9, 136; Nordic 9; planetary 147, 150–151; plant-based diet 29, 51; sustainable 10; and water use 51; *see also* diet-related disease; vegan; vegetarian
diet-related disease 9, 134–137; cancer 137; diabetes 137, 140; heart 73, 137–140, 143, 147; obesity 137–140
disease 61; coffee 9; diet related disease 9, 73, 134–140; livestock 52–54, 94, 142; plant 56, 90, 118; *see also* biosecurity
distribution channels 87, 262; wholesale 125; *see also* food systems
diversification 234
domestic hot water (DHW) 184–185

eating out 15, 30; attitudes to waste 236, 244, 246; consumer decision-making 153; energy consumption 189; sustainability of 25, 273
Ecolabel Index 157; *see also* certification
economic development 23
ecosystem services 15, 47–48
Ecuador 163
education 16, 138, 174, 241, 258, 264, 266; chef 223, 266; community 119, 229–230; sector 1, 2, 3, 127, 131; staff 15, 18, 196, 246–249; waste 196, 216, 223, 224, 240, 241–242, 246–249
Egypt Airlines 20
Eleven Madison Park 28–29
embodied environmental impact 25; emissions 25; water 50–51
emissions 27, 30, 39–40, 184, 204; carbon labels 160–161; and climate friendly food 59–76; and diet 62–65, 66–67, 138, 151, 267–268; from different subsectors 58, 60; environmentally friendly eating 3; food 25, 59–64; growth 57–59; livestock 59–60, 65–66; and local foods 94, 125; offsetting 164; organic food 102; plastics 6, 9; purchasing and supply chains 121–122, 128–130; transportation 74–75, 121, 132, 266; waste 213, 253
energy efficiency 20, 24, 61, 118–119; building 185; kitchen 190–191; sustainable winegrowing 119
Energy Management System (EMS) 204–209
Energy Star 204–205
environmentally friendly eating 3–4
Epicurious 27
erectile dysfunction 7

321

Index

Estonia 92
ethics *see* food ethics
European Union 5, 163; antibbiotics 141; emissions 59–60, 65, 68; employment 35; food waste 4, 213; meat and dairy consumption 44; organic food 94; trade 32
exports 32, 53, 74; livestock disease 53; as part of culinary system 40

fair trade 114–115; coffee 42; cost 103–104; ethics 133; standards 112–115
Fair Trade Labelling Organizations International (FLO) 114
Fareshare 230
farmers' markets 22, 24, 31, 35. 77, 79, 81, 86, 122, 145, 152
farm shops 79
Fat, oil and grease (FOG) 11, 14
Fearnley-Whittingstall, Hugh 169
fertilizers 13, 20, 61, 70, 82, 121, 128–129; in culinary system 40; organic agriculture 91, 99, 112
festivals 251
financial services 41; as part of culinary system 40
Finland 86, 144, 216
fish *see* seafood
fishing 31, 35, 115–118, 128
flexitarian 170, 245; defined 170
foie gras 162
Food and Agricultural Organisation of the United Nations (FAO) 31, 44, 47, 232
food at home (FAH) 25, 217, 229
food away from home (FAFH) 25
food bank 11, 13, 15, 42, 219, 228, 251, 261
food consumption 32, 60; 73, 96, 151, 221, 237–238; emissions 75; emissions reduction 66, 71; externalities 95, 105; generational 237–238; health 9, 151, 165; identity 244; local 85, 86; sustainable 19, 24, 33, 155, 175, 263; system 19, 40; *see also* diet
food delivery platforms 76, 200, 201, 203; alternative 272; and restaurant management system 201–203
food education 258
food ethics 169–171; virtue ethics 170
food expenditure 25, 150
Food for Soul 253–255
food justice 251–252, 261–262
food manufacturing 2, 22, 125; as part of culinary system 40
food media 122, 263; *see also* media
food miles 65, 74–76; local food 78, 86
FoodPanda 201
food production 19, 21, 30–57, 60–61, 69, 74–75, 171, 234, 265; antibiotics 141–142; biodiversity decline 47–50; and culinary systems 39–41; disease 52–54, 141–142; emissions 25, 57–58, 59, 68, 74–75;

environmental impacts 212; food security 44–47; local food 79, 82, 85; organic 90–94, 126, 259; standards 107; structures 31–36; transnational corporations 38–41; and water use 50–52
food quality 22, 94, 112, 190, 229; *see also* quality
food retail 36–37; *see also* supermarkets
food security 19, 44–50, 55, 94; and climate change 33; and community residence 250; and genetic diversity 47; local 266
food service sector 214; defined 214; *see also* catering; hospitality industry; institutional food services
food supply 40, 50; and COVID-19 41–43; local food 78, 81
food supply chain 25, 40, 45, 107, 120, 263, 265; and COVID-19 41–43; defined 39; global 123, 234; local 86, 262; procurement 131; short 86; waste 210–213
food systems 39–44; defined 39; *see also* culinary systems; sustainable culinary systems
Food Use for Social Innovation by Optimising Waste Prevention Strategies (FUSIONS) 210–211
food value chains 80, 218
foodways 19, 23, 235, 268; and attitudes to leftover food 235
For Here Please 177
France 29, 35, 67, 74, 256; bistros 259–260; carbon labels 160; climate change 47; emissions 67; farms 50; organic agriculture 92, 93; retail 36, 37; waste 234
functional foods 22
fungicides 50

game 82
Game Bird 41
gardens 35, 81, 262; community-based 250; as part of culinary system 35, 40; restaurant 81, 93
gastronomy 68, 171, 239
genetic diversity 21, 38, 47, 55; turkey 38; *see also* biodiversity
genetic modification 21, 98, 107
genetically modified food 21, 82, 90
genetically modified organisms (GMOs) 91, 97, 99, 102, 112, 115; and definition of organic 97
The George & Dragon 260
German Commission on Diets (Deutsche Ernährungskommission) 66
Germany 35, 72, 74, 159; climate change 47; cost 104; insect loss 48; organic agriculture 92, 98; organic market 93–94; retailers 36, 37
global food gap 44–45
global food production 33–43, 48, 55, 60, 92

global food system 9, 25, 31, 54, 55, 60, 65, 74, 147, 265; food miles 74
globalization 32, 36, 233, 234, 238, 264; food miles 74; supply chains 123; terroir 88
goat 33, 34, 144; emissions 64; increase in global numbers 60
GO Box 177
grapes 74; organic production 93; transport emissions 74; wine production 118
grazing 63, 83
Greece 87
green growth 19–24
greenhouse gas (GHG) *see* climate change; emissions
greenhouse gas intensity 63–65
Green Seal Standard for Restaurants and Food Services 25
Green Star 29
groundnuts 143; allergies 104, 142, 143; cost of peanut butter 104; emissions 64; planetary diet 150
Guinea 39
GustOrganics 101

Hackney School of Food 257
halal 4, 123
halibut 162
Hartnett, Angela 256
healthy diet 137; defined 137
heating, ventilation and air conditioning (HVAC) 129, 179, 180, 183–185, 188–189
Henderson, Fergus 170–171, 172, 175, 265
herbicides 50
herbs 70
heritage 82; fruit and vegetables 266
herring 83, 173
Herz und Niere 171
Hines, Maria 101
home food delivery systems 76
homogenization 169
Honduras 163
hospitality industry 42; and COVID-19 41–42; and culinary system 40; mental health 269; and sustainability 266; water use 192
100-mile diet 77; and defining local food 78, 80
Hungary 3, 192
hunger 44, 49, 56, 231, 264–265; definition 264; and redistribution of the food system 231; SDG goal 2 45; in USA 264
Hussain, Nadia 253
hygiene 142, 153; allergies 142; cleaning 195; tooth 144

identity 80, 186, 244; cultural 165; and cuisine 165
IKEA 37
Imad'sSyrian Kitchen 256
immigration 235

imports 32, 42, 74, 75, 113; energy use 75; as part of culinary system 40
Impossible beef 73
India 163, 201
Indonesia 39, 163
innovation 19, 21, 22, 168, 243; social innovation 210; technology 239; waste 210
institutional food services 1, 4, 122, 135, 242; government direction 122; health initiatives 135–136; as part of culinary system 40; procurement 122, 135; waste management 219–220
integrated pest management 119
intellectual property 89, 109; geographical indication 89; and place 89; standards 109; *see also* trademarks
International Energy Agency (IEA) 59
International Federation of Organic Agriculture Movements (IFOAM) 91–92, 111, 114
International Fund for Agricultural Development (IFAD) 137, 264
International Land Coalition (ILC) 35–36
Intergovernmental Panel on Climate Change (IPCC) 55, 57–59
Ireland 44, 131
irrigation 21, 50, 52, 70, 129, 193; almonds 70, vineyards 118
Italy 74, 87, 92; organic production 92; seasonal calendar for fruit 225; sustainable winegrowing 118; waste minimisation 243, 253

Japan 201
Just Eat 272

kebab 88, 256
Kenya 74
Kempinski Hotel Corvinus 197
Kerridge, Tom 256
King, Jeremy 270
Kosher 123
KRAV certification 97, 103

La Fourchette de Collserola 253
La Nef 29
labeling 87, 107–120, 158–161; carbon 72, 160–161; fish 115–118; organic 91, 96–101, 112–114; reinforcing local food 89; sustainability 114–115; sustainable wine 118–119; unhealthy foods 146; *see also* appellation; certification; MSC; terroir; trademarks
labour 19, 21, 197, 250, 270; agriculture 35; cost 258; fair trade standards 115; law 119; migrant 119; sustainable restaurants 19, 21
lamb 63, 83, 84, 171; external costs to farm gate 95; greenhouse gas intensity 63; planetary health diet 150

Index

landfill 71, 130, 132, 231; food loss and waste 210, 211; USA 212
landscape 61, 82, 83
Latin America 45, 46, 235
Le Bab 256
Le Manoir aux Quat'Saisons 81
leaf-to-root eating 168–176; empathy for food 168; principles 175–176; see also nose-to-tail eating
leftovers 25, 217, 220, 224, 231, 239, 244, 247, 249; buffet 221, 241; cultural attitudes towards 235–236; donations 11, 13, 228; food containers for 242–243; generational attitudes towards 236; post-kitchen food waste avoidance 217, 219; reuse 223
Leon Restaurants 258
libido 7
Life Cycle Assessment (LCA) 4, 121, 189; food production 121; heat recovery systems 189; menus 4
light-emitting diode (LED) 181–182, 187, 208; economic impacts 187
linear alkylbenzene sulphonates (LAS) 195
living wage 257, 271; as a sustainable restaurant indicator 18
lobbying 49; pesticide use 49
lobster 41
local food 11, 19, 21, 22, 55, 77–89, 251, 266; chef perception 87–88; consumer demand 85–87; definition 78–80; EU 86; as geographical proximity 78; grower definition 80; local food systems 77, 79, 82, 88, 266; relational proximity 79; resilience 56, 266; restaurants 81–85, 87–88; security 266; social, economic and environmental proximity 79; supply chain 122–123, 126–127, 262; values 69, 79–80; wholesalers' role 122, 126–127; see also terroir
Local Food Heroes 77
localism 24, 169; Localism Act 260
Lodi Winegrape Commission 118
London Restaurant Co-operative 256
Lucky Peach 267

machinery 121; as part of culinary system 40
maize 32, 72, 144; carbon footprint 64; cost 148; production 33, 34; water footprint 51
Malaysia 4, 163
malnutrition 56, 137, 143, 149
Malta 87
mangrove 162; destruction 163
Marine Stewardship Council (MSC) 103, 108, 109, 115–118; Aquaculture Stewardship Council (ASC) and MSC Joint Standard 117; Chain of Custody Standard 117; criticisms 117–118; seaweed standard 117
Max Burgers 164
McDonalds 10, 36, 151; McBurger 10

media 23, 45, 72, 77, 136, 153, 156; examples supporting meat-free food choices 161; food and health 146; image of restaurant cooking 122; social media 161–162; and terroir restaurants 89
Mediterranean cuisine 253
Mediterranean diet 9, 136
melons 225, 227
mental health 268–269
menu design 163–165
menu marketing 152–167; certification and labels 158–161; children's menu 154–155, 156–157; choice editing 162–163; consumer decision making 153–155; design 163–165; food choices 152–153; information tools 157–158; online information tools 161–162
Mexico 153, 201; sugar tax 153
Michelin 29; green star 29; Michelin star 29
milk 33, 43, 59, 74, 95, 128, 156; allergies 142; carbon footprint 64, 65, 66, 70; cost 95; energy input 63; global consumption 44; planetary diet 159; waste 213; water footprint 51
mobility 23, 238
modernization 168, 233
Monsanto 39
morality 79, 170, 235; food wastage 249; moral norm change 154
Morrisons 169
mustard greens 165

National Farmers Union 43
National Food Service 261
National Restaurant Association (NRA) 11, 185–186, 201, 202, 251
near zero energy buildings (nZEBs) 183–185
Nestlé 45
Netherlands 35, 37, 87
networks 30, 111, 116, 125; alternative food 78, 79; distribution 32; local food 78, 85; logistics 76; mutual aid 261
net-zero energy buildings (NZEBs) 183–184
New Zealand 75, 80, 118, 126, 163; consumers 174; seasonal fruit 32, 226
Nicaragua 163
Niland, Josh 171–173
NOMA 169, 263
Nordic cuisine 169–170
Nordic diet 9
Norma 41
Norway 221, 240; food waste 216
nose-to-tail eating 168–176; empathy for food 168; perceptions 174–175; see also leaf-to-root
Nossa Familia Coffee 177
nudging 243–244; reducing food waste 243–244

nutrition 16, 108, 163, 261; children's 154; choice-editing 162; guidelines 135–136; health 135–137, 143, 146; labelling 139, 158–159; and organic agriculture 91; *see also* diet

offal 172–175; cultural attitudes 174; fish 172, 173; as waste 172; *see also* nose-to-tail eating
olive 84; embodied water 51; greenhouse gas emissions 64; healthy eating 144; organic production 93; olive oil 64
ONA 29
One Eighty Restaurant 253
onions 256; greenhouse gas intensity 64, 65
oranges 74; cost 104; juice 104; organic 104; water footprint 51
organic agriculture *see* organic farming systems
organic farming systems 20, 22, 90–106, 126, 128, 166; certification 96, 98–99, 103, 111, 114, 158; dairy 70; defined 90–91, 93–94; economics 94–96; emissions 75; environmental impacts 93; fair trade 115; importance 92; labels 97, 158, 160; meat 17; production 70, 92–93, 99–100, 141, 153; standards 96; winegrowing 119; yields 93
organic foods 90–106, 121, 166; certification 96, 98–99, 103, 111, 114, 158; and cost 104; and COVID-19 93; demand 93; distribution 125; economics 94–96; greenhouse gas intensity 75; labels 97, 158, 160; mainstreaming 105; procurement 128–131; purchasing 101–103
organic restaurants 100–101, 103
Origine Non-Animale (ONA) 29
Osteria Francescana 253
Ottolenghi, Yotam 257, 258
Outlaw, Nathan 172

packaging 9, 22–24, 32, 33, 155; chemicals in 5; and COVID-19 42; and culinary system 40; efficient 176–177; emissions 59, 65, 71; environmentally friendly 109–110; intelligent 229; leftovers 247; plastic 5–7; procurement 131; vacuum 249; waste 24, 33, 40, 71, 130, 202, 210
Paraguay 63; deforestation 63
parsnip 169; aesthetics 169
partnerships 15, 18, 115, 262; public-private 24; *see also* collaboration; networks
pasta 121, 255; cost 104; embodied water 51; food waste 4, 239
peach 225, 227; water footprint 51
peachcot 227
peanuts *see* groundnuts
pears 84, 225, 227
per- and polyfluoroalkyl substances (PFAS) 7, 177

permaculture 268
persimmon 227
persistent organic pollutants (POPs) 5, 6
pesticides 10, 11, 20, 49–50, 70, 82; cost of use 95–96; global market 39; and perceptions of sustainable food 10; sustainability practices 13; *see also* organic food
pig 171; emissions 64; increase in global numbers 60; offal 171; *see also* pork
pizza 88, 144, 154, 257
planetary diet 147, 150–151; focused on health 150–151
plant-based diet 29, 51; water footprint 51; *see also* vegan food, vegetarian food
plastic 5–9; chemicals in 5; definition 5; emissions 9; and human health 5–7, 9; packaging 172, 176–177; waste 3, 4, 5–9, 107, 176–177, 243, 246
plate size 135, 239, 240–242
plumbing. 180
plum 225, 227
point of sale 146, 199–200; *see also* restaurant management systems
Poland 87
pollution 47, 91; air 75, 143, 268; cruise ships 222; plastic 9; and water use 128; of waterways 3, 128, 268; *see also* waste
polychlorinated biphenyls (PCBs) 21
polycyclic aromatic hydrocarbons (PAHs) 5, 6
population growth 33–34
pork 27, 83, 165; consumption 151; cost 95; greenhouse gas intensity 27, 63, 65; planetary diet 150; scratchings 63; water footprint 51
Portugal 87
potato 7, 33, 34, 165, 168, 173; aesthetics 42, 169; costs 95; greenhouse gas intensity 64, 65; planetary diet 150; wastage 4, 42–43, 168, 214, 239; water footprint 51
Potato Processors Association 43
poultry 147, 212; cost 95; emissions 27, 64, 65; global production 60; healthy eating 136; planetary diet 150; *see also* chicken and turkey
prawns 162
primary energy consumption (PEC)
private standards 108–109
processed foods 22, 29, 31, 32, 33, 97, 170, 265; costs 265; and diet-related disease 146; and fast food restaurants 9; and food consumption change 37, 45, 60, 235; increase in sales 36–37; labelling 146; and sustainable culinary systems 40
procurement *see* purchasing
Protected Geographical Indication 89
provenance 162
purchasing 11, 17, 110, 121–134, 157; decisions 124–125, 203; home food delivery

systems 76; local 81, 85–88; public service procurement 127–133; waste reduction 168, 200, 223, 229, 249; wholesale distributors 125–127; *see also* supply chain management
purchasing power parity 147

quality 30, 114, 86, 239; labels 98, 103; standards 52, 114; *see also* food quality
quality of life 111, 270
Quo Vadis 173

Rayner, Jay 269–270
real cost of food 106, 270
real food 265
red meat 9, 147, 174; health aspects 140; planetary diet 147; reduction to combat climate change 73; substitutes 164
Redzepi, Rene 169–170, 263
refrigeration 23, 180–181, 183, 190–191, 204, 205, 213, 218, 224; attitudes towards 235
Refugee Community Kitchen 256
REfUSE 230–231
regional produce 157; *see also* local food
regional promotion 23
regional purchasing 124; *see also* local food
regulation 20, 22, 41, 56, 136, 203; building 184; culinary system 40; EU 97; food choices 138, 167; organic 97–99, 105
reindeer 170
resilience 56, 94, 250
resistance to change 257
restaurant management 101, 249; sustainable 180
restaurant management system (RMS) 199–204, 208–209; features 203; relationship to energy system 200; relationship to food delivery apps 200, 201–203
Restaurant Nora 100
restaurateurs 4, 270, 273
retail *see* food retail
rice 4, 32, 33, 34, 67, 72, 73, 121, 144, 148, 150, 239; cost 104; emissions 61, 64; milk 70; water footprint 51
Royal Association of British Dairy Farmers (RABDF) 43
rye 64; emissions 64

St. John 171
Saint Peter 17–22
salmon 32, 53; farmed 266
salt 84
Sat Bains 270
Saudi Arabia 235
Scandic 163; choice editing of giant prawns 163
scavenging 234
Schwarz Group 37

school food 1, 3, 25, 103, 105, 132–136, 139, 146, 179, 257–258; emissions 25, 121; environmental impacts 122; pre-packed school meals 7; procurement 121; waste 2, 4
seafood 83, 124, 125, 147, 151, 165; MSC certification 109, 117; procurement 128; sustainable 109, 117; waste 128, 213
seaweed 84; MSC standard 117
seed production 21; dominance by transnational companies 28
sheep 33, 65, 144; live animal numbers 34, 60; *see also* lamb
shrimp 163; choice editing 163
Sierra Leone 30
Simmons Prepared Foods 212
smoked food 77, 173
Slow Food 77, 82, 84, 263
slow tourism 23
social food services 127, 131; procurement 127
social justice 22, 79, 91, 251, 262
social networking 238
social services 56
soil 20, 47, 61, 82, 90, 119; fair trade 115; fertility 20, 128; management 61, 119; organic farming 90, 91, 93, 94, 111; regeneration 20, 82; terroir 81
Soil Association 94
soul food 165–166
Spain 36, 37, 74, 118, 252; organic agriculture 92
sperm quality 7
The Sportsman 83-5
standardization 23, 81, 114, 168, 209, 239; negative reaction to 169
strawberries 80, 84, 155; seasonality 156
steady-state *see* sustainable consumption
Stuart, Tristam 231
Styrofoam 246
sugar 9, 153; health aspects 9; tax 153
supermarkets 31, 32, 35, 45, 168; carbon labels 160; donations 229, 254; expansion 60; food choice 152; market power 43; and non-aesthetic fruit and vegetables 42, 169; and sustainability 22, 24
supply chain 3, 17, 31; 42–43, 80, 121–133; and COVID-19 41; culinary system 40; defined 39–40; environmentally friendly eating 3; food system 213; management 122–133; security 113, 117; storage 46; transport 79; *see also* procurement
sustainability 1, 4, 102, 136, 151, 156, 238, 246, 263; branding 23, 270; behaviours 4; certification and labelling 112–120; community 250–252; conceptualization 2, 10–27; environmental 79; environmental practices 13; decision-making 125–126; influencers 267; positioning 110; procurement 131–132; product attributes

108, 112–120; purchasing 121; restaurant strategies 12–15, 182, 191; social 261; use of technologies 182, 199–209; *see also* sustainable culinary systems
sustainable consumption 19–24
sustainable culinary systems 19–24, 263, 264–265; approaches to 19–24; biodiversity 21; concept of sustainability 19; control of pests and diseases 20; defined 15; energy use 20; farm size 21; food distribution 22; food manufacturing 22; food storage 23; hospitality and foodservice 23; soil fertility 20; steady-state strategies 19–24; sustainable consumption 19–24; waste disposal 24; water problems 21
Sustainable Development Goals (SDGs) 45, 55; animal welfare 55; food security 44; food waste 210; global food production 55
sustainable lifestyles 238
sustainable restaurant 1, 10–30, 157, 180, 200, 251; assessments 27; certification 114; defined 10–19, 25–30; dimensions 16–19; management systems 200
Sustainable Restaurant Association (SRA) 15, 82
sustainable transition 238
sustainable wine *see* sustainable winegrowing
sustainable winegrowing 118–119; components of certification programmes 119
Sustainable Wine Growing New Zealand 118
Sweden 92, 103, 105, 131, 141, 153, 216; forest fires 47; organics in public kitchens 105, 259; see also KRAV
Swiggy 201

Taiwan 160
Tamimi, Sami 256–257
tea 41–42, 129, 145; cost 104; Fair Trade 115; waste 214; water footprint 51
terroir 81–85, 88; cooking 81–83; defined 81; as intellectual property 89; media attention 89
Tesco 37; carbon labelling 160
Thailand 74, 163
third party certification 110–112
Tilth 101
tomatoes 84; emissions 64, 65; waste 214, 218
Too Good To Go 43
tourism 23, 52; social 127
traceability 79; certification 108, 116; MSC 116
training 119, 168, 192, 252–253, 266; allergies 143; environmental 11, 15, 18; procurement 132, 133, 218; waste reduction 172, 173, 217, 218–219, 222, 224, 246–247
transportation 32, 41, 46, 59, 67, 58, 70, 80, 86, 95, 130, 177, 213, 224; home food delivery systems 76; food miles 74–75; as part of culinary system 40; wholesale distribution 125–126
trout 32
Trussell Trust network 261
tuna 74, 162
Turkey 92, 188; Kocaeli 188
Turkey 38; genetics 38; greenhouse gas intensity 63

Uber Eats 201
UN Human Rights Council (UNHRC) 49–50
Unite 268–269
United Kingdom 42–43, 67, 71, 75, 82–85, 92, 93, 141, 153, 160, 267, 270; community pubs 259–260; energy efficiency 179, 182, 184–185, 189, 190, 192; estimated average cost of food being wasted in the hospitality and foodservice sector 247; external costs to farm gate 95; food justice 261; food waste 2, 46, 169, 172, 230, 239, 247; livestock disease 52; London 41, 230, 270; plastic pollution 9; retail 37, 169; school meals 258, 260; waste distribution charities 230, 251, 256
United Nations Framework Convention on Climate Change (UNFCCC) 57
United Nations International Children's Emergency Fund (UNICEF) 137, 256; healthy diet 137
United States 11, 25, 32, 33, 41, 44, 51, 57, 67, 73, 179, 190, 234, 240, 246; African Americans 165; agricultural chemicals 88; certified organic restaurants in 100; chicken 171; emissions 59, 75; food waste 212–213, 245; industrial food production and contamination-related losses in 212; obesity 138, 165; organic foods 91, 93, 96, 99, 100–101, 112, 158; plastics 5, 7; retailing 36, 37, 124–125; sustainable winegrowing 118
Universo Santi 252–253
urbanization 33, 45, 233; as driver of changes in food system 60, 234; environmental effects 48
Uruguay 92
US Department of Agriculture (USDA) 212; organic standards 91, 99, 101, 158

Vallée, Claire 29
veal 162
vegan food 3, 29, 69, 70, 142, 157, 161–162, 166, 219, 245; attractiveness 3, 161; burgers 67, 73, 164; certification 158; and climate change mitigation 62, 267; eating healthier 136; emissions 267; environmental value 67; ethics 170; meat replacement 72–73; menus 143, 167; veganism 29, 67, 245; water footprint 51; *see also* vegan restaurants

vegenomic market 245
vegan restaurants 29, 161, 245–246; in France 29; in Korea 245–246; soul food 165–166; in USA 165–166
vegetables 9, 15, 28–29, 33, 94, 128, 164, 172, 213; aesthetics 42, 169, 175–176; allergies 142; and dietary implications of climate change 68–69; external costs to farm gate 95; food miles 74–75; food waste 4, 169, 175–176, 194, 221, 229–231; frozen 43; greenhouse gas intensity of various vegetables 65; heirloom and heritage varieties 266; and human health 9, 10, 136–139, 165; local foods 81–84; seasonal 69; terroir cooking 81
vegetarian food 3, 69, 70, 105, 142, 157, 161–162, 219, 245, 259; attractiveness 3, 161; certification 158; eating healthier 136, 144–147; environmental value 67; ethics 170; meat replacement 72–73; menus 143, 167; planetary diet 150; see also vegan food; vegetarian restaurants
vegetarian restaurant 29, 161, 245–246; in Korea 245–246
ventilation 26, 179, 180, 183–185, 188–189; see also HVAC
Vietnam 163
Viking Line 222
vineyard see sustainable winegrowing; viticulture
viticulture 118; see also sustainable winegrowing
voluntary standards see private standards

Walmart 36, 37; carbon labelling 160
walnut 227
water 5, 50–52; bottled 7, 131; conservation 196–197, 207; consumption 130, 180, 189, 192–193, 195, 197, 199; costs 193, 196; definitions of 52; efficiency 180, 196–197; embodied in foodstuffs 51; footprint 51, 52; management 21, 61, 119, 121, 132, 196; meters 207; pollution 128, 268; quality 52; reduction 15, 17, 193; relationship to energy consumption 180; use 50–52; wastage 196
water smart 196
waste 232; behaviour 233–249; on cruiseships 222; distribution charities 230; education and training 246–247; emissions 59; fair trade 60; management 6, 22, 33, 119, 130, 132, 177, 231; minimization 173, 224, 244; monitoring 209–210; plate 241; technologies 210–232; wastewater 130, 211, 221–222; see also food waste
water heating 180, 181, 189
Wey, Tunde 257
wine 84, 118; greenhouse gas footprint 64; sustainable wine certification programmes 118–119; water embodied in 51
winegrowing 118; sustainable 118–119
The Wonston Arms 260
World Health Organization (WHO) 137–138, 140, 141, 153; recommendations for healthy diets 144, 147
World Resources Institute (WRI) 44, 45, 60–62, 221; food loss waste standard 211; recommendations for reducing agricultural emissions 61
WRAP 2, 46, 214, 239, 253

Ying, Chris 267

ZeroFoodprint 267
Zero Waste 177; coffee shop 177
Zomato 201

Lightning Source UK Ltd.
Milton Keynes UK
UKHW052152060622
403871UK00008B/28